Rendezvous with Destiny

A History of

Modern American Reform

"There is a mysterious cycle in human events. To some generations much is given. Of other generations much is expected. This generation of Americans has a rendezvous with destiny."

FRANKLIN DELANO ROOSEVELT, *June 27th, 1936*

Eric F. Goldman

RENDEZVOUS
WITH
DESTINY

 Chicago

IVAN R. DEE, PUBLISHER

RENDEZVOUS WITH DESTINY. Copyright © 1952 by Alfred A. Knopf, Inc. This book was first published in 1952 and is here reprinted by arrangement with Alfred A. Knopf, a division of Random House, Inc. First Ivan R. Dee paperback edition published 2001. All rights reserved, including the right to reproduce this book or portions thereof in any form. For information, address: Ivan R. Dee, Publisher, 1332 North Halsted Street, Chicago 60622. Manufactured in the United States of America.

Library of Congress Cataloging-in-Publication Data:
Goldman, Eric Frederick, 1915–
    Rendezvous with destiny : a history of modern American reform / Eric F. Goldman.—
1st Ivan R. Dee paperback ed.
        p. cm.
    Originally published: New York : Knopf, 1952
    Includes bibliographical references and index.
    ISBN 1-56663-369-9 (alk. paper)
        1. United States—Politics and government—1865–1933. I. Title.

E661 .G58 2001
973.8—dc21
                                                        00-050437

To Jo, who knows why

in Which the Author Seeks a Basis for Rapport with the Reader

IN THE MIDDLE of my work on this book, the *New York Herald Tribune* sent a staff member out to ask, "What is liberalism?" and he came back with the report: "One sure way to have an interview start with a long awkward silence is to ask people who regularly use the word 'liberal' to explain just what they mean." About the same time, the *New Republic* published a collection of definitions of liberalism by Americans prominently associated with "liberal" politics. Some of the respondents escaped behind the phrase "the most good for the most people," most of them emphasized quite different things, and the former trust-buster Thurman Arnold simply threw up his hands and confessed that, so far as he was concerned, liberalism was "deuces wild." As this book goes to press, Harry Truman, Robert Taft, and Henry Wallace each describes himself as a true liberal, and the word is quite obviously headed toward semantic bedlam.

It has all been disconcerting for a person trying to write about modern American reform, I must admit. But certainly the confusion did nothing to diminish my conviction that it was worthwhile to study the movements which have led to the present importance of the word "liberal" and to study them with a recognition that jumbles are often clarified by tying the present to its meaningful past. This book then is a history, first and foremost. It is written, as the Bibliographical Notes indicate, with an attempt to root the volume in all the relevant research. It aims not so much to declare where we are going or ought to go but to present a narrative, the story of the wise and the shortsighted, the bold and the timid, the generous and the grasping human beings who are the eternal stuff of history.

Some readers may wonder why I begin a history of modern American reform in the years immediately after the Civil War. Certainly, it could have started much farther back, with the Jefferson-Jackson tradition of the pre-Civil War period, or with the seventeenth-century European burghers who were demanding rule by representative assemblies, civil liberties, and the separation of church and state, or even with the ancient Prophets who made social justice a fundamental of Christian-Hebrew thinking. But the reform movements that culminated in the New Deal and the Fair Deal, in my opinion, are most directly a reaction to a rapidly urbanizing, industrializing America. I have therefore begun with the late 1860's of American history, when the factory and the city were swiftly taking over dominance of the United States.

In discussing the reform movements, I have labelled them by the terms that they applied to themselves. No doubt, this will bring jolts to the reader. He may be disconcerted, for example, to find Samuel J. Tilden, whose ideology contrasts sharply with Harry Truman's, discussed as a "liberal," while Woodrow Wilson, an ideological father of Truman, is not categorized by that term. Yet the practice, I suggest, helps rescue the narrative from distracting connotations that have become attached to certain phrases in our generation. After all, one of the clarifying gifts of history is that it is over with.

In addition to being a history, this book is, quite openly, a personal interpretation of the facts. I have always considered myself, in thought and in emotions, part of the "liberal" tradition. I have also done my full share of wriggling in those liberal circles where discussion hurries from cliché to cliché and clarion calls are conspicuously lacking in clarity. My personal approach, together with the attempt to obey the dictates of the historical method, results in breakaways from a number of prevailing ideas about people or events treated in this book. I trust that readers who consider themselves liberals, however much they may be jarred by some of the breakaways, will agree that the reform movement cannot fail to be benefited by all honest attempts at interpretative analysis. I trust, too, that my more conservative readers, however much others of the breakaways may irritate them, will go along with the proposition that any movement as powerful as modern American reform should be given more careful and comprehending treatment than the sneers that frequently pass for discussions of the subject in anti-Fair Deal circles.

I should like to ask conservative readers to join me in a special effort not to blur two significantly different ideas. For a good many years, and never more so than at the present, common practice in some conservative circles has made liberalism synonymous or almost synonymous with socialism. In the history of post-Civil War America, reformers have often co-operated with socialists and sometimes they have worked with Communists; modern American reform has been plainly influenced by socialism; at times many reformers have advocated certain specific measures, such as the municipal ownership of power, or TVA developments, which are unmistakably socialist; it may even be, as books like Hayek's *Road to Serfdom* insist, that Rooseveltism ultimately leads to socialism. Yet at least up to the present the ultimate objectives of most American reformers and of socialists have been distinct. The socialist, however much he backed specific reform measures, has sought a society in which the principal means of production would be owned and operated by the state. The more typical reformer, whether or not he approved of particular socialist moves, has sought a society in which the principal means of production would be left in private hands. Indeed, since the rise of fascism and Communism in the world, the "liberal," far from wanting to get rid of capitalism, has increasingly thought of reform as the way to prevent capitalism from collapsing into totalitarianism. (Franklin Roosevelt was expressing a widely held reform attitude when he said: "I am that kind of a liberal because I am that kind of a conservative.") To slur over the distinction between reform and socialist objectives is to miss a key fact about the whole history of modern American dissidence.

I must also ask my liberal-minded reader to join me in a restraint. Because reformers are quite human human beings, they have often given the words "reformer" or "liberal" a connotation which amounts to saying that these types, in contrast with other Americans, are receptive to new ideas and are ready to place the good of society above any selfish interest. Undoubtedly, the virtues have been common among reformers and they have not especially characterized standpatters. The trouble is that the "liberal" and "conservative" types which many people have in mind are just so many stereotypes. Everyone is aware, for example, of labor leaders who have gone down the line for the New Deal and the Fair Deal but who are hardly open-minded or inclined to place the interests of society over their vested concern, organized labor. Conversely, some businessmen who approach apoplexy at mention of the Fair Deal are notably tolerant and unselfish in many ways and prove themselves strong friends of new ideas in a number of their activities. The fact seems to be that over the years the reform movement has included both the flexible-minded and the guardians of the previous generation's dogmas, both people who were in the movement to give as much as they could to the community and those who were in it for what they could get out of it for themselves or their group. As a matter of fact, one of the central questions that has to be answered in any thorough study of modern American reform is whether at times it has not amounted to a drive to bring benefits to a minority at the expense of the majority. The author and the reader are much more likely to be satisfied with the same answers to this and related questions if neither makes the assumption that a reformer, *ipso facto*, is the noblest species of American.

Having made these somewhat lecturish requests, I can ask the reader to share a much more pleasant experience. Writing a book like this inevitably piles up debts to people and to institutions. A Library of Congress Grant-in-Aid for Studies in the History of American Civilization released me from teaching duties at a critical stage in my research; grants from the Princeton University

A Few Words Before

Research Fund have also furthered the project. I am grateful, too, to individuals and publishers who permitted me to quote from documents or printed works, and these instances are indicated in the appropriate footnotes. The men who gave patient hours to reading and criticizing the manuscript are deliberately not named; I have thanked them personally and I want to grant them absolution from my interpretations of highly controversial subjects. I am indebted to many other people who aided me in a variety of ways, ranging from young women who were paid for stenographic assistance and gave an interest money could not have bought, to scholars or public figures who found time for pestering correspondence or interviews. There is no adequate way to speak one's gratitude for this kind of help, and I have succumbed to the defeatism of confining my acknowledgment to those who were most directly involved in research problems and to making that thank-you simply an alphabetical listing at the head of the Bibliographical Notes. One man bears so special a relationship to this book that I would like to express my appreciation here in the front store-window of the volume. Perhaps you will understand what I owe to the late Charles A. Beard when I say that, whatever our differences on some public questions, he has been for me the reform tradition in its full grandeur.

One summer afternoon Mr. Beard was scourging my ideas about foreign policy, pouring out his knowledge of the last half-century of American life, mulling over the proper way to do a history of reform or of anything else. "Tell them," Mr. Beard said, his china-blue eyes alive with memories, "tell them that the old man says that writing any history is just pulling a tomcat by its tail across a Brussels carpet."

Well, I'm passing the word along. And when you have finished this book and the tomcat of modern American reform still sits with cocked whiskers mocking any attempt at full comprehension of the story, I hope you will think that the pages have been worth your effort and mine.

E. F. G.

☼ CONTENTS ☼

xiii

Rendezvous with Destiny

CHAPTER I

"Bejabers, I'm Worth Me Thousands"

"Y OU CAN see it in people's faces, you can feel it in the air,"
the old farmer chortled. "Everybody and everything's goin'
places." [1]

Except in the battered South, everybody and everything certainly seemed on the move. The drain of the Civil War was over,
the backward-looking planters were crushed. The Industrial
Revolution, whirled ahead decades by the five years of war, was
creating new careers by the thousands, stitching the nation together with railroads, turning thistle patches into whistle stops,
towns into cities, cities into metropolises. In the East, a rampant
prosperity touched every venture with the magic of anything-
is-possible. In the West, the tide of migration swept out in proportions unequaled in all man's restless history. West and east,
virtually every index of activity—the number of steel ingots
produced and the number of trees felled, the immigrants arriv-
ing for a farm and the gentlemen leaving for a spin around Europe,
the poems written, the backhouses torn down, the churches built,
the "Devil's Dreams" danced to—almost any statistic showed a
wild surge upward. Somewhere in the middle of it all, the

---

[1] The late Charles Beard, the historian, used to enjoy quoting this remark, made by an Indiana friend of his father, as representing the ebullient
spirit of the immediate post-Civil War period.

rocking-chair was becoming standard equipment for the home. In the North of the late Sixties you moved while sitting still.

The sheer vitality of the period, its unbridled ambition and audacity, were plain in the men who captured public attention. There was the burr-faced Cornelius Vanderbilt, hurling together the largest fortune of the day by buccaneering, and answering his critics with a brazen: "What do I care about the law? Hain't I got the power?" [2] There was the wild-haired Mark Twain, tumbling jumping frogs, river boating, and innocents abroad into a new kind of literature, barging into the hushed sanctuary of the Eastern literary world with the humor of the belly-laugh. There was the huge revivalist preacher Dwight L. Moody, two hundred and eighty pounds of Adam's flesh, every ounce of which, as he would roar, "belonged to God." [3] There was the rambunctious Captain Carver, he of the bellicose mustache and the long black hair flying in the wind, wagering he could kill more buffalo than any other man on earth and riding forth to leave miles of dead animals until his rival's horse dropped from sheer exhaustion. There was, perhaps most symbolic of all, the nondescript Ulysses Grant, who had won the war and now intended to enjoy the peace, hungrily scooping in fine Havana cigars, a fifty-thousand-dollar home complete with the latest tazzas and lambrequins, vacations at fashionable Long Branch, and all the kudos of the Presidency of the United States.

More kudos, more money, the esteem and comforts that more money could bring, the whole congeries of things that to the American meant getting ahead—here was the point of the furious activity. Americans had always believed their country the land of opportunity; the people of the North had never been surer, never raised their sights higher, than in the whirligig years of the late Sixties. The basic conditions that brought confidence before the Civil War continued. Fabulous natural resources were in the early stages of exploitation. Though urbanization and the con-

[2] Quoted in Matthew Josephson: *The Robber Barons* (Harcourt, Brace, 1934), p. 15.

[3] Quoted in Vernon L. Parrington: *Main Currents in American Thought* (Harcourt, Brace, 1930), III, 13.

4

centration of wealth were racing ahead, the society was still predominantly one of small farms, small businesses, and small towns, in which both the hopelessly poor and the overwhelmingly rich were limited in number. A casual camaraderie in economic relations encouraged assuming the next step up in the world. A steel plant of one hundred and fifty workers was exceptionally large, and the more usual factory or store consisted of a boss and a handful of employees, working in close relationship and first-naming each other. In the rural regions, the owner and the farm hand often labored side by side and ate at the same table; since everyone assumed that the hand would soon have his own acres, who thought it strange if he took the boss's daughter to church on Sunday?

Many of the symbols of caste that made Europe's upper-class life seem so unattainably different to groups at the bottom were less conspicuous or nonexistent in the new land across the ocean. A considerable number of wealthy Americans wielded their forks with easily imitated abandon, cooked their own meals and shined their own shoes, and spoke in a manner scarcely distinguishable from the language of the ditch-digger. Even getting shaved, an American journal pointed out in 1866, was a process that underlined the relative lack of caste. In Europe the man with a valet was dewhiskered in style. Only in the United States was everyone who could "raise ten or fifteen cents . . . surrounded during the operation with so much buhl, ormolu, upholstery, and mirrors, and stretched on so easy a chair, and relieved of his beard with so much skill and consideration, and scoured with so many unguents, and 'vivifiers,' and 'invigorators,' and 'purifiers.'" [4]

If the old America of blurred distinctions still appeared very much present, the new America added exciting possibilities. The mushrooming cities, with their receptivity to the novel, their easy forgetfulness of people's pasts, their tendency to look the other way when ambition cut a corner sharply, seemed ideal bases for any man in a hurry. Education, always a boulevard to success in

[4] "Why Are Our Railroads Not Luxurious?" *Nation* (March 22, 1866), II, 361.

the eyes of Americans, was just entering a period of swift expansion. Whirlwind industrial and commercial growth was facilitating movement from the class of those who worked with their hands to the white-collar group—for many, a sign of advancing in the world as important as an increase in income, if not more important. When the census of 1870 was completed, dazed statisticians estimated that the trading classes had grown twenty-one per cent more quickly than the total population.[5]

Of supreme importance to most ambitious men, opportunities to make money were taking on bonanza proportions. For decades, Northern businessmen had maneuvered to get federal legislation favorable to themselves, but most of these efforts had been stopped by the frosty vetoes of an agrarian-minded Washington. The representatives of the Southern planters had hardly stomped out of the Capitol when Washington was taken over by leaders who considered crushing the Confederacy, battling for Negro rights, and passing pro-business laws all part of the same crusade for Progress. During and after the war these "Radical" Republicans erected high tariff walls around American industry, guaranteed a cheap supply of factory labor by authorizing the importation of contract workers, managed finances in a way that invited speculation, and handed out the nation's natural resources in profligate slices.

Industrial workers and white-collar employees had their own encouragements. If obscure statistics proved that real wages were not rising, pay envelopes were certainly growing fatter and the envelopes could seem delightfully thick to the thousands who had been farm hands or penniless immigrants a few years before. Success was in the air; every clerk or factory hand knew of a case like that of the two New York girls who had made roses for milliners before the war and in 1866 sold a business and a trademark for one hundred thousand dollars. The most disgruntled urbanite had before him a pair of ever expanding, ever alluring

[5] Francis A. Walker: "Some Results of the Census," *Journal of Social Science* (1873), V, 95–7.

frontiers: the one, just around the corner, where a new establishment was always offering new jobs, the other, across the country, to the plains that people were calling the Golden West.

For the would-be farmer as well as the farmer, two concerns had always been paramount, cheap land and ample transportation, and these seemed available as never before. The Homestead Law of 1862 and subsequent land legislation offered a farm on terms that resembled a give-away. At the same time, rapid railroad construction was making the long trip west much more comfortable and offering the means to reach distant markets. On May 10, 1869, every telegraph ticker in the nation clicked "One, two, three—done!" in unison with the blows driving down the last golden spike for the transcontinental railroad. To the poet and philosopher, the day might be an occasion for rhetoric on the final consummation of Union. To millions of Americans with their hopes fixed on the land, the golden spike glittered in suggestion of their own economic futures.[6]

For both rural and urban communities, swift technological developments were heightening the sense of burgeoning opportunity by providing cheaply produced markers of each family's advances. The factory worker or clerk could, with careful handling of his money, achieve a succession of signs of his family's rising status—a Sunday dish of salmon shipped all the way from Oregon, one of the wondrous new sewing machines, then, perhaps, an elaborately carved organ for the parlor. Many farm families, after a good year's crop, knew the exhilaration of store-bought clothes for the whirl to a "Devil's Dream," the pride of adding Disraeli's *Lothair* or Greeley's *American Conflict* to the bookshelf, even, if the crop were especially fine, a Pullman trip to Mr. Barnum's "Incredible, Educational Circus," which was sure to be good for admiring mention in the county paper.

And, withal, the whole conception of how far a man could go and how swiftly he could move was taking on a bold new scope.

[6] Quoted in Allan Nevins: *The Emergence of Modern America* (Macmillan, 1927), p. 56.

7

War and pell-mell industrialization seemed to have shaken up the society, weakening if not shattering any crust of caste. A striking number of the figures who won national attention were instances of the miraculously swift rise from obscure origins, poverty, and ignorance. The awesomely rich Cornelius Vanderbilt, a power in New York Society, started life in the one-room cabin of a ferryboat worker and never read a book until he passed his seventieth year. The Reverend Dwight Moody, second only to Jesus in the eyes of millions, came to the pulpit a barely literate shoe salesman, struggling to pronounce the words in his King James Bible. Mark Twain, hailed as a great writer by Boston itself, was the son of a ne'er-do-well and at the age of twelve was out of school, working as an apprentice printer. In the White House, not only President of the United States but the nation's number-one hero, sat the man who had begun his rise a thirty-nine-year-old nobody, his reputation mottled by failure and whisky, his clothing seedy, maneuvering for a clerking post in the ramshackle United States Army.

Even Americans with heavy drags on their feet, the scorned recent immigrants from Catholic Ireland, could dream heady dreams. Irishmen might be accustomed to signs reading "No Irish Need Apply" and to the stock wisecrack that the wheelbarrow was the greatest of inventions because it taught Irishmen to walk on their hind legs.[7] Yet bonanza economics often forgot to ask where you were born or what your church was, and crumbling walls jarred the stoutest foundations of aristocracy. It was an oil speculator a few years from County Cork who could boast: "Yesterday I wasn't worth a cint and bejabers to-day I'm worth me thousands upon thousands."[8] Any Irishman could see the future of his family in terms of the life of Charles O'Conor, son of a ragamuffin immigrant from Dublin, apprenticed to a lamp-black manufacturer at twelve, a lawyer at twenty, a high-priced counsel in his thirties, and now the recognized leader of the New

[7] H. L. Mencken: *The American Language, Supplement I* (Knopf, 1945), p. 604.
[8] Ellis P. Oberholtzer: *History of the United States* (Macmillan, 1917–37), I, 258 n.

8

York bar, the holder of five honorary degrees from universities, and the master of a stately mansion at Nantucket.

"In worn out, king-ridden Europe," Charles O'Conor phrased the day's credo, "men must stay where they are born. But in America a man is accounted a failure, and certainly ought to be, who has not risen above his father's station in life." [9]

[9] *New York Tribune*, May 13, 1869.

CHAPTER II

Thrust from the Top

ULYSSES GRANT and his cronies often used to talk about it, a little puzzled, more than a little annoyed. Here in this wondrous America a certain group kept nagging away, making sniffish remarks about practical politics, likely to denounce almost anything a practical man did. Talk of rampant opportunity left the group cold; the fact that they had special opportunities seemed to make little difference. Most of them came, indeed, from the group that was often called the "Best People," the families a cut above the middle classes, in which, even if great wealth was lacking, money was no daily problem, a good education was assumed, and the next generation did not have to suffer from the nationality, religion, or reputation of a previous one. It must be, Grant's friend Senator Morton said in irritated puzzlement, that some people simply insisted on being "professional reformers." [1]

The Grants and the Mortons would never quite understand these upper-crust dissenters. The very America in which Ulysses Grant could be President left a large section of the men who believed the top belonged to them feeling crowded, buffeted, almost homeless in their own country. They thought of them-

[1] William D. Foulke: *Life of Oliver P. Morton* (Bowen-Merrill, Indianapolis, 1899), II, 218. Mark Sullivan has noted a characteristic conception of the "Best People." Sullivan quoted Rollin Hartt: "It was 'Main Street' that went to the Fair [the World's Fair of 1893]—the 'best people' had a slight disdain for it." *Our Times* (Scribner, 1926–35), I, 189 n.

selves as the natural elite, with the elite's prerogative of fixing standards, and now the nation was gaping in admiration at strange, crude figures out of the earth and the asphalt. They assumed rule by white, Protestant Anglo-Saxons, and the Radical Republicans were clamping Negro control on the South, while every city of the North was feeling the power of political machines built on the Irish Catholic vote. They thought of good government as a tidy piece of machinery, performing a few essential tasks with brisk efficiency, and governments on the federal, state, and municipal levels were becoming leviathans, supporting hordes of officeholders and lumbering far into every citizen's life with legislation in behalf of favored business groups.

Above all, the Best People, comfortable enough not to be tempted by the grosser forms of money-making, raised, for the most part, in a stern Protestant morality that constantly tapped them on the shoulder, expected a reasonable honesty in human dealings. Now, under the toxic of war and boom, a good deal of American business and political life was taking on the morals of the gashouse. Railroad construction sprawled from scandal to scandal; in Pennsylvania's lush "Petrolia," misrepresentation came close to being the standard method of business. Depositing a dollar in a savings bank of the late Sixties could mean putting it where the chances of ever seeing it again were fifty-fifty, and the practices of life-insurance companies led the usually complacent *Commercial and Financial Chronicle* to remark: "The whole chapter is so dark a record of betrayal of corporate trust . . . that if we had the space and the data, we should not have the desire to expose its details." [2] "Big Jim" Fisk, an adventurer with a penchant for mistresses, *opéra bouffe*, and gilded carriages, represented an important part of the new business community. Criticized for a particularly brazen manipulation of other people's money, Big Jim was totally unperturbed. "Nothing is lost save honor," he said with a wave of his fat hand.[3]

[2] Issue of April 19, 1869, quoted in Allan Nevins: *The Emergence of Modern America* (Macmillan, 1927), pp. 193-4.

[3] Quoted in Vernon L. Parrington: *Main Currents in American Thought* (Harcourt, Brace, 1930), III, 13.

Political morality slithered along. Only President Grant's extraordinary naïveté saved him from being a man who deliberately sold the perquisites of his office; so completely did he think of the Presidency as an opportunity to be exploited that he billeted an estimated forty-two relatives on the country. The Crédit Mobilier affair of the late Sixties, in which shares of stock were distributed where they would "protect us" and "do most good to us," involved the Vice President of the United States, a future candidate for the Presidency, and highly influential members of Congress.[4] Ethics could show remarkable flexibility in the Washington of Crédit Mobilier. Once in a while the young United States Senator William Chandler, fresh from conscience-lashed New Hampshire, became disturbed as he distributed bribes of three thousand dollars a month to reporters or negotiated for the purchase by the Republican National Committee of whole newspapers. "Can a man touch pitch and not be defiled?" Chandler would ask himself. But then, in the next moment, he had it all clear. He was "conscious of the correctness and purity of my own motives" and did not "dare turn away" from the opportunity of undermining those enemies of Progress, the Democrats.[5]

The corruption of municipal and state politics was still more flagrant. Boss William Tweed's rule of New York was untypical only in the scope and daring of his grabs. In effective control of the state, in absolute control of the city, Tweed turned the government of both into a vast and succulent barbecue. Safes valued at $3,450 were charged against the city at $482,500; a courthouse that should have cost $3,000,000 swallowed up $11,000,000 and still was not completed. In 1870 the Tweed men certified bills for nearly $16,000,000, of which more than $14,000,000 represented sheer plunder. When Vanderbilt and another freebooter tangled for control of the Erie Railroad, hundreds of thousands of greenbacks arrived in Albany. One of Tweed's state senators, catching the full spirit of the occasion, took $75,000 from the Vanderbilt

---

[4] J. B. Crawford: *The Crédit Mobilier of America* (Calkins, Boston, 1880), pp. 104, 107.

[5] Quoted in Matthew Josephson: *The Politicos* (Harcourt, Brace, 1938), pp. 54-5.

representative and $100,000 from the other side. He preserved the morals of the new politics by voting for the higher donor.

These were the results, but behind them lay the fact that Tweed's operations represented no flimsy arrangement between a handful of scrofulous politicians and a fringe of dishonest businessmen. The people, in the form of the low-income groups that had long roused democratic poets and philosophers to soulful adjectives, were among the Boss's staunchest supporters. Tweed's lieutenants were always at the dock to greet newcomers, and the machine rarely failed to provide any poor man with a free beer, a few dollars to tide over hard times, a helping hand in locating a job or in getting out of trouble with "the law." Thousands of impoverished New Yorkers responded with regular votes for their jovial Boss, sometimes even with an adulation of him as a kind of Robin Hood. "Well, if Tweed stole," people in the slums would say, he was "good to the poor." [6]

With this vote solidly behind him, Tweed was in a position to make regular levies on businesses ranging from Bowery brothels to Fifth Avenue shops, and to arrange deals with a wide variety of New Yorkers. Going along with the Boss meant rich franchises and contracts, positions of prestige and power, and, above all, security from the hostility of William Tweed. When critics became bothersome in 1870, the Boss easily obtained the signatures of six eminent businessmen to a statement that the city's financial affairs were being administered in "a correct and faithful manner." [7] Among the signers were John Jacob Astor III and Moses Taylor, master of a commercial empire and famous for, of all things, his catlike skill in bookkeeping. Always there were understanding professional men. United States Supreme Court Justice Cardozo, of Holmes-Brandeis-and-Cardozo fame, had to live down the fact that his father was one of Tweed's judges, who sold justice, as New Yorkers used to say, as a grocer sold sugar. In 1870 the *New York Times* hailed the Boss as a "reformer"; the

---

[6] Quoted in James F. Rhodes: *History of the United States* (Macmillan, 1928), VI, 403.

[7] Quoted in Ellis P. Oberholtzer: *History of the United States* (Macmillan, 1917-37), II, 587.

next year the New York *Sun,* which could ooze righteousness on the subject of a red-light district, proposed a monument to William Marcy Tweed.[8] The Tweed-type politics, far from being an ephemeral arrangement between a few adventurers, was a deeply entrenched system, in which the politician, with an appropriate profit for himself, sold the United States to its citizens.

Steadily, ineluctably, such politics went to extremes. In 1867 the Tweed practice was to add a fraudulent thirty-five per cent to contracts; in 1870 the addition was more likely to be eighty-five per cent. The plundering became so bold and so systematic that it amounted to a regular graft of a million dollars a month. The contempt for honesty reached the point where, in an election that worried Tweed, the machine dutifully delivered a majority eight per cent greater than the total number of registered voters. The Boss himself, boasting that his income would soon exceed Vanderbilt's, marrying off his daughter in a carnival of champagne, camellias, and birds' nests, publicly grooming his oafish Mayor of New York for the Presidency of the United States, was taking on an arrogance that made the Best People feel they were reliving one of Nero's more rococo moments.

Confronted with an itemized charge of his maraudings in 1871, Tweed was petulant, almost angry. "What are you going to do about it?" he said.[9]

II

THAT FALL, Samuel Tilden, millionaire, distinguished corporation lawyer, figure in Gramercy Park society, trustee of the New York Medical College, honorary member of the American Board of Foreign Missions, and Fellow in Perpetuity of the Metropolitan Museum of Art, proposed to do something quite definite about it. He strode to the rostrum at Cooper Union, straightened his Prince Albert with an emphatic tug, and declared: "The million

[8] Alexander C. Flick: *Samuel Jones Tilden* (Dodd, Mead, 1939), p. 208; Oberholtzer, II, 588.
[9] Quoted in Gustavus Myers: *The History of Tammany Hall* (Boni & Liveright, 1917), p. 239.

of people who compose our great metropolis have been the subject of a conspiracy the most audacious and most wicked ever known in our free and happy land. . . . It is . . . the foremost duty of every good citizen to join with his fellows in the effort to overthrow this corrupt and degrading tyranny." [1]

In Samuel Tilden the Best People had acquired a reform leader cut from an appropriate pattern. He was no shaggy figure suddenly cast up by the commotion of the times. Tilden started life in a comfortable upstate New York home, where the ancestral pictures on the wall ran back to the Revolution and talk of books and public affairs was common at the dinner table. Much of his fortune came from his work as a corporation lawyer, in which he had built an imposing reputation for legal knowledge and for integrity. With it all went a habit of thought and action which the Best People were sure marked the really solid man. He had, Tilden used to say in his quiet way, "a repugnance for dangerous extremes," and no one ever discovered this grayish-looking man in danger from an extreme.[2]

His clothes were of the finest broadcloth but did not fit too exactly; his home was a mansion but contained no tazzas. He was so deliberate in making all decisions, so the story goes, that he invented the phrase, "See you later," and used it to get more time to consider. Never did Tilden forget the Best People's distinction between the duty of a gentleman and a mawkishness that would tear down the character of the working people. To a ragamuffin girl who came to his door with a story of drunken parents, Tilden was all solicitude and charity; to the new clerk in his office who asked about vacation time, Tilden snapped: "Your vacation will begin at once and continue indefinitely." [3]

For more than four years, Tilden, as chairman of the New York State Democratic Committee, presided over the party of Tweed. He fought the Boss and he was never involved in the thieving, but he did not repudiate Tweed. One must be practical;

---

[1] John Bigelow, ed.: *The Writings and Speeches of Samuel J. Tilden* (Harper, 1885), I, 491.
[2] Flick, p. 526.
[3] Ibid., p. 530.

one must be reasonable; "without . . . concession there can be no common action . . . and . . . without the capability of such action, a man is fit, not for society, not even for a state of nature, but only for absolute solitude." [4] When Tweed went too far and the break came, Tilden, still bristling toward any extreme, crusaded for moderation. The Boss must go, to be replaced by an honest, efficient government, but Tilden would entertain no idea that Tweed was the symbol of a need for venturesome political or economic formulas.

National problems were to be handled in the same hardheaded, respectable way. Rebellion was dead and there was no longer any need for military control of the South. "Domination of . . . a 'negro power' " was without moral or practical justification; a people "inferior in morality and intelligence" should never rule. The reformers were "to prepare" the Irish and the rest of the "masses" for their role in political life. Morality and sound economics required ending governmental favoritism to particular groups of businessmen and stopping governmental encouragement of fly-by-night operations. But anyone who urged legislative aid for lower-income groups forgot the rights of the "industrious millions who stay out of the poorhouses." [5]

The general situation, Tilden said in his most sweeping reform statement, resembled the conditions when Thomas Jefferson became President in 1801. "The demoralizations of war—a spirit of gambling adventure, engendered by false [inflationary] systems of public finance; a grasping centralism, absorbing all functions from the local authorities, and assuming to control the industries of individuals by largesses to favored classes from the public treasury of moneys wrung from the body of the people by taxation—were then, as now, characteristics of the period." The chief difference between 1801 and the Seventies, Tilden went on, lay in the fact that the danger was now greater. "The classes who desire pecuniary profit from existing governmental

[4] Bigelow, I, vii.
[5] Ibid., I, 418–19; Bigelow, ed.: *Letters and Literary Memorials of Samuel J. Tilden* (Harper, 1908), I, 271–324; *New York Times*, May 5, 1875.

abuses . . . the myriads of officeholders . . . the beneficiaries of Congressional grants of the public property or of special franchises . . . the corporations whose hopes and fears are appealed to by the measures of the government . . . the rapacious hordes of carpetbaggers who have plundered the impoverished people of the South . . . have become numerous and powerful beyond any example in our country. . . . For the first time in our national history such classes have become powerful enough to aspire to be in America the ruling classes, as they have been and are in the corrupt societies of the Old World."

In 1801 Jefferson had found the solution. "He stayed the advancing centralism. He restored the rights of the States and the localities. He repressed the meddling of government in the concerns of private business, remitting the management of the industries of the country to the domain of the individual judgment and conscience. He not only brought the administration into conformity with principles which lessen the occasions and the motives for corruption, but he enforced, by precept and by example, purity and disinterestedness in official life. . . ."

"The reformatory work of Mr. Jefferson," said Mr. Tilden, ". . . must now be repeated." [6]

III

As TILDEN gained increasing national attention, a good many eyebrows lifted in the drawing-rooms of the Northern states. "Tilden is a Democrat *and* a gentleman," a Philadelphia matron remarked in amazement.[7] Hadn't the Democrats countenanced Rebellion and wasn't the party now existing off Rum and Romanism? Reform, especially reform that would get rid of rum-soaked Irish political machines, was the function of the Grand Old Party.

The party of the respectables was not entirely failing in its function. Because most of better-educated, upper-income America

[6] Bigelow, ed.: *Letters*, I, 321–3.
[7] Mary Remington, quoted in *Philadelphia Evening Star*, September 2, 1872. Italics in the original.

was Republican, that party produced far more reform leaders of the Tilden type than the Democrats did. For the same reason it produced almost all of the reform leaders who came from a special group within the Best People, the patricians. Like Tilden, the patricians were beyond money worries and were men of education and high social status, but there the identity stopped. If Tilden did not start at the bottom of society, the millionaire and figure in Gramercy Park society had nevertheless climbed a long way from his father's modest farm. The patricians, on the other hand, were born at the top. In consequence, they were inclined to think of themselves as the best of the Best People, and to feel, with particular intensity, that they were displaced persons in the America of Ulysses Grant. The feeling was plain in Henry James, escaping to the consoling aristocracy of England; in Henry Adams, wondering through 505 pages of an autobiography how America could so completely ignore an Adams; in the Dutchess County squires who decided, as Mrs. Franklin Roosevelt later described their attitude, that politics was "pollution," unfit for the "men of the older families." [8] And the feeling was no less plain in the disproportionately large number of patricians who, holding their noses at having anything to do with bawdy politics, plunged into the politics of reform in the early Seventies.

The patrician dissidents, though they generally agreed with the specific items in a reform program like Tilden's, often approached the whole problem of government with a different emphasis. The usual aristocrat of 1870 had little direct connection with industrial America. His money was inherited, and had probably been made in land or in commerce rather than from operations associated closely with the factory system. Like his Tory counterpart in England, the American patrician was inclined to doubt whether anyone involved in grimy industrialism—even when the involvement, like Tilden's, was that of a distinguished corporation lawyer—would ever really want a government free from money-minded self-seeking. To the patrician reformer, the ideal govern-

[8] Quoted in S. J. Woolf: "The New Chapter in Mrs. Roosevelt's Life," *New York Times Sunday Magazine*, December 15, 1946, p. 15.

ment tended to be one by men like himself. They, he was sure, would treat all problems with no urge for self-aggrandizement and would mete out to each group a disinterested justice.

In seeking his ideal government, the patrician reformer frequently gave special emphasis to the establishment of a civil-service system. The "chief evil" of the day, explained Charles Bonaparte, a Marylander who had inherited a lofty family name and more than a million dollars' worth of real estate, was "the alliance between industrialists and a political class which thinks like industrialists." Civil-service reform, Bonaparte argued, would end the ability of politicians to entrench themselves in power and to sell the perquisites of power to men "for whom 'success in life' means 'success in money-making,' 'the pursuit of happiness' . . . the pursuit of wealth." These politicians would be replaced by "gentlemen . . . who need nothing and want nothing from government except the satisfaction of using their talents," or at least by "sober, industrious . . . middle class persons who have taken over . . . the proper standards of conduct." [9] The argument of Bonaparte was common in the literature of patrician reform. The whole civil-service movement, as the patrician Theodore Roosevelt later remarked, was decidedly one "from above downwards." [1]

Reform as an unbusiness, almost antibusiness assertion of aristocracy, reform as the program of a business-minded man like Tilden—the dissidence within the Best People started from different bases and aimed toward different goals, but it joined in a drive against what both groups abhorred as "Grantism."

IV

"AN AGE of reform" was under way, the anti-Grant Lyman Trumbull announced in 1871, and so it was. [2]

[9] Bonaparte to Richard M. Jenks, January 13, 1879, MS., Bonaparte Papers, Library of Congress.
[1] Roosevelt, *Autobiography* (Scribner, 1912), p. 146.
[2] *New York Tribune*, September 16, 1871, quoted in Josephson, p. 153.

19

In New York, Tilden's skilled legal blows were driving Tweed into a whining exile and ultimately to the penitentiary. In Pittsburgh, Chicago, Milwaukee, and Philadelphia, similar leaders were organizing crusades against their own Tweeds. The American Free Trade Association, dedicated specifically to tariff reform but pushing a wide attack on the economic policies of the Grant Administration, was founded in 1868; two years later the organization had so many enthusiastic branches that it was staging frequent public meetings from Maine to Minnesota. When a spokesman of the aristocracy went to Washington shortly after the war to advocate civil-service reform, he found United States Senators who were completely incapable of discussing the merit system except to mumble that it was "something Prussian." [3] By the Seventies, Administration stalwarts were reserving their choicest invective for the "oracular censors so busy of late in brandishing the rod . . . these men who are . . . playing schoolmaster to the Republican party . . . the man milliners, the dilettanti and *carpet knights* of politics." [4] Quite clearly, the leaders from the Best People were acquiring a considerable following, one that seemed to reach deep into the middle classes.

Amid the hubbub, outraged respectability found its own special organ in the weekly *Nation*, edited by an import from British upper-class journalism, Edwin L. Godkin. The United States, Godkin would slash away, was "a gaudy stream of bespangled, belaced, and beruffled barbarians. . . . Who knows how to be rich in America? Plenty of people know how to get money; but . . . to be rich properly is, indeed a fine art. It requires culture, imagination, and character." [5] The *Nation* was particularly effective in turning young sophisticates into young rebels. By the early Seventies a large group in the colleges were taking their attitudes from Godkin's editorials, as their counterparts in the

[3] Rollo Ogden, ed.: *Life and Letters of Edwin Lawrence Godkin* (Macmillan, 1907), II, 40.
[4] Roscoe Conkling, quoted in *New York Tribune*, September 28, 1877. Italics in the original.
[5] Godkin: "Waste," *Nation* (March 8, 1866), II, 302; Ogden, II, 14–15.

1920's were to follow the *American Mercury*, and in the 1930's the *New Republic*.

Both major parties felt the surge of opinion. The grimiest Democratic chieftains had their interest in an agitation that attacked Republican rule; Tilden's star was rising as a gubernatorial and even as a Presidential candidate. Among the Republicans, especially in the border states, an increasing number of responsible leaders were talking of a coalition of Democrats, dissident Republicans, and independents against the regular, pro-Grant Republican organization. As early as 1869 such a coalition in Missouri won a United States Senate seat for the prosperous, highly cultivated Carl Schurz, whose earnestly bespectacled face and polished oratory soon became national symbols of reform. As the Presidential election of 1872 approached, Schurz became the prime mover in arranging a convention that aimed to repeat the Missouri triumph on a national scale.

On May 1, 1872 the trim carriages rolled up to the Exposition Hall in Cincinnati. Everything was calmly efficient; within an hour seven thousand people were comfortably seated. There was, the official proceedings could boast, "no mistaking the material of this impressive assembly. As each State marched in, all eyes turned to fasten on the men who gave weight and character to this historic gathering. The foremost men of every section of the country were seated quietly with the less conspicuous Reformers who came to strike for a purified Government." [6] In one row James Ford Rhodes, an iron magnate who was to retire at the height of his earning power and write a nine-volume history of the United States, sat mulling over a resolution on the tariff question. In another row a Pennsylvanian with a soirée wit was ready to move that "it is inexpedient to nominate a candidate for President who is afflicted with a large circle of relatives." [7] Here and there, moving about with dignity, a "Quadrilateral" of famous

[6] *Proceedings of the Liberal Republican Convention* . . . (Baker & Godwin, New York, 1872), p. 3.
[7] Ibid., p. 16.

newspaper editors—Samuel Bowles of the *Springfield Republican*, Murat Halstead of the *Cincinnati Commercial*, Horace White of the *Chicago Tribune*, and Henry Watterson of the *Louisville Courier-Journal*—talked to this or that delegate, trying to make sure that everyone stayed in line, equally interested in having everyone understand that Messrs. Bowles, Halstead, White, and Watterson were amateurs at this grubby business of politicking. The Reverend Laura de Force Gordon and Susan B. Anthony had been accorded the right to sit on the platform, but when Miss Gordon asked permission to make a speech, Chairman Carl Schurz politely but firmly refused. The men of Cincinnati were to concern themselves with nothing so bizarre as woman suffrage.

The convention bespoke the "conscience" of the nation, Schurz declared in the keynote address, his melodious voice filling every corner of the tastefully decorated auditorium. "We saw jobbery and corruption, stimulated to unusual audacity by the opportunities of a protracted civil war. . . . We saw those in authority with tyrannical insolence thrust the hand of power through the vast machinery of the public service into local and private affairs. . . . We saw men in the highest places of the Republic employ their power and opportunities for selfish advantage. . . . We saw part of our common country, which had been convulsed by a disastrous rebellion, most grievously suffering from the consequences of the civil war; and we saw the haughty spirit of power refusing to lift up those who had gone astray. . . . We observed this, and . . . the question might well have been asked, Have the American people become so utterly indifferent to their true interests, to their national harmony, to the purity of their political life, to the integrity of their free institutions, to the very honor of the American name, that they should permit themselves to be driven like a flock of sheep by those who now assume to lord it over them?" The question, Schurz cried out, had "now found an answer. The virtue, the spirit of independence, the love of liberty, the republican pride of the American people are not dead yet, and do not mean to die, and that answer is given in thunder tones by the Convention of American freemen here assembled." [8]

The details of the answer emerged from the brief platform the convention adopted and from the added meaning given to the phrases by the men associated with them. The Jeffersonian, Democratic anger of a Tilden, the un-Jeffersonian, Republican irritation of a Bonaparte, the less partisan, less ideological concern of a considerable section of upper-strata America, found a common focus in the platform's demand for the restoration of "liberty . . . the largest liberty consistent with public order." Political liberty was to be restored by the election of men who "made public station . . . a post of honor"; the institution of civil-service reforms that would smash "partisan tyranny"; and a return to local self-government, which would "guard the rights of all citizens more securely than any centralized power." The South was to be freed by an immediate removal of all federal troops, by the cancellation of political disabilities imposed on former Confederates, and—implicitly, if not in the words of the platform—by the return of white rule.[9] Economic liberty was to come from governmental policies that did not "unnecessarily interfere with the industry of the people." Governmental expenditures were to be trimmed to a minimum; grants of the nation's resources to favored businessmen, ended.

The convention failed to reach quick agreement on only one aspect of "liberty." If a large number of the delegates had come to Cincinnati seeking tariff reductions, another powerful group was much too Republican to tolerate any such Democratic heresy. After the convention's one period of vociferous debate over a platform item and a fruitless all-night session of the Resolutions Committee, the delegates settled for the weasel that "honest but

[8] Ibid., pp. 9–10.

[9] The platform nominally accepted the enfranchisement of Negroes, a political necessity for a group trying to beat the Radical Republicans in the early Seventies. But the "Address" preceding the specific items of the platform spoke of restoring home government to the South, a sure way to reconstitute white rule, and many liberal leaders like Godkin and Rhodes were expressing increasing doubts about Negro suffrage. Merle Curti: *The Growth of American Thought* (Harper, 1951), p. 487; Rhodes, VI, v–vi.

irreconcilable differences of opinion" made it wise to leave "the discussion of the subject to the people in their Congress Districts, and to the decision of Congress thereon." [1]

Except for its failure to call for tariff reductions, the Cincinnati program resembled closely the policies of the liberal parties in western Europe, and the word "liberal" had appeared increasingly in the language of the anti-Grant movement. Before 1872 the reform-minded Republican groups frequently called themselves "Conservative Republicans" to dissociate their faction from the pro-Grant "Radical Republicans," but by the time of the Cincinnati convention, "liberal" was replacing "conservative" as the distinguishing adjective. Both Tilden and Schurz applied the label to themselves, and Godkin freely interspersed his editorials with it. When the men at Cincinnati named their organization the "Liberal Republican" Party, the word was conspicuously launched into American national politics, and with a readily understandable meaning.

"We want a government," said Carl Schurz, catching the meaning down to its last connotation, "which the best people of this country will be proud of." [2]

V

IN THE White House the affable general munched on the delicacies his rich friends were always sending him, handed out more largesse, jovially brushed aside any of his cronies who showed moments of worry.

"It's a bad business," Senator Morton growled. The reformers were filling the country with "just the kind of talk that gets people all stirred up, and our side is likely to come in suckin' the hind tit."

"Not a chance of it . . ." the President said.

"But a good many people would let those men pull 'em around by the nose and think it was an honor."

[1] *Proceedings*, pp. 18–21.
[2] Ibid., p. 11.

Grant stroked his beard and smiled. The situation reminded him, he told Morton, of his days during the Mexican War, when he went hunting in Texas and the coyotes set up a frightful din. "My friend asked me how many I thought there were. . . . I wasn't going to show how green I was, so I took the lowest number there could possibly be and cut it in half. I said, 'Oh, about twenty,' not much interested, like I knew all about coyotes. . . ."

The President stopped to chuckle. "Pretty soon we topped a rise and saw the beasts. . . . There were just two of them . . . sitting back on their haunches with their heads together, and making all that racket." [3]

Ulysses Grant knew his America. The genuine liberal reformers proved so few in numbers and so unrepresentative of the times that they failed to keep control of their own convention. The liberal leaders wanted a ticket consisting of the patrician reformer Charles Francis Adams, and Lyman Trumbull, the Illinois Senator who had broken with the regular Republican organization and was proving himself a rugged dissenter. While Schurz was telling the convention of the importance of nominating candidates of "superior intelligence, coupled with superior virtue," David Davis, a millionaire land speculator with White House ambitions, sat in a near-by hotel suite, seeing to it that no man with convention credentials went thirsty and instructing the five hundred or so "delegates" that he had shipped in from Illinois and the South.[4] The Quadrilateral managed to smash the Davis candidacy with a carefully planned editorial barrage, but the troubles of the liberal leaders were just beginning. Late on the night before the balloting for candidates, a Missouri reformer went hurrying to the hotel where Schurz and his editor-allies were staying. He brought ominous news. B. Gratz Brown and Francis Blair, two Missouri politicians of the Davis type, had suddenly showed up in Cincinnati, "fit for stratagems and spoils." [5]

The strategy had two major motives. Brown and Blair, leery of

[3] Helen Todd: *A Man Named Grant* (Houghton Mifflin, Boston, 1940), p. 447.
[4] *Proceedings*, p. 12.
[5] Quoted in Oberholtzer, III, 24.

Schurz's mounting power in Missouri politics, did not want him to return home the king-maker of the Cincinnati convention. They were also anxious to nominate a Republican who would attract an enthusiastic Democratic following and they were sure that Schurz's candidate, a Beacon Street Adams, would outrage the Irish Democratic strongholds and arouse little enthusiasm in the West. All during the night before the balloting and the next morning, Brown and Blair plotted furiously, making deals with the Davis group, maneuvering pro-Adams men off delegations, luring reformers with the politician's siren call that an Adams-Trumbull ticket could not be a winner. At the crucial moment in the voting, a spontaneous demonstration, blueprinted the night before, turned the convention into a churning, bellowing mob. When the day was over, the Vice-Presidential candidate was none other than B. Gratz Brown, and the ticket was headed by Horace Greeley, the man the cliques of politicians thought could win, who also happened to believe civil-service examinations silly, had long since made plain that any tariff reduction would be a major sin, and had adopted so many isms, ranging from Fourier-ism to a crusade against the evils of drinking tea, that millions of Americans who considered themselves respectable dismissed Greeley as a disreputable crackpot.

That night Schurz and his friends sat staring at each other, tears in their eyes, the long silences broken by the mournful lieder Schurz played on the piano. In New York, Godkin thrashed about bitterly in "this wretched mess." [6] When the Democratic convention joined in nominating Greeley, Tilden, still a loyal Democrat as well as a liberal, accepted the party decision, but with a dead heart; during the campaign he did noticeably little campaigning. Throughout the nation, Henry Adams wrote, the young men of wealth and talent were folding their tents and stealing silently away.[7]

The country, with a passing snicker, kept right on with the

---

[6] Godkin to Schurz, May 19, 1872, in Frederic Bancroft, ed.: *Speeches, Correspondence, and Political Papers of Carl Schurz* (Putnam, 1913), II, 376.
[7] Paraphrased in Josephson, pp. 163-4.

main business at hand. "Leading capitalists," United States Senator John Sherman wrote his brother, were showing "an elevation,
a scope" to their ideas, "far higher than anything ever undertaken in this country before. They talk of millions as confidently
as formerly of thousands." [8] The ideas of little capitalists were no
less expansive, and in the early Seventies, as in the late Sixties,
they spoke confidently of a better job in the city, a white collar
in place of workmen's clothes, a high-school diploma for the son,
a farm or business of their own, a bigger farm or a bigger business
of their own. The statistics of stores and factories being started
and of the money invested in other people's enterprises sky-
rocketed. Cocky farmers clamored for mortgages to buy more
land and more machines until the big certificates with the gilt
edge and the green ink were almost as much a part of farm life
as a washtub. Month after month, in rapidly mounting numbers,
despite Indians, droughts, and locusts, the covered wagons rolled
west, filled with the exultant singing of

> *Come along, come along, make no delay,*
> *Come from every nation, come from every way;*
> *Our lands are broad enough, don't be alarmed,*
> *For Uncle Sam is rich enough to give us all a farm.*[9]

When election day arrived, the nation sent Ulysses Grant back to
the White House by a landslide majority—a majority so decisive
that it was clearly a verdict against anti-Grantism in any form.[1]

"All hail, liberty!" the generation shouted. "All hail, freedom!
. . . All hail freedom general as the air we breathe!" [2] Who but
professional scolders found liberty wanting when the party ruled
that had struck the shackles from four million slaves? Who but

---

[8] Quoted in Nevins, p. 32.

[9] Oberholtzer, I, 277 n.

[1] Some students of the election have argued that a different candidate,
particularly one who stood more consistently for the liberal program, would
have beaten Grant or at least not lost so badly. The other interpretation,
with which I agree, is argued in Earle D. Ross: *The Liberal Republican
Movement* (Holt, 1919), pp. 190–1.

[2] Quoted in Charles A. and Mary R. Beard: *The Rise of American
Civilization* (Macmillan, 1930), II, 35.

rich men and aristocrats forgot that the most exciting part of freedom was the opportunity to get ahead and to get ahead quickly? Who but man-milliners worried about today at all when tomorrow, a gleaming, crimson-shot tomorrow, was close at hand? And all across the careering North and West, the sweat on the back of the poorest farmer, the crick in the arm of the lowliest clerk, brought the exhilarating feel of that better, always better, spectacularly better tomorrow.

CHAPTER III

From the Bottom Up

Early on a September afternoon, 1873, a newsboy yelled an extra about the failure of Jay Cooke's bank, and a policeman promptly arrested the boy. Jay Cooke was one of the most successful of all the new successes, the renowned financier of the war against Rebellion, a man who could sit in his seventy-two-room mansion and casually discuss with "Ulysses" the way to raise children; businesses run by Jay Cookes simply did not close their doors. With the confirmation of the news and the rapid spread of bank failures, people still consoled one another that this was only a panic. Bustling America, guided by tough-minded businessmen, was much too strong to be laid low very long. A few stupefying weeks, banks and businesses going down like dominoes, and the word "panic" lost its power to console. The United States had to face the depression of 1873.

The country had known hard times before, but only when it was overwhelmingly agricultural. Now it learned how much more serious depression could be in a rapidly industrializing society. The six years of economic distress threw a garish light on the whole structure of opportunity. Military control was removed from the South during the depression, but the former Confederacy returned to a nation almost as frustrated by hard times as the South had been by defeat. Millions of industrial workers, confident of a golden future a short while ago, were unemployed or desperately worried about holding their jobs. Many a small investor, once so sure of a brownstone and a carriage, found his life's savings wiped out overnight. Farmers' gilt-edged mortgage certificates turned from bright symbols of hope to nagging reminders of overconfidence. If the hard times boomed migration westward, the new pioneers passed covered wagons dragging east like whipped animals, their covers chalked with "Going back to our wife's folks" or "In God we trusted, in Kansas we busted." [1]

No less disturbing were the large-scale corporations that rose above the shambles of hard times. The industrialization of the United States, like industrialization in all countries, had been marked by the steady combination of businesses into bigger units, but the pressure of hard times made businesses more willing to sell out and less able to resist the consolidators. Before the crash came, the people of Ohio had begun hearing about the son of an itinerant medicine-seller who was gathering into his Standard Oil Company one after another of the state's oil firms. During the depression John D. Rockefeller's combine spread far outside Ohio. By the end of the hard times, the Standard Oil Company had achieved a substantial monopoly of oil refining in the United States, was reaching out for a monopoly over distribution, and was being taken as a model by ambitious men in every basic industry. The spindly, mild-mannered Rockefeller, who rarely missed a week teaching his Baptist Sunday-school class, was also well on his way to being one of the most feared and hated men in American history. In some respects Rockefeller was a good deal more ethical than the usual businessman of his day. He never watered his stock, he kept the quality of his product high, he treated his employees comparatively well. But Rockefeller had built the first American trust, and trusts, a good many of his countrymen were sure, meant a severe squeezing of opportunity for the small entrepreneur.

[1] Quoted in Allan Nevins: *The Emergence of Modern America* (Macmillan, 1927), p. 160.

Still more disturbing, the depression of 1873 gave the United States its first taste of widespread violence caused by economic hardship. At the blackest period of the depression the country was swarming with "tramps," who were usually factory or farm hands looking vainly for a livelihood and drifting into gang life. Here and there bands of these men allied with professional criminals, drinking, stealing, raping, and murdering. In some New England towns, people living on the outskirts abandoned their homes in terror, while in Jacksonville, Illinois, a gang temporarily took over the whole community.

No large city entirely escaped bitter strikes, and in the summer of 1877 the first nation-wide strike produced the first labor rioting that reached into many states. The trouble started when the principal railroads, refusing to decrease high dividends on watered stocks, decreed a ten per cent cut in wages. First on the Baltimore & Ohio lines in West Virginia, then north and west all the way to Canada and California, the workers hit back. Their violent strikes provoked the use of troops by business-minded governments, and the use of troops provoked more violence.

The turbulence reached a climax in Pittsburgh, where 650 soldiers came into collision with a mob of strikers, strike sympathizers, and drifters who were ready for anything that offered a change from their squalid life. Some twenty-five people were killed and many more wounded before the troops took refuge in a roundhouse, and then the mob set fire to the roundhouse by pushing cars of flaming coke against it. Disorder ricocheted across the city. Barrels of liquor were tapped and drunk on the spot; stores were broken into for food, clothing, and furniture; long lines of freight and passenger cars were looted and set on fire. The incendiarism spread until the four-story Union Depot, two thousand cars, the railroad machine shops, a grain elevator, and two roundhouses with 125 locomotives had been destroyed. Two days later the city awoke to its hangover of ashes and caskets. Railroad executives and storekeepers wrathfully estimated their losses at five to ten millions; railroad workers sullenly went back

31

to work with the wage cut intact. The nation, uneasy and irritated, wondered what America was coming to.[2]

In San Francisco a pale, tense young man wrote some more bitter words on his yellow foolscap. For Henry George, the depression was the last straw. As a boy he had listened to Uncle Thomas proclaim that any lad who worked hard was sure to get ahead swiftly in America. From his thirteenth year George had worked hard, as a delivery-boy, seaman, typesetter, gold prospector, clerk, salesman, and editor, only to find himself still an impoverished nobody. In the late Sixties he managed to acquire some standing as a newspaperman and was sent to New York to arrange telegraphic news for a struggling San Francisco paper; the near-monopolistic Associated Press saw to it that he went home once more a failure. A few years later the depression of 1873 engulfed San Francisco, and Henry George had enough. Far into the night, in his rugless, ill-heated room, he piled up the sheets of foolscap, pounding into them the angry eloquence of *Progress and Poverty*.

"The present century," the book began, "has been marked by a prodigious increase in wealth-producing power. . . . It was natural to expect, and it was expected, that labor-saving inventions would lighten the toil and improve the condition of the laborer; that the enormous increase in the power of producing wealth would make real poverty a thing of the past." But "disappointment has followed disappointment. . . . We plow new fields, we open new mines, we found new cities; we drive back the Indian and exterminate the buffalo; we girdle the land with iron roads and lace the air with telegraph wires; we add knowledge to knowledge, and utilize invention after invention; we build schools and endow colleges; yet it becomes no easier for the masses of our people to make a living. On the contrary, it is

[2] The common uneasiness was caught by the historian James Ford Rhodes, who lived through the violence. It "seemed to threaten the chief strongholds of society," Rhodes wrote, "and came like a thunderbolt . . . startling us rudely. For we had hugged the delusion that such social uprisings belonged to Europe and had no reason of being in a free republic where there was plenty of room and an equal chance for all." *History of the United States* (Macmillan, 1928), VIII, 46.

becoming harder. The wealthy class is becoming more wealthy; but the poorer class is becoming more dependent. The gulf between the employed and the employer is growing wider; social contrasts are becoming sharper; as liveried carriages appear, so do barefooted children." [3]

This situation was made worse by depression, George went on, but hard times were not the basic explanation. The United States had been a wondrous land of opportunity only because of its vast area of public lands. "The child of the people, as he grows to manhood in Europe, finds all the best seats at the banquet of life marked 'taken,' and must struggle with his fellows for the crumbs that fall, without one chance in a thousand of forcing or sneaking his way to a seat. In America, whatever his condition, there has always been the consciousness that the public domain lay behind him; and the knowledge of this fact, acting and reacting, has penetrated our whole national life. . . . The general intelligence, the general comfort, the active invention, the power of adaptation and assimilation, the free, independent spirit, the energy and hopefulness that have marked our people, are not causes, but results—they have sprung from unfenced land. This public domain has given a consciousness of freedom even to the dweller in crowded cities, and has been a well-spring of hope even to those who have never thought of taking refuge upon it." But now the United States had used up much of its public domain, either by settlement or by lavishing it on railroads and speculators. With industrialization helping to speed up the concentration of wealth and power, the New World was beginning to repeat the Old World's dismal story. It was re-enacting the European experience not only, as Samuel Tilden had said, by creating a corrupt ruling class; it was headed toward rigid economic and social stratification and a consequent narrowing of opportunity for the masses. [4]

Progress and Poverty, published in 1879, was not out a year before its author was a national figure. Across the country, farmers squinted over the book's fine print. "Tens of thousands of indus-

[3] Henry George: *Progress and Poverty* (Modern Library, 1929), pp. 3, 5, 392–3.
[4] Ibid., pp. 390–4, 550–2.

trial laborers," a well-informed observer noted, "have read *Progress and Poverty* who never before looked between the covers of an economics book." [5] Troubled Americans who were neither factory hands nor farmers helped make *Progress and Poverty* one of the ten or so most widely selling non-fiction works in the history of the United States. The young man who had wanted to get ahead so fervently and had been stopped so often, with his moving arraignment of his times, his warning that America was moving down the weary road of Europe, his summons to re-create opportunity, had caught the mood with which thousands of Americans left the depression of 1873.

II

THE EIGHTIES lumbered ahead, now prosperous, now dragging through months of economic upset. In good years and in bad ones, sometimes even more so during the stretches of general prosperity, the sense of frustrated opportunity continued to gnaw at large numbers of Americans.

During the Eighties huge corporations kept rising like so many portents of a Europeanized future. In the decade after the depression more than five thousand firms were wrought into giant combines, none of which had a capitalization under fifty million dollars and virtually all of which were pushing toward a monopoly in their fields. The trend was the same in every region. In the West the son of the farmer's hero, Abraham Lincoln, played his part in creating utility trusts, while in the South the grandson of that scourge of capitalism, John Calhoun, consolidated a group of railroads into the Richmond Terminal Company. At the end of the decade United States Senator John Sherman, whose basic friendliness to business could not be questioned, spoke the worry of a good many of his countrymen. "If we are unable or unwilling [to take action against the trusts]," Sherman

[5] Richard T. Ely, quoted in Merle Curti: *The Growth of American Thought* (Harper, 1951), p. 616.

told the Senate, "there will soon be a trust for every production and a master to fix the price for every necessity of life." [6]

For most industrial workers of the Eighties, real wages were rising with aggravating slowness, and each year extremes of wealth jutted out more irritatingly. A titan like Marshall Field made five hundred to seven hundred dollars an hour; his non-executive employees were paid twelve dollars a week or less, for a fifty-nine-hour week. Quickly made fortunes were lavished with infuriating conspicuousness—on a mansion in red, yellow, and black bricks, the purchase of a titled husband for the daughter, banquets where the cigarettes were wrapped in hundred-dollar bills or a poodle was draped with a fifteen-thousand-dollar collar. Just around the corner, slums were sprawling out, filthy, heatless, so dark their corners could not be photographed until flashlight photography was invented in 1887.[7]

Along with extremes of wealth came walls of impersonality. By the Eighties a large percentage of factory hands worked in big plants, where the boss was as remote as any feudal lord had ever been from his serfs. The dry-goods shop was becoming the department store, and in department stores the clerk did not first-name the boss or presume to take his daughter to church. Without the familiar relations, callousness was easy, almost inevitable. Failure to climb out of the ranks, sinking into dire want or sickness, brought only harsh unconcern. An inventor remarked that he could sell a time-saving device in twenty places and a life-saving invention scarcely at all. Doctors thought nothing of charging two dollars a visit to workingmen whose wages were a dollar and a half a day. The first move to protect children from the vice and disease of the slums came from the president of New York's Society for the Prevention of Cruelty to Animals, who, as a kind of afterthought, founded the Society for the Prevention of Cruelty to Children.[8] "Land of opportunity, you say," a Chicago

[6] Quoted in Thomas C. Cochran and William Miller: *The Age of Enterprise* (Macmillan, 1943), p. 171.

[7] Review of a Jacob A. Riis photographic exhibit, *Architectural Forum* (July 1947), LXXXVII, 132.

[8] Harold U. Faulkner: *The Quest for Social Justice* (Macmillan, 1930), p. 110; Senate Committee on Education and Labor, 48th Cong., 2nd Sess.:

worker snarled at a spread-eagle speaker. "You know damn well my children will be where I am—that is, if I can keep them out of the gutter." [9]

The newest immigrants, the millions pouring into the United States from southern and eastern Europe, were finding that America was no longer in a come-one, come-all mood. Many of the older settlers, feeling crowded and cornered, had little welcome for any newcomer, and every prejudice in the American collection was roused by immigrants who were predominantly impoverished and unskilled, short and dark in appearance, Catholic or Jewish in religion. Rapidly the national speech was acquiring phrases that carried as much sneer and hiss as any in the language —"wop" and "dago" for the Italian, "bohunk" for the Hungarian, "grease-ball" for the Greek, and "kike" for the Jew.[1]

A member of a Congressional committee, questioning a railroad-construction boss in 1890, asked: "You don't call . . . an Italian a white man?"

The construction boss was surprised that a United States Congressman should ask so silly a question. "No, Sir," the construction boss said. "An Italian is a Dago." [2]

Organized anti-Catholicism, dormant since the Know-Nothing movement of the 1850's, flared up again in the form of the American Protective Association; and anti-Semitism, which had scarcely appeared previously, started on its way to becoming a virulent national disease. Lincoln Steffens never forgot his introduction to what opportunity could mean in the new immigrant slums. A Russian-Jewish woman pulled him up the tenement stairs to point out how her three little girls were watching a prostitute across

---

Report . . . upon the Relations between Labor and Capital (1885), III, 451, 452; William J. Shultz: *The Humane Movement in the United States,* in *Columbia University Studies in History, Economics and Public Law* (1924), CXIII, 11, 162.

[9] *Chicago Evening Post,* August 21, 1887.

[1] H. L. Mencken: *The American Language, Supplement I* (Knopf, 1945), pp. 601–2, 605–6, 610, 613–17.

[2] Quoted in John W. Higham: "European Immigration in American Patriotic Thought, 1885–1925," MS., University of Wisconsin Library, p. 29.

the airway serve a customer. "*Da se'en Sie,* there they are watching, always they watch. They count the men who come of a night. . . . My oldest girl says she will go into that business when she grows up; she says it's a good business . . . and you can dress and eat and live." [3]

For all the discontented of the cities, the frontier was losing much of its ability to keep hopes high. It was not simply that most of the best acres had passed into private hands; Americans were beginning to realize that the land might be cheap or even free, but transporting yourself and the family to the homestead, paying necessary fees, buying essential tools, and sustaining a wife and children during a season or two of sodbusting cost a sum beyond the resources of the usual urban employee. One Fall River worker, asked why he did not go west, expressed the new attitude toward homesteading with savage simplicity. "Well," he said, "I never saw over a $20 bill. . . . If some one would give me $1,500 I will go." [4]

Out among those who had managed to go, in all agricultural areas of the nation, times were hard and growing harder. For the farmer, the Eighties differed from the unbroken depression years of the Seventies only in leaving him worse off economically. The price of manufactured articles the farmer had to buy and the cost of shipping his crop were sky-high; the amount he received for his products was plummeting down; and the policies of a creditor-minded Washington made it more and more difficult for him to escape from his mortgages. Often the farmer lost money by shipping and selling, and for want of a profitable market, apples lay under the trees, hayfields went uncut to be burned over the next spring, milk was fed to the hogs, corn or cotton was used for fuel in place of coal. "Many a time," Vernon Parrington remembered from his boyhood near Pumpkin Ridge, Kansas, "have I warmed myself by the kitchen stove in which ears were burning briskly, popping and crackling in the jolliest fashion. And if while we sat around such a fire watching the year's crop go

[3] *Autobiography of Lincoln Steffens* (Harcourt, Brace, 1931), p. 245.
[4] Quoted in Senate Committee on Education and Labor: *Report . . . upon the Relations between Labor and Capital,* III, 453.

up the chimney, the talk sometimes became bitter . . . who will wonder?" [5]

In both the South and the Midwest, special circumstances increased the difficulties of the farmer. By clinging to the one-crop system, Southerners were making themselves prisoners of the price of cotton. Midwesterners were discovering that methods of agriculture learned in the damp Eastern areas were unsuited to the dry acres of the Great Plains. Worse yet, the reckless destruction of the forests brought a succession of droughts and floods, and periodically the Midwest was ravaged by chinchbugs, corn borers, boll weevils, or, most destructive of all, plagues of grasshoppers. The bugs swirled down in pelting hordes, ruining the heads of grain, chirping and flaring around the helpless farmers, covering everything in sight with brown disaster.

Noneconomic facts thickened the pall over rural America. As urbanization accelerated and the farm regions sank more deeply in debt, the whole prestige of agricultural life skidded down. Once the tiller of the soil, his head raised high in prickly independence, had been the very symbol of the American way. Now the sneer word "hayseed" was coming into common usage and farmers had to watch their own sons and daughters maneuvering to be off to the city. [6]

Life in the less settled regions of the West brought additional aggravations. Many a pioneer had sung his way to a homestead only to settle into an existence of dreary grubbing. Log-cabin living, a long buckboard ride from the nearest town, meant a nagging loneliness and lack of comforts. Not one farmer in three hundred could get a daily newspaper, and families that lived five miles from the village post office were lucky to receive mail once a week. Women especially paid the price of isolation; for want of the simplest medical care, thousands died in childbirth or lost their babies in infancy. Hamlin Garland, a product of the North Dakota frontier, set out to describe the life of backcountry

[5] Parrington: "Autobiography," MS., in the possession of Mrs. Parrington, p. 32.
[6] Mencken, p. 328.

women but confessed, when his book was done, that he had stopped far short of the truth. "Even my youthful zeal," Garland wrote, "faltered in the midst of a revelation of the lives led by the women. . . . Before the tragic futility of their suffering, my pen refused to shed its ink." [7]

In Kansas, a handsome Irish woman, grown sad-eyed watching the blighting of dreams, caught the mounting national restlessness in five volcanic words. What was needed, said Mrs. Mary Ellen Lease, was to raise "less corn and more HELL." [8]

III

THE HELL was raised. The immediate result of the discontent was an enormous increase in the support for liberalism. Reformers of the 1872 type, coming up out of their storm cellars after the Greeley debacle, found a far more receptive audience for their assaults on Grantism. By the Eighties, liberal triumphs were becoming common on the municipal, state, and federal levels. In 1885 and again in 1893, the White House itself was taken over by Grover Cleveland, a liberal's liberal complete with an abhorrence of corruption and a zeal for local rule, decreased tariffs, governmental economy, and economic liberty.

Yet all the while that lower-income discontent was strengthening liberalism against Grantism, more and more of the discontented were thinking along unliberal lines. Theoretically, liberalism of that day offered a government that benefited no one group of its citizens more than another. An honest, efficient government, holding its activities to a policing minimum, was to leave all citizens free and equal in their drive to get ahead. But liberal politicos had to function amid endless pressures, agrarian, laborite, and capitalist, and the pressure from large-scale business interests was easily the most potent. The liberals, moreover, were predis-

[7] Garland: *A Son of the Middle Border* (Macmillan, 1919), p. 416.

[8] Quoted in Solon J. Buck: *The Agrarian Crusade* (Yale University Press, 1920), p. 135.

posed by the very origins of their doctrine toward the more successful groups in society. As a result of these factors, liberalism became increasingly a pro-corporation credo.

Liberal-minded jurists might applaud local rule and uphold it rigidly when the federal regulation of business was proposed; they reacted differently when a local legislature passed legislation regulating the activities of corporations. President Cleveland might be all for keeping the government out of economic life, and he did keep it out so far as most legislation benefiting low-income groups was concerned. He also heartily approved maintaining a gold standard, which favored creditors over debtors, he assumed a tax system that kept the burden off corporations, and he used federal troops to help the Pullman Company defeat a strike of its pitifully squeezed workers. It was all honest enough; no one would have thought of offering Grover Cleveland a satchelful of bribe money. The more important point was that a good many Americans were wondering whether honesty was enough. "Cleveland might be honest," one agrarian leader snapped, "but so were the mothers who threw their children in the Ganges." [9]

Even if liberalism had been able to preserve an exact governmental impartiality toward all groups, it could hardly have satisfied the new discontent. A twelve-dollar-a-week worker, dependent on a twelve-million-dollar corporation for his livelihood, or a small farmer, desperate about a mortgage owed to a J. P. Morgan bank, was hardly interested in having an impartial government. He wanted a government that would be on his side, helping him fight what seemed to him unfair and overwhelming odds. In 1887 Congress appropriated ten thousand dollars to aid drought sufferers in buying new grain seed, and Cleveland vetoed the item with a declaration that "though the people support the Government the Government should not support the people." [1] It was a

[9] William Jennings Bryan, quoted in Wilfred E. Binkley: *American Political Parties* (Knopf, 1943), p. 318.

[1] Allan Nevins: *Grover Cleveland* (Dodd, Mead, 1932), p. 332. (Italicized in Nevins.) It is interesting to note that President Herbert Hoover, a latter-day "liberal," quoted Cleveland's message in vetoing direct federal funds for relief. Ibid., pp. 331–2.

perfect statement of liberal doctrine, and a perfect illustration why liberalism seemed irrelevant or downright evil to thousands who were quite sure that, even if the government should not support them, it should certainly help them support themselves.

With a curse for Grover Cleveland, farmers and workingmen were hurrying into organizations that spoke neither the tone nor the program of liberalism. Three "Farmers' Alliances"—a Western and a Southern organization and a separate Negro Alliance in the South—were growing at a phenomenal rate, and taking on an emotional intensity that recalled the days of the crusade against slavery. The agrarian bitterness came closest to a call for armed revolution in the South, where the farmers' poverty was deepest and where rule by manufacturers and bankers smacked of another Yankee invasion. The official history of the Southern Alliance had the title: *The Impending Revolution*, and the Arkansas author of the book explained: "The spirit of rebellion against the many evils is growing. . . . Thousands of men who have already lost all hope of a peaceable solution of the great question of human rights are calmly waiting the issue." [2]

A wide variety of unliberal movements churned the lower-income districts of the cities. The Eighties had scarcely begun when Terence Powderly, a deaconish machinist who turned to labor organizing only after he was blacklisted during the depression of 1873, found himself the head of half a million belligerent "Knights of Labor." By 1885 the railroad workers in the Knights were powerful enough to force representatives of the mighty Jay Gould to sit down at the same table and discuss a strike settlement, the first such demonstration of union power in American history. When the Knights won something that could be called a victory, their membership leaped another hundred thousand within a few months and encouraged union activity throughout the country.

Urban agitations that had been present even in the halcyon late Sixties took on added impetus—especially the drive for an eight-hour day and the "Greenback–Labor" demand to break the

[2] Quoted in C. Vann Woodward: *Tom Watson* (Macmillan, 1938), p. 143.

control of banks over the currency. A new agitation, the single-tax movement, was having a pervasive effect. To remedy the curse of poverty amid progress, Henry George's book had called for a "single tax" on the increase in the value of land as communities grew up around it. This increase, George argued, was totally unearned; taxing it one hundred per cent would smash concentrated wealth and spread the national wealth around in a way that would reopen opportunity. Few farmers could be attracted by a program of heavy land taxes, but for the urban discontented here was a plan of alluring simplicity. "No man," the official Knights of Labor organ testified in 1887, "has exercised so great an influence upon the labor movement of to-day as Henry George." [3]

The immigrant slums were finding their single-taxism in the old-country doctrines of anarchism and socialism. Anarchism looked as if it might rival the European successes of the "Black International" until a bomb went off during an eight-hour demonstration in 1886 and killed the movement by associating it with black-bearded horror. Socialism showed no such signs of demise. In the years immediately after the Civil War, most of the socialists had been German-born intellectuals, whose knowledge of non-Germans was small and whose understanding of the American workingman was even smaller. But in the late Eighties socialism found a far more effective leadership in Daniel De Leon, an immigrant from the West Indies. De Leon's restless mind frequently ran to enervating dialectics, but he just as often talked a doctrine that had genuine meaning in the sweatshops and he always conveyed some of his own fierce sense of urgency. Before the Eighties were done, socialism, in a Utopian form, was even trickling through to the middle classes. A raft of novels advocating some variety of Utopian socialism appeared, and in 1888 one of these novels, Edward Bellamy's *Looking Backward*, swept together the collectivist yearnings into a far from negligible movement. Within two years after the book's publication, *Looking Backward* was selling at the rate of ten thousand copies a week, a Bellamyite

[3] *Knights of Labor*, January 15, 1887, quoted in Chester M. Destler: *American Radicalism, 1865–1901* (Collegiate Press, Menasha, Wis., 1946), p. 13.

journal was flourishing, and one hundred and fifty ardent Bellamy clubs were gathering in professors, ministers, and tradesmen as well as farmers and industrial workers.

With dissidence permeating both the urban and rural regions, reformers naturally dreamed of a national union of the discontented that would mean sure political power. There were certainly plenty of encouraging facts. Whatever their doctrinal differences, the Farmers' Alliances, Knights of Labor, socialists, single-taxers, even the anarchists, were united by a fear of big business and by an impatience with liberalism's refusal to sanction governmental action in behalf of the poor. Two local elections of the Eighties sent a special thrill of hope through the coalitionists. In 1886, single-taxers, socialists, union members, and thousands of citizens who were just plain irritated supported Henry George with such fervor that he barely missed winning the mayorship of New York; a rising young liberal named Theodore Roosevelt ran third.[4] Then, in the state and national elections of 1890, candidates backed by the Alliances scored a series of striking victories in the South and West. Five United States Senators, six Governors, and forty-six Congressmen championing bold new economic legislation, a single-taxer almost mayor of the nation's metropolis— weren't these facts sure harbingers of a new national party of urban and rural discontent, which would take power as the coalition Republican Party had triumphed in 1860? With the approach of the Presidential election of 1892, more than thirteen hundred delegates converged on Omaha to get under way just such a coalition, the "People's" or "Populist" Party.

IV

HOUR AFTER hour anger swept through the cavernous old Coliseum Building. July 1892 brought as wilting a heat as Omaha had

[4] There is considerable evidence that George was actually counted out. John R. Commons *et al.: History of Labour in the United States* (Macmillan, 1918–35), II, 453; Anna De Mille: *Henry George* (University of North Carolina Press, 1950), p. 152.

ever known, the city frolicked in a Fourth-of-July mood, near-by saloons had laid in an extra supply of liquor. But nothing could distract the delegates from their rounds of furious speeches, wild applause, and fierce resolutions. From all parts of the United States, some bumping along hundreds of miles in buckboards, others using their last folding money for train fare, the Populists had gathered to launch an all-out assault on the political and economic masters of America. They did it with the dedicated wrath of a camp meeting warring on the Devil himself.

Any delegate who strayed from the mood of the convention was promptly hurled back on a wave of emotion. Midway in the proceedings a member of the Resolutions Committee, pointing out that the Union Pacific had not provided the reduced rates usually granted for convention delegates, proposed that the railroad should be asked to rectify this "oversight." Instantly Marion Cannon, of California, was on his feet, his face livid. An oversight? Ask a corporation to be fair? Cannon shouted. The "customary courtesy was denied deliberately and with insolence. I do not want this Convention . . . to go back to the railroad company, hat in hand, and ask for any privileges whatever. The Democrats and Republicans secured half-fare, but we—not connected with railroads, but producers of the earth—have been refused equal terms." The delegates thundered approval as Cannon concluded: "We can stand the refusal." [5]

On the afternoon of July 4, a plump, genial Irishman with a reputation for quips and politicking mounted the rostrum and this day he sounded like a prophet out of the Old Testament. "We meet in the midst of a nation brought to the verge of moral, political, and material ruin," Ignatius Donnelly cried. ". . . Corruption dominates the ballot-box, the Legislatures, the Congress, and touches even the ermine of the bench. . . . Our homes [are] covered with mortgages . . . the land [is] concentrating in the hands of the capitalists. The urban workmen are denied the rights

[5] E. A. Allen: *The Life and Public Services of James Baird Weaver . . . and . . . of James G. Field . . . [with] an account of the first convention of the People's Party at Omaha* (People's Party Publishing Co., 1892), pp. 91-2.

44

of organization for self protection; imported, pauperized labor beats down their wages; a hireling standing army, unrecognized by our laws, is established to shoot them down, and they are rapidly degenerating into European conditions. A vast conspiracy against mankind has been organized. . . . If not met and overthrown at once it forebodes terrible social convulsions . . . or the establishment of an absolute despotism." [6]

This was the kind of language the delegates wanted to hear. When the specific proposals of the platform continued in the same tone, the convention exploded into a demonstration unprecedented in all the turbulent history of American political gatherings. With the last thrust at "tyranny and oppression," the delegates rose in a cheering, stomping, marching mass. Hats, coats, papers, fans, umbrellas went up in the air, leaders were bounced from shoulder to shoulder, every state tried to outdo the next in noise and movement. Texans whooped and beat on coffee cans. Nebraskans chanted: "What is home without a mortgage? Don't all speak at once." New Yorkers hoisted a beaming old man to the platform, thrust a baton in his hand, yelled wildly while he pretended to lead the musicians in hymns and marching songs. "Good-Bye, My Party, Good-Bye," the delegates sang. Then, to the tune of "Save a Poor Sinner, Like Me," they shouted how "the railroads and old party bosses together did sweetly agree" to deceive and exploit "a hayseed like me." And, breaking through the bedlam time and again, came the "People's Hymn," sung to the consecrated music of the "Battle Hymn of the Republic":

They have stolen our money, have ravished our homes;
With the plunder erected to Mammon a throne;
They have fashioned a god, like the Hebrews of old,
Then bid us bow down to their image of gold.[7]

---

[6] Ibid., pp. 96–7. The word "touching," an obvious misprint, has been changed to "touches."

[7] Ibid., pp. 100–2; Frank B. Tracy: "Menacing Socialism in the United States," *Forum* (May 1893), XV, 332–4; Mason A. Green: "Edward Bellamy," MS., Harvard University Library, Chap. xv; *Omaha Bee*, July 5–7, 1892.

Edwin Godkin read the reports from Omaha and erupted in an editorial that was all anger and foreboding. Carl Schurz, proclaiming the Republic near "the precipice," poured out a thirty-four-page letter pleading for Cleveland's re-election. Theodore Roosevelt seized every opportunity to denounce the "wild Farmers' Alliance cranks." [8] In free-trade clubs, in universities, at soirées, wherever liberals gathered, the news from Omaha left men furious and frightened. Here was a drastically, alarmingly different reformism, bursting up from the bottom.

The leaders at Omaha made it emphatically plain that they intended to base their movement on the groups which the Best People were sure represented the worst people. Populism, almost the first words of the Omaha platform declared, was to be a "permanent and perpetual . . . union of the labor forces of the United States. . . . The interests of rural and civic [urban] labor are the same; their enemies are identical." Since the convention was predominantly agrarian, Populist leaders were careful to emphasize their interest in labor's problems, and resolutions adopted by the convention supported the most important labor demands of the day. The delegates condemned "the fallacy of protecting American labor under the present system, which opens our ports to the pauper and criminal classes of the world, and crowds out our wage earners"; cordially sympathized with the efforts of workingmen to shorten their hours of labor; and roundly denounced "the maintenance of a large standing army of mercenaries, known as the Pinkerton system, as a menace to our liberties." No labor convention would have cared to improve on the language of a resolution that condemned "the recent invasion of the Territory of Wyoming by the hired assassins of Plutocracy, assisted by Federal officers." [9]

Another resolution provoked a debate which showed that these

[8] Godkin, in *Nation* (July 7, 1892), LV, 1; Frederic Bancroft, ed.: *Speeches, Correspondence, and Political Papers of Carl Schurz* (Putnam, 1913), V, 87–121; Elting E. Morison, ed.: *Letters of Theodore Roosevelt* (Harvard University Press, 1951), I, 292.

[9] The platform and supplementary resolution, as printed in Allen, pp. 96–100, 107–11, are used throughout this section.

pro-labor statements were no mere contrivances on the part of leaders, slipped by an indifferent rank and file. While the convention met, a Knights of Labor union was engaged in a hard-fought strike against a group of Rochester clothing manufacturers, and the resolution not only expressed support of the strikers against a "tyrannical combine" but called on "all who hate tyranny and oppression" to boycott the goods of the manufacturers. Sympathy for strikers was one thing; a secondary boycott was going far (so far that its legality was decidedly in question). A secondary boycott was going much too far for a Texas delegate, who wanted to table the resolution, and for a New Yorker, who proposed dividing it so that he could vote for the sympathy and against the boycott.

Promptly, two of the most unmistakably agrarian delegates were on their feet in defense of the boycott. "There is no such thing as a boycott," roared "Cyclone" Davis, of Texas. "It only consists in letting your enemies alone and staying with your friends."

Then Ignatius Donnelly, from agricultural Minnesota, took up the fight. "If this resolution was simply to express our prejudice of a class," Donnelly declared, "I should not support it. It is a declaration that free men will not clothe their limbs in the goods of manufacturers of this slave-making oligarchy. [Loud cheers.] It is war to the knife and the knife to the hilt. [Loud cheers.] I trust that those who have staggered away from this resolution because of the opprobrium that a hireling press has applied to the word boycott, will withdraw their opposition, and that the resolution may be adopted by a rising vote. [Tremendous applause.]" A motion to strike out the boycott clause was overwhelmingly defeated, and the whole resolution was adopted by acclamation.[1]

Among the delegates conspicuous in the uproar was a coal-black Negro, marching about the Coliseum Building with an American flag fluttering from a cane and apparently feeling gaily at home. A number of important Populist leaders not only aimed to unite the discontented of the cities and the countryside. They sought

[1] Ibid., pp. 109–11.

something that no American party has achieved before or since: a political coalition of the poor whites and the poor blacks of the South. The Southern Farmers' Alliance was conspicuously friendly to the Colored Farmers' Alliance. Committees of white Southern Populists ceremoniously met with black colleagues, joint platforms were adopted, and Negro delegates were named to local and national Populist conventions. The most important Southern Populist leader, Tom Watson, of Georgia, regularly held mixed meetings, despite violent attempts to prevent them. "You are kept apart," Watson told his audiences, "that you may be separately fleeced of your earnings. You are made to hate each other because upon that hatred is rested the keystone of the arch of financial despotism which enslaves you both." Often Watson would pledge his white listeners to defend the Constitutional rights of the Negro, asking the whites to take an oath that they would not backslide. When Georgians threatened to lynch a prominent Negro Populist leader, the state witnessed an unprecedented sight. At Watson's call, two thousand white Populists assembled to protect the Negro. For two days and nights, their arms stacked on Watson's veranda, the white men grimly carried out the Populist doctrine that the issue was poverty, not color.[2]

The groups on which Populism was depending for support, so different from the most ardent followers of liberalism, were offered an appropriately different program. The Populists took over the liberal demand for honest, efficient political leaders, but the reformed government was to be no reflection of upper-income, better-educated America. Civil-service reform was not emphasized at Omaha; it smacked too much of establishing a permanent ruling group and contradicted the Jacksonian faith that any well-intentioned American was good enough to carry on government for his fellows.[3] Populist government was to be by and

[2] Jack Abramowitz: "The Negro in the Agrarian and Populist Movements," MS., in Mr. Abramowitz's possession; C. Vann Woodward: "Tom Watson and the Negro in Agrarian Politics," *Journal of Southern History* (February 1938), IV, 17–23. The quotation is from ibid., p. 18.

[3] The only mention of civil-service reform in the Omaha platform came in a special instance. In the event of government ownership of the

for "the people," or, to use a more revealing phrase that the Populists borrowed from pre-Civil War reformers, by and for "the producers." The Populist reversion to the practice of dividing the population into producers and nonproducers was the surest indication of their view of America. It indicated their belief that "producers"—those who worked with their hands—were the men who really created the wealth of the nation. In the Populist view, the producers should run the country and should receive a value from their labor which gave little or no return to men whose chief function was providing capital.[4]

In their eagerness to increase the political power of the producers, the Populists urged the secret ballot and endorsed three adventurous techniques for direct democracy: the popular election of United States senators; the initiative, giving the voters the right to legislate over the heads of their representatives; and the referendum, providing the voters with a veto over the actions of the legislature. The initiative and referendum proposals seemed so radical in 1892 that their chief advocate at Omaha, a representative of a New Jersey workingmen's organization, had to argue vigorously for including them in the platform, but he was ultimately successful. Populists could not resist any idea that promised to end the political control of corporations.[5] In fact, so intense was the Populist hatred of politics as it was being prac-

---

railroads, the Populists wanted "civil service regulation of the most rigid character, so as to prevent the increase of the power of the national administration by the use of such additional government employees." Generally, the Alliance platforms had ignored the merit system, and one Alliance document flatly opposed it with the Jacksonian query: "If this is not the people's government, whose government is it?" (Frank M. Drew, "The Present Farmer's Movement," *Political Science Quarterly* [June 1891], VI, 302). The agrarian leader William Jennings Bryan was to show the same tendency during the campaign of 1896. While conceding the importance of merit appointments, he opposed life tenure because "we do not want to build up an office-holding class." *The First Battle* (W. B. Conkey, Chicago, 1896), p. 460.

[4] Arthur M. Schlesinger, Jr.: *The Age of Jackson* (Little, Brown, 1945), Chap. xxiv, and Destler, pp. 25–9. The Omaha platform pushed the "producer" doctrine to its logical extreme by declaring: "Wealth belongs to him who creates it, and every dollar taken from industry [i.e., work], without an equivalent, is robbery."

[5] Destler, p. 24, 63 n.

ticed that the Omaha gathering whooped through a resolution unique in the history of American conventions, conservative or radical. No one who held a federal, state, or municipal office, the delegates decreed, could sit in a future Populist convention.

And all politics or political machinery was but a means; the end was economic and social reform. The Populists swept together the discontent with both Grantism and liberalism into a bold doctrine of continuous state intervention in behalf of the producers. Governments were to stop aiding the corporations, directly or indirectly, and were to start passing legislation beneficial to Americans who had little or no capital. The issue that excited liberals and old-style Republicans so much—the tariff—was just a "sham battle" to the Populists. "We believe," the Omaha platform emphasized, "that the powers of government should be expanded . . . as rapidly and as far as the good sense of an intelligent people and the teachings of experience shall justify, to the end that oppression, injustice and poverty shall eventually cease in the land."

The Populist eye was on the Interstate Commerce Act of 1887, which put controls over railroads, and the Sherman Anti-Trust Act of 1890, which declared combinations in restraint of trade illegal. These the Populists wanted to strengthen and, in strengthened form, to make the models for state and federal interferences in economic life that would regulate all corporations and would splinter into small units those which had reached the monopoly stage. For years the Populists had watched extremes of wealth piling up, unchecked by legislation; the Omaha platform proposed to reverse, or at least halt, the trend by a graduated federal income tax. In the minds of most Populists, one of the chief enemies of the farmer was a rigid currency system, and the delegates demanded "a national currency, safe, sound and flexible, issued by the general government only." Government-operated postal savings banks were to take the savings business out of the hands of private bankers. Federal subtreasuries, "or some other system," should be established to loan money to farmers at no more than two per cent interest and to see to it that the supply of currency fluctuated with the demand for agricultural credits. "All land now held by railroads and other corporations in excess of their actual needs," the Omaha convention added, ". . . should be reclaimed by the government and held for actual settlers only." On the general subject of the railroads, those prime ogres of the farmers, the Populists were ready for the most drastic kind of governmental power. The United States was to own and operate the railroads. It was, moreover, to own and operate the telegraph and telephone systems, which were approaching the monopoly stage and which the Populists felt were being run with an arrogant disregard of the consumer's interest.

The obvious socialism of these last proposals brought the most anguished of all cries from liberals. They were startled and outraged that free men could seriously propose handing over such great powers to the state, and their vehemence underlined the fundamental difference in the liberal and Populist approaches. The liberal, however much his practices might deviate from his doctrine under the pressure of the corporations, kept his principal emphasis on liberty, the freedom of the individual in political, economic, and social relations, either with another individual or with his government. The Populist did not forget liberty, but in the troubled Nineties, no less than in the confident late Sixties, the essence of liberty to a large number of Americans was the freedom to escape poverty and to rise in economic and social status. The Populists stressed opportunity rather than sheer liberty. Feeling the vise of corporate power and class stratification closing in on them, they were frantically reaching out for any ideological tool that promised to pry back the ominous jaws, whether or not it met the severest tests of freedom.

Most of the Populists, like so many of the liberals, found their hero in Thomas Jefferson. This may have been a tribute to the many-sided Jefferson, but it was also an example of the confusion that results from applying a man's thought in a different age. Liberals looked to the Jefferson who feared centralized power;

Populists, to the Jefferson who considered capitalist power the chief enemy of the aspiring masses. Tom Watson, ardent Jeffersonian and bitter opponent of liberalism, caught the heart of Populism when he spoke of the movement's "yearning, upward tendency." Populism's central target, Watson continued, was "monopoly—not monopoly in the narrow sense of the word—but monopoly of power, of place, of privilege, of wealth, of progress." Its battle cry was: "Keep the avenues of honor free. Close no entrance to the poorest, the weakest, the humblest." Re-create an America that said to ambition: "The field is clear, the contest fair; come, and win your share if you can!" [6]

V

IN THE elections of 1892 the Populists became the first third party to carry a state since the GOP started on its way in 1856. The contingent of Populist-minded United States Senators rose to five; the number of Representatives to ten. Populist governors were elected in Kansas, North Dakota, and Colorado, while the number of sympathetic state legislators and county officials mounted to fifteen hundred. In the important Illinois election the Democrats swept the state, but the result was more a defeat for the Populist Party than for its doctrines. At the head of the victorious Democratic ticket was John P. Altgeld, who agreed substantially with every important plank in the Omaha platform. As this burly, tough-minded dissenter led the elegant Inaugural Ball in Chicago, any radical could feel that a new day was swiftly dawning.

The next year the Populists acquired a powerful ally. Hard times settled over the country again, bringing all the jolting effect of a second severe depression in one generation. The twelve months that began in the middle of 1894 have been called the

[6] Woodward: *Watson*, p. 217.

"*année terrible*" of the post-Civil War period, and the phrase is not overly dramatic for the record of savage strikes and brutal labor repression, deepening agricultural distress, and a national atmosphere of foreboding at the top and bitterness at the bottom.[7]

Never before had the nation seemed so restive. The year 1894 made labor history, with nearly 750,000 workingmen out in militant strikes. The leader of the Pullman strikers, sent to jail by Cleveland's liberalism, sat mulling over the situation and came out a full-blown socialist. "We have been cursed with the reign of gold long enough," Eugene Debs told wildly cheering crowds. ". . . We are on the eve of a universal change."[8] In the clay hills of the South, across the scorched prairies, the farmer's agitation was rapidly becoming, as one supporter described it, "a religious revival, a crusade, a pentecost of politics, in which a tongue of flame sat upon every man."[9] It was "a fanaticism like the crusades," a Kansas observer added. "At night, from ten thousand little white schoolhouse windows, lights twinkled back hope to the stars. . . . They sang . . . with something of the same mad faith that inspired the martyr going to the stake. Far into the night the voices rose, women's voices, children's voices, the voices of old men, of youths and of maidens rose on the ebbing prairie breezes, as the crusaders of the revolution rode home, praising the people's will as though it were God's will and cursing wealth for its iniquity."[1] Hamlin Garland, watching the Populist representatives flail away in Congress, was sure that the country was approaching "a great periodic upheaval similar to that of '61. Everywhere as I went through the aisles of the House, I saw it and heard it. . . . The House is a smoldering volcano."[2]

[7] The phrase is from Nevins: *Cleveland* (Dodd, Mead, 1947), p. 649. Italics in original.

[8] Ray Ginger: *The Bending Cross, A Biography of Eugene Victor Debs* (Rutgers University Press, 1949), p. 193.

[9] Elizabeth Barr, quoted in John D. Hicks: *The Populist Revolt* (University of Minnesota Press, 1931), p. 159.

[1] William Allen White, quoted in Walter Johnson: *William Allen White's America* (Holt, 1947), p. 54.

[2] Garland: "The Alliance Wedge in Congress," *Arena* (March 1892), V, 455-7.

In Indianapolis, a ruche-collared lady measured the political situation and went off to see the cathedrals of Europe. "I am going to spend my money," she said, "before those crazy people take it." [3]

[3] Interview with the late Charles Beard, who was remembering the remark of a friend of his family.

✿ *CHAPTER IV* ✿

A Least Common Denominator

THE RUCHE-COLLARED lady, had she been a bit more discerning, might well have been a good deal less precipitate. The structure of Populism was as rickety as the worst of the sharecropper homes.

The attempt of Southern Populists to form a poor-white, poor-Negro coalition proved politically disastrous. As a group, low-income Southern whites were harsh enemies of the Negro, and the Southern conservatives seriously injured Populism by calling it the "nigger's party."[1] That "everlasting and overshadowing Negro Question," Tom Watson believed, was the explanation of his own failure to achieve greater political power, and the day was not distant when he would shift to a fanatic anti-Negro position in an attempt to out-racist his enemies.[2] In most Southern states the race issue thoroughly stifled Populism. Impoverished but anti-Negro farmers clung to the "white man's party," the Democratic, and turned toward the leadership of demagogues like South Carolina's Ben Tillman and Mississippi's James Vardaman, who combined reform and racist attitudes in a formula similar to the one Adolf Hitler was to perfect. Tillman assailed political and

---

[1] Paul Lewison: "The Negro in the White Class and Party Struggle," *Southwestern Political and Social Science Quarterly* (March 1928), VIII, 379–80; Gunnar Myrdal: *An American Dilemma* (Harper, 1944), pp. 67–70.

[2] C. Vann Woodward: "Tom Watson and the Negro in Agrarian Politics," *Journal of Southern History* (February 1938), IV, 1.

economic conservatism in the same speeches that hailed "the triumph of . . . white supremacy over mongrelism." All the while that Vardaman denounced "the concentration of riches in the hands of the few," he lashed out at any proposal to give the vote to a "veneered savage," no matter what his "advertised mental and moral qualifications may be. I am just as much opposed to Booker T. Washington as a voter . . . as I am to the cocoanut-headed, chocolate-colored, typical little coon, Andy Dotson, who blacks my shoes every morning. Neither is fit to perform the supreme function of citizenship." [3]

South or North, the Populist Party was failing to achieve the shape of a genuine urban-rural movement. Under the whiplash of their debts, farmers were increasingly concentrating on demands for inflation, particularly for inflation by the alluringly simple method of free silver, and this emphasis was decidedly counter to the urban trend. Over the decades of agitation, workingmen's organizations had often gone along with the proposition that more money in circulation meant more money in the pockets of poor men, but by the Nineties inflation aroused no great enthusiasm among industrial workers. They were coming to believe that they would be more hurt than helped by any type of inflation, and they generally shared the businessman's feeling that inflation by free silver was something out of a cracked pot.

Again and again Populists with a broad urban-rural approach, like the Chicago intellectual, Henry Demarest Lloyd, warned that concentrating on free silver would wreck Populism.[4] Many Southern leaders, sure that a sweepingly radical approach was needed, joined in the warning. But the Midwestern farmers, the

[3] Frances B. Simkins: *The Tillman Movement in South Carolina* (Duke University Press, 1926), p. 137; Heber Ladner: "James Kimble Vardaman," *Journal of Mississippi History* (October 1940), II, 190, 199; Paul Lewison: *Race, Class, and Party* (Oxford, 1932), pp. 84–5. In the Senatorial primary run-off of 1903, Vardaman almost invariably carried poor-white counties, and he received majorities in 19 out of 23 counties that had polled heavy Populist votes. Ladner, pp. 183–4.

[4] Typical of this group, Lloyd called free silver "a fake" and "the cow bird of the Reform movement. It waited until the nest had been built by the sacrifices and labour of others, and then it laid its eggs in it." Caro Lloyd: *Henry Demarest Lloyd* (Putnam, 1912), I, 264.

most powerful faction in the Populist Party, were not to be swayed. As the elections of 1896 approached, an Iowa leader spoke for much of Midwestern Populism when he said: "I shall favor going before the people . . . with the money question alone, unencumbered with any other contention whatsoever." [5]

On its part, labor was hurrying in a direction that made coalition difficult. By the Nineties the Knights of Labor, which included farmers and tradesmen and stood for a wide variety of reforms, was giving way to the American Federation of Labor, an organization devoted to labor with belligerent exclusiveness. Samuel Gompers, master architect of the federation, had cut his labor teeth in a New York cigarmaker's local, where one group kept the union in chaos by incessant Utopianizing. The hard-headed Gompers was determined to keep the AFL tightly reined to the purpose of larger wages, better working conditions, and shorter hours for industrial labor. "At no time in my life," he insisted in his autobiography, "have I worked out [a] definitely articulated economic theory." Gompers' co-worker, Adolph Strasser, was still more emphatic. "Our organization does not consist of idealists," Strasser boasted. ". . . We have no ultimate ends. We are going on from day to day. We are fighting only for immediate objects—objects that can be realized in a few years." [6] At times Populism seemed to offer so much to labor that Gompers wavered, but he was soon back to his original position. Complete co-operation between the unions and the Populist Party, Gompers wrote in his most thorough discussion of the subject, was impossible because it was "unnatural." The Populist Party consisted mainly of "*employing* farmers," whose "purposes, methods, and interests" diverged from those of the "*employed* farmers of the country districts or the mechanics and laborers of the industrial centres." The American Federation of Labor would be more

[5] James Weaver, quoted in John D. Hicks: *The Populist Revolt* (University of Minnesota Press, 1931), p. 344.

[6] Gompers: *Seventy Years of Life and Labor* (Dutton, 1925), II, 17–18; for the Strasser quote, see Senate Committee on Education and Labor, 48th Cong., 2nd Sess.: *Report . . . upon the Relations between Labor and Capital* (1885), I, 460.

friendly to the Populists than it had been to any previous third party—and there Gompers drew the line.[7]

The strength of single-taxism in the cities added to the difficulties in the way of a national union of the discontented. Henry George, who was always close to believing himself a special emissary of God, showed little of the give-and-take necessary for successful political coalition. In addition, George was opposed on principle to the Populist demand for extensive governmental controls over economic life. He wanted the federal government to take the drastic step of imposing the single tax, but he believed this one move would reopen opportunity without requiring any further governmental interferences. In 1892 George supported Grover Cleveland and urged his followers not to vote the Populist ticket. Even when single-taxers ran for office on the Populist ticket, the leader would not budge. At a high point in the Populist agitation George was prevailed upon to speak at a Chicago rally, and since two fervent single-taxers were running on the Populist ticket, the organizers of the meeting expected at least a nominal endorsement of Populism. Instead, George declared his "indifference, or even hostility" to the Omaha platform and went out of his way to damn the whole Populist effort.[8]

Equally disruptive was the rising strength of socialism in the cities. The principal socialist leader, Daniel De Leon, filled his journal with denunciations of Populism as "one of the most conservative and even retrograde attempts ever recorded in the history of economic evolution." [9] De Leon insisted upon running socialists against Populists, despite the inevitable consequence; in

[7] Gompers: "Organized Labor in the Campaign," *North American Review* (July 1892), CLV, 93. The italics are in the original.

[8] Quoted in Chester M. Destler: *American Radicalism, 1865–1901* (Collegiate Press, Menasha, Wis., 1946), p. 200. George denounced the Populists as "a socialistic party, aiming not at less restriction but at more." He argued that Cleveland's advocacy of low tariffs was a step in the direction of free trade, which in turn was a stride toward the single tax. J. Martin Klotsche: "The 'United Front Populists,'" *Wisconsin Magazine of History* (June 1937), XX, 378–80.

[9] *The People*, April 17, 1892, quoted in George H. Knoles: "Populism and Socialism, with Special Reference to the Election of 1892," *Pacific Historical Review* (September 1943), XII, 299.

the five Eastern states that had both tickets in 1892, the two parties polled approximately equal votes, with complete futility for both. The Populists returned the antipathy in full degree. The typical Populist shared the general American prejudice in favor of men and ideas that could be called old-stock American or, next best, could be associated with western Europe. Socialism was, beyond all argument, an imported doctrine. Most of the socialists were conspicuously European in origin, and a considerable percentage of them were immigrants from eastern Europe. Socialists usually felt no more comfortable at Populist meetings than they would have been among the D.A.R.[1]

The anti-foreign feeling among reformers was so widespread that it split the socialists themselves. One of the few old-stock socialist leaders, Algie Simons, continually and publicly assailed any European orientation of the movement. There were, Simons maintained, two distinct wings in the party. The Western one, he wrote with obvious approval, "is quite largely agrarian in its origin, comes almost wholly from economic development, and is peculiarly American in its make-up." The Eastern one was primarily "urban, arrived at its conclusions quite largely through direct ideological propaganda, and is still (though rapidly losing this phase) formed mainly among those born in other countries." [2] Privately, Simons complained: "In the East, the Socialist Party is run by Jews." [3] Attitudes that were so divisive among socialists were doubly divisive in the relations between socialists and Populists.

[1] David A. Shannon: "The Socialist Party before the First World War," *Mississippi Valley Historical Review* (September 1951), XXXVIII, 280–1.

[2] Simons: "Lines of Division in American Socialism," *International Socialist Review* (August 1902), III, 109.

[3] Interview of the late Mr. Simons with Mr. John J. Harmon, reported to me by Mr. Harmon. See also Harmon: "Algie Martin Simons," MS., Princeton University Library, pp. 53–8. The attitude of Western dissidents, socialist or nonsocialist, was generally hostile toward Jews, in large part because they pictured them as the "money power." The prejudice was so strong that one scholar, Professor Oscar Handlin, has made the agrarianists chiefly responsible for introducing into American thinking the anti-Semitic stereotype of the money-manipulating Jew. "American Views of the Jew at the Opening of the Twentieth Century," *Publications of the American Jewish Historical Society* (June 1951), XL, 323–44.

Apart from this involved psychological factor, Populists and socialists found it difficult to work together for the simple and sufficient reason that the Populists were not socialists. The Populist Party might call for extending the powers of government as far as "good sense" dictated, and it might advocate the socialization of the railroads and the telegraph and telephone systems. But most Populists emphatically did not want a society in which the principal means of production would be owned by the state. They believed in the system of free enterprise, even cherished it as the heart of the American way of life. They considered their program anything but a demand for a new economic system. Populists thought of themselves as engaged in a work of restoration, a restoration of the good old days, when, as they liked to believe, there was open competition and plenty of opportunity for everyone. They sought to control big capital only to break its overweening power, to regulate the few only in order to free the many.

How serious the antagonism between socialist and antisocialist reformers could be was revealed by the important Illinois elections of 1894. At one of the conferences to prepare for the campaign, Thomas Morgan, founder of the Chicago Trades and Labor Assembly, tossed the inevitable bombshell. English-born, socialist-bred, Morgan had none of the typical Populist's faith in capitalism. He proposed that the Populist platform should demand "the collective ownership by the people of all means of production and distribution," and the fight was on. Immediately a Nebraska Populist was on his feet to tell Morgan: "If this is what you came to the people's party for, we don't want you. Go back from where you came with your socialism." [4] Ingenious minds tried to slide around the difficulty with vague wording, but the split in the Illinois Populist ranks would not close. Soon the much heralded labor-farmer front was a façade, and the farmer representation was pulling the party toward concentration on free silver.

However sharp the conflict between rural Populists and urban

---

[4] Quoted in Destler, pp. 169–70.

radicals, the differences were mild compared with the clash between rural Populists and the "middle classes" of the cities. Regardless of occupation or income, the populations of the cities were becoming increasingly middle-class in outlook, and Populism offended a whole congeries of middle-class attitudes. The Populists made politics urgently important; the middle-class approach made politics the resort of the shifty-eyed and the incompetent, who found it easier to be accommodating than to go to work. The Populists were, inescapably, the party of the failures; the middle-class view, more or less consciously, considered associating oneself with movements speaking for the successful a prerequisite to one's own success. The Populists lambasted the successful industrialist and banker; urban people of middle-class attitudes, including slum-dwellers and clerks grubbing to support their families, looked up to the magnate as the man who had made the most of American opportunity, the "captain of industry," the glamour figure to be excused his frailties as a later generation was to excuse movie stars their divorces. Thinking back to the Delaware town of his boyhood, Henry Seidel Canby remembered that if A-B-C marks had been given, the ratings would have run something like this: a radical thinker, E; a contented idler or a lover of the arts, D; a deeply religious person, a scientist, or a journalist, C; a good parent or an honest man, B; a good salesman, retail, B, wholesale, A; a first-rate businessman with all that implied, A ++. Business, Mr. Canby added, "was much more than an occupation,—it was a philosophy, a morality, and an atmosphere," breathed in as naturally "as a Londoner takes in his November fog." [5]

With special emphasis, the middle-class attitude esteemed respectability and modernity, and the most prominent Populist leaders easily left the impression of a howl from the backwoods. The Omaha convention master, Ignatius Donnelly, had a reputation for the kind of theories that too many lonely nights on the prairie can produce. He had founded a community in which ev-

---

[5] Canby: *The Age of Confidence* (Farrar & Rinehart, 1934), pp. 232–3, 241.

erybody was to love everybody else, insisted, through 478 pages of *Atlantis*, that Plato's "lost isle" had really existed, and produced *The Great Cryptogram* to prove that Francis Bacon had written all of Shakespeare's plays, most of Marlowe's works, Montaigne's essays, and Burton's *Anatomy of Melancholy*. The 1892 Presidential candidate of the Populist Party was that ancient warhorse of agrarian agitation, James Weaver. Its other leaders included the cadaverous Tom Watson, with a windmill oratory straight out of the hills of Georgia; "Sockless" Jerry Simpson, the only American to achieve immortality by being accused of going without stockings; the hulking, red-whiskered Norwegian, Kittel Halvorson, always giving off the air of a man in troubled communion with the Infinite; and a band of female orators led by the bony-handed Mary Ellen Lease, speaking with unladylike ferocity about unladylike topics.

In the official history of the Omaha convention the Populist author went far out of his way to write of Candidate Weaver's friends among "the very best circles" of Des Moines, his "neat and tasty" home, the "chic" daughter and the wife who stayed away from public platforms.[6] The Populist author of the history, a Kansas City reporter who knew his middle classes, was trying.

II

THE FAILURE of the Populists to build an effective union of the lower-income groups received its dramatic confirmation in the Presidential election of 1896. Few situations could have seemed more propitious. The country writhed in its third year of depression. Wheat had sunk to ten cents a bushel, cotton to six cents a pound; unemployment had crossed the four-million mark and was still mounting. The long series of local Populist successes had prepared the way for national operations. When the Democrats and the Populists named the same Presidential candidate in the

[6] E. A. Allen: *The Life and Public Services of James Baird Weaver* . . . (People's Party Publishing Co., 1892), pp. 30, 39.

1896 conventions, the reformers for the first time had the machinery of a major party functioning in their behalf. Most important of all, the joint nominee was William Jennings Bryan.

The country had heard many a great orator; they had never heard anything like this thirty-six-year-old Nebraskan. Bryan could be expository, and then his handsome face was all earnestness and the words rippled out in the cadence of good teaching. He could be sly and witty, and the fervid eyes would light up his paleness as the voice rasped and twisted its way under the enemy argument. He could, above all, be apostolic, his stocky frame vibrant, his long, black hair thrown back, the great golden baritone cascading over the audience. Day after day Bryan campaigned, praying to his God on the floor of his sleeping-car at night, sleeping soundly, rising refreshed to speak to twenty or thirty meetings before another sundown. And after the speeches, observers noted, "the poor, the weak, the humble, the aged, the infirm" would rush forward by the hundreds, holding up "hard and wrinkled hands with crooked fingers and cracked knuckles to the young great orator, as if he were in very truth their promised redeemer from bondage." [7]

Bryan, the opposition railed, was a "baby orator," a "slobbering demagogue" talking a creed of "national dishonor, private robbery, the exaltation of anarchy . . . [and] the damnation of the Constitution." [8] Promptly Bryan turned the attacks on his youth and on his doctrines into an identification of himself with the traditional American concern over opportunity. "As a young man," he told an Iowa crowd, "I know . . . the feelings of young men, and I know what it is to have a condition in our political society that makes it difficult for a young man to rise in life. . . . I want our government maintained as the fathers intended it. I want it so that the child of the humblest citizen in this land can aspire to any position in the political or business world to which his merits entitle him. I want it so that if he enters politics he will

[7] Review of Bryan's *The First Battle*, in the *Arena* (April 1897), XVII, 844.

[8] Quoted in Matthew Josephson: *The Politicos* (Harcourt, Brace, 1938), p. 684, and Mark Sullivan: *Our Times* (Scribner, 1926–35), I, 292.

not find arrayed against him all the great financial influences of society unless he is willing to join them and conspire against the welfare of the people as a whole. If he enters business I want him to be able to stand upon his own merits and not stand always in the fear that some great trust will run him out of business." [9]

Bryan was not only the born campaigner; more than any previous Populist leader he had the qualities to bring rural and urban discontent into coalition. Farm-bred, a passionate advocate of the basic Populist demands, he did not have to labor hard to convince agrarian America that he was its friend. A descendant of old Protestant stock, the son of a judge, growing up touched by town influences, college-educated, Bryan could and did present himself as a thoroughly middle-class man. His approach to reform softened and blurred the "producer" class philosophy of Populism—the farmer and industrial worker were businessmen too, Bryan insisted—and he was careful to emphasize that he was no revolutionary. "We cannot insure to the vicious the fruits of the virtuous life," Bryan spoke the authentic attitude of respectability. "We would not invade the home of the provident in order to supply the wants of the spendthrift." [1]

Any affront to the dignity of Mr. William Jennings Bryan was promptly challenged. When Yale students roughly heckled the candidate during a New Haven speech, Bryan stopped his address with a stiff reminder that he did not speak to rowdies. Then he saw to it that every protest at the students' action was widely publicized, every conceivable protest, down to the communication from the Cherokees, Creeks, Choctaws, and Seminoles, who gravely resolved that "we contemplate with deep regret the recent insulting treatment of William J. Bryan by students of a college in the land of the boasted white man's civilization, and we admonish all Indians who think of sending their sons to Yale that association with such students could not but prove hurtful alike to their morals and their progress toward the higher standard of civilization." [2]

[9] Bryan, *The First Battle* (W. B. Conkey, Chicago, 1896), p. 596.
[1] Ibid., p. 316.
[2] Ibid., p. 487.

Simultaneously Bryan was missing no opportunity to make himself the spokesman of all urban workingmen, whether they were middle-class in attitude or not. He defended unions and attacked labor injunctions, announced that he intended to make Samuel Gompers a member of his cabinet, and supported, at least by implication, a long series of specific labor demands. Free silver, Bryan assured his urban audiences, was merely the "first step" in a general "restoration of just conditions in this country." [3] Swept along by the vista of a genuinely national reform movement, Henry George, AFL leaders, Eugene Debs, and a host of unaffiliated dissenters waived their theories and backed the "Great Commoner." Even many urban reformers who had little respect for Bryan personally gave his drive hearty efforts. "I have been thinking over Bryan's speech. What did he say anyway?" John Peter Altgeld growled, but Altgeld vigorously supported the Bryan campaign.[4]

Downcountry, in Emporia, Kansas, William Allen White waddled amiably along Main Street, stopping here and there to chat with an acquaintance. Emporia knew Will White as a nice young man. At Kansas University the rolypoly redhead had frolicked along, a loyal Phi Delt, a good hand at the mandolin, mingling a reverence for God, Republicans, and Anglo-Saxons with genial politicking and giggling buggy rides. As the editor of the *Emporia Gazette*, White continued to prove himself the upstanding citizen. He wrote ringing editorials denouncing Populism, showed a proper diffidence whenever the conversation turned to the subject of his maverick father, worked hard to earn an elegant house for himself and his bride. Now, like any up-and-coming American, White was off to the post office to take care of his mail, and his suit was a spick-and-span white linen.

A block from the *Gazette* office a group of fifteen or twenty Populists saw White coming and could not resist their chance at such immaculate Republicanism. Surrounding him, refusing to let him continue on his way, they jeered at his editorials and

[3] Ibid., p. 464.
[4] Quoted in Irving Stone: *Clarence Darrow for the Defense* (Doubleday, 1941), p. 100.

jostled him until his linen suit was a mess. White's pinkish face went aflame with rage. Finally breaking through the crowd, he stalked back to his office.[5]

"What's the matter with Kansas?" the words sputtered from White's pen. ". . . We all know; yet here we are at it again. We have an old moss-back Jacksonian who snorts and howls because there is a bathtub in the State House; we are running that old jay for Governor. . . . We have raked the old ash heap of failure in the state and found an old human hoop skirt who has failed as a businessman, who has failed as an editor, who has failed as a preacher, and we are going to run him for Congressman-at-Large. . . . We have discovered a kid without a law practice and have decided to run him for Attorney General. Then for fear some hint that the state had become respectable might percolate through the civilized portions of the nation, we have decided to send three or four harpies out lecturing, telling the people that Kansas is raising hell and letting the corn go to weeds.

"Oh, this is a state to be proud of! We are a people who can hold up our heads! . . . We don't need population, we don't need wealth, we don't need well-dressed men on the streets, we don't need cities in the fertile prairies; you bet we don't! What we are after is the money power. Because we have become poorer and ornerier and meaner than a spavined, distempered mule, we, the people of Kansas, propose to kick; we don't care to build up, we wish to tear down. . . .

"Give the prosperous man the dickens! . . . Whoop it up for the ragged trousers; put the lazy, greasy fizzle who can't pay his debts on the altar, and bow down and worship him. Let the state ideal be high. What we need is not the respect of our fellowmen, but the chance to get something for nothing." [6]

White slammed the editorial on the copy spike with tremendous satisfaction. That took care of the "farmer hooligans"; that

[5] Walter Johnson: *William Allen White's America* (Holt, 1947), pp. 31–100; White: *Autobiography* (Macmillan, 1946), pp. 3–278; White, in a letter to me, April 16, 1940.
[6] White: *Autobiography*, pp. 280–3.

66

performed the duty of a right-thinking editor.[7] Having smugly checked the proof on his editorial, White was off down Main Street again, headed for a train to Colorado, where his wife was resting after an illness.

A week later White came home to find himself a celebrity. "What's the Matter with Kansas?" was being quoted, reprinted, praised throughout urban America; letters were streaming in from bankers and workingmen, from housewives and the Speaker of the United States House of Representatives. Just as Henry George, two decades earlier, vaulted to fame by voicing the anger from the bottom, now another writer was winning widespread repute as the spokesman of the middle-class mood. The nice young man in the linen suit had spoken for all those who wanted their politics starched with respectability. The town editor who saw Populist doctrine as the enemy of prosperity had reacted for millions in the urban areas, for clerks and factory hands no less than for professors and manufacturers.

The election returns told the story in detail. Bryan, the Democrat, swept the Democratic South and held much of the normal machine vote. Bryan, the most convenient outlet for protest against business America, carried most of the embittered agrarian states of the West. In all, the Democratic-Populist nominee received more votes than any previous Presidential candidate and came within 600,000 of equaling McKinley's record 7,000,000 ballots. Yet this strong showing did not, by any means, indicate a genuinely national sentiment. At a time when every third American lived in a community of more than four thousand people, Bryan carried only overwhelmingly agricultural states. He did not win a single electoral vote outside the West and the South; he lost every state in the industrializing east-central and middle-Atlantic areas and every county in the most industrialized section of the country, New England. Equally significant, crossing to the wrong side of the railroad tracks in towns or cities brought no relatively greater support for Bryan. The huge slush funds spent

[7] Ibid., p. 283.

by the Republicans and the intimidation of industrial workers practiced by many employers had something to do with the result, but these were hardly the essential story. The essential story was that reform associated with shaggy agrarianism could not carry a swiftly industrializing, swiftly urbanizing nation.[8]

III

LESS THAN two years after the election of 1896, bands were blaring Sousa's "Stars and Stripes Forever" and Colonel William Jennings Bryan, astride a glistening black horse, was using the famous voice to command a regiment of Nebraska Volunteers. The Spanish-American War was on, a war that proved much more personal for most Americans than either World War I or II. Except for a handful of dissenters, the fight to free Cuba from Spanish rule was a national hoopla against fetid Old World tyranny. The brief ten months of fighting even provided a hero to suit every taste—the laconic Admiral Dewey ("You may fire when ready, Gridley"), the pious Captain Philip, of the *Texas* ("Don't cheer, boys, the poor fellows are dying"), blaspheming Bob Evans, of the *Iowa*, General Joe Wheeler, the gallant old Confederate cavalryman who "laid away a suit of gray to wear the Union blue," and, of course, Teddy Roosevelt, Harvard '80, leading cowboys, bricklayers, and farm hands in a pell-mell charge up Kettle Hill. When it was all over, a thousand commentators noted that the nation seemed united as it had not been for years. "The Spanish War finished us," Tom Watson added. "The blare of the bugle drowned the voice of the Reformer."[9]

It was not quite that simple. The Spanish-American War came in the midst of a number of circumstances that were blunting class strife and decreasing the pressure from the bottom of society.

[8] William Diamond: "Urban and Rural Voting in 1896," *American Historical Review* (January 1941), XLVI, 281–305. Looking back over the election in his *Autobiography* (p. 285), White himself commented: "McKinley's victory was due to the fact that he could unite to a political solidarity the American middle class."

[9] C. Vann Woodward: *Tom Watson* (Macmillan, 1938), p. 334.

The election of 1896 was scarcely over when the depression ended and the whole nation was bathed in the soothing sun of prosperity. Unlike the prosperity years of the Eighties, this period's good times did not leave the farmers feeling outrageously cheated of their share. The new cyanide process for separating gold from crude ore and fresh discoveries of the metal flooded the United States with gold and produced an inflationary effect at least equal to the one that free silver would have brought. During the first decade of the twentieth century the prices of agricultural products increased almost fifty per cent while the money value of rural property doubled. The real wages of urban workers were not rising, or at least were not rising appreciably. Yet the philanthropies of the new millionaires—whatever the ethics of the way the fortunes had been made—were bringing benefits to urban lower-income groups that ranged from increased library facilities to better medical care, and tax-supported facilities from which the whole community benefited were rapidly developing. Public education, that traditional avenue of opportunity, was going through a phenomenal expansion that made any previous stage of development seem slow. By 1910 the coveted high-school diploma was accessible to all except the poorest or those living in the least-settled areas. West of the Appalachians, the land-grant colleges were making even a college degree nothing spectacular for the child of a moderately successful farmer.[1]

City and countryside were both receiving balms for their special irritations, largely as a result of long-running developments that were now showing pronounced effects. The factory hand had less of a feeling that he was considered an animal, to be herded at the demand of the front office. Out of expediency, a sense of decency, or a combination of both, some of the older leaders in industrial circles, most notably Mark Hanna, were suggesting that capitalists could act too imperially. ("A man who won't meet his men half-way," said Hanna, "is a God-damn

[1] In 1902 a writer told of going to a tea party in a farmhouse in central Kansas and meeting twenty-four women, of whom eight had college degrees. Charles M. Harger: "The Prairie Woman: Yesterday and To-day," *Outlook* (April 26, 1902), LXX, 1010.

fool." [2]) Contrary to popular legend, the rising generation of business leaders did not consist largely of self-made men.[3] Most of the executives were the sons of successes, and, while no less interested in profits, they were often less crass in their attitude toward their employees. Old and new business leaders were discovering the general public. It was the early 1900's that invented "public relations," and the fresh concern for what the community thought was rapidly softening the public picture of the corporation executive.

In the agricultural areas, loneliness was being relieved by increasing settlement, the rural free delivery system established in 1896, the growth of lodges and church organizations, and the products of onrushing technology. The farm woman who was such a goad to discontent in the Eighties was often, twenty years later, the contented housewife, preening over the frame house that replaced her sod home, using a shiny new mechanical cleaner to get time for an Eastern Star meeting, even, if the farm was not too far from a city, making a place in the budget for one of Mr. Bell's deliciously clanging boxes. Early in the new century Mary Ellen Lease forsook agitation for Brooklyn, and she had no successor on the prairies.

In the more genial atmosphere of the early 1900's, low-status groups and occupations were finding a greater acceptance. When Samuel Gompers turned to labor organizing in the Seventies, his activities brought virtual ostracism to his family; thirty years later, vaudevillians were gaily patting their bellies as they referred to "my Sam Gompers." [4] The farmer, more than ever, was the "hayseed," but he was no longer the "anarchistic Populist."

[2] Thomas Beer: *Hanna* (Knopf, 1929), pp. 132–3. George W. Perkins, the son of a New York Life Insurance executive and a powerful Morgan partner in the early 1900's, typified some of the new business attitudes by his pioneering moves in labor relations, particularly profit-sharing.

[3] William Miller: "American Historians and the Business Elite," *Journal of Economic History* (November 1949), IX, 184–208, and "The Recruitment of the American Business Elite," *Quarterly Journal of Economics* (May 1950), LXIV, 242–53.

[4] Gompers: *Seventy Years of Life and Labor* (Dutton, 1925), I, 115–16; Rowland H. Harvey: *Samuel Gompers* (Stanford University Press, 1935), p. 99.

Middle-class America was dropping its frightened snarling for un-worried, almost kindly condescension toward the backcountry.[5] The new immigrant might still be the "wop" or the "hunky," but a happier nation was less concerned with pushing the new-comer down, and the recent immigrant could more confidently feel, as the Hungarians were saying, that "The President is Mister and I am Mister too." [6]

"In the United States of today," a Boston newspaper greeted the New Year in 1904, "everyone is middle class. The resort to force, the wild talk of the nineties are over. Everyone is busily, happily getting ahead." [7] If the picture was hardly so idyllic, class and regional tensions were certainly relaxing and a good deal of the old bounce, the old faith in America as opportunity, was com-ing back. Once more, most of the nation's families confidently laid plans for the next step up in the world. Once more most of the country could, without feeling foolish, believe in an always better tomorrow.

Yet the early 1900's were not to be a repetition of the late Sixties. The basic economic and social facts had changed, and changed so drastically that few could fail to note the differences. The frontier, so invitingly open in 1870, so worrisomely closing in the Eighties and Nineties, was now definitely a part of history, and the questions Henry George had raised as early as 1879 were real beyond any sneers at radical Jeremiahs.[8] The decades of

[5] Typically, middle-class America was now joshing about the hayseed who stayed at a city hotel and wrote home: "The bathroom here is so nice I can hardly wait for Saturday night." Sullivan, I, 403 n.

[6] Quoted in Emil Lengyel: *Americans from Hungary* (Lippincott, 1948), p. 114.

[7] *Boston Herald*, December 31, 1904.

[8] It is interesting to note that Henry George's *Progress and Poverty*, published in 1879, advanced much the same thesis about the significance of the frontier in much the same words as Frederick Jackson Turner, whose essay was first presented in 1893 (compare *Progress and Poverty* [Modern Library, 1929], pp. 389–90, and Turner: "The Significance of the Frontier in American History," in *Annual Report of the American Historical Association for the Year 1893*, pp. 215–16, 226–7). The thesis attracted little atten-tion when George advanced it, but was picked up immediately from Turner and widely discussed and accepted. Many explanations of this different re-ception suggest themselves, particularly the fact that George made the thesis part of an argument for a radical economic measure whereas Turner

agrarian distress had left their mark. By 1900, more than one third of the American farmers did not work their own acres. The big factory dominated the industrial scene to such an extent that only the most optimistic employee still dreamed of owning his own plant. The concentration of the whole nation's wealth was reaching a state where one per cent of the population owned more than the remaining ninety-nine per cent put together. Most obvious of all, most arrestingly obvious, the trustification of industry was still racing ahead, and taking on a form that made it especially menacing to the ambitious small entrepeneur.[9]

As the century turned, J. P. Morgan and Andrew Carnegie engaged in a few swift maneuvers and the nation's first billion-dollar trust had been created. Here was a United States Steel Corporation substantially controlling the production of steel products from hairpins to cranes; here was a spectacular step forward in the process of transferring the control of industry to bankers or banking syndicates. By 1913, two banking groups, the one headed by Morgan and the other by representatives of the Rockefellers, held 341 directorships in 112 corporations that had an aggregate capitalization of more than twenty-two billion dollars.[1] "It was bad enough to have million-dollar trusts run by a few men," one publicist expressed the widespread feeling, "but what is going to happen to the farmer, the worker, and the small businessman when we have billion-dollar combines maneuvered by a handful of men who have never been in a plant and who think of a factory as just another chip in a gigantic financial poker game?"[2]

---

presented it as a scholarly hypothesis. Yet it is hard to avoid emphasizing the explanation that Turner was talking about the effects of the disappearance of the frontier when it had much more completely disappeared and hence was much more on people's minds.

[9] Fred A. Shannon: *The Farmer's Last Frontier* (Farrar & Rinehart, 1945), p. 418; Jeremiah W. Jenks and Walter E. Clark: *The Trust Problem* (Doubleday, Doran, 1929), pp. 15–21; Harold U. Faulkner: *The Quest for Social Justice* (Macmillan, 1930), p. 21.

[1] House Committee on Banking and Currency, 62nd Cong., 3rd Sess., *Report . . . [on] the Concentration of Control of Money and Credit* (1913), p. 89.

[2] *Chicago Evening Post*, January 31, 1903.

What was going to happen, scores of other commentators answered, was that the United States would find itself under socialist rule. "Grasping and unrelenting monopoly," conservative newspapers were saying, meant inevitable government ownership or governmental controls so stringent that no significant vestige of free enterprise would be left.[3] The fear that the country was careening toward socialism was accentuated by the rapid growth of the party itself. The year after Bryan's defeat, one wing of the socialist movement broke away from the domination of Daniel De Leon, adopted a moderate, flexible program much like that of the British Labour Party, and acquired the leadership of Eugene Debs. In a short time this group had captured most of the people who considered themselves socialists and was developing a national following far larger than any previous socialist strength in the United States. The new socialism had a characteristic that made it especially worrisome to a nation of anti-socialists. Eugene Debs was no easily dismissed outcaste. He was Indiana-born, a crony of James Whitcomb Riley, a heretic who challenged the gods with a homey Hoosier twang. The crucial convention that established the new socialism in 1901 was made up of delegates who were eighty per cent native-born, a percentage higher than the national ratio.[4] Across the country, doctors, professors, pharmacists, and the Chairman of the Committee on Community Problems of the Terre Haute Ladies' Cultural Group were helping to elect an estimated three hundred socialists to local political offices. Socialism, one of the party executives could boast, was no longer "an exotic plant in this country." [5]

[3] *Philadelphia Evening Telegraph, c.* March 1901, quoted in Sullivan, II, 351.
[4] Morris Hillquit: *History of Socialism in the United States* (Funk & Wagnalls, 1903), p. 339.
[5] Hillquit, in ibid., p. 339. David A. Shannon has commented: "Not only did many of the [pre-1914] Socialist leaders come from . . . middle-class backgrounds, but they also had middle-class values, tastes, and ideas in all but their political-economic thinking. . . . Debs evidently saw nothing incongruous in giving a child a book by Elbert Hubbard for a Christmas present, and Bill Haywood celebrated his last night in Chicago before jumping bail . . . by going to a musical comedy and eating ice cream." "The Socialist Party before the First World War," *Mississippi Valley Historical Review* (September 1951), XXXVIII, 284.

Under the circumstances, if all America was becoming more middle-class in outlook, the middle-class outlook was increasingly friendly to reform. Hopeful about tomorrow, men of middle-class views were too hopeful not to want to nudge tomorrow along. Fearful of socialism, they were more ready to bid against the socialists in offering economic and social change. Irritated by the accelerating trustification and the dangers it brought to their own opportunities, they had an additional impulse toward dissent. The early 1900's were no period to produce a bitter Populism, but they were also no period for acquiescence.

For the first time considerable numbers of small businessmen and white-collar workers were joining factory hands and farmers in a restless questioning. At the top of the society, among the Best People, more men and women were talking reform and more of those interested in change were linking demands for clean government with an advocacy of governmental moves to help the lower-income groups. The breakaway from liberalism among upper-class reformers was most marked in patrician circles. A business-minded reformer might be quite happy with a cleaner, more efficient government that operated in behalf of corporations; patrician reformers were hardly satisfied with liberal triumphs that left intact their long-time target, the parvenu plutocracy. Patrician reformers also evidenced an especially strong concern over the growth of socialism, in part because their relatively extensive contacts with western Europe provided a goading reminder of how discontent could swiftly build up movements for government ownership.

Once again a revealing example was provided by the Maryland aristocrat Charles Bonaparte. In the war on Grantism, Bonaparte had thought politically of the impediments to his ideal of rule by an elite. The "one great issue," Bonaparte believed in those days, was "fair or fraudulent elections." By the early 1900's Bonaparte was thinking politically and economically of the obstacles in the way of his system, and he attacked both political bosses and those "big, strong, greedy, over-prosperous animals of the . . . pig order," the trust magnates. Within a decade after the defeat of

Bryan, a patrician President named the patrician Bonaparte his Attorney General, and the intonation of the appointment was caught by a journalist who wrote that Bonaparte, "with his natural hatred of vulgar and greedy rich men," would prove "a terror to every trust magnate in the country who comes under that head." One of Bonaparte's "infirmities," a friend added, was his "hostility to certain forms of economic progress." [6] If this hostility seemed an infirmity to the friend, who was associated with corporation America, it also represented the bridge by which the patrician reformer moved beyond liberalism and brought his wealth and prestige to a fresh movement of dissidence.

IV

AT FIRST the new reformers had no special name for themselves. "Liberal" was too closely associated with Clevelandism. "Populist" called up the dour radicalism of the Nineties. Gradually the term "progressivism" took its place after "liberalism" and "Populism" as the label for another, quite different attempt to reform post-Civil War America.

In many fundamentals progressivism continued Populism. Progressivism revered the Jefferson of Ignatius Donnelly, rather than of Samuel Tilden. For progressives as for Populists, the central problem was opportunity, and to the extent that the two movements concerned themselves with liberty, they shared an emphasis on freeing the avenues of opportunity. Each aimed to "restore" opportunity by much the same program. Government was to be democratized in order to make it more amenable to reform. Reform meant primarily the ending of governmental interventions that benefited large-scale capital and a rapid increase in the interventions that favored men of little or no capital. Many of progressivism's specific proposals came straight from Populism, including the direct election of United States senators, the initiative

---

[6] Eric F. Goldman: *Charles J. Bonaparte* (Johns Hopkins Press, 1943), pp. 130–1.

and the referendum, anti-trust action, a federal income tax, the encouragement of trade-unions, and an eight-hour day. In the spirit of Populism, progressives took up new proposals for direct democracy or the advancement of lower-income groups, most notably popular primaries, the recall of elected officials, workmen's compensation legislation, and minimum-wage and maximum-hour laws.

The new reform also continued Populism's political recognition of women. The cities were producing their own female activists, and these women, for the most part prosperous and well educated, made effective advocates of feminism in the eyes of progressives. Almost every city had its Jane Addams, charming mistress of the Hull House that was turning so many bright young people into bright young rebels, or its Florence Kelley, a wary, hardheaded crusader, who had a major role in putting through Illinois' first factory inspection act and served brilliantly as the state's pioneer factory inspector. The activities of women like these gave great force to the feminist argument that an equal participation of women in the national life would make that life more decent. By 1905 the progressive municipal reformer, Frederic Howe, was writing: "To man the city is primarily a centre of industry. He measures it by commercial standards. . . . Woman, on the other hand, sees the city in the light of the home. The vice, the saloon, the schools, the libraries, the water, gas, and transportation questions are to her questions of the family, of the child, questions of comfort, of happiness, of safety." No move, Howe was sure, would be more likely to produce a general betterment of conditions than satisfying the demands of feminism.[7]

Watching the progressives take over so much of Populism, the nouveau Brooklynite, Mary Ellen Lease, could not restrain herself entirely. "My work in the good old Populist days was not in vain," she gibed a reporter. "The Progressive party has adopted our platform, clause by clause, plank by plank." [8] Yet progressivism was not simply the Populist buggy rolled out for a new cen-

---

[7] Howe: *The City, the Hope of Democracy* (Scribner, 1905), pp. 175-6.
[8] Quoted in Hicks, p. 421.

tury. More urban in its base, progressivism was much more genuinely concerned with the problems of labor and was far more inclined to include small businessmen and white-collar workers in the groups it wanted to help. Equally important, progressivism was developing its own special attitude toward the immigrant.

The progressives did not entirely drop Populism's anti-immigrant feeling. One of the country's best-known progressive spokesmen, the sociologist, Edward A. Ross, publicly denounced "the lower class of Jews of Eastern Europe [who] reach here moral cripples, their souls warped and dwarfed." Many of these Jews, Ross went on, had "a monstrous and repulsive love of gain. . . . The East European Hebrews feel no reverence for law as such and are willing to break any ordinance they find in their way. The fact that pleasure-loving Jewish business men spare Jewesses but pursue Gentile girls excites bitter comment." [9] In 1901 Ross provided the decade's most effective formula for fear of the whole new migration, Jewish or Gentile. Speaking before the American Academy of Political and Social Science, he argued that the immigrants reproduced rapidly because they were willing to live squalidly, while old-stock Americans, clinging to a high standard of living, were calling one or two children a family. "For a case like this," Ross declared in a phrase that caught on in progressive as well as conservative circles, "I can find no words so apt as 'race suicide.' There is no bloodshed, no violence, no assault. . . . The higher race quietly and unmurmuringly eliminates itself rather than endure individually the bitter competition it has failed to ward off by collective action." [1]

But Ross, if a thoroughgoing progressive in most respects, was talking against the trend of the movement in his attitude toward the immigrant. The general relaxation of anti-immigrant feeling was reflected in reform opinion; progressivism sloughed off some of the farmer's extreme suspicion of the newcomer; and a number of urban progressives, newspapermen like Lincoln Steffens or

[9] Ross: *The Old World in the New* (Century, 1914), pp. 150, 154.
[1] Ross: "The Causes of Race Superiority," *Annals of the American Academy of Political and Social Science* (July-December 1901), XVIII, 86, 88.

municipal reformers like Frederic Howe, were having their doubts whether political corruption was especially attributable to the immigrant slums and were saying so in highly effective ways. Many progressives carried over the Populist fear that unlimited immigration kept wage scales down and exceeded the nation's ability to assimilate. Consequently they continued the Populist demand for restriction of the influx. But progressivism was far more friendly than Populism to the immigrants who had already arrived. It was moving toward a genuine acceptance of the newcomer, even toward espousal of an important role for him.[2]

Progressives made up the dominant element in the settlement houses that were undertaking the first systematic "Americanization" work, and the Americanization they advocated was no one-way street. The immigrant was not only to learn, settlement workers emphasized; he was to teach. While assimilating, he was to preserve the parts of his heritage which did not conflict with adjustment to the United States and he was to enrich American culture by bringing to it desirable ideas or customs from his old-country background. This type of Americanization was enthusiastically approved by Israel Zangwill, a British Jew who had become familiar with American settlement work by his labors as head of an organization that helped Russian Jews flee the pogroms to the United States. In 1908 Zangwill wrote his enthusiasm into *The Melting Pot*, one of those occasional literary works that both express and further a social movement.

The chief characters of Zangwill's play were all immigrants in New York City—an Irish Catholic, a Jew-hating nobleman who had personally conducted pogroms in Russia, his daughter, and a young Russian Jew whose parents had been murdered at the order of the nobleman. The theme was the general benefit to be derived from what Zangwill called an "all-around give-and-take," between the various groups of immigrants and between all the new-

---

[2] Walter Weyl, himself an example of the progressive attitude, correctly pointed out that "many of the people who are opposed to a practically unregulated immigration are the very ones who are seeking to promote the welfare of those immigrants who are already in." *The New Democracy* (Macmillan, 1912), p. 347.

comers and the old stock.[3] At the end of the play, as the Jew and the Jew-killer's daughter prepared to marry, the young man looked out to a sunset and proclaimed it "the fires of God round His crucible."

> DAVID: There she lies, the great Melting Pot—listen! Can't you hear the roaring and the bubbling? (*he points east*). There gapes her mouth—the harbour where a thousand mammoth feeders come from the ends of the world to pour in their human freight. Ah, what a stirring and a seething! Celt and Latin, Slav and Teuton, Greek and Syrian,—black and yellow—
>
> VERA: Jew and Gentile—
>
> DAVID: Yes, East and West, and North and South, the palm and the pine, the pole and the equator, the crescent and the cross—how the great alchemist melts and fuses them with his purging flame! Here shall they all unite to build the Republic of Man and the Kingdom of God. Ah, Vera, what is the glory of Rome and Jerusalem where all nations and races come to worship and look back, compared with the glory of America, where all races and nations come to labour and look forward! [4]

"Romantic claptrap," the *New York Times* critic snorted, and Zangwill's gushing prose is certainly hard to read today without wincing.[5] But in a more sentimental era, the play provided for thousands of progressives an exciting expression of their desire for an attitude toward the immigrant that was more generous and hopeful than Populist snarling.

In the political field, progressivism was altering Populism by the greater degree to which it sought centralization. The Populists may not have been afraid of pyramided power, and the progressives certainly did not ignore reform possibilities on the municipal and state levels. But the increasing urge to centralize was showing itself in a number of ways, of which the two most important were

[3] Zangwill: *The Melting Pot* (Macmillan, 1923), p. 203.
[4] Ibid., pp. 184–5.
[5] Quoted in ibid., p. 199.

greater dependence on federal rather than state action and on executives rather than legislatures.

The progressives were men in a hurry, and even at their best legislatures must always seem slow and cumbersome. The legislatures of the turn of the century, reformers constantly learned in additional ways, were hardly legislatures at their best. At the same time, able individuals were showing the prodigies that could be performed by one skillful reformer in an executive position. Under the circumstances, progressives relied increasingly on the "good man" who would bring to reform the decisiveness of a Carnegie and would maneuver, drive, or skirt around a legislature. The desire to provide efficient by-passes heightened progressive enthusiasm for the administrative commission, a device which gave long-time, quasi-legislative powers to a few men appointed by the executive. A similar zeal to free the executive encouraged progressive assaults against the check-and-balance systems so common in American governmental structures.

Simultaneously progressives were becoming discouraged about the potentialities of action by the states. The problem with which the reformers were most concerned, the large corporation, did not yield to state action. No one of the huge businesses operated in only one state, and state regulations usually ended up in creating a maze of conflicting statutes that hindered the efficiency of corporations without exacting from them any real social responsibility. Worse yet, state social legislation was being thrown out almost as fast as it was passed. Time after time progressives battled a law through a legislature only to have a court rule that it violated the state constitution. Reforms that squeezed by this barrier still had to run the formidable gantlet of the Fourteenth Amendment to the federal Constitution.

Quite obviously, Washington was no perfect base for reform. But many of the most effective local reformers were making their way to the national capital, the Constitution did explicitly empower the federal government to regulate interstate commerce, and, above all, national action seemed the logical way to regulate corporations operating on a national scale. In the early 1900's, much more than in the Populist era, reform eyes were focusing on Washington. The trend was so marked that, as one state enthusiast ruefully admitted, some progressive writers were even arguing that the state had no place "in our governmental system. They look upon it as a political vermiform appendix that has outlived the functions it was designed to perform." [6]

If progressivism was going beyond Populism in its attitude toward centralization, it was pulling back in another important respect. Progressivism virtually gave up the Populist attempt to make the Southern Negro an equal citizen. It paid little attention to the Negro problem as a whole, and, to the extent that it worried over the black man at all, gave its support to the program of a Negro whose whole life had been a preparation for compromise.

Born to slavery and to poverty so great that his bed was a bundle of dirty rags, Booker T. Washington had been helped to his education by a series of kindly whites. The Negro school he was invited to run, Tuskegee Institute, was founded on the initiative of Southern whites, and continued white aid permitted Washington to build Tuskegee from a dilapidated shanty for thirty students to forty-six substantial buildings offering thirty trades to fourteen hundred pupils. It is possible to exaggerate the amount of faith in the white man which this background gave Booker Washington. His was a practical, canny mind, operating in a situation that suggested bargaining Negro equality for some Negro advances. ("Actually," W. E. B. Du Bois once remarked, "Washington had no more faith in the white man than I do," [7] which was saying that he had little faith indeed.) But whatever was going on behind that calm, pleasant face of Booker Washington, he spoke no belligerence toward the white man and no call for immediate equality.

When he was asked to address the Atlanta Cotton Exposition in 1895, Washington put his philosophy into sentences that im-

---

[6] Frederic C. Howe: *Wisconsin, an Experiment in Democracy* (Scribner, 1912), p. vii.
[7] Interview with Mr. Du Bois.

mediately became famous as the "Atlanta Compromise." The Negro should accept political inequality, Washington said, provided he was given the opportunity to advance economically and educationally; in time, having prepared himself for the wise use of the vote, he would be granted the privilege. Washington bluntly repudiated any drive for social equality. "In all things that are purely social," he declared in his most widely quoted sentence, "we can be as separate as the fingers, yet one as the hand in all things essential to mutual progress." [8]

In the early 1900's Washington's argument had the force of apparent success. His program was the first to promise any substantial advance for the Negro which the nation as a whole seemed willing to accept. Tuskegee Institute and similar schools were rapidly turning out trained Negroes who could train others and, by supporting themselves in decency, win respect for the whole race. In the decade between 1900 and 1910, Negro illiteracy throughout the country declined from forty-four to thirty per cent, while the number of farms owned by Southern Negroes increased at a rate four times more swiftly than the growth of the Negro population. Progressives interested in the Negro observed all this and remembered the violence and quick failure that had come with Populist attempts at equality. They were inclined to become enthusiastic, to help make Booker T. Washington the first Negro national hero—and to let well enough alone.

In other, less important details, progressivism also moved away from Populism, but the core of the differences between the movements lay in a consideration that no discussion of specific variations would reveal adequately. Agrarian-dominated Populism, with its desperate sense of being left behind, its doubts whether anyone could be both a businessman and a decent citizen, its inclination to suspect the man with well-fitted clothes or polished grammar, was not the only base of progressivism. The new reform was a product of the cities as much as of the farms, an amalgam of the Best People's liberalism and the nobody's Popu-

[8] Basil Mathews: *Booker T. Washington* (Harvard University Press, 1948), pp. 85–9.

lism, a middle doctrine for a nation rapidly committing itself to middle-class ways of thinking. Progressivism accepted business America, even was enthusiastic about it, and aimed merely to correct abuses. It prized cultivation, manner, and efficiency; quite characteristically, progressivism restored liberalism's emphasis on civil-service reform. Above all, progressivism replaced Populist grimness with a gusty, dawn-world confidence, worrying about America, but not worrying about it enough to turn to extremes. Few progressives continued the Populist demand for government ownership, and the belligerent Populist distinction between "producing" and "nonproducing" classes fast disappeared from reform terminology.[9] To the progressive, America was never farmers or industrial workers locked in a class struggle with big capital. America was always "the people," some of whom were richer and more powerful than others, but all of whom could be given back their birthright of opportunity by moderate, practical moves.

The restoration of opportunity by giving stronger powers to more democratized governments, a businesslike restoration with no disreputable caterwauling—such was the least common denominator of the thinking that was rising out of the union of liberalism and Populism. It was a denominator to which each progressive added his own integers; it had its confusions, its vagaries, and its dodges. But it was a sweepingly appealing program, the most national one since the Republican platform that rode Lincoln into the White House, and for most progressives it carried the kind of emotional intensity that whirls political movements ahead.

---

[9] Many progressives did push hard for one variety of socialism: municipally owned traction, gas, and electric companies; yet even here the call was not for a change that seemed drastic. City-dwellers, accustomed to having their mail delivered, their garbage collected, and their streets protected by municipal agencies, were hardly likely to think they were heading toward socialism if their ride to work or their cooking gas was provided through a city-owned company. In the case of one utility, electricity, the agitation for municipally owned central powerhouses did not even provoke serious business opposition. In those pioneer days of electricity, an electric powerhouse seemed so risky a venture that few businessmen wanted to undertake it. R. H. Bacon: "Municipal Power is Coming Back," *American City* (November 1928), XXXIX, 141–3.

"In fact," one progressive journalist has remembered his mood in the early 1900's, "I used to be sure reform would sweep the country, that is, I always used to be sure until I talked to the man next to me on the street car." [1] Throughout progressive America a growing confidence in the program was accompanied by a growing awareness that the program alone was not enough. Progressivism was face to face with a potent set of hostile ideas, ideas that had been tangled up with the middle-class rejection of Populism and that did not quickly wither as the middle-class attitude moved toward dissent. Somehow the progressives had to dissolve away the argument that their whole program was unscientific, contrary to human nature, antidemocratic, unconstitutional, and immoral.

[1] The late Ray Stannard Baker, in an interview with me.

CHAPTER V

Dissolving the Steel Chain of Ideas*

IN THE closing years of his life Henry George listened to a friend bemoaning the poverty and corruption in New York City. "What do you propose to do about it?" George asked.

"Nothing!" the friend replied with a sigh. "You and I can do nothing at all. . . . We can only wait for evolution. Perhaps in four or five thousand years evolution may have carried men beyond this state of things." [1]

There they were, the hostile ideas in a capsule of conversation, spoken with all the finality of a sigh. The ideas, of course, were no deliberate contrivance on the part of evil men. The dominant groups in America had simply done what dominant groups usually do. They had, quite unconsciously, picked from among available theories the ones that best protected their position and had impressed these ideas on the national mind as Truth.

The process found a striking example in the field of anthropology. Late in the depression of 1873 Lewis Morgan, a Rochester lawyer turned anthropologist, published *Ancient Society*, which described primitive man as communist in his property attitudes, a-religious, and polygamous. The family, private property, and religion, Morgan maintained, had developed slowly amid chang-

---

* Parts of this chapter were printed, in somewhat different form, in the *Journal of the History of Ideas*, April 1952. They reappear here with the permission of the *Journal*.

[1] George: *A Perplexed Philosopher* (Charles L. Webster, New York, 1892), pp. 163–4 n.

ing circumstances. Immediately radicals seized on Morgan's book to argue that if these fundamental institutions had developed only through evolution, nothing in the status quo was fixed and all institutions could and should change. Immediately, too, those who liked the status quo were sure that a book susceptible to such interpretation simply could not be sound. They found their anthropology in the writings of Edward Westermarck. When Westermarck's first book appeared in 1891, a preface had to introduce this "hitherto unknown student"; his evidence was often flimsy and he could torture logic, as later anthropology demonstrated. But Westermarck had arrived at the conclusion that the family was as old as man, probably even an inheritance from the anthropoid apes, and he had no disturbing theories about property and religion. Within a few years the "hitherto unknown student" was anthropological truth so far as most Americans were concerned.[2]

Such truths blocked progressives no matter what point in their program they tried to advance. Their central argument, that government should use centralized powers for reform, was repelled by closely linked conceptions of economics, religion, morals, psychology, biology, history, law, and philosophy. In essence these ideas were the preconceptions common to Grantism and liberalism, a little refurbished and now coming to be known as conservatism. Democracy was founded on "self-evident" or "natural" rights, the conservatives argued, and chief among these rights was "liberty"—the liberty of a man to acquire and keep property without the interference of government, and the liberty of a workingman to deal directly with his employer without the interference of a union. Such interferences not only violated "natural rights."

[2] Robert H. Lowie: *The History of Ethnological Theory* (Farrar & Rinehart, 1937), pp. 54-5; V. F. Calverton, ed.: *The Making of Man* (Modern Library, 1931), pp. 1-37. Calverton, a Marxist, was himself a man who used Morgan's work to support his general ideological position. Alfred R. Wallace referred to the "hitherto unknown student" in an "Introductory Note" to Edward Westermarck: *The History of Human Marriage* (Macmillan, London, 1891). For a typical modern criticism of Westermarck, see Lowie, pp. 96-9.

They were certain to fail, for they contravened the "laws of economics." The Ricardian "law" explained that the income of workers always tended to the subsistence level because a raise in wages simply meant that the poor had more children, who ate up the additional income. The Malthusian "law" explained that enough food for everyone was an impossibility since population invariably increased more rapidly than the food supply. It was all that simple—and that final.

When conservative judges threw out reform legislation, they were not interpreting the state or federal Constitution from a particular point of view. Law was law, the conservative credo ran, and the judicial process included no personal opinions on the part of the judge. He was simply applying, with all the detachment symbolized in the black robe, a general law to a specific case. It was not a judge, Republican or Democratic, conservative or progressive, who spoke, but a constitution that spoke through him.

Since all American law rested ultimately on the federal Constitution, the public attitude toward that document had special importance. Until the Civil War the country as a whole had been less devoted to the property-conscious Constitution than to the fervidly equalitarian Declaration of Independence. In the later nineteenth century, with the mounting assaults on capital and the growing recognition that the Constitution was the chief bulwark of property, conservatives bestirred themselves to lift the Constitution in public esteem and to dismiss the Declaration as a collection of windy generalities. They succeeded so well that the Constitution reached a position of near-sacredness. The naïve Mary Baker Eddy spoke for naïve America when she linked God and the Constitution in describing her pillars of faith.[3] The sophisticated Henry Estabrook, outstanding among the able minds of the New York bar, was no less awe-struck. "Our great and sacred Constitution," he intoned, "serene and inviolable, stretches its beneficent powers over our land—over its

[3] Paraphrased in Thomas A. Bailey: *The Man in the Street* (Macmillan, 1948), p. 256.

lakes and rivers and forests, over every mother's son of us, like the outstretched arm of God himself. . . . O Marvellous Constitution! Magic Parchment! Transforming word! Maker, Monitor, Guardian of Mankind!" [4] Such an aura for the Constitution gave a still greater authority to conservative judges, who were assumed to be following the dictates of a political Decalogue when they voided progressive legislation.

Additional bolstering for conservatism came from the prevailing theories of biology, psychology, and morals. The mind and emotions were assumed to be fixed structures, ready-made in the womb, which functioned regardless of the environment. Some people were born to success and goodness, others to squalor and sin, and "you can't change human nature." Progressives might have the laudable desire to lift the standard of living of Negroes and immigrants and to make women partners in the democratic process, but the progressives were fighting genes. The Rockefellers were born to be Rockefellers, and the slum-dwellers to be slum-dwellers; Negroes and women were created intellectually inferior and morally weaker.

Immigrants from southern or eastern Europe, the prevailing theories continued, were inherently lacking in that "instinct for liberty" which was the basis of democracy. The instinct had appeared first in the primitive Teutonic forests and spread from there as a heritage of the "Anglo-Saxon race." Because it was hereditary, it could never be acquired by those who were not "Anglo-Saxon," no matter how long they lived in the United States nor how favorable an environment for the development of democratic attitudes was created around them. The definition of an "Anglo-Saxon" was left usefully vague. Usually it meant an American from western Europe or from anywhere long enough ago unless it was Africa, and in a pinch one need not bother with the question of origins. "Anybody can tell an Anglo-Saxon," declared Professor John W. Burgess of Columbia, who was teaching constitutional law to many men who were to be leading lawyers.

[4] Quoted in Ralph Gabriel: *The Growth of American Democratic Thought* (Ronald, 1940), p. 402.

"An Anglo-Saxon is a man who instinctively knows that liberty cannot survive trade unions and other socialistic schemes from Eastern Europe." [5]

A final sanction for the status quo came from God Himself. Two doctrines drawn from the Christian tradition were especially emphasized: the concept of the individual as a free moral agent, and the doctrine that God has determined the success or failure of each of His children. The two ideas are far from consistent, but both did yeoman service in the conservative cause. Men like James McCosh, president of Princeton University and a power in Presbyterian circles, opposed social legislation on the grounds that God-given abilities were to be used freely and any attempt to interfere with their use was "theft." Equally common was the emphasis of the famous New York preacher Henry Ward Beecher. "God has intended the great to be great and the little to be little," Beecher cried. If this meant that Henry Ward Beecher received forty thousand dollars a year and a laborer one dollar a day, there was no cause for whimpering at God's decisions. A dollar a day, Beecher explained, was not enough to "support a man and five children if a man would insist on smoking and drinking beer. . . . But the man who cannot live on bread and water is not fit to live." Out in the University of Kansas, William Allen White was learning economic predestination in still more direct form. Poverty was "an evidence of sin, or worse, weakness," White heard from his professors. Those who championed the poor were "even worse than the poor themselves, for they would pander to poverty to profit by it." [6]

Often a society of very rich and very poor was given additional justification by a landaued version of St. Paul's doctrine of stewardship. "The Moral Governor has placed the power of *acquisitiveness* in man for a good and noble purpose," the Reverend

[5] Quoted by the late Charles A. Beard, a student of Burgess, in an interview.

[6] Paxton Hibben: *Henry Ward Beecher* (George H. Doran, New York, 1927), p. 326; Walter Johnson, ed.: *Selected Letters of William Allen White* (Holt, 1947), p. 4. The McCosh quote is from Merle Curti: *The Growth of American Thought* (Harper, 1951), p. 637.

D. S. Gregory declared in his popular textbook, *Christian Ethics.*[7] The onetime militiaman, lawyer, editor, immigration agent, and atheist, Russell Conwell, was less restrained. Turning to the ministry at thirty-seven, Conwell built the struggling Grace Church of Philadelphia into the largest Protestant church in the United States by exuberant preaching that money-making was holy because the money could be spent for good causes. More than six thousand separate audiences, an estimated thirteen million people, heard Conwell's celebrated sermon, "Acres of Diamonds." There were things more godly than money, Conwell would boom, but any of them could be enhanced in value by the use of money. For "money is power; money has powers; and for a man to say, 'I do not want money,' is to say, 'I do not wish to do any good to my fellowmen.' " [8]

Whether in religion or any other field, all these ideas shared an important characteristic: they were absolute ideas, assumed to exist apart from the material world, with no relationship to time, place, or the special interests of individuals or groups. They would be as true in 2000 as in 1900, as useful to a laborer as to a banker. In religion, the "truths" were the "laws of God"; in biology or psychology, they were "objective fact"; in philosophy, law, politics, and economics, they were "natural laws." Always they were unchallengeable Truth, an ideological chain protecting America as it was with iron strength.

By the turn of the century the iron was further toughened by an admixture of Darwinism. For a time after the publication of *The Origin of Species* in 1859, leaders of every important religion fought hard against this denial of standard religious beliefs, but they were waging a losing war. By 1900 biological Darwinism had been accepted by a considerable part of the American population, and with its triumphs came an enormous prestige for anything that could be called Darwinian.

The éclat was speedily transferred to the conservative chain of

[7] Gregory: *Christian Ethics* (Eldredge & Brother, 1875), p. 224. Italicized in the original.
[8] Agnes R. Burr: *Russell H. Conwell and His Work* (Winston, Philadelphia, 1926), pp. 414–15.

ideas. One of Darwin's most brilliant popularizers, Herbert Spencer, transformed Darwin's biological laws into social "laws" that made science say precisely what every conservative wanted said. Biological Darwinism asserted that all species of organic life had evolved and were evolving by a process of the survival of the fittest. According to Spencer's "Social Darwinism," society, too, was an organism that evolved by the survival of the fittest. Existing social institutions were therefore the "fittest" way of doing things, and businessmen who bested their competitors had thereby proved themselves "the fittest" to enjoy wealth and power. No wise man would try to interfere with this evolutionary process by social legislation. At best, the social legislation would not work as it was intended to work, and, in any event, it would have baleful results. Poverty and corruption were undoubted evils, Social Darwinism admitted, but they would be cured only by a centuries-long evolution resulting from the survival of the fittest. Meanwhile, as Henry George's friend had said, "nothing, nothing at all" could be done.

The American conquests of Social Darwinism—or of Conservative Darwinism, to use a less confusing term—were as swift and as sweeping as those of biological Darwinism. "Probably no other philosopher," Henry Holt recalled, "ever had such a vogue as Spencer had from about 1870 to 1890." [9] At Yale one of the best-known academic figures in America, William Graham Sumner, made his lectures a holy war against those who would tamper with the laws of nature by reform legislation. "The truth is," Sumner declared, "that the social order is fixed by laws of nature precisely analogous to those of the physical order. The most that man can do . . . by his ignorance and conceit [is] to mar the operation of the social laws." [1] In a thousand pulpits, universities, and newspaper offices, Sumner's antireform words were echoed. A British literary adventurer, Winwood Reade, made himself a figure on both sides of the ocean by the flamboyant Sumnerism of *The Martyrdom of Man*. "In each generation," Reade declared,

[9] Henry Holt: *Garrulities of an Octogenarian Editor* (Houghton Mifflin, 1923), p. 298.
[1] Quoted in Curti, p. 638.

"the human race has been tortured that their children might profit by their woes. Our own prosperity is founded on the agonies of the past. Is it therefore unjust that we also should suffer for the benefit of those who are to come?" [2]

Spencer's visit to the United States in 1882 was an unprecedented triumph. Railroad and hotel executives, grateful for their scientifically proved fitness, competed to give him free services, and a farewell banquet at Delmonico's glittered with big names from American cultural, business, and political life. It was hard to top the tributes, which embarrassed even the vain Spencer, but Henry Ward Beecher, always resourceful, managed it. He would, Beecher suggested, meet Spencer once again in the heaven of those who had proved their fitness for immortality.[3]

"The problem presented to systems of religion and schemes of government," ironmaster Abram Hewitt had pointed out, was to make men who were equal in liberty content with inequality in the distribution of property.[4] Conservative Darwinism not only repeated the answer to the problem which conservatism had long been effectively using; its solution added all the authority of science. Conservative Darwinism created, as it were, a science of selfishness. Now John D. Rockefeller, with the same confidence that he had in his latest laboratory, could explain the Standard Oil trust to his Sunday-school class as "merely a survival of the fittest. . . . The American beauty rose can be produced in the splendor and fragrance which bring cheer to its beholder only by sacrificing the early buds which grow up around it. This is not an evil tendency in business. It is merely the working-out of a law of nature and a law of God." Now the general manager of the Atlas works of Pittsburgh, asked what might be done to raise the wages of employees who made seventy-five cents a day, was able to reply: "I don't think anything could be done. . . . The law

[2] Reade: *The Martyrdom of Man* (Kegan Paul, Trench, Trubner, London, 22nd ed., n.d.), p. 543.

[3] Edward L. Youmans: *Herbert Spencer on the Americans and the Americans on Herbert Spencer* (Appleton, 1883), pp. 21–67; Spencer: *Autobiography* (Appleton, 1904), II, 479; Holt, pp. 50–2.

[4] Quoted in Richard Hofstadter: *Social Darwinism in American Thought* (University of Pennsylvania Press, 1944), p. 32.

of the 'survival of the fittest' governs that." [5] Conservative Darwinism had brought to the iron chain of ideas protecting the status quo all the added strength and modernity of steel.

II

"NARCOTIZING TEACHING and preaching," progressives railed. The whole conservative system, Edward Ross said for the reformers, was nothing more than "a brutal selfishness as old as the Ice Age [which] struts about in phrases borrowed from the Darwinists and bids us see in the prosperity of the wicked the Success of the Adapted." [6] Yet few of the progressives showed any desire for an entirely new system of thinking. They too were sons of the nineteenth century, entranced by science, confirmed Darwinians. Like the conservatives, and quite as unconsciously, they adapted to their own needs ideological possibilities already at hand.

Conservative Darwinism itself suggested the reform reply. After all, Conservative Darwinism was supposedly Darwinism, and the heart of the Darwinian doctrine was continuous evolution in relation to the environment. Conservative Darwinians had recognized evolution up to the present, and then, for all practical purposes, they had called a halt. In the name of environmentalism, they advocated ideas which they called timeless and which were therefore independent of any environment, past or present. Accepting a doctrine that inevitably suggested a relationship between ideas and material things, the Conservative Darwinians nevertheless talked as if truth were absolute.

Each of these phases of Conservative Darwinism pointed to its own obvious question. Why not insist on thoroughgoing evolution and argue that contemporary institutions could and should change

---

[5] Rockefeller is quoted in ibid., p. 31; the Atlas general manager, Thomas M. Miller, in *Senate Committee on Education and Labor*, 48th Cong., 2nd Sess.: *Report . . . upon the Relations between Labor and Capital* (1885), II, 26.

[6] Ross: *Social Control* (Macmillan, 1901), p. 392, and *Social Psychology* (Macmillan, 1909), p. 252.

rapidly? Why not call for thoroughgoing environmentalism and explain away any apparent superiority of a Rockefeller or an Anglo-Saxon by arguing that they had enjoyed favorable environments? Why not consider Conservative Darwinism itself nothing more than an ideology that had developed in an environment of political bosses and trust magnates in order to justify that environment? Why not, in short, work out a Reform Darwinism that would dissolve away conservativism's steel chain of ideas while leaving Darwinism itself intact? Why not—if you were a Darwinian who disliked Conservative Darwinism, if you wanted to replace dreary inevitabilities with a philosophy of flux that justified experiment and change? The attraction of Reform Darwinism was the greater because it could use all the cosmetics of science by which Conservative Darwinism made itself so alluring. As a matter of fact, Reform Darwinism could claim to be, and was claimed to be, a good deal more scientific than Conservative Darwinism because it related more things more continuously to environment.

The men who helped develop Reform Darwinism were not all economic and social reformers. Simply as a way of thinking, the prevailing ideas were enticingly vulnerable. Conservative Darwinism not only used and stopped using concepts with conspicuous convenience. It included obvious absurdities, such as the insistence that ethics was important in a world supposed to be an irredeemable jungle. Conservative Darwinism, moreover, was the doctrine of a generation that was getting old, as unexciting as a long-opened bottle of champagne. Countless restless young minds who were just as ready as Herbert Spencer to lambaste social legislation felt intensely uncomfortable in Herbert Spencer's world. But the conservatives who became iconoclasts were far less numerous than the reformers. More important, conservatives who subjected Conservative Darwinism to a sweeping environmentalism rarely placed great emphasis on the economic environment.

A generation of American scholarship has made plain that reformers of the early 1900's did not invent economic interpretation. The way of thinking goes back to the ancients, and it had been an important part of American political argument in the pre-Civil War period. What has not been made plain is that economic interpretation has seldom been used to argue, without judgment values or emotional connotations, that the ideas of each economic group correlate with the economic interests of the group. Few Americans have been interested in a purely analytical tool. They wanted an interpretation that would function as a corrosive of enemy arguments, and to serve as a corrosive, an economic interpretation had to be constructed in such a way that its acid ate into enemy ideas alone.

The techniques for making economic interpretation a one-way corrosive have varied. Sometimes the interpretationist associated ideas that he approved with an economic group that he endowed with favorable attributes, such as intelligence and public-spiritedness, while opposition ideas were connected with an economic group that was made opprobrious in other respects. Thus Thomas Jefferson, firmly convinced that parties bespoke property interests, described small farmers not simply as small farmers but as "the chosen people of God, if ever He had a chosen people . . . vigorous . . . independent . . . and virtuous"; urban citizens not only represented a different economic interest but were inclined to "corruption." [7] Hamilton, just as vigorous an economic interpretationist, stood Jefferson's usage on its head. In Hamilton's writings, the wealthy were the men of better "character"; the low-income groups, including Jefferson's small farmers, tended more toward "moral depravity." [8] Progressives sometimes employed an economic interpretation that added noneconomic attributes, but they were more inclined toward another method of making economic interpretation work for their purposes. They often attributed to the economic groups they favored additional,

[7] Quoted in Charles A. Beard: *The Economic Origins of Jeffersonian Democracy* (Macmillan, 1936), pp. 424, 425. Beard remarked that Jefferson "accepted the Federalist principle and practise of distrusting the intelligence and character of the section of the people that was opposed to him" (p. 463).

[8] Henry Cabot Lodge, ed.: *The Works of Alexander Hamilton* (Putnam, 1904), II, 27. For discussion of a similar usage in the late nineteenth and early twentieth centuries, see Eric F. Goldman: *John Bach McMaster* (University of Pennsylvania Press, 1943), pp. 137-9, and "J. Allen Smith: the Reformer and His Dilemma," *Pacific Northwest Quarterly* (July 1944), XXXV, 203-4.

95

highly laudable characteristics, while their enemies were spoken of as money-grabbers and little or nothing else.[9]

In this use, the effectiveness of the interpretation obviously depended on the audience's assumption that there was something low about acting for economic ends when the ends could not be ennobled by noneconomic associations. The word "assumption," must be used, for the idea is just that. In cold rationality there is no more reason for considering unadorned economic motivation low than there is for looking askance at a sheer motive of love. But the progressives could depend on the reaction of their public. If making money has always been considered an achievement in the United States, condemnation of the mere moneymaker has been just as much a part of the nation's thinking, deeply set in its most common political and literary traditions, refreshed every year by tens of thousands of sermons, editorials, novels, and Fourth-of-July orations.

Any attempt to analyze how this attitude became so ingrained in the American mind would require another book about the United States, if not an excursion into the intellectual history of the world. Even Karl Marx, who prided himself on the rigidly scientific nature of his economic determinism, could casually divide mankind into the followers of Karl Marx, who were lovers of humanity, and his opponents, who were almost always merely money-seekers.[1] Certainly religious tradition is a large part of the explanation. All of the powerful religions, and none more so than Christianity, distinguished sharply between the spiritual and the material realms and placed the material world in a lower, almost leprous category. The United States, growing up in an intensely Christian atmosphere, could never turn its face to an unadorned Mammon. The Beechers and the McCoshes and the Conwells found a way of accepting the pecuniary drive of their America and even of glorifying it, but the acceptance and glorification were managed only by making money a means to a noneconomic

[9] The methods of a number of important progressives who used these types of economic interpretation are analyzed in Chaps. vi and vii.

[1] Jacques Barzun: *Darwin, Marx, and Wagner* (Little, Brown, 1941), p. 197.

end. The author of "Acres of Diamonds," who was inclined to believe that any rich man was a good man, would still have been outraged by anyone, rich or poor, who advocated a policy merely on the grounds that it enriched people. One had to become rich, if not in a fit of absence of mind, at least in a fit of godliness.

Whatever the sources of the American aversion to the cash nexus, that aversion made economic interpretation the most important element in Reform Darwinism. It gave the progressive a way of saying to the conservative: "Your philosophy, economics, politics, anthropology, everything you call Truth, is a rationalization of your economic interests." More important yet, it gave the reformer a way of making the charge that placed an onus of shame on his opponent. In 1947 the British scholar Edward Carr pointed out that the Soviet impact on the thought of Western civilization was largely attributable to the way Marxism had taken the "supposed absolute values" of democracy and reduced them to "a reflexion of the interests of a privileged class. . . . What was thought of as absolute turns out to be relative to a given social structure and to possess validity only as an adjunct of that structure." Thus Marxism had "called in question the moral authority of the ideals and principles of Western democracy." [2] Long before the Soviet Union existed, American reformers were using a similarly effective economic interpretation in their Reform Darwinian attack.

III

THE EARLIEST important use of Reform Darwinism, and one of the most sweeping applications ever made, was the book that had heralded the rise of the non-liberal discontent. Henry George's *Progress and Poverty* performed a dual role in the history of modern American reform. It not only contributed Single Taxism to the swirl of dissenting doctrines in the Eighties and Nineties; it was responsible for starting along new lines of thinking an

[2] Carr: *The Soviet Impact on the Western World* (Macmillan, 1947), pp. 91, 94.

amazing number of the men and women who emerged as progressive leaders in the early 1900's. Some of these reformers became single-taxers, but most did not or, if they did, they remained single-taxers only a short while. The doctrine's emphasis on the land problem, its hostility to governmental controls, and its revolutionary implications hardly suited the rising generation of reformers. The story of a large number of the group was like that of Clarence Darrow, who, having been jolted out of conservative ways of thinking by *Progress and Poverty*, soon tossed aside its "Problem Solved" chapters. What Henry George did for the Darrows was to point a way, by a Reform Darwinism of cankerous power, through the steel chain of conservative ideas.

George's thesis that abundant land had created the enormous opportunity of the earlier period provided a sweeping economic interpretation of American life, and he pushed on to a specific economic interpretation of Conservative Darwinism. According to that doctrine, George wrote, existing social evils resulted from "fixed laws, inevitable and eternal"; actually the "laws" were merely a rationalization of greed. Conservative Darwinism was a "buttressed" form of Malthusianism, which "parries the demand for reform, and shelters selfishness from question and from conscience. . . . Poverty, want, and starvation are by this theory not chargeable either to individual greed or to social maladjustments; they are the inevitable results of universal laws, with which, if it were not impious, it were as hopeless to quarrel as with the law of gravitation." Having reduced inevitable laws to defenses of economic interest, George quickly made plain why he was anxious to emphasize them as such. Then Americans would know "that the injustice of society, not the niggardliness of nature, is the cause of . . . want and misery." [3]

With similar Reform Darwinism, George went after conservative religion and the conservative conception of democracy. Ministers like Henry Ward Beecher, *Progress and Poverty* maintained, were not expounding the laws of God but were engaged in "a

[3] George: *Progress and Poverty* (Modern Library, 1929), pp. 98–102, 141, 390–4, 478–82, 550–2.

gratuitous attribution to the laws of God." They were interpreting Christianity in a way that made it possible for the "rich Christian [to] bend on Sundays in a nicely upholstered pew to implore the good gifts of the All father without any feeling of responsibility for the squalid misery that is festering but a square away." [4] Conservatives who failed to relate democracy to its economic setting, George summarized his political analysis, were glossing over the "central truth." In an economic situation like the one developing in the United States, democracy as conservatives defined it became "the liberty to compete for employment at starvation wages." Political conceptions, if they were to retain their original effect, had to evolve with changing conditions.[5]

The purport of George's approach was plainest in his treatment of the differences between individuals. Neither the success of a trust magnate nor the political competence of an "Anglo-Saxon," he argued, came from hereditary traits, as the Conservative Darwinians claimed. "The great differences . . . cannot be explained in this way. The influence of heredity, which it is now the fashion to rate so highly, is as nothing compared with the influences which mold the man after he comes into the world." In emphasizing the point, George described how he himself had been converted from the belief that Negroes were innately inferior. Negro children, George wrote, were fully as bright as white children until they were ten or twelve years old, but then they slumped. He had accepted this as proof of a racial inability to keep up with white standards until a Negro Bishop started him on a different line of thinking. Negroes, George quoted the Bishop approvingly, fell behind for a reason that had nothing to do with native ability. " 'As soon as they get old enough to appreciate their status—to realize that they are looked upon as belonging to an inferior race, and can never hope to be anything more than cooks, waiters, or something of that sort, they lose their ambition and cease to keep up.' " [6]

George was too much a product of the nineteenth century not

[4] Ibid., pp. 99, 150.
[5] Ibid., pp. 299–300, 340, 544–52.
[6] Ibid., pp. 489, 490.

to consider Jews very different, and he showed no inclination to call the difference good. He did insist that the difference came from intensive intermarriage, and that the intensive intermarriage resulted from an environmental fact. "It is the Hebrew religion—and certainly religion is not transmitted by generation, but by association—which has everywhere preserved the distinctiveness of the Hebrew race. This religion, which children derive, not as they derive their physical characteristics, but by precept and association . . . has, by engendering suspicion and dislike, produced a powerful outside pressure which . . . has everywhere constituted of the Jews a community within a community. Thus has been built up and maintained a certain peculiar environment which gives a distinctive character. Jewish intermarriage has been the effect, not the cause of this." [7]

And why all this involved explanation of a group for whom George clearly felt no warmth? Even in the case of these peculiar people, he obviously wanted to stress, even when inescapable laws seemed plainly at work, inescapable laws were not the correct explanation. Environment, an environment that had been made by human beings and could be changed by human beings, determined the characteristics of Jews, as it determined all men, institutions, and ideas. Therefore the Conservative Darwinian argument that social progress was possible only through slow race improvement was an unnecessary and brutal fatalism. Legislating a better environment, particularly a better economic environment, could bring about a better world, and bring it about before unconscionable centuries. [8]

IV

HENRY GEORGE did not invent Reform Darwinism. His book, however influential, was only the most rounded and powerful note in a growing chorus. In the generation after the depression

[7] Ibid., pp. 497–8.
[8] Ibid., pp. 478–81.

of 1873, as the progressive program was emerging from liberalism and Populism, parts of Reform Darwinism were developed and made important by all kinds of men in every section of the country. From the bench of the Massachusetts Supreme Court, Justice Oliver Wendell Holmes looked down his patrician nose and told all apostles of inevitability: "The mode in which the inevitable comes to pass is through effort." [9] In New York a half-hungry lodger at the Art Student's League, Stephen Crane, borrowed money from his brother to publish *Maggie: A Girl of the Streets* and sent a copy to a Baptist minister with the note: "It tries to show that environment is a tremendous thing in this world, and often shapes lives regardlessly. If I could prove that theory I would make room in heaven for all sorts of souls (notably an occasional street girl) who are not confidently expected to be there by many excellent people." [1] In Georgia, in the days when he was still at the height of his Populist enthusiasm, Tom Watson would get off sweeping Reform Darwinian interpretations of politics. What of this cry of "class legislation"? Watson asked. "What has this country ever had but class legislation? The second law Congress ever passed was aimed to build up commerce and manufactures at the expense of agriculture. Our statute books are filled with legislation in behalf of capital, at the expense of labor. . . . If we must have class legislation, as we have always had it and always will have it, what class is more entitled to it than the largest class—the working class?" And at these words, an observer reported, "a glad shout of approval . . . rang through the wood"—from a clay-hill crowd most of whom would have reached for their guns at being called a Darwinian.[2] Under any name, for pauper or patrician, Reform Darwinism was the natural approach of Americans who were angry at their America.

An incidental fact made the professor peculiarly susceptible to Reform Darwinism. Before the Civil War many American schol-

[9] Oliver Wendell Holmes, Jr.: *Collected Legal Papers* (Harcourt, Brace, 1920), p. 305.
[1] Quoted in Malcolm Cowley: "Dos Passos and His Predecessors," *New York Times Sunday Book Review*, January 19, 1947, p. 1.
[2] C. Vann Woodward: *Tom Watson* (Macmillan, 1938), p. 178.

101

ars went to Europe for advanced study because of the superior, or what were thought to be superior, universities there. The Civil War halted this trend, but it was soon revived, and by the Nineties a large proportion of the ambitious young men in each academic field were seeking European degrees. Some went to England, where the attack on Spencerianism was far more advanced than in the United States. Most went to Germany, and there they came under influences equally likely to prepare them for Reform Darwinism. The leading German scholars were teaching the "Historical" approach, a way of viewing institutions that was George-like in its emphasis on continuous evolution in relation to environment. Study in Germany also meant living in a country where Bismarck's anxiety to undermine socialism was bringing about an exciting series of state-sponsored reforms. To a generation that has lived through Hitler and learned the continuity between Bismarck and Hitler, it may seem ironical that Bismarck's Germany should have served as a catalytic of American progressive thought, but in the case of many American scholars that is precisely what happened. They returned to the United States, to use the words of the German-trained psychologist G. Stanley Hall, "fairly loathing . . . the narrow, inflexible orthodoxy" of their country.[3]

Of course there was no mass upsurge in the American universities. Most academics were satisfied to march in step with the dominant opinion, and manufacturers and bankers on boards of trustees did their best to see that the professors kept in step—so much so that almost every one of the important dissenting academics was fired from at least one college. Particularly in the years surrounding the election of 1896, the colleges were so relentlessly purged that the reform sociologist Edward Ross can be pardoned for having spoken of a "net of tyranny."[4] Heretical professors who were not dismissed were likely to find their classes scheduled at hours when compulsory courses in other fields were given, their promotions blocked, their teaching loads so

[3] G. Stanley Hall: *Life and Confessions of a Psychologist* (Appleton, 1923), p. 223. "Loathed" has been changed to "loathing."
[4] Ross: *Seventy Years of It* (Appleton-Century, 1936), p. 52.

heavy they often resigned in despair. Yet a significant number of academics, spurred on by European and American influences alike, continued to think and write reform, and within a decade after the Bryan election, five universities had emerged as foci of attack on conservatism's chain of ideas.

First to become prominent as such was Johns Hopkins, founded in 1876 with a German-trained president and German-trained scholars manning most of the key professorships. Particularly in economics and religious studies, Hopkins became so associated with adventurous thought that long after its most rambunctious days, in the 1930's, the witch-hunting presidency of Isaiah Bowman still seemed decidedly incongruous. In New York, where industrialism had shown its ugliest possibilities, ancient Columbia University developed its own band of rebels, most notably in political science, history, philosophy, and anthropology. The new University of Chicago, made rich by John D. Rockefeller, went bidding for talent and soon found its solemn array of big names interlarded with obstreperous free thinkers. The state universities beyond the Appalachians were particularly sensitive to the winds of reform, and two of these institutions, Wisconsin and Washington, completed the five major storm centers in the country. At Madison, university professors became an intimate part of Governor La Follette's drive to remake Wisconsin. The University of Washington, born in the midst of a Populist upheaval, quickly added to its faculty Vernon Parrington, whose youthful discontent had been intensified by study in England, and J. Allen Smith, a fierce critic of conservative political science and a victim of the 1896 purge of Marietta College in Ohio. No university, not even the ancient citadels of conservatism in the East, went untouched. Divinity schools like Rochester Theological Seminary, where thought had long tiptoed from one serene absolute to another, suddenly heard the yawp of Reform Darwinism. And many a doughty old heretic was ready to believe anything when he considered that the Woodrow Wilson who talked so sweeping a Reform Darwinism in the election of 1912 was only a few years removed from the presidency of Princeton University.

The professors did not always think the Henry Georges were very sound; the Henry Georges did not always think the professors were very useful. But seminal reform minds in and outside the universities were one in working away at Conservative Darwinism. Between the depression of 1873 and the beginning of World War I, and especially during the early 1900's, these thinkers developed ideological acids capable of dissolving every link in conservatism's steel chain of ideas.

CHAPTER VI

"The God That Answereth by Low Food Prices . . ."

WHEN *Progress and Poverty* was published, one of Henry George's first acts was to hurry off a copy to his father with an exultant note. He had written, George was sure, "a great book," but he did not say that the work was great as political, economic, or social thinking. George was deeply troubled because he felt that millions of Americans were finding it difficult to reconcile a faith in God with the belief that the laws of God condemned so many to poverty and frustration. *Progress and Poverty* was "a great book" because the single tax, by reopening opportunity, would restore religious faith.[1]

George's attitude was not unusual, except in its intensity. America of the late nineteenth century, whether reformist or standpat, was a religious America, and probably the key link in the conservative chain of ideas was the religious sanction for the status quo. If it was hard to argue against Ricardo and Spencer when people believed them to have formulated absolute truths, it was still harder to argue against "the laws of God." Until God was brought over to reform, the walls of Jericho would stand against a thousand progressive trumpets.

[1] Henry George, Jr.: *Life of Henry George* (Doubleday, Page, 1911), II, 321; George: *Progress and Poverty* (Modern Library, 1929), Conclusion.

English influences strongly encouraged the development of a reform-minded Protestantism in the United States. Industrialized earlier, England more quickly sensed the incongruity of pious manufacturers who worked men sixteen hours a day for a pittance. Before the Civil War, and increasingly with each passing year, English churchmen, novelists, and settlement workers were sounding an international call for a Christianity that could stand the test of the society it helped create. Especially influential in the United States were the writings of the Englishmen William Morris and John Ruskin, who insisted, in prose of stained-glass beauty, that true Christianity meant working for economic and social change. A reformer as little sentimental as Charles Beard carried Ruskin's *Unto This Last* around with him for years. The books of William Morris, especially his Utopian novel *News from Nowhere*, brought to thousands of sensitive minds the catalysis that Vernon Parrington experienced. "The flame of radicalism was making ready to leap up within me," Parrington recalled of his youth. "It wanted only further fuel, and William Morris came bringing that fuel. In lovely prose . . . he laid bare the evils of industrialism. . . . It was a message that stirred me to the quick and convinced me . . . that the business man's society, symbolized by the cash register and existing solely for profit, must be destroyed to make way for another and better ideal." [2]

In the midst of this churning, American churchmen worked out the Reform Darwinian interpretation that would tie religion to reform. The publication of *Christianity and the Social Crisis* in 1907 and of *Christianizing the Social Order* in 1912 gave the leadership of the movement to Walter Rauschenbusch, a slender, trimly goateed professor at the Rochester Theological Seminary. The seventh in a line of ministers, Rauschenbusch had started his preaching career with the traditional emphasis on saving individ-

[2] Parrington: "Autobiography," MS., in the possession of Mrs. Parrington, p. 49. Professor William Savery, of the University of Washington, a long-time friend of Parrington, has written (in a letter to me, January 17, 1944): "Parrington told me at one time that the main influence upon his thinking had been that of William Morris." And certainly, Professor Savery added, while Parrington was writing his *Main Currents in American Thought* he was "primarily a follower of Morris."

ual souls. But his pastorate raised questions none of his ancestors had to face. The Rauschenbusch church was located on the edge of "Hell's Kitchen," a despairing side-alley of New York's swagger and glitter. "One could hear human virtue cracking and crushing all around," Rauschenbusch wrote of the slum, and yet there were always a host of ministers to sigh inevitability. Feverishly the young preacher read in the dissident literature of the day. He devoured Bellamy's *Looking Backward*; whole chapters of *Progress and Poverty* clung to his troubled mind; John Ruskin, he said admiringly, was "the most Christlike thinker in all literature." [3] A visit to England, where Rauschenbusch stayed with Beatrice and Sidney Webb, and several trips to Germany, where he did advanced work in the "Historical" study of Jesus, heightened his sense of what could be achieved if men's thoughts were redirected. By 1897, when Rauschenbusch left his pastorate for a professorship at the Rochester Seminary, he was well on his way toward the Reform Darwinian Protestantism that made his books so rousing a message.

"We cannot join economic inequality and political equality," Rauschenbusch argued, much in the manner of Henry George. "Progress slackens when a single class appropriates the social results of the common labor, and fortifies its evil rights by unfair laws. . . . Then there is a gradual loss of productive energy, an increasing bitterness and distrust, a waning sense of duty and devotion to country, a paralysis of the moral springs of noble action." Such was the condition of America, and it had been sanctified by dogmatizing the laws of God into support of "an unregenerate economic system." The truth was that Christianity affirmed no unchanging economic system. "Translate the evolutionary themes into religious faith, and you have the doctrine of the Kingdom of God," Rauschenbusch declared in a sentence that was quoted and paraphrased across Protestant America.[4]

---

[3] Rauschenbusch: *Christianity and the Social Crisis* (Macmillan, 1907), p. 238; Donald R. Come: "Sources of the Kingdom of God of Walter Rauschenbusch," MS., in Mr. Come's possession, p. 19.

[4] Rauschenbusch: *Christianity and the Social Crisis*, pp. 254, 284, and *Christianizing the Social Order* (Macmillan, 1914), pp. 90, 257, 322.

Rauschenbusch's own translation of the evolutionary themes varied in details. At the turn of the century he emphasized co-operatives, a single tax, and trade-unions. By 1912 he was calling for a Christian socialism which would so improve men's morals by eliminating poverty that dance halls, resorts, and excursion steamers would give way to "quieter and higher pleasures," and women would stop wearing "indecent skirts, adapted to the professional needs of harlots." But always change was justified by the arguments that the prevailing Christianity was simply a rationalization of irresponsible wealth; that Jesus' teachings should be continually reinterpreted to apply to changing circumstances; and that Christianity meant, not dogma, but Christianizing the environment in which children grew up and men and women worked. Even Rauschenbusch's own Christian socialism was not to be above the incessant challenge of material welfare. "Unless the ideal social order can supply men with food, warmth, and comfort more efficiently than our present economic order," he was sure, "back we shall go to Capitalism. . . . 'The God that answereth by low food prices, let him be God.' " [5]

The year before Rauschenbusch graduated from theological seminary, nineteen rabbis from various parts of the country assembled in Pittsburgh to draw up the first comprehensive statement of "Reform Judaism." By reform these men primarily meant changes in custom and dogma, such as the abolition of the ancient prohibition on the eating of pork, the use of English prayers in synagogue services, and the denial of the doctrine that Jews should restore a Jewish state in Palestine. Such changes, said the rabbis, who were almost all of German background and dominated by German evolutionary thinking, were necessary to bring

---

A striking instance of the long-running influence of Rauschenbusch was provided in 1951 when Mrs. Myron W. Cowen, wife of the American Ambassador to the Philippines, lashed the irresponsible wealthy of the Philippines in a Manila speech that closed with a lengthy quotation from *Christianity and the Social Crisis. New York Herald Tribune*, February 10, 1951.

[5] *Christianizing the Social Order*, pp. 257, 330, 440. Rauschenbusch emphasized this approach to the point of insisting: "I am not a theologian and never shall be." Dores R. Sharpe: *Walter Rauschenbusch* (Macmillan, 1942), p. 322.

Judaism into accord with "the modern discoveries of scientific researches in the domain of nature and history." But the demands of evolutionary science did not end with a call for altered religious ideas. "We deem it our duty," Point Eight of the Pittsburgh declaration stated, "to participate in the great task of modern times, to solve, on the basis of justice and righteousness, the problems presented by the contrasts and evils of the present organization of society." [6] Although the prosperous professional and business men who dominated most Reform synagogues managed to keep Point Eight de-emphasized, they did not entirely succeed. As early as 1904 the central body of Reform Judaism had an influential committee which, under a succession of names, went ahead defining the mission of Judaism in a way basically similar to Rauschenbusch's conception of Protestantism.[7]

Well before the establishment of this committee, Reform Judaism had even produced an influential figure who was bent on reforming Reform Judaism into a social-service organization. Early in the depression of 1873 Felix Adler returned from Germany with a Ph.D. and a crusading conviction that theological exegesis or concern over any custom was hopelessly outdated by the new revelation of Darwinism and the new problems of society. Eloquent, prodigiously learned, with the face and manner of a third Isaiah, Adler seemed destined to succeed his father as rabbi of Temple Emanuel, in New York, the cathedral church of Reform Judaism and of all American Judaism. The offer came, but Adler turned it down. Instead he founded the Society for Ethical Culture, which considered itself neither Jewish nor Christian, ignored theology, called its church a "meeting-place" and its clergymen "leaders." Greatest emphasis was placed on intellectual and ethical development, and the harnessing of both to social amelioration. By 1914 Ethical Culture had an influential, if small

[6] Quoted in David Philipson: *The Reform Movement in Judaism* (Macmillan, 1931), p. 357.

[7] Bernard J. Bamberger, ed.: *Reform Judaism* (Hebrew Union College Press, Cincinnati, 1949), pp. 18–19; interviews with the late Rabbi Edward L. Israel, a leader in Reform Jewish circles. The committee first appeared in 1904 under the name Committee on Social Religious Union, and later acquired its present-day title, the Committee on Social Justice.

following, but Adler's hope for a creed that would transcend religious and social divisions was not fulfilled. Most of the devotees were upper-income, highly assimilated Jews. Ethical Culture consequently functioned as a kind of advance guard of Reform Judaism, more social-minded as a result of its doctrine, if somewhat artificial because so many of its members had joined, at least in part, as a way of ceasing to be Jews without going through the embarrassment of declaring themselves Christians.[8]

Craggy obstacles stood in the way of a Catholicism that openly appealed for a Darwinian reinterpretation of the church's doctrines. In 1864 the Papal "Syllabus of Errors" had taken a markedly dim view of "progress, liberalism, and civilization as lately introduced," and a 1907 declaration continued the papal pressure against any argument that "scientific truth" required a change in church attitudes or doctrine.[9] The American church, mass-based on a conservative Irish group and wedded to the status quo at the top by a thousand political and economic ties, was rocky soil for reform thought.[1] Yet so pervasive was the religious trend that Catholicism produced, under other rames, its own forceful band of Reform Darwinians, most notably the burly, blunt-spoken Irishman Father John Augustine Ryan.

Ryan had grown up amid the agrarian discontent of the Eighties and Nineties. Home was a hundred and sixty acres near Dakota County, Minnesota, where every crop was a gamble against tornadoes and grasshoppers and the only variation in the mortgage was whether the interest was six or twelve per cent. *Progress and Poverty* electrified the young man, while out of a neighboring Minnesota town came the voice of his fellow Irishman, Ignatius Donnelly, converting the general message of George into the planks of the Populist platform. No one in the Ryan family, es-

---

[8] The Ethical following is discussed in James Waterman Wise: *Jews Are Like That!* (Brentano's, 1928), pp. 133–6.

[9] D. Carl Mirbt: *Quellen zur Geschichte des Papsttums und des römischen Katholizismus* (J. C. B. Mohr, Tübingen, 1924), pp. 454, 508.

[1] Richard J. Purcell: "John A. Ryan, Prophet of Social Justice," *Studies* (Dublin, June 1946), XXXV, 155; Henry J. Browne: *The Catholic Church and the Knights of Labor*, in *Catholic University of America Studies in American Church History* (1949), XXXVIII, *passim.*

pecially John, had doubted that he was to be a priest, and his ardor for Populism, which most of the hierarchy denounced, would have troubled him deeply had his seminary teachers not assigned the reading of Pope Leo XIII's new encyclical, *Rerum Novarum*. There Ryan found the highest authority of the church declaring that "a small number of very rich men have been able to lay upon the masses of the poor a yoke little better than slavery itself. . . . No practical solution of this question will ever be found without the assistance of religion and the church." [2] This encyclical, Ryan was telling his co-religionists almost as soon as he won the right to wear the black robe, was "a clear challenge to and condemnation of all those selfishly interested persons and all those sincerely ignorant persons who say or think that the Church ought to keep to spiritual matters and not meddle with business or industrial matters." [3]

Soon transferred from parish work to study and teaching, Ryan proceeded to apply the *Rerum Novarum* in a way scarcely distinguishable from the Reform Darwinism of Protestants and Jews. Year after year he fought conservatives in and outside the church, insisting that the responsibilities of Catholicism evolved with changing economic circumstances. It was an uphill battle, accompanied by charges of socialism and daily excursions close to excommunication, but the Irish had not gained a reputation as politicians for nothing. After Ryan had been hurling the *Rerum Novarum* at his enemies for years, a reform-minded rabbi achieved a masterpiece of superfluity by saying to the priest: "You have a very great advantage over men in my position. . . . You can hang your 'radical' utterances on a Papal encyclical."

"Yes, I suppose there is something to that," said Father Ryan, smiling.[4]

[2] *"Rerum Novarum,"* translated in Joseph Husslein, ed.: *Social Wellsprings* (Bruce Publishing Co., Milwaukee, 1943), pp. 168, 175. The sentences are italicized in Husslein.

[3] Ryan: "The Teaching of the Catholic Church," *Annals of the American Academy of Political and Social Science* (September 1922), CIII, 77. This article well summarizes many earlier statements.

[4] The rabbi was the late Edward L. Israel, who told the story to me.

II

RYAN'S FIRST book contained a laudatory introduction written by Richard T. Ely, professor of economics at the University of Wisconsin, and the endorsement of the Catholic clergyman by the Protestant professor was natural.[5] For Ely was arguing the same view of society to American economists that Ryan was preaching to American Catholics.

Solemn, pink-cheeked, looking like nothing so much as the minister of a prosperous parish, Ely came from a solid New England background, but the background was not simply pedigree. It included a father with a Yankee nose for reform, who, though a busy civil engineer, was forever writing angry letters to the county paper or leading a protest meeting. Indignation against evil was bred into the boy no less deeply than family and God.

The outside world that Ely first knew did not seem to give indignation much point. First at Dartmouth, then at Columbia, he was taught the inevitabilities of conservative economics. All economic truth was assumed to be contained in books like the *Political Economy* of Mrs. Fawcett, which explained that charitable relief to keep women and children from starving to death was a "striking example of the harm that may be done by interfering with the operation of competition." When Ely won a fellowship for study abroad in 1876 and made the usual choice of Germany, he assumed that he was going merely to learn more about the "absolute" truths of life.[6]

Ely was not in Germany a year before the absolute truths were melting into a wondrously fluid world. At Heidelberg he came under the influence of Karl Knies, a professor with a passionate sympathy for the German workingman, who taught a "Historical," evolutionary, economics which argued the possibility and wisdom of social reform. After three years of Germany, indigna-

<hr>

[5] Ryan: *A Living Wage* (Macmillan, 1906), pp. vii-ix.
[6] Ely: *Ground under Our Feet* (Macmillan, 1938), pp. 34, 126.

tion seemed anything but pointless to Ely. He returned to the United States vowing to work for a different America through a different economics. "If this world was to be a better world," Ely was sure, ". . . we must have a new economics." [7]

Teaching at Johns Hopkins until 1892 and then at the University of Wisconsin, Ely helped make those universities centers of dissidence by his pioneer work in developing a Reform Darwinian economics. Ely's economics was the Historical system of Professor Knies, with a still heavier emphasis on evolution and on environment. The prevalent "natural laws" of economics, Ely maintained, were actually products of an environment of extremes of wealth and were "used as a tool in the hands of the greedy and the avaricious for keeping down and oppressing the laboring classes." Since the alleged laws were merely man-made rationalizations, they could and should evolve into a new economics. The sensible kind of new economics would be based on the assumption that "to upbuild human character in men you must establish for them right social relations"; that right social relations come from a healthy economic environment; and that environments can be quickly made more healthy by state action and by permitting the underprivileged to act in their own behalf through trade-unions or similar organizations.[8]

Early in his career, in 1885, Ely and a little band of rebel economists converged on a parish house near Saratoga Springs to form the association that was to spearhead the Reform Darwinian attack on orthodox economics. The American Economic Association, now a staid academic organization, was anything but staid in its origins. Its prospectus was an assault on conservative economists who dealt in "final statements," and on their theories, which were declared not only "unsafe in politics" but "unsound in morals." Reporting on the organization, Ely bluntly tied the new

[7] Ibid., p. 154.

[8] Ely: *The Past and Present of Political Economy*, in *Johns Hopkins University Studies in Historical and Political Science* (1884), II, 64, and *The Social Law of Service* (Eaton & Mains, New York, 1896), p. 140. "The most fundamental things in our minds," Ely wrote of his group, "were, on the one hand, the idea of evolution, and on the other hand, the idea of relativity" (*Ground under Our Feet*, p. 154).

economics to a demand for reform by governmental actions. "The avenues to wealth and preferment," he stated, "are continually blocked by the greed of combinations of men and by monopolists. . . . We hold that there are certain spheres of activity which do not belong to the individual, certain functions which the great co-operative society, called the state—must perform to keep the avenues open." [9]

Yet the new economics of Ely and his group had its limits. They did not entirely cease to think in terms of fixed institutions and for them, too, competition kept an aura of beneficent inevitability. At the 1900 meeting of the American Economic Association, no one was surprised when President Ely spoke on "Competition: Its Nature, Its Permanency, and Its Beneficence." [1] There was room for a further step, and it was soon taken by the restive mind of Thorstein Veblen, who had no reason to want permanence for anything in his world.

The son of Norwegian immigrants at a time when "Norskie" ranked with "kike" and "dago" as a sneer word, raised in the dour isolation of a pioneer farm, a heap of rough clothing hanging from an anemic body, Veblen never reached rapport with his America. His try at a professorial career was conspicuous for its firings and slow promotions, finally grinding down to a "lectureship" at $2,400 a year in a town that seemed to him "a woodpecker hole" in a "rotten stump called Missouri." [2] His two marriages and his extramarital adventures were only different varieties of incompatibility. The most trivial custom of the everyday world could send Veblen into bizarre revolt. In his house children slept until they woke, no matter how many times the principal protested their lateness, and beds simply had their sheets turned down because making beds every day was deemed

[9] Ely: "Report of the Organization of the American Economic Association," *Publications of the American Economic Association* (March 1886), I, 6–7, 16.

[1] Published in ibid. (1901), 3rd Ser., II, 55–70.

[2] Joseph Dorfman: *Thorstein Veblen and His America* (Viking, 1934), p. 306.

a useless ostentation. Late in life, Veblen published an essay on the Jews in which he argued that their sense of separation from the Gentile world gave "them a degree of exemption from hard-and-fast preconceptions, a skeptical animus . . . [a] release from the dead hand of conventional finality." [3] Seeing introspection in the statement is inevitable despite the fact that Veblen was a Protestant, for his alienation from contemporary life can hardly be disconnected from his animus against it.

His way of expressing the animus was to try to undermine all the conventional finalities of its central interest, the economic. To Veblen, economists like Ely, just as much as the older school, were "pre-Darwinian." Both were committed to the fundamentals of the status quo, and both defended them by incomplete and distorted Darwinisms which assumed certain laws of society. The pre-Ely economists had formulated "ultimate laws and principles," which were "laws of the normal or the natural, according to a preconception regarding the ends to which, in the nature of things, all things tend. In effect, this preconception imputes to things a tendency to work out what the instructed common sense of the time accepts as the adequate or worthy end of human effort. It is a projection of the accepted ideal of conduct." The Ely group had recognized some movement of ideas in relation to a changing environment, but they still left man "a lightning calculator of pleasures and pains, who oscillates . . . under the impulse of stimuli that shift him about the area, but leave him intact." [4] Real Darwinism, Veblen argued, would have men and their institutions in a continuous flux, changing each other under no law except the lack of laws. It would show that business enterprise, far from operating under laws of any kind, was a chaotic clawing for profit. Hence no one need have the slightest fear that the clumsy hand of human intervention would disturb some principle. "A reform adopted," a present-day economist has

[3] "The Intellectual Preëminence of Jews in Modern Europe," *Political Science Quarterly* (March 1919), XXXIV, 39.

[4] "Why is Economics Not an Evolutionary Science?" *Quarterly Journal of Economics* (July 1898), XII, 382, 388, 389.

summarized Veblenism, "is a way of supplying a measure of order to a system that is characterized by disorder." [5]

Having dissolved away the businessman's economics by completely evolutionary argument, Veblen went after the businessman's mores by economic interpretation. His famous book, *The Theory of the Leisure Class,* correlated with fundamentally economic drives and thereby condemned many characteristic features of America's business civilization. An interest in smart clothes was "an expression of the pecuniary culture"; the well-trimmed lawn bespoke "pecuniary canons of taste"; the higher education a manufacturer sought for his son was a form of "conspicuous leisure" and "conspicuous consumption." A classical education was especially prized, Veblen added, because it showed that one was wealthy enough to be able to waste so much money on something so useless. Almost nothing in that hated world outside Veblen's office escaped his relentless reduction of the reputable to the pecuniary. Did people assume that at least loving a dog had nothing to do with money and money's prestige? The dog, Veblen wrote, "is the filthiest of the domestic animals in his person and the nastiest in his habits. For this he makes up in a servile, fawning attitude towards his master, and a readiness to inflict damage and discomfort on all else. The dog, then, commends himself to our favour by affording play to our propensity for mastery, and as he is also an item of expense, and commonly serves no industrial purpose, he holds a well-assured place in men's regard as a thing of good repute." [6]

In most of his writings Veblen professed to take no stand on the issues he was discussing; he was simply the scholar laboring out of "idle curiosity." [7] Yet even if the implications of Veblen's doctrine had not made plain his ardor for change, his language alone would have stamped him an enemy of the status quo. That

[5] John S. Gambs: *Beyond Supply and Demand* (Columbia University Press, 1946), p. 17.
[6] *The Theory of the Leisure Class* (Modern Library, 1934), pp. 133-4, 141, 167, 363-400.
[7] Quoted in Herbert W. Schneider: *A History of American Philosophy* (Columbia University Press, 1946), p. 394.

curious vehicle, as tortured as the man himself, winding through melancholy lucubrations into phrases of startling tartness, always managed to make the world in which he lived silly and sinister. Veblen's America was too sinister for most of his contemporaries, reformers or conservatives. But from the time *The Theory of the Leisure Class* was published in 1899, his way of thinking pushed ahead with the force of a slowly moving icecap, and after the crash of 1929, when reform was ready to use its toughest tools, Veblen came into his own. Then the bumbling, mumbling professor, who had never known what to do when someone complimented him, was widely hailed as the most penetrating thinker of modern American dissidence.

III

OF MORE immediate importance was the way the economics of the Ely school and the religion of men like Rauschenbusch combined to produce a Reform Darwinian definition of good and evil. The most direct contributions to this new morality were made by Edward A. Ross, the professor of sociology who has kept appearing in so many parts of the reform story. Farm life around Marion, Iowa, and schooling at backwater Coe College had given Ross the usual indoctrination in the absolutes of conservatism. "The tight little intellectual world we were led into," he remembered, "was bounded by Presbyterianism, Republicanism, protectionism and capitalism." But his youth also provided the usual opportunity to learn dissent. A professor who expressed horror of *Progress and Poverty* led Ross straight to that exciting reading. Advanced study in Germany was "a colossal intellectual spree," his youthful mind churning so much that the opinions he wrote in his diary one week seemed strange, almost incomprehensible the next. By the time Ross finished his graduate work among the German-trained rebels at Johns Hopkins, the tight little intellectual world of his youth was unraveling into criticism, even mockery.

At his doctoral examination a professor asked: Who are the railroad stockholders of the nation?

"If we are to believe the railroad attorneys, virtually all are widows and orphans," Ross answered, and laughter floated him to his degree.[8]

When Ross began teaching, in 1891, only a handful of Americans called themselves sociologists. Ross, who was rapidly developing both the build and the belligerence of a truck-driver, barged crusadingly into the field, helping to give it the orientation of a man who admired Bryan, got himself fired from Stanford University, and was a natural addition to Richard Ely's omnibus department at the University of Wisconsin. Ross's sociology was typical Reform Darwinism. Having dismissed Conservative Darwinism as a rationalization of greed, he called for "real Darwinism," "pure environmentalism," "methods of analyzing society which recognize that relationships to property have something to do with what men think." [9] But Ross's bulky sociological works were no purer Reform Darwinism than his one slim volume on morals, and nowhere near as influential.

The trouble was, Ross declared in *Sin and Society*, that morals had stood still. The public condemnation of what was evil had not broadened to cover new forms of sin. A businessman, provided he went to church, did not steal his neighbor's lawn-mower, and confined his sexual activities to his wife, was a good man—even if, in his office, he watered the stock of his business, refused to install safety devices, and beat down his workers' wages. "People are sentimental," Ross wrote in his pungent way, "and bastinado wrong-doing not according to its harmfulness, but according to the infamy that has come to attach to it. . . . They chastise with scorpions the old authentic sins, but spare the new. They do not see that boodling is treason, that blackmail is piracy, that embezzlement is theft, that speculation is gambling, that taxdodging is larceny, that railroad discrimination is treachery, that the factory labor of children is slavery, that deleterious adultera-

---

[8] Ross: *Seventy Years of It* (Appleton-Century, 1936), pp. 15, 27, 45.
[9] *New York Times*, January 3, 1901.

tion is murder. It has not come home to them that the fraudulent promoter 'devours widows' houses,' that the monopolist 'grinds the faces of the poor,' that mercenary editors . . . 'put bitter for sweet and sweet for bitter.' " This variance between individual and social morality, Ross contended, had become one of the most effective props of the status quo. To achieve economic and social betterment, the public had to realize that "sin evolves along with society. . . . Our social organization has developed to a stage where the old righteousness is not enough. We need an annual supplement to the Decalogue." [1]

The vigor of Ross's writing added to the reading public of *Sin and Society*, but vigor alone does not explain why the book sold so widely and was praised or damned by so many important people. *Sin and Society* carried the impact of the first systematic effort to recapture morality from the conservatives. An ardent progressive hit the point squarely when he wrote admiringly to Ross: "You show that the worst evils we have to combat have inevitably evolved along with the evolution of society itself, and that the perspective of conduct must change from age to age [if we are] more effectively to hold to account the really dangerous foes of our present civilization." [2]

Both Ross and his progressive friend, when they talked about morality evolving in relationship to a changing environment, assumed that there was one kind of evil that had nothing to do with evolution and environment. The ordinary criminal, the thief, the murderer, the rapist, was born, not made.[3] Overwhelming opinion accepted this view, and the curbstone dictum was supported by the conclusions of the first systematic student of crime, Cesare Lombroso, an Italian, who saw the criminal as a special biological

[1] *Sin and Society* (Houghton Mifflin, 1907), pp. viii, 14–15, 40.
[2] Theodore Roosevelt, well after he had passed over from liberalism to progressivism, in an Introduction to *Sin and Society*, p. x.
[3] One of the leaders in settlement work of the period, the late Mary Simkhovitch, made the interesting comment (in an interview): "Ordinary criminality, I think, is the last field in which people will ever really accept the explanation of economic environment. It takes too much away from the self-satisfaction of the man who, by years of work and living within the constraints of respectability, has acquired his own bit of prestige."

119

type.[4] But the opinion was not overwhelming enough to stop some humanitarians from wondering, and as early as the Seventies, the wonderings were headed toward a Reform Darwinism that could free thought even about the ordinary criminal.

Richard Dugdale, in the course of his work as an inspector for the New York Prison Association, had been struck by the consanguinity of many of the criminals, and particularly by one family for which he used the name Juke. In 1877, after careful research into the history of each member of the family, Dugdale published *The Jukes*. The volume created an immediate sensation, and little wonder. Of 1,200 persons of Juke blood, it reported, 280 had been in the poorhouse or received outdoor relief for a total of 1,150 years; 140 had been convicted of criminal offenses and 60 more were habitual thieves, convicted or unconvicted; 50 were prostitutes; 40 women venereally diseased had infected approximately 400 other persons, and 30 prosecutions in bastardy had been lodged against the family. "Over a million and a quarter dollars of loss in 75 years, caused by a single family 1,200 strong," Dugdale added up, "without reckoning the cash paid for whiskey, or taking into account the entailment of pauperism and crime of the survivors in succeeding generations, and the incurable disease, idiocy and insanity growing out of this debauchery and reaching further than we can calculate. It is getting to be time to ask, do our courts, our laws, our alms-houses and our jails deal with the question presented?"[5]

To most readers of the book, the question presented was the one they had always asked about people like the Jukes: how could society best protect itself against hereditary criminality, hereditary pauperism, and hereditary degeneracy? The very nature of the study seemed to emphasize the connection between genes and failure in society. But the tender-minded, hopeful Dugdale was not ready to surrender the Jukes completely to the inevitability of heredity. "I am informed," he wrote with all the

---

[4] Lombroso's basic work, *L'Uomo delequente*, was published in 1889. In subsequent writings he modified his conclusions but he did not depart from his fundamental emphasis on heredity.

[5] *The Jukes* (Putnam, 1895), pp. 68–70.

anger his diffident pen could show, "that $28,000 was raised in two days to purchase a rare collection of antique jewelry and bronzes recently discovered in classic ground, forty feet below the *debris.* I do not hear of as many pence being offered to fathom the *debris* of our civilization, however rich the yield." [6] Amid all the sordidness which one family had produced, Dugdale nowhere committed himself to the proposition that the Jukes were hopeless debris. And the over-all conclusions of his book, largely ignored in the furor over its spectacular details, actually were:

"1. Where the organization is structurally modified, as in idiocy and insanity, or organically weak as in many diseases, the heredity is the preponderating factor in determining the career; but it is, even then, capable of marked modification for better or worse by the character of the environment.

"2. Where the conduct depends on the knowledge of moral obligation (excluding insanity and idiocy), the environment has more influence than the heredity, because the development of the moral attributes is mainly a post-natal and not an ante-natal formation of cerebral cells. The use to which capacity shall be put is largely governed by the impersonal training or agency of environment, which is itself very variable.

"3. The tendency of heredity is to produce an environment which perpetuates that heredity: thus, the licentious parent makes an example which greatly aids in fixing habits of debauchery in the child. The correction is change of environment." [7]

The correction is change of environment—in Denver the words checked with what a country judge was learning in the day-by-day business of his courtroom. Throughout the Nineties Ben Lindsey, remembering a boyhood so miserably poor he once tried to commit suicide, had been battling greed and corruption in the Colorado legislature. In 1900 the Democrats, with the aid of Populist sentiment, swept the state, and Lindsey was rewarded for his ardent campaigning by a judgeship in Denver. For a while he seemed just another reform-minded magistrate, understanding

[6] Ibid., p. 4. The italics are Dugdale's.
[7] Ibid., p. 65.

and humane but practicing no especially new philosophy. Then one day an urchin was brought into Lindsey's court, charged with stealing lumps of coal from the railroad tracks.

Lindsey performed his duty under the law and sentenced the boy to the state reform school. The words were scarcely out of his mouth when the mother, a toothless old woman, rushed down the aisle, her arms flailing the air, her face horribly contorted, screaming in anguish—"the most soul-piercing scream of agony," Lindsey recalled in his autobiography, "that I ever heard from a human throat." [8] When the bailiff tried to lead the mother from the room, she broke away and beat her head against the wall as if to batter down the courthouse and bury all who were responsible for what was happening to her boy. Lindsey, badly unnerved, stopped the proceedings, got an agreement from the district attorney to suspend the sentence, and set out to investigate. He discovered that the boy's father was a smelting worker dying from lead poisoning without one penny's compensation. Home was a tenement, where coal was desperately needed to heat the frigid room. Was this boy a "bad" boy, bad by heredity, so dangerously bad that the community had to protect itself by treating him like an adult criminal? Lindsey could not believe it. He left the tenement convinced that some different way had to be found to handle juvenile offenders.

While Lindsey searched the statutes for a loophole, he began visiting the reform schools and jails where the youthful delinquents were sent. In the city jail he found boys waiting trial in filthy, vermin-ridden cells. In the reformatories and the county jail he found boys locked in cells with older criminals, subjected to beatings and homosexual advances, worshipfully lapping up stories of big-time crime. More and more Lindsey was convinced that rarely, if ever, was a child innately "good" or "bad." Children were made good or bad by their economic environments, and, once they had turned bad, made worse or better by the new environment. At last, in the period of his deepest disturbance,

[8] Lindsey and Harvey J. O'Higgins: *The Beast* (Doubleday, Page, 1917), pp. 80–1.

Lindsey found a clause in a Colorado school law which could be taken to mean that juvenile delinquents were wards of the state, to be corrected by the state as *parens patriæ*. Using this clause to the hilt, Lindsey began transforming his court into a "juvenile court," which avoided the concept of punishment and set up a system to bring child offenders into an environment of good care and educational opportunities.

At first all Denver cheered the "Kids' Judge." Lead and copper magnates joined ministers and schoolteachers in backing his drive for slum-clearance, playgrounds, public baths, and industrial schools. But Lindsey's conception of changing the environment had the full sweep of Reform Darwinism, and the judge was soon in the forefront of Colorado progressive battles to hedge business about with social legislation. The support from the magnates turned into ruthless hostility. Both political parties rejected Lindsey, and when he was elected as an independent, corrupt judges forced him to run again. Social ostracism closed over him; prostitutes were bribed to name him as one of their customers; when his mother was operated on for a cataract, stories were spread that her bandaged eyes came from the beatings the son inflicted in drunken rages. The charges hurt, but when the going became roughest, Lindsey could always march before the public unreformable children whom his methods had reformed. "Only the plain people stayed with him," one Denver newspaperman remembered of Lindsey's battles, "but their votes kept him in office year after year." [9] Sanctioned by success, Lindsey's emphasis on the economic environment as the explanation of juvenile delinquency spread steadily over the United States, most notably to Judge Julian Mack's court in Chicago.

That city, long a center of crime, had long been developing its own economic environmentalists in criminology. More than a decade before Lindsey broke off on his new path, in 1884, John Peter Altgeld published *Our Penal Machinery and Its Victims*, a passionate argument that poverty lay at the bottom of most crime, adult or juvenile. Altgeld's rapidly increasing political prominence

[9] George Creel: *Rebel at Large* (Putnam, 1947), p. 121.

(his election as Governor of Illinois came shortly) alone would have given his book wide attention. To make sure that it caught all possible eyes, the wealthy reformer sent out copies at his own expense to every legislator, judge, warden, minister, teacher, writer, lecturer, social worker, and club president he could find on a mailing list.

In Ashtabula, Ohio, a police magistrate leafed through his copy, yawned, and handed it to a string-bean of a country lawyer who was always shambling around the court talking about strange books like something or another by a man named Henry George. Clarence Darrow was already weary of Ashtabula, where Protestantism was "inspired, the Republican party and all its doctrines came as a divine revelation, [and] . . . all pleasure was sinful and all suffering righteous." [1] Naturally skeptical of finalities, with a Lincolnian sense of the community of men in the ridiculousness of things, Darrow was enormously excited by the flexible environmentalism of Altgeld's argument. A short time after reading *Our Penal Machinery*, Darrow was off to Chicago, to shake the hand of the man who wrote the book and to start forty years of propagandizing its main point in and out of courtrooms. Crime, the shirt-sleeved spellbinder told a thousand different audiences in a thousand different ways, resulted from "the unjust condition of human life." [2] Speaking at the Cook County penitentiary, Darrow defiantly pushed economic environmentalism to its farthest limit. "There is no such thing as crime as the word is generally understood," he said to the gaping prisoners. ". . . If every man, woman and child in the world had a chance to make a decent, fair, honest living there would be no jails and no lawyers and no courts." [3]

[1] Irving Stone: *Clarence Darrow for the Defense* (Doubleday, 1941), pp. 24–5.
[2] Darrow: *Resist Not Evil* (C. H. Kerr, Chicago, 1903), p. 177.
[3] Stone, p. 170.

IV

ON ANOTHER occasion, when Darrow was chatting with a group of Virginia lawyers, one of the group took him to task for advocating the equality of races. "Mr. Darrow," the man challenged, "what about the purity of the Anglo-Saxon race?"

"Purity of the Anglo-Saxon race," Darrow snorted. "The greatest race of sons of bitches that ever infested the earth. Mind you, if there is such a race, I am one of them. . . . But I do not brag about it; I apologize for it." [4]

The irritation of humane environmentalists like Darrow was never greater than when it met racism. Here Darwinism had offered special opportunities to those who sought scientific bolstering of their prejudices, and the opportunities were fully exploited to reduce the Negro and "non-Anglo-Saxon" immigrants to a position of permanent inferiority. Conservative Darwinism was particularly triumphant in this field because so large a part of the population, including a good many of the progressives, wanted it to be triumphant.[5] Yet as a greater sympathy for the Negro and the new immigrant entered reform thinking, progressives cast about for a Darwinian formulation that would give their attitude effectiveness.

The formulation was already there, half worked out, obscurely presented, in the writings of two generations of scientists and publicists who had squirmed under the almighty Aryan. In the early 1900's the formulation was completed with prodigious authority by Columbia University's professor of anthropology, Franz Boas. Born and educated in Germany, looking, lecturing, and writing like the American's conception of the *Herr Professor Doktor*, Boas never produced a sentence with the rousing quality of the whole of *Progress and Poverty* or the goading mockery of any one of a dozen of Veblen's phrases. But if Boas could bring

[4] Ibid., p. 103.
[5] Carl Krummel: "The Attitudes of Some of the Leaders of the Progressive Movement, 1890–1914, toward Negroes," MS., in Mr. Krummel's possession.

to the emerging reform philosophy neither eloquence nor wit, he could and did bring an anthropology that cut ground from under all absolute ideas, particularly from under racism.

A number of technical considerations stayed Boas from becoming a thoroughgoing economic environmentalist, but he took over the parts of Reform Darwinism which had greatest significance for progressivism. In 1908, in one of his earlier generalizations, Boas argued that anthropology is important in the everyday world because it "teaches better than any other science the relativity of the values of civilization. It . . . [makes] the differences between our civilization and another . . . appear less as differences in *value* than as differences in *kind*. This broader outlook may also help us to recognize the possibility of lines of progress which do not happen to be in accord with the dominant ideas of our times." [6] Equipped with this broader outlook, Boas lumbered into the serene fastness of Anglo-Saxonism. Race, he wrote in his most influential book, *The Mind of Primitive Man*, could mean to a scientist only common descent, and according to this definition there was no such thing as an Anglo-Saxon race. Moreover, no group of human beings was more or less advanced than the others. Their developments, coming about in different environments, represented specializations in different directions, some features of each development being closer and some features farther away from the apes. Culture was a cumulative evolutionary product, not a function of racial heredity. "A Magna Charta of self-respect for the 'lower races,' " admirers called *The Mind of Primitive Man*.[7]

Year after year Boas trained his anthropological guns on Americans who assigned inherent inferiority to the Negro, and in 1911 he launched a massive assault on the detractors of the new immigrants. The United States Immigration Commission had asked him to make an anthropological study of immigrants, and Boas did it with a thoroughgoing environmental approach. Instead of

[6] Boas: *Anthropology* (Columbia University Press, 1908), p. 26. The italics are Boas's.

[7] Quoted in "Environmentalist," *Time* (May 11, 1936), XXVII, 39.

comparing "Anglo-Saxons" and "non-Anglo-Saxons," he measured the changes that occurred in immigrants as their environment changed from Europe to the United States. He concerned himself primarily with eastern European Jews and Sicilians, groups that were generally considered most hopelessly "non-Anglo-Saxon," and he gave greatest attention to the cephalic index (contour of head), a physical characteristic assumed to be exceedingly stable. His principal conclusions were:

1. Cephalic indices did alter in a changed environment. The cephalic index of Sicilians born in Sicily averaged 78; of their children born in the United States, 80. The cephalic index of Jews born in Russia averaged 83; of their children born in the United States, 81. In both cases, the longer the parents lived in the United States before the birth of the children, the greater the alterations in the indices of the children.

2. Cephalic indices not only changed, but changed toward a uniform type. In one generation in the American environment, the round-headed Russian Jews became more long-headed, and the long-headed Sicilians became more round-headed.[8]

All this was set down in a maze of statistical charts. Then, in his dull, stubborn English, Boas pounded home the revolutionary meaning of his figures. Anthropologists had long since agreed that environment could affect physical development, but the dominant school denied the possibility of any change in basic bodily traits like the cephalic index. Boas's statistics showed precisely such a change, he pointed out, and if a change in bodily type could appear "under the influence of environment, presumably none of the characteristics of the human types that come to America remain stable." And then, the direct use of Reform Darwinian anthropology against the conservative argument that "non-Anglo-Saxons" were incapable of adapting to democracy. "The adaptability of the immigrant," Boas wrote, "seems to be very much greater than we had a right to suppose before our investigations

[8] *Changes in Bodily Form of Descendants of Immigrants*, 61st Cong., 2nd Sess., Sen. Doc. 208 (1911), pp. 1–3. But see Boas's qualification of the second point in ibid., p. 76.

were instituted. . . . We are compelled to conclude that when these features of the body change, the whole bodily and mental make-up of the immigrants may change." [9]

"This environment business is beginning to worry the lordly Anglo-Saxon," Clarence Darrow could chortle in 1913. "Everywhere I go people are poking into his ribs sentences about, 'You've just had more opportunities.' Asking how people grew up may make all men equal yet." [1]

V

ASKING HOW people grew up could make women equal, too, and the feminists were rapidly discovering that fact. Reform Darwinism appeared sporadically in the literature of women's rights during the Nineties; rested quietly beneath the argument of the most carefully formulated feminist book of the early 1900's, Anna Spencer's *Woman's Share in Social Culture;* and burst stridently into the foreground in the raft of novels about women that appeared in the years immediately around World War I.

The trend was clearly marked in the day's most widely selling feminist fiction, the novels of David Graham Phillips. Like most progressives, Phillips at first was little concerned over the woman's problem. His early working years were spent in muckraking business and politics, including the writing of the sensational "Treason of the Senate" series. But also like most urban progressives, Phillips got to women's rights before he was done, and in his case feminism became all-absorbing. Phillips was a bachelor, a man who was rarely comfortable at a social occasion, an inseparable companion of an adoring sister; for him the relationship between the sexes was never normal enough to permit him to forget it. After 1905, when he made his first venture in feminist fiction, Phillips devoted the rest of his life to novels about women. To

[9] Ibid., pp. 2, 5.
[1] Interview with the late Charles Beard.

Phillips, the novels were a continuous call for the same justice. From the perspective of a half-century, they are an accurate mirroring of the change in argument which was developing in this phase of progressivism.

The first six novels, appearing between 1905 and 1911, contained little emphasis on environment as the explanation of any apparent inferiority in women. Instead the novels argued that what was wrong with women was men. It was the men, Phillips had his stories say, who insisted that a woman should be educated to be "a doodle-wit . . . playing with a lapful of artificial flowers of fake culture," and it was the men who then viewed with condescension, if not contempt, the product of their own demand.[2] To make the point more strongly, Phillips usually picked, not a boor, but an intelligent, well-educated, likable male to portray as the oppressor of his wife. The hunger in *The Hungry Heart* was created by just such a male, whose smile for his wife was "like a parent's at a precocious child. He kissed her, patted her cheek, went back to his work." When the wife grew restless, the husband had an easy explanation: "A few more years'll wash away the smatter she got at college, and this restlessness of hers will yield to nature, and she'll be content and happy in her womanhood. A few more children would have an excellent effect. She's suffering from the storing up of the energy that ought to have outlet in childbearing. As grandfather often said, it's a dreadful mistake, educating women beyond their sphere."[3] All of this may have been exciting in the long-skirt 1900's—it was exciting enough to get Phillips assassinated by a lunatic who believed the novelist was "trying to destroy the whole ideal of womanhood." But blaming men for doodle-wit women was doing little to convince a man's world that women were not doodle-wits to begin with.

Two weeks before he was murdered, Phillips mailed a huge manuscript to his old friend Joseph H. Sears, president of D.

[2] Eric F. Goldman: "David Graham Phillips," in Willard Thorp, ed.: *The Lives of Eighteen from Princeton* (Princeton University Press, 1946), p. 325.
[3] *The Hungry Heart* (Appleton, 1909), p. 67.

Appleton & Company. With the manuscript went a note asking Sears to telephone when he had read the book.

The call came soon. The novel, Sears said, was "terrible."

At breakfast the next day, with the adoring sister at his side, Phillips began pleading to Sears the case for *Susan Lenox: Her Fall and Rise.* "You haven't kept up with the times," the novelist told his publisher. "You think all arguments about women should be in terms of Thomas Jefferson, and kitchen *vs.* career. Emancipation will never go forward that way. What woman has been and can be is a product of the environment around her, particularly her economic environment. We are changing to that kind of thinking more every day." [4]

Certainly *Susan Lenox* was emphatically different from Phillips's own earlier writings about women. Susan, an unhappy prostitute, was no victim of men or of kitchens but of poverty. Without resources or opportunities, she first turned to prostitution to earn hospital expenses for a friend who was desperately ill. Thereafter economic environmentalism explained her from bed to bed. A job as a fashion model required sleeping with a Chicago buyer to guarantee his order. Revulsion at this forced her into sweatshops where she made less than five dollars a week, and, when she could tolerate the sweatshops no more, back to prostitution. Always harried by economic fear, Susan ran the gamut of prostitution from streetwalking to serving as the jeweled mistress of a Tenderloin gang leader. At the end of the 964 pages, Phillips brought his heroine to triumph by a supremely economic fact. A wealthy dramatist, Robert Brent, was murdered out of jealousy over Susan, and Susan fell heir to all of Brent's money. With ample economic resources, she emerged an actress of great talent and impeccable morals.

When *Susan Lenox* was finally published by Appleton in 1917, it was taken up as a Bible by the advance wing of feminists. They recognized the book for what Phillips had intended it to be, a dramatic presentation of the way that economic environment explained any failure of a woman, even a descent to the streets.

[4] Interview with the late Mary Simkhovitch.

Phillips had been right. The urbane president of D. Appleton & Company, who had no particular desire to crusade for anyone, did not understand the importance of Reform Darwinism to progressives who were chafing to free women, along with everyone else, from conservatism's steel chain of ideas.

CHAPTER VII

"*God-Dammit, Let Them Build It*"*

Sooner or later the issue always came round to "democracy." There was a time, at the end of the eighteenth century, when an important part of the population reacted to the word with horror. There was to come a time, after World War I, when "democracy" had a tin ring for thousands. But in the early 1900's, saying "democracy" was semantic magic. One argued for or against anything on the grounds that it did or did not represent the truly democratic way.

Basic to the American's conception of democracy was his view of law and of the Constitution, where conservatism had scored so sweeping a triumph. Nine out of ten lawyers, Richard Ely angrily estimated, were educated in a way that made them hostile to economic or social reform.[1] Their minds grooved by Blackstone's fears of state intervention, their adulation fixed on the resplendent corporation attorneys, they nodded vigorous assent when speakers told the American Bar Association that the "duty" to stop "so-called social legislation . . . devolves primarily upon our

---

* Parts of this chapter were printed, in somewhat different form, in the *Journal of the History of Ideas*, April 1952. They reappear here with the permission of the *Journal*.

[1] Quoted in Alpheus T. Mason: *Brandeis* (Viking, 1946), p. 102.

profession " [2] As for the Constitution and Constitutional interpretation, those awesome subjects were beyond debate. A president of the American Bar Association expressed the opinion widespread among lawyers when he declared that attorneys should unite in "setting their feet upon and their hands against all efforts . . . to make it [the Constitution] at all the subject of political discussion." [3]

Reformers had their own idea of what was having feet put upon it and hands set against it. Did a state legislature attempt to restrain the manufacture of cigars in filthy tenements? The legislation, the Supreme Court declared, was unconstitutional because it "arbitrarily" deprived cigarmaker Peter Jacobs "of his property and of some portion of his personal liberty." Did a legislature decide that ten hours a day was long enough for bakers to remain at their stoves? The ten-hour law was unconstitutional because it was a "meddlesome interference with the rights of individuals"; the Constitution guaranteed workers "the right" to labor more than ten hours if they so "desired." And always the decisions were not those of conservative justices speaking conservatism but of the revered Constitution speaking through impartial judges.[4]

The process of removing the legal link in the conservative chain of ideas went ahead on two levels, but along essentially the same line of Reform Darwinism. Lawyers and legal scholars worked away at the conception of unchanging principles of law. Law was and should be a constantly evolving set of ideas, the dissident legalists argued. The evolution came about through interpretation of the law by a judge, and the interpretation was likely to satisfy the economic group which had conditioned the thinking of the court. The Supreme Court decisions throwing out social legisla-

---

[2] Frederick N. Judson: "Liberty of Contract under the Police Power," *Report of the Fourteenth Annual Meeting of the American Bar Association* (1891), pp. 258, 259.

[3] E. J. Phelps, quoted in Charles E. Merriam: *The Role of Politics in Social Change* (New York University Press, 1936), p. 65.

[4] Quoted in Merriam: *American Political Ideas* (Macmillan, 1920), p. 159, and Mason, p. 247. Mason pointed out that the judge who delivered the majority decision in the bakers' case said in so many words that it was the Constitution that compelled invalidation of the act.

tion therefore indicated merely the pro-business prejudices of the justices. With no less legal sanction, a Supreme Court interested in "the people's" welfare would uphold social legislation.

The second level of attack came primarily from social scientists. Reform-minded lawyers, historians, and political scientists toppled the Constitution off the pedestal of eternal truth by making an economic interpretation of the way it was written and of the purposes for which it was written. The Framers had not been codifying inalienable rights, the progressives argued. The Framers were propertied men who were quite consciously setting up a system that would protect a minority of the rich from "the people." Hence if judges were not going to be antidemocratic, a reform interpretation of the Constitution was essential. Much in the manner of a Rauschenbusch or an Ely, reform social scientists and lawyers were placing on their opponents the onus of thinking in a pre-Darwinian way and of defending greed.

II

THE FIRST important steps toward legal Reform Darwinism were taken by the redoubtable Oliver Wendell Holmes, Jr. A natural skeptic, Holmes had always been uncomfortable in the presence of dogma. A patrician to the core, he never had any difficulties piercing through the rationalizations of business. "I always think of a remark of Brooks Adams," Holmes commented in his genial way, "that the philosophers were hired by the comfortable class to prove that everything is all right. . . . When I say that a thing is true, I mean that I cannot help believing it. . . . I therefore define the truth as the system of my limitations, and leave absolute truth for those who are better equipped." [5]

In 1881 Holmes's book *The Common Law* presented the first distinguished statement of a sweeping Darwinism in law. "The

[5] Mark De Wolfe Howe, ed.: *Holmes-Pollock Letters* (Harvard University Press, 1941), I, 139, and Holmes: *Collected Legal Papers* (Harcourt, Brace, 1920), pp. 304–5.

life of the law has not been logic: it has been experience," he declared in some of the most widely quoted sentences ever written by an American lawyer. "The felt necessities of the time, the prevalent moral and political theories, intuitions of public policy, avowed or unconscious, even the prejudices which judges share with their fellow-men, have had a good deal more to do than the syllogism in determining the rules by which men should be governed. The law embodies the story of a nation's development through many centuries, and it cannot be dealt with as if it contained only the axioms and corollaries of a book of mathematics." In 1897, in his famous address entitled "The Path of the Law," Holmes bluntly denied the possibility of avoiding judge-made law. "The language of judicial decision is mainly the language of logic. And the logical method and form flatter that longing for certainty and for repose which is in every human mind. But . . . behind the logical form lies a judgment as to the relative worth and importance of competing legislative grounds. . . . There is a concealed, half conscious battle on the question of legislative policy, and if any one thinks that it can be settled deductively, or once for all, I only can say that I think he is theoretically wrong, and that I am certain that his conclusion will not be accepted in practice." [6]

Yet if Holmes swept away the absolute truths of conservative law in a flood of skepticism, he was scarcely less questioning about reform. At heart he was a Spencerian—a reluctant one, but a Spencerian nevertheless—believing that everything was a tooth-and-fang struggle and wistfully wishing that the animals would conduct themselves with a touch of gentlemanliness. A trust magnate appeared to Holmes an inevitable survival of the fittest, and attempts to control large-scale capital, such as the Interstate Commerce Commission and the Sherman Antitrust Act, were just so much "humbug." The reformers were "upward and onward fellows," unconvincing, if interesting. "I agree with you in liking to see social experiments tried," Holmes commented to one

[6] Holmes: *The Common Law* (Little, Brown, 1881), p. 10, and *Collected Legal Papers*, pp. 181, 182–3.

of his friends who had turned upward and onward, "but I do so without enthusiasm because I believe that it is merely shifting the place of pressure and that so long as we have free propagation Malthus is right in his general view." To such a kindly doubter nothing was left as a criterion for a good law except what the majority seemed to want. When a friend asked Holmes if he had ever worked out any general philosophy to guide him in the exercise of the judicial function, the Justice answered: "Yes. Long ago I decided that I was not God. When a state came in here and wanted to build a slaughter house, I looked at the Constitution and if I couldn't find anything in there that said a state couldn't build a slaughter house I said to myself, if they want to build a slaughter house, God-dammit, let them build it." [7]

The same Darwinism that Holmes used merely to free the law permitted other, more reform-minded men, to free the law for progressive purposes. In the universities the leadership was taken by Roscoe Pound, whose naturally questioning mind had been prodded by a period of courtroom practice and of politics in the turbulent Nebraska of the Nineties. Mild-mannered, intensely ambitious, never able to get himself to stop voting a respectable Republican ticket, Pound did not leap to heresy. At the University of Nebraska, where he did his apprentice teaching, he was still bothered by reformers who brought the courts too close to the struggle between capital and labor. When Edward Ross would grind away at lunch on the failure of the courts to protect society from greed, the law professor struck back irritably. But gradually Pound's absolutism weakened. Shortly after he became dean of the University of Nebraska Law School, he shocked the American Bar Association by delivering a speech which argued that good reasons existed for the "more than . . . normal amount of dissatisfaction with the present day administration of justice in America." [8] By 1910, when he was called to the Harvard Law School, Pound was emerging as the leader of a school of "so-

[7] Howe, I, 163, 167; interview with the late Edwin M. Borchard; Mason, pp. 572–3, 574.
[8] Paul Sayre: *Roscoe Pound* (State University of Iowa Press, 1948), p. 148.

ciological jurisprudence," another name for law that was sensitive to the movement for social reform.

Even more than Holmes, Pound's sociological jurisprudence insisted that "the judge makes the actual law" and that law is therefore continually evolving. Where the skeptical, Spencerian Holmes had left the process of evolution to a bare clash of wills, Pound argued that it was the judge's duty consciously to shape law to the needs of the day. "Law is not scientific for the sake of science," he maintained. "Being scientific as a means to an end, it must be judged by the results it achieves, not by the niceties of its internal structure. . . . The sociological movement in jurisprudence is a movement . . . for the adjustment of principles and doctrines to the human conditions they are to govern rather than to assumed first principles. . . ." A sweeping economic interpretation of law was too much for Pound, whose reform enthusiasm continued to have its limits and who was deeply impressed by psychological considerations. But he paid high tribute to economic interpretation for having encouraged jurists "to picture a legal ordering of the satisfaction of wants" and for having provided "a stimulus to faith in the efficacy of effort." [9]

What Pound was saying in partial form to the limited audience of legal scholars, Louis Brandeis trumpeted full-blast to the whole nation by a sensational new technique of arguing a case. No one in the United States was in a better position to understand how law was serving the dominant group. The son of a Kentucky grain merchant who was neither rich nor Anglo-Saxon, Brandeis knew ruling America not only because he became part of it but also because he had quite consciously made himself part of it. "In this age of millions," Brandeis early decided, "the man without some capital can only continue to slave and toil for others to the end of his days." [1] Having romped through Harvard Law School with a record no one has ever bettered, he soon used the éclat to make

[9] Pound: *The Spirit of the Common Law* (Marshall Jones, Boston, 1921), p. 176; "Mechanical Jurisprudence," *Columbia Law Review* (December 1908), VIII, 605, 609–10; *Interpretations of Legal History* (Macmillan, 1923), pp. 114–15.

[1] Mason, p. 77.

extensive social and business contacts in and around Boston. Having gained his entree into the upper world, he rapidly solidified his position by establishing a reputation as a lawyer who knew more about business than any of his businessman clients. On his fortieth birthday, in the mid-Nineties, Brandeis was a near-millionaire, one of the most sought-after corporation lawyers in the United States, a man who counted among those who counted.

Yet additional thoughts stirred behind that dark face and the piercing gray eyes. Mother and father Brandeis were "forty-eighters," Germans with a passion for reform which had been developed fighting autocracy in the homeland. This passion they passed on to their son, whose restless mind was always ready for fresh ideas. Even in his days of intense preoccupation with winning cases for corporations, Brandeis's thinking roamed far afield, to the connections between law and economics and between economics and democracy. This quality led the president of the Massachusetts Institute of Technology, a former professor of economics, to ask Brandeis to lecture at the Institute on Business Law, and this quality made the lectures a landmark in Brandeis's life. Halfway through preparation for them, he read in his newspaper of the bitter strike at the Homestead plant of Carnegie-Illinois Steel and of the way in which the courts were backing the company all down the line. Quite clearly, Brandeis told himself, the prevailing conception of law provided no adequate protection for workers. He threw away the lecture notes he had prepared and began approaching his subject from "new angles." [2]

The nature of the new angles was implicit in the battles that Brandeis soon undertook, as the "People's Attorney," against intransigent capitalists, traction and railroad machinators, boodling politicians, and a dozen other favorite targets of reform. The new angles became explicit, and of enduring importance, in 1908, when he defended Oregon's ten-hour law for women before the United States Supreme Court. The National Consumer's League, chief sponsors of the law, had first sought the services of Joseph

[2] *Ibid.*, p. 87.

Choate, a warhorse of conservatism but a lawyer whose great reputation would have made him an impressive spokesman for their cause. Choate would have nothing to do with the case. He could see no reason why "a big husky Irishwoman should not work more than ten hours a day in a laundry if she and her employer so desired." [3] The next day the Consumer's League invited Brandeis, and he jumped at the chance to put his new angles to work in the most critical type of case before the highest court of the land.

The argument Brandeis made was as unconventional as a six-foot judge in a two-foot robe. His brief was 104 pages long, and only two of the pages dealt with legal logic and precedents. The existing law, Brandeis said, made clear that the right to purchase or sell labor was part of the "liberty" protected by the Constitution and that this liberty was subject to such reasonable restraints as a state government might impose, in the exercise of its police power, for the protection of health, safety, morals, or general welfare. Therefore the question at issue was whether Oregon's ten-hour law was a restraint necessary to protect the health, safety, morals, or general welfare of the people of Oregon. At that point, after a scant thousand words, Brandeis ended his purely legal argument.

The Justices leaned forward, puzzled, expectant. Why had Brandeis, who was as much a master of legal logic as anyone in the United States, made his legal argument so brief? The Justices promptly found out. The question of whether Oregon's law was a necessary restraint, Brandeis maintained, could not be answered by legal logic; it could be answered only by facts. And then Brandeis poured out the facts, more than 75,000 words of facts, facts drawn from ninety reports of factory inspectors, commissioners of hygiene, and special committees in Europe and the United States, squalid, jolting facts, all making it seem very evident that a ten-hour law for women was necessary to protect the health, safety, morals, or general welfare of the people of Oregon.

[3] Ibid., p. 248.

Five weeks later Brandeis awoke to find himself denounced as a dangerous anarchist by men who only a few years before had paid him fortunes to represent their businesses. The Supreme Court had unanimously voted that Oregon's ten-hour law was Constitutional. For the first time in an important case a majority of the United States Supreme Court had taken the position that the meaning given to law should evolve, and evolve in relation to social needs.

III

DESPITE THIS and other spectacular victories that soon followed, conservative legalism was far from demolished. As Brandeis ruefully remarked a decade later, "the living law" was still often frozen by the prepossessions of judges; when "stubborn facts were confronted with stubborn theory," the theory frequently won.[4] So the reform-minded lawyers fought on and found themselves aided by progressive social scientists who were applying economic interpretation to the history of the framing of the Constitution. The aid was of no small importance. What better way to make the Constitution a living document than to write of it as representing not fixed law but the ideas and interests of a particular group of men at a particular time? What better way to smash the sanctity of the doctrines conservatives had made identical with the Constitution than to make the whole document a product of antidemocratic, intensely property-conscious thinkers?

The movement toward economic interpretation of any phase of American history was given a strong shove forward in 1893, when Frederick Jackson Turner published his essay "The Significance of the Frontier in American History." The most characteristic American institutions and attitudes, Turner maintained, had been produced by a constantly receding area of free land. Henry George may have advanced much the same thesis in much the same words fourteen years before, but it was Turner's statement

4 Ibid., p. 143.

of it that caught on and was soon winning wide acceptance.[5] Turner was not much of an economic interpretationist and he was even less of a reformer. The Wisconsin professor of history was irritated, for his own nationalistic, Midwestern, and scholarly reasons, at the standard view of American institutions, which had them originating in Europe and transplanted via New England. His frontier was more a place and a process than an economic setting; it split America vertically, not horizontally. But the vogue of Turner's idea pulled men away from thinking in terms of political abstractions and shifted their minds to a concept that was close to the economic. On and around the Turner thesis more reform-minded men were to build interpretations that were more strictly economic.[6]

Not unexpectedly, the first thoroughly economic interpretation came from a student of Turner and Richard Ely, Algie M. Simons. Fresh from a farm in the Wisconsin woods, Simons's study at the University of Wisconsin moved him gradually left through the frontier thesis of Turner to the greater heresies of Ely. Simons's job after graduating, working for the Chicago Bureau of Charities, completed his education in dissent. He was the first of his family to go up to the big city, and doing charity work among the thousands caught in the depression of 1893 overwhelmed him with pity and anger. All of Simons's spare time went to collecting materials on working conditions in the stockyards. He produced his own bitter pamphlet about "Packingtown," then turned his materials over to Upton Sinclair, who was in Chicago writing *The Jungle*. When newspapers scoffed at some of the lurid scenes in Sinclair's book, Simons could retort: "I knew the family whose child drowned in the gutter; I have helped to treat dozens of cases of infection and blood-poisoning of Yard workers; I have known men . . . who have fallen into the rendering vats . . . ; I have

[5] Compare George: *Progress and Poverty* (Modern Library, 1929), pp. 389–90, and Turner, in *Annual Report of the American Historical Association for the Year 1893*, especially pp. 226–7.

[6] For example, Charles Beard, who was to write the most effective economic interpretation of the Constitution, named Turner as the man who had influenced him most. Malcolm Cowley and Bernard Smith, eds.: *Books That Changed Our Minds* (Doubleday, Doran, 1939), pp. 61–71.

seen things in the lives of the workers in Packingtown more terrible than any depicted in 'The Jungle.' " [7] Three years in stockyard charity work, three years trying to fight "that poverty business," and Simons's swarthy, finely chiseled face took on the
yellow haggardness of strain.[8] He turned for a while to socialism,
and for the rest of his life to a reinterpretation of the American
past that would clear the way for change.

Simons's most comprehensive reinterpretation first appeared as
a pamphlet in 1903 and was revised and enlarged until it emerged
in 1911 as a book, *Social Forces in American History*. With an
eye fixed steadily on the cash nexus, Simons ran through all
American history. "Political struggles," he generalized in the first
words of *Social Forces*, are "based upon economic interests." The
American Revolution was "one battle of a great world-wide struggle between contending social classes. . . . The industrial life of
the colonies had reached the stage where it was hampered and restricted by its connection with England. Large classes of the population required an independent government to further their interests." The Civil War, far from being a struggle over the
moral issue of slavery, was basically a drive by the "capitalist class"
of the North to free itself from the rule of Southern agrarians, and
the years after the war brought the politics of "dollarocracy."
With special emphasis, Simons applied his economic interpretation
to the Constitution. "The organic law of this nation was formulated in secret session by a body called into existence through a
conspiratory trick, and was forced upon a disenfranchised people
by means of a dishonest apportionment in order that the interest
of a small body of wealthy rulers might be served." [9]

Social Forces in American History was written during Simons's
period of socialist enthusiasm, and, like a good Marxist, he sprin-
kled the book with protestations that he was being completely ob-

[7] Simons: "Packingtown, 'The Jungle,' and Its Critics," *International Socialist Review* (June 1906), VI, 714.
[8] John J. Harmon: "Algie Martin Simons," MS., Princeton University
Library, p. 12.
[9] Simons: *Social Forces in American History* (Macmillan, 1911), pp. vii,
69, 70, 99, 263, 307.

jective and amoral, simply tracing out "the stream of social evolution." His economic interpretation of the American past, Simons maintained, imputed no moral condemnation of the capitalist groups; their rise to power was an ineluctable part of evolutionary progress. But Simons's "objectivity" was precisely the kind that enraged Conservative Darwinians. He did not stop at associating capitalism with evolutionary progress. In *Social Forces* the Darwinian concept of progress through evolution was neatly extended, by Reform Darwinism, into a dictate for further change. Businessmen may have once formed the class that was essential to progress, but—the telltale *but* of Reform Darwinism—the time had arrived for further evolution, and that was to be carried forward by labor, which had now become, in its turn, "the embodiment of social progress, and is fighting for victory with a certainty of success before it. . . . It is impossible to draw the lines of social forces through all the perspective of the past and then stop them short at the present." One-sided attribution of economic drives constantly appeared in Simons's writing, making the capitalist greedy, and the worker oppressed and noble. In the midst of his economic interpretation of the Constitution, the reformer paused to emphasize the point of his "objectivity." "There was nothing particularly sacred about the origins of this government," Simons nudged the reader, "which should render any attempt to change it sacrilegious." [1]

Social Forces had its influence, but the book was not the type to leave a deep impress on the early 1900's. Conspicuously Marxist, skimpy in research and lecturish in style, sweeping over the whole American past rather than concentrating on the focus of reform interest, the Constitution, the book's chief function seems to have been the spurring on of more effective writers. America heard far more of a chunky little volume directed squarely at the Constitution and written with no trace of Marxism, J. Allen Smith's *The Spirit of American Government*.

Smith's career once provoked a battle-weary reformer to re-

[1] Ibid., pp. 1, 99, 300, 317. It is especially revealing to compare Simons's treatment of businessmen in Chap. xxiii with his treatment of workers in Chap. xxiv.

mark: "If you want to become a reform leader in the United States, you'd better have money, or, next best, marry it." [2] J. Allen Smith grew up with little money and a series of provocations to doubt. The conservatism he was taught on a land-poor Missouri farm was shaken by the early Populist campaigns; reading *Progress and Poverty* in Kansas College raised more questions; practicing law in Kansas City kept him fuming against the way the city was run. Law, he told his friends, had disgustingly narrow limits when it amounted to a daily rationalization of what the stockyard masters wanted to do. Yet Smith remained a stockyard lawyer for almost a decade and apparently would have gone on being one had he not been part of an exceedingly capitalistic situation. Mrs. Smith had brought into the marriage a substantial sum of money. Watching her husband wriggle in discontent, she prodded him: "Why don't you give up your office and spend your time getting to the bottom of all this? " [3] Mrs. Smith did not have to prod long. After a few more years of the law, in his thirties, Smith was off to study economics under Henry C. Adams, an Ely-trained professor at the University of Michigan.

Quickly Smith's thought shaped into the progressive pattern. Adams warned his idealistic protégé that a Ph.D. dissertation attacking conservative economics would face hard going before the university's board of examiners. Too excited to bother, Smith pushed ahead with his study, produced a plan for a government-controlled money system which became the basis for Irving Fisher's much-vaunted "managed currency," and managed to slip by the university's watchdogs of the status quo. Two years later, in one of the incidents of the 1896 purge, Smith learned what Professor Adams had been talking about. His first teaching post was at Marietta College, where most of the board of trustees was connected by blood or business with the Dawes family that was to produce Calvin Coolidge's Vice President. The Dawes group, controlling gas, traction, and other monopolies throughout Ohio, were in no mood to employ a professor, particularly an exceed-

[2] The late Charles A. Beard, in an interview.
[3] Interview with Mrs. James Falconer (the former Mrs. J. Allen Smith).

ingly popular professor, who denounced the postulates of their economics. In the election of 1896 Smith announced that he was voting for William Jennings Bryan, and the board of trustees announced that unfortunately the need for economy required them to dispense with Professor Smith. While the trustees proceeded to install another professor at a higher salary than Smith's had been, the heretic took a train for the University of Washington, where a Populist board of trustees loved him for the enemies he had made.

Seattle soon heard from the new professor. A few months after Smith arrived at the university, the Seattle Electric Company applied for a franchise that was to run for fifty years and contained no provisions for free transfers or for commuters' rates. The city council was ready to grant the franchise when a citizens' committee took up the fight. Granted two hours by the city council to state its case, the committee gave half its time to Smith for a report on the limitations on franchises in other American cities. Largely as a result of his carefully documented and vigorously argued statement, the franchise was limited to thirty-five years, free transfers were granted, and books of one hundred tickets were sold at a twenty-five per cent reduction. "I guess I am a hopeless radical," Smith told the city council with an enragingly straight face. "I keep thinking that ten percent is enough profit for a company, even for a company with a municipal franchise." [4]

Year after year the gusty, sardonic professor intervened in public affairs, tangling with political bosses, pouring cold pacifist water on imperialist passions, standing with labor on many a touchy issue, and battling for public ownership of power utilities. His influence in the public-ownership movement became so great that Harry M. Kenin, of the Bonneville Dam Administration, attributed to Smith a large part of the gains that public ownership made in the Northwest in the first decades of the twentieth century. [5] Inside the state of Washington, reformers of a dozen va-

---

[4] Interview with the late Edward McMahon, a close friend of Smith.
[5] Kenin, in a letter to me, March 6, 1945.

rieties recognized a leader. Only Smith's strong discouragement stopped a powerful movement to get for him both the Democratic and Progressive gubernatorial nominations in 1912.

In the midst of this furious activity, in 1907, Smith published *The Spirit of American Government*. In tone and often in points, the book was similar to much of the dissident literature of the day. It attacked the alliance between big business and politics, criticized with special sharpness the conservatism of the federal judiciary, assailed the type of economics that rationalized monopoly. The feature that made the *Spirit* distinctive was its analysis of the root of the problem. Smith fixed the responsibility for the major ills of America squarely on the Constitution and argued that "conservative approval of the Constitution under the guise of sympathy with majority rule . . . has perhaps more than anything else misled the people as to the real spirit and purpose of that instrument. . . . It is to call attention to the spirit of the Constitution, its inherent opposition to democracy, the obstacles which it has placed in the way of majority rule, that this volume has been written." [6]

To understand the real spirit and purpose of the Constitution, Smith went on in the authentic manner of a Reform Darwinian, Americans had to get over the idea of laws fixed by nature. "Laws, institutions and systems of government are in a sense artificial creations, and must be judged in relation to the ends which they have in view. They are good or bad according as they are well or poorly adapted to social needs." [7] The Constitution, Smith maintained, was such an artificial creation, written by a particular group of men with a particular economic end in mind. The framers represented a minority of large property-holders intensely concerned with preventing a majority of have-nots from getting control of the government, and the framers had brilliantly achieved their purpose. Despite a century's changes in the operation of the Constitution, Smith argued, its system of checks and balances continued to check and balance so well that the majority

[6] Smith: *The Spirit of American Government* (Macmillan, 1907), p. vii.
[7] Ibid., pp. 400–1.

still found it exceedingly difficult to get social legislation by the three hurdles of the President, the Congress, and the judiciary.

In working out his economic interpretation of the Constitution, Smith did not neglect to bend the interpretation in a way that brought down upon the framers, and upon Smith's contemporaries who sanctified the framers, the onus of greed. His technique was made plain by his use of historical sources. The historian on whom Smith relied most heavily for facts was the arch-conservative, John Bach McMaster. McMaster had described the Constitution as the work of men of large property and had included mention of the opposition to the Constitution by the debtors. But McMaster's wealthy people were "decidedly the more respectable" group, men of "close reasoning" and "careful statements," and his poor were a rabble given to "such reasons for hating the Constitution as were every night hiccoughed out in the taverns." [8] Smith took McMaster's facts and turned his economic interpretation upside down. In *The Spirit of American Government* the framers were profit-minded and little else. The small farmers and city poor were not directly associated with economic interests, and they were endowed with all the idealistic connotations clustering around the phrase "the people."

By applying the same type of economic interpretation, Smith arrived at the same emotion-arousing analysis of state and municipal constitutions. In the state constitutions, he argued, checks and balances had been deliberately used to create conditions under which "the people" found it difficult to fix the blame for official misconduct. Hence the state constitutions made it easy for those "private interests which are ever seeking to control the government for their own ends." In the cities the "real source of misgovernment—the active cause of corruption—is to be found, not in the slums, not in the population ordinarily regarded as ignorant and vicious, but in the selfishness and greed of those who are the recognized leaders in commercial and industrial affairs. . . . The powerful corporate interests engaged in the exploitation of mu-

[8] McMaster: *History of the People of the United States* (Appleton, 1883–1913), I, 201, 490.

nicipal franchises are securely entrenched behind a series of constitutional and legal checks on the majority which makes it
extremely difficult for public opinion to exercise any effective
control over them." [9]

In his most unusual use of the progressive economic interpretation, Smith blamed the business orientation of both political parties on the checks-and-balances system. The divided authority
brought about by checks and balances, he maintained, meant that
the party of the executive in the municipal, state, or federal government was rarely in control of all the policy-making divisions of
the government. The political parties, knowing that they could
usually blame some opposition-controlled branch, were inclined to
make promises with no intention of carrying them out. As a result,
ordinary citizens lost interest in political organizations and the
parties fell prey to organized business interests. "In practice,"
therefore, political parties had become "an additional and one of
the most potent checks on the majority." [1]

The Spirit of American Government had not appeared in book
form when the *Seattle Times*, getting hold of the proof sheets,
quoted under a front-page headline the section containing Smith's
vigorous attack on the Supreme Court. Immediately the city's
legal leaders were up in arms. "The man writes like an anarchist,"
rang the denunciations. "Lawyers all over the country will repudiate his doctrine. . . . In a case in the criminal courts . . . Smith's
attack on the Supreme Court would make good evidence to sub-
stantiate a plea of insanity." [2] The University of Washington's
board of trustees, long past its Populist interlude of the Nineties,
squirmed uneasily at the thought of what was going on in its
Political Science Department. A Dr. Henry Suzzalo was brought
from Columbia to head the university, apparently on the understanding that his first duty was to get rid of J. Allen Smith. Smith's
dismissal was repeatedly threatened, his teaching was harassed by
every means known to irritated administrators. But there was al-

[9] *Spirit of American Government*, pp. 247, 288–9.
[1] Ibid., p. 208.
[2] Quoted in Eric F. Goldman: "J. Allen Smith: The Reformer and His
Dilemma," *Pacific Northwest Quarterly* (July 1944), XXXV, 205.

ways an army of former students to make removing the professor politically dangerous, and he went on teaching an approach to the Constitution that was tremendously useful to progressives.

The Smith thesis was avidly taken up in reform circles. Scores of progressive journalists were soon working it into their writings. Oscar Ameringer, trying to bring a moderate socialism to Oklahoma, found the *Spirit* a powerful weapon. Senator Robert La Follette of Wisconsin directed his party organization to give away hundreds of copies of the book as part of his campaign to make the state more progressive. "It was awful," Mrs. Smith remembered with an impish smile; "there I was, raised by my mother to be a lady, and I had helped Allen become a hero to all kinds of trouble-makers." [3]

IV

Six years after the publication of *The Spirit of American Government* a still more powerful storm of economic interpretation broke out of the East. This time the heretic was not only impeccably American in his arguments but a product of the kind of family on which conservatism took its stand. William Henry Harrison Beard, as his son, Charles, used to chuckle, was "about as solid a citizen as Indiana ever produced." [4] He owned Knightstown's bank, newspaper, and mill, and his farm holdings stretched far across the countryside. Once in a while neighbors grumbled about a streak of iconoclasm in Knightstown's leading citizen. When a Negro bishop visited the town and the local hotel denied him admittance, William Beard shook the county with his fulminations and installed the Negro in his own guest room. But such acts were simply in the tradition of idealistic Radical Republicanism and had little or nothing to do with the deeper issues disturbing the country. In 1894 the son, Charles, went off to DePauw

[3] Falconer interview.
[4] Unless otherwise identified, all quotations in this section come from interviews with the late Charles Beard.

University serenely sure that all questioners of Republicanism were obvious allies of the Devil.

Then, gradually, it happened. Little DePauw, a product of the Methodist zeal for keeping young people on the godly path, was hardly a hotbed of radicalism, but it did include professors, particularly one Colonel James Riley Weaver, who delighted in shaking up youthful minds. As a field trip for a DePauw course, Beard went up to Chicago, and seeing the city during hard times brought him the same sense of outrage which Algie Simons was experiencing. This was not the America his father extolled, Beard was telling his friends; things had never been like this in Indiana, even when the locusts came. Soon he was an avid participant in the discussions at Hull House, listening to Populists arguing with socialists and Clarence Darrow arguing with both, trying this or that heresy for himself, daily moving farther from the certitudes of Knightstown.

After his graduation from DePauw, at the turn of the century, Charles Beard spent most of two years in Europe, and this period capped his dissidence. He left Germany amused at the pretensions of German professors and fuming at Prussian soldiers who forced him into the gutter rather than share the sidewalk, but more convinced than ever that America was lagging far behind in social legislation. Most of Beard's period abroad was spent in England, where he was swirled along on a dozen streams of dissidence. Deeply affected by Ruskinism, he helped set up the workingman's Ruskin College at Oxford; he beered and argued and worked with trade-unionists, Tory reformers, suffragettes, single-taxers, and socialists.[5] Lecturing before labor audiences throughout the Midlands and the North, dashing off a belligerent pamphlet, *The Industrial Revolution*, hobnobbing at Labour Party councils, the young American became so prominent in the Labour coterie that Ramsay MacDonald had an eye on him for the Labour government which they all thought was around the corner. But Beard

[5] During his stay in England, Beard was especially close to an Oxford professor, Frederick York Powell, who was intensely concerned with reform questions, if in a somewhat off-beat way. Powell's general ideas are expressed in his preface to Beard's *The Industrial Revolution* (Swan Sonnenschein, London, 1901). See also Oliver Elton: *Frederick York Powell* (Clarendon, Oxford, 1906), I, 312–14.

was not interested in a British Cabinet post. He was interested in returning to the United States and stirring it as his English friends were stirring their country.

Returning for graduate work at Columbia University, a copy of Ruskin's *Unto This Last* still in his pocket, Beard hurried through his doctoral dissertation and joined the little band of faculty rebels who were turning Columbia into a major focus of dissidence. Year after year the rugged, red-headed Indianan, who never stopped looking like a farmer even when he began resembling a Roman philosopher, became more of a campus storm-center. Columbia students packed "Uncle Charlie's" lectures, delighting in his tightly disciplined erudition, his bold theorizing, his quinine wit. "There was no one at Columbia in the second decade of this century," Beard's colleague, John Erskine, reminisced, "who could rival Beard as an orator. . . . More than once I heard him address the student body on some question about which I disagreed with him, but while he spoke I could feel persuasion creeping over me, as it crept over the boys." [6] The most exciting things his audiences heard, Beard was mulling over on trips to Washington, where he invaded the dust-covered records in the old Treasury Building with a vacuum cleaner and a theory. The rest of the country heard, too, when *An Economic Interpretation of the Constitution* was published in 1913.

At the close of the *Economic Interpretation*, Beard set down his conclusions about the Constitution in a series of trip-hammer sentences:

"The movement for the Constitution of the United States was originated and carried through principally by four groups of personalty interests which had been adversely affected under the Articles of Confederation: money, public securities, manufactures, and trade and shipping.

"The first firm steps toward the formation of the Constitution were taken by a small and active group of men immediately interested through their personal possessions in the outcome of their labors.

[6] Erskine: *My Life As a Teacher* (Lippincott, 1948), p. 93.

"No popular vote was taken directly or indirectly on the proposition to call the Convention which drafted the Constitution.

"A large propertyless mass was, under the prevailing suffrage qualifications, excluded at the outset from participation (through representatives) in the work of framing the Constitution.

"The members of the Philadelphia Convention . . . were, with a few exceptions, immediately, directly, and personally interested in, and desired economic advantages from, the establishment of the new system.

"The Constitution was essentially an economic document based upon the concept that the fundamental private rights of property are anterior to government and morally beyond the reach of popular majorities. . . .

"The Constitution was ratified by a vote of probably not more than one-sixth of the adult males. . . . The leaders who supported the Constitution in the ratifying conventions represented the same economic groups as the members of the Philadelphia Convention; and in a large number of instances they were also directly and personally interested in the outcome of their efforts. In the ratification, it became manifest that the line of cleavage for and against the Constitution was between substantial personalty interests on the one hand and the small farming and debtor interests on the other.

"The Constitution was not created by 'the whole people' as the jurists have said; neither was it created by 'the states' as Southern nullifiers long contended; but it was the work of a consolidated group whose interests knew no state boundaries and were truly national in their scope." [7]

Quite obviously, Beard's *Economic Interpretation* was little different from Simons's and Smith's books in its statements of key facts. It also continued the Reform Darwinian approach, the air of scientific neutrality, the economic interpretation that cut against conservatism.[8] But Beard's book was infinitely more influ-

[7] Beard: *An Economic Interpretation of the Constitution* (Macmillan, 1913), pp. 324–5.
[8] Although Beard did not specifically associate the lower-income group with ennobling characteristics, he achieved the customary anticonservative

ential than its predecessors, and the reasons are clear. Smith's *Spirit of American Government* may have been much better buttressed and considerably less dogmatic than Simons's *Social Forces*, and it drew its economic interpretation from American, non-Marxist sources; it was still little more than a suggestive essay, written with a conspicuous Jeffersonian bias. In contrast, Beard's book rested on prodigious research; it argued with disarming reasonableness; and, probably most important, it avoided all apparent Marxism or Jeffersonianism, all isms, all tone of special pleading or even eloquence. For a man like Charles Beard, who could write with either shillelagh or stiletto, the *Economic Interpretation* was a triumph in dullness. Not a single departure from catalogue organization, not a single bright sentence, enlivened the book, which carefully described itself as an "arid survey." [9] Max Lerner, who believes the *Economic Interpretation* influenced his own thinking enormously, has described the volume's strategy of flatness. "Beard must have had a premonition of the desperate resistance he would run into," Lerner commented. ". . . It is almost as if the author had set out with a deliberate severity to strip the book of every adornment, on the theory that a plain woman would be less suspected of being a wanton than an attractive one." [1]

The *Economic Interpretation* was plain enough to win a hearing in the most respectable circles, and the division between those who hailed it and those who scorned it showed how much economic interpretation of the Constitution had come to mean in the struggle between conservatism and progressivism. Almost without exception, those who assailed the book were standpatters like William Howard Taft, who promptly lumped Beard with "all the fools I have run across." Would Beard have been better satisfied, Taft hrrumphed, if the Constitution had been drafted by "dead bodies, out-at-the-elbows demagogues, and cranks who never had

---

impact of progressive economic interpretation by detaching the framers of the Constitution from any concern over "the vague thing known as 'the advancement of general welfare' or some abstraction known as 'justice.'" Ibid., p. 17.

[9] Ibid., p. 324.
[1] Quoted in Cowley and Smith, p. 76.

any money?" [2] An angry committee of the conservative New York Bar Association summoned Beard to appear before it and, when he declined, treated his declination as a kind of contempt of court.

"Have you read Beard's last book?" Columbia's high-Tory president, Nicholas Murray Butler, was asked.

"I hope so," Butler replied.

A few years later, when Beard resigned from Columbia over an issue of academic freedom, Butler accepted the resignation with unaccustomed efficiency. The *New York Times*, then in one of its most conservative moods, was so happy to see Beard de-robed that, according to Beard, it permitted Butler to write the unsigned editorial that trumpeted "Columbia's Deliverance." [3] The *Marion* (Ohio) *Star* was more direct. On May 3, 1913 Warren G. Harding's paper pushed aside a story of an Elks convention and a pitchfork murder for the headline: "SCAVENGERS, HYENA-LIKE, DESECRATE THE GRAVES OF THE DEAD PATRIOTS WE REVERE." The story nominated Beard for "the place of Chief Hyena. His book . . . is libelous, vicious, and damnable in its influence and every patriotic citizen of the United States, every lover of liberty in this land, should rise to condemn him and the purveyors of his filthy lies and rotten perversions." [4]

For every snarl from the right, there was a gleeful shout from the left. An overwhelming percentage of the favorable reviews of *An Economic Interpretation* appeared in reform publications, and the farther west the place of publication, the closer to the territory seeded by Populism, the more favorable the review was likely to be. [5] In *La Follette's Magazine* a Wisconsin reviewer stated precisely the progressive's interest in the book. "The time has come,"

---

[2] Henry F. Pringle: *Life and Times of William Howard Taft* (Farrar & Rinehart, 1939), II, 860.

[3] *New York Times*, October 10, 1917.

[4] Marion (Ohio) *Star*, May 3, 1913.

[5] It is interesting to note that Justice Holmes's lack of ardent social reformism combined with a skepticism about conservative law was reflected in an ambivalent attitude toward economic interpretation of the writing of the Constitution. He did not brush it aside but he objected to the "covert sneer." After all, he wrote his friend, Sir Frederick Pollock, "you and I believe that high-mindedness is not impossible to man." Howe, I, 237, II, 222–3.

he wrote, "when all of us, who are looking toward a wider national life, must realize that the Constitution, which has ever been the retreat of privilege, must be changed. When we once realize that this was a human document, written by men acting in many cases under human impulses, we shall have achieved the initial attitude necessary to change it. Professor Beard's book, scholarly and incisive, will do more than any other volume to set us right." [6]

V

CHARLES BEARD had a different nominee for the progressive thinker whose volumes were doing most to set Americans straight. "He's the quiet one," Beard used to say, "my friend who looks like your milquetoast uncle and who is undermining the whole world of the nineteenth century with his pragmatism." [7]

John Dewey's pragmatism, like all the parts of the emerging Reform Darwinism, had a mixed origin. Some of its basic features were worked out as early as 1878 by Charles Peirce, a brilliant logician whose eccentricity of habits was matched only by his unconcern over public affairs. In the Nineties William James expanded Peirce's fragmentary suggestions into a system, applied the system to the everyday world in alluringly graceful language, and began popularizing the succinct name "pragmatism."

The trouble with the prevailing thought in philosophy and psychology, James declared in good Reform Darwinian style, was that it was really pre-Darwinian while it claimed to be scientific. It assumed an absolute distinction between material things and activities of the mind; it assumed that in the realm of thought the human mind was a fixed structure, which, by logic or intuition, arrived at certain truth. Such a closed system, James maintained, ignored the central meaning of the doctrine of evolution. Nothing was absolutely distinct or absolutely fixed. Both the mind and the material things it thought about were constantly

[6] George Middleton, in *La Follette's Magazine* (May 24, 1913), V, 7.
[7] Beard interview.

evolving, and evolving in relation to each other. Any proposition could find meaning only in relation to the consequences that came from believing the proposition. "Grant an idea or belief to be true," James summarized, "what concrete difference will its being true make in any one's actual life? How will the truth be realized? What experiences will be different from those which would obtain if the belief were false? What, in short, is the truth's cash-value in experiential terms?" [8]

The philosophy and psychology that John Dewey built on James's work varied in a number of ways, but Deweyism was a fundamentally similar attack on closed systems. Both men, as Dewey wrote admiringly of James, were seeking "an open universe in which uncertainty, choice, hypotheses, novelties and possibilities are naturalized." The important difference between Dewey and James lay in the uses to which they put pragmatism. James, a patrician who was scarcely a patrician reformer, had come to his revolt against absolutes with no reform urge except a vague irritation against "the bitch-goddess, success" and a compassion in thinking of human problems. In general, the politics and economics of Conservative Darwinism met James's own pragmatic test. His problem was a personal one, the sense of suffocation that "block universe" philosophies brought to a high-spirited individual of acute intellectual and æsthetic sensitivities.[9] As a young man, the idea of living and thinking under the dictates of a philosophy that had everything finished and executed, impervious to chance or choice, brought him close to a nervous collapse. For William James, pragmatism was, first and foremost, a way of freeing William James.

John Dewey had his youthful upset at closed systems, too. As a junior at the University of Vermont, he was assigned a reading from an English Darwinian, and the quiet, painfully shy student, who had seemed as leery of ideas as he was of girls, came to life.

[8] James: *Pragmatism* (Longmans, Green, 1907), p. 200.

[9] Quoted in Richard Hofstadter: *Social Darwinism in American Thought, 1860–1915* (University of Pennsylvania Press, 1944), p. 103, and Joseph Ratner, ed., John Dewey: *Characters and Events* (Holt, 1929), I, 115, 121.

Here was a seemingly unanswerable statement of the overwhelming power of material forces in the world. But what happened, then, to the teachings of his home, and the Congregationalist Sunday-school class he taught, and everything he had ever known, which argued just as unanswerably the overwhelming power of pure ideas and ideals? Suddenly Dewey's house of thought, which had never seemed complicated enough to be worth fussing over, showed a disturbing gap between the cellar of things and the roof of thought, the same gap that had almost unbalanced James. Dewey was upset and confused, but in Vermont U. one did not have nervous collapses. You decided whether you were going back to work in your father's grocery store in Burlington or whether you were going to find some other way of making a living. Dewey did not go back to the grocery store. Much to the bewilderment of his neighbors, who had always thought him such a sensible boy, he decided to become a professor of philosophy. Somehow he was going to close that gap.

Dewey's road to becoming a professor of philosophy kept him constantly amid scenes that raised questions about his America. Home meant his kindly, whimsical father, the grocery-store keeper in Burlington who never thought enough of business success to push collecting bills very hard. Burlington itself was shot through with the small town's distrust of big-city capitalism. ("Where I was raised," Dewey once remarked, "the Hoovers and the Mellons would have had a hard time passing for Americans." [1]) To earn funds for graduate work, he taught elementary school in a Pennsylvania oil town that was about as grimy an example of industrialism as the United States could offer. Graduate work at Johns Hopkins, then teaching that included ten years at the University of Chicago and brought him finally to a professorship at Columbia—as much as any academic of his day, Dewey's professional life followed the circuit of university reform centers. William James had to reach out to touch social problems, but John Dewey would have had to run away to avoid them.

[1] Sidney Hook: *John Dewey* (John Day, 1939), p. 6.

The reedy Vermonter, still so shy that even an audience of one seemed to embarrass him, was not the man to run away. Every teacher, he declared, "is a social servant," and then proceeded to define service by aiding reformers ranging from socialite suffragettes to labor leaders locked in battle with corporations. In 1903, in the *Studies in Logical Theory*, Dewey laid down the technical bases of his thought, but at the same time he was hitching pragmatism to reform. "The ultimate refuge of the standpatter" in every field, he argued, was the notion that thinking could produce only one kind of truth, for then existing institutions, produced by the thinking of a past generation, were beyond challenge. But, actually, thinking "is a kind of activity which we perform at specific need, just as at other need we engage in other sorts of activity. . . . The measure of its success, the standard of its validity, is precisely the degree in which thinking actually disposes of the difficulty and allows us to proceed." [2] Difficulties could not be disposed of by using a limited idea of evolution or by ignoring the environment. A valid conception of thought assumed continuous evolution and depended on environment. Ideas could and should change to give men what they sought; ideas would give men their goals when the ideas called for creating an environment favorable to the achievement of the goals.

Here was a philosophy and a psychology perfectly tailored to progressive needs. From Henry George to Charles Beard, reform thinkers had been feeling their way toward specific pragmatisms in their own fields. In religion, economics, morals, criminology, anthropology, law, history, and political science, each had denied that the prevailing ideas could be eternally true, fixed by the nature of man and of the universe. Each had insisted that conservatism be tested by its political, economic, and social results. Applying the test and finding conservatism wanting, each had proposed substantially the same change in ideas. Clergymen or economists, anthropologists or lawyers, reform thinkers wanted to replace an

[2] Quoted in Hofstadter, p. 117, 58 n.; Dewey: "The Need for Social Psychology," *Psychological Review* (July 1917), XXIV, 273; Cowley and Smith, p. 123.

evolution that stopped at the present with an evolution that raced on; an environment that predetermined men and women with an environment that human beings manipulated to meet their needs; the dreary inevitabilities of Conservative Darwinism with the radiant hopefulness of Reform Darwinism. And now John Dewey had swept all their specific pragmatisms into a system from which each reformer, working away in his own field, could draw comfort and strength. "We were all Deweyites before we read Dewey," J. Allen Smith phrased the fact, "and we were all the more effective reformers after we had read him." [3] Dewey was the Herbert Spencer of Reform Darwinism, and if there were no banquets at Delmonico's, a thousand other signs pointed to the fact that he was rapidly becoming the most important philosopher in the United States.

This vogue can hardly be explained except in terms of the fact that a good many Americans were weary of ways of thinking which froze them in a society they did not like. Dewey wrote at least thirty-six books and 815 articles and there is scarcely a lively sentence in the whole mass of words. The man himself, allergic to publicity, stumbling through his lectures, ill at ease at his own cocktail parties, continued to be the least colorful of leading reform thinkers. His system offered none of the assurances and certainties for which men usually turn to philosophies. Pragmatism was, as the Italian, Giovanni Papini, remarked, less a philosophy than a method of doing without one.[4] But the troubled Papini, tangled in Europe's ancient war between reason and mystique, was missing the point so far as reformers on the other side of the Atlantic were concerned. For them the great attraction of pragmatism lay precisely in the fact that it was a method of doing without the conservative philosophy.

The progressive thinkers had not failed the progressive activists. Reformers of the early 1900's who were producing an appealing workaday program were simultaneously being provided the ideo-

[3] Quoted by the late Edward A. Ross, in an interview.
[4] Translated from Papini: *Sul Pragmatismo* (Libreria Editrice Milanese, Milan, 1913), p. 66.

logical means to dissolve away conservatism's steel chain of ideas. For Reform Darwinism, with its overarching pragmatism, made the whole progressive program quite consistent with human nature, enticingly scientific, thoroughly democratic, Constitutional, and moral.

CHAPTER VIII

A Condition of Excitement
and Irritation

IN THE year in which John Dewey was working on the *Studies in Logical Theory*, while Edward Ross prodded Roscoe Pound toward legal heresy at the University of Nebraska, a short period after Thorstein Veblen questioned "The Preconceptions of Economic Science" in the *Quarterly Journal of Economics*, the funeral train carried President McKinley's body back to Ohio. Mark Hanna slumped glumly in his parlor chair. "I told William McKinley it was a mistake to nominate that wild man at Philadelphia," Hanna growled. "I asked him if he realized what would happen if he should die. Now look, that damned cowboy is President of the United States!" [1]

For a while no one was quite sure about the policy of the new President; no one was ever quite sure what Theodore Roosevelt would do. Yet there was a pattern in Roosevelt's life, scattered and cross-stitched but a pattern nevertheless, and the pattern was that of patrician reform. Roosevelt had entered political life in the Eighties with a demand for clean government and arguments against labor legislation drawn straight out of Malthus and Ricardo. As late as 1896 he was combating the whole idea of using governmental powers to aid lower-income groups, even hinting darkly,

[1] Quoted in H. H. Kohlsaat: *From McKinley to Harding* (Scribner, 1923), p. 101.

so the story goes, that he expected to have to meet the Populist leaders across a barricade.[2] Then, in the late Nineties, friends noted troubled thinking beneath the oratorical certainties. Like his friend and Harvard classmate Charles Bonaparte, Roosevelt had a patrician's disdain for greedy businessmen, a patrician's sense of *noblesse oblige* toward the downtrodden, and a patrician's fear of socialism or some other "riotous, wicked" surge from the bottom groups.[3] Much more than Bonaparte, Roosevelt was politically ambitious, and he had not run behind Henry George in a New York mayoralty election without mulling over the vote-getting appeal of social reform. By 1900, when Roosevelt had served a term as Governor of New York, his economic conservatism was so uncertain that the New York bosses were maneuvering him out of their state and into the Vice Presidency. A few years after an assassin's bullet made Roosevelt President, Mark Hanna knew full well what horse his cowboy was riding. Out of an urge to reform and a fear that some reformers would go too far, Theodore Roosevelt was emerging the first President of the United States who represented the progressive movement.

The appearance of this progressive reformer in the White House was no historical accident. In the early 1900's the growing concern of the middle and upper classes over social problems, the rapid development of a dissident program of moderation and respectability, and the effectiveness of the Reform Darwinian assault on old ways of thinking were converting progressivism into a powerful political movement. The patrician-turned-progressive in the White House presided over a nation that was hurrying, as swiftly as respectable reform could hurry, away from conservatism.

[2] Henry F. Pringle: *Theodore Roosevelt* (Harcourt, Brace, 1931), p. 164.

[3] Quoted in Mark Sullivan: *Our Times* (Scribner, 1926–35), III, 249. Roosevelt spoke an attitude characteristic of patrician reformers of the day when he remarked late in his Presidency: "If I am fighting against plutocracy it is because I am the enemy of Socialism, of Anarchism. . . . Plutocracy is the best ally of Socialism and Anarchism. I am in my way a conservative, and that is the reason why I attack plutocratic abuses." André Tardieu: "Three Visits to Mr. Roosevelt," *Independent* (April 16, 1908), LXIV, 862.

II

As PRESIDENT, Roosevelt was certainly no paragon of reform. He could be brutally militaristic, evasive about trusts, compromising on social legislation, purblind to the merits of reformers who did not equate reform with Theodore Roosevelt. Yet the bouncing Teddy, with his bold grasp of the possibilities in change, his instinct for workable political combinations, his teeth-gnashing phrases, was the most tremendous thing that could have happened to American progressivism. Before a dazzled country, Roosevelt preached the progressive doctrine of executive leadership. The leadership, however much it wobbled, moved in the general direction of the use of federal powers to promote clean, efficient government, to check exploitation by large-scale capital, and to strengthen the bargaining position of lower-income groups.

Lashing out at "malefactors of great wealth," Roosevelt revived the Sherman Antitrust Law and employed it in a way that made trust magnates more careful even if the general concentration of industry was not appreciably slowed. By persistent conservation propaganda, he secured from Congress sweeping powers to remove public lands from the possibility of plundering operations, and used the powers to withdraw 148,000,000 acres of forest lands, 80,000,000 acres of coal lands, 4,700,000 acres of phosphate lands, and 1,500,000 acres of potential waterpower sites. With Presidential co-operation, often with Presidential goading, Congress forbade railroad rebates, strengthened the Interstate Commerce Commission, passed a meat-inspection act and a pure food and drug law, and brought the federal government into the workmen's compensation field for the first time. When intransigent owners produced a national coal strike, the country witnessed an unprecedented scene. Cracking down on the operators and forcing them to arbitrate, Roosevelt pulled the federal government far from its accustomed business-is-always-right position.

A whole new attitude permeated the White House. Since the days of Grant, the typical visitor had been a politician with a state in his pocket or a banker come to deal on equal, if not superior terms with the President. Roosevelt was openly sniffish about big businessmen; they needed "education and sound chastisement." [4] While never neglecting the politicians, he always managed to convey the impression that he found them a decidedly inferior lot. He didn't want the Vice-Presidency, Roosevelt kept telling the delegates who were making him Vice President with no real effort on his part to stop them. "I couldn't stand those damned Senators. I'd be throwing the gavel at them." [5] During the Roosevelt Administrations the White House calendar was crowded with the names of artists, writers, professors, anyone with an idea, particularly a new and startling idea. The President wrote introductions to dissident books like Ross's *Sin and Society*, named that persistent nonconformist, Oliver Wendell Holmes, to the Supreme Court, and, for the first time in the history of American cabinets, appointed a Jew to his official family.[6]

These Roosevelt attitudes ran all up and down the spine of the federal government, attracting to its service men of the honesty, abilities, and broad social view, for which reformers had pleaded so long. Until 1906 the federal District Attorney's office in southern New York, the most important in the United States, had usually been manned by lawyers of so little talent that the government hired outside attorneys when an important case was involved. He wanted, Roosevelt shrilled, the legal help of some of "my type of men," and the call was answered by Henry L. Stimson and a group of able young assistants, including Felix Frankfurter. On a total budget that was less than Stimson alone had earned in private practice, the new group converted the

[4] Pringle, p. 251.

[5] Sam Koenig, a delegate to the 1900 convention, interviewed in *New York Times*, June 24, 1948.

[6] The Jew was Oscar Straus, named Secretary of the Department of Commerce and Labor in 1906. In telling Straus of his decision, Roosevelt gave as one of the reasons: "I want to show Russia [where pogroms were then raging] and some other countries what we think of the Jews in this country." Oscar S. Straus: *Under Four Administrations* (Houghton Mifflin, 1922), p. 210.

Southern New York office into the equal, if not the superior, of any corporation legal staff in the country.[7]

For thousands who did not enter the government, Roosevelt was a bombshell. America of the early 1900's did not easily dismiss an agitator who bore one of the nation's most aristocratic names, who could charm a Sunday-school class or lead a regiment, turn out historical essays or lasso a steer, and who, in addition, happened to be President of the United States. In Emporia, Kansas, subscribers to the *Gazette* were reading strange doctrine. What was the matter with Kansas, William Allen White was saying now, was not reformers but "special privilege," and White was going down the line for the whole progressive program. "I was a young arrogant protagonist of the divine rule of the plutocracy," White recalled in 1934. Roosevelt "shattered the foundations of my political ideals. As they crumbled then and there, politically, I put his heel on my neck and I became his man."

"Teddy," White added, "was reform in a derby, the gayest, cockiest, most fashionable derby you ever saw."[8]

III

ALL ACROSS the nation the lanterns of reform were lighting up. In unlikely Cleveland, long a submissive fief of robber barons, progressives suddenly found their municipal Roosevelt. Tom Johnson

---

[7] Henry L. Stimson and McGeorge Bundy: *On Active Service* (Harper, 1948), pp. 3–7.

[8] Walter Johnson, ed.: *Selected Letters of William Allen White* (Holt, 1947), p. 7; White, in a letter to me, September 21, 1942. One of the soundest estimates of Roosevelt's place in history was provided by the journalist Norman Hapgood, who wrote in 1920: "When I was a boy . . . hostility to the first faint protests of the less fortunate was confident and decisive. . . . Mark Hanna's era marked the climax of this easy defiance by the strong. I well remember the charming, bulldog manner in which Hanna took up the defense of unlimited private monopoly in reply to Mr. Bryan's attacks on the trusts. It was a note that can never be sounded quite so fearlessly again. . . . Surely history will be just to Col. Roosevelt. It will call him the first American of enormous popularity and ability to question the modern industrial system." *The Advancing Hour* (Boni & Liveright, 1920), pp. 76–7.

possessed his own special kind of prestige: he had met the captains of industry on their terms and met them so successfully he emerged a magnate. Johnson was still a boy, selling newspapers on the streets of Louisville, when he learned the beauties of monopoly. Rolypoly and jolly, the youngster made friends easily and the conductor of the street-car that brought the newspapers to his part of town decided to do him a favor. "See here, Tom," the conductor said. "I like you and I'm going to boost your business. Hereafter I'll bring papers only for you. You'll have a monopoly and can charge what you like." [9] Young Tom did not forget the lesson. For his field he chose the traction business, which lent itself easily to combinations. Before he was out of his thirties Johnson had built a fortune by manipulations in street-car systems and was extending his holdings into the related steel industry.

One day a train butcher tried to sell Johnson a copy of Henry George's *Social Problems*, and the traction magnate was emphatically not interested. But a conductor passing down the aisle heard the conversation and joined in the urging. Johnson had a soft spot for conductors. He bought and read the book, went on to *Progress and Poverty*, and found a thousand demons dancing in his head. Henry George was having his usual effect on an active mind; besides, the points of George fitted in with too much else Johnson had read or seen. Soon he carried *Progress and Poverty* to his lawyer and demanded: "I want you to answer that book for me. I can't. And I must. For if that book is right I am all wrong." [1] The lawyer's answer did not satisfy Johnson. In a few years this tremendously successful businessman was up to his big, bull-like neck in fighting successful businessmen.

Johnson's enemies said they did not understand. He went to Congress and battled high tariffs all the while that tariffs were fattening the dividends he received from his steel holdings. He appealed for the public ownership of street-car systems at the same time that he was extending his own interests, sometimes even preaching municipal ownership to the city councils from which

[9] Quoted in Lincoln Steffens: *Autobiography of Lincoln Steffens* (Harcourt, Brace, 1931), p. 474.
[1] Quoted in ibid., p. 475.

he was soliciting franchises for himself. Johnson, always genial, patiently explained that so long as "privilege" existed, he along with most people would seek to take advantage of it, and progressives gladly accepted the explanation. Three times, from 1901 to 1909, they saw that Johnson was elected Mayor of Cleveland, delighted that he knew the connections between business and politics so well, delighted with the methods he used in breaking the connections.

Johnson conducted the city government with the same shrewdness and showmanship he had used in building his business empire. Political callers were glided through his office, swiftly but with no appearance of haste, decisively but always with a laugh. His administrations were featured by outdoor meetings in a huge tent, where Johnson joshed his opponents and made his constituents feel as if they were important stockholders in a prospering business. The quickest way for a Johnson lieutenant to get dismissed was to fail to show the utmost consideration to some housewife who was stumbling through a question to the Mayor in a crowd of two or three thousand people.

Cleveland's oldsters still chortle at Johnson's handling of the perennial vice problem. He summoned the madams to his office and told them that if they would rob no customers, pay off no policemen, and keep reasonably quiet houses, he would let them do business. To a committee of irate clergymen who called this conniving at vice, Johnson replied that he did not know how to abolish prostitution, but he did know he would not permit vice to corrupt politics during his stay in office. Progressive clergymen stepped in to explain Brother Johnson to their colleagues. The Mayor, said the Reverend Mr. Williams, who had also read his Henry George, was "trying, not to enforce Christianity, but to make it possible." [2]

With these methods and a sweeping progressive program, Johnson won for Cleveland the reputation of being the best-governed city in the United States. During his administrations he started a score of civic improvements, put through more equitable

---

[2] Quoted in ibid., p. 480.

tax laws, came close to ridding the government of all graft, checked the political influence of corporations, and made his office a power for municipal reform throughout the country. Newton D. Baker, Johnson's City Solicitor and later President Wilson's Secretary of War, recalled how Johnson was "guide, counsellor and friend to all other American cities [and] was visited almost daily by men from everywhere who were interested in rescuing city government." [3] No other city quite achieved a Johnson, but by 1912 municipal reform was so general that Charles Beard could write enthusiastically: "Out of the combined gains in our common municipal experience have come some of the finest achievements in our political life." [4]

IV

WHAT JOHNSON was to the cities, Robert M. La Follette was to the states. The Wisconsin reformer did not come to progressivism through business success or aristocracy. Born in a two-room log cabin, he grew up in circumstances that were barely respectable, and, at an age when Roosevelt was frolicking in New York Society and Johnson was well on his way to a fortune, La Follette was happy to make eight hundred dollars a year as a horseback district attorney. Nor did La Follette come to dissidence slowly. His region in Wisconsin was shot through with rural discontent; he read his Henry George as a boy and grew up with a full equipment of indignation. Yet La Follette did not leap to any extreme political or economic position that would have disqualified him for progressive leadership. He served as a district attorney and a Congressman for ten years without advancing much beyond the thought that honesty was good and railroad-owners were evil. Like a sound young man with a due regard for money, La Follette was even considering giving up politics for private law practice when, as La Follette told the story, he was offered a bribe by

---

[3] Quoted in Sullivan, III, 475 n.
[4] Beard: *American City Government* (Century, 1912), p. 30.

Philetus Sawyer, a pine timber baron who doubled as United States Senator from Wisconsin. That, La Follette always insisted, was the making of the progressive.[5] Jumping back into politics, he lashed out at both political parties, declaring that political democracy was meaningless as long as money controlled its machinery. With Johnson and the whole progressive movement, La Follette called for facing the "momentous" issue of the day: "Shall the American people become servants instead of masters of their boasted material progress and prosperity?" [6]

What Wisconsin reformers remember as the "holy war" was on. Conservatives in both parties joined to ruin La Follette's law practice and to stop him from becoming governor. But the state had long been restless under a corrupt conservatism and now the old leaders faced a politician who knew crowds as an artist knows colors. Direct, sarcastic, savage, jutting his powerful jaw at its most belligerent angle, banging home his points until his fists sometimes trickled blood, "Battling Bob" made speeches men did not forget. More melodramatic than either Johnson or Roosevelt, carrying the prestige neither of a patrician nor of a millionaire, La Follette was exposed to conservative charges that he was a throwback to Populism. But a friendly Wisconsin paper could make the satisfactory answer: "We challenge . . . his enemies to cite one line in which Bob La Follette has ever arrayed class against class, one speech in which he has not been as concerned for the civic-minded rich man as for the poor, one politician in Wisconsin who, in his personal life, better represents the great middle classes that are the backbone of this state and this nation." [7]

In La Follette's 1898 battle for the Republican gubernatorial nomination, his opponent made him an invaluable gift—a politically potent cow. The incumbent, Edward Scofield, had made

[5] La Follette's story of the bribe, on which he based his subsequent career, was, of course, sharply challenged by Sawyer. Compare *La Follette's Autobiography* (La Follette Publishing Co., Madison, 1920), pp. 138–58, and Richard N. Current: *Pine Logs and Politics* (State Historical Society of Wisconsin, Madison, 1950), pp. 260–2, 264–5.

[6] Ellen Torelle, ed.: *The Political Philosophy of Robert M. La Follette* (La Follette Co., Madison, 1920), p. 155.

[7] *Milwaukee Free Press*, November 3, 1901.

full use of the railroads' generosity to politicians, and a reform-minded express clerk put in La Follette's hands a copy of Express Order No. 2,169, which showed that Scofield had shipped free of charge:

> *2 boxes, 2 barrels;* JANUARY 7, 1897
> *3 barrels, 1 box;* JANUARY 8, 1897
> *2 boxes, 200 pounds;* JANUARY 9, 1897
> *2 barrels, 2 boxes, 1000 pounds;* JANUARY 11, 1897

And, finally,

> *1 cow (crated);* JANUARY 13, 1897.

Within a week the face of "Scofield's Cow" was looking accusingly from the front page of every La Follette newspaper, outdoing in public interest the stormy face of the candidate himself. The Scofield machine managed to stop the celebrated cow in 1898, but not for long. Two years later she slogged with La Follette to victory.

Swiftly, the new Governor hammered his program through an opposing and tricky legislature. An industrial commission—the first of its kind in the nation—was established "to control and regulate the most difficult questions of sanitation, safety, health and moral well-being which affect the workers of the state."[8] A newly constituted railroad commission slashed rates, while the taxes on the railroads were increased more than $600,000 a year. Wisconsin became the pioneer in adopting the direct primary for all nominations, and more than a hundred other laws reached into corrupt practices, public utility controls, education, workmen's compensation, and conservation. The University of Wisconsin, given special attention by its alumnus in the statehouse, welcomed to its faculty Richard Ely, Edward Ross, and a host of lesser Reform Darwinians, who in turn served as a brain trust for the state government. One of Ely's students, Charles McCarthy, set up the nation's first Legislative Reference Bureau in the university library, and conservatives were soon furious at the imposing array

[8] La Follette, p. 311.

of facts that were always at hand to support a La Follette bill. By 1906, when the Governor took the train for Washington as United States Senator-elect, the La Follette name was magic in Wisconsin. "If I owned Pennsylvania as Bob La Follette owns Wisconsin," Pennsylvania's old-guard boss, Boies Penrose, growled, "my life would be a perpetual holiday. All that he has to do before election is to telephone home and send his latest photograph. . . . He would have to get out an injunction to stop them from electing him." [9] Outside the state, the "Wisconsin Idea" was rapidly becoming a program and an inspiration. By 1910 New York, California, New Jersey, Michigan, Iowa, North Carolina, and Texas were going through decidedly progressive phases, and no state was entirely unaffected.

V

LINCOLN STEFFENS was watching it all from the offices of the *New York Commercial Advertiser,* and he smiled wearily. Not that this gifted reporter, whose artist's string tie went along with an artist's sensitivities, was conservative or cynical. Study in Germany, covering Wall Street, all-night wanderings in the Tenderloin had amply convinced Steffens that "the struggle for existence is very animal-like" and that something better than the jungle must be possible.[1] It was simply that Steffens had his doubts about the rising heroes. He knew Roosevelt well, knew him well enough to detect the broad streak of opportunism in the President's make-up. After all, Steffens asked his excited progressive friends, hadn't Tom Johnson discovered reform only after he made his own fortune? Wasn't La Follette building a political machine that had all the authoritarianism of Tweed's organization? So Steffens coasted along, a little sad and more than a little tired, a fiftyish man at thirty-five. In 1901 he made an unenthusiastic

---

[9] Walter Davenport: *Power and Glory, the Life of Boies Penrose* (Putnam, 1931), p. 225.
[1] Quoted by the late Ray Stannard Baker, in an interview.

decision, leaving newspaper work to become an editor of *Mc-Clure's Magazine*.

S. S. McClure was part genius, part madman, and part inexplicable. He once spent hours telling an explorer what the explorer had seen in the Antarctic and so fascinated S. S. McClure by the telling that the man was immediately signed up for a long series of articles. When the McClure editors received this high-priced mass of dullness, S. S. was off to Europe. He was always off to some place, and always coming back with a valiseful of incomparable, world-shaking, history-making articles. One time the valise would contain Kipling's *Kim*; another time, a year's headaches for his staff. But if the editors failed to dissuade S. S. from an obvious mistake, the obvious mistake often turned into a triumph. McClure would put to work the technique he had learned peddling merchandise on the Mississippi, and the housewives would be sure they were abysmally behind the times until they read that article.

In 1902 McClure's antennæ told him that something was astir in the United States which no magazine was covering and which would make the housewives feel very much up to date. He was not sure what it was, but he was certain, after watching Steffens for a while, that his new editor would never discover it in a New York office building.

"Get out of here, travel, go—somewhere," McClure told Steffens. "Go out in the advertising department. Ask them where they have transportation credit. Buy a railroad ticket, get on a train, and there, where it lands you, there you will learn to edit a magazine." [2]

McClure's had an advertising bill against the Lackawanna Railroad and Steffens headed west. In Chicago he heard of a quiet old German named Weyerhaeuser who was gathering into his possession much of the best timberland of the United States. Steffens went to St. Paul, brashed his way into the confidence of Weyerhaeuser, and left with a fascinating story of a millionaire who did not know how much money he had or why he had acquired it.

[2] Steffens, p. 364.

Unfortunately, it was all off the record. In St. Louis, Steffens had better luck. There a wispy Southern Puritan, Joseph Folk, having stumbled into the District Attorney's office by an accident of machine politics, was creating a storm by insisting on performing the duties of District Attorney. Folk desperately needed publicity to help him. The Missouri papers were hostile or afraid, and h? poured out his story to the editor from New York.

He was hardly seated in his office, Folk told Steffens, when the St. Louis boss sent a representative to tell him whom he was to make his assistants, whom he was to prosecute, and whom he was to let off. When Folk ignored the boss and pushed ahead, he found that the trail of corruption led from politicians straight to businessmen, many of them honored figures in St. Louis. Folk's pinpoint eyes spurted anger as he added: "It is good business men that are corrupting our bad politicians; it is good business that causes bad government. . . . It is the leading citizens that are battening on our city." [3]

Steffens left Folk's office in a froth of excitement. All weariness, all skepticism were gone. Here was the kind of story, timely, detailed, sensational, that would certainly pull the housewives from *Ben-Hur* and really score against corruption. The October 1902 issue of *McClure's* carried "Tweed Days in St. Louis." In the November issue Ida Tarbell, a sweet young woman out of the oil regions of Pennsylvania, began her devastating "History of the Standard Oil Company." By January 1903 McClure knew he was getting what he had been fumbling for. He was ready for an editorial, "Concerning Three Articles in this Number of McClure's, and a Coincidence that May Set Us Thinking."

Here was Steffens extending his municipal studies into "The Shame of Minneapolis," another chapter of Tarbell's history of Standard Oil, and an article by Ray Stannard Baker on abuses by the labor union during the recent coal strike. Three articles that seemed quite different, McClure asked his readers to note, but really all on the same theme: the corruption of American life.

[3] Ibid., p. 371.

"Capitalists, workingmen, politicians, citizens—all breaking the law, or letting it be broken. Who is left to uphold it? The lawyers? Some of the best lawyers in this country are hired, not to go into court to defend cases, but to advise corporations and business firms how they can get around the law without too great a risk of punishment. The judges? Too many of them so respect the laws that for some 'error' or quibble they restore to office and liberty men convicted on evidence overwhelmingly convincing to common sense. The churches? We know of one, an ancient and wealthy establishment, which had to be compelled by a Tammany hold-over health officer to put its tenements in sanitary condition. The colleges? They do not understand.

"There is no one left; none but all of us. . . . We all are doing our worst and making the public pay. . . . We forget that . . . while each of us . . . can shove off on the rest the bill of to-day, the debt is only postponed; the rest are passing it on back to us. We have to pay in the end, everyone of us." [4]

McClure and Steffens did not invent muckraking—a dozen other writers and editors, jealous of their place in history, have made that quite plain. But *McClure's*, by common admission, was the most influential pioneer in the sudden vogue for indignant, fact-packed articles of exposure. *Collier's*, the *American Magazine*, the *Cosmopolitan*, *Munsey's*, *Hampton's*, the *Independent*, *Everybody's*—scarcely a mass-circulation magazine failed to follow the trend. *Everybody's* ran Thomas Lawson's lurid analysis of stock-market practices and Charles Edward Russell's sensational exposure of the beef trust. *Collier's* published Samuel Hopkins Adams on patent-medicine frauds, and the *Cosmopolitan* commissioned David Graham Phillips's "Treason of the Senate." Judge Ben Lindsey assailed the administration of law, Burton Hendrick took on the life-insurance companies, and George Turner's series on prostitution directly connected corrupt politics and the white-slave traffic. Nothing was immune to the rake. In thinly disguised fiction as well as factual magazine articles, many of the best-known writers of the day rummaged their way into every major

[4] *McClure's* (January 1903), XX, 336.

industry, into all parts of the political machinery, even into the women's clubs, the universities, and the churches.

"Time was," Mr. Dooley pointed out to Mr. Hennessy over his Archey Road bar, when the magazines "was very ca'ming to the mind. Angabel an' Alfonso dashin' f'r a marriage licence. Prom'nent lady authoresses makin' pomes at the moon. Now an' thin a scrap over whether Shakespear was enthered in his own name or was a ringer, with the longshot players always agin' Shakespear. But no wan hurt. Th' idee ye got fr'm these here publications was that life was wan glad sweet song. . . .

"But now whin I pick me fav-rite magazine off th' flure, what do I find? Ivrything has gone wrong. . . . All th' pomes by th' lady authoresses that used to begin: 'Oh, moon, how fair!' now begin: 'Oh, Ogden Armour, how awful!' Read th' horrible disclosures about th' way Jawn C. Higgins got th' right to build a bay-window on his barber-shop at iliven forty-two Kosciusko Avnoo, South Bennington, Arkansaw. . . . Read Idarem on John D.; she's a lady, but she's got th' punch. Graft ivrywhere. 'Graft in th' Insurance Companies,' 'Graft in Congress,' 'Graft be an Old Grafter,' 'Graft in Its Relations to th' Higher Life,' be Dock Eliot; 'Th' Homeeric Legend an' Graft; Its Cause an' Effect; Are They th' Same? Yes and No. . . .'

"An' so it goes, Hinnissy . . . till I don't thrust anny man anny more. I niver did much, but now if I hear th' stealthy step iv me dearest frind at th' dure I lock th' cash dhrawer. I used to be nervous about burglars, but now I'm afraid iv a night call fr'm th' prisidint iv th' First National Bank."

Mr. Hennessy, having read his magazines too, thought he sniffed a revolution and Mr. Dooley had to explain further. "Th' noise ye hear is not th' first gun iv a rivolution. It's on'y th' people iv th' United States batin' a carpet." [5] Peter Dunne, the creator of the Dooley series, was as shrewd a political commentator as the United States has ever produced, and he had his muckrakers just right. Far from being revolutionists, they were the journalistic and literary voice of progressivism, expressing its indignation at

[5] Quoted in Sullivan, III, 87–8.

corruption which cut down opportunity and its faith that moderate reform would remedy the situation. At a time when the country as a whole was awakening to the enormous possibilities of publicity, the muckrakers were the publicity men for reform. By 1909 muckraking was dying out, a victim of public fickleness and of a crackdown on the magazines by advertisers and bankers, but in its six rambunctious years, it brought the progressive case to thousands who would never have been reached otherwise. Many a machine politician feared a Steffens article more than he worried about his opponent. The furor created by Upton Sinclair's muckraking of the stockyards helped materially in riding the Pure Food and Drug Act through Congress, and Phillips's explosive "Treason of the Senate" series gave new power to the long-time demand for the popular election of senators.

Among the muckrakers one story kept making the rounds and their progressive friends were ready to forgive it. The story was about the wealthy Alaskan miner who walked into an editor's office and demanded a crusade.

"Well!" the editor remarked, "you certainly are a progressive, aren't you?"

"Progressive!" the miner roared. "Progressive! I tell you I'm a full-fledged insurgent. Why, man, I subscribe to thirteen magazines." [6]

VI

AT THE height of muckraking, Ray Stannard Baker, having finished with the railroads, did a series on the conditions of Negro life. The articles, ending with a plea for the Booker T. Washington policy, were much like other progressive statements on the subject and provoked the usual praise from pro-Negro reformers and the usual raps from Negrophobes. But this time there was an additional reaction, vigorous criticism from some pro-Negro progressives. Baker was puzzled, entered into a correspondence with a few of his critics, and soon had the answer. Gradually, by

[6] Quoted in Louis Filler: *Crusaders for American Liberalism* (Harcourt, Brace, 1939), pp. 357–8.

troubled steps, a significant group of progressives were turning to new solutions for the problems of the Negro.[7]

The changed attitude was developing from dissatisfaction with the results of the Washington policy. That policy was obviously producing gains for the Negro, yet the gains were pathetically slow and the position of the Negro was worsening in deeply disturbing ways. If the Southern Negro was advancing educationally and economically, his very advances were making him a more dangerous competitor to the whites, and Southern anti-Negro feeling was mounting. The early 1900's were the period when the Southern Negro was finally clamped into second-class citizenship by laws concerning voting and segregation. President Cleveland had invited the Negro leader, Frederick Douglass, to the White House several times without creating any particular furor—and Douglass brought along his white wife—but when President Roosevelt ate dinner with Booker Washington in 1901, the South screamed hysterical protests for months. "Entertaining that nigger," Senator Tillman, of South Carolina, shouted, would "necessitate our killing a thousand niggers in the South before they will learn their place again," and in the next decade the South filled more than half of Tillman's quota.[8] Throughout the country, race tensions were increasing. The first wave in the large-scale migration of Southern Negroes to Northern cities was under way, producing segregation ordinances and race riots on the other side of Mason and Dixon's line. And to all this Booker T. Washington answered only: learn, work, win the respect of the white man. In Russia, Kropotkin, the anarchist, laughed long and hard at being told that American Negroes had a "conservative" Negro leader. "What on earth do they have to conserve?" Kropotkin wanted to know.[9]

[7] The articles, published in *McClure's* and the *American Magazine* during 1907 and 1908, were collected in the book *Following the Color Line* (Doubleday, Page, 1908). Their reception was described by Baker, in the interview.

[8] Quoted in Sullivan: *Our Times*, III, 136. The number of Negroes lynched in the South from 1901–11 is estimated from the tables in Walter White: *Rope and Faggot* (Knopf, 1929), pp. 230–5.

[9] Quoted in Filler, p. 276.

In Atlanta's tumbled-down Negro university, Professor William Du Bois wanted to know, too. Unlike Washington, Du Bois had never learned to think of the white man as a benefactor. Du Bois was born, of a comfortable mulatto family, in Great Barrington, Massachusetts, where a residue of Civil War enthusiasm gave him an education with no tuition in condescension. At seventeen he was bundled off to Fisk University in Tennessee, and there a sudden introduction to discrimination cut him so deeply that for the rest of his life he had to check the thought that all white men were scoundrels. By the time Du Bois shifted to Harvard in 1888, he was defiant. He accepted racial segregation, even insisted on it, determined "to disdain and forget as far as . . . possible that outer, whiter world." He "asked no fellowship of my fellow students"; he stopped dating a girl because she "looked quite white." Brilliant and quite aware that he was brilliant, Du Bois made every scholastic competition a war between the Negro and the white. When he was chosen as one of the six commencement speakers, he picked "Jefferson Davis" for his subject and handled it, a reporter noted, with an "almost contemptuous fairness." [1]

The contempt was a thin veil for Du Bois's real feelings. In the anguish of his first son's death, he cried out the "awful gladness in my heart. . . . No bitter meanness now shall sicken his baby heart till it die a living death, no taunt shall madden his happy boyhood. . . . Well sped, my boy, before the world had dubbed your ambition insolence, had held your ideals unattainable, and taught you to cringe and bow. Better far this nameless void . . . than a sea of sorrow for you." To this fiercely proud man, with a poet's sensitivities and an agitator's impatience, Booker Washington's gradualism seemed an insufferable doctrine of "submission . . . that practically accepts the alleged inferiority of the Negro races." [2]

The clash between Washington and Du Bois was not simply

[1] Du Bois: *Dusk of Dawn* (Harcourt, Brace, 1940), pp. 35, 42, 101.
[2] Du Bois: *The Souls of Black Folk* (A. C. McClurg, Chicago, 1903), pp. 50, 213.

a question of temperament. Washington, the older man, accepted industrialism uncritically. Du Bois, coming to maturity in the progressive era, approached all problems with an assumption that the big businessman had to be watched. He noted that Washington emphasized the training of Negroes for manual labor, concerned himself little with opening college opportunities, and was ardently supported by a number of powerful industrialists. Putting these facts together, Du Bois saw the whole Washington program as a mechanism by which a cheap, submissive supply of labor would be provided for a rapidly industrializing South. "Unconsciously or not," Du Bois believed, Washington was providing "a voteless herd to run the machines and wash the dishes for the new aristocracy. Negroes would be educated enough to be useful but not enough, or not in the right way, to be able to assert self-respect." [3]

In the early 1900's Washington was the towering figure in Negro America. Not only was his program for the Negro widely accepted by whites and Negroes; to an extraordinary extent Negro projects, especially Negro schools, were given white funds only after Washington approved them. Atlanta University had received the imprimatur, and Washington did not like the reports about Atlanta's new professor of sociology. Apparently Washington's first thought was that it would be a good idea to have this rambunctious young professor closer at hand, where he could absorb sounder doctrine. Twice Du Bois was offered a place on the Tuskegee faculty, the second time at a salary that more than doubled his Atlanta income; twice Du Bois brusquely refused. Then the president of Atlanta University called Du Bois to his office. He did not question the value of a Department of Sociology, the president said, but certain developments made it likely that Atlanta would have to retrench. Unfortunately, either the Sociology Department or the university's experimental kindergarten would have to go.

"Of course, we can't let a kindergarten go," Du Bois snapped.

[3] Interview with Mr. Du Bois.

And the president said yes, well, perhaps, and let's talk about it some other time.[4]

Meanwhile Du Bois was beginning to speak out against Washington in print, most notably in his 1903 publication, *The Souls of Black Folk,* and these statements were attracting excited approval from other young Negro intellectuals.[5] Encouraged, Du Bois spearheaded a series of meetings that climaxed in a demonstration at Harper's Ferry, scene of John Brown's raid to free Negro slaves. At dawn, in bare feet, a small group of Negro professors, writers, and doctors marched to the spot from which John Brown had started, and there they adopted resolutions that Du Bois correctly called "some of the plainest English" ever spoken by American Negroes. The resolutions declared:

"We want full mankind suffrage, and we want it now, henceforth and forever.

"Second. We want discrimination in public accommodation to cease. Separation in railway and street cars, based simply on race and color, is un-American, undemocratic, and silly. . . .

"Third. We claim the right of freemen to walk, talk, and be with them that wish to be with us. No man has a right to choose another man's friends, and to attempt to do so is an impudent interference with the most fundamental human privilege.

"Fourth. We want the laws enforced against rich as well as poor; against Capitalist as well as Laborer; against white as well as black. We are not more lawless than the white race, we are more often arrested, convicted and mobbed. . . . We want the

---

[4] Ibid. Ray Stannard Baker, who interviewed Washington during the period, confirmed Du Bois's story in an interview with me. One student of American Negro history, basing his statements on research in the Washington correspondence, maintains that the opposition to Negroes who opposed his policy went to the point of buying out newspapers and suppressing mention of the opposition charges. Jack Abramowitz: "Origins of the NAACP," *Social Education* (January 1951), XV, 23 n.

[5] James Weldon Johnson, himself one of the rebellious young Negro intellectuals at the time, has said of *The Souls of Black Folk*: "I think . . . [it] has had a greater effect upon and within the Negro race than any other single book published in this country since *Uncle Tom's Cabin*." *Along This Way* (Viking, 1933), p. 203.

Constitution of the country enforced. We want Congress to take charge of the Congressional elections. We want the Fourteenth Amendment carried out to the letter and every State disfranchised in Congress which attempts to disfranchise its rightful voters. . . .

"Fifth. We want our children educated. . . . And when we call for education, we mean real education. We believe in work. We ourselves are workers, but work is not necessarily education. Education is the development of power and ideal. We want our children trained as intelligent human beings should be, and we will fight for all time against any proposal to educate black boys and girls simply as servants and underlings, or simply for the use of other people. They have a right to know, to think, to aspire.

"These are some of the chief things which we want. How shall we get them? By voting where we may vote; by persistent, unceasing agitation; by hammering at the truth; by sacrifice and work. . . ." [6]

The delegates went home, Du Bois returned to more conferences with his president, and most white progressives who concerned themselves with the Negro at all continued to plead the Booker Washington policy. The Harper's Ferry call seemed a cry in the wilderness. But the mixed reception of the Baker articles, published in the years surrounding the Harper's Ferry meeting, indicated that some progressives were having their doubts, and two years after the meeting an event of almost incredible poignance stirred many reformers to a new scrutiny of their doctrine.

Well outside the South, in the centennial year of Lincoln's birth, in his home town of Springfield, Illinois, a race riot careened on for two days. Two Negroes—one eighty-four years old—were lynched; Negro stores were raided or burned and scores of Negroes were driven from their homes in terror. This time the most widely read progressive article had no Booker Washington tone. "Either the spirit of the abolitionists . . . must be revived and we must come to treat the negro on a plane of

[6] Du Bois: *Dusk of Dawn*, pp. 89–92.

absolute political and social equality," William English Walling declared in the muckraking *Independent*, "or Vardaman and Tillman will soon have transferred the race war to the North." [7]

Mary Ovington, a white student of Franz Boas who was engaged in a study of the Harlem Negroes, read the article and she was soon conferring with Walling on ways to do something. A "Call" for a conference went out, signed by forty-nine well-known names. No person on the list could have been described as an out-and-out conservative; only a few were socialists, moderate socialists; the overwhelming majority had been associated with typical progressive activities. From this "Call" came the National Association for the Advancement of Colored People. When the Association began operating, in 1910, its eight top officers included one Negro, Director of Publicity and Research William Du Bois, and the selection of Du Bois symbolized its policy. A significant group of American progressives, white and colored, were rejecting Washington's gradualism and were demanding immediate political, economic, and social equality for the Negro.

Du Bois promptly resigned from Atlanta University and gave all his energies to advancing the NAACP. But another idea, an idea quite different from the NAACP program, was also growing in his mind. Du Bois had always felt a sense of "racial solidarity" as he listened to Negroes singing or looked at Negro women, who seemed to him a much more beautiful type than the white female. [8] The sense of solidarity became stronger as his hope of winning real acceptance for the Negro waned. Bitterly he noted that the activities of the NAACP were accompanied by a flood of discriminatory legislation and by extra-legal, but no less meaningful, acts of discrimination. Du Bois was particularly affected by an incident connected with Harvard. That university had been one of the few white institutions which occasionally gave Du Bois the feeling he could drop his guard, but three years after the NAACP

[7] Walling: "The Race War in the North," *Independent* (September 3, 1908), LXV, 534.
[8] Du Bois interview.

was founded, a group of Northern alumni almost succeeded in a move to bar Negro members from the annual dinner.

Did he have any real ties to this hostile white America, Du Bois was beginning to ask. Or didn't his ties actually run to the Negro people, to the "fatherland of Africa," which had given all black men, in and outside the United States, "common traditions"? Discrimination and hopelessness about checking it were producing the usual introversion. America didn't want the Negro—and the Negro world was separate and better anyhow. Du Bois and a number of Negro progressives, more or less consciously, were moving beyond the program for immediate integration of the Negro into American life and toward a full-blown Negro racialism or nationalism. Here and there white progressives, discouraged in their efforts to win opportunities for the Negro, were beginning to slur the demand for opportunity into an acquiescence in Negro nationalism.[9]

In the case of the Jews a similar trend was still more marked. Jews, and progressives friendly to Jews, rarely had to pass through a Booker T. Washington stage; their program had always been immediate equal status. Nor did Jewish Nationalism have to be invented out of the American social tensions of the late nineteenth century. For more than eighteen hundred years the idea of a separate Jewish people, centered in a Palestinian state, had been kept alive in Talmudic lore, and in 1897 this nationalism was given organizational form when 204 delegates from many nations convened in Basel to form the Zionist Organization of the World.

At the time Du Bois led his militant group to Harper's Ferry, Zionism was still a negligible movement in the United States, confined largely to uninfluential recent immigrants and ignored or assailed by most Jewish and Gentile progressives. Virtually all of the leading spokesmen for American Jewry, whether progressive or conservative, were successful, highly assimilated men of western European origins who wanted nothing to do with a movement that smacked of the eastern European ghetto. "We have fought

[9] Du Bois and Baker interviews. Du Bois has interestingly discussed the process of introversion in *Dusk of Dawn*, pp. 132–3.

our way through to liberty, equality, and fraternity," the financier Henry Morgenthau, Sr., said for these leaders. ". . . No one shall rob us of these gains. . . . We Jews of America have found America to be our Zion. Therefore I refuse to allow myself to be called a Zionist. I am an American." [1]

But this leadership was soon to be overwhelmed. Despite the general relaxation of anti-immigrant feeling, the masses of recent Jewish immigrants from eastern Europe were finding no Zion in America. They were learning English, shaving off their beards, throwing away their skullcaps, hurrying away from all the ways of the East Side ghettos only to be sharply rebuffed. Quickly they discovered that they were accepted in little except the game of making money, and there mostly in the cloak-and-suit field, which earlier German-Jewish immigrants had deserted for occupations of greater status. A little frightened, more than a little bitter, thousands of them drew back in clan-consciousness and veered toward the Zionist movement, which offered a solace of pride in what they had failed to escape. [2]

In rebuffing these new-migration Jews, the United States became more generally anti-Semitic. As the first decade of the twentieth century closed, the *American Jewish Yearbook* noted the mounting number of clubs and resorts that were adopting a "No Hebrews" policy, the increase in classified ads ending with "Gentiles Only," the plainer streaks of anti-Semitism appearing in every field of American life. [3] "No Hebrews" could mean no Morgenthaus as well as no cloak-and-suiters; the new discrimina-

[1] Quoted in James Waterman Wise: *Jews Are Like That!* (Brentano's, 1928), p. 42.
[2] The introversion was not confined to Jewish immigrants, as Oscar Handlin has made plain in his moving work: *The Uprooted* (Little, Brown, 1951). But Zionism was to prove the most important single result.
[3] Carey McWilliams: *A Mask for Privilege* (Little, Brown, 1948), pp. 23–30. The Chicago employment situation was studied in detail by A. L. Severson, who pointed out that from 1872 to 1911 virtually no discriminatory want-ads appeared but that the discriminatory ads increased from 0.3 per 1,000 in 1911 to 4 per 1,000 in 1921. "Nationality and Religious Preferences as Reflected in Newspaper Advertisements," *American Journal of Sociology* (January 1939), XLIV, 541.

tion produced self-consciousness in Jews who had long insisted that being a Jew was simply a religious affiliation, requiring no greater sense of separation from the community than membership in the Baptist or Presbyterian church. For fifty-four years Louis Brandeis had been such a Jew, and in 1905 he roundly condemned anyone, Jew or Gentile, who encouraged "habits of living or of thought which tend to keep alive differences of origin or to classify men according to their religious beliefs." Such ways of thinking, he said, "are inconsistent with the American ideal of brotherhood, and are disloyal." Seven years later Brandeis became the first wealthy, distinguished, non-eastern European Jew to publicly associate himself with Zionism. The Jews were no longer simply a religious group to Brandeis. They were a "nationality," a special "blood," "peculiarly fitted" to contribute to the "ideals of democracy and social justice," and non-Zionist Jews were "against their own people." [4]

Influenced by the action of the much-admired Brandeis, upset by the continually increasing discrimination, a wide variety of Jewish and Gentile liberals were finding a new sympathy for Zionism. Even more than in the case of the Negroes, the line between demanding greater opportunity within the nation and minority nationalism was blurring.

VII

BLURRINGS, TENDENCIES, trends—but in the first decade of the twentieth century the main current of progressivism was the one on which Teddy Roosevelt bobbed along so gaily. He might scourge minority nationalists, but Du Bois and Brandeis were both admirers as his Administrations drew to a close. He might suddenly turn on the muckrakers, even, on occasion, thwack the unions or help the United States Steel trust, but for the over-

---

[4] Alpheus T. Mason: *Brandeis* (Viking, 1946), p. 442; *Brandeis on Zionism* (Zionist Organization of America, Washington, 1942), pp. 14–15, 21, 35.

whelming number of American reformers Roosevelt was progressivism incarnate, and that progressivism was bringing an
all-excusing sense of achievement. The new reform not only ruled
the White House and hundreds of state and local governments.
Progressives could take deeper satisfaction in the way that economic and social change was becoming the central subject of
the day, the exciting, even the glamour subject, replacing the
older generation's awed discussions of captains of industry with
ebullient talk about the goodness, the inevitability, the sheer fun
of re-doing America.

Late in 1904 Mrs. Sarah P. Decker took her ample self to the
rostrum of the General Federation of Women's Clubs, turned a
carefully coiffured head to the delegates, and said: "Ladies, you
have chosen me your leader. Well, I have an important piece of
news to give you. Dante is dead. He has been dead for several
centuries, and I think it is time that we dropped the study of his
Inferno and turned our attention to our own." [5] It was that way
everywhere in the country, on all social levels. In Chicago an immigrant worker walked up to her boss and demanded better toilet
facilities with the statement: "Old America is gone. There is new
times." In middle-class New York, pretty young Frances Perkins
was reading the reform books the President was always recom-
mending and vowing that "the pursuit of social justice would be
my vocation." In Baltimore a socialite horseman turned the city
upside down with full-page advertisements preaching Rauschenbusch's dictum that "the greatest thing a millionaire can do is to
make the rise of future millionaires impossible." [6] Thirty-three
Protestant denominations joined in a Federal Council dedicated
to Reform Darwinian Christianity, Walter Lippmann proudly
took over the presidency of the Harvard Socialist Club, a muckraking novelist, Winston Churchill, led both Rex Beach and *The
Trail of the Lonesome Pine* on the best-seller lists, and Clarence

---

[5] Quoted in Filler, p. 261.

[6] *Chicago Evening Post*, August 17, 1905; Frances Perkins: *The Roosevelt I Knew* (Viking, 1946), p. 10; Ray Stannard Baker: "The Rich Young
Man Who Began to Believe in Jesus Christ," *American Magazine* (July
1914), LXXVIII, 79.

Darrow was invited to address the Ulysses S. Grant Chapter of the Daughters of the American Revolution in Ashtabula, Ohio.

There was, said Theodore Roosevelt in the only understatement of his entire career, "a condition of excitement and irritation in the public mind. . . ." [7]

[7] Pringle, p. 413.

CHAPTER IX

Mr. Croly Writes a Book

O N A dazzling spring morning of 1909 Roosevelt, wrapped in the greatcoat of a colonel of the Rough Riders, rumbled down to the Hoboken pier. The strenuous Teddy, always a little ahead of the game, was an ex-President of the United States at fifty. For two hours he shook hands with a mob of admirers, resummoned his countrymen to the "life of strenuous effort," skittishly supervised the porters who were loading the S.S. *Hamburg* with books, guns, and safari clothing. A cornetist from Governor's Island played "There'll Be a Hot Time in the Old Town Tonight," and Roosevelt was off for "the joy of wandering through lonely lands, the joy of hunting the mighty and terrible lords" of Africa, "where death broods in the dark and silent depths." [1]

Everything was bully. When the near-sighted colonel leveled his gun, three other guns leveled at the same instant. "Mr. Roosevelt had a fairly good idea of the general direction," the safari leader explained, "but we couldn't take chances with the life of a former president." [2] Delighted with his nine lions, five elephants, thirteen rhinoceroses, and seven hippopotamuses, Roosevelt swung off on a grand tour, lecturing Egyptian nationalists on the beneficence of British imperialism, dining with the King and Queen

[1] *New York Times*, March 24, 1909; Hermann Hagedorn, ed.: *Works of Theodore Roosevelt* (Scribner, 1923–6), V, xxv.

[2] Quoted in George Creel: *Rebel at Large* (Putnam, 1947), p. 90.

of Italy and finding their etiquette something like that of "a Jewish wedding on the East Side," spending five rapturous hours astride a charger while the troops of the German Empire goose-stepped in review.[3] Somewhere in the course of it all, he whisked through dozens of books, including Herbert Croly's *The Promise of American Life,* which an ardent Rooseveltian, Justice Learned Hand, had mailed to Africa.

It is doubtful whether Roosevelt read many of Croly's 454 pages, which include a good deal of labyrinthine analysis and even more tedious writing. (Alfred Zimmern was fond of describing how Roosevelt hailed his *Greek Commonwealth* as a great book, invited Zimmern to lunch to talk about it, and then spent the hour repeating an *Encyclopædia Britannica* article on the subject, including the mistakes.[4]) But Roosevelt certainly read enough of *The Promise of American Life* to get its main point, and that point cut through his mind like a knife specially honed for the purpose. The *Promise,* he announced, was "the most profound and illuminating study of our national conditions which has appeared for many years."[5] Soon after Roosevelt's ship had docked, and the wildest reception New York had ever known was over, Croly received the inevitable call to come out to Oyster Bay for lunch.

II

THE MAN Roosevelt saw across the table was the antithesis of the strenuous life. Pale and fragile, ugly to the point where he was acutely aware of his looks, speaking with an impediment and so quietly that he could hardly be heard, Croly would have been utterly ridiculous on a safari and completely lost in the hurly-burly of politics. But a penetrating mind and an all-absorbing concern with public affairs were bred into this waterish little man.

[3] Henry F. Pringle: *Theodore Roosevelt* (Harcourt, Brace, 1931), p. 516.
[4] Interview with Mr. Horace M. Kallen, to whom Zimmern told the story.
[5] Hagedorn, XIX, 86.

Croly's mother, a brilliant woman of an English Chartist background, set up a whole series of American feminist firsts—the first regularly working newspaperwoman in the United States, the first to write for out-of-town newspapers, the first to be syndicated. Angered because of the refusal to admit women to a Dickens reception in New York, "Jenny June," as Mrs. Croly liked to be called, founded Sorosis, the first important women's club, and she later aided in establishing the pioneer Woman's Press Club of New York City. The father, David Goodman Croly, rose to be editor of the crusading *New York Daily Graphic*, and was never without a passionate cause.

David Croly was the principal author of a pamphlet called *Miscegenation*, which, in the course of giving the word to the language, had a not unimportant role in the Presidential election of 1864.[6] A few years later he was badgering New York leaders with a plan to set up, in the manner of ancient Rome, a board of censors over the city's political life.[7] Then he was feverishly at work getting under way the *Modern Thinker*, "An Organ for the Most Advanced Speculation," which appeared a blaze of purple print on yellowish paper. "This is no mere whimsey," Editor Croly explained. "The eyes of the present generation have been seriously injured by white paper and black ink. . . . The human eye is an extremely defective machine. . . . As in the case of the male and female organs of generation, where, in nine cases in ten, the 'key does not fit the lock' . . . , the human eye is peculiarly liable to derangements. . . . Artificial protections [are needed] and this is why the MODERN THINKER calls attention to the color question."[8]

Behind all the fervid activity of mother and father Croly was

---

[6] The pamphlet was an amazing literary hoax. Appearing anonymously just before the election of 1864, it argued, as if from a pro-Negro, Republican point of view, for miscegenation. It was widely read and discussed, much to the detriment of the Republicans, and thus advanced Croly's own anti-Negro, Democratic cause. Sidney Kaplan: "The Miscegenation Issue in the Election of 1864," *Journal of Negro History* (July 1949), XXXIV, 274–343.

[7] Croly: "Organizing Public Opinion," in *Northern Monthly*, February 1868, reprinted in the *Modern Thinker* (1873), No. 2, pp. 107–14.

[8] Ibid., p. 157.

a devotion to the ideas of Auguste Comte, the French thinker who had given to an American coterie the faith that rigorously scientific living, infused with moral aspiration, would regenerate mankind. Comte's "Positivism" was half philosophy and half religion, and the Crolys gave it their emotions as well as their minds. Brushing aside the standard creeds as muddled supports of the outmoded, David and Jane Croly turned their home into the country's best-known salon of Positivism. The son, Herbert, was certainly the first, and perhaps the last, American infant to go through the Positivist "Ceremony of Presentation" into the "Religion of Humanity." He went off to Harvard with a stern parental injunction to remember that the chief point of living was advancing the welfare of mankind.

The welfare of mankind was hardly the major concern of the freshman. In two months he spent most of his two years' allotment of money on beer and dates, and then, trying to dredge himself out by playing poker, he lost the rest of the funds. The next year David Croly was still more shocked to receive a letter which said, with a minimum of circumlocution, that Auguste Comte was a pompous fool. But all this was a schoolboy revolt, the more violent because Herbert Croly was doing and saying things that were quite unnatural for him. By his junior year his evenings were devoted to vast plans for the study of man, and his manner was taking on the tortured intensity of his later years. Every word he spoke, people began to note, seemed to fight its way through an exacting morality and intellectualism; "Crolier than thou," one irritated acquaintance put it.[9] For a few years after graduation Croly did editorial work for the *Architectural Record*—architecture was always a delight to him—but something that he enjoyed was not to be permitted to stand in the way of the main business of life. In the mornings before he went to the office, at lunch hours, and then so far into the night that his body wasted to a wraith, Herbert Croly worked out his blueprint for a better United States. It came, in 1909, in the agonized pages of *The Promise of American Life*.

[9] Quoted in Robert Morss Lovett: *All Our Years* (Viking, 1948), p. 179.

The *Promise* has often been called one of the few genuinely important political studies written by an American in the early twentieth century, and when the volume has been given such high rank, it has generally been considered an expression of progressivism.[1] In essence the book certainly was a statement of the progressive program and philosophy. It identified wide opportunities to get ahead with the American dream; pointed with indignation to narrowing opportunities; called for evolving ideas and institutions to meet the changed circumstances; restated the progressive demand for the use of executive leadership and of federal powers to broaden opportunity; and approved many of the specific proposals reformers were pushing. The very title of the book captured so well the expansive mood of the new reformism that the phrase, "the promise of American life," soon became a cliché.[2]

Yet if the book was an expression of contemporary reformism, it was also something else, something a good deal more important. The Croly home had always been a European island in New York, and Herbert Croly's thinking, far more than the ideas of most progressives, was heavily influenced by European patterns; his Comtean background, in particular, inclined him to emphases uncommon among reformers of his day.[3] His severe intellectualism and inordinate shyness cut him off from progressives who swept each other over ideological difficulties in a tide of emotion. These facts tended to make Croly write about American progressives the way foreign ambassadors often talk about American baseball games. He was there, he wanted to be part of it all, but

[1] The Bibliographical Notes to this chapter indicate how little work has been done on Herbert Croly, and the neglect has left a serious hole in the intellectual history of modern America. For indications of his great significance, see the essays of Felix Frankfurter and Walter Lippmann in "Herbert Croly," *New Republic* (July 16, 1930), LXIII, Pt. II, pp. 247–52.

[2] It continued to be used by reformers in the grim 1930's, and, with a poignant change of tense, became the title of one of Archibald MacLeish's more widely read poems, "America Was Promises" (*New Republic* [November 8, 1939], CI, 46–8).

[3] Croly's prime aim in all his work seems to have been the erection of a kind of Comtean social science. This is interestingly illustrated not only in *The Promise of American Life* but in his Introduction to Eduard Lindeman: *Social Discovery* (Republic Publishing Co., 1924).

he remained an outsider who could not help wondering at some of the antics he saw. Part of Croly's criticism of the progressives was made directly, in a chapter on "Reform and the Reformers." Still more came in the course of his criticism of general American thinking, so much of which the progressives had taken over. A final part emerged by implication. From the total, the *Promise* turns out to be not only a major expression of American progressivism but also a perceiving and disturbing critique of it. Equally disturbing were the possibilities inherent in the proposals that Croly himself made.

III

THE IMPORTANT differences between Croly and contemporary progressivism all revolved around that perennial symbol, Thomas Jefferson. Jefferson might be a hero to most reformers of the day, but to Croly he was a man of "intellectual superficiality and insincerity . . . [who had] perverted the American democratic idea." [4] Croly granted that Jefferson had done a great deal to infuse American thought with democratic aspirations, and that Jefferson's doctrines had considerable value in the earlier period of American history. But Jeffersonianism, he insisted, was basically unsound at any time, and it was dangerously inadequate in the twentieth century, for the country in general or for its reform movement.

The central error of Jeffersonian progressivism, Croly maintained, was the way it went about trying to expand opportunity. "Equal rights for all and special privileges for none," the progressive credo ran, and by "restoring" this condition, America was to be taken back to a happy state in which individuals competed freely and fairly for advancement. But in Croly's view, "our earlier political and economic condition was not at its best a fit subject for any great amount of complacency. It cannot be re-

[4] *The Promise of American Life* (Macmillan, 1909), p. 29. Quoted by permission of The Macmillan Co.

stored, even if we would; and the public interest has nothing to gain by its restoration." The attempt to practice equal rights, Croly was sure, inevitably defeated reform aspirations. "The strong and capable men not only conquer, but they seek to perpetuate their conquests by occupying all the strategic points in the economic and political battlefield. . . . Thus in so far as equal rights are freely exercised, they are bound to result in inequalities; and these inequalities are bound to make for their own perpetuation, and so to provoke still further discrimination." [5]

The fallacious desire to restore free competition, Croly went on, showed itself in the great number of reformers who were avid for trust-busting. The large-scale corporation, tending toward monopoly, was endemic to industrialism, Croly was sure. Moreover, breaking up trusts would not benefit the general public. Some huge corporations had undoubtedly been guilty of abuses, but in general big businesses "contributed to American economic efficiency." They constituted "an important step in the direction of the better organization of industry and commerce." They meant "cooperation, and it should be the effort of all civilized societies to substitute cooperation for competitive methods, wherever cooperation can prove its efficiency." The Sherman Act, with its attempt to protect the small enterprise, was a serious mistake. In certain fields the little entrepreneur could hold his own, "but where he is not able to hold his own, there is no public interest promoted by an expensive attempt to save his life." [6]

Croly was no more enthusiastic about reform proposals to create conditions of free and fair competition by the setting up of administrative commissions. "The efficient conduct of any complicated business," he argued, ". . . always involves the constant sacrifice of an occasional or a local interest for the benefit of the economic operation of the whole organization. But it is just such sacrifices of local and occasional to a comprehensive interest which official commissions are not allowed by public opinion to approve.

[5] Ibid., pp. 148–54, 189.
[6] Ibid., pp. 358–9.

Under their control rates will be made chiefly for the benefit of clamorous local interests." What's more, under commission rule the economic life of the country would become the "victim of routine management," and "the flexibility and enterprise, characteristic of our existing national economic organization, would disappear." In place of pleas for the restoration of competition, Croly proposed a "reconstruction" of American attitudes. Corporations should be permitted to go through their "natural" growth, and sweeping, continuous federal powers should be used to rein their activities to the national interest. In the event that any corporation achieved a monopoly detrimental to the country, it should be gradually nationalized.[7]

The Jeffersonian call for free competition carried an implication that disturbed Croly almost as much as the call itself. If government could preserve free and fair competition, then government had to be able to pass laws that were partial to no citizen or no group of citizens. Most reformers considered the Sherman Antitrust Act such an impartial law. In cold fact, Croly insisted, there was no such thing as impartial legislation; every law, of necessity, discriminated for and against some interest. The Sherman Antitrust Act discriminated for small business at the expense of big business—and, most significant of all, it discriminated for small business at the expense of the general good. Croly saw in the taxation proposals advocated by most progressives a similar failure to recognize that all laws discriminated and a consequent failure to choose between taxes that discriminated for and those that discriminated against the general interest. They lumped inheritance and income taxes together as legislation beneficial to "the people," he argued, but the two taxes had opposite results. The inheritance tax contributed to the general good because "the preservation intact of a fortune over a certain amount is not desirable either in the public or individual interest." On the other hand, the income tax discouraged a type of individual initiative that was beneficial to the whole country, made no "edifying dis-

---

[7] Ibid., pp. 362-3, 369-81.

crimination" as to the different types of investments that produced income, and confused plans for bringing corporate profits under federal supervision.[8]

The Jeffersonian "cant" concerning equal rights, Croly pushed his analysis ahead, led to a serious misunderstanding of trade-unions. The unions were not really seeking "fair play," as so many progressives believed. They were after "special opportunities. . . . The demand for fair play is as usual merely the hypocritical exterior of a demand for substantial favoritism." The average union member "has no respect for traditional American individualism as applied to his own social and economic standing. Whenever he has had the power, he has suppressed competition as ruthlessly as have his employers. . . . His own personality is merged in that of the union. . . . The unionist . . . has come to depend upon his union for that material prosperity and advancement which, according to the American tradition, was to be the inevitable result of American political ideas and institutions. His attachment to his union has come to be the most important attachment of his life—more important in most cases than his attachment to the American ideal and to the national interest." [9]

In Croly's analysis, most of the reformers, along with the whole nation, were failing to realize that "the large corporations and the unions occupy in certain respects a similar relation to the American political system. Their advocates both believe in associated action for themselves and in competition for their adversaries. They both demand governmental protection and recognition, but resent the notion of efficient governmental regulation. They . . . both are opposed to any interference by the Federal government —except exclusively in their own behalf." It was true, Croly conceded, that at the time unions were needed to protect labor and that consequently unions should be encouraged. But in the present as in the future it was dangerous to proceed on the Jeffersonian assumption that any group of individuals could be left un-

[8] Ibid., pp. 357-9, 382, 384-5. The point concerning the effect of the income tax on initiative is deduced from Croly's points on p. 384 and his general emphases; e.g., p. 115.
[9] Ibid., pp. 127, 386.

checked by the national government without turning into "powerful and unscrupulous . . . special interests." [1]

The progressive political program was run through the same meat-chopper of anti-Jeffersonianism. Some of Croly's most unusual passages commented on the reformers' apotheosis of "the people." Any failure of the democratic process was assumed to be a result of some betrayal of "the people" by a man or a party; the more "the people" ruled, the more democracy would serve the general good. "It is never the people who are at fault," Croly summarized. But who were "the people" as they had manifested themselves in American history, Croly challenged. They were individuals, and groups of individuals, pursuing their own interests. Big businessmen and political bosses had been distinguished from "the people" by "peculiar ability and energy" rather than "by peculiar selfishness." [2]

Initiatives and referendums and primaries would not magically transform "the people" into selfless patriots, Croly was sure. Besides, he predicted, the direct primary was actually likely to increase the power of political bosses by creating more elections and therefore more need for professional politicians. The whole democratic process would be improved not by more direct participation of "the people" but by encouraging leadership that would lead toward the national interest and by giving this leadership greater powers. "The way to make votes important and effective," Croly argued, "is not to increase but to diminish their number. A democracy has no interest in making good government complicated, difficult, and costly. It has, on the contrary, every interest in so simplifying its machinery that only decisive decisions and choices are submitted to the voter. . . . The cost of government in time, ability, training, and energy should fall not upon the followers but upon the leaders; and the latter should have every opportunity to make the expenditure pay." Out of his concern for leadership, Croly had harsh words for the kind of civil-service reform being promoted by progressives. "The civil service laws,"

[1] Ibid., pp. 126, 131, 385–98.
[2] Ibid., pp. 165, 320.

he emphasized, "have been designed . . . to a very considerable extent for the purpose of protecting the subordinates against their chiefs; and that is scarcely to be conceived as a method of organizing administrative employees helpful to administrative efficiency." [3]

In calling for powerful officials operating a powerful state, Croly realized that he was staking his whole system on the possibility of creating an officialdom and a public opinion reasonably free from selfish interests. That, he emphasized again and again, was precisely the point. "The principle of democracy *is* virtue"; reform did depend on bringing "the feeling of human brotherhood . . . into possession of the human spirit." In modern America this feeling could be effectively promoted only by a "New Nationalism," which directed individual efforts away from self-aggrandizement and toward the collective solution of national problems.[4]

Croly's New Nationalism, by plain implication, warned against the trend toward inward-looking thinking among America's minority groups, and any progressive acquiescence in that trend. If reform was to be advanced by a sense of joint movement toward the solution of joint problems, encouragement to vote as a member of a special group with special interests obviously would prove detrimental. Group-centered voting not only militated against concern over the community interest. It made more likely situations in which a low-income minority, driven by a religious, racial, or nationality emotion, voted for conservatism. A good many candidates so loyally supported by poor Catholics, Negroes, or Jews were all for the upbuilding of Palestine, or reverence for the Pope, or honor to Booker T. Washington, but against or unconcerned with slum-clearance or eight-hour laws. "When the question is food or clothing," Algie Simons once sadly remarked, "the vote is determined by who is persecuting somebody's cousin three thousand miles away. Conservatives can easily get Americans to vote against reform by identifying the conservative side of the

[3] Ibid., pp. 320–7, 335–6, 342–3.
[4] Ibid., pp. 169, 279–88, 403–9, 453, 454 (the italics are Croly's).

issue with the special interests of some self-conscious minority." [5] Herbert Croly would have agreed, and seen this danger to reform as an especially important one in heterogeneous America.

Croly's insistence that, at bottom, the reform hope rested on simple, absolute morality pointed to troublesome possibilities in the general philosophy of the progressives—their Reform Darwinian argument that all ideas must be submitted to the pragmatic test, particularly the pragmatic test of asking what economic interest is served by believing the ideas. Pragmatism, as one of John Dewey's disciples, Horace Kallen, has pointed out, is not a philosophy that most men can live with comfortably. It "dissolves dogmas into beliefs, eternities and necessities into change and chance, conclusions and finalities into processes. Men have invented philosophy precisely because they find change, chance and process too much for them, and desire infallible security and certainty. Pragmatism . . . calls for too complete a disillusion." [6] Reformers of the early 1900's were in no mood for philosophical discomfort, not to say disillusionment. They were, with few exceptions, men of the most absolute judgments. When they said that all ideas must be related to economic interest, they did not really mean *all* ideas; they meant only their opponents' ideas. So conservatism became a rationalization of greed, while the tenets of progressivism were "scientific," "objective," and "moral," the same kind of absolute Truth and Good that has immemorially given men enthusiasm for a cause. A Rauschenbusch compared his "scientific" Christianity with a Protestantism that was merely an unscientific defense of the rich. "My book," Ross wrote of *Sin and Society*, "hailed as ethical, is in fact sociological," in contrast to Conservative Darwinians, who were, in violation of true social science, providing a blind for "the dog-eat-dog practices of current business and politics." [7]

The danger in such thinking is like the danger in inflation. It

[5] Interview with the late Algie M. Simons.

[6] Kallen: "Pragmatism," *Encyclopedia of the Social Sciences* (Macmillan, 1930–5), XII, 311.

[7] Walter Rauschenbusch: *Christianizing the Social Order* (Macmillan, 1914), pp. 118–19; Edward A. Ross: *Seventy Years of It* (Appleton-Century, 1936), pp. 55, 107.

often achieves what you are seeking if it can be controlled, but it is exceedingly difficult to control. When men keep insisting that all ideas are relative to economic interests, there is a natural tendency for their disciples to begin believing it, especially when their disciples are a generation hungry for emancipation from all fixedness. Once your own movement as well as the other fellow's is stripped of the Truth and the Good, once thinking has entered a phase of sweeping relativism, the troubles come.

Relativism encourages the most blatant kind of self-aggrandizing politics; if all ideas reflect economic interests, why not advocate the program that most directly serves yourself or your group? Relativism breeds ideological eunuchs, their ardor castrated by the feeling that, after all, they are being asked to act upon temporary, class-angled truth. Relativism easily turns into a doctrine of expediency. Asserting the impossibility of absolute standards removes any very compelling check on the choice of means to an end, thus encouraging a practice that usually needs little encouraging anyhow—justifying the means by the end. But justifying means by the end brings a difficulty which has been emphasized as long as men have taken thought about their mental processes. Means not only lead to an end; they can change the end; they can even, as John Dewey himself has pointed out, "become the end." [8] A special feature of Reform Darwinian relativism produced its own special danger. By heavily emphasizing environment as the factor that makes men what they are, Reform Darwinism opened the way to using the environment as an excuse for any failure of ability or of will power. Eat, drink, and be antisocial, for tomorrow the environment explains us. "The apostle of relativity is destined to be destroyed by the child of his own brain," Charles Beard warned years later, after relativism had plainly damaged reform.[9] In 1909 Herbert Croly's argument that progressivism should be tied to an absolute morality was also a portent, no less important because it was unintended.

[8] Quoted in Upton Sinclair, review of Manes Sperber: *The Burned Bramble*, in *New York Times Book Review*, March 18, 1951, p. 1.

[9] Beard: "Written History as an Act of Faith," *American Historical Review* (January 1934), XXXIX, 225.

Mr. Croly Writes a Book

Doggedly, conscientiously, far more concerned with expounding the New Nationalism than with criticizing other reformers, Croly ground ahead with the description of his system. The program advocated by *The Promise of American Life* amounted to the establishment of a tremendously powerful national state that would regulate corporations, unions, small businesses, and agriculture in the "national interest." That national interest would be defined by leaders who were to guide public opinion far more than they were guided by it and who were to have all the powers necessary for "efficiency." The New Nationalist state would speak for "much more than a group of individuals." It would represent "the nation of yesterday and to-morrow, organized for its national historical mission," and it would bind leaders and people into a continuous rapport by their joint obedience to "a morally authoritative Sovereign will." Most Americans, Croly summarized in his curious, off-beat language, would no doubt consider his program "flagrantly socialistic . . . and if any critic likes to fasten the stigma of socialism upon the foregoing conception of democracy, I am not concerned with dodging the odium of the word. The proposed definition of democracy is socialistic, if it is socialistic to consider democracy inseparable from a candid, patient, and courageous attempt to advance the social problem towards a satisfactory solution. It is also socialistic in case socialism cannot be divorced from the use, wherever necessary, of the political organization in all its forms to realize the proposed democratic purpose. On the other hand, there are some doctrines frequently associated with socialism, to which the proposed conception of democracy is wholly inimical; and it should be characterized not so much [as] socialistic, [but] as unscrupulously and loyally nationalistic." [1]

[1] *The Promise of American Life*, pp. 209, 265–88, 399–454.

IV

"Unscrupulously and loyally nationalistic," a state that was more than the people who made it up, a "national" socialism that encouraged huge combinations of labor and capital and attempted to make them serve an interest defined by the state, a society given cohesion by a sense of "the nation of yesterday and to-morrow" —the 1920's found another name for such systems and that name was fascism. Yet it would be inaccurate and extraneous to apply the fascist label to the New Nationalism. Croly was writing in a different cultural climate, he was devoted to democracy, and his program varied in important respects from the system of a Mussolini.[2] The significance of *The Promise of American Life* is rather that it suggested pointedly, and at an early date, the troubles into which modern American reform could get itself. This first systematic expression of American progressivism had indicated serious inadequacies in the beliefs of most reformers, but in the course of trying to improve the program, it offered a system with still graver deficiencies. The New Nationalism, when placed beside the more typical progressive thinking of the day, presented a series of on-the-one-hand, on-the-other problems, problems so difficult to escape that they approach being dilemmas.

If progressivism went on with its Jeffersonian faith in "the people," Croly challenged, was it not relying on special interests to defeat special interests? Would not all the bright hopes of reform turn into greedy rule by some special interest, or group of special interests? On the other hand, if progressivism subordinated "the people" in a New Nationalism, could it preserve the political freedom that Croly, along with the whole progressive movement,

[2] Though it is interesting to note that Comte once remarked of his American disciples: "The principal Conservatives of the United States of America have nobly invoked the Positive religion as their one systematic defense against the subversive tendencies of the most anarchical of Western populations, in a world which makes any material repression quite out of the question." Quoted in Frederic Harrison: "August Comte in America," *Positivist Review* (June 1, 1901), No. CII, p. 122.

thought essential, so essential that they assumed its continuance?

If progressivism tried to break up the trusts, Croly asked, was it not attempting the impossible and the unwise? But if trusts were permitted to develop, on the assumption that federal power would regulate them in the national interest, what was to assure that corporations so powerful would not control the controls? Did not the policy of encouraging the growth of giant labor combines and attempting to control them run the same danger? For centuries students of government have pointed out that centralized power, when it falls into the hands of self-interested groups, simply gives self-interest that much more power. The conservatives themselves could find important advantages in the controls set up by reformers. There were always the haunting words of the astute railroad attorney Richard Olney, commenting on the Interstate Commerce Commission. Olney told a railroad baron to cheer up, for the commission "is, or can be made, of great use to the railroads. . . . [It could be employed as] a sort of barrier between the railroad corporations and the people and a sort of protection against hasty and crude legislation hostile to railroad interests. . . . The part of wisdom is not to destroy the Commission, but to utilize it." [8]

If progressivism sought to increase opportunities for racial, nationality, or religious minorities, its efforts were in constant danger of sliding over into an acquiescence in minority chauvinisms that created more special interests and might work against the general effectiveness of the reform movement. But Croly's American "unity" easily became a totalitarian nationalism, offering nothing or worse than nothing to those who did not fit the dominant white, Protestant, "Anglo-Saxon" pattern.

Without Reform Darwinism, how was conservatism's steel chain of ideas to be effectively attacked? With Reform Darwinism, how were progressives to be held back from a dangerous relativism?

[8] Quoted in Matthew Josephson: *The Politicos* (Harcourt, Brace, 1938), p. 526.

V

THE DIFFICULTIES are plain in the 1950's. In 1909 they were mercifully obscured. A few progressives protested Croly's anti-Jeffersonianism. Most reformers who managed to struggle through his tortuous prose emerged with a confirmation of what they already believed. "A brilliant study," Henry Stimson called the *Promise*, and used a few of its points in a typical progressive campaign for the Governorship of New York.[4]

The book's most important reader was not done with it so quickly. The invitations to Oyster Bay became fewer and farther between; Theodore Roosevelt did not cotton long to a man who would sit in owlish silence while an ex-President of the United States discoursed on the state of the world. But *The Promise of American Life* kept jangling around in Roosevelt's head. If the book had been deliberately planned for the purpose, much of it could not have been better designed to capture Oyster Bay. It showed its good judgment by extolling Theodore Roosevelt as the soundest of the contemporary reform leaders. Before and during his White House days Roosevelt had written his own denunciations of that "incompetent," Thomas Jefferson, with "his nervous fear of doing anything that may seem to be unpopular with the rank and file of the people." In the course of being President, Roosevelt had come to his own emphatic conclusion that not all trusts were "bad" and not all unions were "good." Having been the state for seven and a half years and, by his own admission, done magnificent things for the people while he was the state, Roosevelt was no man to fear powerful leadership. Hadn't Croly said what the ex-President had always wanted to say when he praised the Roosevelt Administrations for abandoning "that part of the traditional democratic creed which tends to regard the assumption by the government of responsibility, and its endowment with power adequate to the responsibility as inherently dangerous and undemocratic," for

[4] Henry L. Stimson and McGeorge Bundy: *On Active Service in Peace and War* (Harper, 1948), p. 59.

realizing that "any efficiency of organization and delegation of power which is necessary to the promotion of the American national interest must be helpful to democracy"? And wasn't Croly right when he spanked Roosevelt for retaining streaks of Jeffersonianism? [5]

The Croly points not only settled easily into Roosevelt's mind. They took on added attractiveness from arguments that other, quite different men were making at Oyster Bay. While progressivism was rushing ahead in the early 1900's, the thought of the new generation of businessmen had not been standing still. A small but influential group was beginning to drop the argument that an economic system dominated by great corporations represented free competition. Openly proclaiming the end of free competition, they argued that big businesses, including the trusts, were the best hope of promoting the general welfare, because of the greater efficiency of large industrial units. Some of the new business thinkers argued that corporations should be held in line with the national interest by self-policing trade associations. Others—especially those who were impressed by the way Germany was using state controls to combat socialism—wanted some degree of federal supervision. All agreed on the cessation of antitrust activity.[6] Two years after Croly announced his New Nationalism, a Chicago lawyer, Arthur Eddy, won considerable favorable attention in the business world by a call for the "New Competition." "Competition is war," Eddy declared, "and 'war is hell.'" The road to heaven was repeal of the Sherman Antitrust Act and an amalgam of trade associations and federal supervision.[7]

Two of the ablest exponents of the new business thought, George W. Perkins and Frank Munsey, were friends of the ex-

[5] Croly: *The Promise of American Life*, pp. 167–71, 172–5; Joseph B. Bishop: *Theodore Roosevelt and His Time* (Scribner, 1920), II, 71; Pringle, p. 369.
[6] Gordon M. Jensen: "The Growth of a Sense of Social Awareness upon the Part of Capital in America," MS., in Mr. Jensen's possession, *passim*; interview with Mr. Herbert Hoover; Milton N. Nelson: *Open Price Associations*, in *University of Illinois Studies in the Social Sciences* (June 1922), X, 24–40.
[7] Eddy: *The New Competition* (Appleton, 1912), pp. 19, 333–43.

President. Perkins, a Morgan partner and a key figure in the International Harvester and United States Steel trusts, had long been interesting Roosevelt with his public-spirited activities and his reforms inside firms that he controlled (Perkins assumed most of the responsibility for setting up the Palisades recreational park, stopped the New York Life Insurance Company from buying highly speculative stocks, and worked out the first large-scale profit-sharing system that proved successful). Shortly after Roosevelt left the White House, Perkins resigned most of his directorships and his Morgan partnership to devote himself to public affairs, and Oyster Bay was soon deluged with copies of articles and speeches hailing a new era of progress based on the retention, expansion, and federal supervision of the great corporations. "Competition is over," Perkins was sure. "If regulation fails, then government ownership." [8]

Munsey, a publishing tycoon and a heavy investor in United States Steel, had been drawn into the Oyster Bay circle by his close friendship with Perkins. Now Munsey was advising the ex-President that the United States should stake its future on "good" trusts and sweeping federal supervision of the nation's whole economic life. "My observation and reasoning as I study these problems at home and abroad," Munsey told Roosevelt, "leads unerringly to the conclusion that the state has got to . . . take on a more parental guardianship of the people. The people need safeguarding in their investments, their savings, their application of conservation. They need encouragement, the sustaining and guiding hand of the state. They need the German system of helping them to save money for their old age. It is the work of the state to think for the people and plan for the people—to teach them how to do, what to do, and sustain them in the doing." [9]

The thought of Munsey and Perkins was fundamentally different from that of Croly. They saw the corporation as the center of American life and fitted everything else around that focus. To

[8] Quoted in Harold Kellock: "A Pioneer of Big Business," *Century* (April 1915), LXXXIX, 953.

[9] Quoted in William B. Hesseltine: *The Rise and Fall of Third Parties* (Public Affairs Press, Washington, 1948), p. 25.

Croly, political, economic, and social change was paramount and the corporation was to be manipulated to serve that end. But the different ideological roads crossed at one critical junction: the common opposition to the Jeffersonian reform program of "restoring" an America of small, freely competing economic units. "The great question of the day," Perkins said for all three men, "is whether we shall go on with a war between corporations and the people which is certain to do neither any good." [1]

That question, urged on him from such diverse sources, continually bobbing up from a thousand memories of his own experiences as President, was in the forefront of Roosevelt's mind during the months after his return from Africa. There was also the question of the unemployment of Theodore Roosevelt. He was still only fifty-one, he had not served two elective terms in the Presidency, and William Howard Taft was in his chair in the White House, impudently refusing to be merely a lieutenant, hrrumphing and bumbling, infuriating the progressives and not pleasing the conservatives. If Roosevelt could only strike out with a rousing new approach. . . .

All during the summer of 1910, as he edged closer to declaring his candidacy, Roosevelt fumbled for the new approach. There were Jeffersonian enthusings over direct primaries and a cordial conference with that rampant trust-buster, Robert M. La Follette. There were Croly-like utterances on business and on reformers.

Then, in August 1910, Roosevelt publicly took over the New Nationalism, phrase, key doctrine, and difficulties.

[1] Quoted in *New York Times*, April 10, 1910.

CHAPTER X

Honeymoon

OSAWATOMIE, KANSAS, forgot its grimy railroad shops, its dust, even the stifling heat that August 31. Main Street, where "Old Osawatomie" John Brown had made a bloody stand against slavery, was gay with Sears Roebuck gingham and fresh blue denim. The whole town, and thousands from near by, had declared a holiday to hear Teddy Roosevelt get off one of his thumping speeches, and they were not disappointed. There was a yip and kyoodle for John Brown and "the great deeds of the past." There were all the familiar themes of progressivism, rousingly summarized in the first use of the phrase: "I stand for the square deal." This was the Roosevelt the farmers, grocers, and workingmen had worshipped for so long, "the modern Tom Jefferson," as a local speaker remarked in welcoming the ex-President.[1]

But then, as the speech neared its climax, it veered off in a new direction. Herbert Croly's pale eyes must have sparkled as he read the next day: "I mean not merely that I stand for fair play under the present rules of the game, but that I stand for having those rules changed so as to work for a more substantial equality

---

[1] Hermann Hagedorn, ed.: *Works of Theodore Roosevelt* (Scribner, 1923–6), XIX, 11, 16; *Kansas City Star*, September 1, 1910.

of opportunity. . . . The American people are right in demanding that New Nationalism, without which we cannot hope to deal with new problems. The New Nationalism puts the national need before sectional or personal advantage. It is impatient of the utter confusion that results from local legislatures attempting to treat national issues as local issues. It is still more impatient of the impotence which springs from overdivision of governmental powers. . . . This New Nationalism regards the executive as the steward of the public welfare. . . . [It] rightly maintains that every man holds his property subject to the general right of the community to regulate its use to whatever degree the public welfare may require it." With respect to the trusts, government regulation was to have an especially important function. "Combinations in industry," Roosevelt declared, "are the result of an imperative economic law which cannot be repealed by political legislation. The effort at prohibiting all combination has substantially failed. The way out lies, not in attempting to prevent such combinations, but in completely controlling them in the interest of the public welfare." [2]

The "New Nationalism"—Croly's very phrase. Putting the "national need" before any other concern, the subjection of property to the "public welfare," the exaltation of the executive and the acceptance of trusts—the heart of the Croly demands on Jeffersonian liberalism. The Osawatomie speech did not take over all the specific points of *The Promise of American Life*, but in fundamentals and in tone it amounted to a popular restatement of the book.

Quickly the new doctrine became a matter of practical importance for all progressives. At the 1912 Republican convention the Taft forces quashed the Roosevelt candidacy, and the Roosevelt faction, which included most of the reformers in the party, walked out to cries of "robber" and "thief." Two months later they returned to the Chicago Coliseum to launch the "Bull Moose," or "Progressive," Party. The Bull Moosers were clearly a reform party—more sweepingly and more belligerently reform-

[2] Hagedorn, XIX, 16, 18, 24, 27.

209

ist than any important party since the Populists. But the top Bull
Moose leadership had no use for Jeffersonian trust-busting. The
candidate, almost the god of the party, was the Roosevelt of the
Osawatomie doctrine; George Perkins was named chairman of
the Executive Committee; the principal financial angels of the
movement were Perkins and Frank Munsey. The Progressive convention was keynoted by ex-Senator Albert J. Beveridge, chief
author of the Pure Food and Drug Act, who proceeded to flail
the Sherman Antitrust Act as legislation that struck at "big business itself," not at "the evils of big business." The Bull Moose aim,
Beveridge told the delegates, was "to make little business big and
all business honest, instead of striving to make big business little
and yet letting it remain dishonest." In his "Confession of Faith"
the next evening, Roosevelt was less direct; he had been in the
White House much too long not to know the emotion that the
Sherman Antitrust Act called up for millions of Americans. Roosevelt said he favored retaining the law and making it more effective "where it is applied." But, he added, the basic solution
for the problem had been phrased in an "important volume"
recently published by the president of the University of Wisconsin, Charles R. Van Hise. Once again Roosevelt was restating
Herbert Croly. President Van Hise, Roosevelt put it, was "unquestionably right" in his main thesis that "concentration, co-
operation, and control are the key words for a scientific solution of the mighty industrial problem which now confronts this
Nation." [3]

It was all an extraordinary performance. Presidential candidates
do not usually quote three lengthy paragraphs from a scholarly
book to a fervid convention crowd. No other ex-President has denounced both the party that elected him and the other major organization as two "husks, with no real soul within either, divided
on artificial lines, boss-ridden and privilege-controlled." Rarely

[3] "First National Convention of the Progressive Party," typed from
the shorthand notes of J. M. Striker, MS., Harvard University Library,
pp. 24, 27; Roosevelt: *Address . . . before the National Progressive Party
in Chicago* (n.d.), pp. 16, 18. Roosevelt was quoting from Van Hise: *Concentration and Control* (Macmillan, 1912).

has any politician aroused enthusiasm so close to religious frenzy that a Michigan delegation chanted:

> *Follow! Follow!*
> *We will follow Roosevelt*
> *Anywhere! Everywhere*
> *We will follow on!*

and the New York delegation, led by an elderly Jewish philanthropist, launched the convention into passionate renditions of "Onward, Christian Soldiers." [4]

The Bull Moose meeting was startling in still another respect, one that became plain as soon as the Resolutions Committee tried to write a platform. A clear-cut majority of the committee were Jeffersonian progressives. With little disagreement, it adopted a long list of traditional reform planks, ranging from the initiative and referendum to the eight-hour day, and then the head of Wisconsin's Legislative Reference Bureau, Charles McCarthy, phrased the majority opinion in a stern antitrust plank. The resolution not only called for strengthening the Sherman Antitrust Act; it was menacingly specific about what constituted an antitrust violation. Immediately George Perkins was up in arms. All that night he hurried back and forth from the hotel room in which the committee was wrangling to the near-by bedroom in which Roosevelt was getting no sleep. Finally Perkins was satisfied that the committee accepted his version, which declared "the concentration of modern business, in some degree . . . both inevitable and necessary for National and international business efficiency," and contained no mention of strengthening the Sherman Antitrust Act. The next day the chairman of the Resolutions Committee— whether deliberately or by mistake, no one is sure yet—read the discarded antitrust plank to the convention, which enthusiastically accepted it. This time Perkins did not bother with conferences. He shoved back his chair with a loud noise and stomped out of the hall, followed by several of his wealthy friends. Roosevelt quickly

[4] Roosevelt: *Address*, pp. 3, 17–18; Claude G. Bowers: *Beveridge and the Progressive Era* (Houghton Mifflin, 1932), p. 425.

saw to it that the press reported the Perkins version, and when that draft appeared in all the official party literature, Perkins was mollified.[5]

Conservatives and anti-Bull Moose progressives enjoyed a laugh together. When Perkins threatened to leave, they snickered, he took the pocketbook of the Progressive Party with him. Some of Roosevelt's warmest admirers complained that his attitude toward the trusts was being influenced too much by Perkins and his trust-magnate friends. Other admirers rejoined that, after all, the Perkins plank represented Roosevelt's deep conviction about economic organization. Whatever the involvements of the situation, a powerful American progressive party, led by the most popular reform leader in the country, was going into the campaign with a platform that a friendly newspaper described as "recognizing the permanence and beneficence of the trust organization." [6]

No more spankings, however gentle, came from Herbert Croly. "At last," he said, "America has a reform party which can lead to reform. Whether the United States is ready to face the real present is not at all clear. But the Progressives are now talking a doctrine that is certain to cast a shadow across all our to-morrows." [7]

II

THE DEMOCRATS orated and snarled, took unalterable stands and altered them, ground through ballot after ballot in a steaming Baltimore armory. There were all kinds of candidates, but as the voting went on, the two men who broke into the lead both represented a suspicion of corporate power. On the forty-sixth ballot, with William Jennings Bryan using to the hilt the last great strength he was to wield in a Democratic convention, the party named a man to whom trusts seemed downright immoral.

[5] The Perkins version, and ultimately the official version, appeared in the *Platform of the Progressive Party* (1912), p. 6.
[6] *Los Angeles Tribune*, September 9, 1912.
[7] Interview with the late Philip Littell.

One Maryland politician took his measure of the candidate and told the bartender: "He gives me the creeps. The time I met him, he said something to me, and I didn't know whether God or him was talking." [8] People had been having that trouble with Woodrow Wilson for a long time. All the while he climbed the academic ladder, first as a successful professor of jurisprudence and political economy, then as a spectacular president of Princeton University, this granite-faced son of a minister had given the impression of the reverend in an academic robe. Wilson's undoubted power over men did not come from any striking originality of thought or any great ability in reaching rapport with other human beings. It came from God-lashed energies, a contagious self-righteousness, a talent for finely chiseled oratory which carried a constant implication that only the Devil would disagree.

Well into his Princeton presidency, as late as 1907, Wilson was defining the Devil much like any other conservative Southern Democrat. He was against high tariffs without calling tariffs breeders of trusts, and he was for clean government without being for economic and social reform. He lauded combinations and trusts, attacked the initiative, referendum, and recall, proclaimed himself a "fierce partizan of the Open Shop," and uttered a fervent wish that some "dignified and effective" way could be found "to knock Mr. Bryan once for all into a cocked hat." Then, in the space of a few years, the Devil became a conservative. In the period after 1907 Wilson took over one item after another in the progressive program, stumped Princeton alumni clubs calling for a "democratic regeneration" of the colleges, swept into the Governorship of New Jersey on a tide of reform feeling, and jammed through a program drawn straight from the Wisconsin Idea.[9]

[8] The ward leader was William Kelly, quoted by Mr. B. H. Hartogensis, a Baltimore lawyer, in an interview with me.

[9] William Diamond: *The Economic Thought of Woodrow Wilson*, in *Johns Hopkins University Studies in Historical and Political Science* (1943), LXI, 70–1, 74, 85, 88 n.; Arthur Link: *Wilson, the Road to the White House* (Princeton University Press, 1947), p. 84.

Cynics commented what wondrous changes the Presidential bee could bring. Friends pointed out that, after all, Wilson had a mind, and torrential shifts in thinking were going on around him. Some historians have emphasized the jolt that must have come to Wilson from having his Princeton policies opposed and ultimately defeated by men who spoke the credo of entrenched status. Whatever the explanation, Woodrow Wilson emerged in 1912 a Presidential candidate who preached a fervent Jeffersonian progressivism.

Wilson took naturally to the ideas of the inveterate trust-buster Louis Brandeis, and during the campaign the Jeffersonian candidate and the Jeffersonian lawyer developed a close intellectual and personal relationship. In the course of their correspondence Brandeis sent Wilson a set of "Suggestions" for campaign materials, which, despite the partisanship and extremity of some of the language, provide the clearest expression of the line that can be drawn between Rooseveltian and Wilsonian progressivism. The Democratic position, Brandeis wrote, "insists that competition can be and should be maintained in every branch of private industry; that competition can be and should be restored in those branches of industry in which it has been suppressed by the trusts; and that, if at any future time monopoly should appear to be desirable in any branch of industry, the monopoly should be a public one—a monopoly owned by the people and not by the capitalists." On the other hand, the Roosevelt party "insists that private monopoly may be desirable in some branches of industry, or at all events, is inevitable; and that existing trusts should not be dismembered or forcibly dislodged from those branches of industry in which they have already acquired a monopoly but should be made 'good' by regulation. . . . The New Party does not fear commercial power, however great, if only methods for regulation are provided. We believe that no methods of regulation ever have been or can be devised to remove the menace inherent in private monopoly and overweening commercial power." The difference between the policy of the two parties, Brandeis concluded, was "fundamental and irreconcilable. It is the difference between industrial liberty and industrial absolutism, tempered by governmental (that is, party) supervision." [1]

Taking over the essence of the Brandeis formula, Wilson invented the slogan the "New Freedom," to distinguish between the New Nationalism and his call for the restoration of "free enterprise." Trust legislation, tariff reduction, and banking reform were the three principal issues emphasized by Wilson, and all three were tied into an attack on monopoly. High tariffs, Wilson stressed again and again, were a form of special privilege which encouraged the growth of monopoly; banking reform was necessary to free credit for small businessmen and farmers from the "money trust." With increasing directness Wilson lashed out at the New Nationalism's attitude toward trusts. "When you have thought the whole thing out," he told an audience of workingmen in Buffalo, ". . . you will find that the programme of the new party legalizes monopolies and systematically subordinates workingmen to them and to plans made by the Government, both with regard to employment and with regard to wages. By what means, except open revolt, could we ever break the crust of our life again and become free men, breathing an air of our own, choosing and living lives that we wrought out for ourselves? Perhaps this new and all-conquering combination between money and government would be benevolent to us, perhaps it would carry out the noble programme of social betterment, which so many credulously expect of it, but who can assure us of that? Who will give bond that it will be generous and gracious and pitiful and righteous? What man or set of men can make us secure under it by their empty promise and assurance that it will take care of us and be good?" [2]

Roosevelt hit back hard, and in the authentic manner of the New Nationalism. Wilson was simply preaching "rural toryism," which carried over the old agrarian fear of corporations and of governmental power. "We are for liberty," Roosevelt insisted.

---

[1] Quoted in Link, p. 492.
[2] Link, p. 491. "General," an obvious misprint, has been changed to "generous."

"But we are for the liberty of the oppressed. . . . It is idle to ask us not to exercise the powers of government when only by that power . . . can we exalt the lowly and give heart to the humble and downtrodden." [3]

In all the hubbub the issue often became confused. Wilson, a shrewd as well as an idealistic politician, was anxious to remove any impression that he was entirely out of sympathy with the trend toward large-scale economic organizations. His New Freedom speeches, read consecutively, leave the impression that he thought bigness inevitable, that bigness led to wicked monopoly, and that bigness, in and of itself, was not the issue. On his part, Roosevelt was acutely conscious that his new party was seriously hurt by the charge that it was a façade for the trusts. On occasion he slurred over the Bull Moose acceptance of the trust so thoroughly that the distinction between his and Wilson's program was lost in the fog of oratory. The similarity of most specific planks in the Bull Moose and Democratic platforms increased the confusion.

Yet from the perspective of another generation, the significance of the campaign is clear. Of the three candidates, one was quickly eliminated as a possible winner. "I have no part to play but that of a conservative," William Howard Taft sighed early in the campaign, and then awaited defeat with resigned dignity.[4] The contest was between the New Nationalist Roosevelt and the New Freedomite Wilson. For the first time the two major candidates for the Presidency were progressives, and for the first time a major split in reform doctrine was being argued before a national audience.

III

THE DEBATE lasted just about as long as the campaign. It is exceedingly doubtful whether any large number of Bull Moosers

[3] George E. Mowry: *Theodore Roosevelt and the Progressive Movement* (University of Wisconsin Press, 1946), p. 278.

[4] Henry F. Pringle: *Life and Times of William Howard Taft* (Farrar & Rinehart, 1939), II, 823.

accepted Roosevelt's doctrine on the trusts. Most of Roosevelt's following supported him because they were Republicans and progressives, because of the exciting reform air of the Progressive Party, and, above all, because the Progressive Party was Teddy Roosevelt, whom they no doubt would have supported if he had decided that theosophy was essential to the nation's welfare. A Jeffersonian suspicion of big business was so deeply ingrained in American dissent that even socialists like Algie Simons, whose theory demanded that they accept the trend toward business concentration, were uncomfortable at the thought of tolerating trusts. "I accept the doctrine that concentration is inevitable," Simons confessed during the campaign of 1912, "but I simply don't like monopolies and cartels." [5]

Once Wilson had won the election, progressives were soon thrilled into further unity. If under Roosevelt social reform had taken on all the excitement of a circus, under Wilson it acquired the dedication of a sunrise service. Wilson's inaugural address was the most moving statement of progressivism the United States had ever heard. "No one," the new President told a profoundly hushed crowd, "can mistake the purpose for which the Nation now seeks to use the Democratic Party. It seeks to use it to interpret a change in its own plans and point of view. . . . The Nation has been deeply stirred, stirred by a solemn passion, stirred by the knowledge of wrong, of ideals lost, of government too often debauched and made an instrument of evil. The feelings with which we face this new age of right and opportunity sweep across our heartstrings like some air out of God's own presence, where justice and mercy are reconciled and the judge and the brother are one. . . .

"This is not a day of triumph," Wilson concluded. "It is a day of dedication. Here muster, not the forces of party, but the forces of humanity. Men's hearts wait upon us; men's lives hang in the balance; men's hopes call upon us to say what we will do. Who shall live up to the great trust? Who dares fail to try? I summon

[5] Interview with Simons by Mr. John J. Harmon, reported to me by Mr. Harmon.

all honest men, all patriotic, all forward-looking men, to my side. God helping me, I will not fail them, if they will but counsel and sustain me!" [6]

Reformers were scarcely done thrilling to the President's words when they were given a rapid-fire of reasons to applaud his actions. Long before he was a progressive in most other ways, Wilson had ardently espoused the doctrine of executive leadership. Now he put the doctrine to work. To dramatize executive leadership, Wilson revived a custom defunct since 1801 and personally appeared to address Congress. In nine spectacular months he whiplashed through Congress the Federal Reserve Act, which satisfied much of the long-running demand for breaking up the "money trust," and a tariff reduction so injurious to a number of corporate interests that lobbyists fought with unprecedented activity in an attempt to block it. With Wilson's ardent encouragement, many another reform bill tumbled through Congress—most notably the La Follette Act, improving the ordinary sailor's well-being, the appropriation of millions for farm demonstration work and more millions for vocational and agricultural education, a workmen's compensation act for federal employees, the Adamson Act, decreeing an eight-hour day on all interstate railroads, and the exclusion from interstate commerce of the products of child labor.

Wilsonianism was not without its streaks of the New Nationalism. The President was expressing a basic attitude as well as talking the language of political expediency when he declared that he wanted no part of an "antagonism between business and Government." The Administration's key legislation concerning corporations, the laws clustering about the Clayton Antitrust Act, departed in important respects from traditional Jeffersonian trust-busting; under this legislation, as one recent study has remarked, "the trust was no longer an ogre . . . to be bludgeoned into submission with . . . a dissolution suit, but rather the result of a number of malignant growths each of which must be cauter-

---

[6] *The Messages and Papers of Woodrow Wilson* (Review of Reviews Corp., New York, 1924), I, 1, 5.

ized." Wilson also could draw a Croly-like distinction between legislation in the "national interest" and laws that benefited "special interests." If he saw no such clash in a number of pro-labor proposals, he flatly opposed legislation for direct federal loans to farmers because of his "very deep conviction that it is unwise and unjustifiable to extend the credit of the Government to a single class of the community." But in most fundamentals and in tone, to Wilson and to the nation, Wilson's program was the New Freedom, "the restoration of free competition," as he said repeatedly, "the application of Jefferson's principles to our present-day America." [7]

Just before the end of his first Administration, Wilson capped the symbolism of the New Freedom by nominating Louis Brandeis to the Supreme Court. Reformers and conservatives had long agreed that the Supreme Court was crucial battleground; naming an unyielding progressive like Brandeis was certain to provoke a savage fight and took genuine political courage. When Wilson doggedly stood by his man, with many a sharp reminder to the opposition that the world was changing, most progressives were sure they had found their leader. Exhilarated as they had not been since the most exciting days of Roosevelt, they forgot about the issue that had divided their old and new idols, frequently forgot about the old idol himself. Roosevelt could only thrash about in impotent fury, suing an obscure editor for calling him a drunk, chasing after his adolescence in the Brazilian jungle, shrilling to friends who had a hard time keeping an interested look that Wilson was the greatest menace the United States had ever known. The New Freedom was obliterating the New Nationalism, the questions it raised as well as its doctrine.

[7] Ibid., I, 49; H. C. F. Bell: *Woodrow Wilson and the People* (Doubleday, Doran, 1945), p. 161; Baker: *Woodrow Wilson* (Doubleday, Doran, 1927–39), IV, 365; *New York Times*, January 13, 1914.

IV

THE BATTLE over the Brandeis appointment had another significance, the way it pointed up the ever increasing progressive
acquiescence in minority nationalisms. Brandeis was not only the
first progressive to be appointed to the Supreme Court; he was
also the first Jew. The anti-Semitic innuendoes that some conservatives used in an attempt to block his confirmation disgusted
reform circles and accelerated the progressive tendency to identify defending Jews with defending Zionism. "If the reactionaries
had simply denounced Brandeis' politics, they would have turned
thousands of Jews into Zionists," one Zionist leader has recalled.
"But when they attacked his politics *and* his religion, they won
friends for Zionism among all Americans who were concerned
with fairness." [8]

Without a dramatic Brandeis case, other minority groups were
hurtling toward their own chauvinisms and sweeping progressive
opinion along with them. Naturally, the process was most marked
in New York City's crazy-quilt of races, religions, and nationalities. In 1915 the able young progressive, Horace M. Kallen, a
Jewish immigrant to New York, published a blunt repudiation of
the whole idea of an assimilated American community. "Democracy versus the Melting Pot" was Kallen's title, and he summoned
all those who really understood democracy and reform to the acceptance of an America that would be "a federation or commonwealth of nationalities." [9] The next year a similar thesis was stated
with arresting brilliance by another, non-Jewish product of the
New York area, Randolph Bourne.

Bourne was brought up a five-cent commuter's ride from the
city, in a New Jersey town that was its own unhappy jumble of
immigrant workers, aggressive parvenus, and resentful old families
with little money. In Bloomfield no family was more impeccably
ancient and Protestant than the Bournes, but the income was

[8] The late Stephen Wise, in an interview with me.
[9] *Nation* (February 25, 1915), C, 219.

meagre and at seventeen Randolph Bourne began discovering how America could look from a vantage other than the top. In near-by Morristown a musician had a machine for perforating the music rolls used on player-pianos. From eight to five each day Bourne perforated the rolls, getting five cents a foot, while the musician collected fifteen cents a roll from the manufacturer and diddled away the days composing bad symphonies. All went well until Bourne became too skilled at his job; then the musician announced that the piece rate was cut to four and a half cents. If he was worth five cents as a learner, Bourne demanded, why was he worth less as an experienced hand? The musician folded his arms and, with the majesty of John D. Rockefeller, announced that Bourne could stay or go—he was "perfectly free." Bourne returned "cravenly to my bench." [1]

But he was learning. Soon he was off to New York, to exhilarating conversations about Henry George and immigrants, to study at Columbia under Boas, Dewey, and Beard. A few years after graduating, Bourne walked into the office of the *Seven Arts*, an *avant-garde* journal that James Oppenheim had talked an intellectualish lady into financing by selling her Whistler paintings. "I shall never forget," Oppenheim has written, "how I had first to overcome my repugnance when I saw that child's body, the humped back, the longish, almost medieval face, with a sewed-up mouth, and an ear gone awry. But he wore a cape, carried himself with an air, and then you listened to marvelous speech, often brilliant, holding you spellbound, and looked into blue eyes as young as a Spring dawn. His coming was the greatest thing that happened to the *Seven Arts*." [2]

Bourne was soon busy writing a series of scintillating literary and philosophical essays for the *Seven Arts*, but he did not forget the Italian and Slavic workers of Bloomfield or the potpourri of nationalities among his fellow students at Columbia. About the same time that he began publishing in the *Seven Arts*, Bourne

[1] Louis Filler: *Randolph Bourne* (American Council on Public Affairs, Washington, 1943), p. 18.

[2] Quoted in James Oppenheim: "The Story of the *Seven Arts*," *American Mercury* (June 1930), XX, 163.

poured out his thoughts on the immigrant in an *Atlantic Monthly* essay. The melting-pot, Bourne declared, had not worked. What's more, it was a good thing that it had not worked. Those who discouraged immigrants or native minorities from holding to their old ways were not creating Americans; they were creating "detached fragments of peoples . . . the flotsam and jetsam of American life, the downward undertow of our civilization with its leering cheapness and falseness of taste and spiritual outlook." The sound approach, Bourne contended, was to work toward making the United States, not a nation, but "a trans-nationality," "a cosmopolitan federation of national colonies." And this should be done as no hangdog acceptance of a *fait accompli*. It was a goal to be consciously sought, for it would bring "the more creative America." [3]

Bourne's philosophical and literary essays produced a trickle of congratulatory letters from friends. His appeal for "trans-nationalism" brought a flood of approving correspondence, from friends and strangers, whites and Negroes, scions of ancient families and men and women who still wrote with a touch of the old country in their syntax. "I have," Bourne concluded quite accurately, "tapped a vein of interest that is going to more and more characterize the reform thinker." [4]

Pragmatism, too, was charging ahead to extremes. The progressive leader in the White House may have talked the moral absolutes of a Roosevelt or a Croly, but in younger reform circles relativism ran rampant. In the year of Wilson's inauguration Walter Lippmann's *Preface to Politics* presented the first conscious, all-embracing relativism in the discussion of public affairs. Fresh out of Harvard, where he had taken deep draughts of William James, Lippmann had received postgraduate training in pragmatism by working as an assistant to Lincoln Steffens. The cocky, science-minded Lippmann was deeply impressed by Steffens's growing tendency to avoid being moral about anything

---

[3] Bourne: "Trans-National America," *Atlantic Monthly* (July 1916), CXVIII, 91, 93, 96.
[4] Interview with the late Mary Simkhovitch.

they saw. "We were looking not for the evils of Big Business," Lippmann wrote proudly, "but for its anatomy." [5]

A Preface to Politics scorned all moral absolutists, reformers or conservatives. Any social philosophy was, consciously or unconsciously, the servant of "men's purposes. . . . We find reasons for what we want to do. . . . Men desire first, then they reason." A reformer who did not act on this assumption was a "routineer . . . simply working for another conservatism, and not for any continuing liberation. . . . The type of statesman we must oppose to the routineer is one who regards all social organization as an instrument. Systems, institutions and mechanical contrivances have for him no virtue of their own; they are valuable only when they serve the purposes of men." Lippmann was sure that if only "we think in terms of men, find out what really bothers them, seek to supply what they really want, hold only their experience sacred, we shall find our sanction obvious and unchallenged." Talk of moral or ethical bases for action was simply irrelevant. "No moral judgment can decide the values of life. No ethical theory can announce any intrinsic good." [6]

The book was received with enormous enthusiasm in progressive circles. In part this was a tribute to Lippmann's boyishly exuberant style and his ability to expound any doctrine so lucidly that doubters had the feeling their thinking must be muddled. In greater measure, it was a sign of the extent to which Lippmann's relativism expressed the trend of reform thinking. "How do we know what instruments to use if morals don't tell us what we want? How do we know what to justify if we can justify anything?" Croly asked a group of friends who were extolling the *Preface to Politics*. The friends indicated a polite interest and went on with their praise of Lippmann.[7] 1914 was no time to talk moral yardsticks to reformers.

1914 was a time to be free of all arbitrary yardsticks, progressive or conservative, to be free of everything that smacked of the

[5] Lippmann: *A Preface to Politics* (Mitchell Kennerley, New York, 1913), p. 19.
[6] Ibid., pp. 8–9, 200, 202, 213, 215.
[7] Littell interview.

old America. The prim Presbyterian in the White House, far more than he intended, caught the reform mood when he called for a New Freedom. The New Freedom spawned a hundred other shimmering escapes from the past—the New Poetry, the New History, the New Democracy, the New Art, the New Woman, the new anything so long as it was new and gave an intoxicating sense of freedom. In every field the pattern of the *avant-garde* became a revelry of nose-thumbing. Duchamp's cubist nude zigzagged down the stairs of the New York Armory show, while in Chicago Harriet Monroe's journal, *Poetry*, began its hectic career with Ezra Pound proclaiming: "To Hell with *Harper's* and the Magazine Touch." In a whirl of freely flowing robes Isadora Duncan revolutionized the dance, and announced, after the birth of her second illegitimate child, that marriage was an oppressive superfluity.[8] Little theaters popped up everywhere to talk of sex and labor and politics with a tolerance for anything except the conventional. Alfred Stieglitz freed the camera from the daguerreotype, Emma Goldman preached anarchism to church audiences, Harvard founded a Men's League for Women's Suffrage, and Vassar girls broke dates with Harvard students to picket in New York's garment district.

The quest for newness and freedom found a national symbol in the cramped, twisted streets of Greenwich Village. At the turn of the century the area was just another decaying region of New York City, so many old brownstones settling into tenements. Then a group of enterprising real-estate men, noting the picturesqueness of the neighborhood, saw the possibilities of luring artists and writers by low rents. The artists and writers attracted artists and writers, and by the days of the New Freedom the Village was becoming an American Left Bank. "Everybody was freeing themselves and the world," the Village writer Floyd Dell has recalled, "and everybody was freeing the world faster than everybody else."[9] It was not quite that cultish. In the batik-hung

[8] Quoted in John A. Kouwenhaven: "Personal & Otherwise," *Harper's* (October 1950), CCI, 8; Duncan: *My Life* (Boni & Liveright, 1927), p. 247.
[9] Simkhovitch interview.

studios surrounding MacDougal Street, the ultra-respectable Lippmann wrote his *Preface to Politics*, Eugene O'Neill kept the hours of a bank clerk writing his early plays, and Frances Perkins continued her family's tradition of gracious living. But the Village had an air, and the air was emancipation. Some eccentricity was *de rigueur*, if only a shirt that shouted dissent from convention. There was a variety of freedom for everyone. Henrietta Rodman, a lanky schoolteacher from upper Manhattan, escaped the textbooks by donning a mealsack gown and appointing herself hostess of the "Liberal Club," which functioned over the Neighborhood Playhouse on MacDougal Street. The entirely legitimate son of a Chicago newspaperman, who insisted that he was a bastard, worked off years of frustration by calling everyone he met a "bourgeois pig." Even the moralizing Herbert Croly had his few years in the Village and his hours in the Old Grapevine Bar on Eleventh Street and Sixth Avenue, which that ancient rebel, William Dean Howells, boasted he had discovered.

Almost single-handed the Village discovered Sigmund Freud. The Viennese had visited the United States in 1909 and gone home convinced that any nation which paid so little attention to him was a "miscarriage" of civilization.[1] But wasn't Freud, too, calling for the new and the daring? Within five years every third Villager was being psychoanalyzed and every second one was viewing his luncheon companion with that knowing concern.

V

"THE THING that constantly amazed me," William Allen White has reminisced in his jovial way, "was how many people were with us."[2] Despite the Greenwich Villages, despite the powerful undertow of conservatism, progressivism was whirling ahead. The Roosevelt era, quite clearly, had been a period of beginnings, of

[1] Quoted in Max Eastman: *Heroes I Have Known* (Simon & Schuster, 1942), p. 271.
[2] William Allen White in a letter to me, July 12, 1940.

a scattering of pioneer legislation and a mounting favorable opinion. The Wilson era, building on this foundation, was a period of sweeping achievement.

Every success in Washington was accompanied by a score of successes on the local level, and almost any field illustrated the speed-up of the progressive march. For years reformers had urged Constitutional amendments to force the popular election of United States senators and to permit a federal income tax; within the four months surrounding Wilson's inauguration both amendments were ratified by the required number of states. The tendency to depend on direct-democracy techniques and to exalt the executive was reaching the point where political scientists wondered if "it will ultimately prove worthwhile to retain an expensive legislature to exercise its small residue of petty powers." [3] Between 1900 and 1911, four states had enacted employer liability acts containing workmen's compensation features; between 1912 and 1915, twenty-four states adopted workmen's compensation legislation.

"It must be bewildering," Walter Lippmann wrote, "to men brought up, let us say, in the Hanna school of politics. For here is this nation which sixteen years ago vibrated ecstatically to that magic word 'Prosperity'; to-day statistical rhetoric about size induces little but excessive boredom. If you wish to drive an audience out of the hall tell it how rich America is; if you wish to stamp yourself as an echo of the past talk to us young men about the Republican Party's understanding with God in respect to bumper crops." [4] Few shrewd politicians let themselves be stamped as echoes of the past, as Frances Perkins learned when she joined in a campaign to write factory-building legislation into the New York statutes. Expecting a curt refusal of support, she climbed the stairs of the old Tammany Hall on Fourteenth Street to ask the aid of Charles Murphy, a political boss straight out of the school of Mark Hanna.

[3] James Q. Dealey: "General Tendencies in State Constitutions," *American Political Science Review* (February 1907), I, 211.
[4] Lippmann, p. 89.

Miss Perkins had recently led a fight for a maximum-hour law for women, and Murphy greeted her: "You are the young lady, aren't you, who managed to get the fifty-four-hour bill passed?" Miss Perkins admitted she was.

"Well, young lady, I was opposed to that bill."

"Yes, I so gathered, Mr. Murphy."

"It is my observation," Murphy said, "that that bill made us many votes. I will tell the boys to give all the help they can to this new bill. Good-by." [5]

The most barricaded areas of American life felt the power of the progressive drive. Women were storming the colleges and the professions, raising their skirts a daring few inches above the shoe, winning the vote in state after state, turning every political occasion into a demonstration for national suffrage. In 1914, when Father Ryan applied to the church authorities for permission to found a "social questions" journal that would "stress social doctrine," he was refused. Three years later he was permitted to establish the *Catholic Charities Review*, which ranged far beyond charity in its interests, and the American Catholic Church was soon announcing a "Bishops' Program of Social Reconstruction," which Ryan had written almost to the last comma. In the full Wilsonian manner the program called for the restoration of "genuine competition in business," minimum wages, unemployment, sickness and old-age insurance, slum-clearance, the legal enforcement of labor's right to organize, and "heavy taxation" of incomes, inheritances, and "excess profits." [6]

During the same years, even the friends of the scorned Negro could claim a victory in the battle for public opinion. In 1915 D. W. Griffith released his movie *The Birth of a Nation*. The picture was based on a novel by Thomas Dixon, a North Carolina preacher who boasted of the fact that his uncle had been the Grand Titan of the Ku Klux Klan, and the film made Reconstruction in the South a story of heroic Ku-Kluxers defending

[5] Frances Perkins: *The Roosevelt I Knew* (Viking, 1946), pp. 24-5.
[6] Richard J. Purcell: "John A. Ryan," *Studies* (June 1946), XXXV, 162; Ryan: *Social Reconstruction* (Macmillan, 1920), p. 236.

white womanhood from lecherous black men. The situation was touchy. *The Birth of a Nation* undoubtedly represented a tremendous advance in the new art of movie-making; Du Bois himself was worried about asking progressives to call for censorship of a form of expression. Pushing aside these worries by the arguments that human beings were more important than techniques and that the Negro lacked equally effective means of counterexpression, the National Association for the Advancement of Colored People undertook a campaign to bar *The Birth of a Nation* from the screen.

At the first sign of trouble Dixon hurried to Washington to see the Southern-born President Wilson, whose attitude toward the Negro was, to say the least, equivocal.[7] Wilson, according to Dixon's autobiography, quickly consented to see the movie, had it shown in the East Room of the White House with the whole Cabinet present, and when it was over, offered his enthusiastic congratulations. Then Dixon hastened to see the Chief Justice of the United States Supreme Court, Edward White. The Chief Justice had a reputation of being the most bearish man in Washington, and as quickly as possible Dixon got in his statement that he wanted the Supreme Court to see a movie about the Ku Klux Klan which the President had seen and praised. At the mention of the Ku Klux Klan, Dixon recalled, White's manner changed magically.

" 'You tell the true story of the Klan?'

" 'Yes—for the first time—'

"He removed his glasses, pushed his book aside and leaned back in his big swivel chair. His strong lips contracted and then relaxed into a curious smile. He leaned toward me and said in low tense tones:

" 'I was a member of the Klan, sir. . . . Through many a dark night, I walked my sentinel's beat through the ugliest streets of New Orleans with a rifle on my shoulder. . . . You've told the true story of that uprising of outraged manhood?'

[7] Link, p. 502; W. E. B. Du Bois: *Dusk of Dawn* (Harcourt, Brace, 1940), p. 235; Oswald Garrison Villard: *Fighting Years* (Harcourt, Brace, 1939), pp. 236–41.

" 'In a way I'm sure you'll approve.'

" 'I'll be there!' he firmly announced." [8]

Now the NAACP really had a problem. Whenever it applied to a licensing bureau or a court to stop the showing of the movie, Dixon was on hand, brandishing the statement that the President and the Chief Justice had not only seen the picture but lauded it, and no denials came from the White House or the Supreme Court. "The silly legal opposition of the NAACP," Dixon sneered, ". . . will make me a millionaire if they keep it up." [9] But the organization, supported by many progressives, kept right on hounding *The Birth of a Nation* with every device of law and propaganda it could command, and within a year the pro-Negro reformers had their day. Griffith produced another technically brilliant movie and its name was *Intolerance*.[1]

The exuberant progressive sense of achievement was heightened by the feeling that all civilization was moving in the same direction. "The most hopeful sign of the times," William Allen White rejoiced, "lies in the fact that the current is almost world-wide. The same stirring to lift men to higher things, to fuller enjoyment of the fruits of our civilization, to a wider participation in the blessings of modern society." [2] Other countries were showing as much interest in American reform leaders as they were in American technological geniuses or captains of industry. By 1914, John Dewey was well on his way to being an international schoolmaster. Delegations from many countries of Europe were visiting Judge Ben Lindsey's court to observe his methods of handling juvenile delinquents, and when the Japanese came, they even added a photographer so that the courtroom furniture might be exactly reproduced in Tokyo. Germany, on its part, was sending

[8] Thomas Dixon: "Southern Horizons," MS., in the possession of Mrs. Madelyn Dixon, pp. 432–5. White was a Catholic from Louisiana. He had served in the Confederate Army and during Reconstruction was active in state Democratic politics.

[9] Quoted in Filler, p. 283.

[1] In a subsequent film, *The Greatest Thing in Life*, Griffith had a white soldier kissing his wounded Negro comrade. *The Birth of a Nation* has continued to be shown and the NAACP has continued to fight it.

[2] White: *The Old Order Changeth* (Macmillan, 1909), p. 30.

"Historical"-minded Ph.D.'s back to America by the hundreds, while the sons of men who had been excited by Ruskin and Morris now had available the still more heady wine produced by Graham Wallas, George Bernard Shaw, and, above all, H. G. Wells. "We who are over sixty," Sinclair Lewis wrote when Wells died, in 1946, "have remembered all that he meant to us from 1910 to 1930, in Greenwich Village or Pekin or Sauk Centre or Twitterton-on-Twit. For here was a man who, more than any other of this century, more even than Shaw or a whole tribe of Huxleys, suggested to our young minds the gaudy fancy (which conceivably might also be fact) that mankind can, by taking thought, by real education, acquire such strange, crimson-shot, altogether enchanting qualities as cheerfulness, kindness, honesty, plain decency, [and a] refusal to make ourselves miserable and guilty just to please some institution that for a century has been a walking and talking corpse." [3]

In their giant-killing mood the progressives founded a magazine, and before it was on the news-stands, the journal showed how many different kinds of reformers could be sure that something called reform was triumphant. About the time Theodore Roosevelt made his Osawatomie speech, a copy of Herbert Croly's *Promise of American Life* found its way into the hands of Mr. and Mrs. Willard Straight, a couple with that combination of wealth and zeal to make the world over which has constantly refueled American reformism. The wealth was that of the wife, Dorothy Whitney, a daughter of the William Collins Whitney who had married Standard Oil millions and established a reputation as the gay blade of the Cleveland Cabinet. On her deathbed Mrs. Whitney exacted from a friend a promise to see that Dorothy Whitney was brought up to the "good and useful life," and the friend, Miss Beatrice Bend, proceeded to carry out the promise with uncompromising tenacity. She hovered over the girl's every activity, disregarding friends who shook their heads at the thought of what would happen to the reputation of a woman who was in

[3] Lewis: "A Generation Nourished on H. G. Wells," *New York Herald Tribune Weekly Book Review*, October 20, 1946, p. 1.

the home of William Collins Whitney so much. Miss Bend guided Dorothy Whitney through settlement-house work, the Consumers League, and the New York Junior League, which, under the leadership of young women like Frances Perkins, was concerned less with debuts than sweatshops. Then she took her charge on an educational trip to the Far East, where Dorothy Whitney promptly fell in love with Willard Straight, a handsome, able young man who was half missionary and half promoter in his attitude toward China.

After the marriage Willard Straight soon emerged an important Wall Street figure, but the couple also intensified each other's interest in religion as social service. "Use your wealth to put ideas in circulation," Straight urged his wife. "Others will give to churches and hospitals." [4] As soon as the Straights read Croly's *Promise,* they were convinced they had found the way to put ideas in circulation. They provided the money for a weekly "journal of opinion," to be edited by the obviously provocative Herbert Croly. In 1914 the offices of the *New Republic* opened in New York City, located, by some coincidence of symbolism, on the edge of the Village, next door to a home for wayward girls and across the street from the General Theological Seminary.

It was notable enough to have a Wall Street banker and the daughter of William Collins Whitney financing a journal which announced that its purpose was "less to inform or entertain its readers than to start little insurrections in the realm of their convictions." [5] On top of this, the staff of the *New Republic* seemed to be an attempt to make beef stew out of pork and lamb. The two chief assistants of the anti-Jeffersonian, absolutist Croly were the strident pragmatist Walter Lippmann, and Walter Weyl, a thoroughgoing Jeffersonian progressive. The *New Republic* had not been functioning six months when Weyl added a fervent Zionism to his differences from Croly. Francis Hackett, the journal's first literary editor, was indifferent to Zionism, skeptical about pragmatism, and an ardent Jeffersonian.

---

[4] Quoted by Miss Frances Perkins, in an interview with me.
[5] Herbert Croly: "The New Republic Idea," *New Republic* (December 6, 1922), XXXIII, Pt. II, p. 3.

To a category-minded socialist like John Reed, the *New Republic* line-up at first made no sense. Then, after attending some of the luncheons at which the *New Republic* was planned, Reed went away impressed more by agreement of the editors than by their differences. The editors, Reed admitted, were one in their "poised and aggressive" attack on "this damned shambles of a country which is finally admitting it has bugs." Editor Croly, always decorous, made the point more sedately. "No free country," he told a friend, "will ever produce vigorous thinkers who entirely agree on what should be done with it. But the editors of the *New Republic* agree that things should be done, they agree on many important specific measures, and what's more, they agree that the country is ready to have them done."

"That," Croly added with the confidence of all 1914 progressivism, "is no small thing to be able to say." [6]

[6] Littell interview.

CHAPTER XI

Internationalists in War

A SHORT WHILE before the *New Republic* offices opened, a fanatic Serb nationalist shot the heir to the Austro-Hungarian throne, and World War I was under way. The progressives working on plans for the new magazine had discussed domestic issues in infinite detail. They had scarcely mentioned foreign policy. Now, overnight, they had to find a foreign policy.

For the *New Republic* editors, as for most of the nation, the immediate answer was simple enough. The proper foreign policy was to stay out of foreign complications. From the Civil War to 1914 the country had fixed its attention on building factories and staking out homesteads, on careering and debating the ways to keep the avenues for careering open. In an age of comparatively slow transportation and communication, the countries of Europe seemed far off and, at that, hopelessly given to kings and armies and squabbles. Even these decadent nations were assumed to have passed beyond the stage where they would commit the folly of a war big enough to involve the United States. In 1910 Andrew Carnegie, in the process of cutting up his fortune for good works, earmarked the comparatively modest sum of ten million dollars "for the abolition of international war." When ten million dollars failed and the European countries obstinately set about hacking one another to pieces, most Americans were ready to sigh with the *Wabash Plain Dealer*: "We never appreciated so keenly as now the foresight exercised by our forefathers in emigrating from Europe." [1]

The usual progressive not only shared this attitude; he was under isolationist influences from which the conservative was comparatively free. From the Samuel Tildens, down through the Henry Georges and the reformers of the early 1900's, American discontent had been deeply concerned with preventing the United States from going the way of Europe, and consequently any involvement with Europe raised fears in reform circles. The involvement that was the practical issue after 1914—fighting alongside England and against Germany—had a special repugnance for many Midwestern progressives. In their eyes, Britain was the center of international financial machinations, and they wanted no part of the "Wall Street" activities they had been assailing for so long. West or east, the whole progressive movement had a soft spot for Germany. Hadn't that country led the world in using national powers to promote reform and in writing specific social legislation into its statutes? At the time that World War I began, American reformers frequently called their model state, Wisconsin, "the Germanic state," and they did not simply mean that Wisconsin contained many inhabitants of German origin.

Reform Darwinism contributed other pressures toward isolationism. According to the Conservative Darwinian theory, the "instinct for liberty" first appeared in the primitive "Anglo-Saxon" forests, then developed into the representative institutions of western Europe and was transplanted and expanded into the American democracy. Hence the United States was bound, and proudly bound, to western Europe by a common heritage of freedom. Pro-war conservatives had their difficulties with the primitive Anglo-Saxon forests, most of which happened to have been in Germany, but the great strength of the Anglo-Saxon doctrine has always been its flexibility in defining who is an Anglo-Saxon at any given time. The Kaiser's Germany simply

[1] Quoted in Mark Sullivan: *Our Times* (Scribner, 1926–35), IV, 161, and V, 32.

had its membership in the great race of liberty-lovers suspended while the sense of a common Western civilization went on. In contrast, Reform Darwinism took its conception of American development from thinkers like Frederick Jackson Turner and Charles Beard. Turner may have emphasized the role of the frontier, Beard the importance of the clash of economic groups, but they emphatically agreed that the explanation of American democracy was not an "Anglo-Saxon" past. For the progressive, much more than for the conservative, America was made in America, and fewer ideological ties stretched across the ocean.

The economic interpretation of Reform Darwinism directly militated against involvement in war, even against participation in the ordinary operations of power politics. A conservative used words like "power politics" or "balance of power" in the matter-of-fact way that he discussed any of the political or economic arrangements that were part of workaday life. To the full-blown Conservative Darwinian, war itself was a necessary method for bringing about the survival of the fittest among people within a nation and among the nations of the world. Even conservatives who did not take Darwinism that seriously usually considered wars inevitable, if ugly, occurrences, occasionally necessary to defend an ideal, preserve national interests, or satisfy the sheer cussedness of human beings. For many progressives, nothing in the world of diplomacy or war could be calmly inevitable. In 1914 the reformer was reading his Charles Beard and learning that the Spanish-American War resulted from "the present economic system." Factories seeking markets and capital seeking investment, Beard explained, were "shaping" the foreign policies of all major nations.[2] Progressives were applying their characteristic economic interpretation to power politics and it was emerging a scene of evil men in black coats deceiving the people at the behest of bankers and manufacturers. They were applying economic interpretation to war itself and it was reduced to a blood-spattered grab for profit. In no field does economic interpretation

[2] Beard: *Contemporary American History* (Macmillan, 1914), p. 202, and James Harvey Robinson and Beard: *Development of Modern Europe* (Ginn, 1907–8), II, 328.

carry a heavier emotional charge than in foreign affairs. Large groups of men have never been willing to kill or risk being killed, or to engage in the power politics that can lead to killing, if they believe that the issue is primarily one of economic gain.

Above all, many reformers were leery of intervention in the European war precisely because they were reformers. Men humane enough to worry over the hours of factory hands were much too humane to contemplate machine-gun slaughter without horror. Moreover, most progressives were sure that war would bring an end of reform. They remembered that the Civil War had been followed by the Grant era and that during the Spanish-American War, to use Beard's phrasing, "for a time appeals to patriotism subdued the passions of the radicals." "If the country went to war" again, Ray Stannard Baker was asking for many of his fellow progressives, "would not all the hopeful advances that had been made in recent years go by the board? . . . How develop a constructive program in such a time of passion?" William Allen White found a more succinct expression of the mood. "War," he wrote, "brings men down to beasts quicker than whiskey, surer than women, and deadlier than the love of money." [3]

II

MONTHLY, THE news from Europe filled a larger part of the front pages. Monthly, progressive concern over foreign affairs deepened, and reform opinion, instead of clustering in a general isolationism, began reshaping itself into opposing groups.

An important minority continued a stubborn, dramatic isolationism. William Jennings Bryan, now shorn of his agrarian frenzies and sitting in Wilson's Cabinet as Secretary of State, pushed aside domestic reform in a constantly heightening offensive for peace. As the Administration took an increasingly anti-

---

[3] Beard: *Contemporary American History*, p. 198; Baker: *American Chronicle* (Scribner, 1945), p. 301; Walter Johnson, ed.: *Selected Letters of William Allen White* (Holt, 1947), p. 15.

German position, the Secretary's scrawl became larger and more agitated, his Scriptural admonitions more pointed, his anger higher until on one occasion he forgot himself to the point of denouncing his Cabinet colleagues as pro-Ally. When the *Lusitania* was sunk in 1915 and President Wilson asked his Secretary of State to sign a stern note of protest, Bryan made the most selfless act of his career in behalf of peace. Thrice a Presidential nominee but never before even the lowliest member of a national administration, Bryan gave up his cherished premiership of the Cabinet because he believed that signing the note might well lead to war. At a luncheon after his last Cabinet meeting, the aged Galahad of discontent showed the depth of his feelings. "I must act," Bryan began, "according to my conscience. I go out into the dark. The President has the Prestige and the Power on his side—" Then Bryan broke down and finally added: "I have many friends who would die for me." [4]

He had thousands of reform-minded friends, who, if they might hesitate at dying for him, raised a terrific din in support of his demand for peace. Jane Addams was busy launching a Woman's Peace Party, which by 1916 was powerful enough to bring both major parties assiduously courting its leader, while her reformist friend Rosika Schwimmer was just as busy talking Henry Ford into financing a "peace ship." At this time the quixotic millionaire was telling the newspapers: "Do you want to know the cause of war? It is capitalism, greed, the dirty hunger for dollars," and many well-known reformers showed an intense interest in Ford's peace ship until it took on the plain lines of a psychopathic ward. [5] Every month brought a new reform book arguing against intervention; every city had its band of progressive intellectuals, analyzing, assailing, counterattacking any move that seemed to lead toward war.

In Greenwich Village, Randolph Bourne went hopping around like some misshapen visage of idealism, shaking a bony hand in the faces of progressives who were wondering if the time had not

[4] Quoted in Walter Millis: *The Road to War* (Houghton Mifflin, 1935), p. 190.
[5] Keith Sward: *The Legend of Henry Ford* (Rinehart, 1948), p. 86.

come to do something, sending out of his littered garret essays that will disturb reformers as long as reformers go to war. Bourne's impassioned stand was to cost him most of his friends and his income. The well-paying magazines lost interest in his articles, the lady who had sold her Whistler paintings to finance the *Seven Arts* decided that she had better uses for her remaining money. Soon the proud cripple's food and lodging had to be provided by friends, but when pneumonia struck down his twisted body he was working away at an angry analysis of war. Calling upon the Beardian economic interpretation of the American Constitution, on Marx and on Freud, on the whole panoply of new approaches that progressives were making their own, Bourne fashioned them into a presentation of war versus progressivism. War was "the health" of the predatory groups, Bourne repeated over and over in his essay, like some chant of doom for decency.[6]

The stormy April evening on which Wilson read his war message to Congress brought into lurid focus the opposition to war existing among reformers. When the President came to the phrase: "We will not choose the path of submission," Chief Justice White dropped the big soft hat he was holding, raised his hands high in the air, and brought them together with a heartfelt bang. Instantly the packed chamber was on its feet, obliterating the thunder and the rain in a roar of applause, which died down, then rose louder than ever. But the man whom thousands considered an incarnation of progressivism, Senator Robert La Follette, sat motionless, his arms folded tight and high on his chest, chewing gum with a sardonic smile.

In the debate that followed, George Norris, the Nebraskan who was already a Senatorial symbol of reform second only to La Follette, took the floor in the angriest speech of his forty years in Congress. Years later Norris remembered how he had felt powerless "to stop the flow of words coming from my heart." What was all this high-flown talk about "a duty to humanity,"

[6] James Oppenheim, ed., Bourne: *Untimely Papers* (B. W. Huebsch, New York, 1919), pp. 140–230.

Norris demanded to know. Actually, the war sentiment had been whipped up by "munition manufacturers, stockbrokers, and bond dealers," who would make "enormous profits" by American intervention. "We are going into war upon the command of gold. . . . We are about to put the dollar sign upon the American flag." [7]

Promptly Senators were on their feet to tell Norris that he was speaking near-treason, and one of them paid unintentional tribute to the importance of economic interpretation in anti-war thinking. In March 1917 Senator James Reed, of Missouri, had been against intervention. "I refuse, and will in the future refuse," he told the Senate, "to be a party to sending our Nation to war to protect munition makers in their unholy business of piling up tremendous dividends." A month later Reed had swung over, and he was saying to Norris: "The Senator from Nebraska, I fear, is so obsessed with a fear of 'money' and of 'profits' and of 'fortunes' that all that it is necessary to suggest is that some wealthy concern may have an interest, remote, contingent, or direct, in the subject matter under consideration in order to confuse his mental vision. . . . Sir, this war is not being waged over dollars. It is not being waged over commerce. It is not being waged over profits and losses. It is a war for the maintenance of the sovereign rights of the American Republic and for the preservation of American dignity in the councils of the nations of the earth." [8]

La Follette, of course, depended heavily on the reformer's economic interpretation. The year before, in fighting the preparedness program, he had made the cause of the European war the same factor that "was back of all modern war . . . financial imperialism. . . . The interests that are behind this preparedness program in the United States do not fear Germany, do not fear England, do not fear any nation on earth; but they do want a large army, they do want a large navy. It fits into the commercial, industrial, and imperialistic schemes of the great financial

---

[7] Norris: *Fighting Liberal* (Macmillan, 1945), p. 197; *Congressional Record*, 65th Cong., Spec. Sess., LV, Pt. 1, pp. 213–14.

[8] Ibid., pp. 7, 215–18. In the phrase "business of piling up," "or" has been changed to "of" as an obvious misprint.

masters of this country." Bitterly, *La Follette's Magazine* cried: "If a man dares to intimate that he is unwilling to swallow the whole program for preparedness—a Big Army, a Big Navy, Big Contracts for Munitions of War—that man is a fool or a coward or a traitor. Who are the real Patriots of the Country? . . . They are the Morgans, the Rockefellers, the Schwabs, the Garys, the DuPonts and [those] . . . who are back of the thirty-eight corporations most benefited by war orders. . . . Shades of Lincoln! What a band of patriots!" [9]

In his grim four-hour oration on the war resolution itself, La Follette continued his assault on "selfish ambition and cruel greed" and added all the other points in the usual progressive argument against American intervention. Joining the Allies had nothing to do with democracy, La Follette insisted in the authentic manner of an anti-war Jeffersonian reformer. If the United States really wanted to act like a democracy, it would never fight except after a popular referendum, and a referendum would go "more than ten to one" against war. Far from encouraging reform at home or abroad, American intervention would produce soaring prices, limitations on civil liberties, and a general psychology of reaction. How could a better world order be established, La Follette sneered, by fighting alongside nations that had long since proved their addiction to ways of the "old order"? The pro-German, anti-English tone of much of 1917 progressivism emerged with La Follette's attack on Britain as "a hereditary monarchy, with a hereditary ruler, with a hereditary House of Lords, with a hereditary landed system, with a limited and restricted suffrage for one class and a multiplied suffrage power for another, and with grinding industrial conditions for all the wage-workers." In sharp contrast, the Germans were a nationality who "wherever they have lived . . . have left a record of courage, loyalty, honesty, and high ideals second to no people which have inhabited this earth since the dawn of history." What's more, it "will be generally conceded" that Germany had led Eu-

[9] Quoted in Ellen Torelle, ed.: *The Political Philosophy of Robert M. La Follette* (La Follette Co., Madison, 1920), pp. 194, 195, and Millis, p. 236.

rope "in the solution of municipal problems and in securing social and industrial reforms." [1]

The lights were on when La Follette finished. There were no more anti-war speeches, only snarls at the "verbal eternity" of La Follette, some magniloquent pledges of the "sons of Dixie" to the firing lines, and a befuddled explanation by Senator Warren Gamaliel Harding of his vote for war.[2] The Senate and the country were in no mood for argument. Five of the seven Senators who refused to go along with the war resolution came from the Midwest; four of the seven, from states with exceptionally large proportions of the German-born and of the Scandinavian-born, who tended to be pacifist or pro-German.[3] Quickly the anti-war group was explained away as "Midwestern isolationism" or as the reflection of immigrant prejudices. There was little notice of the fact that the opposition was as much marked by its progressivism in domestic affairs as it was by any other characteristic.[4]

The reception of the war resolution in the House of Representatives was a re-take of the Senate scene. The most bitter anti-war speech was made by Representative William La Follette, from the state of Washington, who had fully lived up to his name in his support of progressive legislation and who now moved that munitions-makers, pro-war editors, and "the J. Pierpont Morgans and their associates" should offer themselves or their sons as soldiers or should give "one-half of all their worldly goods to make good their patriotic desire for our entering the European war."

---

[1] *Congressional Record*, 65th Cong., Spec. Sess., LV, Pt. 1, pp. 223–34.
[2] Ibid., pp. 234, 250.
[3] The seven Senators were Gore, of Oklahoma, Gronna, of North Dakota, Lane, of Oregon, Stone, of Missouri, La Follette, of Wisconsin, Norris, of Nebraska, and Vardaman, of Mississippi. All of these states except Mississippi and Oklahoma contained a population of German background considerably higher than the national average, and all except Mississippi, Oklahoma, and Oregon had a population of Scandinavian background well above the national average. Four of the states—Missouri, Nebraska, Oregon, and Wisconsin—had sizable percentages of Irish-Americans, but these percentages do not stand out so conspicuously above the national average.
[4] This statement is based on a study of the voting records of the anti-war Senators (except Gore, who rarely voted and did not formally oppose the war resolution). The voting study is described on p. 463.

The most important anti-war speech was made by Claude Kitchin, of North Carolina, the Democratic floor leader, who had enthusiastically steered through New Freedom legislation.[5] The roll-call showed that in the House, as in the Senate, anti-war sentiment was strongest in the Midwest and consequently in a region where hyphenate tendencies were anti-English, pro-German, or pacifist. Even more clearly than the Senate vote, that of the House showed a strong progressive bent among the group voting against the war resolution.[6] Close analysis of the total House-Senate vote spotlights the progressivism of the anti-war group so much that it raises the question whether the long-assumed "Midwestern isolationism" of 1917 was not primarily a progressive-nationality isolationism which happened to concentrate in the Midwest—a product of background and ideology rather than of distance from the oceans.

The final negative vote in the House was made in a way that poignantly expressed the wrench that war meant for so many progressives. Jeannette Rankin, of Montana, was the first woman to sit in either the House or the Senate, a former social worker, an ardent suffragette, and now a no less ardent advocate of the New Freedom. When her name was called, she made no reply and the clerk droned on. Cadaverous "Uncle Joe" Cannon, dean of the House, hurried over to Miss Rankin.

"Little woman," Cannon was understood to whisper, "you cannot afford not to vote. You represent the womanhood of the country in the American Congress. I shall not advise you how to vote, but you should, one way or another."

On the second roll-call there was again, for a long few seconds, no answer. Then Miss Rankin stood up, staring straight ahead. "I want to stand by my country," she said in a quavering voice, "but I cannot vote for war." Her words could hardly be heard as she added: "I vote 'No.'"

Astonished tally clerks looked to the Speaker for instructions.

[5] *Congressional Record*, 65th Cong., Spec. Sess., LV, Pt. 1, pp. 332-3, 372.
[6] See p. 463.

For one hundred and forty years no Representative had deviated from the House rule barring explanation or comment during a roll-call. "One negative vote," Speaker Champ Clark said in a kindly way, and Miss Rankin, pressing her hand to her forehead, fell back in her seat.[7]

People did not forget the scene. Many times in his later life Fiorello La Guardia was asked whether it was true that the dignified Jeannette Rankin had stood before the Congress of the United States with tears filling her eyes. La Guardia was never able to satisfy his questioners. "I could not see," the Congressman who himself favored war had to reply, "because of the tears in my own eyes."[8]

III

AT OYSTER BAY there were no tears. Theodore Roosevelt was so happy to see the United States in the war that he was even willing to look for something good to say about that "damned Presbyterian hypocrite," Woodrow Wilson.[9] Roosevelt, the long-time reform demigod, was the most important spokesman of a foreign policy that was advocated by a significant group of progressives and that directly combated progressive isolationism.

From his first emergence on the national scene at the time of the Spanish-American War, Roosevelt had insisted that the United States should continuously concern itself with the rest of the world. "American politics," he declared, "is world politics," and even at the high point of his absorption in domestic reform, during the campaign of 1912, Roosevelt paused to chastise progressives who forgot international affairs. The nature of Roosevelt's own concern with the rest of the world varied. On occasion he

---

[7] This incident is put together from slightly variant accounts given in *New York Times*, April 6, 1917; Fiorello La Guardia: *The Making of an Insurgent* (Lippincott, 1948), pp. 140-1; and an interview with the late Ray Stannard Baker, who was present.

[8] La Guardia, p. 141.

[9] Quoted in Harold L. Ickes: *Autobiography of a Curmudgeon* (Reynal & Hitchcock, 1948), p. 217.

called for American participation in building an international organization for peace. Most of the time his foreign policy was standard turn-of-the-century aggressiveness. How expansionist Roosevelt could be was suggested by a speech in which he hoped "to see the day when not a foot of American soil will be held by any European power." If such a program led to war, that was not necessarily a drawback. As a matter of fact, war encouraged "the soldierly virtues," and soldierly virtues were "the most valuable of all qualities." Roosevelt's contempt was never greater than when he described "the futile sentimentalists of the international arbitration type," who would bring about "a flabby, timid type of character, which eats away the great fighting qualities of our race." During most of his seven years in the White House, this apostle of strenuousness kept the United States roaring across the world in approved imperialist fashion.[1]

Roosevelt's imperialism was shared by a variety of progressives, ranging from the political-minded Albert Beveridge, who orated on "The March of the Flag," to the bookish Herbert Croly, whose chapter on foreign policy in *The Promise of American Life* was a schematization of Roosevelt's most belligerent thoughts. "The isolation which has meant so much to the United States, and still means so much, cannot persist in its present form," Croly wrote. ". . . Its standing as a nation is determined precisely by its ability to conquer and to hold a dignified and important place in the society of nations." In recognizing its international "responsibilities," America should end any questioning of "the validity of colonial expansion." As for regions like China, where the United States had traditionally asserted its interests, "it is wholly improbable that China can be protected . . . without a great deal of diplomacy and more or less of fighting." In all foreign affairs, there should be no mollycoddle tendency toward peace for peace' sake. "If America wants peace," Croly declared, "it must be spiritually and physically prepared to fight for it. . . . [It is

[1] Quoted in André Tardieu: "Three Visits to Mr. Roosevelt," *Independent* (April 16, 1908), LXIV, 862; Hermann Hagedorn, ed.: *Works of Theodore Roosevelt* (Scribner, 1923-6), XIX, 438-9; and Henry F. Pringle: *Theodore Roosevelt* (Harcourt, Brace, 1931), pp. 166-7, 168, 172.

probable] that the road to any permanent international settlement will be piled high with dead bodies, and will be traveled, if at all, only after a series of abortive and costly experiments." [2]

The German troops had hardly swept through Belgium before Roosevelt emerged as the leader of a get-tough faction, which advocated a policy that became increasingly indistinguishable from a demand for war. The ex-President spared no epithets in assailing attempts at continued neutrality. President Wilson's hesitancies along the road to intervention proved him "a silly doctrinaire . . . an utterly selfish and cold-blooded politician" who was "trailing the honor of the United States in the dust." Jane Addams, who only a few years before had seconded Roosevelt's Bull Moose nomination for the Presidency, was now "poor bleeding Jane Addams" and a "Bull Mouse." The popular song "I Didn't Raise My Boy to Be a Soldier," Roosevelt sneered, was comparable to singing "I Didn't Raise My Girl to Be a Mother." [3] In his frenzy for "sound Americanism," Roosevelt subordinated all considerations of domestic reform, even trying to win the 1916 Republican nomination for the conservative but bellicose Henry Cabot Lodge. It is impossible to say how many progressives moved as swiftly as Roosevelt toward war, but he was certainly no solitary crusader. The Bull Moose convention of 1916, still representing a segment of reformers, flatly refused to consider any nominee other than Roosevelt. When the symbol of belligerence declined the nomination, the party quickly disintegrated.[4]

Without accepting Roosevelt's extreme position or his imperialism, progressives of many types were far ahead of the Administration in urging drastic action. The legal-minded Henry Stimson insisted that the "Prussian doctrine of state supremacy" had to be

---

[2] Croly: *The Promise of American Life* (Macmillan, 1909), pp. 307-12.

[3] Quoted in Sullivan, V, 204; William Allen White: *Autobiography* (Macmillan, 1946), p. 531; the Baker interview; and Preston W. Slosson: *The Great Crusade and After* (Macmillan, 1930), p. 10.

[4] Other factors, of course, had a good deal to do with the collapse of the party. See George E. Mowry: *Theodore Roosevelt and the Progressive Movement* (University of Wisconsin Press, 1946), Chaps. xiii–xiv, and Harold L. Ickes: "Who Killed the Progressive Party?" *American Historical Review* (June 1941), XLVI, 306–37.

halted, no matter what the cost. The ideological Harold Ickes, as he has recalled in his autobiography, "early became of the opinion that we ought to jump in and help Great Britain and France. Every democratic nation in the world was in danger—or so I thought." Tears may have come to La Guardia's eyes as Congress voted for war, but he had believed the move inevitable and wise almost from the start of the conflict in Europe.[5] Studying the American press during the first years of the fighting, Walter Millis was struck by the conspicuousness of reformers among those who were vehement in asserting that the conflict was America's war. "It was not, in those early days, the conservatives . . . who saw in the Allied cause a holy crusade," Millis stated. ". . . It was . . . the progressives, the leaders of reform."[6]

IV

SOMEWHERE BETWEEN the quick interventionists and the isolationists most of the progressives worried along. With La Follette, they hated war, considered it a result of ugly nationalism and greed, thought that the United States should devote itself not to killing but to domestic reform. With Roosevelt, they believed that there were things worse than fighting, felt an intense pride in American national honor, and became increasingly pro-Ally as Germany showed little respect for human life, international law, or the rights of small countries.

Woodrow Wilson, of course, was the key figure among these anti-war, pro-"humanity" progressives. The reform President had shared most of the ideas that La Follette hurled at him in the debate on the war resolution. During the campaign of 1912 Wilson had clamped an economic interpretation on the foreign policies of Roosevelt and Taft, and Wilson's most important diplomatic moves before the European war emphasized hostility to "dollar

[5] Henry L. Stimson and McGeorge Bundy: *On Active Service* (Harper, 1948), p. 89; Ickes, p. 184; La Guardia, pp. 114–15.
[6] Millis, p. 56.

diplomacy." He handled a proposed loan to China in a way that could be called a "knockout for Wall Street"; through all his statements on the Mexican situation ran an insistence that his Administration would avoid the diplomacy of "material interest." [7]

News of Sarajevo came to Wilson as a shocking intrusion. He was just completing his basic reform legislation, and the domestic road stretched invitingly ahead, offering opportunities to consolidate gains already made and to push progressivism in other fields. Wilson read the reports on the sudden holocaust across the ocean a little unbelievingly and more than a little angrily. He would have none of it for America. His Neutrality Proclamation was the most sweeping such injunction ever issued by the head of a large nation, and his first important message to Congress after Sarajevo warned: "This is the time above all others when we should wish and resolve to keep our strength by self-possession. . . . To engage in extensive preparedness would mean merely that we had lost our self-possession, that we had been thrown off our balance by a war with which we have nothing to do, whose causes cannot touch us." [8]

Privately, Wilson filled in the details of his attitude. To friends, he wrote that greed and folly characterized both sides in the European war, and "the more I read about the conflict across the seas, the more open it seems to me to utter condemnation." He agreed with his closest foreign-policy adviser, Colonel House, that victory by either side offered nothing beneficial to the United States. A German victory meant "the unspeakable tyranny of militarism for generations to come," House and the President concurred, but an Allied triumph was likely to result in Russian domination of Europe. In a conversation with his Secretary of the Navy, Josephus Daniels, Wilson added: "If war comes, we shall have to get the cooperation of the big businessmen and, as a re-

[7] Quoted in Harley Notter: *The Origins of the Foreign Policy of Woodrow Wilson* (Johns Hopkins Press, Baltimore, 1937), pp. 197–8, and Ray Stannard Baker: *Woodrow Wilson* (Doubleday, Doran, 1927–39), IV, 72, 283.

[8] *Messages and Papers of Woodrow Wilson* (Review of Reviews Corp., New York, 1924), I, 77, 78–9.

sult, they will dominate the nation for 20 years after the war comes to an end." No element in progressive thinking was lacking in Wilson's reluctance to go to war, not even flashes of the racism that was still so prevalent among reformers. David Houston, a member of the Wilson Cabinet, has described a session at which the President spoke of his duty to the white race. "He would say frankly," Houston paraphrased Wilson, "that, if he felt that in order to keep the white race or part of it strong to meet the yellow race—Japan, for instance, in alliance with Russia, dominating China—it was wise to do nothing, he would do nothing, and would submit to anything and any imputation of weakness or cowardice." [9]

Wilson never lost the reformer's horror of war *per se* and as an enemy of reform. By Saturday, March 31, 1917, the President had decided to ask Congress to declare war, and the forty-eight hours that remained before he read his war message were a nightmare to him. Through most of Saturday night, he held himself to his battered old typewriter, pecking out the fateful words in fretful solitude. Sunday, while ministers across the nation cried war and vengeance and editors readied exultant editorials, Wilson fidgeted in the White House, weary, haggard, despondent. Suddenly he felt the need for talk, not the sympathetic words of Mrs. Wilson or the soothing admiration of Colonel House, but robust, questioning talk. The President dispatched an urgent invitation to Frank Cobb, of the New York *World*, who more than once had asked questions about policies of Woodrow Wilson.

Cobb arrived at the White House at one o'clock of the morning the President was to address Congress, and the two men sat talking away the last night of peace. But it was not Frank Cobb who spoke the disturbing thoughts. Germany had forced America's hand, Cobb was sure. Wilson agreed.

But do you know what war means? Cobb reported the President's conversation. "He said war would overturn the world we

[9] Quoted in David Loth: *Woodrow Wilson* (Lippincott, 1941), p. 124; by Jonathan Daniels, in Henry Wallace: "Report on the South," *New Republic* (July 14, 1947), CXVII, 14; and in David F. Houston: *Eight Years with Wilson's Cabinet* (Doubleday, Page, 1926), I, 229.

had known. . . . It would mean that we should lose our heads along with the rest and stop weighing right and wrong. It would mean that a majority of people in this hemisphere would go war-mad, quit thinking and devote their energies to destruction. . . . It means an attempt to reconstruct a peace time civilization with war standards."

Wilson cherished no hope that a war could be fought in a progressive atmosphere. "When a war got going," Cobb paraphrased the President, "it was just war and there weren't two kinds of it. It required illiberalism at home to reinforce the men at the front. We couldn't fight Germany and maintain the ideas of Government that all thinking men shared. He said we would try it but it would be too much for us."

"Once lead this people into war," Cobb remembered Wilson's grim conclusion, "and they'll forget there ever was such a thing as tolerance. To fight you must be brutal and ruthless, and the spirit of ruthless brutality will enter into the very fibre of our national life, infecting Congress, the courts, the policeman on the beat, the man in the street. Conformity would be the only virtue, the President said, and every man who refused to conform would have to pay the penalty." [1]

Some historians, emphasizing the three years during which Wilson gave powerful reasons for not going to war, have seen in his change of mind considerations of domestic politics and an ambition to be a world figure. Certainly the state of public opinion made a declaration of war politically expedient, and American intervention did give Wilson the opportunity to become a haloed figure to millions around the globe. Yet if selfish motives were operating in the President's mind, they could hardly have been operating consciously. The conscience-lashed minister's son had to move to a war position in terms of his responsibilities as President of the United States and his general ideals. More specifically, the progressive pro-war Wilson had to be able to answer the progressive anti-war Wilson.

[1] Quoted in John L. Heaton: *Cobb of "The World"* (Dutton, 1924), pp. 267–70.

The reformer's case against American intervention had boiled down to two main points: any nation participating in the conflict would be joining a greedy struggle for power and wealth, and much more harm than good would come to the United States from entering the war. Wilson's argument for war directly answered both points. The United States was entering a contest of principle, not greed, he maintained. The actions of Germany, climaxed by its unrestricted submarine warfare, had proved it a government without "compassion or principle," engaged in "a warfare against mankind." In taking arms against it, the United States had "no selfish ends to serve. We desire no conquest, no dominion. We seek no indemnities for ourselves, no material compensation for the sacrifices we shall freely make." The United States was entering the war, Wilson emphasized, only because "the right is more precious than peace." [2]

Wilson's argument that more good than harm would come to America from fighting naturally rested on the premise that Prussianism was a menace to all free peoples. But once beyond this fundamental, he gave less emphasis to an existing danger than to the coming peace. "We are at the beginning of an age," Wilson declared, "in which it will be insisted that the same standards of conduct and responsibility for wrong done shall be observed among nations and their governments that are observed among the individual citizens of civilized states." [3] America could remain a peaceful democracy in the future only if the world remained at peace, and to prevent wars the United States had to be present at the peace table to see that a lasting settlement, a just rather than a vindictive peace, was written. Such a peace had to rest on the Fourteen Points, and the call for national self-determination, the spread of democracy, and the immediate establishment of a league of nations.

In one of the unending accidents of history, the phrase that was to symbolize the Wilsonian case received its impetus because a near-deaf man heard it. Toward the end of his message asking

---

[2] *Messages and Papers of Wilson*, I, 373, 374, 381, 382.
[3] Ibid., I, 378.

for the declaration of war, in the midst of statements of grave importance, the President said: "The world must be made safe for democracy." Mississippi's master orator, Senator John Sharp Williams, had been leaning forward, his hand cupped to his ear. Williams knew a natural slogan even when it had to fight its way through his deafness. At the words "safe for democracy," the Senator began to clap all alone and kept it up until others had joined in and the sentence was called to the attention of reporters. Making the world safe for democracy—what could be more certain to produce good that outweighed the evils of war, what could be freer of the taint of national self-seeking?

Wilson did not invent out of whole cloth his justification for intervention. Some of it was implicit in traditional American attitudes. Other parts had been originated and given currency by individuals or organizations working independently of the Administration. But the President who denounced war the night before he asked Congress to pass a war resolution was peculiarly qualified to justify fighting to an anti-militarist nation, and the anti-war progressive who had to answer himself was precisely the man to persuade other anti-war reformers. The Wilson formula, conceived out of his own doubts and stated with rousing artistry, became the ideological bridge by which most of the progressive group moved with their leader from neutrality to intervention.

The way in which the Wilson formula served as the progressive rationale found a striking example in the *New Republic*. Suddenly forced to devise a foreign policy, the journal zigzagged for two years. Sometimes the *New Republic* proclaimed the end of isolation so sweepingly that it sounded as if it were marching with Theodore Roosevelt. On other occasions, it qualified its militancy to such an extent that interventionist papers denounced it as pro-German and an ugly break came between Roosevelt and the chief editors, all of whom had grown up politically in the Bull Moose movement. The colonel stomped into the office, tried to straighten out his erring children, and, failing, stomped out with the physiologically interesting statement that the *New Republic* was "a negligible sheet, run by two anæmic Gentiles and two uncircumcized Jews." [4]

But in the later phases of the debate the *New Republic* moved steadily toward war, and as it did, the journal talked the Wilson formula. In increasing cadence with the President, it answered the arguments that war was a big businessman's plot and that intervention would bring more harm than good. It was Charles Beard himself who was now writing in the *New Republic* of war aims that made the conflict "not at bottom, or even potentially, a capitalist war for colonies, markets, and concessions." It was John Dewey himself who described how making culture pragmatically consonant with the needs of the day led toward intervention. "Few really desirable ends can be achieved by war," the editors took up the theme," but there are some that can be. . . . If the end is clear and certain, there cannot be much doubt about the means. . . . That which distinguishes constructive progressivism from mere pious wishing is the use of present means to bring one forward to one's end." The ends that justified the present means of war were substantially those of Wilson—the destruction of German militarism, the spread of free institutions and national self-determination, the establishment of a just peace and of a league of nations to preserve the just peace.[5]

The thinking of the reform President and that of the nation's leading reform publication were so increasingly similar that a spontaneous relationship between the two appeared. Ideas would bubble up at the brilliant luncheon discussions of the *New Republic* editors and would reach the White House, either through

[4] Interview with Mr. Alvin Johnson, then a member of the *New Republic* group.

[5] Quoted from Beard: "The Perils of Diplomacy," *New Republic* (June 2, 1917), XI, 137; Louis Filler: *Crusaders for American Liberalism* (Harcourt, Brace, 1939); and an interview with the late Philip Littell. Of course the *New Republic*, edited by a group of exceedingly restless and critical minds, was often at variance with the President or defended the same case with a different emphasis, most notably in the famous editorial, "The Defense of the Atlantic World." This argued American concern with the Allied cause primarily in terms of "a profound web of interest" which joined together an "Atlantic community." *New Republic* (February 17, 1917), X, 59–61.

the President's reading of the magazine or through his contacts with Walter Lippmann, who gave the ideas all the additional allure of his semantic magic. Often the White House was interested. The most notable liaison was in the case of the famous phrase, " peace without victory." The idea of a peace that would avoid vindictiveness and would not leave the Germans bitterly spoiling for revenge was widespread among progressives, and the *New Republic* had long urged it. In the course of editorializing on a somewhat different point, the journal coined the phrase "peace without victory," and soon a startled and none too pleased world heard the President of the United States using it in the more general progressive sense. A few more instances of this sort of thing and word got around that the *New Republic* was an inside source for developments in Administration policy. For a while, until the rumors proved mere rumor, copies of the austerely intellectual magazine were snatched from the news-stands, and speculators seeking market tips made detective-story attempts to lay their hands on advance proofs.

The *New Republic* editors had their laugh, but they were more interested in a less melodramatic development. Of all the journal's staff, only one member, the unreconstructable Irishman Francis Hackett, was to remain impervious to the war enthusiasm. Next to Hackett, Walter Weyl was slowest in moving with the trend. A personality of paper-thin sensitivity, Weyl could be moved to tears by the sight of a European casualty list; a tough, skeptical mind, he kept cutting through the President's rhetoric with embarrassing questions. But the appeal of the Wilson formula to the progressive mind did not fail. Shortly after the President made plain his idealistic intent in his "peace without victory" speech, even Weyl was ready to lower his cocked eye. "American isolation ends," Weyl announced, "not in confusion, but with purposes defined, which we can justify to our own consciences and to the world." [6]

[6] Weyl: "A History of Three Months," *New Republic* (February 10, 1917), X, 35.

V

AMERICA WAS scarcely in the war before it was taxing the con-science of Weyl and thousands of other progressives. All the dis-mal predictions Wilson had made to Frank Cobb rapidly came true. Reform stopped dead, large-scale business swiftly increased its profits and its powers, inflation began its ravaging. Civil lib-erties were twisted, narrowed, virtually abolished in the tradi-tional American meaning of the phrase. Excited by the powerful opposition to war that had shown itself in the three years of for-eign-policy debate, the Administration and Congress rushed through sweeping legislation dealing with espionage, sedition, and trading with the enemy, and many local governments followed suit. These laws created a situation in which virtually any criti-cism of the Wilson Administration could be ruled illegal.[7]

The administration of the laws was no less oppressive. Wilson was never a man to take criticism calmly, and his long-running reluctance to ask for war seems to have made him the readier to permit the crushing of criticism once he had made the decision. The President may have blanched but he did not intervene while a nationwide spy system was created which used many of the weapons dear to the Czarist police. "According to authentic evi-dence," the pro-war progressives, Charles and Mary Beard, have recorded, " 'tools' were planted among organizations . . . sup-posed to have dangerous tendencies, and were instructed to incite them to unlawful acts; meeting places of such associations were raided without proper warrant, property was destroyed, papers

[7] Zechariah Chafee, Jr.: *Free Speech in the United States* (Harvard University Press, Cambridge, 1941), 38–42, 98, 102 n.; La Guardia, pp. 150–4. La Guardia presented striking evidence of the effects of inflation in *Con-gressional Record*, 65th Cong., 1st Sess., LV, Pt. 4, pp. 4014–16. The *Harvard Law Review*, speaking of the federal Espionage Act alone, declared that it left "little room for any public discussion adverse to the war policies of the national government. The question of constitutionality seems alone to re-main, and if the amended act is held to be constitutional, the power of Congress to abridge the time-honored right of freedom of speech will seem well established." "The Espionage Cases," *Harvard Law Review* (February 1919), XXXII, 417.

seized, innocent bystanders beaten, and persons guilty of no discernible offense rushed off to jail, subjected to police torture, held without bail, and released without recourse." [8]

Not untypically, Wilson's Postmaster General, A. R. Burleson, denied mailing privileges to the anti-war radical journal, the *Masses,* on the ground that it contained treasonable passages, and then refused to name the offending passages when the publisher offered to delete the material. A federal judge, Theodore Roosevelt's friend, Learned Hand, overruled Burleson, and the Postmaster General promptly found another technique of suppression. The *Masses* had missed an issue because of the original suppression. Hence, Burleson decreed, it was no longer a regularly issued periodical and was not eligible for second-class privileges. The Postmaster General cracked down on an issue of *Public,* which urged that more money be raised by taxes and less by loans; suppressed Thorstein Veblen's *Imperial Germany and the Industrial Revolution,* which the President's own Committee on Public Information had recommended; and contemplated moving against the *New Republic,* as Walter Lippmann has bitterly recalled, "for advocating a Wilson peace in the mad days of 1918." [9]

Many prosecuting and judicial officers operated in the same spirit. The persons indicted or imprisoned included a woman who had received a Red Cross solicitor in a "hostile" manner, a socialist who had written a letter to the *Kansas City Star* charging wartime profiteering, and an editor who printed the statement: "We must make the world safe for democracy even if we have to 'bean' the Goddess of Liberty to do it." A Californian went to jail for laughing at rookies drilling on San Francisco's Presidio, a New Yorker served ninety days for spitting on the sidewalk near some Italian officers. In Los Angeles a former associate of D. W. Griffith was sentenced to ten years and a five-thousand-dollar fine for trying to produce a *Birth of a Nation* about the American Revolution. The

[8] Charles A. and Mary R. Beard: *The Rise of American Civilization* (Macmillan, 1930), p. 642. See also Chafee, p. 273, and Baker, VII, 165 n.
[9] Lippmann, in "Herbert Croly," *New Republic* (July 16, 1930), LXIII, Pt. II, p. 252; Chafee, pp. 42–5, 98–9.

film, the judge said, "tended to make us a little bit slack in our loyalty to Great Britain in this great emergency." [1]

Outside the government, the contagion of suppression spread rapidly. Radical labor leaders were tarred and feathered, ministers were unfrocked for emphasizing the Sermon on the Mount, clubs expelled members who questioned the omniscience of the Administration, college professors were dismissed or bludgeoned into resigning for pacifist leanings or for ardent pro-war statements that also criticized the home front. From Outagamie County, Wisconsin, where the large population of German-Americans made the situation especially tense, came the sworn statement of John Deml, illustrating another form of the hysteria. Late one Sunday night a crowd of men came pounding at Deml's door, demanding that he sign up for Liberty Bonds. Deml told the crowd he had already done his share by buying $450 in bonds, and then "all at one time . . . [they] closed in on me like a vise; some grabbing my fingers or wrist, others my legs, and several of them were shouting, holding a paper before me, 'Sign up.' I said, 'I will not sign up at this time of night.' Then a man shouted, 'Get the rope!' The first I knew was when the rope was about my neck and around my body under my arms. Someone then gave a sharp jerk at the rope and forced me to my hands and knees; at the same time some of them jumped on my back, and while bent over someone struck me in the face, making me bleed; then a man . . . said, 'Boys, you are going too far. . . .' " [2]

Both the unofficial and the official hysteria fell more and more under the control of conservatives, who were just as interested in silencing reform agitation as they were in suppressing friends of Germany. Sometimes the witch-hunt appeared primarily a reform-hunt. Cases were numerous like the dismissal of Professor

---

[1] Quoted in Chafee: "Freedom of Speech," *New Republic* (November 16, 1918), XVII, 67; National Civil Liberties Bureau: *War-Time Prosecutions and Mob Violence* (National Civil Liberties Bureau, New York, 1919), pp. 19, 23, 29, 32, 34; Chafee: *Free Speech in the United States*, p. 55.

[2] Quoted in Charles D. Stewart: "Prussianizing Wisconsin," *Atlantic Monthly* (January 1919), CXXIII, 101–2. See also ibid., pp. 99–105; *War-Time Prosecutions*, pp. 5–13, 44–6; Oswald Garrison Villard: *Fighting Years* (Harcourt, Brace, 1939), pp. 302–60.

J. McKeen Cattell, a well-known psychologist, by the Columbia board of trustees. Cattell had opposed American entrance into the war, but he was doing nothing that could remotely obstruct the war effort. On the contrary, his son, with the father's approval, had volunteered for combat service, and the psychologist himself was at work on plans to guide the War Department in its selection of aviators. But Cattell was a long-time critic of the board of trustees' autocratic control over the Columbia faculty and of its refusal to improve slum property that the university owned. Twice before the United States entered the war, the trustees tried to maneuver Cattell's dismissal and retreated only when the faculty sharply protested. Now, Cattell could charge, "the trustees have hid behind the flag to assassinate." [3]

Progressives were quite aware of this technique of assassination. Many of them, recognizing it for what it was, refused to be intimidated and kept up a vigorous fight to protect the standard of living of lower-income groups and to preserve all freedoms compatible with a full war effort. Anti-war and pro-war progressives both had their crusades. It was Jeannette Rankin who staged one of the most publicized reform coups of the war period. Employees of the Bureau of Engraving and Printing had long been complaining to the Treasury Department that the head of the Bureau made passes at a number of the female employees and, despite the eight-hour rule, worked his staff twelve, fourteen, and even sixteen hours without extra pay. The head of the Bureau had powerful political connections; the complaints were ignored and a number of Congressmen who were approached refused to touch the matter. Then, in July 1917, the employees got to Miss Rankin. At her own expense she sent a private investigator into the Bureau for two weeks, collected a mass of material supporting the employees' claims, and marched over to the Treasury Department with her

[3] Interview with the late Charles A. Beard. Beard, a colleague of Cattell, publicly said of the general Columbia situation: "It was the evident purpose of a small group of the trustees (unhindered, if not aided, by Mr. Butler) to take advantage of the state of war to drive out or humiliate or terrorize every man who held progressive, liberal, or unconventional views on political matters in no way connected with the war." "A Statement by Charles A. Beard," *New Republic* (December 29, 1917), XIII, 250.

evidence. If the Bureau head was not fired before the end of the day, she assured the Department, she would make her evidence public. That evening the *Washington Post* brought out an extra to announce the dismissal; in all American history, the *Post* chortled, no government bureau had ever moved so swiftly.[4]

The agitation by pro-war reformers brought to national attention the first of the important progressive politicians who came from the immigrant groups of the cities, New York's chunky spitfire, Fiorello La Guardia. La Guardia was born only a few years after his parents passed through Ellis Island. His father's job as leader of an Army band gave Fiorello an Arizona boyhood, but the father's early death brought the family back to a more usual habitat for immigrants. It was on New York's East Side that La Guardia learned his politics, and came to hate what he learned. As a Deputy Attorney General, he quickly discovered that he was considered decidedly queer for wanting to enforce the law equally against both the powerful and the weak. One day State Senator Jimmy Walker, who had the kindliness of a thoroughgoing cynic, tried to set the excitable young man straight. "Fiorello," Walker said, "when are you going to get wise? . . . What are you in politics for, for love?" That was enough to confirm La Guardia in his suspicion that he could never be a member of Walker's party, the Democratic.

The local Republicans, by sounding just as bad, gave La Guardia his chance. Republicans were rarely elected from an East Side district, and the machine concentrated on deals with Democratic factions, wasting little time on such fripperies as the democratic process. La Guardia, a Republican precinct captain, was visiting the clubhouse when it was discovered that no one had bothered to pick a Republican nominee for Congress.

"Who wants to run for Congress?" the district boss bellowed

"I do," said La Guardia, who certainly did.

---

[4] *Washington Post*, July 3, 1917; letter of Belle F. Winestone, Miss Rankin's assistant at the time, to John Gillette, January 23, 1949, lent to the author by Mr. Gillette.

"OK, put La Guardia down," the boss dismissed the matter, disappearing into the back room.[5]

On his second try, in 1916, La Guardia became the first Republican ever to go to Congress from his district. He did it by shrewd politicking, by providing street-corner crowds with clowning that was not excelled in Maurice Schwartz's famous Yiddish theater round the corner, by speaking Yiddish to the Jews and Italian to the Italians, and by talking to all his audiences a reformism that was directly related to their ambitions and their fears. Once in Congress, La Guardia gave to progressivism the combination of the actor, the adventurer, and the statesman that was peculiarly his own. In arguments brilliantly uniting general economic considerations and appeals to New York special interests, he proposed shifts in the war taxes, including greater exemption from income levies for low-income groups. In a performance that skated the edge of demagoguery, he attacked inflation and proposed a Constitutional amendment to give "power to the National Government at all times to regulate and control the production, conservation, and distribution of food supplies." The Espionage Act La Guardia assailed in torrential apostrophes to democracy, never neglecting to emphasize that it might prevent any criticism of the War Department and melodramatically offering to draw a sample indictment of himself to prove his point. Except for one revision of the Espionage Act and a minor tax change, La Guardia got little that he demanded, but the old-guard leaders were discovering that they still had progressivism very much on their hands.[6]

Outside Congress, reformers and reform journals kept up a relentless supporting fire. No profiteering went unscourged; no dismissal of a minister or a professor went uninvestigated. Cattell's removal at Columbia provoked an incident that has become something of a landmark in the history of American academic freedom. A week after the dismissal Professor Charles Beard finished his customary afternoon lecture, then added coolly: "This is my last

---

[5] La Guardia, pp. 103, 113; interview with the late Fiorello La Guardia.
[6] La Guardia, pp. 149–52; *Congressional Record*, 65th Cong., 1st Sess., LV, Pt. 2, pp. 1700–1; Pt. 3, pp. 2298–9, 2488, 2609–10, 2694; Pt. 4, pp. 4014–16.

lecture in Columbia University. I have handed in my resignation this afternoon to take effect at 9 a.m. I thank you." A stunned silence was followed by a roar of applause that defied all efforts to quell it for fifteen minutes.

The next day, progressives throughout the nation were cheering Beard's militant letter of resignation. "Having observed closely the inner life at Columbia for many years," he declared, "I have been driven to the conclusion that the university is really under the control of a small and active group of trustees who have no standing in the world of education, who are reactionary and visionless in politics, narrow and mediæval in religion." These trustees, Beard went on, by attempting to force conformity on the faculty, were not only checking free thinking but checking it at the worst possible time. "If these were ordinary times one might more readily ignore the unhappy position in which the dominant group in the board of trustees has placed the teachers, but these are not ordinary times. We are in the midst of a great war and we stand on the threshold of an era which will call for all the emancipated thinking that America can command." The country desperately needed arguments addressed to "reason and understanding. . . . Such arguments, however, must come from men whose disinterestedness is above all suspicion, whose independence is beyond all doubt. . . . I am convinced that while I remain in the pay of the trustees of Columbia University I cannot do effectively my humble part in sustaining public opinion in support of the just war on the German Empire or take a position of independence in the days of reconstruction that are to follow." [7]

VI

YET BEARD'S very letter of resignation underlined his own support of the war. La Guardia soon voluntarily left Congress for combat flying service. The *New Republic* backed Wilson the war leader

[7] Beard to Nicholas Murray Butler, October 8, 1917, printed in *New York Tribune*, October 9, 1917.

all the while that it assailed Wilson the inquisitor. The anti-progressivism accompanying the war in no way diminished progressive enthusiasm for the war. If anything, it increased the addiction to the Wilson formula. War, the reformers consoled one another, was a necessary evil to open the way to unending peace and reform. "I am personally opposed to militarism, imperialism, and all manner of oppression," La Guardia explained to his constituents, many of whom were anti-war socialists. "I am against war, and because I am against war I went to war to fight against war. I don't think we can end war by merely talking against war on the corners of the East Side." [8]

As the Wilson formula sank more deeply into reform thought and feeling, something important seemed to be happening to American progressivism. From the first decades after the Civil War the movement had felt European influences, drawn strength from the thought that it was part of a world-wide trend, even attempted international liaison on occasion. But at bottom progressivism had been as exclusively national a movement as the United States ever knew. It sprang directly from American problems and went about solving them with only an infrequent glance beyond the nation's borders. American reform was assumed to be an American problem.

Now, most progressives were convinced that the future of American reform, of America itself, depended on events occurring three thousand miles away. The Wilson formula stated a doctrine of world relationships. Americans not only had to fight to make the world safe for democracy in 1917; after peace they had to continuously engage in a league of nations to keep the world safe for democracy and progress. With the acceptance of this formula by most progressives, the movement that had functioned on isolationist assumptions for half a century was suddenly taking on a sweeping internationalism.

[8] La Guardia, p. 200.

CHAPTER XII

Isolationists in Peace

T HE NEWS of the Armistice arrived in the middle of the night, and by dawn carnival was sweeping the United States. For the progressives there was special joy. The war they had never felt at home with, the hatreds they had hated, the iron hand on reform were gone. The day of reward was at hand. Hadn't the Armistice been signed on the basis of the Fourteen Points and wasn't the New Freedom leader to be the most powerful figure in converting the Armistice into a permanent peace? [1]

The reception of Woodrow Wilson in Europe heightened progressive expectations. Cæsar and Genghis Khan and Napoleon had known adulation, but nothing like the reception that came to the schoolmasterish President who visited the Allied capitals talking peace and democracy. In Rome, pictures of *il Presidente* were in every shop-window, quotations from his speeches on every wall; thousands milled before the palace in which he stayed and waited six hours to see him walk out of a door and into a limousine fifteen feet away. In Brussels, men and women tugged idolatrously at Wilson's coattails. In Paris, two million throats roared "Wilson *le Juste*" as his carriage moved down the avenue of France's glory.

[1] For the necessary qualifications concerning the extent to which the Fourteen Points were actually accepted by both sides as the basis of peace, see Thomas A. Bailey: *Woodrow Wilson and the Lost Peace* (Macmillan, 1945), pp. 44–54.

Around the globe, in Poland, China, and South Africa, peasants and workingmen tacked up the President's picture beside those of Confucius or Jesus Christ. American reformers read the accounts of all this and were quite ready to agree with the *New Republic*'s dictum: "In making a just peace Mr. Wilson has on his side one fact of overwhelming importance. He has engaged the attention, and can depend upon the support, of the people." [2]

Details of the Versailles Peace Treaty trickled back to the United States in unofficial, semifinal form. Germans in the know, who were not bound by the Allied agreement to release only the final form, hawked a preliminary draft throughout Europe. The *Chicago Tribune* bought and published a copy, and Senator William E. Borah had the draft inserted in the *Congressional Record*. Progressives pondered and worried, but they still hoped. After all, semifinal terms were not final, and everybody knew that the *Chicago Tribune* and Senator Borah hated the idea of a League of Nations so much that any move they made concerning the President's foreign policy was suspect.

On the afternoon of July 10, 1919, Wilson appeared before the Senate carrying the official terms of the treaty under his arm. The President presented the document in what was probably the worst speech of his career, failing, except at the very end, to achieve eloquence, stumbling over words now and then, appearing like a man talking to an uncomprehending and hostile crowd. If anxiety over the treaty's reception was the explanation of Wilson's ineptitude, he had judged the situation correctly. For as the facts of the treaty seeped into the public mind, the President was assailed with a savagery seldom equaled in American history, not only by his customary enemies but by progressives who had marched with him in peace and war and who had hailed his foreign policy as inspired.

It is impossible to speak with any high degree of accuracy about progressives' attitudes toward the Versailles Peace. The rapid shifts in opinion during the war make it difficult to determine

[2] "Let Us Have Patience," *New Republic* (January 18, 1919), XVII, 328.

just which men and women should be placed in the progressive category once the war was over. The situation was further confused by the fact that the League of Nations and the specific peace terms were incorporated in one treaty, and the terms were defended by Wilson on the grounds that the League would take care of any difficulties created by them. What can be said with certainty is that only a small percentage of the Americans who were unquestioned progressives in domestic affairs showed enthusiasm for the Versailles Treaty. A large number were lukewarm or bitterly hostile, some toward the League as well as a number of specific settlements, some with varying types of approval for the League. Progressives were an important unit in the coalition that brought about American rejection of the whole treaty—the more important a unit because conservatives could point out that Wilson's strongest admirers were deserting him.[3]

II

To SOME extent progressive opposition to the treaty was a recrudescence of progressive isolationism. Whatever his ineptitude in presenting the Versailles Peace, Wilson had left no doubt that in his opinion the League of Nations was inextricably entangled with the whole settlement and that the clauses setting up the League were the most important provisions. Progressives who had been opponents of the internationalism implicit in Wilson's appeal for war had no intention of accepting the internationalism woven into the treaty he was sponsoring. A good deal of anti-League progressive opinion was shot through with suspicion of an international "superlegislature," to use La Follette's angry phrases, which would "draw upon the lusty man power and the rich material resources of the United States."[4] No opponent of the

[3] These and subsequent statements concerning general progressive opinion are based on a sampling technique described on p. 463.

[4] Ellen Torelle, ed.: *The Political Philosophy of Robert M. La Follette* (La Follette Co., Madison, 1920), pp. 252, 253.

Versailles settlement was more vituperative or more effective than the reform bulldozer, the new California Senator, Hiram Johnson, who had long since made plain that he did not like the rest of the world and to hell with it.

Yet most progressive opponents of the treaty were not attacking from an isolationist position. To them the treaty was bad because it did not sufficiently carry out the Fourteen Points. Four of these points primarily concerned questions to be worked out in the Austrian and Turkish settlements. Of the ten points most at stake, progressive publicists generally scored the results somewhat as follows:

Four points were put down as definitely achieved:

(1) and (2) Adequate provision was made for the evacuation and restoration of Belgium and France.

(3) An independent Poland with access to the sea was created.

(4) A league of nations was formed.

Two points were put down as partially achieved:

(1) The Versailles Treaty was an open covenant, openly arrived at, in the sense that full reports of the plenary sessions were available and the entire final document was published. But the treaty was partially a secret document because many of the most important conference decisions were made behind locked doors.

(2) Concern over improving the lot of colonial populations was shown by setting up the mandate system of the League of Nations. But colonial claims were hardly adjusted in a "free, open-minded, and absolutely impartial" manner, with as much weight given to "the interests of the populations concerned" as to "the equitable claims of the government whose title is to be determined."

Four points were put down as completely or substantially unfulfilled:

(1) Freedom of the seas was not achieved, nor even defined.

(2) The removal of economic barriers was not furthered.

(3) The reduction of armaments was agreed upon only in a statement of general intention. No "adequate guarantees" were provided that the intentions would be carried out.

(4) Whether "all Russian territory" was evacuated depends on the definition of "Russian territory." Certainly "all questions affecting Russia" were not settled in a way that would "secure the best and freest co-operation of the other nations of the world in obtaining for her an unhampered and unembarrassed opportunity for the independent determination of her own political development and national policy and assure her of a sincere welcome into the society of free nations under institutions of her own choosing; and, more than a welcome, assistance also of every kind that she may need and may herself desire." [5] At the moment Wilson presented the Versailles Treaty to the Senate, the United States and other Allied countries were using economic pressure against the Bolshevik regime, and Allied troops were fighting Red troops in an attempt to overthrow the new Russian government.

Four points won, two partially achieved, four substantially lost—hardly a rousing score. Of the four points won, three were the kind of provision that might well have been written into an old-fashioned peace.[6] Of the points lost, one—reaching rapport with Russia—Wilson himself had called the "acid test" of the settlement. Specific territorial changes made at the conference, especially the virtual cession of Shantung to Japan and the drawing of the eastern boundaries of Germany, flatly violated the Wilsonian principle of national self-determination. And this was to have been a "peace without victory." Yet the Versailles Treaty attributed to "the aggression of Germany and her allies" sole responsibility for the war, and Germany was saddled with heavy reparations to expiate its guilt. The establishment of the League of Nations may have been an exciting departure in a direction that most progressives had made their own, yet even this proposal brought little enthusiasm in reform circles. Could a league tied to such a treaty, Clarence Darrow phrased the widespread feeling,

[5] *Messages and Papers of Woodrow Wilson* (Review of Reviews Corp., 1924), I, 468–70.

[6] Points 1 and 2, the evacuation and restoration of Belgium and France, were merely carrying out the immemorial practice of making the loser pay. The Polish settlement—like so many previous Polish settlements—was one that met traditional French security concerns.

prove anything except "the machinery for fastening an unjust and war-breeding peace on the world"? [7]

The whole settlement, many progressives charged, was permeated with hatred and vindictiveness, the kind of kicking of a fallen enemy which has immemorially left the victim spoiling to strike back. The fight against ratification of the treaty created weird alliances—the *New Republic* and the *Chicago Tribune*, Robert La Follette and Warren G. Harding—and sometimes it was difficult to distinguish between the arguments in the extraordinary collection of distortion and billingsgate which made up much of the debate. Yet one line of division was usually clear. Most conservatives who opposed the treaty argued that it was too soft on Germany and did not adequately protect American national interests. Most progressive opponents said that the treaty was too hard on Germany and betrayed the idealism of the Wilson formula.

The most common progressive attitude was summarized, and enormously encouraged, by a book published in the middle of the Senate debate over ratification. John Maynard Keynes, a Cambridge economist, had been serving as a British expert at the peace conference, and he resigned as soon as he was sure what the main outlines of the settlement would be. Angry and dejected, Keynes wrote to General Smuts his feeling that "one ought to do something about what was happening in Paris—revelation, protestation." The South African shared Keynes's unhappiness at the treaty and suggested that Keynes should write "a clear connected account of what the financial and economic clauses of the Treaty actually are and mean, and what their probable results will be. It should not be too long or technical, as we may want to appeal to the plain man more than to the well informed or the specialist." [8]

The book Keynes hastily wrote, *The Economic Consequences*

[7] *Messages and Papers of Wilson*, I, 469; *Papers Relating to the Foreign Relations of the United States* (Government Printing Office, 1947), XIII, 413; Darrow, quoted in an interview with the late Charles A. Beard.

[8] Sarah G. Millin: *General Smuts* (Faber & Faber, London, n.d.), II, 255–6.

of the Peace, was neither long nor technical. It had so much appeal for the general reader that it became a best-seller on both sides of the ocean, and in time exerted an extraordinary influence over thinking in Western civilization. Keynes gave the peace conference all the drama of a struggle between Good and Evil. Good was represented by the Fourteen Points; Bad was the policy of the vindictive peace, incarnate in Georges Clemenceau, the cynical old Frenchman who had "one illusion—France; and one disillusion—mankind, including Frenchmen, and his colleagues not least." Evil had won, Keynes declared, and produced a treaty that was "a web of sophistry and Jesuitical exegesis," an expression of "senseless greed overreaching itself." The stupidest and most outrageous parts of the treaty, Keynes argued, were its economic clauses, particularly the type and extent of reparations imposed on Germany. These reparations would lead to immediate economic misery in the defeated country, would prove so onerous that the Allies could collect only by forcing Germany into servitude, and would serve as a continuing unsettling influence in the economy and the peace of the world.[9]

Keynes was no less sure of the reason for Evil's triumph; Woodrow Wilson had ignominiously failed to uphold the Fourteen Points. In some of the most savage polemical passages in English literature, Keynes pictured the President as a "blind and deaf Don Quixote," talking pious platitudes while he was outmaneuvered by hardheaded Old World diplomats. The President's näive self-righteousness, Keynes flailed away, not only permitted Clemenceau and Lloyd George to turn the treaty into a document of vengeance. It even blocked consideration of the German protest about the peace, and thus any chance to retrieve mistakes. For Wilson to entertain the idea of revisions meant that he had previously accepted imperfections, and "this was exactly what the President could not admit; in the sweat of solitary contemplation and with prayers to God he had done *nothing* that was not just and right. . . . The President was set. His arms and legs had been

---

[9] Keynes: *The Economic Consequences of the Peace* (Harcourt, Brace & Howe, 1920), pp. 32, 51, 103.

spliced by the surgeons to a certain posture, and they must be broken again before they could be altered. To his horror, Mr. Lloyd George, desiring at the last moment all the moderation he dared, discovered that he could not in five days persuade the President of error in what it had taken five months to prove to him to be just and right. After all, it was harder to de-bamboozle this old Presbyterian than it had been to bamboozle him; for the former involved his belief in and respect for himself." [1]

General Smuts was shocked at this assault on Wilson in a book he had encouraged, but he did not miss the reason why so few other people were shocked. "The truth is," Smuts later remarked, "America wanted a reason for denying Wilson. The world wanted a scapegoat. At that opportune moment Keynes brought out his *Economic Consequences of the Peace*. There were a few pages about Wilson in it which exactly suited the politics of America and the world's mood . . . and they led a fashion against Wilson that was adopted by the Intelligentsia of the day." [2] Of the American intelligentsia in 1919, an overwhelming percentage were progressives. No group had been more idolatrously attached to Wilson's Fourteen Points; none felt more crushed at reading the peace terms. Most American progressives were desperately anxious to deny Woodrow Wilson and they embraced Keynes's book with the delight of an apostate watching the desecration of his old god. [3]

Once again the *New Republic* capsuled the general reform situation. The confidence that Wilson was going to create a shimmering new world died hard with the journal's three major editors, two of whom had overcome their repugnance for war only by their ecstatic expectations concerning the peace. As

---

[1] Ibid., pp. 41, 53–5. The italics are Keynes's.

[2] Millin, II, 174.

[3] George Soule remarked in 1946: "Keynes's brilliant and engaging book has, ever since its publication in 1919, determined the attitude of liberals throughout the world" (review of Etienne Mantoux: *The Carthaginian Peace*, in *New Republic* [October 28, 1946], CXV, 559). Though 1946 is a somewhat late date to make the statement (World War II naturally had an important effect on progressive attitudes toward Germany), the observation certainly checks with general progressive literature and statements up to 1939.

reports of deals and compromises drifted back from Paris, Croly, Lippmann, and Weyl canceled each worry about Wilson with blasts at "the machinations of the Tories, the imperialists, and the exponents of an international order founded on power instead of justice and good faith." [4] They chastised Wilson, they warned him, but they stuck by him. Then, on a lilting spring day, the full telegraphic text of the treaty arrived at West Twenty-first Street, and spring disappeared from the office of the *New Republic*. Lippmann took the leadership in denunciation of the President for having brought back a treaty that broke faith both with Germany and with America's moral obligations to the world. That week, the dignified beige cover of the *New Republic* carried tabloid-type print. It read:

THIS IS NOT PEACE

Americans would be fools if they permitted themselves to be embroiled in a system of European alliances. America promised to underwrite a stable peace. Mr. Wilson has failed. The peace cannot last. America should withdraw from all commitments which would impair her freedom of action.

A short while later the *New Republic* started serializing Keynes's *Economic Consequences of the Peace*.[5]

III

BUT WAS it all the fault of the old Presbyterian? Had it been simply a battle between Good and Evil, in which Good faltered at the critical moment?

Shortly before it came out against the Versailles Treaty, the *New Republic* carried a revealing editorial. As if in apology for the repudiation it was about to announce, the journal explained that it had guided its course "by the light of one fixed principle.

---

[4] Ibid. (December 7, 1918), XVII, 146.
[5] Robert Morss Lovett: *All Our Years* (Viking, 1948), p. 172; interview with the late Philip Littell; *New Republic* (May 24, 1919), cover. Keynes was serialized in the issues of December 24, 1919 to January 21, 1920.

We insisted upon the fundamentally political and moral significance of the controversy between Germany and her opponents. . . . We were . . . accepting the major premise of the pro-Ally propaganda which had proclaimed from the start the superior political righteousness of the Allied cause." [6] The "fundamentally political and moral significance," the "superior political righteousness"—this was interesting language for progressive intellectuals to be using. For a long time progressives had been intensely suspicious of just such phrases and had been demanding that all political and moral ideas must be subjected to the pragmatic test: what results from believing them? They had especially emphasized that abstractions brought forward out of the past were likely to justify the status quo. Could it be that the old Presbyterian, who was shocked to discover so wicked a world in Paris, had not brought it any very new preachment? Could it be that American progressives, in the stress of a war situation, had accepted precisely the type of ideas which, in domestic affairs, they had insisted upon reinterpreting by Reform Darwinism? Could it be that progressives had proclaimed an essentially conservative peace program and then were indignant when they got an essentially conservative peace?

At the bottom of the Fourteen Points and the whole Wilson formula were the three ideas of national self-determination, democracy, and international law and order. Each of these phrases can mean very different things, but in the Wilson formula accepted by most American progressives the meanings were carried over from the nineteenth century. In dealing with the whole nationality question Wilson quite correctly said of himself that he depended on "tradition and habit." [7] "National self-determination," in his use of the word, did not call for a nationalism especially adapted to progressive purposes. It was essentially the same nationalism conservatives had been preaching for years. Every language, so far as it could be arranged, was to have its own state; that—simply that—was the important thing.

[6] "The Test of Events," *New Republic* (April 5, 1919), XVIII, 290.
[7] Quoted in Ray Stannard Baker: *American Chronicle* (Scribner, 1945), pp. 495–6.

As the Wilsonian plea for national self-determination caught fire around the globe, it raised formidable obstacles in the way of achieving some of the most important points in the larger Wilsonian program. A world in the throes of an enormously stimulated nationalism had little inclination to make peace without victory, to reduce armaments, to cut down tariffs, or to consider colonies in the genuine spirit of the mandate system. The Versailles settlement as a whole was notably successful in achieving national self-determination, so much so that Winston Churchill could write in 1929: "Probably less than 3 per cent. of the European population are now living under Governments whose nationality they repudiate; and the map of Europe has for the first time been drawn in general harmony with the wishes of its peoples." [8] It was significant that the high-Tory Churchill considered this achievement important, and that Europe in 1929 seemed to most American reformers a tragedy of snarling nations, overworked peasants, underfed industrial workers, and a middle class that was in danger of proletarianization. [9]

The Wilsonian cry for "democracy" did not carry a totally conservative impact. Its influence was progressive to the extent that it encouraged change, and change in the direction of representative institutions, civil liberties, and the separation of church and state. To a certain extent the drive for democracy was an ally of economic and social reform, for the kind of government it encouraged was more likely to put through progressive legislation. Yet the major influence of the democracy called for by the Wilson formula was conservative. Its emphasis was on parliaments, votes, and civil liberties, and from Henry George through Wilson's New Freedom period, reformers had been pointing out that a conception of democracy which was largely political could easily be subverted to the purposes of powerful vested interests. The political democracy glorified by Wilsonianism certainly

---

[8] Winston S. Churchill: *The Aftermath* (Scribner, 1929), p. 11.

[9] Harold L. Ickes has remarked of his fellow progressives: "In the early Nineteen-Hundreds, the reform element was inclined to ignore Europe; in the Twenties, the general tendency was to look down your nose at it as an utter failure, especially because of its rampant nationalism and its failure to solve economic problems." Interview with the late Mr. Ickes.

helped create the peace that American progressives condemned as reactionary. In the name of protecting such democracy, England and France imposed the economic terms on Germany which Keynes denounced so angrily. Wilson himself, appealing only for political democracy, was unable to rally world lower-income opinion to back the one important economic change the Fourteen Points advocated, the reduction of tariffs. And even while the peace conference met and gave its blessings to emerging political democracies, the new governments were falling under the control of economic cliques that made the new Europe strongly resemble the old America of the Eighties.

Most importantly, the kind of democracy that Wilson and the progressives were talking had a lot to do with the failure of the peace conference in the "acid test," the handling of Russia. At the time Wilson first used the phrase, Russia was undergoing a change toward a democratic system, the Kerensky revolution, and the test could have been easily met if Russia had stopped there. But before the peace conference assembled, the Bolsheviks seized control and announced that true democracy meant drastic economic change brought about under a dictatorship of the proletariat. Wilson and even Lloyd George wanted to continue to treat the Russians as if they had a right to do what they pleased within their own borders, but every conservative voice in the world, shouting Wilson's slogans concerning the glories of political democracy, demanded the quarantining and quick extermination of the "Bolshevik plague." Wilsonianism was buried under the onslaught of anti-Wilsonians flaunting Wilson's democracy. The anti-Bolshevik fury sat at every conference meeting, driving every decision farther right. At home, American progressives had long since learned how appeals to sheer political democracy could serve conservatism, but their perception seems to have vanished at the ocean's edge.

The most striking deviation of American progressivism in foreign affairs from its attitudes in domestic affairs was the enthusiasm for international order in the form of the League of Nations. The League was based on the assumption that the nations of the world had a harmony of interest in the general good of peace, and that this harmony could be reached by each country's pursuing its own interest within the framework of the League. This assumption was precisely the premise of laissez faire in domestic affairs, which the progressives had attacked so vigorously. They had argued that no harmony of interests between the units in a society can be assumed; that phrases like the "general good" usually cloak the interest of some dominant group or groups; that general good in any real sense cannot be reached by the untrammeled pursuit of individual interest. Had the American progressives applied the same method of thinking to Wilson's League, they could hardly have emerged with a favorable attitude.

In 1939 the British scholar Edward H. Carr applied the same method of analysis and concluded: "The doctrine of the harmony of interests . . . is the natural assumption of a prosperous and privileged class, whose members have a dominant voice in the community and are therefore naturally prone to identify its interest with their own. In virtue of this identification, any assailant of the interests of the dominant group is made to incur the odium of assailing the alleged common interest of the whole community, and is told that in making this assault he is attacking his own higher interests. The doctrine of the harmony of interests thus serves as an ingenious moral device invoked, in perfect sincerity, by privileged groups in order to justify and maintain their dominant position." Thus, Carr maintained, the kind of internationalism represented by the League of Nations was a method through which the nation or nations on top organized to stay on top and threw the onus of "disturbing the peace" on underdog nations that wanted to challenge their supremacy. It called for no surrender of any national interests in behalf of the international good, any more than John D. Rockefeller's laissez faire called for the surrender of Standard Oil interests in behalf of the national good. It set up an international system dominated, through Big Four control of the all-important League Council, by the powers that had won the war, and it called that domination peace.

In striking argument for his thesis, Carr carried the analysis into the period after World War I and traced the trend of fiercely nationalist fascist countries toward the use of extra-national conceptions as they began to see themselves dominant in Europe. After Munich, Hitler depicted Germany as the leader in a "New Order" that would prove a bulwark of peace, while Mussolini borrowed the British formula concerning the possibility of settling all disputes by peaceful means. "This is the symptom," Carr wrote, "not of a change of heart, but of the fact that the Axis powers are now approaching the time when they may become strong enough to espouse internationalism. 'International order' and 'international solidarity' will always be slogans of those who feel strong enough to impose them on others." [1]

For the peace of mind of pro-League American progressives, it was probably a good thing that the United States did not join the organization. Their own customary methods of analysis suggested that their disillusionment could only have been more complete. For the peace of mind of American progressives, it was also probably a good thing that Wilson did not win all his Fourteen Points and thereby keep progressive support behind his foreign policy. The Wilsonian approach not only contained a self-defeating emphasis on nationalism and political democracy. The whole program, with its nationalist basis and its call for political democracy, its limitation of economic change to tariff reduction, and its laissez-faire League, was a replica in international affairs of the domestic liberalism advocated by men like Tilden and Schurz. The best possible world it could have created would have been the society of Grover Cleveland, which progressives of 1917 found so woefully inadequate. Wilson and the reform movement of his time might be full-blown progressives in domestic affairs. In their thought about foreign affairs they were a full generation behind, back of the New Freedom and the New Nationalism, back of Populism, all the way back to the severely limited liberalism of 1872.

[1] Carr: *The Twenty Years' Crisis* (Macmillan, London, 1939), pp. 102–12.

IV

THE YOUNG progressive intellectual, Harold Stearns, mulled the situation over in his Greenwich Village flat and decided it was time for a book. When the volume appeared, in 1919, it bore the sweeping title: *Liberalism in America*, and in fact the work takes its place along with Croly's *Promise of American Life* as a broad-ranging study of modern American reform.

Personally, Stearns was no Croly, agonizing out his thoughts in the loneliness of shyness and of an austerely intellectual background. Stearns came to reform by being the son of a widowed mother who never made quite enough money as a nurse and by working at odd jobs in plants where discontent was epidemic. Romping through his Harvard years on a slipshod of finances, he played poker not to exorcise Auguste Comte but because he liked to play poker. He had his try at every pretty girl in Cambridge, his period with every off-beat thought, his general conclusion that change could hardly fail to be an improvement. On graduating, he promptly joined the *avant-garde* of New York and Chicago, earning his living writing or editing for progressive journals. Stearns was quite handsome, quite devoted to the better world, quite troubled, and when Woodrow Wilson decided that democracy required a war, he reached for another drink. Exempt from the draft because of his now dependent mother, he was soon working with unaccustomed concentration on the book that pondered why so many of his reform friends did not share his skepticism of the Wilson formula.

Much of Stearns's *Liberalism in America* was standard progressive anti-war argument, presented with a kind of contemptuous charm and an insight that kept the discussion above the level of a La Follette polemic. When Stearns attempted a synthesis of reform thought, as he did in the early chapters, his points were so general and so obviously tied to his isolationist views that he half-apologized for them in his Preface. The man who always thought of reform as "so many men and women acting very much like men and women" really reached his milieu when he discussed the human problem involved in the progressive's reaction to the war.[2]

Ordinary timidity, Stearns argued, was important in persuading many progressives that the Wilson program would further progressive ends. Being persuaded was far more comfortable than doubting; it permitted a person to keep the feeling that he was a reformer while avoiding the costs of criticizing the official interpretation of the war. These costs, Stearns emphasized, could be great. In the frenzied atmosphere of 1918 they might well include a man's job and were almost certain to include most of his friends and much of his prestige in the community.

Along with timidity there was ambition, often combined in the same reformer. The Administration, Stearns charged, deliberately played on the *arriviste* psychology. "Many young men with radical inclinations who might otherwise have been irritating 'outside' critics, many college professors who were known to possess to an uncomfortable degree a mind of their own, were seduced from their independence by being invited into the service of the government and by the hint that possible careers were in store for them. Hundreds dreamed so ardently of being invited to the peace conference that they ignored the unpleasant realities around them. . . . In New York I wondered if all my acquaintances were in some branch of government service; indeed, there was one period when in self-protection one had to pretend one was on some mysterious government mission in order to avoid the suspicion of one's friends that one was in the secret service." With obvious hyperbole, Stearns added: "The bold critics were committed to prison; the more amenable ones were taken into the government and committed to keeping their mouths shut." [3]

Yet whatever the importance of these factors, Stearns recognized, they could hardly have been the whole explanation. Many reformers had amply proved that they were not timid and that they were not ambitious to the point of permitting their thinking

---

[2] Quoted in the Littell interview.

[3] Stearns: *Liberalism in America* (Boni & Liveright, 1919), pp. 109, 110. Quoted by permission of the Liveright Publishing Corp.

to be subverted to personal aggrandizement. The more important question, then, was how men and women who were courageous, sincere, and intelligent progressives accepted so easily a formulation of war aims that helped defeat their purposes. It was in trying to answer this question that Stearns produced his most perceptive points, some of them certainly true, others revealingly half-true. Most difficult to challenge was Stearns's basic contention. An onrush of events, he argued, hurtled the United States toward war, and in the confusion and tension of such a decision any man was likely to show his weakest powers of analysis. Progressives were rendered especially uncritical of war ideology by their customary habit of thinking, the pragmatism of Reform Darwinism.

Criticism of pragmatism had to be inferred from Croly's *Promise of American Life*. Stearns, writing after the way of thinking had rushed ahead to extremes and after it had been subjected to the harsh test of war, went at pragmatism with savage directness. He began with the fact that pragmatism denied absolute truth, thus stripping ideas of any compelling emotion and encouraging a state which Stearns was already willing to call spiritual ennui. This ennui, he maintained, prepared them to accept simple war slogans with a sense of relief, for a simple slogan made war a battle between Good and Evil to which a man could give his unconstrained emotions. The reform thinkers, Stearns stated in one of his brilliant half-truths, "intensely wanted something to believe in, something worth fighting, and if need be, dying for. And, I believe, we here have the reason why the masses, after the first emotional wave of excitement and change, usually sickened of the war much more quickly than the intellectuals who were conducting it from the top. They at least were not wholly corrupted by the spiritual malaise of the era; unlike their intellectual betters, they still believed in something." [4]

Whatever the truth of this point, it could, of course, apply only to intellectuals. Stearns's analysis took on broader application when he moved to the second difficulty inherent in pragmatism, the way it can turn into a doctrine of expediency. Moral con-

[4] Ibid., p. 176.

siderations, more and more progressives had come to argue, are relative to time, circumstance, and the goal you want to reach; the test of a means is whether it achieves the end that is sought; the end, in short, justifies the means, or at least puts up a powerful argument for it. The pragmatic attitude toward ends and means, Stearns argued, greased the way to acceptance of the Wilson formula.

The emphasis of the pragmatic-minded reformer, Stearns pointed out, was on "utility" and "efficiency" in achieving the end that he had decided was good—in this case, military victory over the Central Powers. Making the world safe for democracy might be a vague and dangerous expression of progressive purposes, but it was an "effective" slogan. The extreme suppression of civil liberties might contravene the core of progressive doctrine, but it "contributed to the war effort." The Wilson formula might be inadequate, but going along with it was more "useful" than opposing it. In illustration of the way pragmatic methods of thinking gave practical reasons for acquiescence, Stearns described what happened when he asked his reform friends whether they were worried by the Wilson formula. Often Stearns got the answer that the friend certainly was worried. "When I asked why he did not come out in the open with his fears and doubts the retort invariably was . . . 'Is it not better to keep quiet, to select from the Administration's activities those which are in a liberal direction, emphasize them, call public attention to them, and attempt to strengthen the hand of the government wherever it is liberal, possibly influencing it and giving it enough courage to go even further?' " [5]

"Can there be much doubt," Stearns went on, "that during the war the pragmatists gave almost as much of a sacrosanct glamour to the word utility as the militarists in their turn did to the word preparedness? When you said that a certain method of action, a certain way of doing things in the political field, a certain technique of controlling public opinion, had a higher utility value than any other corresponding method, way, or technique, had

[5] Ibid., p. 107.

you not said the most valuable thing about it? Had not you given it the highest praise? " Actually, Stearns countered, "the pragmatists were always talking about utility when they really were talking about processes. For as you could usually floor the militarists by asking them plainly what the preparedness was 'for,' similarly the pragmatists were dreadfully embarrassed when you suggested that the utility of a method had absolutely no meaning until a previous question had been answered, 'utility for what?' . . . The plain truth is that method and technique are subsidiary to ends and values in any rational philosophy of politics or life, and that the pragmatists were so busy studying method that they had small time left for studying the purposes to which that method was to be applied." [6]

Such an approach, Stearns concluded in a phrase that was to haunt the reform movement, was "the technique of liberal failure," the practice of being very analytical until further analysis becomes embarrassing. "Succinctly, it was the method of compromise; and it might be maliciously described as the method whereby one hopes to control events by abandoning oneself to them. . . . Pushed to extremes, indeed, it becomes a justification for almost anything. . . . It is a philosophy so enamoured of mingling with the warm living stream of everyday that it turns with ferocity upon any claims for ethical resistance to the main current of events. It is typically American in the sense that it is a philosophy which is afraid to be alone." [7]

All of this was disturbing enough, but the most disturbing point made by Stearns's *Liberalism in America* was not inside the covers of the book. The author had practiced no limited technique in his own thinking about the war and the peace. He had subjected Wilsonianism to a thoroughgoing economic interpretation and he had come out where any such thinker had to come out—antiwar, skeptical of the League of Nations, isolationist with respect to the issues of 1919. A second important attempt at a general treatment of modern American reform had turned out precisely

---

[6] Ibid., pp. 179-80.
[7] Ibid., pp. 183-4.

like Herbert Croly's *Promise of American Life*, more significant as criticism than as synthesis, more disquieting than hopeful. Directly or by implication Croly's book had pointed up four tortuous difficulties in progressivism's approach to domestic affairs. Stearns's *Liberalism in America* suggested other difficulties, this time in the field of foreign affairs, and they were also so difficult to solve that they approached being dilemmas. No nation ever has been able, or ever will be, to embark on a positive foreign policy completely detached from considerations of markets, investments, and raw materials. Hence, if a progressive applied the economic interpretation of Reform Darwinism to foreign policy, as Stearns did, how could he fail to emphasize the economic factors that produced the revulsion and isolationism of a Stearns? But most reformers, at the moment of international crisis, had not wanted to be isolationists. They were convinced that national and humanitarian considerations beyond any economic interpretation called for war and the League of Nations. Pushing aside economic interpretation, seeking to bring about the greatest possible national unity, encouraged to be expedient by their own pragmatism, how could they avoid being swept into acceptance of essentially traditional ideas, which, because they were traditional, helped produce a conservative peace?

V

THIS WAS an especially complex difficulty. Any suggestion of it immediately aroused disturbing thoughts of responsibility for the thousands of young men who had died in battle. Stearns's book flared briefly in reform circles, then fizzled out on the twenty-five-cent shelves of bookstores. Progressives were in no mood for an intricate, disturbing dilemma. They were disillusioned, angry, filled with a self-righteous sense of betrayal. They were interested not in difficulties within but in devils without.[8]

[8] One interesting exception to the rule that progressives tended to look for the troubles without was Walter Lippmann's review of Stearns, in *New Republic* (December 31, 1919), XXI, 150-1. Lippmann emphasized progres-

Progressives who condemned both the specific terms of the Versailles Treaty and the League found their chief devil in Woodrow Wilson. The Keynesian portrait of the sanctimonious fool being bamboozled by Old World cynics was repeated in a hundred different forms, each variation adding its own vehemence. Progressives who hated the peace terms but who favored American entrance into the League had their own variety of blaming Wilson. Out of stubborn egotism, they charged, the President turned down all compromise with the Senate opposition and thus made rejection of the League a certainty. These progressives were also inclined to attach horns to the Senate opposition to the League, particularly the opposition leader, Henry Cabot Lodge, a choice target for reformers because of his general conservatism and narrow partisanship. The corporal's guard of reformers who supported the whole Versailles Peace naturally had the widest variety of devils. They could blame most politicians or publicists, conservative or progressive.

Whatever their special devils, an overwhelming majority of the progressives were done with Wilsonian internationalism. More and more they reverted to their pre-1917 emphasis. Domestic affairs became the central interest; to the extent that international affairs were thought about, the concern was for freedom from entanglement with "power politics" or "imperialism," for disarmament, above all for peace, almost for peace at any price. Economic interpretation reasserted its primacy in progressive thinking. This, of course, made American entrance into World War I a blunder and any similar intervention, an unthinkably repetitious folly. A shrug of hopelessness usually greeted talk of a world organization that would be anything more than a façade for greed and chauvinisms.

Progressives throughout the United States smiled understand-

---

sivism's "apathy about administration, its boredom about the problem of organization, its failure to make its own what may be called roughly the constructive tradition of Alexander Hamilton," and the closely allied habit of "a shrinking from intellectual effort . . . [an] urban temper and tolerance . . . [which] easily confuses itself with something very close to indolence."

ingly at the story of Charles Beard's last venture in internationalism. In 1928 the new Yugoslav nation was being racked by
quarrels between its Serbian and Croat populations, and the government asked Beard to come over and blueprint a solution. After
weeks of intricate labor he worked out an administrative set-up
that was approved by both the Serbian and Croatian leaders. The
next day a Serbian deputy rose to his feet in the Yugoslav Parlia-
ment, pulled out a pistol, and shot the Croatian leader and two of
his followers. Beard packed his bag with a definitive snap of the
lock.

"Let Dorothy Thompson settle the problems of Europe," he
rasped as he returned to his concern with the United States. "I
can't." [9]

In this climate of opinion, progressives who had opposed the
war acquired the garland of I-told-you-so. The *Nation*, editorializing on Croly's death at the end of the Twenties, smugly pointed
out how it had never made "the grave mistake of yielding to the
belief that if only the United States entered the war it could
dictate the peace and thereby assure a much better world." [1]
Among intellectuals, admiration for the martyred Randolph
Bourne took on the extremes of a cult; among all types of progressives, reform Congressmen who had voted against the war
achieved a new authority. In 1924 the progressive movement came
as close as it had ever come to naming an official leader. That
year the American Federation of Labor, the Railroad Brother-
hoods, the moderate socialists, the *New Republic*, the *Nation*, and
hundreds of progressive organizations joined in sponsoring a third
party. And the candidate of this coalition, its unifying force, was
Robert M. La Follette, who believed in 1924 as in 1917 that
American entrance into any war or any international organization
was a betrayal of progressivism. [2]

---

[9] Beard interview.
[1] "Editorial on Herbert Croly," *Nation* (May 28, 1930), CXXX, 613.
[2] Naturally, however, there was some tug-and-pull over foreign policy.
See Kenneth C. MacKay: *The Progressive Movement of 1924* (Columbia
University Press, 1947), especially p. 146.

CHAPTER XIII

The Shame of the Babbitts

IT WAS shortly before Christmas 1920, and William Allen White was writing to his old friend Ray Stannard Baker, but the best the genial White could manage in the way of season's cheer was: "What a God-damned world this is! . . . If anyone had told me ten years ago that our country would be what it is today . . . I should have questioned his reason." [1]

Something or somebody had certainly damned the world of reformer William Allen White. In the White House a bitter, broken Wilson awaited death and Harding. Too ill to know much of what was going on, too changed to care very deeply, the one-time progressive hero headed a country that was racing to the right. Congress whooped through pro-corporation legislation, the courts interpreted New Freedom laws in a way that harassed unions and encouraged trusts, official and unofficial Red-hunts hounded reformers even more relentlessly than the wartime inquisition. In the midst of it all, the crowning symbol of the drive for conformity, the nation decreed that anyone who drank a liquid containing as much as one two-hundredth part of alcohol was a criminal. From the sickroom in the White House came a weakly worded veto of the Prohibition enforcement act. It was the last gasp of Wilsonian progressivism.

[1] Walter Johnson, ed.: *Selected Letters of William Allen White* (Holt, 1947), p. 213.

The Shame of the Babbitts

A few months later Warren Harding's amiable smile broke over the inaugural crowd. The new President's father once spoke a three-sentence biography of his son. "Warren, it's a good thing you wasn't born a gal," the old man said. ". . . You'd be in the family way all the time. You can't say No." [2] Harding couldn't say no to politicians wheedling privileges for corporations. He couldn't say no to jobseekers like the Reverend Heber H. Votaw, whose qualifications to be Superintendent of Federal Prisons consisted of having been a missionary in Burma and a Republican in Ohio. He couldn't say no to a gang of thieves that swept into Washington with him, including jolly Jesse Smith, who used to hum "My God, how the money rolls in" while he sold federal favors from the notorious little green house at 1625 K Street. Jesse Smith's friend in the White House did manage three positive achievements. The President, according to his mistress, left behind an illegitimate daughter, conceived in the Senate Office Building shortly before his nomination.[3] He added "back to normalcy" to the American language because he misread the correct phrase that a professor had written for him.[4] And he took a firm stand on the tariff. "We should," the President of the United States told a reporter, "adopt a protective tariff of such a character as will help the struggling industries of Europe to get on their feet." The reporter rose and left the room, speechless.[5]

After Harding there was Coolidge and after Coolidge there was Hoover. As President, Coolidge permitted no flagrant boodling, made no additions to the language or to the population. Hoover was not only virtuous and grammatical; he was intelligent. He had,

[2] The story was told by the President himself in an off-the-record National Press Club speech. Quoted in Samuel H. Adams: *Incredible Era* (Houghton Mifflin, 1939), pp. 7–8, and, in a slightly variant form, in Cabell Phillips *et al.*, eds.: *Dateline: Washington* (Doubleday, 1949), p. 61.

[3] Adams, pp. 232, 234–41, 262–3; Nan Britton: *The President's Daughter* (Elizabeth Ann Guild, New York, 1927), *passim.*

[4] Interview with the late Jacob Hollander, professor of political economy at Johns Hopkins and a long-time adviser to Republican Presidents. Hollander had written the speech, which included the correct phrase: "back to normality."

[5] The reporter was Bruce Bliven. Quoted in Stewart H. Holbrook: *Lost Men of American History* (Macmillan, 1946), p. 329.

besides, entered the White House something of a darling among reformers. He wore the garland of a humanitarian for his war relief work, and had shown his interest in new thinking by offering to purchase stock in the *New Republic*. Hoover's Presidential candidacy was first pushed by progressive journalists, against the strong opposition of old-guard Republicans (even Mary Ellen Lease, in the early Twenties, was hailing Hoover as "one sent by God").[6] But reformers soon discovered that intelligence, or respectability, or even feeding the Belgians was not quite the point. Under Hoover and Coolidge, no less than under Harding, government proved increasingly responsive to the will of corporations.

Economists have long since made plain the real nature of the prosperity of the Twenties. The national income was fabulously high, unemployment was relatively low, but the control of the country's industries was steadily concentrating and the returns from the increased national wealth were not proportionately distributed. The Twenties were another intensive period of trust-building, new combines constantly forming, old combines gaining new power through the holding-company device or through establishing links with international cartels. By their ability to control prices, these giants brought unprecedented wealth to a few and substantial gain to thousands of skilled workers and white-collar employees, while small business was also generally prosperous. For the rest of the nation the glow of prosperity was largely reflected heat. Statisticians with no strong ideological bent have agreed that about $2,000 was the minimum necessary to provide a family with the decencies during the Twenties, and almost one third of the breadwinners received less than $2,000—one fifth, less than $1,000. Child labor was increasing; all industrial laborers had to face new dangers to their health from the speed-up of mass

---

[6] Letter of Robert M. Lovett to me, February 23, 1945; Walter Lippmann in "Herbert Croly," *New Republic* (July 16, 1930), LXIII, Pt. 11, p. 252. John Gunther has written: "One interesting story is that FDR tried to make Hoover declare himself as a Democrat in the early 1920's because he thought he would be a perfect candidate to succeed Wilson" (*Roosevelt in Retrospect* [Harper, 1950], p. 272). The Lease quotation is from the *Kansas City Star*, March 29, 1931.

production and new risks of unemployment from the onrushing technology.

To the farmers the Twenties brought another disaster. In the years immediately after the Armistice farm prices took the sharpest drop in American history. In 1919 a bushel of corn bought five gallons of gasoline; a year later it bought one gallon; one year more and it bought half a gallon. Throughout the Twenties, farm prices never went up enough to stop an ominous increase of tenant farming in the South and in the Midwest. The distress of the farmers was so great and their political power so concentrated that a number of governmental moves were made to aid them. But even the farmers never got the legislation they wanted most, the McNary-Haugen bill, and the general reaction of government to the maldistribution of prosperity was to aid in distributing it still more unequally.

Business triumphant, of course, included a reconquest of the American mind by conservatism. With no widespread protest, an official United States Government publication defined democracy as "a government of the masses. . . . Results in Mobocracy. Attitude toward property is communistic—negating property rights. Attitude toward law is that the will of the majority shall regulate, whether it be based upon deliberation or governed by passion, prejudice, and impulse, without restraint or regard to consequences. Results in demagogism, license, agitation, discontent, anarchy." Conservative Darwinism reasserted itself in a thousand sleek apostrophes to the economic jungle. Walter Rauschenbusch's Jesus of low food prices had become Bruce Barton's Jesus as the prototype of the go-getting businessman. Magazines that only a few years before were deploring the unbridled competitiveness of the marketplace now featured articles on "It Is Up to You," "What a Whale of a Difference an Incentive Makes," and "The Bookkeeper Who Refused to Stay Put." [7]

---

[7] Quoted or cited in Merle Curti: *The Growth of American Thought* (Harper, 1951), pp. 696, 699. Barton's *The Man Nobody Knows* remained a best-seller for two years.

If any one man was the American folk hero of the Twenties, unquestionably the man was the winner in the race for automobile millions, Henry Ford. The peevish, erratic manufacturer did his best to fray the halo. He conducted his business with a coarse tyranny. He succumbed to a whole menagerie of fads, announcing that crime could be cured by changes in diet, and that cows, which were lazy besides being crime-breeding, "must go." He proved himself an ignoramus by financing assaults on a supposed Jewish conspiracy to rule the world, and a coward by wriggling for weeks to avoid appearing in the libel trial that ensued. The halo simply would not fray. The American people played mah jong, devoured five million telegraphed words on the murder of the Reverend Mr. Hall and his choir-singer mistress, repeated with M. Coué: "Day by day in every way I am getting better and better," and made Henry Ford a major threat for the Presidency of the United States.[8]

For progressives, here was certainly a post-Civil War all over again, only worse. Reform in the Seventies and Eighties had the buoyancy of a movement that was just taking the offensive. Progressivism of the Twenties was a beaten army, muscles aching, its ranks seriously depleted. As the new era opened, so the story goes, Herbert Croly went home and refused to see anyone for three days. On the fourth day he summoned his editors to his office and told them that progressivism was finished. "From now on we must work for the redemption of the individual." Then Croly began bringing to *New Republic* luncheons a bearded Englishman named Orage, who explained that what the world needed was the self-discipline of yoga. Croly's death in 1930, some of his friends believed, was hastened by forcing his frail body through the rigors of the cult.[9]

[8] Keith Sward: *The Legend of Henry Ford* (Rinehart, 1948), pp. 107–9, 125–31, 146–60, 305–27; Frederick L. Allen: *Only Yesterday* (Harper, 1931), pp. 79–84. It was characteristic of Ford's prying paternalism that he tried to foist his anti-nicotine and anti-alcohol opinions on his employees. Sward, pp. 107–8, and "Smoke Rings at Ford," *Newsweek* (November 10, 1947), XXX, 61.

[9] Interviews with Mr. Alvin Johnson and the late Philip Littell. Orage, a British editor, was connected with an establishment near Fontainebleau

Others found a less strenuous escape. Thousands were like the progressive the authors of *Middletown* talked to in Muncie, Indiana. With witch-hunters thrashing through the state, this man was no longer signing petitions or making speeches at the town meeting. "I just run away from it all to my books," he explained resignedly.[1] Still other progressives turned to the cushion of cynicism, or to expatriation, which offered the delights of disillusionment on a devaluated franc, or to the exhilaration of Socialism or Communism. The varieties of Marxism that were winning American converts before 1917 were certainly not made less attractive by the progressive debacle at Paris and at home. Besides, as Robert Morss Lovett has remarked in his autobiographical account of the Twenties, only from Russia did there seem to be any light breaking on the world.[2]

In the middle of the Twenties, the remaining progressive aspirations, ignored by the leaders of both the Republican and the Democratic organizations, found their natural outlet in the third-party effort headed by Robert La Follette. The election of 1924 was La Follette's last campaign, and pathos surrounded the exit of the gallant old battler. Two generations of reformers swung to his support; the famous pompadour, now totally gray, bristled as belligerently as ever, flame still leaped from his words. But when the votes were counted, the ticket had polled only seventeen per cent of the total—about ten per cent less than Roosevelt's third-party vote in 1912. In seven months La Follette was dead, finally exhausted by his thirty years' crusade, scarcely concealing his bitterness that progressivism had become a nagging aunt unwanted in the cozy rendezvous of business and America.

---

called the "Gurdjieff Institute for the Harmonic Development of Man," which emphasized attaining spiritual regeneration through ritualistic extreme physical activities. A number of well-known people became devotees, including Dorothy Caruso, the singer's wife, and Katherine Mansfield. Isabel C. Clarke: *Katherine Mansfield* (Beltane Book Bureau, Wellington, Australia), pp. 16, 39–49; J. Middleton Murry: *Journal of Katherine Mansfield* (Knopf, 1927), pp. 246–55; Dorothy Caruso: *Dorothy Caruso: A Personal History* (Hermitage House, 1952), pp. 145–91.

[1] Robert S. and Helen M. Lynd: *Middletown* (Harcourt, Brace, 1929), p. 494.

[2] Lovett: *All Our Years* (Viking, 1948), p. 178.

Why the failure of progressivism in the Twenties, reformers asked themselves then and have continued to ask. The most common explanation boiled down to two points: the effects of the war and of an atmosphere of general prosperity. Unquestionably these factors were important. In the modern history of many countries war has frequently exalted the large-scale businessman and smothered discontent; hard times certainly have increased the appeal of programs for change. But it is possible to make these explanations carry too heavy a load, as Professor Arthur M. Schlesinger has suggested in an essay on "The Tides of National Politics." From the beginnings of political parties in the United States to the anti-Fair Deal Congressional landslide in 1946, Professor Schlesinger maintained, the country has shifted eleven times from "conservative" governments to those which represented an inclination for change. Analysis of the eleven instances indicates that "the worsening of material conditions invariably disturbs the political waves, but, unless reinforced by other factors, does not affect the deeper waters." Foreign wars, he continued, offer no more satisfying an explanation. "These conflicts have taken place about equally in conservative and liberal periods, sometimes coming at the start, sometimes at the end and sometimes midway." [3]

What's more, explaining progressive weakness in the Twenties by prosperity and war suggests the same type of incomplete analysis as explaining the progressive debacle at the peace conference by blaming Woodrow Wilson. Both explanations were the natural kind for progressives to make—they assigned the whole fault, or almost the whole fault, to factors external to progressivism. But placing Jeffersonian, New Freedom progressivism alongside Crolyite, New Nationalist progressivism has revealed important deficiencies in both varieties of reform. Going at the problem in this way suggests that war and prosperity, in addition to being causes of the progressive decline in the Twenties, provided the circumstances that brought out progressivism's own inner difficulties. These difficulties lost followers for reform, rendered less effective

[3] Arthur M. Schlesinger: *Paths to the Present* (Macmillan, 1949), pp. 87, 88.

certain factors on which the progressives had depended heavily, and made the rule of conservatives more disastrous to progressive purposes.

II

AT THE heart of traditional, Jeffersonian progressivism had been a faith in the people, or, more specifically, in the majority. The trouble with America was that the people did not really rule, most reformers had argued; democratize government, and government would really serve the whole community. The years immediately surrounding the war brought climactic successes in the drive for more democracy. By the time of the Armistice, the direct election of United States senators had been made mandatory by a Constitutional amendment. Direct primaries were in operation in all but four of the states; the initiative and referendum, in almost a half; the recall, in scores of state and municipal governments. Within a year after the Armistice, and partly as a result of the war, the woman-suffrage amendment was ratified. With that, a far larger percentage of American citizens could participate in the processes of government than ever before in the history of the country. And the results that appeared during the Twenties in no way justified the hopes and the claims of the progressives.

The most conspicuous result was the lack of any result. The initiative, referendum, and recall were invoked sparingly, and to a lessening extent. When the techniques were used, they produced no significant change in the political and economic situation. The experience of California, probably the most active direct-democracy state during the Twenties, was revealing. The initiative was employed in attempts to license "naturopaths," to close barbershops on Sunday, and to create the Klamath Fish and Game District; referendums were staged in efforts to get rid of laws enforcing the Volstead Act, to increase the registration fee on trucks, and to prohibit shingle roofs in incorporated places. A wide variety of groups, practical-minded and crackpot, turned to the new devices. But when the decade was over, two political scientists reviewed the California experience and emerged with this "indubitable fact": direct democracy had changed California very little.[4]

No more perceptible effect came from the direct elections of senators, unless it was in increasing the chances of a candidate with a talent for demagogy. As early as 1912 the reform-minded political scientist Charles Merriam had sighed: "Some bosses are wondering why they feared the law; and some reformers why they favored it." [5] The primary did seem to make political bosses interested in picking a candidate who could appeal to the general public more than the rival faction's candidate. But one of the shrewdest and most intensive students of democratic processes, Professor V. O. Key, Jr., has concluded that in general the direct primary left elections where they had always been, in the hands of party managers. If reform forces were strong enough to make the bosses recognize them within the primary, Professor Key pointed out, they were also strong enough to force approximately the same degree of recognition under any nominating system.[6]

Woman suffrage made the most spectacular lack of difference. Elections became no cleaner, no glow of motherly kindness spread over the industrial scene. In election after election large numbers of women failed to use their hard-won ballots. (In 1924 the estimated percentages of males and females voting were sixty-five and thirty-five, respectively.) When women did vote, the fact that they were women did not seem to matter particularly. Using the data available after a decade of woman suffrage, observers concluded that sex had less to do with determining a vote than place of residence, wealth, occupation, race, nationality, or religion.[7]

[4] V. O. Key, Jr., and Winston W. Crouch: *The Initiative and the Referendum in California*, in *Publications of the University of California at Los Angeles in Social Sciences* (1939), VI, 462–3, 475, 496, 572.
[5] Quoted in Evans Woolen: "The Direct Primary Experiment," *Atlantic Monthly* (July 1912), CX, 43.
[6] V. O. Key, Jr.: *Politics, Parties, and Pressure Groups* (Crowell, 1948), pp. 350–72. "With the exception of the 1912 campaign," Harold Faulkner added, ". . . [the Presidential preferential primary] has been of little significance." *The Quest for Social Justice* (Macmillan, 1930), p. 87 n.
[7] Hugh L. Keenleyside: "The American Political Revolution of 1924," *Current History* (March 1925), XXI, 839; Stuart A. Rice and Malcolm M.

The Shame of the Babbitts

The history of the woman's movement itself suggested how right the observers were. Hardly had the suffrage been won when some organizations, speaking largely for upper-income women, began pushing an Equal Rights Amendment, which removes from the statute books all laws that distinguish between males and females. Promptly the Women's Trade Union League filled the air with feminist hair. Workingwomen were more workingwomen than they were equalitarians. They wanted those laws saying that *women* could not be worked more than a certain number of hours, or that *women* had to be given a minimum of one day's sick leave each month.

Where were "the people" of the progressives, those individuals who, if they were only given the opportunity, would vote into law the interests of the majority, male and female, worker, farmer, and manufacturer? Such a people, as Herbert Croly had long since emphasized, never really existed; "the people" were a collection of special-interest groups. Whatever reality there may have been in the progressive conception of the people was almost completely dissipated as a result of developments climaxing in the decade of World War I. For years the increasing specialization of society had been encouraging occupational groups of all types to organize for the protection and advancement of their interests, and now the trend was tremendously accelerated. By creating a need for the speedy recruitment of specialists, the war put the government in a situation where, for the first time, it dealt with large numbers of people not as uncategorized citizens but as doctors, or historians, or cement experts. By speeding up the urbanization and mechanization of American society, both the war and the years immediately around it made the unorganized individual far more a cog in the wheel, far more conscious of being alone in a complex and potentially cruel maze. Occupational organizations

Willey: "American Women's Ineffective Use of the Vote," ibid. (July 1924), XX, 641–7. But there is also some evidence that women tended to the conservative or "moral" side of issues. Malcolm W. Willey and Stuart A. Rice: "A Sex Cleavage in the Presidential Election of 1920," *Journal of the American Statistical Association* (December 1924), XIX, 519–20.

leaped up in importance. Where they existed, they acquired new powers and prestige, within the occupation and with respect to the general community. Where they did not exist, their formation was greatly encouraged.

During the Twenties, these guilds functioned with the mixture of social and antisocial attitudes that has always impelled such groups. In the controls they established over admission to the occupation, there was an element of wanting to guarantee qualified personnel—and an element of limiting competition. In their efforts to establish codes of proper practice, there was concern for good craftsmanship—and concern to restrain the maverick who might forget the interests of the occupation in his eagerness to serve the community. By the end of the Twenties the seventy-five-year-old American Medical Association, exalted to enormous power and prestige during the war, was providing a classic example of how "the people" manifested themselves through an occupational organization. Only extreme critics doubted that a good deal of AMA policy was motivated by a desire for good doctoring. Only the AMA doubted that a good deal of its policy was also motivated by concern over the fees and the éclat of doctors.[8]

The trend was still plainer in the groups on which progressives had depended so heavily as "the people"—the industrial workers and the farmers. The only organization that could pretend to speak for any large body of workers during the Twenties, the American Federation of Labor, had always stood, as President Gompers said, for getting "more and more—and then more" for the particular minority it represented, the organized skilled workers.[9] But before the war the AFL contained a powerful faction

[8] In his thorough study of the increasing gildification of American society, Prof. J. A. C. Grant has emphasized that the occupational groups have often revealed their self-interestedness most importantly by their exercise of control over the state regulations affecting them. "We may take it for granted," he concluded, "that unless they are curbed, regulation will be primarily in the interests of the group rather than of the public as a whole." "The Gild Returns to America," *Journal of Politics* (August 1942), IV, 336.

[9] Quoted in Edward Levinson: *Labor on the March* (Harper, 1938), p. 7.

which kept pushing it toward policies that were concerned with a group broader than its own membership. After the war, and partly as a result of the war, the AFL suffered serious reverses, its membership plummeting down twenty-five per cent between 1920 and 1923, its ability to organize unions and win strikes hamstrung by injunctions and hostile public opinion. Under these circumstances, concern over anybody else seemed a luxury even to many a long-time idealist in the ranks of the organization. With increasing ease, Gompers pushed aside the dissident members as "visionaries" and "ideologues."

In the election of 1924 the AFL flabbergasted thousands of progressives by acting like the AFL. Both the Republican and the Democratic conventions had ignored labor so contemptuously that rank-and-file resentment ran high, and the AFL executive committee endorsed the La Follette ticket. Before the week was out, headquarters began hearing from local AFL chiefs, who saw their carefully constructed arrangements with Democratic or Republican political machines endangered. Bit by bit Gompers whittled away the force of the endorsement. First he announced that the AFL backed only the candidacy of La Follette, and not his third party. Then he added that the AFL did not necessarily agree with the reasons any other group might have for backing La Follette. As the campaign went on, Gompers did nothing while large units of the AFL publicly repudiated La Follette or privately knifed his candidacy as their part of deals with old-party organizations. By election day AFL support amounted to little more than the Gompers statement that "Bob La Follette is a great American," a statement that is assigned its proper force by recalling that, shortly before, Gompers called the Atlantic City bathing-beauty contest "the greatest treat I was ever afforded." [1] Watching the AFL performance during the election, a British Labour spokesman suggested that the whole matter of cooperation between American labor unions and reform intellectuals had resolved itself into the question of "whether, or how far, the in-

---

[1] Quoted in *New Republic* (September 20, 1922), XXXII, 82.

tellectuals can afford to recognize the vested interests of the labor movement." [2]

A month after the election the octogenarian Gompers called his chief lieutenants to his deathbed and spoke a final message to his old friend James Duncan, head of the granite-cutters. "I have kept the faith," Gompers murmured. "Tell them I expect them to keep the faith." [3] The lieutenants solemnly nodded, and when one of the group, William Green, took over the presidency of the AFL, he not only kept the faith but improved upon it. The plump, mild-mannered Green, fervent Baptist, Odd Fellow, and Elk of Coshocton, Ohio, looked like a small-town businessman, and he was a businessman whose business happened to be the AFL. The policy most associated with Green permitted the AFL to operate still more effectively for its own interests. He brought to a stage of high development the practice of presenting his unions to businessmen as a bulwark against "radicals" with plans to reform society in general. This service the AFL was glad to perform, the Green line ran more or less explicitly, in return for better terms for such human beings as might be members of the AFL. The philosophy of the AFL, explained President Green, "is not academic. It is practical." [4]

The principal organization of farmers was no less practical. As part of the New Freedom legislation for the farmer, the federal government had begun providing funds for county agents, whose statutory function was to set up local farm bureaus through which knowledge of modern agricultural methods could be spread. Shrewd farmers quickly saw the possibilities of building political organizations around these bureaus. The prerequisites were more money to use in building the bureaus and the means of attracting farmers to them. The war brought the money. "Food Will Win the War," the government proclaimed, and the appropriation for county-agent work was trebled by the time of the Armistice.

[2] William Orton: "American vs. British Progressivism," *New Republic* (March 11, 1925), XLII, 62.
[3] Quoted in Levinson, p. 3.
[4] Quoted in V. O. Key, Jr.: *Politics Parties and Pressure Groups* (Crowell, 1942), p. 78.

Agricultural hard times after the war brought the farmers to the bureaus in droves and added large sums for bureau work from manufacturers of agricultural implements, who knew well that poor farmers made poor customers. By the end of 1921 the state bureaus had been welded into the powerful American Farm Bureau Federation, under the presidency of James R. Howard.

The portly Howard had no yearnings to remake society. He grew up on a comfortable Iowa farm, graduated from the University of Chicago without learning to place the farm problem in any national setting, then returned to his 480-acre tract single-mindedly devoted to the proposition that the political role of the farmer was to get high prices and cheap credit for the farmer. With this attitude, he naturally modeled the Farm Bureau after the American Federation of Labor. The organization concentrated its membership drives among the more successful farmers, corresponding to the skilled craftsmen of the AFL. In further parallel to the AFL, the Bureau showed little interest in the rest of rural America and avoided issues that had to do with general reform. "I stand as a rock against radicalism," Howard said in an address that could have been a paraphrase of any one of a number of William Green's speeches.[5] In his eagerness to show that the Farm Bureau was "practical," Howard liked to point out that his organization was actually set up in the offices of the Binghamton Chamber of Commerce in Broome County, New York. Progressive publicists sourly agreed. They charged an understanding between the Farm Bureau and the National Association of Manufacturers: the Bureau would go along with demands for inflated industrial prices, the NAM would go along with demands for inflated farm prices, and both would attack labor.

The Farm Bureau was so completely a representative of one group among the farmers that two smaller organizations, representing different categories of farmers, continually fought it. The venerable Grange, its membership narrowed largely to the Northeast, spoke the special interests of farmers whose produce

[5] Quoted in Orville M. Kile: *The Farm Bureau Movement* (Macmillan, 1921), p. 118.

was sold mostly in the domestic market. The National Farmer's Union, its membership centered in Oklahoma, Kansas, Nebraska, the Dakotas, and Colorado, represented men operating near-marginal lands. During the Twenties a number of other agricultural groups organized on a commodity basis and pushed their own interests with the ideological blinders of a Henry Ford or a William Green.

The farmer's participation in the campaign of 1924 was a caricature of "the people" fighting for general reform. At the opening of the campaign, agricultural distress was so great that all indications pointed to a tremendous vote for La Follette in the rural areas. But even at the height of the enthusiasm, speakers trying to argue the importance of a progressive program for the nation as a whole were interrupted by shouts of "What's all that got to do with the price of hogs?" Halfway through the campaign, food prices swerved suddenly upward, and thousands in the agricultural regions forgot all about their interest in reform. In James Howard's Iowa the farmers themselves revived an ancient wisecrack and gave it the terminology of the Twenties. "When corn is $1.00 a bushel," they chuckled, "the farmer is a radical; when it's $1.50 a bushel, he's a progressive; and when it's $2.00 a bushel, he's a conservative." [6]

The question of Herbert Croly came back hauntingly. In relying on "the people" to promote national reform, wasn't the progressive asking special interests not to act like special interests?

III

A FEW YEARS before La Follette was defeated, Bagdasar K. Baghdigian walked up to the registration desk of a Kansas City school and struggled through an application for courses. The teacher glanced at the Armenian name and snapped: "Oh, give that up and change your name to Smith, Jones or a name like that and be-

---

[6] Quoted in Arthur Garfield Hays: *City Lawyer* (Simon & Schuster, 1942), p. 270, and from an interview with the late George W. Norris.

come Americanized. Give up everything you brought with you from the Old Country. You did not bring anything worth while anyway."

Baghdigian froze into group consciousness. "The Turkish sword," he told himself, "did not succeed in making me become a Turk, and now this hare-brained woman is trying to make an American out of me. I defy her to do it." After that, Baghdigian recalled later, "I was more of an Armenian patriot than I had ever thought of being." [7] And after that he was a perfect symbol of the rapid accentuation of another type of special interest in the United States.

The trend had been spurred on by two quite different developments. Wilson's appeal to nationalism during the war had an electric effect within the United States. Czech, Slovak, and Polish immigrants, pouring funds into movements for the creation of an independent Czechoslovakia and Poland, became a good deal more nationality-conscious in all their attitudes, and every other American group felt the surge of nationality feeling. This positive effect of Wilsonianism, important as it was, proved less significant than the kickback from another wartime phenomenon.

Until 1917, most Americans, progressive or conservative, had glided along in the happy illusion that the melting-pot was working with great efficiency. But as soon as the foreign-policy issue became acute, the country split into a babble of groups, many of them obviously influenced by Old World ties. Suddenly it was plain that the melting-pot had failed in important respects, and this revelation provoked the campaign that made sure the melting-pot would fail still more. After the Armistice a call for "Americanization" sounded across the country. To informed and humane people, Americanization might still mean the old progressive policy, the two-way procedure of bringing all the American people into a common community. But for an overwhelming percentage of the Americanizers, the campaign quickly turned into the process that Baghdigian met; the whole population was to be insulted

[7] Bagdasar K. Baghdigian: *Americanism in Americanization* (Burton Publishing Co., Kansas City, 1921), pp. 17–18.

and browbeaten into "one-hundred-per-cent Americanism," which meant what the local guardians of Americanism defined as the ways of white, Protestant Americans who were not recent immigrants. Such Americanization stimulated all racial, religious, and nationality prejudices, and the resulting discrimination hurried all minorities along the way to minority chauvinism.

The Twenties saw the reaction of Bagdasar Baghdigian repeated time and again. Scores of organizations sprang up to assert that their members, no matter how much the Americanizers shrilled, were still Armenian patriots, Irish patriots, or Scandinavian patriots. In the previous generation it was not difficult to find prominent Catholics who were so leery of marking out Catholics from the general population that they opposed parochial schools; by the mid-Twenties the newly created National Catholic Welfare Conference was busily co-ordinating the segregation of Catholics, hurrying them toward parochial schools, a Catholic Boy Scouts, a Catholic Daughters of America, and a Catholic Total Abstinence Union, not to speak of the election of a Catholic Mother of the Year.[8] Among the Jews and Negroes, the groups hit hardest by the intolerance of the Twenties, the long-running trends toward inward-looking minority feeling speeded up two- or three-fold. "Until the Twenties," one Zionist leader, Stephen Wise, has recalled, "we were a movement. Then we became an avalanche, and we tumbled along with us many a boulder of Jewish respectability." [9]

Negro nationalism leaped ahead to its own full-blown Zionism. The leader was a chubby, elegantly mustached immigrant from the West Indies, Marcus Aurelius Garvey, who had organizational abilities worthy of a Gompers and a flair for publicity which no muckraker had excelled. Establishing himself in Harlem in 1916, Garvey summoned his fellow Negroes to have done with

[8] For a pre-World War I instance of opposition to parochial schools by a prominent and Church-approved Catholic, see Charles J. Bonaparte: *The Catholic Church and American Institutions* (no pub., 1889). (Bonaparte was subsequently awarded the coveted Laetare Medal by the University of Notre Dame.) I have been unable to find any similar instance during the Twenties.

[9] The late Stephen Wise, in an interview.

The Shame of the Babbitts

"boot-licking" organizations like the National Association for the Advancement of Colored People, and mulattoes like William Du Bois, who could not possibly understand the national glories of the black man. "As much as the white man may boast of his glorious deeds to-day," Garvey blustered, "the fact remains that what he now knows was inherited from the original mind of the black man who made Egypt, Carthage and Babylon, the centres of civilization, that were not known to the unskilled and savage men of Europe." So glorious a race deserved its own home. The immediate necessity for the Negroes was a "Back to Africa" movement, which would give all the black men of the world their "motherland." When "the Jew said, 'We shall have Palestine,' " Garvey added, "we said, 'We shall have Africa.' "

Soon Garvey had churned black America into a chauvinistic froth by his inflammatory speeches, wild receptions for Negro dignitaries, and resplendent parades in which uniformed troops and "Black Cross" nurses chanted:

> *Oh, glorious race of mighty men*
> *The homeland calls to you.*

An estimated one hundred thousand Negroes were buying subscriptions to Garvey's journal, and, according to Garvey's wife, ten million dollars poured in to pay for the "Black Star" ships that were to carry the American Negroes "home." At the height of Garvey's influence, about 1921, his organization boasted the largest membership of any Negro society in American history: four million dues-paying enthusiasts. In Europe, nervous chancelleries pondered the possible effects of the "Back to Africa" movement on their delicate colonial arrangements.[1]

---

[1] Quoted from Truman H. Talley: "Marcus Garvey—the Negro Moses? " *World's Work* (December 1920), XLI, 163; Garvey: *Aims and Objects of Movement for Solution of Negro Problem Outlined* (Press of the Universal Negro Improvement Association, New York, 1924), p. 8; Garvey: "The Negro Race," *The Blackman* (May–June 1934), I, No. 5, p. 16 (a succinct expression of a point Garvey made from the beginning of his agitation); Amy J. Garvey, ed.: *Philosophy and Opinions of Marcus Garvey* (Universal Publishing House, New York, 1923), p. 52; Rollin L. Hartt: "The Negro Moses," *Independent* (February 26, 1921), CV, 206.

The leader never quite got around to mundane details. He was too busy making his ornate offices still more ornate, supporting a bevy of very nationalistic and very good-looking women, equipping, gazetting, and knighting the aristocracy of the coming black empire. The United States Government, skeptical about Garvey's use of the mails, sent him to Atlanta Penitentiary in 1925, but even this did not entirely quash him. Negro political pressure secured Garvey's release in return for his deportation, and he went on agitating in the freedom of Jamaica. When Garvey died, in 1940, the decorous *Journal of Negro History*, which lived conspicuously above sex and parades, chose to point out that if Garvey was a criminal, "he was no more a criminal . . . than thousands of other persons in the business world." Besides, he was the only well-known American Negro who did not owe his prominence "mainly to white men." [2]

Few educated Negroes were captured by the rococo Garvey, but many went on sympathetically reading W. E. B. Du Bois, who, in one important sense, was an honest and a sophisticated Marcus Garvey. Though the brilliant official of the NAACP showed no sympathy for "repatriating" Negroes to Africa, he was increasing his emphasis on the point that Negroes were a separate people and should act as one. For all of Garvey's scurrilous attacks on him, Du Bois could never quite get himself to repudiate the Negro Zionist completely. Garvey's methods were "bombastic, wasteful, illogical," but he was also a "sincere" leader, speaking for "one of the most interesting spiritual movements of the modern world." Du Bois's intense racialism became most clear in 1919, when he began organizing "Pan-African Congresses," where representatives of Negroes from all nations were to plan "concerted thought and action." The trouble with progressivism among white Americans, Du Bois declared, was that it "did not envisage Africa and the colored peoples of the world. They [the progressives] were interested in America and securing American citizens of all and any color, their rights." Most Negroes made

[2] "Marcus Garvey," *Journal of Negro History* (October 1940), XXV, 592.

the same mistake. "They felt themselves Americans, not Africans. They resented and feared any coupling with Africa." [3]

Pan-Africanism easily blended into the more general movement that is often called the "Black Renaissance." On the surface, this Renaissance was simply an exciting and long overdue recognition of Negro talent. Publishers suddenly found that Negroes could write highly salable books, Negro musicals became the vogue, night-rounders discovered that many ebony clubs offered a better show than the monotonous gyrations of white thighs on Broadway. But in the mind of the Negro, the Renaissance increasingly became an expression of the chauvinism that was marking all minority life. Negroes complained about the white invasion of "our" night clubs, campaigned to have Negroes deal only in Negro stores and read only Negro newspapers, and started a drive to substitute the term "Afro-American" for "American Negro." An Association for the Study of Negro Life, headed by a man who announced that he hated "interracialists," made rapid progress among Negro intellectuals.[4]

The psychology of many of the Negro writers was expressed by James Weldon Johnson, a major literary figure in the Renaissance as well as the executive secretary of the NAACP. The writing of which Johnson was most proud was his "Negro National Hymn," which he wrote in a "feverish ecstasy" and could never hear performed without reliving the ecstasy. Editing a group of Negro poems in 1922, Johnson asserted that the Negro was "the creator of the only things artistic that have yet sprung from American soil and been universally acknowledged as distinctive American products." When some readers were aghast at the statement, Johnson compounded his racialism by adding a footnote in

---

[3] W. E. B. Du Bois: *Dusk of Dawn* (Harcourt, Brace, 1940), pp. 275, 277–8.

[4] Interviews with the late Fiorello La Guardia and Ray Stannard Baker; Carter Woodson: "An Accounting for Twenty-five Years," *Journal of Negro History* (October 1940), XXV, 425-6. The most recent student of Garveyism itself has pointed out that its widespread influence came not so much from its promised-land feature as from its credo of racial chauvinism. Robert M. Brisbane, Jr.: "Some New Light on the Garvey Movement," ibid. (January 1951), XXXVI, 59.

the second edition which conceded, perhaps, that skyscrapers were of some importance and not an invention of Negroes. Nor did Johnson fail to get around to the argument that always seems to creep into embittered chauvinisms—our women are better-looking than your women anyhow. Writing his autobiography at the end of the Black Renaissance, Johnson paused to emphasize that Negroes too often accepted white ideals of beauty. He had once actually compared the types, said Johnson, and it was clear that "the Negro woman, with her rich coloring, her gayety, her laughter and song, her alluring, undulating movements—a heritage from the African jungle—is a more beautiful creature than her sallow, songless, lipless, hipless, tired-looking, tired-moving white sister." [5]

And the progressive in the midst of all this? By the Twenties, urban influences had marked reform so deeply that the progressive who spoke Anglo-Saxonism was rare and was promptly denied the label "progressive" by most reformers. Edward Ross, still alive, was already history, and was bluntly told so every time he bemoaned "race suicide." The progressive of the Twenties was outraged by the blatant bigotry of the period, and out of outrage, his sympathies, his admiration, went to the Negro or Jew or Armenian immigrant who reared back and tried to declare his self-respect. Since declaring self-respect so often took the form of minority chauvinism, the progressive's emotions easily swept him toward acceptance of, or at least failure to attack, the mounting glorification of group.

The effect of this acquiescence on progressivism during the Twenties was mixed. To the extent that minorities identified the interests of their group with a reform cause, the reform received the additional impetus of powerful clan feelings. Al Smith, a much more progressive candidate than Herbert Hoover, was aided in the Presidential election of 1928 by thousands of conservative Catholic votes, which went to him only or primarily because he

---

[5] James W. Johnson: *Along This Way* (Viking, 1933), pp. 121, 155; Johnson, ed.: *The Book of American Negro Poetry* (Harcourt, Brace, 1922), p. viii, and 1931 ed., p. 10 n.

was a Catholic. La Guardia was ardently backed in his campaigns for Congress by many slum-dwelling Italians and Jews, whose fervor for him was compounded of an approval for his program and an enthusiasm for his descent.[6]

But the available evidence on the point suggests that progressivism was hurt rather than helped by the rising group consciousness. The more employees felt identified with the homeland or a particular race or religion, the easier it was for employers to divide and conquer them. "We want you," the United States Steel Corporation displayed the pattern in sending out instructions during a strike, "to stir up as much bad feeling as you possibly can between the Serbians and the Italians. . . . Call up every question you can in reference to racial hatred between these two nationalities."[7] In the political field, closer identification with a nationality group, the Negro community, or the Catholic Church —the minority attachments that were, numerically, the most important in the Twenties—brought the citizen more under conservative influences. The popular picture of the immigrant community as more inclined to radicalism than the older settlers was incorrect, and came from a few conspicuous exceptions. Both Negro and Catholic leadership were markedly conservative. (Clarence Darrow, with pardonable hyperbole, called the hierarchy "the right wing of the right wing," and when the depression struck, it was not surprising that the only Negro Congressman, De Priest, of Chicago, fought federal relief funds.)[8] Most important from the long-range view, the increased tendency toward religious, racial, and nationality feeling was a tendency toward thinking which asked not the progressive question: what is good

[6] La Guardia interview; William F. Ogburn and Nell S. Talbot: "A Measurement of the Factors in the Presidential Election of 1928," *Social Forces* (December 1929), VIII, 175–83; Gilbert C. Fite: "The Agricultural Issue in the Presidential Campaign of 1928," *Mississippi Valley Historical Review* (March 1951), XXXVII, 670.

[7] Commission of Inquiry, Interchurch World Movement: *Report on the Steel Strike of 1919* (Harcourt, Brace & Howe, 1920), p. 230.

[8] Schlesinger, pp. 68–9; Herbert J. Seligman: "The Negro's Influence as a Voter," *Current History* (May 1928), XXVIII, 230; Harold F. Gosnell: *Negro Politicians* (University of Chicago Press, 1935), pp. 319–20, 371. The Darrow quotation is from the Beard interview.

for "the people" as a whole? but rather: what is good for us special few? The question could, by coincidence, aid reform, but movements do not keep their power by coincidence.

IV

NEXT TO "the people," the progressives had put most faith in the federal government. Get Washington more into the national life, they had argued, and because the federal government best represented the general interest, its intervention would further a progressive program. The period of the New Freedom and of World War I gave the federal government great powers and accustomed the public to look to Washington for leadership. The postwar period did not undo the basic developments. And in this field, too, the results hardly fulfilled progressive expectations.

Before 1917 both progressives and conservatives had assumed that leadership from Washington would be leadership by progressives; that was precisely why reformers fought for it and why conservatives fought against it. But the federal actions of the war and immediate postwar years came under a Wilson who had lost interest in progressivism and under a Harding who had never had any. As the government-approved "Red purge" threw opprobrium on any variety of dissent, a decidedly uncomfortable fact became plain: Washington, darling of 1914 progressivism, was proving one of its most dangerous enemies.

By 1923 the hysterical days of hounding readers of the *New Republic* were over, only to highlight another trouble of the reformers. Progressives had been especially enthusiastic about federal economic controls. Yet rule by conservatives made the very conception of controls and the very instrumentalities the progressives had set up work against reform. The conservative administrations of the Twenties abolished none of the regulatory commissions established before the war, and they did not call for the repeal of either the Sherman or the Clayton Antitrust Act. On the contrary, when a new industry, radio, became of importance, Calvin Coolidge's Administration took the leadership in having a federal commission set up over it. What the conservatives did do was to staff the commissions, the antitrust enforcement division, and the courts with men sympathetic to corporations—to "bore from within," in the angry phrase of Senator Norris.[9] The result was not simply that the reform purposes of regulatory legislation were nullified; business was more immune than ever, as the shrewd railroad attorney Richard Olney had predicted, because the paper existence of the laws mollified discontent. Commenting on the Interstate Commerce Commission and the Federal Trade Commission, William E. Humphrey, a decidedly conservative member of the latter, was enthusiastic, and little wonder. The commissions, Humphrey could report, had "reversed" their attitude. They had become "the bulwark instead of the oppressor" of industry.[1]

Businessmen were even taking over the progressive doctrine of putting the government still further into business and were using it for their own purposes. During the war, Wilson had delegated his near-dictatorial economic controls to the War Industries Board, a group dominated by dollar-a-year business executives. Many of the dollar-a-year men went back to their fifty-thousand-dollar-a-year jobs with an idea buzzing in their heads. Perhaps their decades-old battle for "free competition" and against "government in business" had not been wise. They had been given striking proof that federal activity need not be anti-business, and they had seen the advantages that could come from joint operations carried on under federal ægis. The kind of thinking that a few Eastern businessmen like George Perkins and Frank Munsey had been doing in the heyday of Roosevelt's New

---

[9] Norris: "Boring from Within," *Nation* (September 16, 1925), CXXI, 297.

[1] Quoted in Samuel E. Morison and Henry S. Commager: *The Growth of the American Republic* (Oxford, 1942), II, 534. Marriner Eccles, chairman of the Federal Reserve Board during the New Deal, has written of the system during the Twenties: "Private interests, acting through the Reserve banks, had made the System an effective instrument by which private interests alone could be served." *Beckoning Frontiers* (Knopf, 1951), p. 166.

Nationalism now began to seep through chambers of commerce all over the country.

Why not give up the talk about competition and draw firms together in trade associations, which would standardize products, pool information, advertising, insurance, traffic, and purchases, and draw up codes of proper practices? Why not stop fighting the government and work with it in setting up these trade associations? Few of the new business thinkers went so far as Munsey and Perkins had gone. They rarely called for repeal of the antitrust acts, but rather implied that the acts should not be permitted to stand in the way of the fullest functioning of trade associations. Still less rarely did they speak of government regulation; government and industry were to "co-operate." But whatever the importance of these emphases, vanguard thinking among businessmen in the postwar period was not opposed to governmental intervention in economic life. The new thinking was all for intervention—provided that businessmen or business-minded politicians conducted the intervention.

The war had also given ideas to the Farm Bureau leaders. Most of them might continue to believe that anything called government intervention smacked of a horrendous Populism. But the lavish governmental aid to agriculture during the war pointed up the possibilities in government interference which interfered in a way that the Farm Bureau leaders liked. Soon the Bureau was pushing the McNary-Haugen bill, which represented the new type of "co-operation" between government and economic groups applied to agriculture. The bill provided that the federal government would raise certain agricultural prices by arranging the dumping of surpluses abroad, and the arrangements were to be made in a way that might well have had the Farm Bureau functioning as a kind of trade association for its membership.

If the business-minded Republican administrations of the Twenties killed the McNary-Haugen bill with frosty vetoes, they certainly did not oppose the larger philosophy behind it. Despite the White House phrases about "getting back to normalcy" and "rugged individualism," neither Harding, Coolidge, nor Hoover represented the old idea of free enterprise. In particular, Herbert Hoover, as Secretary of Commerce from 1921 to 1929 and then as President, systematically pushed the businessman's type of governmental intervention. The prevailing impression of Hoover as an apostle of economic individualism is not only wrong; it fails to recognize his role in a major ideological development. His engineer's sense of efficiency was outraged by the waste that came with competition, and he emerged from wartime service in Washington with enthusiasm for "a new era of national action, in which the federal government forms an alliance with the great trade associations and the powerful corporations." More specifically, he believed that the federal government should encourage the formation of trade associations and, once they were formed, work with them in the preparation of codes for co-operative activities among the member firms. In 1920 only an estimated dozen trade associations were functioning; when Hoover left the White House, more than two thousand were in existence and many of them had worked out, in association with Hoover or his successor as Secretary of Commerce, codes of close co-operation which virtually ignored the antitrust laws. "We are passing," Hoover proudly announced, "from a period of extreme individualistic action into a period of associational activities." [2]

"Associational Activities"—a new twist to the doctrine of centralization and a new phrase to add beside conservatism, the New Freedom, and the New Nationalism. The reformer's long-standing plea for federal activity in economic affairs was coiling back upon the progressives. Glumly, Vernon Louis Parrington made the point in a letter to a friend: "Wherever power is lodged, a great struggle for control and use of that power follows. . . . Have you been able to convince yourself that the corporate wealth of America will permit a centralized political state to pass out of its control and become an agent to regulate or to thwart its plans? . . . [In the event of corporation control], the stronger

---

[2] Quoted from an interview with the late Hugh Johnson, and Charles A. Beard: *Jefferson, Corporations and the Constitution* (National Home Library Foundation, Washington, 1936), p. 79.

the state, the more . . . serviceable it becomes to the exploiting class. . . .

"You see the dilemma in which I find myself," Parrington concluded. "We must have a political state powerful enough to deal with corporate wealth, but how are we going to keep that state with its augmenting power from being captured by the force we want it to control?" [3]

V

PARRINGTON USED to mull over this problem with J. Allen Smith, his colleague at the University of Washington, and Smith agreed that it was a stickler. But Smith, the doughty old moralist, had his own special worry. "The real trouble with us reformers," he would say, "is that we made reform a crusade against standards. Well, we smashed them all and now neither we nor anybody else have anything left." [4]

Smith had his point; there were enough difficulties developing in progressivism for almost any critic to have his point. Well before 1917, progressive intellectuals had pushed Reform Darwinism far toward the argument that all codes are relative to time, place, and what somebody or some group wants. When war placed thousands in situations where the old sexual morality seemed to have little to do with where they were and nothing to do with what they wanted, many of them were ready for an entirely new approach to the subject of sex. The new approach was at hand, in the doctrine that had so excited Greenwich Village in the Wilsonian heyday. During the Twenties Freud moved up from the Village to the colleges, the art colonies, and the cocktail parties of the nation—to all the better-educated groups, but especially to the circles that had been prepared for the new doctrine

[3] Parrington to Ross L. Finney, January 23, 1929, MS., Parrington Papers, in the possession of Mrs. Parrington.

[4] Quoted from an interview with the late Edward McMahon, a friend of Parrington and Smith.

by Reform Darwinism. "A German scientist can explain perfectly," Sherwood Anderson had one of his characters express the attitude in 1925. "If there is anything you do not understand in human life consult the works of Dr. Freud." [5]

Freud himself thought of his system as a way by which men could better understand themselves and thereby bring their acts under control. But Freud, like many seminal thinkers, was less important for what he meant to say than for what he was said to mean. To many postwar progressives, Freud said that what happens when a male and a female are placed in proximity has nothing to do with any code but results from impulses over which human beings have little or no control. In short, he gave a very scientific-sounding reason for doing what you please and leaving to the psychiatrist the solution of any troubles that might follow. Having been interpreted into this convenient view of sex, Freudianism was applied the more rapidly in all fields of progressive thought and thus provided a capstone to relativism. The Darwinism of progressives had related all men and ideas to the environment. Economic interpretation had emphasized the relationship to economic class. Now Freudianism added the relationship to the unconscious. [6]

"It's all relative," the advanced thinkers chorused, and so it was. Human attributes? Obviously a product of environment. The actions of human beings? Clearly the result of economic and psychical compulsions. Political or religious ideas? Naturally the reflection of property relationships and of mass psychology. Everything was "explained" or "understood" in the bright light of science. The only trouble was that, with everything so thoroughly explained, the human will was reduced to some excrescence out of Victorianism, anything could be justified, and flinging yourself into a cause with the total fervor of a La Follette became obvious proof that you simply hadn't read the latest literature. Here was freedom from all absolutes, from all codes,

[5] Anderson: *Dark Laughter* (Boni & Liveright, 1925), p. 230.
[6] Freud was said to have foreseen the Freud craze in the United States, and to have been sure that most of his American devotees would misunderstand him. Fritz Wittels: *Sigmund Freud* (Dodd, Mead, 1924), pp. 137–8.

and like all such freedom, it brought an enslavement to nothingness.

Dimly, amid the gin vapors and the flights to Reno, a few of the new thinkers began realizing where they had arrived. Like some kind of irritating portent, the novels of F. Scott Fitzgerald kept breaking into the conversation at cocktail parties. This favorite of the progressive intelligentsia, suddenly tumbled through the Army after seventeen years of Midwestern and three more of Princeton certitudes, was in no mood to leave any traditional standard intact. But Fitzgerald lounged amid the smashed pieces with an acute sense of discomfort. "All the stories that came into my head," he recalled later, "had a touch of disaster in them." His brash young men kept turning into "the beautiful and damned" and "all the sad young men." His heroines kept murmuring: "I'm hipped on Freud and all that, but it's rotten that every bit of *real* love in the world is ninety-nine percent passion and one little soupçon of jealousy." [7]

As the Twenties ended, Walter Lippmann, still producing the book for the day with uncanny timing, published his *Preface to Morals*. In 1913 Lippmann's *Preface to Politics* had heralded the glories of the coming emancipation from conservative ways of thinking. Now, in melancholy retrospect, his *Preface to Morals* surveyed freedom's shambles. "We are living," Lippmann wrote, "in the midst of that vast dissolution of ancient habits which the emancipators believed would restore our birthright of happiness. We know now that they did not see very clearly beyond the evils against which they were rebelling. . . . The evidences of these greater difficulties lie all about us: in the brave and brilliant atheists who have defied the Methodist God, and have become very nervous; in the women who have emancipated themselves from the tyranny of fathers, husbands, and homes, and with the intermittent but expensive help of a psychoanalyst, are now enduring liberty as interior decorators; in the young men and

---

[7] Quoted in Arthur Mizener: "F. Scott Fitzgerald," in Willard Thorp, ed.: *The Lives of Eighteen from Princeton* (Princeton University Press, 1946), p. 333, and from Fitzgerald: *This Side of Paradise* (Scribner, 1920), p. 255. The italics are Fitzgerald's.

women who are world-weary at twenty-two. . . . These are the prisoners who have been released. The prison door is wide open. They stagger out into trackless space under a blinding sun. They find it nerve-wracking." [8]

Lippmann had his solution. The difficulties in pragmatism had to be gone at pragmatically; from such an approach would emerge a new code of living, even a new religion, the credo of the "disinterested." Progressive-minded reviewers caressed the *Preface to Morals* in an ecstasy of relief, but the same year, in unintentioned comment on Lippmann's book, Joseph Wood Krutch brought out *The Modern Temper*. With the sensitive thinking that characterized his writing for the *Nation*, Krutch traced the creation of the modern progressive intellectual—his progress through "scientific" Darwinism, economic interpretation, and Freudianism to the belief that all beliefs were fictions agreed upon for particular purposes. That such an approach had been needed and was still needed to combat conservatism, Krutch readily admitted. That beliefs were fictions agreed upon, Krutch did not deny. Then, why not, with Lippmann, consciously agree upon the fiction of a pragmatic code for the laudable purpose of freeing pragmatism from its debilitating results? Krutch's answer was simple—and devastating. "Fictions," he reminded his readers, "served to guide and to control many rebellious generations, but they could do so only because they were not known to be fictions, and they lose their power as soon as we recognize them as such." [9]

VI

But what were the alternatives? Krutch was only too aware that, wherever Reform Darwinism led, conservatism could not

---

[8] Lippmann: *A Preface to Morals* (Macmillan, 1929), pp. 6–7.

[9] Krutch: *The Modern Temper* (Harcourt, Brace, 1929), p. 226. Krutch has sometimes been categorized as a despairing conservative, but in my opinion, his writings do not justify this classification. In 1929 he seems to have approved most of the specific parts of the progressive program and to have gone along with much of Reform Darwinism. His disturbance came from considering where the latter was leading.

be analyzed away, and kept analyzed away, without Reform Darwinism. Vernon Louis Parrington had described the progressive difficulty connected with centralization quite as discerningly. "We must have a political state powerful enough to deal with corporate wealth," but how, his words had hit the point squarely, how "are we going to keep that state with its augmenting power from being captured by the forces we want it to control?" If a progressive assailed minority chauvinisms, how did he avoid giving aid to anti-progressive Americanizers? And if "the people" were acting less and less like the progressives' "people" during the Twenties, what other conception could one turn to, except some variety of totalitarianism?

One or another of these difficulties engaged a good many progressive minds during the Twenties. Yet most reformers, continuing to act very much like human beings, kept right on finding the cause of their failures outside themselves. There were always war and prosperity to explain away the progressive debacle. There were, moreover, at least two ways a reformer could live in reasonable happiness with his difficulties. He could look at them and not see them. Or he could, whether seeing them or not, crusade fiercely for something that did not involve them.

Oblivious of problems within their own movement, flailing the enemy the harder because of their fury of frustration, a corporal's guard of progressives fought on. They filled their journals with scathing analyses of the Henry Fords, manned the old organizations and set up new ones advocating the same type of program, tried to reinforce the little band of reform-minded Congressmen who sometimes showed surprising strength in Washington.[1] In the House, Fiorello La Guardia, clowning, cannonading, and politicking with increasing skill, was occasionally able to build some crazy-quilt coalition into a formidable opposition. In the Senate, the old stand-bys, Robert La Follette, George Norris, and Hiram Johnson, held their seats, their influence increased by seniority and by their votes against the war. There were even

[1] Probably the most important of the new organizations was the American Civil Liberties Union, which emerged from the wartime National Civil Liberties Bureau.

reinforcements—the lean, roistering foeman of Montana copper companies, Burton K. Wheeler, who walked into the Senate so green he had to be cautioned not to smoke in the chamber and six weeks later forced the Attorney General of the United States to resign in disgrace; Wheeler's colleague, the gaunt Thomas J. Walsh, prying off the lid on corruption and then, characteristically, weeping at the sight of the depravity that was making him famous; and, above all, shaggy William E. Borah, of Idaho, as good an orator as Bryan, as rousing a showman as La Follette, as canny a politician as Roosevelt, a one-man party who, through a process no one ever quite understood, usually ended up voting with the progressives. A redoubtable crew, but one which, as La Guardia himself remarked, "were hardly the men to engage in complicated self-criticism." [2]

The progressive practice of not seeing progressivism's inherent difficulties reached a high point in the La Follette campaign of 1924. A few leaders in the third party effort, like the attorney, Donald Richberg, worked hard to have the campaign based on something beyond the traditional reform cries, but their efforts were wasted. The La Follette campaign song, Richberg remarked as he looked back at the election, should have been "Tenting Tonight on the Old Camp Ground." [3]

Simultaneously, many urban progressives of the better-educated group were giving their enthusiasm to a cause that involved no nagging difficulties. Even before the campaign of 1924 was over, they were neglecting La Follette's speeches for the invective that came once a month in a newly founded journal, the *American Mercury*. The magazine's editor, Henry L. Mencken, was hardly in the usual progressive tradition. He looked like a German burgher out of the eighteenth century and, in many ways, he thought like one. Suspicious of anything new, even New York, Mencken valued Pilsner, Beethoven, a sharp sally, or a workmanlike job of bricklaying far more than any plans to change society. Violently contemptuous of ordinary men, he pronounced de-

---

[2] La Guardia interview.

[3] Richberg: *Tents of the Mighty* (Willett, Clark, & Clay, Chicago, 1930), pp. 135–6.

mocracy "the worship of jackals by jackasses," and the American people, "the most timorous, sniveling, poltroonish, ignominious mob of serfs and goose-steppers ever gathered under one flag in Christendom." He flayed all reformers and their "bilge of idealism," lauded "free competition . . . to the utmost limit," advocated wars, aristocracy, and a frank recognition that it made no difference whether the union or the employer won a strike. The *Nation*, Mencken merely "deplored"; the *New Republic*, because it was subsidized by the Straights, had coined for it the famous sneer "kept idealists." As for the *American Mercury*, the first issue made emphatically plain that "the Editors have heard no Voice from the burning bush. . . . The world, as they see it, is down with at least a score of painful diseases, all of them chronic and incurable." [4]

Of course, Mencken, who was at least half Puck, loved to hear the rumble of his own hyperboles, and at bottom he was as much of a reformer as any cornfield Populist. No one outside an insane asylum ever stayed so vitriolic for so long out of sheer cussedness, and Mencken was anything but crazy. He simply had no use for much of the program that had become associated with American progressivism. He was devoted, and passionately so, to the essence of the 1872 liberalism which had been assumed with little discussion by succeeding generations of reformers until the ruthless standardization of the Twenties placed it in real jeopardy—the freedom of the individual to think and act as an individual. Simeon Strunsky was quite right when he suggested that the Mencken approach was really a kind of latter-day muckraking, exposing and assailing The Shame of Prohibition, The Shame of Comstockery, The Shame of the Babbitts. [5]

With powers of scorn unexcelled in American letters, Mencken flailed away at Prohibitionists, Fundamentalists, book-censors,

---

[4] Quoted in Ernest Boyd: *H. L. Mencken* (McBride, 1925), pp. 42–3, 64; Allen, p. 231; interview with the late Philip Littell; Lillian Symes and Travers Clement: *Rebel America* (Harper, 1934), p. 288; and from "Editorial," *American Mercury* (January 1924), I, 27.

[5] Henry S. Harrison: "Last Days of the Devastators," *Yale Review* (Autumn 1928), XVIII, 96–7.

Rotarians, Ku-Kluxers, farm-bloc leaders—anyone who wanted to cajole or force anyone into a pattern. The existence of Prohibition gave Mencken's bastinado a daily workout. The Scopes trial in Tennessee brought his campaign to a rollicking climax. Here was a state forbidding by law the teaching of a doctrine that more than two generations of scientists had accepted. Here was William Jennings Bryan, a three-time nominee for the Presidency of the United States, defending the law to the cheers of thousands. Mencken hurried down to Tennessee, agonized through the insistence that all schoolchildren should accept as literal truth every word in the Bible, and wired back descriptions of rule by "gaping primates" which brought him an avalanche of invitations to leave the United States on the next boat.

Mencken's china-blue eyes took on their most ingenuous softness. Why did he continue to live in America, he catechized himself. "Why do men go to zoos?"[6]

After a few years of the *American Mercury*, Walter Lippmann could call Mencken "the most powerful influence on this whole generation of educated people," and not a few of these educated people were men and women who in 1914 had been busy pushing the political and economic program of progressivism.[7] Reform in the Twenties, as always, included an enormous variety of dissidents, but unquestionably the group that was most articulate and most effective were those who adopted the Mencken-type emphasis. Unlike Mencken, the typical reformer of the Twenties did not actually oppose the political and economic program of progressivism; he simply gave less stress to these problems and more stress to the battle against conformity. Appropriately enough, with the change in emphasis came a change in title, and the group that had called itself "progressive" was now more and more using the old term "liberal." In part, this shift was attributable to a desire to shake free from the clammy aftermath of Wilsonianism. In part, it reflected concern over getting rid of any connection

[6] Quoted in Edgar Kemler: *The Irreverent Mr. Mencken* (Little, Brown, 1956), p. 186, and from Mencken: *Prejudices, Fifth Series* (Knopf, 1926), p. 304.

[7] Quoted in Allen, p. 232.

that could play into the hands of the witch-hunters. (Vernon Louis Parrington, coming to appreciate the well-aged respectability of the term "liberal," went through his manuscript substituting it for "radical." [8]) But most significantly, the revival of the term "liberal" corresponded to the revival of the major concern of dissidence in the late Sixties and early Seventies. Whatever the squeezings of opportunity in the days of Ulysses Grant and of Calvin Coolidge, lack of opportunity was not the problem that protruded most conspicuously. In both periods individual liberty was in danger, and plainly so.[9]

Prewar and entirely new reform figures now engaged in a brilliantly varied campaign for personal and intellectual freedom. The effort was most noticeable in the literary field. Harold Stearns, restless in "the shadows . . . of intolerance," delayed his European exile long enough to edit *Civilization in the United States*, which made each aspect of American life a self-convicting pursuit of sameness.[1] Sherwood Anderson, a puzzled manager of a paint factory before the war, emerged in the Twenties a mordant analyst of the village twisting under respectability. The cherubic W. E. Woodward, a frolicsome socialist in 1912, a restless employee of the Morris Plan Bank in 1920, invented a word and a

---

[8] Parrington to S. Kahan, February 24, 1928, MS., Parrington Papers.

[9] Writing at the beginning of the Twenties, Walter Lippmann attributed the use of the word "liberal" to "that group who were Progressives in 1912 and Wilson Democrats from 1916 to 1918. They wished to distinguish their own general aspirations in politics from those of the chronic partisans and the social revolutionists. They had no other bond of unity. . . . American liberalism is a phase of the transition away from the old party system. But it is an early phase and there is no agreement as to ends or methods. Intellectually it is still more transitional. If it has any virtue at all it is that many who call themselves liberals are aware that the temper of tolerant inquiry must be maintained" (*New Republic* [December 31, 1919], XXI, 150). The substitution of "liberal" for "progressive" in the reform vocabulary had gone ahead steadily during the war, and by the mid-Twenties the use of "liberal" was commonplace (the one notable exception being the use of "progressive" by the third-party effort in 1924). In 1930 a group met in New York City to organize another third party, which would emphasize freeing the nation from "a strangling grip by powerful groups of men and women, narrow and fanatical of mind," and appropriately they called their organization the "Liberal Party." Samuel H. Church: *The Liberal Party in America* (Putnam, 1931), p. 3.

[1] Stearns: *The Street I Know* (Lee Furman, 1935), p. 202.

profession by gaily "debunking" all the icons of the Rotaries and the ladies' clubs.[2] Theodore Dreiser, grimly portraying Sister Carrie in the early 1900's, was grimmer still in his 1925 *American Tragedy* of a boy, a girl, and an illegitimate baby in Lycurgus, New York. Most widely read of all, as savage as Mencken, as wistful as Fitzgerald, as impish as Woodward, Sinclair Lewis came out of a socialist past to assail the Twenties in terms of the pathetic conformity of George F. Babbitt.

"I really didn't have any answers to it all," Lewis once said of his thinking in the Twenties. "I only knew that the answers could come only from free men."[3] The dominant liberalism of the Twenties offered few answers, except from those who found an answer in despair, but at that it served a vital function in the history of American reform. It fought a magnificent delaying action, staving off the complete triumph of the Babbitts, trading positive thinking for sorely needed time.

[2] The word "debunking" originated in Woodward's novel *Bunk* (Harper, 1923), p. 2.
[3] Interview with the late Sinclair Lewis.

✻ *CHAPTER XIV* ✻

Second Honeymoon

IT STARTED like 1873. On October 29, 1929, scrambling, yelling traders dumped 16,410,000 shares of stock on the New York Stock Exchange, and the United States refused to believe what it was watching. A nation returned to the cult of captains of industry did not expect its gods to fail it. "Wall Street may sell stocks," thousands chorused with the *Saturday Evening Post*, "but Main Street is buying goods." After a period of collapsing businesses, people still grinned with the billboards: "Wasn't the Depression Terrible?" Then, as unemployment mounted at the rate of four thousand a week, confidence gave way to worry, worry to bitterness. By 1931 Amos was asking Andy: "Did you hear about the fellow who registered at the hotel and the clerk said, 'For sleeping or jumping, sir?' " [1] The Thirties, like the Seventies, had finally admitted that the captains of industry did not have the situation in hand.

But having started so much like '73, the new depression soon took on far grimmer lines. All the things that had shocked the country in the Seventies reappeared in doubly disturbing form. Small businesses were going down at a rate never before approached, and the number of farmers losing their lands was near-

[1] Quoted in Dixon Wecter: *The Age of the Great Depression* (Macmillan, 1948), p. 13, and Don Ross: "Blue Anniversary," *New York Herald Tribune*, October 30, 1949.

ing the three-quarters-of-a-million mark. Henry George may have been horrified by so much poverty amid so much technological advance. He did not live during a decade when, on the one hand, the New York World's Fair unveiled television, the Rust brothers devised a mechanical cotton-picker, and Clarence Birdseye's frozen foods entered mass production, while, on the other hand, as soon as the truck pulled away from the Chicago garbage dump, "men, women and children . . . started digging with sticks, some with their hands, grabbing bits of food and vegetables." [2] The pillaging and bloodshed of the strike of 1877 had been disquieting, but in the early Thirties, food riots were becoming common, 15,000 angry veterans milled around the national Capitol, and in the Midwest, where the Seventies had produced nothing more violent than Greenback speeches, farmers dragged from his bench a judge who tried to foreclose mortgages, beat him, then strung him up until he fainted.

As the depression ground past its third year, an unprecedented fear seeped through the nation. Would the old America, the America of bountiful opportunity, ever reappear? Men had asked the question before; this time the questioning was much more widespread, much more persistent. Didn't all the violence and talk of violence mean that the United States had reached the iron class lines of Europe? Hadn't the onrush of labor-saving inventions made large-scale unemployment permanent under any system approximating free enterprise? How could the country ever escape the consequences of the final settlement of the West? [3] Perhaps an eighty-year-old Californian had hit it right when

[2] Quoted in Wecter, p. 13.

[3] In an interesting passage Franklin Roosevelt later remarked that when he took office, "millions of people, gripped by . . . fear, had begun to feel that the machinery of modern American economics and Government had broken down so completely under the strain of the new demands placed upon it by modern civilization, that an entirely new type of mechanics for existence would have to be invented. They were not clear in their own minds as to what type they should seek; but their confidence and morale were so shaken that many of them would have been willing to accept any form of specious glittering guarantee of a chance to earn a livelihood." Samuel I. Rosenman, ed.: *The Public Papers and Addresses of Franklin D. Roosevelt* (Random House, 1938), II, 3.

he told his story to the State Unemployment Commission. The depression of 1873 had cost him his job as a machinist, the old man said, but "at that time the whole West was open to Homesteaders. At that time the mountains were honeycombed with . . . new mines. . . . Railroads had been building all over the country. . . . New towns were being opened." A railroad hired him as a section hand, then he went on to the grocery business, until by the Nineties he was prospering. The hard times of 1893 ruined him again, and once more, by homesteading, he climbed back. But now, he was sure in his old bones, there was no way back for him or for millions of younger men. "There isn't an acre of decent land to be had for homesteading," he told the Commission. "There isn't a railroad to be built anywhere. There isn't a chance for a new factory. . . . Years ago Horace Greeley made a statement, 'Young man, go West and grow up with the country.' Were he living today, he would make the statement, 'Go West, young man, and drown yourself in the Pacific Ocean.' " [4]

Gloomy and restive, the nation watched its President finding reasons for hesitating, mincing ahead to small measures, mumbling promises of recovery. Few were sure what should be done; millions were sure that, whatever should be done, this Administration was not likely to do it. As unemployment crossed the thirteen-million mark and corn sank below thirty cents for the first time since the Civil War, the voters swept into office the man who was running against Herbert Hoover. [5]

II

THE VOTERS were reaching desperately into the dark. They knew little about Franklin Roosevelt beyond the luster of his family name, the fact that he had made a good if unspectacular record as

[4] Quoted in California State Unemployment Commission: *Report and Recommendations* (San Francisco, 1932), pp. 94–5.

[5] Estimates of unemployment varied widely. Frances Perkins, Roosevelt's Secretary of Labor, stated that the estimates at the time Roosevelt took office ranged from 13,300,000 to 17,900,000. *The Roosevelt I Knew* (Viking, 1946), p. 182.

Governor of New York, his obvious pleasantness and energy. Roosevelt's campaign speeches hardly filled out the picture. He spoke kindly of "the forgotten man at the bottom of the economic pyramid" and made clear that he proposed a "New Deal" for the nation. But some of the campaign sounded as if he intended to use the old cards of government economy, sound currency, and antitrust action, while other speeches suggested a crisp new pack.[6] He was sure Roosevelt was against Prohibition, Elmer Davis wrote after listening to the candidate define the New Deal. "For the rest, you could not quarrel with a single one of his generalities; you seldom can. But what they mean (if anything) is known only to Franklin D. Roosevelt and his God." Then Davis contributed his vote against Hoover and kept on wondering, with the rest of the country, what kind of a man he was backing into the White House.[7]

Promptly, on Inauguration Day itself, the country decided one thing about its new President. Early on that bleak morning the creeping paralysis of bank closings touched the nerve center of New York; by eleven a.m., the nation's financial system had come to a dead stop. Hoover, half-sick from worry, began the day with a despairing "We are at the end of our string." [8] Roosevelt, hatless and coatless in the chill March air, his voice strong and clear, his jaw jutted out, told the United States: "This great Nation will endure as it has endured, will revive and will prosper. So, first of all, let me assert my firm belief that the only thing we have to fear is fear itself—nameless, unreasoning, unjustified terror which paralyzes needed efforts to convert retreat into advance."

[6] Rosenman, I, 625, 659. In one address—the Commonwealth Club speech —Roosevelt did clearly anticipate a sweeping progressive program (Rosenman, I, 742–56), but the purport of this speech was blurred by other utterances.

[7] Quoted in Frederick L. Allen: *Since Yesterday* (Harper, 1940), pp. 81–2. Mr. Davis has added: "I had hopes after Roosevelt's Commonwealth Club speech in September, but he said so many other things during the campaign that I didn't know till Inauguration Day whether he meant it or not." (Letter to me, October 31, 1951, quoted by permission of Mr. Davis.)

[8] Quoted by Arthur M. Schlesinger, Jr.: "The First Hundred Days of the New Deal," in Claire Leighton, ed.: *The Aspirin Age* (Simon & Schuster, 1949), p. 275.

Heartfelt cheers, the first real cheers Washington had heard since 1929, roared up from the crowd. Roosevelt paused, calmly brushed a speck from his manuscript. "We do not distrust the future. . . . The people of the United States have not failed. In their need they have . . . asked for discipline and direction under leadership. They have made me the present instrument of their wishes. In the spirit of the gift I take it." [9] As the new President drove away, he responded to applause by shaking his hands over his head like a cocky prizefighter. It was all wonderful theater; it could have been little more. But in that yearning hour most Americans were sure they had stumbled upon a leader who was totally devoid of fear that closed frontiers, labor-saving devices, or anything else need alter the fundamental way of American life.

Almost as soon, and beyond anyone's questioning, the new President revealed another characteristic. Franklin Roosevelt was the most complete devotee of playing by ear the White House had ever known. Restless and mercurial in his thinking, a connoisseur of theories but impatient with people who took theories seriously, he trusted no system except the system of endless experimentation. "I have no expectation of making a hit every time I come to bat," the President flipped in an early Fireside Chat. Or more seriously, in an address at Oglethorpe University: "The country needs . . . bold, persistent experimentation. It is common sense to take a method and try it: If it fails, admit it frankly and try another. But above all, try something." [1]

Yet even the most casual doctrinaire has his ideological guide-

---

[9] Rosenman, II, 11, 15–16. The astounding number of 460,000 citizens wrote to the President as a result of the speech. Rexford G. Tugwell: "The New Deal in Retrospect," *Western Political Quarterly* (December 1948), I, 378.

[1] Rosenman, I, 646, and II, 165. Tugwell has suggested that Roosevelt's apparent casualness about programs was, at least in part, a desire to avoid telegraphing his punches—to his supporters as well as his enemies. Roosevelt, according to Tugwell, was wary of letting his progressive support know too much of his plans because, disliking some feature or other, they would be likely to denounce them. Roosevelt liked to repeat some remarks made to him by Wilson: "Roosevelt, we progressives never beat the conservatives because they, wanting to disturb nothing, and maintaining a purely defensive position, have the cohesiveness and resistance of a closed

posts, and Roosevelt's thinking acquired its direction in one of the tiny number of families that fit precisely the definition of the American patrician. There were the ancestral acres at Hyde Park, the income connected with business America largely by coupons handled in a distant broker's office, the tutors, Harvard, the trips to Europe, and presiding over it all, Sara Delano Roosevelt, serenely sure that she and her kind were the natural custodians of the nation's destiny. At Harvard, Roosevelt showed an upperdog concern for the underdog, avoided the doubtful taste of either flunking or getting too near the top of the class. When marrying time came, no one was surprised that the bride was a female counterpart of Franklin, or even, considering the exclusiveness of the circle in which the Roosevelt family moved, that she was a distant relative.

At the wedding the bride and the bridegroom did not receive anywhere near their due. Among their common relatives was the President of the United States, and "Uncle Ted" so completely stole the show that another relative growled: "When he goes to a wedding, he wants to be the bride, and when he goes to a funeral, he wants to be the corpse." [2] The shadow of Uncle Ted stretched far across the earlier years of Franklin Roosevelt. The older man had a considerable affection for his handsome, high-spirited fifth cousin and nephew-in-law. The youth, in turn, respected and admired Uncle Ted, and the relationship brought Franklin Roosevelt a continuous suggestion that politics was a permissible career for a patrician, that a patrician's politics should be reform, and that reform meant broad federal powers wielded by executive leadership in the pattern of the New Nationalism. [3]

fist; but we, being determined to make progress and each knowing best how it should be done and being therefore utterly unable, any of us, to support any others of us, have about as much striking power as you'd expect from the fingers of an open hand, each pointing in a slightly different direction." "The New Deal: the Progressive Tradition," *Western Political Quarterly* (September 1950), III, 395–6.

[2] Quoted in Gerald W. Johnson: *Roosevelt: Dictator or Democrat* (Harper, 1941), p. 69.

[3] But F. D. R. could disagree with his senior relative, and one such disagreement has its amusing aspect in view of F. D. R.'s own actions as Presi-

Until the time of Theodore's father, all the Roosevelts had considered themselves as much Democrats by birth as they were Dutchmen or Episcopalians by birth. Under the extreme provocation of the Civil War, Theodore Roosevelt's branch of the family turned Republican, but the Dutchess County wing stuck to the traditional allegiance. Having a family like the Roosevelts in the Democratic Party of that day had its amusing aspects (when Franklin ran for office the first time, politicians had to caution him not to campaign in a riding habit), but it soon brought significant consequences. Young Roosevelt was the first New York Democratic politician of importance to support Wilson's Presidential candidacy, and shortly after Wilson entered the White House, Roosevelt was offered his reward. Passing by assistant secretaryships in the State and War Departments, he chose Uncle Ted's old office of Assistant Secretary of the Navy, and in a few months Washington veterans were chuckling at the reincarnation they were watching, even to the frequent use of "Bully!" But the Assistant Secretary was also soaking up the New Freedom of the man he called "the Chief," in genuine if somewhat distant admiration. Given the Democratic Vice-Presidential nomination in 1920, Roosevelt's campaigning on domestic issues often sounded unmistakably like the Wilson of 1912.

The election of 1920 over, and the Democratic candidates unemployed, Roosevelt was ready for new jobs and new ideas. He was much more ready than many other patrician reformers for the idea of Associational Activities that the new business thinkers were developing. The New Nationalism he had imbibed from Uncle Ted contained its own acceptance of big business. Moreover, Roosevelt's wartime Navy work had brought him into contact with a good many of the advocates of Associational Activities, including a man named Herbert Hoover, who, with

---

dent. In 1902, when he was at Harvard, he wrote of T. R.'s intervention in the coal strike: "In spite of his success in settling the trouble, I think that the President made a serious mistake in interfering—politically, at least. His tendency to make the executive power stronger than the House of Congress is bound to be a bad thing, especially when a man of weaker personality succeeds him in office." Elliott Roosevelt, ed.: *F. D. R.: His Personal Letters* (Duell, Sloan & Pearce, 1947-50), I, 481.

his wife, frequently dined with their good friends the Roosevelts. Part New Nationalist when the war began, increasingly sympathetic to Associational Activities during the war, entering a decade when the New Freedom seemed almost irrelevant, Roosevelt in 1921 accepted a position that made him, for a brief period, a key figure in the new business ideology.

The position grew out of a legislative investigation of the New York building industry. Construction work in New York, the investigation revealed, was a sorry mess of outmoded techniques, corrupt relations with the unions, and ravenous competitive tactics that hurt both the companies and the public. Worried into a new approach, the principal firms set up the American Construction Council in 1922, with the declared purposes of giving the industry a code of ethics, modernizing its practices, and providing "a unification of effort"—to use the Council's phrase for industry-wide understandings that could easily turn into by-passes around the antitrust laws.[4]

The American Construction Council was one of the first major trade associations of the Twenties, and its founding provoked a great deal of excitement among men interested in luring business away from its old tooth-and-fang ideas. "The tremendous possibilities of such an organization," the Council preened itself in a brochure, "induced Mr. Herbert Hoover to consent to preside at the formal organization meeting and Mr. Franklin D. Roosevelt to accept the presidency of the organization." The Council, Hoover told the organizational meeting, "is a step I have long looked for. . . . You are taking one of the most important steps ever taken in the history of this nation." Roosevelt, enthusiastically agreeing with Hoover, added: "The tendency lately has been toward regulation of industry. . . . But Government regulation is not feasible. It is unwieldy; it is expensive. It means employment of men to carry on this phase of the work; it means higher taxes. The public doesn't want it; the industry doesn't want it. . . . There has been no system, no co-operation, no intensive

---

[4] *The American Construction Council* (American Construction Council, Washington, 1922), p. 11.

national planning. The time was ripe for an organization such as that being formed." [5] How much the Council intended to "co-operate" with government in working out its program, the record does not reveal, but it is clear that the Roosevelt of the early Twenties had little of the traditional reformer's feeling against the drawing together of industries into larger organizations and even less of the nineteenth-century businessman's apotheosis of competition.

Roosevelt had been president of the Council only a short while when the infantile paralysis struck. He did not return to full-time work for seven years, and then it was to the kind of position most likely to submerge any interest in Associational Activities. Roosevelt's election to the Governorship of New York in 1928 not only directed his attention toward state problems and away from concern over nationally organized business. It also meant that he had to function in the shadow of Al Smith, who was out of the statehouse only because he left to run for the Presidency and whose New Freedom administrations had won him enormous popularity in the state. The Wilsonianism in Franklin Roosevelt came to the fore again, and he swung easily into the Smith tradition.

A Wilsonian—that was the impression Roosevelt gave most people who were willing to venture a classification as he entered the White House. But beneath surface appearances he was something far less predictable—a patrician reformer whose mind was a potpourri of the three major programs that had emerged in the previous half-century: the New Freedom associated with Wilson, the New Nationalism of Theodore Roosevelt, and the Associational Activities of the Twenties.

III

THE DAY after the Inaugural the new President proclaimed a four-day bank holiday, summoned Congress into special session, and

[5] Ibid., Title page and p. 6; *New York Times*, June 4, 1922.

started day-and-night White House conferences on emergency banking legislation. The bill was ready seventy-two hours later. The House of Representatives debated it thirty-eight minutes. The Senate debated it three hours. That night the President signed it. The Hundred Days were under way, the most controlled, directed, overpowered period in all the history of Congress.

Many of the bills whisked through Congress bespoke the central idea common to both principal reform traditions, the New Freedom and the New Nationalism—the belief that the best solution for economic and social ills was action by the federal government under strong executive leadership. The powerful leadership of Franklin Roosevelt set up federal protections for bank depositors and for all investors in stocks. Federal credit eased the burden of debt on farmers and householders, and federal guidance reorganized the railroads. A variety of federal devices made phony bankruptcy proceedings more difficult, imposed excess-profit and dividend taxes, created the Civilian Conservation Corps for the youthful unemployed, and raised prices by taking the country off the haloed gold standard. "Liberal" measures, the country called them, and quite clearly liberalism had come to mean not the Mencken-type emphasis of the Twenties but a full-blown revival of economic and social reformism. Talk of liberty in reform circles now was likely to produce a yawn, if not a scowl; opportunity, at least opportunity for the millions to have jobs, was the point.

The New Deal handling of the desperate unemployment problem produced the most sweeping reaffirmation of general progressive doctrine. For three years Herbert Hoover and the conservative press had been arguing against the outright gift of large-scale federal funds for unemployment relief. Such a practice, they contended, would bring about a dangerous political centralization, tear down the character of the recipients, and violate the economic law that the national debt cannot go beyond a fixed point without bankrupting the government. To these arguments, liberals of a dozen schools of thought made substantially one set of replies. Unemployment on its 1933 scale was too big a problem for the states and cities, and handling it required tremendous federal funds and centralized administration; environment shaped human character, and federal relief funds, by helping to remove squalor, would build character rather than injure it. The conservative appeal to economic laws was met by a barrage of Reform Darwinism, even by a fresh Reform Darwinian formulation of economics.

Well before the depression began, a number of economists had been developing theories which brushed aside the alleged economic law standing in the way of large-scale public spending. During the Thirties the long-time leader in world reform thinking, John Maynard Keynes, was rapidly developing these ideas into a persuasive system. The supposed economic law, Keynes argued in the authentic manner of Reform Darwinism, was simply the rationalization of upper-income groups who did not want to pay heavy taxes. There was nothing dangerous about running up a government debt. On the contrary, when private expenditures of money fell off, a sensible government would start compensatory spending. "A dollar spent on relief by the government," Keynes summarized his theory to an American friend, "was a dollar given to the grocer, by the grocer to the wholesaler, and by the wholesaler to the farmer, in payment of supplies. With one dollar paid out for relief or public works or anything else, you have created four dollars' worth of national income." [6]

Franklin Roosevelt, together with a large segment of the liberal movement, distrusted the Keynes-type argument in the early New Deal days. At heart they hankered for a balanced budget. Yet the idea of large-scale federal spending on relief, with its implied contempt for rigid economics, its assignment of a key role to the national government, and its promise of quick alleviation of human distress, was a natural for the President and his following. Amid the roar of the Hundred Days, Congress passed a half-billion-dollar relief bill, and the President gave the administration of the money to a *de facto* Keynesian whose economics

[6] Paraphrased by Frances Perkins, p. 226.

consisted largely of an urge "to feed the hungry, and Goddamn fast." [7]

Harry Hopkins had always been in a hurry. He was already in a hurry when his father, a convivial jack-of-all-trades, finally settled the family in Grinnell, Iowa, and the homely youngster hustled his way to the title of "Big Man of the Class" at Grinnell College. On graduation, Hopkins almost took a job on a Montana newspaper; he almost did a dozen things; and somewhere in the midst of it all, a professor urged him to sign up as counselor in a boys' camp in New Jersey. A charitable boys' camp sat well with the son of a pious Methodist mother, who had bundled her five children off to church every Sunday and made them repeat the minister's points afterward. A boys' camp sponsored by influential people and near New York City had special attractions for the ne'er-do-well's son who was determined to find a place for himself in the exciting world of power. The professor did not have to urge long.

Nor did Hopkins remain long in the camp organization. Quickly he was off to a series of successes in the social-work profession. By 1933 Hopkins had attained the number-one social worker's position in the nation, director of emergency relief in New York State, and a striking if somewhat mixed reputation. Associates knew him as a man who thought more swiftly than anyone working for, with, or against him, a first-class administrator with a habit of cutting through red tape like so much confetti, a wraith of quick cigarettes, frayed suits, curt sarcasms,

---

[7] Quoted by the late Harold Ickes, in an interview. There is considerable dispute as to when, and to what extent, Keynesianism influenced the New Deal. Certainly his ideas were not the only ones pushing New Deal thinking in the direction of deficit spending, and all varieties of the idea were more influential in the later stages of the New Deal. A good deal of what has been called Keynesianism was simply the result of an attempt to solve a practical problem. For example, Marriner Eccles, one of the leading advocates of deficit spending in the New Deal, later commented: "The concepts I formulated, which have been called Keynesian, were not abstracted from books. . . . My conceptions were based on naked-eye observation and experience. . . . Moreover, I have never read Keynes's writings except in small abstracts up to this day." *Beckoning Frontiers* (Alfred A. Knopf, 1951), p. 132.

and a highly developed ability to confuse advancing mankind with advancing Harry Hopkins.

Transferred to Washington to direct the New Deal relief program, Hopkins sat down at his desk before the workmen had moved it out of the hallway and in two hours spent more than five million dollars. During the ensuing months Hopkin's shabby little office in the old Walker-Johnson Building, with the faded paint and the water pipes running up and down the walls, became the most swift-acting agency in all frenzied Washington. When somebody brought in a plan that "will work out in the long run," Hopkins snapped: "People don't eat in the long run—they eat every day." When inspectors from the Budget Bureau came around to see the "organizational chart," they heard that Hopkins had ordered: "I don't want anybody around here to waste any time drawing boxes. You'll always find that the person who drew the chart has his own name in the middle box." [8] Out of the fury came striking new practices of unemployment relief, a devil for conservatives to flay, and an application of liberal doctrine so personal that its effects sank deep into the national mind.

Roosevelt's close friend, the level-headed businessman Frank Walker, discovered just how personal the application was when the President sent him on a tour to inspect the workings of the relief program. In his home state of Montana, Walker found former businessmen digging ditches and laying sewer pipes in their old business clothes because they had no money to buy overalls and rubber boots. And one of the ditch-diggers spoke for millions when he said to Walker: "I hate to think what would have happened if this work hadn't come along. The last of my savings had run out. I'd sold or hocked everything I could. And my kids were hungry. I stood in front of the window of the bake-shop down the street and wondered just how long it would be before I got desperate enough to pick up a rock and heave it through that window and grab some bread to take home." [9]

[8] Robert E. Sherwood: *Roosevelt and Hopkins* (Harper, 1948), pp. 49, 52.
[9] Quoted in ibid., p. 54.

I V

IN THE White House the lights burned late six or seven nights a week. Wearing out assistants by his energies, amazing intimates by his ability to toss off worries, Roosevelt kept prodding, brain-picking, quipping, politicking the Hundred Days ahead. Federal relief would alleviate distress; it could hardly cure a depression.

There was no lack of advice on the cure. The president of the Chamber of Commerce, a charwoman from Butte, the head of the AFL, Harvard classmates of Roosevelt, the third vice-president of Kiwanis, and some five thousand other people all brought or sent the President sure-fire remedies. Immediately around the President was the group of brilliant and contentious minds that the country had been calling the Brain Trust since the early phases of the campaign of 1932. Yet amid all the babble the proposals from informed and responsible people revealed a striking fact. Many business leaders and labor officials, Farm Bureau men and liberals, Brain-Trusters and Kiwanians, agreed on certain fundamentals of a recovery program.

Some agreement from supposed ideological opposites was not surprising. During the Twenties the New Nationalist type of thinking had not entirely lost its influence and, while the New Nationalism and the Associational Activities outlook had important differences, they agreed on encouraging the formation of large economic units and on an important role for government in economic life. The depression of 1929, by presenting free enterprise in its most chaotic and inhumane form and by raising serious doubts about its ability to get back on its feet, brought an onrush of converts to the general idea of national planning of national economic units. New Freedomite reformers, who had so long battled any program that accepted the concentration of industry, now forgot their old battle in their concern with getting government controls over the existing situation. Businessmen who had railed at any system restricting their independence besought the government to tell them what to do to avoid bankruptcy.

(According to Herbert Hoover, during the campaign of 1932 a "leading industrialist" brought him a plan for over-all federal controls of industry, and when Hoover rejected the plan as "fascism," the industrialist and many of his friends gave campaign contributions to the Democrats.[1]) As the banks closed and the abyss seemed near in March 1933, free enterprise virtually abdicated. "There was hardly an industrial, economic, financial, commercial, reform, or agricultural leader who did not advance some idea of governmental intervention," one Washington insider has recalled. "A snowfall of paper plans drifted about the Capitol, and there was not one of them that would not, in some measure, have modified the Anti-Trust Acts." [2]

The merger of Associational Activities ideas and New Nationalist thinking in a demand for national planning of large-scale economic units was plain in the Brain Trust. Raymond Moley, chief of the group, perfectly represented the coalescence in his own amiable, hardheaded self. As a boy in Berea, Ohio, Moley wept at the 1896 defeat of William Jennings Bryan, and as a young man he made a hero of Tom Johnson. Then, while the trust-busters kept on thundering and the trusts kept on growing, Moley began to wonder whether traditional, anti-big-business reform was not trying to change the tides of economic development. He turned down an offer to plunge into the progressive politics of the New Freedom era; he decided he was not a "professional reformer"; and, as a professor of political science, first in the Midwest and then at Columbia, Moley sought solutions of the nation's ills that assumed the necessity of a battle against "ignorance" rather than against "sin." The nature of the proper enlightenment was not always clear. But the Professor Moley who became important in the Roosevelt circle was a man who talked easily with people of an Associational Activities persuasion and whose own doctrine, if it was contained in any one place, was found in the Crolyite book that Theodore Roosevelt had quoted to the Bull Moose convention, Van Hise's *Concentration and Con-*

[1] Interview with Mr. Herbert Hoover.
[2] Hugh S. Johnson: *The Blue Eagle from Egg to Earth* (Doubleday, 1935), p. 189.

trol. The Moley of 1933, eschewing trust-busting, had sidled toward national economic planning, by self-governing action if possible, by planning under federal compulsion if necessary. The essential was to end "the thoughtlessness and aimlessness" of free competition.[3]

The merger of the New Nationalism and Associational Activities was no less striking in the relations of two of the important figures who gathered around Moley in the Brain Trust. No human beings could have seemed more different than Hugh Johnson and Rexford Tugwell. Johnson learned to spell to the whinnying of cavalry horses and the bawling of top sergeants at Fort Scott, Kansas, yelling to anyone who would listen to him: "Everybody in the world is a rink-stink but Hughie Johnson and he's all right!" Tugwell, the son of a prosperous farmer and cannery-owner in Sinclairville, New York, was raised to a genteel tradition of concern with community problems, almost to a Rooseveltian *noblesse oblige.* West Point remembered Johnson as the most talented hazer and the possessor of the biggest nose in the history of the school. The University of Pennsylvania recalled Tugwell as a handsome, smartly dressed ideologue, a gourmet with a special pride in his elaborate salads, who was given to practicing his sharp wit on bourgeois America and was more than likely to steer his date to a reform soiree. While Johnson was doing a hell-roaring border patrol along the Rio Grande, Tugwell was showing intimates a poem that included the lines:

> *I am sick of a Nation's stenches;*
> *I am sick of propertied Czars;*
> *I have dreamt my great dream of their passing.*
> *I have gathered my tools and my charts;*
> *My plans are fashioned and practical:*
> *I shall roll up my sleeves—make America over!* [4]

The mature careers of the two men showed no more similarities. Johnson swashbuckled his way to a brigadier general's star,

[3] Raymond Moley: *After Seven Years* (Harper, 1939), pp. 4–5.
[4] Quoted in *Current Biography 1940* (H. W. Wilson), p. 431, and *1941*, p. 874.

interrupting his military life only for tossing off children's books that were chock-full of carnage and last-minute touchdowns. Somewhere along the line, the Army discovered that its leathery-faced cavalryman, a perfect Captain Flagg in his tough talk and his sentimentality, also had a mind, a quick, perceptive instrument that expressed itself in curiously effective off-beat phrases. The Army sent Johnson to law school, then made him its principal representative on the War Industries Board of World War I. Excited by his contact with industry, Johnson resigned from the Army after the Armistice and entered business, first as an officer of the Moline Plow Company, later as one of the men who helped Baruch manage his web of interests. Still clattering across any room in a roar of Army attitudes, deeply involved with large-scale industry and finance, Johnson in 1933 seemed a caricature of the traditional reform type. Tugwell was close to being a type-case of the liberal professor. Settled at Columbia, he was entrancing classes by his iconoclasm, making a national reputation as a heretical agricultural economist, visiting the Soviet Union and coming back with the declaration that Russian rural life was entering a "renaissance" even if Bolshevik totalitarianism was objectionable.[5] It was hardly surprising that at early Brain Trust sessions the relations between Tugwell and Johnson were a study in hostility, Tugwell holding Johnson off with witticisms, Johnson snapping and snarling at his debonair torturer.

Yet with the passage of a few months, Tugwell and Johnson were soon bending happily over the same charts and memoranda. Johnson had emerged from his service with the War Industries Board and his work with Baruch an ardent advocate of Associational Activities, though he added to Hoover's reliance on co-operation between government and economic units the belief that some degree of governmental compulsion should be used. Tugwell had emerged from his books and his indignation a highly involved economic thinker but fundamentally a New Nationalist. The line between Johnson's planning by partial co-operation and

[5] Tugwell: "Russian Agriculture," in Stuart Chase *et al.*, eds.: *Soviet Russia in the Second Decade* (John Day, 1928), p. 101.

Tugwell's planning by over-all compulsion was a wavering one, much too wavering not to be pushed aside by the impact of depression. The common denominator of their thinking in 1933, and of his own, was described by Moley when he wrote of the Brain Trust's "rejection of the traditional Wilson-Brandeis philosophy that America . . . could once more become a nation of small proprietors, of corner grocers and smithies under spreading chestnut trees. . . . We believed that any attempt to atomize big business must destroy America's greatest contribution to a higher standard of living for the body of its citizenry—the development of mass production. . . . We recognized that competition, as such, was not inherently virtuous; that competition . . . created as many abuses as it prevented." So the Brain-Trusters, Moley summarized, turned "from the nostalgic philosophy of the 'trust busters,'" turned to national economic planning.[6]

This was the kind of thinking swirling around the President during the Hundred Days, and it did not disturb him. In the period immediately preceding his election Roosevelt had begun to submerge the New Freedom element in his own thinking; he too could find little in trust-busting liberalism that seemed to apply to the emergency at hand. The real question for him, the real quarrel among his advisers, was not national planning versus free competition. The issue was: should the planning hew closer to the Associational Activities pattern, with its emphasis on noncompulsory relations between the government and economic life, or should it follow more the New Nationalist pattern of powerful federal controls?

V

NEXT TO feeding the hungry, the most urgent problem was agriculture. Another good crop was on its way and, with farm prices already perilously low, another good crop could mean disaster. Even during the campaign of 1932, while most of his program

[6] Moley, p. 24.

was still a cloud of generalities, Roosevelt edged toward a specific program of national planning for agriculture. Shortly before the nominating convention, Tugwell began urging on Moley a plan that was the product of many minds but had been most actively propagandized by Professor Milburn L. Wilson, of the Montana State College. Wilson's proposal assumed that the American farmer could no longer depend on the foreign market. Instead of calling on the federal government to arrange dumping abroad, as the McNary-Haugen bill had done, Wilson argued that the government should plan crop-control at home by an elaborate procedure known as the "Domestic Allotment Plan." The Wilson program appealed to the planner in Moley; when Moley arranged a conference between Roosevelt and Tugwell, the plan appealed no less to the planner in Roosevelt. Roosevelt wanted to know more, and just as the convention was about to vote on the nomination, Tugwell wired Wilson to meet him in Chicago. The two men talked for a day in a hotel room; then Tugwell reported to Hyde Park on the long-distance phone. Roosevelt was sufficiently impressed to slip into his acceptance speech an endorsement of the basic Wilson principle that the federal government should make itself responsible for ridding the farmer of the curse of surpluses without resorting to attempts at dumping abroad.

But just how was the responsibility to be fulfilled? Advocates of an Associational Activities tendency—most notably Hugh Johnson's crony George Peek—urged as little compulsion as possible. Peek argued long and ably that the chief mechanism for raising farm income should be a payment to the farmer for whatever money he lost by having to sell at a low price in foreign markets; only in years of superabundant yield should the actual size of his crop be curtailed, and then not until the crop was actually in growth. Professor Wilson, backed by a group including Tugwell, proposed crop curtailment, even in normal years and before planting, by offering attractive rentals to farmers on acreage taken out of production. The final legislation, the bill establishing the Agricultural Adjustment Administration, made the execution of either or both plans possible. But the Triple A plainly contained ample provisions to make it the boldest use of national agricultural controls in the modern history of Western civilization.

The next week or so, the already famous Roosevelt smile was especially radiant. The President was busy with the final stages of a bill which, of all the New Deal legislation, was his labor of love. The idea of a Tennessee Valley Authority lit fires in a dozen cubicles of Roosevelt's mind. A TVA would provide a yardstick for power costs; it would mean a giant stride in conservation, an enthusiasm of Franklin no less than of Theodore Roosevelt; it would chain a capricious, destructive river to the development of one of the most depressed areas of the country.

Shortly before the bill went to Congress, its chief sponsor, Senator George Norris, came to dinner at the White House, and the two men, the Dutchess County patrician and the son of a Nebraska dirt farmer, sat talking enthusiastically over TVA's possibilities.

"What are you going to say when they ask you the political philosophy behind TVA?" Senator Norris laughed.

"I'll tell them it's neither fish nor fowl," Roosevelt laughed back, "but, whatever it is, it will taste awfully good to the people of the Tennessee Valley."

Until midnight that evening the President squeezed dry his interlude, talking of forests and schoolhouses and the future, far away from the nagging present of hungry men and warring policies.[7]

Congress was just beginning debate on TVA when the present returned with the jarring report that the Senate had passed the Black bill. In the bleak months of 1932 Senator Hugo Black, like so many other Americans, had become convinced that a return to the 1929 level of prosperity was impossible. Sure that technology had reached the point where there would never be enough jobs to go around unless everybody worked less, he introduced a bill decreeing a thirty-hour week.

To Roosevelt the bill seemed a menace. It assumed a closed economy, with no room for expanding production and oppor-

[7] Interview with the late George W. Norris.

tunity. It contained no minimum-wage provisions and would almost certainly result in a wholesale slashing of take-home pay. It was completely rigid, allowing for no seasonal variations or the special hours required by some occupations. How could you order farmers up in his country to work their hired hands thirty hours, the President asked. "There have to be hours adapted to the rhythm of the cow." [8] But there it was, a piece of legislation already approved by the Senate of the United States and, because of its patness and its appeal to the fears of the day, a bill that was soon likely to end up on the President's desk.

Quite clearly, the practical alternative to the Black bill was different legislation that also promised escape from industrial unemployment. Roosevelt had not wanted to rush industrial-recovery legislation. He felt that, though there was general agreement on the need for national planning, too much disagreement over key points still existed among important economic leaders. One school believed that industrial reorganization alone would bring recovery; another school, reflecting the growing influence of the ideas of Keynes and similar thinkers, insisted that industrial reorganization had to be accompanied by a pump-priming public-works program. There were also serious differences over the degree of governmental compulsion that should be involved. The President was reluctant to force the decisions. But now, with the Black bill close to final Congressional approval, Roosevelt could no longer wait. Soon after the legislation passed the Senate, Roosevelt summoned the proponents of the more important plans to his office, listened to them wrangle, then told them to go lock themselves in a room until they could agree on one bill.

The order quickly produced a draft. After two days the conferees emerged with a bill, and the President accepted it with only minor modifications. With respect to the pump-priming issue, the National Industrial Recovery Act compromised, providing for public works as part of the general program but appropriating for them a sum much smaller than the ardent pump-primers wanted. The heart of the bill, the machinery for industrial plan-

[8] Quoted in Frances Perkins, p. 194.

.ing, was less of a compromise. The codes were to be originally drafted by representatives of industry, which meant the trade associations in most cases; the antitrust laws were suspended; and no prohibition was placed on price-fixing. All of these provisions had been major goals of business-minded planners since George Perkins's day. But the codes of hours, wages, and conditions of competition were to be written under the supervision of a federal administrator, they had to be approved by the President as the representative of the national welfare, and, once given White House approval, they carried the force of federal law. Herbert Hoover, speaking up from the deepest oblivion any living ex-President has ever known, was horrified. "Fascism, pure fascism," the advocate of Associational Activities called the enormous governmental powers granted to the National Recovery Administration.[9]

Raymond Moley was jubilant. His Brain-Trusters, representing quite different approaches, had joined in giving the nation blueprints for both industry and agriculture which brushed aside the Wilsonian hostility to large-scale economic units and brought all enterprises, large and small, into a government-sponsored national planning. To the program of Associational Activities had been added the idea of federal compulsion, which men like Croly and Van Hise had long been advocating. The appointments of the top personnel of the Triple A and the NRA emphasized the way in which the New Deal was sweeping Associational Activities into a bolder pattern. None other than Bernard Baruch's World War I assistant, George Peek, accepted the post as head of the Triple A. Another Baruch protégé, Hugh Johnson, not only moved into the top position of the NRA; he promptly began talking federal power in a way that made businessmen feel like so many captured peasants herded before the Czar.

Happily, Moley worked away on the draft of the Fireside Chat in which Roosevelt was to present the Triple A and the NRA to the public, working into the speech a huzza to the coming era of national planning. The President seemed to like the passage, and

9 Hoover interview.

Moley pressed his advantage. Having spent two years in almost daily conversation with Roosevelt, Moley was keenly aware of the President's many minds, his zest in playing by ear.

Did the President, Moley asked, realize to its fullest significance the "enormous step" he was taking? Did he realize that the Triple A and the NRA were committing him to a sharp break not only with the conservative adulation of free enterprise but with the appeal for a return to the free enterprise of New Freedom liberalism? Did he really approve, in its deepest meaning, this passage extolling national planning?

Roosevelt was quiet for a few minutes, then he replied solemnly: "I never felt surer of anything in my life than I do of the soundness of this passage." [1]

Uncle Ted, thrashing out his last years in impotent fury at Woodrow Wilson, had died too soon. For in the clear import of basic legislation and in the mind of the President of the United States, the nation was close to the repudiation of trust-busting and the dependence on compulsory federal planning which Theodore Roosevelt had appealed for under the name of the New Nationalism.

VI

FOR ONCE, Franklin Roosevelt admitted he was tired. Hastily signing the National Recovery Act, he climbed aboard the little *Amberjack II*, put on his oilskins, and went sailing up the New England coast to Campobello.

He left behind an enormously relieved nation. Across the country, the doubts of 1932 were disappearing with the swiftness of a summer shower. Businessmen, coming out of their storm cellars, drove up the index of manufacturing production from 56 in March, when the Hundred Days began, to 65 in April, then up to

---

[1] Quoted in Moley, p. 189. The similarity in over-all conception of the NRA and the Triple A is underlined by the fact that one important part of the Triple A, the marketing agreements, was the direct forerunner of the NRA codes.

77 in May and 93 in June. Labor, losing the wildness of despair, hurried into unions and turned the frantic violence of 1932 into businesslike strikes. With the flood of Triple A checks starting out of Washington, the farm areas were regaining hope in the old America, even to the extent of a few furtive elections of Republicans once again. The technological wonders of a World's Fair no longer seemed entirely ironical, and as families roamed around the exhibits, planning when they could buy a Mixmaster or a car with free wheeling, those who were up on the latest movies were whistling, "Who's Afraid of the Big Bad Wolf?"

Hard times were still grimly present, but a liberalism that had been able to conquer fear seemed the obvious program to conquer a mere depression. In the years immediately after 1933, New Deal liberalism gained a hold on the American mind such as no previous reform movement had known. Among the educated, the Shame of the Babbitts was being forgotten in the horror of poverty. Writings in economic and social reform shoved Mencken and Fitzgerald into the farthest stacks of libraries, and Sinclair Lewis kept a toehold on the front shelves only by *Ann Vickers*, portraying a social worker, and *It Can't Happen Here*, a fictionalized warning that unemployment was the seed-bed of fascism. During the Hundred Days, Prohibition was repealed with only a few hiccups of excitement, and the next year the Catholic Legion of Decency began its censorship of the movies amid the merest scattering of protest. The news about sex, *Fortune* reported after surveying the colleges, was that sex was no longer news. "I am now definitely ready to announce," the postgraduate Robert Benchley added in his dramatic column, "that Sex, as a theatrical property, is as tiresome as the Old Mortgage. . . . I am sick of little Southern girls who want 'to live.' . . . I am sick of rebellious Youth and I am sick of Victorian parents, and I don't care if all the little girls in all sections of the United States get ruined or want to get ruined or keep from getting ruined." [2]

Among educated and uneducated alike, millions were rejecting

[2] "Youth in College," *Fortune* (June 1936), XIII, 155–6; Benchley: "Hail to the King," *The New Yorker* (November 29, 1930), VI, 36.

conservatism with the vehemence of men trying to forget their pasts. New Deal critics stormed and threatened. But when the Congressional elections of 1934 came, and the only discernible issue was the New Deal, the overwhelming Democratic majority of 1932 became still more overwhelming (an especially emphatic endorsement because it is phenomenal in American politics when the party in power increases its strength in an off-year election). In the cities and states, public pressure was bringing an avalanche of social legislation—more in the first two years of the New Deal than in the administrations of Theodore Roosevelt and Woodrow Wilson combined. Symbolically, the nation's metropolis chose for its Mayor none other than Fiorello La Guardia, chunkier and more reform-minded than ever. "They didn't elect me for my looks," said La Guardia. "They wanted things done and they knew damn well I'd do them." [3]

And above it all, rapidly approaching a popularity unexceeded in American history, was the President of the United States who believed that his party's function was to be "the party of militant liberalism." [4] The voters may have sent Franklin Roosevelt to the White House as a pleasant man who could hardly be worse than Hoover. Now they were cheering him as the most effective of American reform leaders. A good part of the nation had respected Wilson, as they respected their ministers, and delighted in Teddy Roosevelt, as they delighted in a dashing Sunday-dinner uncle. They found Franklin Roosevelt delightful too, and far removed from ordinary politicians in the respect he called up, but there was also something else—an intangible mass feeling that converted attacks on him into intensified support. A man who remained so jaunty under heavy strain would not fail to pull things through somehow; a reformer so skillful at political deals would know how to get reforms effected; a President who had suffered so much himself would understand and care about all the nagging todays and worrisome tomorrows of ordinary men and women. In North Carolina a reporter from an anti-Roosevelt paper ap-

[3] Interview with the late Fiorello La Guardia.
[4] Rosenman, VII, xxxi.

proached a mill worker and grilled him about his enthusiasm for the President. Did he realize, the reporter asked, that the New Deal was based on crackpot theories and was certain to bankrupt the country? The mill worker squirmed and reddened. Then, finally, he managed to get out his answer. "Mr. Roosevelt," the mill worker said, "is the only man we ever had in the White House who would understand that my boss is a sonofabitch." [5]

In Washington, paunching old Harold Ickes, who had known all the delights of reform achievements in the early 1900's, delivered himself of a historical judgment from his new post as a member of the President's Cabinet. "By God," Ickes declared, "I never thought I'd live to see this. Why this is a second honeymoon." [6]

[5] Interview with the late Stephen T. Early, who was told the story by the North Carolina worker.
[6] Ickes interview.

CHAPTER XV

Liberalism, and Then Some

"HUGH," said Harry Hopkins, "your codes stink."
Hugh Johnson's face reddened, partly in anger, even more in surprise. When he took the job as NRA Administrator, Johnson knew that he was in for a rough time, but he did not expect sharp criticism from New Dealers, especially from so loyal a New Dealer as Harry Hopkins.[1] Now, when the NRA was scarcely six months old, Hopkins proved only the first of many reformers who denounced the codes, and the criticism was increased by groups that liberals had long considered two of their prime concerns, the small businessmen and labor. Seven Cleveland grocers spoke for thousands of grocers, druggists, and small manufacturers when they wired the President: "NRA is the worst law ever passed by Congress." A Baltimore picket line expressed a common labor feeling with placards reading: "NRA means National Run Around."[2]

By March 1934 the discontent was so great that President Roosevelt set up a National Recovery Review Board, under the chairmanship of Clarence Darrow. The seventy-six-year-old veteran of reform threw himself into the task as if it were his first case in Ashtabula. For four months, in the cramped heat of a Washing-

---

[1] Quoted in an interview with the late Harold L. Ickes.
[2] *New York Times*, January 21, 1934.

ton hotel suite, he drove his board through hearings on some three thousand complaints, only the infrequency of the old man's quips suggesting that this was to be his final important effort. And when Darrow sent his bulky three reports to the President, Hugh Johnson knew full well that he had lost much of liberal America.

"[In] virtually all the codes we have examined," the final Darrow report stated, "one condition has been persistent, undeniable and apparent to any impartial observation. . . . The code has offered an opportunity for the more powerful and more profitable interests to seize control of an industry or to augment and extend a control already obtained. In Industry after Industry, the larger units, sometimes through the agency of what is called an Institute [a trade association], sometimes by other means, have for their own advantage written the codes, and then, in effect and for their own advantage, assumed the administration of the code they have framed. Thus privilege has exerted itself to gather more privilege. . . . To deliver industry into the hands of its greatest and most ruthless units when the protection of the anti-trust laws had been withdrawn was a grave error. It may safely be said that not in many years have monopolistic tendencies in industry been so forwarded and strengthened."[3]

The specific sections of the reports were an angry documentation of "bold and aggressive . . . monopolistic practises." Citing the motion-picture distributors' code as a typical case, the Darrow Board charged that the code had been written largely by representatives of the chain movie houses, though 13,571 of the nation's 18,321 theaters were independent. The chain representatives did their work so well, the reports went on, that the large-scale distributors were now able to arrange priorities on the more popular pictures, to determine the allocation of shorts, to fix minimum admission prices, and, by these and other devices, to put the independents at a tremendous disadvantage.[4]

[3] U.S. National Recovery Review Board: "Third Report to the President," MS., Princeton University Library, pp. 35, 39. The reports were never published beyond mimeographed form.
[4] Ibid., "First Report," MS., pp. 5, 79–123.

The lumber code brought a flash of the old courtroom Darrow into one of the most technical sections of the reports. The code, Darrow snorted, was annihilating the small distributors and yet Administrator Hugh Johnson denied that the little fellows had any cause for concern. "Perhaps . . . [the small] proprietor ought to sing a jubilee. He is ruined, but thank God, his big competitor is thriving at the old stand. And·as he pursues his way to the Relief Station . . . let him console himself by recalling the Administrator's precious assurance that annihilation is not oppression. . . . Should . . . [this] fail, let him reflect that . . . [the lumber code] is what is called 'A Code of Fair Competition,' a fact that should be enough to cheer almost any doubting soul." [5]

The wrathful Darrow reports contained many overstatements or inaccuracies, and Hugh Johnson immediately boomed corrections across the nation. But the general's loudest roars could not drown out the fact that Darrow's basic contention was correct. Most of the codes had been written primarily by big business and were decidedly advantageous to big business. As a matter of fact, Darrow overlooked one choice subject for his sarcasm: in most important respects, the cotton, woolen, carpet, and sugar codes were copies, down to the last comma, of the trade-association agreements written during the Administration of Herbert Hoover.

The story of Triple A was less clear-cut. Industry was more completely dominated by large-scale producers than was agriculture, and the trade associations were more prepared, by their experience and by the nature of their field, to bend national planning to their own purposes. Yet the Triple A revealed the same tendency as the NRA. From the beginning of its operation, big-scale processors and distributors saw to it that their interests were generously protected. During the first three years of the New Deal, the total earnings of farmers leaped up, twenty-five per cent in 1933, fifteen per cent more in 1934, an additional sixteen per cent in 1935. But the new prosperity was not evenly spread. Large-scale farmers, organized in powerful associations, had their crops placed on the list for curtailment on highly favorable terms, while smaller

[5] Ibid., "Third Report," MS., pp. 27–8.

and more weakly organized producers often were not on the lists at all or, if they were, benefited little from the program. Moreover, the Triple A assumed most of the risks of production for the landowner, but did not provide safeguards to prevent the landowner from passing on to tenants any unfavorable effect of the reduced acreage. "Proportionately at least," one historian of the Triple A has commented, "the principle—or application—of the AAA seemed to be: to him that hath it shall be given." [6]

Still more disturbing, the Triple A was speeding up what the farmers called "tractoring" workers off the land. Displacing men by machines certainly was not the intention of anyone who had a part in conceiving the program. Yet this effect of the Triple A, just because it was so unintended, provided an especially striking instance of the way national planning can be converted into planning that benefits the better-established. By putting cash in the hands of farmers and encouraging receptivity to modern methods, the Triple A helped turn the Thirties into a decade of spectacular mechanization for agriculture—a seventy per cent jump in the purchase of tractors, a large-scale shift to electrified dairying, a rapid increase in the use of mechanical corn-pickers, and more and more planting of the recently developed hybrid corn which, because of its "standability," facilitated mechanical picking. The profits of the farmer with money for mechanization soared, but jobs became increasingly scarce for farm laborers and the sharecropper often found that he had no share to crop. "In '34," an Oklahoma landlord summarized the trend, "I had I reckon four renters and I didn't make anything. I bought tractors on the money the government give me and got shet o' my renters." [7]

More and more, liberals who were concerned with agriculture began to sound like the Darrow Reports in their comments on the Triple A. Their indignation climaxed in the spring of 1935, when a group resignation removed from the Agricultural Adjustment Administration some of its most devoted reform figures. To the

[6] Dixon Wecter: *The Age of the Great Depression* (Macmillan, 1948), pp. 145–6.
[7] Quoted in ibid., p. 146.

liberal journals this was a "purge," a purge that, to use the phrasing of the *Nation*, spelled "the defeat of the social outlook in agricultural policy." The Triple A had succumbed to the "triumphant greed of the processors, distributors, and big producers," groups whose interests are "oftener than not diametrically opposed to the public interest, or the interest of the small producer." The *Christian Century*, an organ of liberal Protestantism, added: "What it all boils down to is that the old divergence between the NRA and the AAA—a matter of much conservative criticism a year or so ago—has been done away with. Both now . . . represent recovery programs . . . controlled by the big corporations involved, giving a subsidiary attention to the interests of the labor element, and hoping that the consumer will be satisfied with a few kind words and a seat out in the alley." [8]

What had happened to all the glowing hopes of 1933? Liberal critics found a wide variety of explanations. Hugh Johnson was such a bad administrator that the NRA quickly became a chaos in which big business did much as it pleased; or both Johnson and George Peek were big-business types, naturally inclined toward the interests of large-scale enterprises; or important administrative mistakes had been made, like the NRA's attempt to write codes for hundreds of industries instead of confining itself to a few basic codes, a decision that made it impossible to give pinpoint consideration to the documents that were being accepted. Each of these points had its truth, but they did not add up to an impressive explanation. If Johnson was undoubtedly a horrible administrator, George Peek was recognized as an exceptionally efficient executive by friends and enemies alike. Both Johnson and Peek may have been big-business types, but Johnson, at least, was also filled with an intense zeal for the public welfare. Trying to produce 546 industrial codes in a hurry was no doubt a mistake. Yet the lumber code, which turned out to be one of the most complete triumphs for big business, was mulled over to the point where, as Darrow

[8] R. G. S.: "The Purge at the AAA," *Nation* (February 20, 1935), CXL, 216–17; "What Has Happened to the AAA?" *Christian Century* (March 6, 1935), LII, 294.

himself remarked, "everybody in on it—and everybody seemed to be in on it—was repeating the damn thing in his sleep." [9]

Hardheaded George Peek approached a more basic explanation when he wrote of his Triple A experience: "I learned that Americans think of their government as something above and beyond the people of the United States, as something which can control groups at its will. The truth is that no democratic government can be very different from the country it governs. If some groups are dominant in the country, they will be dominant in any plan the government undertakes." [1] Peek, of course, was simply restating a difficulty that was latent in Croly's first description of the New Nationalism and became blatantly clear once a form of this New Nationalism was put into practice. Under the New Deal, national planning was called upon as the obvious way to seek the national interest. But the machinery set up to control business and agriculture in the national interest was being used by the larger units to further their own interests, and since the machinery was more powerful than any the United States had ever known, the benefits to the larger units were commensurately great.

Clarence Darrow, called before a Senate committee investigating the NRA, was melancholy and confused. "The concentration of wealth is going on," he told the Senators, "and it looks almost as if there were nothing to stop it. . . . I think this movement is going on faster then it ever did before, much faster. . . . If we do not destroy it there will be nothing but masters and slaves left before we get much further along." Darrow implied that the antitrust laws should be restored in full force; he also argued that "something like a socialistic system" was necessary.[2] What the old warrior said was obviously contradictory, and it was obviously the struggle of a liberal caught in liberalism's worst domestic trouble.

The liberal in the White House was disturbed too. Though Roosevelt brushed aside the Darrow Reports, he soon moved to

---

[9] Quoted in the Ickes interview.

[1] *New York Times*, December 13, 1936.

[2] U.S. Senate Committee on Finance, 73rd Cong., 1st Sess.: *Hearings . . . on the National Recovery Administration* (1933), Pt. 2, pp. 300, 308.

bar price-fixing from future industrial codes, to set up an Industrial Appeals Board, which was to hear the complaints of small businessmen, and to get under way studies directed toward helping the low-income farmer. But the discontent with the NRA and the Triple A, particularly the irritation at the NRA, did not quiet. Worse still, the perversion of the purpose of New Deal planning meant that the whole structure was adding little to the nation's purchasing power, and recovery was stalling. Suddenly fate, in the form of a Brooklyn chicken-dealer, intervened. The Schechter poultry firm wanted to know what happened to its Constitutional rights if the Live Poultry Code told it how much it had to pay chicken-killers and which chickens were fit to sell. In May 1935 the Supreme Court answered by unanimously decreeing the NRA unconstitutional. Seven months later the Court knocked the other leg from under Roosevelt's New Nationalism by invalidating the crop-control sections of the Triple A.

II

THE PRESIDENT was furious. The wording of the decisions was so sweeping, Roosevelt felt, that the whole recovery effort stood in danger of judicial nullification. Publicly he denounced the Supreme Court decisions as "horse-and-buggy" law, and privately he was testy in a way he had not been since he entered the White House.[3]

At a particularly irascible luncheon, an old friend decided it was time to interject a different tone. "Governor," he ventured, "did you see this morning's *Times?* You don't have a thing to worry about. The Communist Party has decided to pat you on the head." [4]

The venture was a success. Franklin Roosevelt threw back his big head and roared at the news of Communist friendliness. Ever since he took office, the *Daily Worker* had categorized Roosevelt

[3] Samuel Rosenman, ed.: *The Public Papers and Addresses of Franklin D. Roosevelt* (Random House, 1938), IV, 221.
[4] Quoted in an interview with the late Stephen T. Early.

as that most despicable of leaders, worse than a conservative or even a fascist, a "social fascist" who blocked real change by offering hypocritical reforms. The kindest Marxist treatment of the New Deal had been a 1935 book by Benjamin Stolberg and Warren Vinton which concluded: "There is nothing the New Deal has so far done that could not have been done better by an earthquake." [5] But while Stolberg and Vinton sneered, the Politburo in Moscow was watching Adolf Hitler proclaim himself the defender of the world against Bolshevism, and the Politburo decided that, for the time being, winning military allies was more important than building revolutionary parties. Two months after the Supreme Court invalidated the NRA, the Communist International proclaimed the "Popular Front," ordering Communist parties throughout the world to cease open revolutionary activities and to work with all "antifascist" organizations and governments, including the New Deal of former social fascist Franklin Roosevelt.[6]

From the beginning of the depression, Communism had been gaining in influence among American liberals. The world trend toward fascism encouraged support for the Soviet Union, which appeared to be the most active foe of Hitlerism. The liberal enthusiasm for national planning gave heroic stature to the Stalin regime, which was already entering its second Five-Year Plan. American liberals who came from minority groups could not fail to notice the Communists' militant stand against discrimination of any kind. Above all, the Communist Party, dominating people's personal lives as well as their minds, filled nagging voids for men and women whose thinking was a jumble of personal frustrations and social sensitivities.

Miss Joy Davidman, a young woman from the Bronx who joined the party in the Thirties, has provided a revealing description of her road to Communism. Chunky and wearing glasses,

[5] Stolberg and Vinton: *The Economic Consequences of the New Deal* (Harcourt, Brace, 1935), p. 85.
[6] It should be noted, however, that the Communists did not directly back Roosevelt. The support was given by a sidewise technique that better suited their purposes. See Benjamin Gitlow: *The Whole of Their Lives* (Scribner, 1948), pp. 260-3.

Miss Davidman was sensitive about her looks; precociously bright and ambitious to become a writer, she was restless under the routine of a schoolteacher's job; a Jew and a liberal, she was depressed by the mounting tide of anti-Semitism in the United States, the world-wide surge of fascism, the brutal results of hard times which she saw in the faces of the children she taught. With increasing sympathy, Miss Davidman listened to friends who argued that Russia had faced these problems boldly and was hammering out a decent society. One day, mulling it all over on a long walk, she told herself: "If I keep on thinking like this I'll be a Communist." She stopped short as the full revelation swept home. "By God," she said, "I am a Communist." [7]

Yet whatever the attractions of Communism before 1935, approval of it meant association with a revolutionary organization that was disreputable in the eyes of the community and was flagrantly at variance with liberalism in its thinking. The new Popular Front party line of 1935 swiftly reduced these barriers. It made Communism seem, as the Communists were now fond of saying, simply a continuation of the Jefferson-Jackson tradition of militant reform, a kind of supercharged New Dealism, "Twentieth-Century Americanism," no less.[8] As Popular Front activities brought the Communists into increasingly respectable associations, the movement acquired status, even fashionableness. For a liberal to show sympathy for Communism hardly seemed extreme when the Baltimore *Sun* was reporting: "Wearing a black ensemble with orchids at the shoulder, Mrs. William A. Becker, national president of the Daughters of the American Revolution, attended the reception at the Soviet Embassy last night to celebrate the twentieth anniversary of the Russian Revolution." [9]

Under the circumstances, if the new Communist Party line did not lure any large number of liberals into actually taking out membership cards, it did produce an enormous amount of fellow-

[7] Quoted in Oliver Pilat: "Girl Communist," *New York Post*, November 1, 1949.
[8] Earl Browder: *The People's Front* (International Publishers, New York, 1938), p. 235.
[9] Baltimore *Sun*, November 8, 1937.

traveling after 1935.[1] No one, especially the people affected, will ever be able to estimate accurately the number of liberal minds that commuted on the Moscow subway. Sometimes the fellow-traveling went far. The State Department employee Henry Julian Wadleigh gradually came to the fervid opinion, as he testified later, that "the Communists were practically the only people . . . putting up a determined resistance against fascism" and without joining the party he served it by sneaking out secret documents to have copied for passing on to the Soviet Union.[2] The more usual fellow traveler simply joined Communist-front organizations, "understood" the Soviet Union, dismissed criticism of Communism as Red-baiting, and took over more or less consciously parts of Communist ideology. Westbrook Pegler, who considered himself a liberal in the Thirties, certainly typified much of the movement in one respect. He did not repudiate a *Daily Worker* story that quoted him as strongly endorsing the Communist plan for a "progressive" farmer-labor party.[3]

In every field, well-known reformers gave evidence of the trend. The liberal's most beloved journalist, Heywood Broun, carried on an open flirtation with the Communists in his Newspaper Guild, while W. E. B. Du Bois published *Black Reconstruction*, a belligerently Marxist interpretation of that pivotal period. The *New Republic* and the *Nation* published sympathetic reports on Soviet activities, and John Haynes Holmes, the revered leader of liberal Protestantism, adopted an attitude he later described as one that "defended, or at least apologized for, evils in the case of Russia which horrified us wherever else they appeared." [4] While standards of "proletarian literature" rose to importance in many of the leading critical reviews, the League of American Writers, an offshoot of the International Union of Revolutionary Writers,

[1] According to the party's estimates, the C.P. had a total of only 75,000 members at its high point in 1938, with 20,000 in the Young Communist League. Arthur M. Schlesinger, Jr.: *The Vital Center* (Houghton Mifflin, 1949), p. 103.
[2] *New York Times*, June 17, 1949; *New York Post*, June 17, 1949.
[3] *Daily Worker*, June 18, 1936.
[4] Quoted in Eugene Lyons: *The Red Decade* (Bobbs-Merrill, 1941), p. 356.

could command for its manifestoes liberal names of the prominence of Van Wyck Brooks, Erskine Caldwell, John Dos Passos, Theodore Dreiser, Clifton Fadiman, Waldo Frank, Granville Hicks, Langston Hughes, Robert Morss Lovett, Lewis Mumford, Lincoln Steffens, Edmund Wilson, and Richard Wright.[5]

More than any other book, Lincoln Steffens's *Autobiography* brought the first jabs of political excitement to college students in the Thirties, and the *Autobiography* was a description of Steffens's transition from muckraking to his growing enthusiasm over Soviet Russia. By 1936 Steffens was calling Lenin "the greatest of liberals" and was telling *New Republic* readers: "It is, I admit, heart and head-breaking to see the job begun and carried on over there by a dictator and a small minority using force when they don't know how otherwise to govern. . . . [But we] can rejoice that the deed was done and a path blazed for us." Now, even if everything else failed, "you and I and the world, if it please, can always lie down and say: 'Oh, well, anyhow, there's Russia.' " [6]

In time, this fellow-traveling was to have many important effects on American liberalism, but one of its most immediate effects was in the realm of patterns of thinking. For two generations Reform Darwinism had been opening liberal minds to the doctrine of expediency, and now fellow-traveling added an additional influence in the same direction. Sympathetic interest in Communism meant some degree of acceptance for a doctrine that put economic change before all else, a doctrine expressed in Lenin's call for a morality "entirely subordinated to the interests of the class struggle of the proletariat"—in short, a doctrine completely given to arguing that the end justifies the means.[7] For any

[5] The names are from the "Call" for the first Congress, which was to consist of those "who have clearly indicated their sympathy with the revolutionary cause." (Henry Hart, ed.: *American Writer's Congress* [International Publishers, New York, 1935], pp. 11–12.) In subsequent years the names fluctuated, but many remained the same until 1939.

[6] *Lincoln Steffens Speaking* (Harcourt, Brace, 1936), p. 256; Steffens: "Bankrupt Liberalism," *New Republic* (February 17, 1932), LXX, 15–16.

[7] Lenin, quoted in Edward E. Palmer, ed.: *The Communist Problem in America* (Crowell, 1951), p. 47.

humane, democratic-minded liberal, praise for Communism as it was practiced in the Soviet Union required the actual use of justifying means by the end. As John Haynes Holmes went on to say of his own fellow-traveling days, "We liberals . . . permitted ourselves to condone wrongs that we knew must be wrongs. . . . We accepted covertly, if not openly, the most dangerous and ultimately disastrous idea that can lodge within the human mind, namely, that the end justifies the means." [8]

How much liberals were coming to accept this dangerous way of thinking was revealed in 1937 when President Roosevelt translated his anger against the Supreme Court into action. There were a number of direct ways to go at the problem of a high court that ruled social legislation unconstitutional. One was to propose a Constitutional amendment clearly empowering Congress to pass such laws. Another was to challenge the right of the Supreme Court—a right that is certainly not clear in the Constitution—to nullify a law passed by Congress. Roosevelt used neither of these approaches in the press conference at which he announced his plan. Ostensibly, the program he laid before the reporters did not concern the Supreme Court's opinions about the New Deal, or even the Supreme Court alone; it did not "raise any issue of constitutional law." The point was, Roosevelt explained, that almost ten per cent of the total number of federal judges were over seventy years old, and, apart from their age, the amount of work piling up was too great for so small a personnel. "Delay in any court," he declared solemnly, "results in injustice." Hence Roosevelt urged a bill that would permit the President to appoint an additional justice for each federal judge who served ten years and did not retire at seventy. It was all very simple, Roosevelt assured the reporters, and the newsmen agreed as they rushed for their phones.[9] It was as simple as guaranteeing a New Deal majority on the Supreme Court by forcing enough conservative justices into retirement or by offsetting their votes.

The indications were overwhelming that the Administration

[8] Quoted in Lyons, p. 356.
[9] Rosenman, VI, 35–50.

was trying to put something over on the country. The over-age argument was rendered completely evasive by the fact that the President's most consistent supporter on the Court was the eighty-year-old Louis Brandeis. Either judges beyond seventy were capable of sound decisions, or the eighty-year-old man who supported the President was thinking unsoundly. The argument that the Court was too small to handle its burden of work sounded like filigree over lace after a detailed public statement by Chief Justice Hughes. Most important, a Roosevelt move against the Supreme Court, though it was being seriously considered in the White House before the election of 1936 and affected one of the most controversial of all political issues, was never publicly mentioned until the election was over. In fact, so opposite an impression was conveyed that Senator Ashurst, a staunch New Dealer and chairman of the Senate Committee on the Judiciary, heatedly defended Roosevelt from the "ridiculous, absurd, and unjust" charge that he planned to enlarge the Supreme Court. When the Supreme Court began approving New Deal legislation but the Court enlargement bill was killed by Congress, the President himself indirectly admitted the disingenuousness of his proposal. He had lost a "battle," Roosevelt cracked, but won the "war." [1]

As the fight over the Court plan had gone on, a good many liberals joined conservatives in denouncing the deviousness of the method. The Court proposal, in fact, brought the first serious split in New Deal ranks, and some reformers who were shocked by Roosevelt's technique never again followed him with full-hearted enthusiasm. Yet a large part of the liberal movement went along, some wincing at the means but accepting them, many openly justifying deviousness as "smartness" or "practical politics."

At the beginning of the Court fight, Raymond Moley was discussing the issue with one of the younger men around the President. Moley expressed his concern that Roosevelt, in order to assure the support of Senate Majority Leader Joe Robinson,

[1] Quoted in Wesley McCune: *The Nine Young Men* (Harper, 1947), p. 18, and in Basil Rauch: *The History of the New Deal* (Creative Age Press, 1944), p. 283.

had made an implied promise of a Supreme Court place to the Senator, who was hardly a leading light of liberalism. Wouldn't the President have to honor this promise if the bill passed, Moley asked.

"There aren't any binding promises in politics," Moley remembered the reply of the young New Dealer. "There isn't any binding law. You just know that the strongest side wins." [2]

Moley was aghast, but he had not yet had a chance to read *The Deflation of American Ideals*, soon to be published by another young liberal, this one just out of training for government work at the Littauer School of Harvard. Under the New Deal, Edgar Kemler exulted, "the progressive ideal has been changed from a race horse into a mule, whose value lies, not in its beauty and morality, but in its practical usefulness. . . . With the repeal of Prohibition, sin was returned to the jurisdiction of the churches where it belongs, and the present administration has shown little inclination to reclaim it." Machiavelli had suggested the "wise" course for progressives, Kemler was sure. "We progressives are simply one kind of animal engaged in a struggle with other animals, dragons or capitalists, as the case may be. . . . We must show our worth in the only sense in which the word has meaning—by developing superior strength and skill in combat." [3]

A "rather original book," the *Nation* reviewer commented calmly, and the attitude was appropriate. Max Lerner, editor of the *Nation* during the Supreme Court fight and a powerful influence among the liberal intelligentsia, had made quite plain his own impatience with concern over means. He could not understand, Lerner wrote in 1938, what people meant by saying that liberals were faced by an "ethical crisis," that "they must not at their soul's peril use means that are justified only by the ends sought. . . . It puzzles me because I should have thought that means were never justified by anything except ends." [4]

[2] Quoted in Raymond Moley: *After Seven Years* (Harper, 1939), p. 354.

[3] Kemler: *The Deflation of American Ideals* (American Council on Public Affairs, Washington, 1941), pp. 16, 29, 33.

[4] *Nation* (August 9, 1941), CLIII, 126; Lerner: *It Is Later Than You Think* (Viking, 1938), p. 126.

The casualness about means was probably plainest in the general liberal unconcern over ordinary problems of political morality. Kemler was right when he categorized New Deal reformism as a movement that had relegated political sin, in the old sense, to the churches. Liberalism of the Thirties was little concerned with the clean government crusade which had conspicuously marked pre-World War I progressivism. The enormous increase in federal employees was brought about so largely outside the merit system that foes, with considerable justification, spoke of a new spoils system. When the Hatch Act, confining the political activities of federal employees, was proposed, it received noticeably little support from ardent New Dealers. Harry Hopkins's political uses of WPA funds are plain in the biography by his admirer Robert Sherwood.[5] And the leader himself, with a blandness that would have shocked the muckrakers, did business with the Hagues and the Kellys and the Pendergasts.

In part this attitude was the result of a genuine concentration on desperately pressing economic and social problems. In part, too, New Deal liberalism relied on the outstanding integrity and social-mindedness of its devotees, ranging from the incorruptibles on the highest levels, like Harold Ickes, down through the thousands of young men and women to whom government work in the Thirties was a dedicated service. Yet the attitude of New Deal reformism toward clean government was also, quite clearly, a product of the growing casualness about means, with its assumption that one should not be finicky about aid from Boss Hague if that aid would help put through social legislation.

Gloomily, another Clarence Darrow caught in another liberal difficulty, the aging Charles Beard fretted: "These people are talking the relativism which will ruin liberalism yet. Don't they know that the means can make the ends? Don't they realize that

[5] Sherwood quoted, with a stark poignance, Hopkins's surrender to expediency: "I thought at first I could be completely non-political. Then they told me I had to be part non-political and part political. I found that was impossible, at least for me. I finally realized there was nothing for it but to be all-political." So, Sherwood added, "the altruistic social worker—the lover of Keats—developed into one of the toughest of politicians." *Roosevelt and Hopkins* (Harper, 1948), p. 68.

their method of arguing can justify anything? I wish we could find some way of getting rid of conservative morality without having these youngsters drop all morality." [6]

III

IN THE White House, testiness had long since disappeared. Only a short while after the invalidation of the NRA, Roosevelt was musing to Secretary of Labor Frances Perkins: "You know the whole thing is a mess . . . [and] we have got the best out of it anyhow. Industry got a shot in the arm. Everything has started up. . . . I think perhaps NRA has done all it can do. . . . I don't want to impose a system on this country that will set aside the anti-trust laws on any permanent basis." [7] The President was back to his old self, impatient at the thought of permanence for the New Nationalism or any other ism, happily playing by ear.

Roosevelt could hardly improvise on the keyboard of American reform thought without hitting one chord constantly. Use the power of the federal government to smash concentrated wealth and to restore free enterprise; use it simultaneously to lift the standard of living of the country's less favored groups; and, by both these moves, make opportunity more abundant—in short, the reform program conceived in the depression of 1873, erected into a powerful political force by decades of agitation, given effectiveness and respectability by the early Theodore Roosevelt and by Woodrow Wilson, kept alive even during the complacent Twenties. When Uncle Ted's New Nationalism failed, there was always the Jeffersonian New Freedom of the Chief.

Even in the middle of Roosevelt's New Nationalist period, two quite different facts had been reopening his mind to the New Freedom. The Roosevelt of the early Thirties had considerable sympathy for big business, and thought of government controls less as a crackdown than as a partnership between government and

[6] Interview with the late Charles A. Beard.

[7] Quoted in Frances Perkins: *The Roosevelt I Knew* (Viking, 1946), pp. 252–3.

business in working out socially useful regulations. But during the NRA period the President discovered that corporation executives could prove highly unsatisfactory partners. Many openly flouted or skirted around all provisions of the NRA which were not entirely favorable to them, assailed most of the other New Deal measures, and spent millions of dollars trying to convince the country that Roosevelt was an egomaniacal Communist. By the time the President had to consider substitutes for the NRA, his irritation with big-business men had reached the point where he was remarking to intimates: "I get more and more convinced that most of them can't see farther than the next dividend." [8]

Simultaneously, the President's mind was being moved in an anti-big-business direction by a push from the left. The shrewd, unscrupulous Senator Huey Long, clawing his way toward the Presidency, was not asking his audiences to wait for the workings of elaborate reforms, or to understand that there might be some point in co-operating with trust magnates. He was flailing his arms, pointing to his pockmarked face as evidence of the way the rich ground the poor, and announcing that after the election of 1936 "your Kingfish, Huey, asittin' in the White House, will know how to handle them moguls." [9] By late 1935 the Kingfish had demagogued himself to a political strength which, if it could not move him into the White House, might possibly move Roosevelt out. A secret poll taken by the Democratic National Committee indicated that Long at the head of a third-party ticket would poll three to four million votes. This strength was not confined to the area around Louisiana, but reached into pivotal Northern states—including a potential one hundred thousand votes in New York State, which could swing that big group of electors to the Republicans. Before the election an assassin's bullet ended the Long threat. But Roosevelt had learned to worry about what could happen to a reform President who did not reckon sufficiently with the anti-big-business feeling rooted in decades of American agitation. From the demagogic left and from the

[8] Quoted in the Early interview.
[9] *New York Times*, November 17, 1935.

uncooperative right, the Jeffersonian reformer in Roosevelt was being pushed to the fore.[1]

The New Deal never did pass over to a strict New Freedom pattern. The Social Security Act, one of the most important bills passed after the invalidation of NRA, was no more Jeffersonian than it was New Nationalist; if it belonged to either pattern, it probably fitted better the Crolyan conception of the protective state. Nor did any one date or action mark the transition from the New Nationalism to the New Freedom. The shift came, in a blurred gradualism, after the invalidation of the NRA and the Triple A in 1935.

The change was marked by a slow turnover in the President's Brain-Trusters. By 1938 Washington was saying: "Moley is in opposition; Tugwell is in the city-planning business; and Hugh Johnson is in a rage," and the place of the early Brain-Trusters was being filled by a much larger group who shared an enthusiasm for New Freedom liberalism.[2] Some of these men had been in the Administration almost from its start—most importantly, Harold Ickes and Harry Hopkins—and were now moving into the inner circle. Others were new figures, working together in shifting combinations, rising and falling in importance, men like Robert H. Jackson, Herman Oliphant, of the Treasury Department, Leon Henderson, a WPA economist, Commissioner of Labor Statistics Isador Lubin, and a half-dozen or more brilliant young graduates of Harvard Law School who had been placed in New Deal posts through the influence of the day's leading Jeffersonian legalist, Felix Frankfurter.

Early in the Hundred Days, one of these young lawyers showed up at a White House reception, maneuvered a friend into asking him to perform, and enchanted the President for two hours by singing Irish ballads, sea chanteys, and mountain laments. "You

---

[1] Moley, p. 305; James A. Farley: *Jim Farley's Story* (McGraw-Hill, 1948), pp. 50–1; Harnett T. Kane: *Louisiana Hayride* (Morrow, 1941), Chap. v. Moley asserted that F. D. R. spoke directly of the need to "steal Long's thunder."

[2] Quoted in Joseph Alsop and Robert Kintner: "We Shall Make America Over," *Saturday Evening Post* (October 29, 1938), CXI, 5.

certainly stole the show, Tommy," the friend congratulated him. "I always steal the show," said Tommy Corcoran, and he always did.[8] Springing somehow from a humdrum Rhode Island merchant family, Corcoran left Brown University loaded with prizes, and then proceeded to equal Brandeis's record at Harvard Law School, a record that had seemed about as vulnerable as Babe Ruth's sixty home runs. The Hundred Days were not over before Corcoran was the unquestioned leader of Frankfurter's protégés, ranging airily through the government bureaus, making droves of friends and bringing the friends together for a session of songs and denunciations of big business, calling them all "my kids" or "my little chicks" from the senescence of his thirty-three years.

By 1934 Corcoran began admitting that one of his kids was his full equal, and at first friends were amazed at the choice. The anointed of the handsome, ebullient Tommy was a pale, shy ascetic, completely oblivious of pleasure or even comfort, who was shepherded around by Corcoran like a child at his first visit to an Automat. But Ben Cohen, Corcoran kept telling everyone, was something special, and everyone soon agreed. Cohen's legal powers aroused an admiration akin to worshipfulness, and his selfless absorption in public service won for the Corcoran-Cohen team a respect that Corcoran's pyrotechnics could never have achieved alone.

The team enjoyed a moment of importance in early New Deal days when, through Frankfurter's recommendation, Corcoran and Cohen were called on to draft the Securities and Exchange Act and the Securities Tax Bill. The President was impressed with their skill and there were more songs at the White House, but these were not the days for militant Wilsonians. Moley was wary of Corcoran's efforts "to grind the Wilson-Brandeis little-business ax," and he saw to it that the President's taste in music was not extended to other matters.[4] Corcoran and Cohen gained their real admission to the inner circle in 1935, when Roosevelt made one of the first important moves of his New Freedom period, the

[8] Quoted in the Ickes interview.
[4] Moley, p. 333.

attack on holding companies in the power utilities field. The President asked the long-time trust-buster, Secretary of the Interior Harold Ickes, to supervise the working out of a bill, and, through Ickes's office, Corcoran and Cohen were assigned the detailed work.

The pair went at the task in a manner that was soon to be famous—all-night furies of work, with endless cups of sticky-sweet black coffee—and the bill that went to Congress would have delighted the heart of any trust-hating Populist. All holding companies in the power field, the "death sentence" clause provided, had to prove their social usefulness within five years or dissolve. When the provision provoked a savage battle in Congress, Corcoran bobbed up in the middle of the fight, artfully explaining and defending, dangling patronage before the eyes of reluctant Congressmen, rushing back and forth to the White House for reports and instructions. The holding companies were partially reprieved before Congress passed the bill, but the Corcoran-Cohen team was made. From then on, few important White House conferences did not include one or both of the men, at least four key laws were products of their legal wizardry, and "Tommy the Cork," as the President was soon affectionately calling the front man of the team, emerged as one of the two or three most inside New Deal insiders.

Shortly after the Holding Company Act went to Congress, Roosevelt sent to Congress a tax bill that was truculently anti-corporation. The President's "State of the Union" address of January 1936 bristled with phrases about "our resplendent economic autocracy" and the men of "entrenched greed" who sought "the restoration of their selfish power." [5] All suggestions to revive the New Nationalist aspects of the NRA and the Triple A were brushed aside. Instead, the Administration pressed ahead with key legislation that bore the unmistakable New Freedom stamp. It went along with the Wagner-Connery Labor Act, probably the most bluntly anti-corporation legislation the United States has ever known, and pressed the Fair Labor Standards Act, with its

[5] Rosenman, V, 13, 14, 16.

ironclad provisions of minimum wages and maximum hours. A modified Triple A and other agricultural legislation, dropping much of the national-planning aspect of the original Triple A, aimed directly to improve the economic position of farmers and took especial care to promote the interests of the lowest-income group.

Amid this churn of legislation, the most symbolic of all New Freedom moves was made. In October 1937 a recession declared itself to the roar of crashing stocks, and the Corcoran group, attributing the recession to greedy price-fixing by monopolistic combines, urged on the President a series of bold steps, among them a general trust-busting campaign. Roosevelt was a willing listener, but the New Nationalist in him had not entirely disappeared. For the moment, the President decided, he would ask for a new housing act, hoping that this would stimulate employment. Beyond that, he would sit tight.

But Tommy Corcoran had no intention of sitting tight. The Administration was now being assailed on all sides, by conservatives for having caused the recession and by liberals for not ending it. To Corcoran it seemed as if the whole New Deal was on the run and something had to be done quickly. In a council of war instigated by Corcoran, a group of the new Brain-Trusters decided to gamble. They would go ahead on their own trust-busting campaign, hoping to stir the President into joining them but leaving him free to repudiate them at any time.

Assistant Attorney General Robert Jackson opened the campaign. In a radio speech written by Corcoran and Cohen, Jackson charged: "By profiteering, the monopolists and those so near monopoly as to control their prices have simply priced themselves out of the market, and priced themselves into the slump." [6] In the excitement that followed, Corcoran asked Harold Ickes to speak. The Secretary of the Interior had been impressed by Léon Blum's assault on France's "Two Hundred Families" and he had been reading Ferdinand Lundberg's *America's Sixty Families* and

[6] Quoted in Joseph Alsop and Robert Kintner: *Men around the President* (Doubleday, Doran, 1939), p. 135.

Sinclair Lewis's *It Can't Happen Here.* Ickes answered Corcoran's request with two assaults on big capital, "It Is Happening Here" and "Sixty Families Revisited." Washington was in a tumult. Conservative Senators demanded that Roosevelt immediately repudiate Jackson and Ickes. Ickes told his friends he slept with his hat hanging ready on the bedpost.

But the business indices were fighting on the side of the New Freedom trust-busters. Industrial production plummeted from 120 in July 1937 to 84 in March 1938; factory employment, from 89 to 81. As the spring of 1938 came on, Uncle Ted's New Nationalist nephew was overwhelmed by the Chief's disciple; Roosevelt, too, had become convinced that the whole New Deal was threatened by selfish and shortsighted big capital. In March he reinvigorated the antitrust division of the Justice Department, naming as its chief the able Thurman Arnold, whom Jackson gleefully characterized as "a cross between Voltaire and a cowboy, with the cowboy predominating." [7] The next month the President sent to Congress a strong message urging "a thorough study of the concentration of economic power in American industry and the effect of that concentration upon the decline of competition." [8]

IV

AT THE high tide of the New Deal shift from the New Nationalism to the New Freedom, Franklin Roosevelt attempted a little essay on the place of his Administrations in American history. No matter what the specific program of the moment, the President wrote, the Democratic Party which he led was the "liberal" party, and throughout American history there had been two key differences between liberals and conservatives. "One great difference . . . has been that the liberal party . . . believed in the wisdom and efficacy of the will of the great majority of the people, as

---

[7] Quoted in *Current Biography 1940* (H. W. Wilson), p. 28.
[8] Rosenman, VII, 315.

distinguished from the judgment of a small minority of either education or wealth. . . . The other great difference between the two parties has been this: The liberal party is a party which believes that, as new conditions and problems arise beyond the power of men and women to meet as individuals, it becomes the duty of the Government itself to find new remedies with which to meet them. The liberal party insists that the Government has the definite duty to use all its power and resources to meet new social problems with new social controls." [9]

Roosevelt's definition of liberalism certainly fitted the New Deal in general, even if conservatives could rightfully question how much of a role its New Nationalist phase left to "the people." But the statements of the President are of little use for the purpose of close analysis. His description of the reformer would have been acceptable to a Populist, to a progressive of the early 1900's, and to most of the widely variant liberal groups in the Thirties. There was something more to New Deal liberalism in both its New Nationalist and New Freedom phases, and the something more, as always, was connected with the climate of national opinion.

In the hundreds of articles and books that treated the thinking prevailing in the United States during the Thirties, one note was persistently struck. The New Deal, though it had given the nation a way of coping with fear, had not entirely conquered it, and the common attitude was to go along with the New Deal enthusiastically, but warily. If it could produce, fine; but there was always the reservation, enormously accentuated by the recession of 1937, that it might not solve the problem. "Here we come, WPA!" the college boys wisecracked, and millions beyond college age smiled understandingly.[1]

[9] Ibid., VII, xxix, xxx. Roosevelt had another definition, his favorite. "A reactionary," he liked to say, "is a somnambulist walking backwards. A conservative is a man with two perfectly good legs with both feet planted firmly in the air. And a liberal is a man who uses his legs and, simultaneously, his head." Quoted in Grace Tully: *F. D. R., My Boss* (Scribner, 1949), p. 98.
[1] Quoted in Charles A. and Mary R. Beard: *America in Midpassage* (Macmillan, 1946), p. 902.

The depression not only created a continuing uneasiness that another crash was round the corner; it brought into frightening focus a number of long-time trends that also spelled insecurity. Every year of increased urbanization and mechanization left thousands of individuals feeling more like an easily replaceable cog in the wheel, more alone in the impersonal crowd. By the late Thirties students of American society were also writing of "the specter of insecurity" raised by the steadily mounting percentage of the population who depended on someone else for a job, the growing proportion of women supporting themselves or contributing a vital portion to the family income, the ineluctable decline in independent farming. "Even the heads of our large industrial corporations have no security in their jobs," one authority added. "No longer the owners of their businesses . . . they have become merely paid employees of their respective firms with the accompanying insecurity of tenure inherent in all jobs, high or low." [2] Above all, the average age of the population was rapidly changing, with the age curve moving ever farther beyond the confidence of youth. It was the 1930's that, poignantly, kept Walter Pitkin's *Life Begins at Forty* at or near the top of the best-seller list for two solid years.

The general sense of insecurity was accompanied by a special restiveness among America's minority groups. They were not only, in fact, the least secure—the "last hired, the first fired," as the Negroes put it. By the 1930's the Negroes were more than half a century from slavery, and thousands of the newer immigrant families were raising a second or third generation on American soil. Often these later products of minority origins had the education and the manner to compete successfully for higher prestige positions and to move in higher-status circles, and the general liberal atmosphere of the Thirties encouraged their aspirations. Just because of this encouragement and the increased adaptation to the ways of the dominant groups, the enormous obstacles still standing in the way were the more frustrating.

Despite these developments, there is little evidence that any

[2] Abraham Epstein: *Insecurity* (Random House, 1938), p. 13.

considerable part of the population gave up the faith in America as the land of opportunity. Too many generations had rooted their whole way of life in the belief; too many facts still proclaimed that the United States, more than any other country, did actually throw open the road for ambition. What happened was that millions of Americans were supplementing the credo of opportunity with a demand for laws that would guarantee them greater economic security and more equality in the pursuit of economic and social status. In case—just in case—economic opportunity did not knock, they wanted to be sure that the mailman would be around with a social-security check. In case—just in case—the social ladder proved too steep, they wanted laws which would guarantee that they would not be left on too humiliating a rung.

These trends showed themselves plainly in liberal thinking. Previous generations of reformers had been little concerned with equality or security brought about by law. The emphasis, whether in the bitter period of the late nineteenth century or in the expansive early twentieth century, had been simply on creating a situation in which men could compete with some approximation of fairness of terms. Far from seeking security, earlier reformers had been inclined to agree with Edward Ross that "security, as a goal, is essentially un-American because it implies a willingness to sacrifice the possibility of a great future for a safe present." [3] Far from wanting an equality enforced by law, most of the reformers would have gone along with Ray Stannard Baker's dictum that "the Great Teacher never preached the flat equality of men, social or otherwise." Improving one's position in society, he explained, was no subject for legislation but rather a matter of winning higher status by individual attainment. [4]

Now, during both the New Nationalist and the New Freedom phases of the New Deal and increasing in intensity, a drive was being made to bring about greater security. The President himself laid down the line in 1934 when he placed "the security of the

[3] Interview with the late Edward A. Ross.
[4] Baker: *Following the Color Line* (Doubleday, Page, 1908), p. 307.

men, women and children of the Nation" first among the objectives of his Administration, and went on to specify that security included "decent homes . . . [located where men could] engage in productive work . . . and some safeguard against misfortunes which cannot be wholly eliminated in this man-made world of ours." [5] The Social Security Act of 1935, of course, was the keystone of the Administration's security legislation, but a similar purpose marked a variety of New Deal legislation, ranging from the creation of the Home Owner's Loan Corporation in 1933 to the establishment of the Farm Security Administration in 1937. How far New Deal liberalism was ready to go in guaranteeing security was far from clear. Conservatives could only gloomily note the portents. The President spoke of a security program "which because of many lost years will take many future years to fulfill"; both the Farm Security and Resettlement Administrations were bringing group security ideas even into that sanctuary of individual relations, the medical field; and many New Dealers were ready to agree with Eleanor Roosevelt when she declared: "In the nineteenth century . . . there was no recognition that the government owed an individual certain things as a right. . . . Now it is accepted that the government has an obligation to guard the rights of an individual so carefully that he never reaches a point at which he needs charity." [6]

The New Deal made no concrete moves toward enforced equality, unless it was in its none too vigorous steps against segregation in public housing and against discrimination in employment on government contracts, but it smiled sympathetically on a liberal movement that was hurrying in that direction. The very tone of the New Deal was far more aggressively equalitarian than that of either Populism or progressivism. The Populists had never been able to win the workingman; all during the decades from 1865 to 1936, most of the Negroes had been voting Republican while most of the newer immigrants were voting Democratic. The New Deal, for the first time, brought all the low-status

[5] Rosenman, III, 288.
[6] Ibid., IV, 17; Eleanor Roosevelt: "If You Ask Me," *Ladies' Home Journal* (July 1948), LXV, 44.

groups into one camp and produced an economic and social cleavage in voting unprecedented in the history of the country. Under the circumstances, New Deal liberalism naturally represented leveling to an unusual degree.[7] It was the New Dealer's President who told the Daughters of the American Revolution: "Remember, remember always that all of us, and you and I especially, are descended from immigrants." [8] It was his wife who was photographed while being escorted by two Negro R.O.T.C. cadets.

Over much of previous progressivism had hung an air of patronizing the unfortunate, of helping the group that reformers often called "the little people." The attitude of the new liberalism was spoken with classic tartness when Joseph Mitchell presented his stories of "McSorley's Wonderful Saloon." The phrase "little people," Mitchell declared, was "repulsive. . . . There are no little people in this book. They are as big as you are, whoever you are." [9] The point was carried to its further significance by a discerning, upper-income liberal, who added: "For quite a while I have lived in a commuter community that is rabidly anti-Roosevelt and I am convinced that the heart of their hatred of Roosevelt is not economic. The real source of the venom is that Rooseveltism challenged their feeling that they were superior people, occupying by right a privileged position in the world. I am convinced that a lot of them would even have backed many of his economic measures if they had been permitted to believe the laws represented the fulfillment of their responsibility as 'superior people.' They were not permitted that belief. Instead, as the New Deal went on, it chipped away more and more at their sense of superiority. By the second term, it was pressing hard on a vital spot and the conservatives were screaming." [1]

To many liberals, it was just these variations in reform that gave

7 Polling figures, whatever their error, still indicated the startling new line-up of American politics. See, for example, William A. Lydgate: *What America Thinks* (Crowell, 1944), Chap. ix.

8 Rosenman, VII, 259.

9 Mitchell: *McSorley's Wonderful Saloon* (Duell, Sloan & Pearce, n.d.), Author's Note.

1 For an obvious reason, this person is not identified.

the New Deal its great strength. "This isn't a do-gooder tea club, patching things up here and there," one of the President's close associates exulted. "This is a real people's movement getting at the heart of the great modern problem, insecurity—insecurity in jobs and insecurity in feelings." [2] Other liberals were not so confident. Even with the new concerns over economic security and social equality, American liberalism of the late Thirties was still fundamentally the New Freedom, and once it was tested over any considerable period of time, it could easily develop all the serious difficulties inherent in the New Freedom.

The New Deal was to have time only to begin the test of its variety of the New Freedom. For just as it was really swinging into its new phase, frenetic men across the oceans, whose interest in liberalism had always been minimal, decided to shove a different issue to the fore.

[2] The person prefers not to be identified.

CHAPTER XVI

"... *Much of What Not to Do*"

T HE FRENETIC men had been worrying Franklin Roosevelt
for quite a while. A long-time naval enthusiast, an ardent,
if somewhat erratic, collective-security advocate, a cosmopolite
who took an enormous zest in international affairs, the President
was no man to let aggression rumble in Europe and Asia without
his attention. He was sure that the security of the United States
required keeping in friendly hands the Atlantic beachheads of the
British Isles, France, the Iberian Peninsula, and the north and west
coasts of Africa, and, in the Pacific area, the Netherlands East
Indies, the Philippines, and the Marianas. By late 1936, Axis
aggressions in Europe and Asia threatened so many of these posts
that the President was becoming, to use the phrase of Under
Secretary of State Sumner Welles, "obsessed" with the dangers
confronting the United States.[1] In the following three years,
while the domestic New Deal was taking on the New Freedom
shape, he moved forcefully to meet the foreign situation, sum-
moning the United States to join in a "quarantine" of aggression,
pushing a huge rearmament program, and attempting a revision of
the neutrality legislation which would have permitted nations
attacked by aggressors to buy American-made arms.

As Administration foreign policy emerged in the late Thirties,

[1] Welles: *Where are We Heading?* (Harper, 1946), p. 3.

liberal opinion split into three groups quite similar to those of pre-1917 days—the collective-security faction, the die-hard isolationists, and the middle group, isolationist in its yearnings but ready to be persuaded that collective security, perhaps even war, was the wise course. But there was an important difference between the liberal situation of 1914–17 and that of the late Thirties. As American entrance into World War I came on, both the reform President and most of the reform movement were middle-of-the-roaders in foreign policy. In the late Thirties the reform President was leading the collective-security faction while most of the liberals were convinced anti-interventionists, tending strongly toward a genuine isolationism.

All the old impulses toward liberal isolationism were operating in full force—the way the reformers' economic interpretation made any active foreign policy seem a servant of greedy businessmen, their fear that war meant the end of reform, their abhorrence of its carnage. Now, in the Thirties, there were also potent extra factors creating a fear of entanglement. General American opinion was far more consciously isolationist, and liberals naturally reflected this national attitude. The reformer of the Wilson period had scarcely looked toward Asia; the liberal of the late Thirties was quite aware of the Far East, and saw across the Pacific the discouraging spectacle of an arrogant Japan and a corrupt China locked in a seemingly interminable warfare. In 1914–17 France and England, the two natural allies of the United States in the event of war, were both under reform-minded governments. In the late Thirties the Prime Ministers were Chamberlain and Daladier, both routine conservatives and men whose foreign policies, many liberals believed, were motivated largely by a desire to preserve fascist Germany as a buffer against the Soviet Union. The Munich appeasement of Hitler in 1938, while it increased the liberal fear of fascism, also increased the liberal contempt for Chamberlain and Daladier. If any one book summarized the American reform attitude toward the English and French governments after 1938, the book was G. E. R. Gedye's *Betrayal in Central Europe*, an argument that both governments represented a clammy reaction, tending toward fascism themselves, assuming that the choice for the Continent had to be Hitler or Stalin, and showing by their every move their preference for Hitler.

Above all, the liberal of the late Thirties was pushed toward isolationism by the deep-seated disillusionment with Wilsonianism. In 1917 the La Follettes and the Bournes had told reformers that collective security and preparedness led to war, and that war would mean the end of reform, a stifling of civil liberties, a peace that left the world no better than it was before. They had not listened, and they got the Versailles Treaty, the Palmer raids, and Warren Harding. Once burned so badly, most liberals were in no mood to expose their fingers again. Herbert Croly's successor as chief editor of the *New Republic,* Bruce Bliven, spoke the feeling precisely when he remarked in 1938: "I remember vividly the days before April, 1917, when a country that did not want to go to war was tricked and bullied and persuaded into doing so. . . . I feel, as I watch the motion picture of events unreeling on the screen of time, that I have seen it all before. This is where I came in." [2]

In such an atmosphere the liberal economic interpretation of diplomacy and war continued in full vigor. The Senate Munitions Investigating Committee of the mid-Thirties, which gave great vogue to the argument that the United States was pushed into World War I by greedy businessmen, was largely a liberal performance. An outpouring of newspaper and magazine articles by reformers had a good deal to do with getting the investigation under way.[3] The chairman of the Senate Committee and its chief figure was Senator Gerald Nye, then something of a liberal

[2] Bliven: "This Is Where I Came In," *New Republic* (January 5, 1938), XCIII, 245–6.

[3] Typical of the literature, and one of the most influential samples, was *Merchants of Death* (Dodd, Mead, 1934), of which the chief author was H. C. Engelbrecht, associate editor of the liberal-minded *World Tomorrow.* Liberals, of course, were not alone in the interest. One of the most influential articles appeared in *Fortune* ("Arms and the Men" [March 1934], IX, 53–7, 113–26), then a magazine with an editorial board of quite mixed political views.

hero for his efforts in domestic affairs; its head counsel was Stephen Raushenbush, the son of Walter Rauschenbusch and a persistent reformer in his own right. It was the liberal-minded journalist Walter Millis who expressed much of the attitude of the Nye Committee in his enormously influential *Road to War*, and it was the dean of the reform historians, Charles Beard, who broadened the findings of the committee into a widely imitated liberal economic interpretation.

Basically, Beard argued in *The Devil Theory of War*, America went to war in 1917 "apart from the uproar of propagandists, sentimentalists and the intelligentsia." Businessmen had leaped to supply the Allies with goods, and when the Allies no longer could pay for the goods, bankers stepped in to provide the funds. Thus American prosperity was so mortgaged to an Allied victory that the United States had to intervene when that victory was in danger. The whole development was "like a Greek tragedy. . . .

ACT I. AUGUST 10, 1914–OCTOBER 22, 1914. THE GOVERN-
MENT OF THE UNITED STATES BLOCKS POWERFUL IN-
TERESTS EAGER TO MAKE MONEY FOR THEMSELVES
AND OTHERS. . . .

ACT II. OCTOBER 23, 1914–MIDSUMMER, 1915. BANKERS PUT
THE GOVERNMENT OF THE UNITED STATES IN A
DILEMMA AND WIN APPROVAL FOR CREDITS TO BEL-
LIGERENTS. . . .

ACT III. AUGUST 14, 1915–AUGUST 26, 1915. BANKERS PUT THE
GOVERNMENT OF THE UNITED STATES IN ANOTHER
DILEMMA AND OBTAIN APPROVAL FOR LOANS TO
BELLIGERENTS. . . .

ACT IV. SEPTEMBER, 1915–APRIL, 1917. DEEP IN THE MIRE OF
WAR THROUGH LOANS, CREDITS, AND SALES, THE GOV-
ERNMENT OF THE UNITED STATES ENTERS THE WAR." [4]

And the way to prevent a re-enactment of the tragedy? The United States, Beard stressed again and again, should cling to the

[4] Beard: *The Devil Theory of War* (Vanguard, 1936), pp. 27, 32, 40, 55, 89.

Neutrality Acts, and combine with the legislation a vigorous reform at home that would raise American consuming power to the point where no foreign trade would be essential to prosperity. The United States had "the setting for a continental power. . . . We should concentrate our attention on tilling our own garden. It is a big garden and a good garden, though horribly managed and trampled by our greedy folly. Tilling it properly doubtless involves many drastic changes in capitalism as historically practised. Well, with all due respect to the enterprise and virtues of capitalism, I never regarded that 'system' as sacred, unchanging and unchangeable." [5]

The actual beginning of World War II in 1939 did little to alter the strength of liberal isolationism. The attitude, if it varied at all, may well have intensified. The months of "Phony War" stripped away any sense of urgency and made the Chamberlain and Daladier governments seem still less the crusaders for democracy. If the Soviet-Nazi Nonaggression Pact at the beginning of the war cost the Communists much of their influence over liberal thinking, the influence that did continue was stridently isolationist. Both sides in the conflict, the Communists argued, were "reactionary, imperialist" powers, and the Americans, like the Russians, should have sense enough to remain neutral and devote their energies to raising their own standard of living.

These points, so close to the traditional trend of American reform thinking, slid easily into liberal minds. Shortly after the war began, the Communist-dominated District No. 2 of the Maritime Federation of the Pacific published a pamphlet, *The Yanks Are Not Coming*, which had been written by one of its Communist-minded members, Mike Quin. "This is a war of bankers and the people have no stake in it whatever," the pamphlet proclaimed. ". . . We've got a first class job on our hands straightening out this civilization we have right here." [6] Here was the language of Robert La Follette, of Senator Nye and Charles Beard,

[5] Ibid., pp. 119, 120.
[6] Quin: *The Yanks Are Not Coming* (Maritime Federation of the Pacific, San Francisco, n.d.), pp. 4, 10.

of generations of American reformers. Within a short while, three hundred thousand copies of the pamphlet had been sold, numerous unions were distributing it, and the title was becoming a favorite slogan at reform meetings and on non-Communist picket signs. Quite typically, the strongly anti-Communist liberal, William Allen White, oblivious of the source of the phrase, wrote: "If I were making a motto . . . it would be 'The Yanks Are Not Coming.' " [7]

Never, on any other issue, had the liberal in the White House and most of his liberal support been so little in rapport. The general isolationism of the country, and especially the isolationism of the people who were usually Roosevelt's strongest supporters, left the President feeling stymied at a time when he believed that drastic action was needed for the very security of the nation. On their part, millions of liberals viewed the President suspiciously on the issue which they knew was the crucial one of the day. Roosevelt, they told one another warily, would go down in history as one of the greatest of Presidents if only he would "keep out of Europe." [8]

II

DENMARK TOOK one day; Norway, a little over two weeks; Belgium and the Netherlands, eighteen days; France, another fifteen days. Within seventy days after Adolf Hitler ended the Phony War, the Nazis were masters of western Europe, England was in mortal peril, and American isolationism, liberal or conservative, was collapsing.

Roosevelt, like a fighter with his hands suddenly untied, leaped forward in a rat-a-tat of executive blows. But the White House alone could not meet the most urgent problem. England was desperately in need both of funds and of shipping, and American

[7] Quoted in Walter Johnson: *The Battle against Isolation* (University of Chicago Press, 1944), p. 182.

[8] The statement is from a close friend and supporter, quoted in Bruce Catton: *The War Lords of Washington* (Harcourt, Brace, 1948), p. 15.

aid in these respects was barred by the cash-and-carry provisions of the Neutrality Acts, so cherished by the remaining isolationist sentiment. Two months after the fall of France, the President, his private secretary, "Missy" LeHand, and the Ambassador to France, William Bullitt, sat mulling over the situation. After dismissing endless alternatives as too likely to be blocked by opposition in Congress, Roosevelt scratched his head, cocked his cigarette-holder, and spoke out the thought that had been slowly forming in his mind.

"Bill," he said, "if my neighbor's house catches fire and I know that fire will spread to my house unless it is put out, and I am watering the grass in my back yard, and I don't pass my garden hose over the fence to my neighbor, I am a fool. How do you think the country and the Congress would react if I should put aid to the British in the form of lending them my garden hose?" [9]

The country, together with its liberal movement, reacted to Roosevelt's proposal for Lend-Lease just as he wanted. Liberal isolationism did not disappear. In the Senate, Robert La Follette, Jr., kept the hearings on the bill under a machine-gun fire of hostile questions, and he was joined in his opposition by Senator Nye and two other men who had commanded widespread liberal admiration, Hiram Johnson and Burton Wheeler. Here and there, outside of Congress, well-known reformers resolutely held to their isolationism. Most notably, Charles Beard's contribution to the Lend-Lease hearings was an assault on the bill which called on all American history to support his claim that Lend-Lease was both unconstitutional and a dishonest maneuvering of the country into war.[1] But most liberals were in no mood for discussions of

[9] Quoted in William C. Bullitt: "How We Won the War and Lost the Peace," *Life* (August 30, 1948), XXV, 88.

[1] Reading aloud the official title of the Lend-Lease bill, "An act to promote the defense of the United States," Beard declared: "It should read: All provisions of law and the Constitution to the contrary notwithstanding, an Act to place all the wealth and all the men and women of the United States at the free disposal of the President . . . to authorize him to wage undeclared wars for anybody, anywhere in the world, until the affairs of the world are ordered to suit his policies, and for any other purpose he may have in mind now or at any time in the future, which may be remotely related to the contingencies contemplated in the title of this Act." U.S.

history or of the intricacies of Constitutional law. They were horrified and frightened and looking for leadership. A liberal President was giving that leadership, boldly and ingeniously, and they rallied behind him.

The *New Republic,* so accurate a weathervane of reform opinion in the Wilson era, again gave a correct indication of the shift. Ever since its repudiation of the Versailles Treaty, the journal had opposed Rooseveltism in foreign affairs with such vigor that, as one of its favorite contributors, Max Lerner, remarked, it seemed to be atoning for its sin of 1917 by its isolationism in the next generation.[2] But the Nazi blitz of western Europe was too much for the *New Republic.* Its editors swung behind Lend-Lease and handed his hat to John T. Flynn, a columnist who refused to support the bill. Flynn hit back with the charge that he was simply continuing the attitude that the *New Republic* had represented for years, and the editors made no strenuous effort to deny his argument. Instead, they spoke the 1941 liberal's feeling of the urgency of the moment.

"There are times," the *New Republic* declared, "when to stand still is to change, and that is what Mr. Flynn has done. . . . The collapse of France and the danger of a possible British defeat suddenly brought home to all sensible Americans the fact that the peril was much greater and more imminent than we had previously believed it could be. We do not see how anyone with eyes in his head can dispute the fact that Hitler is a menace to this country and that, to this extent, England's battle is our own. . . . The editors of The New Republic . . . are willing to admit that they may be wrong; but they feel that when the existence of the country is at stake, it is better to be sure than sorry." [3]

The Congressional vote on Lend-Lease showed how many other liberals were determined not to be sorry. Analysis of the

---

Senate, Committee on Foreign Relations, 77th Cong., 1st Sess.: *Hearings . . . [on] a bill further to promote the defense of the United States* (1941), p. 309.

[2] Lerner: *Ideas for the Ice Age* (Viking, 1941), p. 10.

[3] "Mr. Flynn Speaks for Himself," *New Republic* (February 3, 1941), CIV, 150.

ballots in the House and the Senate and supplementary evidence
indicates that, as in the case of the opposition to entrance into
World War I, the vote against Lend-Lease concentrated in the
Midwest and in regions where hyphenate tendencies were pacifist,
pro-German, or anti-Ally. But the evidence also makes plain that
the 1917 and 1941 votes were emphatically different in an important respect. The vote against entrance into World War I came
from a group that had a significant strain of progressivism in its
thinking. The Representatives and Senators who opposed Lend-
Lease were overwhelmingly conservative in domestic affairs.
Equally striking, of the three most widely publicized "liberal"
Congressmen who opposed Lend-Lease, Senators La Follette,
Nye, and Wheeler, the latter two were rapidly ceasing to support
reform in domestic affairs.[4]

As liberal opinion swung away from the Nye Committee
attitude, it naturally de-emphasized the liberal economic interpretation which tainted any collective-security policy by connecting
it with the greedy finaglings of imperialism. Appropriately
enough, the author of *Road to War*, Walter Millis, led the way,
and two months after Hitler invaded Poland, Millis was eating his
words in the front window of *Life*. He had never intended that
his book should make any one factor, economic or noneconomic,
the major explanation of American entrance into World War I,
Millis declared. As for World War II, "few things seem to me
more certain than that, if the United States does become a belliger-

[4] The domestic and foreign-affairs votes of the Congressmen who voted
against entrance into World War I and of those who voted against Lend-
Lease have been correlated by the process described on pp. 463-4.
Of the 31 Senators who voted against Lend-Lease, 19 indicated their
attitude on 10 or more of the domestic measures that were used as the
test of degree of liberalism. Of these 19 men, only 6 indicated that they
approved three quarters or more of the measures, and 5 out of the 19 were
on the liberal side less than 60 per cent of the time. The conservatism of
the opposition to Lend-Lease is additionally confirmed by the fact that
many of the New Deal measures used in the test, particularly the earlier
ones, were backed by huge, almost nonpartisan majorities. In the House,
the Lend-Lease opposition was even more conservative in domestic affairs.
Of the 74 Representatives who indicated their attitude on 9 or more of
the 18 test measures, 35, or slightly less than half, approved 6 or less of
the measures.

ent, it will not be for business reasons or under the impulse of an industrial and financial community." [5]

Liberals of a more leftish persuasion, for whom economic interpretation was a deeply set way of thinking, sloughed it off less easily. If the general breakaway can be dated, it was marked by the passionately eloquent article of Archibald MacLeish, unofficial poet laureate of the New Deal, which appeared in the *Nation* as the blitz hit France. The American intellectual, MacLeish contended in "The Irresponsibles," had sought objectivity with little concern over moral values; he had been "a refugee from consequences, an exile from the responsibilities of moral choice," and consequently was ill-equipped to meet the basic challenge of fascism. The MacLeish article, however oblique its approach to the Nye Committee attitude, released the floodgates. The *Nation*, asking a variety of liberal intellectuals to comment on "The Irresponsibles," received replies that were summarized in Professor Hans Kohn's denunciation of the "general indifference to, or contempt of, moral values, a complacent belief in economic and social factors as the prime motivation in man's life." [6] Thereafter the liberal intelligentsia hurried into an anguish of revaluation. A few of the more smug whiplashed all liberals except themselves. More were critical of themselves as well as of the movement.[7] Whatever the approach, the liberal economic interpretation of diplomacy and war was done. The tenaciously economic-minded and isolationist Charles Beard, only a few years before a savant of liberal foreign policy, was now a lonely old man, glooming out his last years on his Connecticut hill.

"Well," Beard would remark snappishly, "so now it's all morals and no economics, and we all rally behind the leader. And just which Roosevelt do we rally around—the Roosevelt who is going

[5] Millis: "1939 Is Not 1914," *Life* (November 6, 1939), VII, 96.

[6] MacLeish: "The Irresponsibles," *Nation* (May 18, 1940), CL, 622; "On the 'Irresponsibles,'" ibid. (June 1, 1940), CL, 680.

[7] One of the most interesting manifestations of the new attitude was John Dos Passos's *The Ground We Stand On* (Harcourt, Brace, 1941), which discussed what he called the generation's confusion between "self-government as a political method" and "a particular phase of the economic setup of production." P. 9.

to keep us out of war by Lend-Lease or the Roosevelt who knows full well that Lend-Lease is the sure path to war?" [8] The question was bothering liberals. Much as they had swung over to the collective-security position, they were sharply divided, among themselves and often in their own minds. Did they favor collective security only in so far as it would keep the country out of the shooting war or did they favor collective security up to, if necessary, the complete joining in the Allied cause? [9] Roosevelt was of little help in clarifying the situation. His Administration persistently presented its foreign policy, including Lend-Lease, as the best way to stay out of war. Yet the Lend-Lease policy, which plainly implied the convoying of American arms across the Atlantic, opened wide the probability that the United States would find itself in full-fledged hostilities.[1] Liberals fretted and snarled over the situation, dividing principally between those who were ready to fight and those who were ready to do everything up to fighting. Then suddenly, on that December Sunday afternoon, Japan settled the question.

As the bombs fell on Pearl Harbor, American reform opinion reached near-unanimity in foreign affairs. An attack admitted of no discussion; a nation that was attacked, liberals and conservatives, fought back. The votes on the resolutions recognizing a state of war with Japan, Germany, and Italy were perfunctorily unanimous in the Senate. In the House, by a peculiar irony, Jeannette Rankin, the woman who had cast so dramatic a vote against American entrance into World War I, had just returned to Con-

---

[8] Interview with the late Charles Beard.

[9] The debate was reflected in the breakaway of the increasingly prowar Fight for Freedom Committee, which included many liberal leaders, from the more hesitant Committee to Defend America by Aiding the Allies, also representing many liberals.

[1] The confusion was climaxed by Roosevelt's famous 1940 campaign statement that "your boys are not going to be sent into any foreign wars." The statement was taken to mean quite different things, as perhaps Roosevelt intended it to be. Strictly speaking, it amounted to saying only this: American troops would not fight unless, as a result of American policy or regardless of American policy, some nation attacked the United States and thus started a war that was not "foreign." It therefore completely skirted the nub of the controversy: was Lend-Lease likely to bring about a "foreign war"?

gress after twenty-two years' absence. Her firm "No" was the only opposition to the Japanese resolution, and even she voted a nervous, noncommittal "Present" when the resolutions concerning Germany and Italy were put to the ballot. A handful of important liberals, like Charles Beard, received the news of Pearl Harbor unconvinced that it was not all a plot of Roosevelt's, but their grumblings were lost in the general acceptance of hostilities.[2] After Pearl Harbor not a single anti-war liberal figure commanded anywhere near the respect that dozens of reform-minded isolationists were given during World War I. There was no Robert La Follette in politics, no Randolph Bourne among the intellectuals. In a few short years a predominantly isolationist liberalism, divided from its leader by an unprecedented abyss of suspicion, had been brought to support him in an unprecedentedly unified acceptance of war.

III

SAMUEL GRAFTON, the liberal columnist, was looking for some music on his radio when the Pearl Harbor flash came. He felt the need for friends. They arrived, a group of fifteen by suppertime, and sat around in skittish conversation, trying to comprehend the incredible. "Then," Grafton remembers, "the news came that local Japanese aliens were being rounded up. A couple of liberals automatically hoped we would be fair and decent with them." [3]

The hope for fairness and decency—having accepted a war they could not avoid, liberals set about trying to make sure that it would be a liberal's war. The signs were not promising. There might be no hysteria comparable to that of 1917, no call to change the name of sauerkraut to "liberty cabbage" and no wholesale invasion of civil liberties. But didn't this, liberals asked warily,

[2] Beard summarized his attacks in *American Foreign Policy in the Making* (Yale University Press, 1946), and *President Roosevelt and the Coming of the War* (Yale University Press, 1948). These books have served as a jumping-off place for a "revisionist" interpretation of American entrance into World War II, which is already acquiring importance.

[3] Grafton: *An American Diary* (Doubleday, Doran, 1943), p. 140.

simply reflect the fact that Pearl Harbor had obliterated any really potent opposition to American participation in the war? When a situation touched war emotions, action could be disturbingly drastic. More than one hundred thousand people of Japanese descent on the west coast were summarily removed from their homes to detention camps, without individual inquiry into their loyalty, concern over their property, or regard for the fact that two thirds of them were American citizens with a claim to full Constitutional rights.

On the basic economic front, trends were still less encouraging. Roosevelt himself, as war came closer, had increasingly talked "national unity," that familiar slogan of conservatism; after Pearl Harbor he bluntly told a press conference that "Old Dr. New Deal" had to be replaced by "Dr. Win-the-War." [4] "And somehow, as he described them," wrote Jonathan Daniels, an ardent New Dealer, "Doc New Deal seemed an old-time practitioner who came with his bags and his goodness to the bedside. Dr. Win-the-War seemed a precise scientific gentleman to be seen by appointment only in the midst of the finest scientific apparatus, efficient undoubtedly but a colder individual expecting a much bigger fee—and getting it." [5] Now, unquestionably, the closest adviser to the President was Harry Hopkins, not the business-phobe social worker of WPA days but a war-driven man who snapped at "those goddam New Dealers" and was maneuvering into top policy positions his "tame millionaires," men like Edward Stettinius, of United States Steel, and William L. Batt, president of S. K. F. Industries, Inc. [6]

In the center of it all was the telltale reappearance of the dollar-a-year men. A back-bench New Dealer, suddenly coming to prominence as the chairman of the Senate Committee Investigating the Defense Program, tried hard to stop the practice. Why,

[4] Samuel Rosenman, ed.: *The Public Papers and Addresses of Franklin D. Roosevelt* (Macmillan, 1941), IX, 9, and (Harper, 1943), XII, 569–75.
[5] Quoted in Jack Goodman, ed.: *While You were Gone* (Simon & Schuster, 1946), p. 115.
[6] Robert E. Sherwood: *Roosevelt and Hopkins* (Harper, 1948), pp. 110–11, 280.

asked Senator Harry Truman, should young men be compelled to risk their lives while industrialists entering the government were not even asked to give up their large salaries, particularly when retaining corporate connections could easily lead to decisions colored by the connections? But Donald Nelson, the Sears Roebuck executive who headed the key War Production Board, insisted that the practice must go on; business executives had standards of living adjusted to high incomes. "I am laboring," Truman could only retort, "and have been, under the delusion, maybe, that if the Government has the power to take these young men away from their jobs and their outlook on life for the purpose of this emergency, the dollar-a-year men could face the same situation and face it adequately, and would be glad to do it. However, if that is not the case, and their morale won't stand it—and you say it won't—we want to win the war. Therefore, we are not going to hamper you in that effort and in your manner of handling it." [7]

The decision to keep the dollar-a-year men was fundamentally a decision to fight the economic war much as World War I had been fought on the home front. The Administration did not revive the War Industries Board of 1917, which had directly delegated huge powers to committees of industrialists and kept the antitrust laws in virtual suspension. That was too much for Roosevelt, and he supported John Lord O'Brian, general counsel to the successive top production agencies, a mild-mannered Republican in most respects but a tigerish crusader in insisting that sweeping economic powers should not be delegated to industrialists or the antitrust laws generally suspended. Then the President, as war Presidents have a way of doing, became more concerned with other problems. Gradually the economic controls took on much of the 1917 pattern, with much the same consequences.

The results were reflected in the fury of ex-Congressman Maury Maverick, a La Guardia with a Texas drawl, whose de-

[7] Quoted in U.S. Senate, Special Committee Investigating the National Defense Program, 77th Cong., 2nd Sess.: *Additional Report . . .* (1942), pp. 7–10, and in ibid., 77th Cong., 1st Sess.: *Hearings . . .* (1941–8), Pt. 10, p. 4030.

votion to general liberalism was exceeded only by his conviction that Roosevelt's wartime reliance on captains of industry was catastrophic. (It was Maverick who coined the term "gobble-degook" for government jargon and managed to substitute for it an eloquent profanity when discussing most dollar-a-year men.) First Maverick, as head of a War Production Board unit, tried to set up machinery to see to it that wartime patents were not channeled to big-scale industry after the hostilities. Then, as chief of the Smaller War Plants Corporation, he labored to prevent further concentration of industry by spreading the contracts around. Shortly after the war ended, Maverick issued a report describing his almost total failure in both efforts. Concentration, he wrote, had reached a spectacular high, and, of the nearly one billion dollars spent for scientific research in industrial laboratories, two thirds went to the sixty-eight largest firms. Over ninety per cent of the contracts made between the government and corporations placed the ownership of patents with the contractor, the government receiving merely a royalty-free license for its own use.[8]

The stocky, irascible Maverick was never so happy as when in a slugfest, but he knew when he was licked. Invited to send a communication to a WPB meeting in 1944, Maverick ground the telephone receiver into his ear, hitched his chair forward, and exploded: "You know what they're doing to me, don't you? They started on the roof, and they took rubber hoses and beat me, on top of the roof, and then they threw me down the steps to the third floor, and then they kicked me, on that escalator, and I got a leg cut off and both of my ears. . . . So I don't know what the hell I could talk to them about."[9]

In perfect symbolism of the new era, the first wartime elections, those of 1942, brought the most conservative results since the days of Herbert Hoover. Down to defeat went scores of New Dealers as Republicans or anti-New Deal Democrats won control of both houses of Congress, took over enough state governments to repre-

---

[8] Catton, p. 138.
[9] Quoted in ibid., p. 290.

sent a majority in the Electoral College, and moved the right-wingers' new hero, Thomas Dewey, and the neanderthalic John Bricker into the politically significant Governorships of New York and Ohio. Even George Norris, who had held Nebraska like a fief for thirty years, was shoved out of office, and the victor was "Lightning Ken" Wherry, Ford dealer, mortician, and enemy of the phrase "democratic processes" because it is "too close to socialism." Bewildered and heartbroken, Norris was ready to pronounce the requiem for reform which so many liberals felt. "I have done my best to repudiate wrong and evil in governmental affairs," he told reporters. ". . . I have lived according to my philosophy of government and now . . . the flag of that philosophy [is] trailing in defeat."[1]

IV

FIVE DAYS after the disastrous election, liberals received a still worse shock. The Allies landed in North Africa, and reports of this first offensive action were accompanied by the news that a deal had been made with the scrofulous Admiral Jean Darlan, a Nazi collaborator. Worse yet, Secretary of State Cordell Hull soon defended the move in a statement which could be interpreted as meaning that the United States was willing to make virtually any deal in order to achieve military victory.[2]

Liberals had been increasingly restive under wartime foreign policy. After the sudden unanimity brought by Pearl Harbor, when they paused to consider the war aims that were being offered, the fare seemed anything but enthralling. The two major statements of potential war aims which Roosevelt had made before the bombs fell—his "Four Freedoms" declaration and the Roosevelt-Churchill Atlantic Charter—were hardly the kind of documents to arouse liberal ecstasy. The sentiments were noble enough,

[1] Quoted in William S. White: "Portrait of a 'Fundamentalist,'" *New York Times Sunday Magazine* (January 15, 1950), p. 27, and in "'I Have Done My Best,'" *Time* (November 16, 1942), XL, 20.

[2] Quoted in "Expediency," ibid. (December 14, 1942), XL, 32-3.

the reform-minded agreed; there was even an exciting vista in the inclusion of "freedom from want" in the Four Freedoms. But what was deeply disquieting, as *Commonweal*, the liberal Catholic journal, remarked in discussing the Atlantic Charter, was "the emphasis placed on restoring the status quo. . . . [The points] seem too exclusively conceived in terms of the world as it once was, too oblivious of the fact that modern capitalism will never again have the character it did in the twenties and thirties. They fail to make allowance for the fact that the world is at a turning point, and that it is undergoing a revolution—not, to be sure, what Axis leaders mean by that term—but the ending of nineteenth century colonial exploitation, of expansion of mass production, of seeming national economic independence and many other things."[3]

After Pearl Harbor, liberal disquietude was not diminished when the President did little to expound the war as a crusade for a new world. Instead he usually talked about it in defensive, negative terms—a fight, as he described it in a 1942 speech before the Pan-American Union, for the "survival of what we have all lived for, for a great many generations." In the same speech Roosevelt suggested that the name for the struggle should be "The Survival War."[4] If the general public yawned at the suggestion and went on talking about "World War II," liberals were especially disturbed by the implications of the phrase.

Nor was it simply a matter of phrases; the President's actions were proving equally worrisome. On two occasions since Britain, the Soviet Union, and the United States became allies against the Axis, Roosevelt had met with Churchill in important conferences and Stalin was not present. Reformers might share the general American admiration for Churchill's war leadership, but they did not forget that the doughty old aristocrat was a Tory of Tories, an intransigent imperialist, an ancient enemy of the Soviets. What kind of world would it be, liberals asked, if it were

[3] "The Roosevelt-Churchill Eight Points," *Commonweal* (August 29, 1941), XXXIV, 435–6.
[4] Rosenman, XI, 193, 194, 196–7.

planned in partnership with Churchill and without the Soviet pressure in behalf of economic and social change? Was it not Churchill's desire for an invasion through the Balkans, motivated by British imperial concerns in the Mediterranean, that slowed up the launching of a second front? And didn't this delay leave the Russians slugging it out without diversionary relief and endanger American-Soviet co-operation in the postwar world?

Liberal restiveness was the greater because, once Russia had begun its spectacular resistance to the Nazis and even Herbert Hoover was talking about Stalin's "gallant armies," many reformers began again to "understand" the Soviet Union. After all, as Eleanor Roosevelt was saying, the Nazi-Soviet pact had been "defensive" on Russia's part, and the Soviet seized Polish territory only to make her boundaries "secure." [5] The new attitude was both expressed and greatly encouraged by *Mission to Moscow*, the 1941–2 best-seller written by Joseph E. Davies, who had gone from a progressive background to serve as Ambassador to Russia. The Soviet Union, Davies's book maintained, was moving toward a kind of humanized capitalism. Its purges had been simply a drastic cleaning-out of pro-Nazi elements, and the Russian armies were fighting not only "for their own homes and their own liberties, but . . . also . . . for the homes and liberties of all free men upon earth—ourselves not least among them." As for questioning the integrity of the Stalin government, that was "bad Christianity, bad sportsmanship, bad sense. . . . The Soviet government has a record of keeping its treaty obligations equal to that of any nation on earth." [6]

And now liberals looked up from their reading of Davies to confront the Darlan deal. Here, they testily told one another, was the epitome of Churchillism; the sort of thing that would make working with Stalin impossible; the harbinger of a postwar world built on shabby deals with reaction, perhaps even with a Göring in Germany or a Matsuoka in Japan. A storm of liberal protest

---

[5] Quoted in Arthur M. Schlesinger, Jr.: "What Made Them See Red?" *Look* (August 1, 1950), XIV, 70, and in Eleanor Roosevelt: *If You Ask Me* (Appleton-Century, 1946), pp. 71–2.
[6] Davies: *Mission to Moscow* (Simon & Schuster, 1941), p. 550.

broke over the country, and the storm took on gale proportions when the Darlan deal was followed by news that Marcel Peyrouton, a collaborator who had made a particularly brutal record as Minister of the Interior in the Vichy Government, was going to Algeria as a top administrator. Disgruntled as they had not been since 1933, with all their pre-Lend-Lease doubts about Roosevelt in foreign affairs returning, thousands of liberals were listening eagerly to the words of two men who seemed to be calling for a genuinely new world.

"Henry's the sort," an old-line politician once remarked of Vice President Wallace, "that keeps you guessing as to whether he's going to deliver a sermon or wet the bed." [7] There was a broad streak of the messianic in Wallace, no doubt. The angular face could take on a glazed pallor; the flopping shock of reddish-brown hair recalled the frenzy of Populist days; the speeches throbbed with references to the Bible and a tendency to see everything, including the price of corn, in terms of its "spiritual" effect on America and its possible role in bringing about "a reformation even greater than that of Luther and Calvin." [8] More and more as Wallace discussed the war, he saw it as an Armageddon of liberalism, with a necessity for drastic action on the part of the Lord's host.

The world had failed at the close of World War I, Wallace declared in his most important speech, "Toward a Free World Victory," because it did not build the peace on "the fundamental doctrine of the people's revolution." This revolution had been going on for more than a hundred and fifty years, through the American Revolution of 1776, the French Revolution of 1789, the Latin-American revolutions of the Bolivarian era, the German revolution of 1848, and the Russian Revolution of the World War I period. Now the revolution was reaching the most backward continents, and a peace that did not recognize it would be meaningless or worse than meaningless. To recognize it required, specifically, the ending of all imperialism, military or economic;

[7] Quoted in George Creel: *Rebel at Large* (Putnam, 1947), p. 313.
[8] Wallace: *Statesmanship and Religion* (Round Table Press, New York, 1934), pp. 120, 132.

a sustained effort on the part of the more prosperous countries, especially the United States, to industrialize the backward countries; the subjection of all cartels to international control; and, above all, the recognition that the people's revolution would not stop until world-wide freedom from want had actually been attained.

"Half in fun and half seriously," Wallace hammered his point, "I said the other day to Madame Litvinoff: 'The object of this war is to make sure that everybody in the world has the privilege of drinking a quart of milk a day.' . . . The peace must mean a better standard of living for the common man, not merely in the United States and England, but also in India, Russia, China and Latin America—not merely in the United Nations, but also in Germany and Italy and Japan. . . . I say that the century on which we are entering—the century which will come of this war— can be and must be the century of the common man. . . . The people's revolution is on the march, and the devil and all his angels can not prevail against it. They can not prevail, for on the side of the people is the Lord." [9]

Here was a sweeping, emotion-charged declaration that World War II was not simply a war for survival but a crusade to carry liberalism around the world, a pursuit of war aims far removed from any attempt to restore the status quo. A good many liberals might blanch at Wallace's religiosity, but they delighted in the bold reformism of what he was saying. Raymond Clapper, then at the height of his influence as a liberal columnist, pronounced "Toward a Free World Victory" comparable to Lincoln's Gettysburg Address; an "inspiring address . . . the greatest speech on this war which has been delivered by any public man of the United Nations," rang the words of approval from other reformers.[1] The febrile Vice President, commingling generations of the Protestant ethic, the New Freedom and the New Nationalism, all the hopes of the Thirties and all the doubts after Pearl Harbor, was emerging the New Dealer's New Dealer in foreign

[9] Wallace: *The Price of Free World Victory* (L. B. Fischer, New York, 1942), pp. 14, 15, 22.
[1] Quoted and paraphrased in ibid., pp. 26–7, 28.

affairs, "the conscience," as one high-placed enthusiast remarked, "of Roosevelt and of liberalism." [2]

The second figure coming to prominence as a liberal hero in foreign affairs was a good deal more of a surprise. During the Thirties Wendell Willkie, then head of the Commonwealth & Southern power company, had proved himself one of the most dangerous critics of the New Deal. When he was nominated for the Presidency in 1940, he had seemed to most liberals just a corporation executive affecting a New-Dealish homespun for political purposes, "a simple barefoot Wall Street lawyer," as Harold Ickes sneered.[3] But Willkie, like Louis Brandeis, came from the crusading German Forty-eighter tradition, and both his parents were eternally agitating about some failing of Elwood, Indiana. One year it was saloons and prostitution; the next year it was slums; always books, argument, and uplift were the dominant notes in the Willkie home. As a college student, the son fancied himself a socialist and fought to have a course in Marxism put in the curriculum. All the while Willkie was climbing in the business world, colleagues were upset by flashes of attitudes that seemed about as proper in an up-and-coming captain of industry as his rumpled appearance and helter-skelter manner. The jumbled "me-too-ism" of Willkie's 1940 Presidential campaign ("Willkie agreed with Roosevelt's entire program of social reform," the wags said, "and felt that it was leading to disaster") was only in part the politicking of a corporation executive trying to beat Franklin Roosevelt.[4] It was also the genuine confusion of a restless, leftward-tending mind that was nearing a break with an uncongenial conservatism.

By 1941, when liberals were making support of Lend-Lease a major test of a man's liberalism, Willkie passed the test magnificently—so magnificently that Roosevelt later assigned him an important share of the credit for passage of the bill—and his state-

[2] The late Harold L. Ickes, quoting a person who must remain unidentified, in an interview with me.

[3] Quoted in *Current Biography 1940* (H. W. Wilson), p. 875.

[4] Quoted in Irving Stone: *They Also Ran* (Doubleday, 1945), pp. 355–6.

ments on domestic affairs were moving rapidly in the same direction.[5] Thousands of former supporters fumed and ranted, including the heavy contributor to Willkie's 1940 campaign fund who wrote him: "I know not what others may think of you, but as for myself, it would take an act of Divine Providence to raise you to the level of moral degradation."[6] Liberals, loving Willkie more and more for the enemies he was making, listened with increasing admiration to his statements.

Just before the North African invasion, Willkie took off on a 31,000-mile trip to Africa, the Middle East, China, and the Soviet Union. In Moscow, Willkie chided the Allies for failure to open a second front; in Chungking, he issued a statement that called on the Allies to recognize that the war was not "a simple, technical problem for task forces. It is also a war for men's minds." The Allies were not winning the second war, Willkie warned. Everywhere, and especially in Asia, "the common people" were skeptical of Allied war aims, wondering whether the defeat of the Japanese and the Nazis would not mean simply rule by Western imperialism. "No foot of Chinese soil, for example, should be or can be ruled from now on except by the people who live on it. And we must say so *now*, not after the war. . . . Some say these subjects should be hushed until victory is won. Exactly the reverse is true. Sincere efforts to find progressive solutions now will bring strength to our cause. Remember, opponents of social change always urge delay because of some present crisis. After the war, the changes may be too little and too late."[7]

The Chungking statement electrified liberal circles, but Willkie was just beginning. On his return to the United States he went

---

[5] It is difficult, of course, to estimate how far or how deep Willkie's liberalism went by the time of his death in 1944. Morris L. Ernst has stated that Willkie went so far as to regret his whole fight on TVA. Review of John P. Frank: *Mr. Justice Black*, in *New York Times Book Review* (January 9, 1949), p. 6.

[6] Quoted in Walter White: *A Man Called White* (Viking, 1948), p. 200.

[7] Willkie: *One World* (Simon & Schuster, 1943), pp. 181–3. The italics are Willkie's.

on a nationwide network to repeat his Chungking message around a haunting phrase. The United States had a vast "reservoir of good will" in the world, he declared, but the reservoir was being rapidly drained primarily because of doubts about Anglo-American war aims. When Secretary Hull defended the Darlan deal, Willkie blasted back: "The United States has lost moral force . . . and by it, we may lose the peace. . . . With all my soul I hate this false finagling with expediency. . . . The peoples of the world must be given again the conviction that the banners Americans fight under bear bright clean colors." [8]

At the height of the liberal discomfiture over Darlanism, Willkie brought out his book *One World*. The volume repeated his previous arguments with a wealth of human, moving detail, but it also added other vigorous points. In speaking of the Soviet Union, Willkie told the United States that it had better accept three facts:

"First, Russia is an effective society. It works. It has survival value. The record of Soviet resistance to Hitler has been proof enough of this to most of us, but I must admit in all frankness that I was not prepared to believe before I went to Russia what I now know about its strength as a going organization of men and women.

"Second, Russia is our ally in this war. The Russians, more sorely tested by Hitler's might even than the British, have met the test magnificently. Their hatred of Fascism and the Nazi system is real and deep and bitter. And this hatred makes them determined to eliminate Hitler and exterminate the Nazi blight from Europe and the world.

"Third, we must work with Russia after the war. At least it seems to me that there can be no continued peace unless we learn to do so." [9]

In a chapter called "Our Imperialisms at Home," Willkie bluntly maintained that "the attitude of the white citizens of this country toward the Negroes has undeniably had some of the

---

[8] Quoted in "The Great Challenge," *Time* (November 2, 1942), XL, 21, and in "Expediency," ibid. (December 14, 1942), XL, 32-3.

[9] Willkie, pp. 53-4.

unlovely characteristics of an alien imperialism—a smug racial superiority, a willingness to exploit an unprotected people. We have justified it by telling ourselves that its end is benevolent. And sometimes it has been. But so sometimes have been the ends of imperialism. And the moral atmosphere in which it has existed is identical with that in which men—well-meaning men—talk of 'the white man's burden.'" This domestic imperialism, Willkie emphasized, was not only incompatible with professed American ideals. It was casting doubts on our sincerity abroad, impeding the war and likely to wreck the peace.

For the peace, Willkie concluded, could only be lasting if it were based on the concept of one world in the broadest meaning of the phrase—one world without regard to size of nation, color of skin, amount of wealth, or size of army. "Our Western world and our presumed supremacy are now on trial. Our boasting and our big talk leave Asia cold. Men and women in Russia and China and in the Middle East are conscious now of their own potential strength. They are coming to know that many of the decisions about the future of the world lie in their hands. And they intend that these decisions shall leave the peoples of each nation free from foreign domination, free for economic, social, and spiritual growth." [1]

The publishers of *One World*, Simon & Schuster, who are not noted for underestimating sales possibilities, figured that, at most, they could sell 250,000 copies of the book. Within two months after its publication, its sales topped a million; within two years, two million. No book in American publishing history—not *See Here, Private Hargrove* or even *Gone with the Wind*—had ever sold more swiftly. If *One World* was exciting reading for thousands of the general public, for the liberals it marked the final emergence of a new leader. More surely than Henry Wallace, and without the Vice President's disquieting air of frenzy, Willkie had caught up the liberal yearnings, and he had said, with all the firmness of the man of affairs: "Now!" Henceforth Wendell Willkie was no simple, barefoot Wall Street lawyer. He was, to

[1] Ibid., pp. 190, 204.

397

use Samuel Grafton's characterization, "the first United Nations statesman."[2]

And never, as Willkie's book went on with its missionary work, did its message seem more sorely needed. Roosevelt and Churchill conferred again, this time at Casablanca, and again Joseph Stalin was not present. The fall of Mussolini in July 1943 once more raised the question whether the United States was going to deal with a Darlan. The answer was that the United States accepted the continuance in office of King Victor Emmanuel, who had worked with Mussolini for more than two decades, and the elevation to the Premiership of Pietro Badoglio, the Duce's commander-in-chief in the brutal invasion of Ethiopia. As the full details of the Italian settlement reached America, liberal anger was unrestrained.

Using a speech of Willkie for his text, Max Lerner, now a columnist for the leftish *PM*, spoke the feeling in the sharpest criticism of Roosevelt he had ever written. "It is tragic," Lerner declared, "that FDR should make big concessions to reaction, especially in this area. I do not say this in a spirit of wide-eyed naïveté . . . I know that you can not strike twelve at once, that all good is tempered with evil, and all the other platitudes. But there is a gap wide as the poles between this knowledge and the plain evidence that—whatever be the character of the war we are fighting—the peace we are making is old and weary and cynical. To make shrewd compromises in order to retain the substance of your principles is one thing. To raise cynicism into a principle in itself is quite another."[3]

V

THE PRESIDENT publicly hit back at Willkie only once ("typewriter strategists," he said when the roar for a second front became especially loud), and he shrugged off Darlanism with a Balkan proverb. You can let the Devil himself help you over the

[2] Grafton, p. 195.
[3] Lerner: *Public Journal* (Viking, 1945), p. 237.

bridge, the President laughed, as long as you drop him on the other side.[4]

Roosevelt, as usual, was sure that he had the situation well in hand. As early as 1937, he had told the country: "Remember that from 1913 to 1921, I personally was fairly close to world events, and in that period, while I learned much of what to do, I also learned much of what *not* to do."[5] As wartime White House intimates listened to Roosevelt's frequent references to World War I and observed his face when his eyes fell on the big portrait over the mantelpiece in the Cabinet room, they became increasingly conscious of what the President, above all, did not want to do. He did not want to repeat the mistakes of Woodrow Wilson.

In Roosevelt's view, Wilson had made four especially serious errors. His peace program had been developed too swiftly for public opinion to adjust to it. He had not checked in time a wartime rightist reaction in domestic affairs. He had taken insufficient steps to see to it that the coalition of the Allies would continue into the peace. And, most important of all, he had failed in the respect that Wilson himself had called the "acid test"—bringing about a genuine understanding with Russia. Of these four Rooseveltian criticisms of Wilson, three were obviously much the same as the errors that liberals of the World War II era were attributing to Roosevelt himself. The fourth point—that Wilson had de-

[4] Quoted in Sherwood, p. 635, and paraphrased in John Gunther: *Roosevelt in Retrospect* (Harper, 1950), p. 331. At the same press conference at which he spoke of "typewriter strategists," the President gibed Willkie by imitating his Indiana pronunciation of "reservoir." Willkie was furious, and Roosevelt, who had an affectionate regard for his opponent of 1940, knew he had gone too far. He promptly dispatched a letter that may well take its place among the most human of Presidential documents. The letter read:

"Dear Wendell: When you sit in the chair where I sit, and I hope you will soon, you will learn that the President has few friends, and fewer relaxations. And I, even fewer than most, bound as I am to a wheel chair as well.

"One of the relaxations I speak of, is kidding with the reporters at my press conferences. But, Wendell, some days I go too far—and afterwards thoroughly regret what I let slip on the spur of the moment. Well . . . yesterday, I did." Quoted by Bartley Crum in *New York Herald Tribune*, September 10, 1951.

[5] Rosenman, VI, 438. The italics are Roosevelt's.

veloped his peace program too swiftly—explains the curious situation. Roosevelt, who was never a man to race ahead of public opinion, was especially anxious to keep only a bit in front of it in matters of foreign policy. "In time," he would caution his more impatient intimates, "all things, in good time." [6]

Near the close of 1943, after American public opinion had been to school in internationalism for two years and as the end of the European war became visible, Roosevelt decided that the time was propitious. Suddenly, out of a long silence of military security, came a communiqué which said something that most liberals had been longing to hear. Churchill and Roosevelt had faced the problem of the millions of Asia; they had met with Chiang Kai-shek at Cairo, disavowed "any thought of territorial expansion," and hinted at sympathy for the nationalist ambitions of the Asiatic lands. The news of Cairo was immediately followed by a still more spectacular communiqué. Roosevelt and Churchill had held a second top-level meeting, at Teheran, and this time the conference included Joseph Stalin. The Big Three had "concerted our plans" to launch the second front. They had, in all respects, shaped a "common policy. We express our determination that our nations shall work together in war and in the peace that will follow." And it was not only what the Teheran communiqué said; the document had a tone unusual for diplomatic papers. It spoke in emotional terms, of the "heart and mind," of "consciences," of "free lives, unfettered by tyranny." It concluded: "We leave here, friends in fact, in spirit, and in purpose." [7]

As the less formal news of the Teheran conference trickled out, a dozen personal details seemed to confirm all the words. For the four days of the conference the Big Three had lived and worked never more than two hundred yards away from each other, and apparently with the greatest amiability. At a tea, the Soviet leader had troubled himself to serve as an anxious host, constantly moving around to look after the comfort of the guests.

---

[6] Interviews with two Presidential intimates, who prefer not to be named. Roosevelt's leeriness of Wilson's mistakes is touched upon in Sherwood, pp. 227, 263, 360, 507, 697, 757, and in Rosenman, XIII, 32, 36.

[7] Rosenman, XII, 530–1, 532, 533.

The British leader had invited everyone to a birthday party and thrown himself into readying it like a girl preparing for her first date. Stalin had toasted "My fighting friend Roosevelt" and "My fighting friend Churchill," and Churchill—Winston Churchill!— had toasted "Stalin the Great." Shortly after returning to the United States, Roosevelt delivered a Christmas Eve Fireside Chat on Teheran which glowed with all the good-fellowship of the season. Of Stalin, the President said: "He is a man who combines a tremendous, relentless determination with a stalwart good humor. I believe he is truly representative of the heart and soul of Russia; and I believe that we are going to get along very well with him and the Russian people—very well indeed." [8]

Liberals were scarcely done cheering Teheran when Roosevelt summoned old Doc New Deal. With a sharp reminder to the country that the Wilsonian postwar should not be repeated, he called on Congress to begin enactment of an "Economic Bill of Rights." The rights were to apply to "all—regardless of station, race, or creed," and they were sweeping:

"The right to a useful and remunerative job in the industries or shops or farms or mines of the Nation;

"The right to earn enough to provide adequate food and clothing and recreation;

"The right of every farmer to raise and sell his products at a return which will give him and his family a decent living;

"The right of every businessman, large and small, to trade in an atmosphere of freedom from unfair competition and domination by monopolies at home or abroad;

"The right of every family to a decent home;

"The right to adequate medical care and the opportunity to achieve and enjoy good health;

"The right to adequate protection from the economic fears of old age, sickness, accident, and unemployment;

[8] Quoted in "The Big Parade," *Time* (December 31, 1943), XLII, 27–8, and in Rosenman, XII, 558. In their enthusiasm for Teheran, liberals had an extra joy, a kind of well-we-weren't-so-foolish-anyhow feeling. See, for example, "Four Men Reshape the World," *New Republic* (December 13, 1943), CIX, 835–7.

"The right to a good education."

"All these rights," the President said, "spell security. And after this war is won we must be prepared to move forward, in the implementation of these rights, to new goals of human happiness and well-being." [9]

In the fourth-term Presidential campaign of 1944, Roosevelt reiterated the Economic Bill of Rights, militantly pledged that "we are not going to turn the clock back! We are going forward," and, when the campaign seemed to lack the old New Deal fervor, brought his liberal following to its feet by the most extraordinary tour de force in the history of American politics. In a tone of grave injury, Roosevelt told how Republican leaders were saying that "my little dog Fala" had been left behind on an inspection trip to the Aleutians and was brought back to Washington at huge cost to the taxpayers, "two or three, or eight or twenty million dollars." Fala's "Scotch soul was furious. . . . Well, of course, I don't resent attacks, and my family doesn't resent attacks, but Fala *does* resent them. He has not been the same dog since." [1] This was the F. D. R., frolicsome, cocky, festooning reform in the gayest of trappings, who had led liberals so long and so effectively. Their confidence was flooding back and they enthusiastically helped to re-elect the President and to increase Democratic strength in both houses of Congress.

Three months after the election the Yalta communiqué was released. Teheran had brought Britain, the United States, and the Soviet Union into a working coalition and proclaimed agreement on broad fundamentals. The Yalta communiqué not only announced agreement on every point taken up, but, on the most difficult points, the declaration broke down the agreement into hard specifics. Germany was to be politically and economically disarmed, once and for all, and she was to be occupied in four zones controlled by the United States, Britain, the Soviet Union, and France. An Allied commission, sitting in Moscow, would

[9] Rosenman, XIII, 41–2.
[1] Ibid., pp. 290, 371, 378. The italics are Roosevelt's.

work out reparations, which Germany was to pay to "the greatest extent possible." Russia was to get Poland up to the Curzon line (with some minor adjustments "in favor of Poland"), and Poland was to acquire "substantial accessions" of German territory to the west and north. In Poland, as in other "liberated" countries, the Big Three declared their "mutual agreement to concert during the temporary period of instability in liberated Europe the policies of their three Governments in assisting the peoples liberated from the domination of Nazi Germany and the peoples of the former Axis satellite states of Europe to solve by democratic means their pressing political and economic problems." In the case of Poland, the guarantee of democratic procedures was doubly specific. The prevailing Communist government was to be broadened by taking in "democratic leaders from Poland itself and from Poles abroad," and this provisional government was, "as soon as possible," to be subjected to "free and unfettered elections." Plans for world organization were pushed to an exceedingly practical point. A conference of the United Nations was summoned, to meet at San Francisco, on April 25, 1945, for the purpose of preparing a charter of an international security agency, and announcement was made—though the exact terms were not given—that the Big Three had reached agreement on the crucial question of voting procedure.[2]

Striving to lay another ghost of Wilsonianism, the President, while still abroad, made unmistakably plain that American entrance into the United Nations was to be a bipartisan move. Among the chief delegates he named to represent America at San Francisco were Senator Arthur Vandenberg, who for years had been opposing Democratic measures, including Lend-Lease, as if they were concoctions out of hell, and Harold Stassen, the rising G.O.P. hopeful from Minnesota. On the way back, at a press conference held on the ship, the President talked in a way that seemed light-years from Versailles. The people in outlying regions "are not educated, do not get enough to eat, cannot cope

[2] Ibid., 531–48.

with health problems"; something had to be done for them. As for Churchill's attitude toward nationalist ambitions in Asia, "Yes, he is mid-Victorian on all things like that." [3]

"There's never been anyone quite like F. D. R.," one liberal remarked as the Yalta story came in. "You wonder, you doubt, you think he's let you down. Then, suddenly, he's leading you right where you want to go." [4] Many of the reform-minded still had their worries. They wondered querulously when the President was going to come down from the cosmos to do something specific about the Economic Bill of Rights. They did not entirely forget Darlan and Badoglio. They scrutinized Yalta, and they had questions. Was the confirmation of the Russian seizure of a chunk of Poland in accord with the high-sounding phrases of the Big Three? How, specifically, would Churchillism be handled? Revelations that spurted out soon after the Yalta communiqué—about votes for White Russia and the Ukraine in the United Nations Assembly and certain side agreements of the Big Three—revived misgivings of another Wilsonian debacle. But for most liberals three facts were transcendent: the President of the United States was very much aware of the importance of continuing domestic reform and was forcefully saying so to the country; the Soviet Union and the United States were working together closely in war and were pledged to continue the co-operation in peace; an international organization was being set up, with the United States in it, before the close of the war. Still a bit warily—the once-burned never expose themselves again with quite the same abandon—but relieved and generally confident, liberals of Yalta days settled back to await a peace that would be no Versailles, and a postwar that would be no twenties.

[3] Ibid., 558, 563.
[4] The person, an intimate of the President, prefers not to be identified.

�֎ CHAPTER XVII ✖

Down, Down, Down

A BARBER IN Cleveland stopped in the middle of a shave, took a slow drink of water, sat down, and stared for nearly ten minutes. At a San Francisco cocktail party the glasses were suddenly placed on the table and the guests, with murmured thanks, went off to their homes. A girl in New York City clutched at her friend's arm and cried out: "Oh, my God!" That evening and the next day, night clubs darkened, restaurants were shuttered, hand-lettered signs appeared on stores: "Closed out of Reverence for F. D. R." [1]

To a whole nation that had lived through its grimmest depression and its most frightful war with Franklin Roosevelt in the White House, the news of his death came with the force of personal shock. Liberals were not only stunned. Suddenly they realized to what extent their confidence in the postwar had rested on one man. Suddenly all their long-running fears of another debacle swirled back. In the hours following Roosevelt's death, rumors rampaged through liberal circles. New Dealers were being scuttled from high government posts; the San Francisco Conference would be called off; all economic controls were to be scrapped immediately.

[1] Quoted in "'A Soldier Died Today,'" *Time* (April 23, 1945), XLV, 17, and Donald P. Geddes, ed.: *Franklin Delano Roosevelt* (Pocket Books, 1945), p. 22.

After the first shock, reassurances came. Publicly before Congress and privately to New Dealers, the new President declared his determination to carry on both the domestic and foreign policies of "that noble soul . . . with all my strength and with all my heart." [2] The whole impression of Harry Truman's first address as President was comforting to liberals. Stoutly controlling his nervousness, radiating modesty, sincerity, and a quiet strength, he made plain that the grand strategy of the war would go on unaltered, that the San Francisco Conference would meet as scheduled, and that domestic reform would be pushed. Within twenty-four hours Truman could even announce a coup important for keeping the United Nations united. The Russians, who had been threatening to snub the San Francisco Conference by sending a second-ranking diplomat, agreed to dispatch Foreign Affairs Commissar Molotov.

In the glow of these events, liberals began looking up the Truman record and found further encouragement. His votes in the Senate had been largely pro-New Deal in domestic affairs and almost unanimously pro-Roosevelt in foreign affairs. His watchdog committee on the defense effort had been the most respected in many years, prodding and scourging with a conspicuous lack of timidity before big business or big brass. And, after all, Franklin Roosevelt himself, who surely must have known that four terms might be too much, had named Truman his heir apparent.

Soon the rush of world news was obscuring the transition from the dazzling Hyde Park patrician to the grayish little county judge from Independence. Twenty-six days after Roosevelt died, the Chief of Staff of the German Army signed his name to a document in a Reims schoolhouse, stood up stiffly, then in a strangled voice, like a sob, said: "With this signature the German people and the German armed forces are, for better or for worse, delivered into the victor's hands." [3] Two months later the new President was off for a Big Three conference in Potsdam, and

---

[2] *New York Times*, April 17, 1945.
[3] Quoted in "How It Ended," *Time* (May 14, 1945), XLV, 20.

the headlines told both of the upset Labour victory over Winston Churchill and of the loosing of the atomic bomb on Hiroshima. While people were still writing letters to the White House addressed to President Franklin D. Roosevelt, the lights were on again in London and the Japanese were signing surrender papers under the guns of the U.S.S. *Missouri* and the glare of Douglas MacArthur. The infinitely analyzed postwar, so longingly awaited and feared for so long, was at hand.

II

THE POSTWAR looked very much like a postwar. In 1946, the first full year of peace, the President and Congress wrangled endlessly over price-controls, and prices kept going up; by the end of the twelve months, you could pay $2.75 for a hamburger plate and $17.50 for a shirt. More than four million workers, feeling the inflationary squeeze, walked off their jobs, the President of the United States proposed the peacetime drafting of workers to break a strike, and the White House was doing nothing to check assaults on freedom of thinking which approached the hysteria of the days of Attorney General Palmer.

Around the President were gathering a personal circle that Warren Harding would have found thoroughly congenial—the Babbittish John Snyder, hail-fellow George Allen, a master at rowdy stories and at collecting business directorships for himself, the hulking Edwin W. Pauley, who thought politics another, and a lesser, branch of the oil business, and brassy Harry Hawkins Vaughan, always ready to suggest: "You guys will want favors at the White House some day. . . ." [4] New Dealers were fleeing or being pushed out of Washington almost at the rate the gloomiest rumors had predicted. After ten months of the new Administration, old Harold Ickes, for years a symbol of uncorruptible liberalism, rumbled out with a blast at Pauley that stopped just

[4] Quoted in "The General Opens His Mouth," ibid. (July 18, 1949), LIV, 14.

short of calling him a crook and went the full way of calling him a liar. Seven months later, Henry Wallace, still very much the New Dealer's New Dealer, was gone from the Cabinet, gone from Washington, spending his days convincing *New Republic* readers of their lifelong convictions. On the lower levels the exodus was still more marked. "There isn't any fun working for the government any more," the lesser New Dealers said in their farewells. "No inspiration. . . . No bold adventures."[5]

Congress was hurried into step. In the election of 1946, for the first time in sixteen years, Republicans took over both houses, and a considerable percentage of the new majority were the kind of Republicans who saw dark premonitions of socialism in a bill for free school lunches. Now the Senatorial powerhouse was unquestionably Robert A. Taft, the best mind in the Senate, as liberals wryly commented, until he made it up.[6] The new House was led by Joseph W. Martin, he of the puffed eyes and the policeman's shoes and the glummings about dictatorship, a droning voice straight out of the era of William McKinley. "We have just begun to fight," said the CIO politico, Jack Kroll, bravely whistling as he passed the cemetery.[7]

The 80th Congress, once functioning, was so many months of anguish for liberals. It undercut the Wagner Act with the Taft-Hartley bill, killed effective rent-control, slashed funds for soil conservation and for crop storage, and trimmed all federal pay rolls to the point of forcing the discharge of tax-collectors who took in twenty dollars for each dollar they cost. It tried to enact tax legislation and a tariff that smacked of post-Civil War bonanza days. It ignored the 800,000 displaced persons begging for admittance into America, the estimated 6,000,000 Americans desperate for housing, the demands for extended social security, and an ominous increase of monopoly in the major industries. "This Congress," one liberal newspaperman exploded, "brought back

[5] Quoted in Tris Coffin: *The Missouri Compromise* (Little, Brown, 1947), p. 64.
[6] Liberals also assigned Taft the slogan: "Come weal, come woe, my status is quo."
[7] *New York Times*, November 7, 1946.

an atmosphere you had forgotten or never thought possible. At first, even the vested interests themselves couldn't believe it. And then you saw them, the Neanderthal Men, lurching forward on hairy feet—the sugar lobby, the wool lobby, the rail lobby, the real estate lobby, the Power trust—tiptoeing back again, fingering things tentatively and then more boldly. Victories fought and won years ago, like the TVA, were suddenly in doubt. Everything was debatable again." [8]

If domestic affairs were dismal for liberals, foreign relations were downright frightening. The San Francisco Conference had no sooner begun than it made public an ominous split between the Soviet Union and the Western powers, and each month seemed to make the division deeper and more dangerous. The Soviet Union went ahead violating its wartime agreements, flatly rejected the American plan for international control of atomic weapons, and talked the blunderbuss language that has so often marked the preparation of totalitarian states for war. The Truman Administration, on its part, turned to the openly anti-Soviet Truman Doctrine in 1947, added the more effectively anti-Soviet Marshall Plan, and began matching the Politburo epithet for epithet. More and more, the violent East-West quarrels threatened to kick the legs from under the young United Nations. And over the flimsy peace played the ghastly knowledge that another world war would be an atomic war.

Hiroshima, more than any other fact in modern history, tore at the minds and hearts of American liberals. It presented in the most urgent possible form the problem that had beset reform-minded men and women since the beginnings of the Industrial Revolution—the enormous difference in the speed of technological development and the rate at which men learn ways to use industry and science for the benefit of the general population. Liberals poured out a tremendous literature underlining the significance of Hiroshima, articles, speeches, and books which reached temporary climaxes in Norman Cousins's rousingly emotional *Modern Man*

[8] T. R. B.: "Neanderthal Men," *New Republic* (August 4, 1947), CXVII, 3.

Is Obsolete and John Hersey's factually jolting *Hiroshima*. Like soldiers backed into a ravine, the reform-minded threw themselves into the fight to keep control of the development of atomic energy in the United States out of military hands, and when the fight was won, they greeted the victory with the air of men who had been snatched, at the last moment and probably only temporarily, from disaster.

Around everything clung the miasma of another Twenties. These were the years when Republicans rediscovered Herbert Hoover and swimmers refilled the English Channel; when Preston Tucker spent twenty-five million dollars of other people's money not producing a car with a rear motor, and Vincent Sheean embraced Gandhism; when the socialite Elinor Frothingham, shopping for a trousseau with her fiancé's former wife, said, "I think Peggy is sweet to give me the benefit of her marital experience with George," and the amount of child labor suddenly doubled; when a man named Joseph McCarthy ended the half-century of La Follette victories in Wisconsin, and bearded, besandled eden ahbez (capital letters were reserved for God) was annoyed because his song "Nature Boy" led the Hit Parade for eighteen weeks; when Mrs. Christine G. Fochak, 37, sat on a flagpole in Cleveland for 29 days, 11 hours, 3½ minutes, and former Air Force Lieutenant David Downey, having strangled his bride and then beaten her on the head with a rock, explained: "She liked labor unions."

At least, said the *Progressive*, "please, no bathtub gin. Pretty please." [9]

[9] For the revival of Hoover, see Eugene Lyons: *Our Unknown Ex-President* (Doubleday, 1948), Chap. ii; for Tucker, Lester Velie: "The Fantastic Story of the Tucker Car," *Collier's* (June 25, 1949), CXXIII, 13–15, 68–72; for Sheean, John Gunther: "John Gunther Interviews Vincent Sheean," *New York Herald Tribune Sunday Book Section* (July 31, 1949), p. 2; for Frothingham, *New York World Telegram*, November 29, 1948; for child labor, Harold L. Ickes, in *New York Post*, February 21, 1949; for ahbez, Powers Moulton: " 'Nature Boy' Meets City Life," *PM* (June 1, 1948), p. 15; for Fochak, *New York Daily News*, August 21, 1947; for Downey, "Open Season," *New Republic* (August 4, 1947), CXVII, 5; for the *Progressive* remark, *Progressive* (January 12, 1948), XIV, 377.

410

III

FOR EACH hellish period, its devil, and with every passing month more liberals were placing the horns squarely on Harry Truman's head. Now they were looking at his pre-White House activities and interpreting the record quite differently from their reassuring conclusions immediately after Roosevelt's death. Wasn't the President a loyal product of the notorious Pendergast machine? Wasn't his voting record as a Senator, however pro-Roosevelt, fundamentally that of an old-fashioned party man? Hadn't he been picked for the Vice-Presidential nomination as a nonentity who would alienate fewer people, and taken up the Presidency a frightened man, publicly protesting that the job overwhelmed him? A hundred things, little and big, seemed to confirm the impression that an illiberal fate had tumbled another Harding into the White House—not only his precipitate retreat before the new Republican Congress, not only the Missouri cronies, but the stumbling speeches and the quoted sniping at "New Deal crackpots," the daughter who took her nice choir girl's voice on a national hook-up and the public s.o.b.ing and the grinning marches with World War I buddies and the frequent trips to see Mother while crises battered at the White House.[1] "I look at him," one high-placed liberal phrased the feeling, "and I say to myself, 'Yes, he is in Roosevelt's chair, yes he is, yes he is.' And then I say, ' Oh no, no, my God, it's impossible.' "[2]

A whole liberal literature rapidly appeared bewailing the loss of Roosevelt and decrying his successor, including *As He Saw It*, an account of the major wartime conferences by the late President's second son, Elliott. Franklin Roosevelt, the son maintained, had built his peace plans on Big Three unity, and on the ending of the British, French, and Dutch colonial systems. On his way

---

[1] Quoted in Joseph and Stewart Alsop: "Candidate Truman's Magic Brew," *Saturday Evening Post* (December 31, 1949), CXXII, 12.

[2] The person prefers not to be identified.

toward such a peace, Roosevelt had continually to combat the British and especially Winston Churchill, who aimed to retain the colonial systems and was so anti-Bolshevik that he thought of all moves in terms of containing and, if possible, smashing the Soviet Union. "You see," Elliott Roosevelt had his father say, "what the British have done, down through the centuries, historically, is the same thing. They've chosen their allies wisely and well. They've always been able to come out on top, with the same reactionary grip on the peoples of the world and the markets of the world, through every war they've ever been in." [3]

After President Roosevelt's death, the son contended, American foreign policy shifted radically. Little or no attempt was made to break up the colonial systems. For example, Queen Wilhelmina had announced that, as soon as the hostilities were over, the Dutch East Indies would be given dominion status with a swift opportunity to vote themselves independence. What actually happened was that "the British—mindful of the effects of Javanese independence on their own colonial peoples—shot into the Dutch East Indies as though out of a gun and used American Lend-Lease material to suppress most ruthlessly the struggle of those peoples for independence, while in America we did—precisely nothing." The whole handling of colonial problems, *As He Saw It* charged, was characterized by the attitude: "Quick! While the time is ripe! Give it back to the same imperialist interests, while no one is looking!" [4]

Simultaneously, Elliott Roosevelt went on, Big Three unity was being scuttled. The Kremlin had good reason to be suspicious of the United States and Britain because it was they "who first shook the mailed fist, who first abrogated the collective decisions." American and British troops had not withdrawn promptly to the occupation zones agreed upon at Yalta, and the occupation forces of the two countries were making "no particular effort" to fulfill the reparations schedules established at the conference. The United States lined up in back of Britain when her soldiers "cold-

[3] Roosevelt: *As He Saw It* (Duell, Sloan & Pearce, 1946), p. 121.
[4] Ibid., p. 251.

bloodedly shot down Greek anti-fascists" and her Foreign Office staged an election that was a "mockery" of democracy.

So far as China was concerned, President Roosevelt had made an agreement with Chiang Kai-shek. The agreement was conditional on two Russian actions—the Soviet return of Manchuria to Chinese sovereignty and a Soviet guarantee of abstention from Chinese affairs—and on an American promise that extraterritoriality would end, to be reinforced by barring British warships from Chinese ports when Japan was defeated. "The performance?" Elliott Roosevelt asked. ". . . All the necessary assurances were received from the Soviets, who in fact have lived up to the letter and spirit of their agreement since that time. It then devolved on the United States to fulfill *its* conditional responsibility. We did not. The first warships to enter Chinese ports were British warships. . . ." All the while, the United States was further destroying Big Three unity by dangling the bomb over Russia's head. "If there was one single factor magnificently calculated to breed suspicion of rich, powerful America in the minds and hearts of the countries who were our Allies for peace, it was that we were concealing the world's most devastating weapon. Why? For use against whom?" [5]

And the explanation of these American policies? Elliott Roosevelt was sure how they came about. "I am writing this book," he declared bluntly, ". . . to you who agree with me that Franklin Roosevelt was the wartime architect of the unity of the United Nations, who agree with me that Franklin Roosevelt's ideals and statesmanship would have been sufficient to keep that unity a vital entity during the postwar period. . . . If Father had lived . . . British colonial policy would be a dead duck, British attempts to dominate world trade would be a dead duck, and British ambitions to play off the U.S.S.R. against the U.S.A. would be a dead duck." [6]

Liberal reviewers of *As He Saw It* rarely accepted the book totally. They wondered if Elliott Roosevelt's memory had not

[5] Ibid., pp. 249–50, 252, 254, 255. Italics in the original.
[6] Ibid., pp. xviii, 42.

failed him in some of the opinions he attributed to his father; they were inclined to be much less critical of Britain and much more critical of Russia; some of them were suspecting what soon was revealed to be a fact—that Roosevelt was becoming suspicious of Soviet intentions before his death and might well have shifted his policy soon.[7] Yet whatever the reservations, *As He Saw It* evoked at least emotional concurrence from virtually all liberal reviewers on its central point: if only *he* had lived. . . .

Apparently the late Forties were to repeat the Twenties even in the way liberalism took disappointment. Woodrow Wilson, living into the postwar, had been made the victim of disillusionment. Truman, taking over when liberals were once more looking for a scapegoat, was flayed with all the mercilessness of the invidious comparison.

IV

IN NEW YORK CITY, Henry Wallace was settling down in the crowded offices of the *New Republic* on East Forty-ninth Street. The editors, having captured their big name, were bustling about with an elaborate program, changing personnel, retaining a public-relations man, slicking up the typography of Herbert Croly's staid-appearing journal. The big name performed his functions dutifully. He went out of his way to explore advertising possibilities for the magazine; he met regularly with the other editors, usually sitting, hand in vest, listening. But sometimes in the middle of an editorial conference Wallace's eyes would close and he would seem to be far away in thought.

What Wallace was thinking quickly emerged in the editorials and articles he wrote for the *New Republic*. The central problem of the day was preserving the peace, Wallace declared, and the peace could not be kept without Big Three unity, independence for the colonial areas, and a world-wide lifting of the standard of

---

[7] The first authoritative revelation came the next year, in James F. Byrnes: *Speaking Frankly* (Harper, 1947), pp. 54-5.

living. This was the Roosevelt approach, and at the beginning of Truman's Administration the new President "really believed" in it. But Truman, unlike Roosevelt, "looked up to . . . the wealthy and the powerful . . . and was taken in by them." Becoming the creature of "the Big Brass and the Big Gold," he wrecked Big Three unity by promulgating the anti-Soviet Truman Doctrine and Marshall Plan, and he did nothing to aid the just aspirations of colonial areas.[8]

In domestic affairs Wallace hammered hard on the necessity for immediate reforms, but he emphasized especially the preservation of civil liberties and the ending of discrimination against minority groups. "The almost incredible invasions" of civil rights were threatening to stifle any genuine discussion of public affairs; the prevailing attitudes toward Negroes, Jews, and recent immigrant groups were causing peoples around the world to laugh at American pretensions to democracy. "My field," Wallace declared in the most sweeping of his *New Republic* editorials, "is the world. My strength is my conviction that a progressive America can unify the world and a reactionary America must divide it. My enemy is blind reaction. . . . My friends . . . all who believe in true democracy. If I have importance, it is because of the ideas that I have come to represent. They are major ideas, indestructible and on the march." [9]

Editor Wallace would have had to be singularly obtuse not to note the very special place he held in the dreary political scene of 1947. For fourteen years he had been an important figure in the New Deal, for four of them only a heartbeat from the Presidency of the United States. His wartime speeches had given him so enthusiastic a following in liberal groups that old-line politicians had to maneuver frantically to stop his renomination for the Vice-Presidency in 1944.[1] Now, once more, he was boldly speak-

[8] Wallace: "Farewell and Hail!" *New Republic* (July 19, 1948), CXIX, 18.

[9] Ibid., and Wallace: "Jobs Peace Freedom," *New Republic* (December 15, 1946), CXV, 789.

[1] Edwin Pauley, then treasurer of the Democratic National Committee and a self-described "conspirator" for Truman's nomination as Vice President, later remarked that the pressure for Wallace was so great that if a

ing the worries, hopes, and fears of thousands. "Wallace's strength," wrote Samuel Grafton, "is that he is emotionally right; his logical rightness is another question. In fact, if there were no Henry Wallace we might have to invent one." Harold Ickes added: "My own analysis of the undoubted and widespread enthusiasm which has attended Mr. Wallace is that the people are looking for leadership. More than this, they are looking for leadership that has at least the appearance of ideality. They are looking for leadership with courage. Whether the qualities that the mine run of American citizens want do exist to the degree that many people believe they do in Mr. Wallace or whether they exist at all, is beside the point. Thousands of people believe that Mr. Wallace possesses the qualities they are looking for." [2]

The inevitable came quickly. Thousands of troubled liberals, particularly those from the restive urban minority groups, saw in Wallace an ideal leader. The American Communist Party and its fellow travelers, their line now calling for a repudiation of the Democrats, saw in Wallace an ideal leader. And Henry Wallace, as messianic as ever, saw in Henry Wallace an ideal leader. In the summer of 1948, at a cheering, chanting, stomping convention that recalled the Populist frenzy at Omaha, the delegates named Wallace the Presidential candidate of a new third party. Once more, the "Battle Hymn of the Republic" was refurbished with new words and this time the delegates sang:

> *From the Bay of Massachusetts*
> *Out into the Golden Gate*
> *Henry Wallace leads his army*
> *'Gainst destruction, fear and hate.*
> *We Americans will save the*
> *Precious land that we create*
> *For the people's march is on.*

Wallace man, instead of himself, had been "in charge" of the convention, Wallace might well have been renominated. Quoted in Jonathan Daniels: *The Man of Independence* (Lippincott, 1950), pp. 237, 251–2.

2 Quoted in Kenneth Stewart: "Wallace the Symbol," *PM Sunday Magazine* (November 9, 1947), p. 5.

Down, Down, Down

Glory, glory, hallelujah,
For the people's march is on.[3]

The platform of the latest "Progressive" party made plain that the people were to march toward sweeping economic and social changes, including the nationalization of basic industries. It called for an end to "the suppression of dissent" and for the immediate abolition of the segregation of any minority anywhere under the American flag. But greatest emphasis, in the platform and in the convention as a whole, was given to foreign policy. The Progressives assailed the leadership of both the Republicans and the Democrats as warmongers, called for scrapping the Truman Doctrine and the Marshall Plan, advocated the destruction of all atomic stockpiles, and insisted that American foreign policy was needlessly racing the world toward a conflict "between east and west [that] will mean fascism and death for all." [4]

"The choice," said the keynote speaker of the Progressive convention, "is Wallace or war." [5]

V

MIDWAY IN the convention proceedings, James Loeb, Jr., executive secretary of a new liberal organization called Americans for Democratic Action, appeared before the Resolutions Committee with some blunt remarks. The Progressive Party, Loeb charged, was Communist-dominated; it concerned itself with freedom in every place except the Soviet Union, and it made opposition to the Marshall Plan its "basic tenet" because wrecking the plan was the chief Soviet concern of the day. Obviously referring to the Stalinist tactic of encouraging reactionaries so as to bring about a better setting for revolution, Loeb reminded the Progressives that the practical effect of their movement would be to split the liberal

---

[3] *New York Times*, July 23, 1948.
[4] "Progressive Party Platform," printed in *Congressional Record*, 80th Cong., 2nd Sess., XCIV, Pt. 12, pp. A5091, A5092.
[5] *New York Times*, July 24, 1948.

vote and thus to aid the more conservative candidates. "We know," Loeb concluded in the name of Americans for Democratic Action, "that we speak for the great non-Communist liberal and labor majority when we state our conviction that your movement is a dangerous adventure undertaken by cynical men in whose hands Henry A. Wallace placed his political fortunes." [6]

Indications were certainly plentiful that the Progressive Party was deeply influenced by men who had long thought along Communist or fellow-travelerish lines. The two most powerful figures at the convention were Representative Vito Marcantonio, whose votes in Congress followed virtually every twist in the party line, and Lee Pressman, who later admitted that he had been a Communist Party member in 1934–5 and had not broken ideologically with the movement until two years after the Wallace candidacy. Among the prominent delegates were a number of people who for years had shown little inclination to oppose Communist thinking, including Jo Davidson, Lillian Hellman, Rockwell Kent, Paul Robeson, and Harlow Shapley. On the surest test issue of the day, foreign policy, the convention acted like a Communist Party cell.[7] When Wallace's old friend Rexford Tugwell tried to win approval of the Marshall Plan in the Resolutions Committee, he was summarily voted down; Lee Pressman deftly took care of a floor resolution that would have put the convention on record as denying "blanket endorsement to the foreign policy of *any* nation." [8] No informed person seriously believed that Henry Wallace had become a Communist. But in the months surrounding the convention period, he quite clearly was fellow-traveling, avoiding any criticism of Soviet foreign policy, expressing a

[6] Ibid., July 23, 1948.

[7] *New York Herald Tribune*, August 29, 1950; Victor Lasky: "Who Runs Wallace?" *Plain Talk* (June 1948), II, 1–13.

[8] *New York Times*, July 23, 1948; "The Pink Façade," *Time* (August 2, 1948), LII, 12–14. (Italics in the original.) Tugwell, commenting on the battle in the Resolutions Committee, said of the other faction: "I certainly don't know whether they are Communists, but they act as though they are" (*New York Post*, August 20, 1948). Tugwell ended his support of the Progressive Party before the election.

preference for Taft, "the most reactionary candidate of the most reactionary party," and cozily welcoming Communist support ("If they want to help us out on some of these problems, why God bless them, let them come along").[9]

If Loeb was at least partly correct in calling the Progressive Party a Communist front, he was totally right in his prediction that the liberal movement as a whole would not support Wallace's candidacy. The refusal was not easy. Max Lerner expressed the mood when, after the Progressive convention, he wrote of Wallace as "a great political figure of our time and a profoundly moving democrat with a small *d*. . . . To people who have felt the lash of injustice and glimpsed the promise of equality—to Negroes and Jews, workers and sharecroppers—he has been a leader. To many of the youngsters who fought a war to achieve lasting peace, he is with all his weaknesses a symbol that evokes intense loyalties. And to many simple people, young and old, who are weary of the war talk and frightened at its ugliness, Wallace's passionate belief in peace transcends everything else." But Lerner, however reluctantly, was taking a different path. Wallace had proved himself "too naïve about the Russians and the nature of their foreign policy; he does not recognize the extent to which the ruthlessness of the police-state has led to a Communist imperialism."[1]

Nor was it simply that the Progressive Party was operating with little suspicion of Stalinism. The Wallaceites thought of themselves as the true internationalists, and in a sense they were internationalists. But in another, more important sense they bespoke a reform-minded isolationism. They wanted the United States to stay out of European and Asiatic affairs and to disarm, and they defended their position with the economic interpretation that traditionally accompanies liberal isolationism. The whole approach represented by the Marshall Plan, the Progres-

[9] Quoted in *New York Post*, December 11, 1947, and in Arthur M. Schlesinger, Jr.: *The Vital Center* (Houghton Mifflin, 1949), p. 119.
[1] Lerner: *Actions and Passions* (Simon & Schuster, 1949), p. 227.

sives liked to argue, was a "Wall St." machination, "a sucker plan to spend billions of the taxpayer's dollars to help monopolists and cartelists to control the markets of the world." [2] Instinctively Wallace's running-mate, Senator Glen Taylor, seeking a historian's estimate of the situation, telephoned the Nestor of isolationist economic interpretation, Charles A. Beard. Most liberals were as little interested in the isolationism as they were in the pro-Russianism of the Wallace approach. Two World Wars and a Cold War had made the least international-minded of them, as one Chicago liberal professor remarked of himself, "an unwilling internationalist, but an internationalist nevertheless." [3] Under the circumstances, they brushed aside the liberal economic interpretation of diplomacy and war. The issue, the Americans for Democratic Action said for the liberal movement, was not Wall Street. It was not even a clash between capitalism and socialism. "The issue is between those who believe in personal rights and individual dignity and those who do not." [4]

The story was the same when the United States Senate considered the great questions of postwar foreign policy. Analysis of the Senate votes reveals no tendency on the part of men who were liberals in domestic affairs to show an isolationist or a fellow-travelerish reluctance to take strong measures against Russian aggression. Of the twenty-three men who voted on the liberal side eighty per cent or more of the times when domestic issues were at stake, all but four also cast two thirds or more of their votes for such foreign-policy measures as the Atlantic Pact and the sending of American soldiers to General Eisenhower's Western European Command. The difference between the main body of liberal thinking and the Wallace deviation is emphasized by pulling out one specific comparison. The voting record of Claude Pepper, a fairly representative liberal Senator at the time, was 9 out of 11 on the reform side in domestic affairs, 4 out of 5 in

[2] Quoted from Wallace, Radio Address, July 29, 1948 (mimeographed), and Glen Taylor, Wallace's running-mate, in *New York Times*, July 23, 1948.

[3] William T. Hutchinson, quoted in *New York Times*, August 7, 1950.

[4] *New York Post*, December 5, 1947.

favor of measures for the containment of Russia. The record of Senator Glen Taylor was 9 out of 11, and 1 out of 5.[5]

The Progressives were failing to move with the trend of liberalism in one final important respect. Henry Wallace and much of his following were inclined to think in a Thirties fashion about civil liberties. Economic and social change came first; "liberty" was a catch phrase of the reactionaries. Besides, the real menace to civil liberties came from the right, not the left.[6] But most liberals, appalled by McCarthyism and Communism alike, were done with a cavalier attitude toward liberty or with a double standard in judging leftist or rightist dangers to it. They were moving civil liberties to the forefront of their interests, and denouncing Marxist totalitarianism with the same vigor they used for the fascist-minded. Unlike many reformers of the Twenties, they did not subordinate economic questions to a battle against conformity. The liberal of the early 1950's was, more than ever before in modern American history, a composite of his tradition. Like the men of 1872, he was deeply concerned with liberty; like the progressives of the New Freedom era, he was eager to expand opportunity; like the New Dealers, he added a quest for security. Liberty, opportunity, and security—all vital and all equally vital.

VI

1947, then 1948, and nothing seemed to change but the calendar. President Truman, swinging to the left, went before Congress with a belligerent liberal program; Congress yawned. The United Nations kept meeting and the Soviet kept vetoing. Witch-hunters thrashed across the nation, chasing freedom down back alleys like a fugitive crap game. Prices went on rocketing, gangster

[5] The determination of "liberal" voting in domestic affairs and the comparison of domestic liberalism with foreign-policy attitudes have been made by the process described on pp. 463-4.

[6] These attitudes were most clearly revealed in Wallace's press conference at the Progressive convention, reported in *New York Times*, July 24, 1948.

Jimmy Moran showed up in pants with a diamond-studded zipper, Elizabeth Bentley found God, and Mushkig, the seven-hundred-pound moose, said moo on the radio without even rehearsing.

As if to underline the gloom of all those who had dreamed of a postwar of splendid progress, the reports on the Bikini atom test were revealing the full horror that could come from man's technological wizardry and his social primitiveness. A young doctor attached to the Radiological Safety Section at Bikini led the way in a little book with an awesomely apt title, *No Place to Hide*. At first, Dr. David Bradley wrote, "Operation Crossroads" seemed something of an anticlimax to Hiroshima. Bombs exploded both above and below the water had left an extraordinary number of ships afloat. But then tests began to reveal the extent and persistence of the deadly radioactive fission particles. The most improbable objects turned out to be thoroughly charged—a ship's bell of brass, some chemicals from a first-aid locker on a deck, a bar of soap that had been caught in a stream of neutrons. Rocks miles away were found tainted by fission products. Fish that had been near the fleet area and fish that had eaten the deadly fish spread over huge areas of the Pacific. On the ships themselves, nothing—soap, scrubbing, the best of Navy profanity—nothing short of sandblasting off the whole outer surface got rid of the deadly material.

"The question," wrote Dr. Bradley, "is not political so much as biological. It is not the security of a political system but the survival of the race that is at stake. . . . [The] problems are self-evident. . . . Among them are: 1) There is no real defense against atomic weapons. 2) There are no satisfactory counter-measures and methods of decontamination. 3) There are no satisfactory medical or sanitary safeguards for the people of atomized areas. 4) The devastating influence of the bomb and its unborn relatives may affect the land and its wealth—and therefore its people—for centuries through the persistence of radioactivity." Dr. Bradley added: "When one considers that one millionth of a gram of radium contained within the body may be fatal one is inclined to turn from calculus to Christianity for comfort." [7]

Liberals, rarely content to be comforted by Christianity alone, looked at the little man in the White House, watched him getting nowhere with the Tafts and the Wherrys, reversing, then re-reversing himself on the Palestine issue, and they were sure they had enough of Harry Truman. "TRUMAN SHOULD QUIT," the cover of the *New Republic* shouted in blue ink. "The President of the United States is today the leader of world democracy. Truman has neither the vision nor the strength that leadership demands." [8]

Down went liberal morale. First, leading liberal politicians maneuvered to get the President out of the race. Harry Truman said, firmly, that he was a candidate to succeed himself. Then ADA leaders frantically tried to get Dwight Eisenhower to contest the Democratic nomination, apparently impelled by the thought that since the General had said virtually nothing on domestic affairs, he had said nothing conservative. George Allen, the friend of both the General and the President, hurried to Columbia University, and Eisenhower issued a resounding "No." Frenzied telegrams went out to a cabin on the edge of the Oregon woods, where the ardent New Dealer, Supreme Court Justice William Douglas, was vacationing. The Justice took off his cowboy hat, turned on his best horse-wrangler's accent, and told reporters: "I never was a-runnin', I ain't a-runnin' and I ain't goin' tuh." Desperate signs went up: "Claude Pepper, the People's Choice for President." The People's Choice could not get the backing of his own Florida delegation. [9]

Down, down went liberal morale. Perhaps the Vice-Presidential nomination? Wouldn't Douglas take that to give the liberals at least the bottom of the ticket? The Justice smiled and disappeared into the Oregon woods. Nobody, it seemed, wanted to be Vice President to a man who wasn't going to be President. Things reached the point where William P. Lane, Jr., humdrum Governor of little Maryland, announced a lofty "No, thank you" to the

---

[7] Bradley: *No Place to Hide* (Little, Brown, 1948), pp. 88, 165.

[8] Michael Straight: "Truman Should Quit," *New Republic* (April 5, 1948), CXVIII, cover.

[9] Quoted in "Lucky Star," *Time* (July 19, 1948), LII, 22.

Vice-Presidential offer. Finally a sacrificial victim was found—the faithful party wheelhorse, Alben W. Barkley.

Down, down, down went liberal morale. Whatever Truman's failings, reformers infinitely preferred a Democratic victory to the return of Republicanism. Wasn't there a chance, just the barest chance, that the Truman-Barkley ticket might make it? Two months before the election Elmo Roper stopped taking public-opinion polls; science had declared the election over. Leading Democratic politicians, students of another science, publicly offered their Washington homes for sale. The 80th Congress, which was not given to underwriting Democratic celebrations, appropriated a record quarter of a million dollars for the coming inauguration. On Election Day 1948, a day of clammy cold in the East and of drizzling mists through the West, American liberalism grimly, resignedly awaited Dewey and doom

CHAPTER XVIII

That Rendezvous

THE FIRST liberal reaction, of course, was one vast gloating. So Dewey was a sure victory, eh? So reform was done? Samuel Grafton was at his radio again on election evening, and this time he needed no friends to comfort him. "It was wonderful," he chuckled. "I shall never forget the night when the thousand smoothies suffered sudden heartburn, the night when the masterminds saw their neat little artificial conceptions kicked over . . . the night when those who had persuaded themselves that the American people would echo what had been taught them, listened for the expected chirp, and heard instead a roar. . . . It must cause a great astonishment to be so surprised, and I—I am in love with my fellowmen all over again." [1]

A few week's rest, with the triumphant President dimming the Florida sun by his pink-and-purple sport shirts, and Truman was back in Washington outlining a militant "Fair Deal" program in his State of the Union address to Congress. The applause was loudest at some of the most liberal passages in the message, including his recommendations of Taft-Hartley repeal, a higher minimum wage, wider social security, tougher antitrust laws, federal medical insurance, and federal aid to education. A "fifth term" for Roosevelt, people were saying. Liberal journalists

[1] *New York Post*, November 3, 1948.

could add: "The discriminating aim with which the public knocked off congressional reactionaries is a rather awe-inspiring sign of political maturity. . . . Truman has a stronger New Deal Congress today than FDR had at any time after '36." [2]

Inaugural Day dawned properly; the weatherman had predicted clouds, and the skies were brilliantly clear. Harry Truman had an old-home breakfast with his buddies of Battery D (after the Inaugural speech "I don't give a damn what you do, but I want you to stay sober until then"), and donned his tall silk hat for the ride to the Capitol. His address, concerned largely with foreign affairs, spoke the same forthright liberalism as his State of the Union message. The United States would have no truck with the "deceit and mockery," the "poverty and tyranny" that marked the "false philosophy" of Communism. But America would not simply oppose Russian expansionism by diplomacy and by rearmament. In the climax of his address Truman announced the "bold new program" of Point Four, to rid the world of poverty and to help colonial areas to a self-supporting independence. "The old imperialism—exploitation for foreign profit—has no place in our plans," the President declared firmly. "What we envisage is a program of development based on the concepts of democratic fair-dealing." [3]

With the end of the speech, Washington broke into the biggest, most folksy celebration the capital had ever seen. For seven and a half miles, almost three hours of marching time, the parade stretched out. Up front was the President's car, flanked by an honor guard from Battery D, at the tail end was a calliope tooting "I'm Just Wild about Harry," and in between were cowboys and pretty girls and Missouri mules and a Virginia band that played "Dixie" over and over again, switched to a few bars of "Hail to the Chief" at the reviewing stand, then hurried back to "Dixie." The President grinned; he was almost always grinning and raising his paper cup of coffee in acknowledgment of a

[2] Quoted in John Gunther: *Roosevelt in Retrospect* (Harper, 1950), p. 378, and T. R. B.: "Washington Wire," *New Republic* (November 22, 1948), CXIX, 3.

[3] *New York Times*, January 21, 1949.

salute. And the crowd, well over a million men, women, and children, yelled "Hi, Harry," " 'Ray, Harry" as if they were welcoming the local boy who had hit the big one out of the park.

When the car of the Dixiecrat candidate, Governor J. Strom Thurmond, approached the reviewing stand, Truman suddenly discovered that he had something very important to say that required turning to the man beside him. A Presidential guest, Tallulah Bankhead, hardly a woman for indirection, let out a foghorn of boos. It was all quite appropriate. On orders from the White House, for the first time in American history Negroes were invited to the top social events of the Inaugural, including the dinner given by the President and Vice President-elect and the grand ball. Even some of the attempts at unofficial Jim Crow were defeated. The New York delegation, including fifteen Negroes, was shunted from hotel to hotel, and when it finally made arrangements at the Roosevelt, the rooms assigned to the Negroes immediately developed grave telephone difficulties. New York City's white Deputy Commissioner of Housing and Buildings, Frank Jones, had an idea. Noting that the owners of the Roosevelt also controlled several New York hotels, he began to wonder out loud if the civic interest of New York did not require an exhaustive reinspection of these hotels. Suddenly all the telephone difficulties disappeared. The assaults on racial segregation at the Inaugural, Walter White, head of the NAACP, enthused, were "a miracle . . . almost as incredible as the spectacular re-election of President Truman." [4]

While the liberals celebrated, the Republicans meditated, and their conclusions made them just so many more floats in the triumphal parade for Fair Dealer Harry Truman. "Does the Republican Party Have a Future?" asked the grandson of Henry Cabot Lodge, and his answer was affirmative only if the party established a "liberal record." The *Saturday Evening Post*, of all magazines, stripped away the main argument Deweyites had been using to console themselves; a heavier vote, the *Post*'s analyst argued, would have meant only a more resounding victory for

[4] *New York Herald Tribune*, February 13, 1949.

the Democrats.[5] Nobody, it seemed, was a conservative any more. Ex-Speaker Joe Martin discovered that the G.O.P. was too full of "plutocrats." Senator Taft lectured a Republican caucus on the wisdom of backing "welfare measures," and Senator Wherry let it be known that "fundamentalist" rather than "conservative" was the proper adjective for his philosophy. Thomas Dewey used the occasion of his first major statement after the election to tongue-lash Republicans who "try to go back to the 19th Century, or even to the 1920's." They "ought to . . . try to get elected in a typical American community and see what happens to them," said Dewey, who spoke with considerable authority on the subject.[6]

Through all considerations of the election ran one dominant note. This was no liberal victory in a depression period, by a dazzling patrician leader. This was a reform triumph in a boom, in what had seemed an era of postwar reaction, by Harry Truman, graduate of the Kansas City Business School, haberdasher, deacon of the Second Baptist Church, Shriner, Elk, Moose, Lion, Eagle, and devotee of the Society for the Preservation and Encouragement of Barber Shop Singing in America, Inc. The time of the triumph, the background and interests of Truman, the very folksiness of the Inaugural proceedings, in the middle of which the President spoke and acted a sweeping liberalism, gave liberals vistas of an entirely new place in American society for their movement. "It was not an election . . . it was a revolution," their expectations rang out. "Liberalism used to be the exception; now it's become as commonplace as Harry. . . . From this election we learn that whereas the people used to have a Roosevelt tradition, the Roosevelt tradition now has a people." [7]

[5] Lodge: "Does the Republican Party Have a Future?" *Saturday Evening Post* (January 29, 1949), CCXXI, 23; Samuel Lubell: "Who *Really* Elected Truman?" ibid. (January 22, 1949), CCXXI, 15–17, 54–63.

[6] For Martin, see *New York Herald Tribune*, November 7, 1948; for Wherry, William S. White: "Portrait of a 'Fundamentalist,'" *New York Times Magazine* (January 15, 1950), p. 14; for Taft, *New York Herald Tribune*, April 14, 1949; and for Dewey, "High Roads & Dead Pigeons," *Time* (February 21, 1949), LIII, 25.

[7] Harold Ickes, in *New York Post*, November 10, 1948; a Washington official, who prefers not to be named, in an interview with me; Samuel Grafton, in *New York Post*, November 4, 1948.

II

As PRESIDENT on his own, Truman made most of his public utterances statements of a belligerent liberalism. He held foreign policy to the main outline of his Inaugural address. He managed to get through the 81st Congress important parts of the Fair Deal, including a considerable grant of powers to cope with inflation, an extension of social security that brought an estimated ten million additional people under its protection, an increase in the minimum wage from forty to seventy-five cents, and the authorization of a large-scale housing program. At times the President wielded his veto power with rousing boldness. He killed a price-raising natural-gas bill that powerful Democrats were ardently sponsoring, and assailed the McCarran "Anti-Subversive" Act, which had such hysterical support in Congress that it was immediately re-passed over his veto by majorities of 286 to 48, and 57 to 10.[8]

McCarthyism, in any form, was now provoking from the White House a magnificent indignation. "True Americanism needs defending—here and now," the President told the American Legion in a voice that snapped with anger. ". . . The growing practice of character assassination is already crushing free speech and it is threatening all our other freedoms. I daresay there are people here today who have reached the point where they are afraid to explore a new idea. How many of you are afraid to come right out in public and say what you think about a controversial issue? How many of you feel that you must play it safe 'in all things'—and on all occasions? . . . I want to warn . . . [the people of the United States]. Slander, lies, character assassination—these things are a threat to every single citizen

---

[8] Among the powerful Democratic supporters of the natural-gas bill were its author, Senator Robert Kerr, a Vice-Presidential possibility when Truman was nominated, Tom Connally, chairman of the Senate Committee on Foreign Affairs, and Speaker Sam Rayburn, who left his dais to plead for the bill. "God bless the President of the United States," the liberal leader, Senator Paul Douglas, said when he heard of the veto. *New York Times*, April 16, 1950.

everywhere in this country. When even one American—who has done nothing wrong—is forced by fear to shut his mind and close his mouth, then all Americans are in peril. It is the job of all of us . . . to rise up and put a stop to this terrible business." [9]

Yet there was an obverse side to the coin. The President talked liberalism a good deal more than he acted it. His stand that had most impressed liberal circles in the election period—the insistence on a sweeping civil-rights program—turned into an acceptance of Dixiecrat blockage. While prices rocketed, Truman avoided using some of the more important anti-inflation weapons that Congress had given him, and his first appointments to the Supreme Court, Burton, Minton, Vinson, and Clark, sounded to liberal ears ominously like Martin, Barton, and Fish. Month after month the President permitted cronies to smirch the Administration with favor-selling, and when the criticisms came, he reacted with irascible statements that no friend of Harry Truman was a dishonorable man.[1] Only late in 1951, as evidence of flagrant corruption in the federal service steadily mounted, did he begin to act. At that, Harry Vaughan still had his bourbon in the White House.

The history of Congress during the period was no more clear-cut than the activities of the President. The House and Senate elected in 1948 may have put through some of the Fair Deal, but they stalled so much on the rest of the program that reform-minded journalists called them the "ho-hum" Congress.[2] In 1950 the voters sent back a Congress that was controlled by an anti-Fair Deal, Republican-Dixiecrat coalition. From the reform point of view, there was only one salient difference between this 82nd Congress and the 80th, which had been swept out in 1948: the 80th did illiberal things and the 82nd did very little at all.

Near the halfway point in the Truman Administration, the

[9] *Congressional Record*, 82nd Cong., 1st Sess. (unbound), XCVII, pp. 10265–6.

[1] President Truman summarized his attitude in a press conference, at which he was paraphrased as saying that "all" his associates were "honorable men," and that he confidently waited for history to judge his Presidency. *New York Herald Tribune*, March 16, 1951.

[2] Quoted from an ADA member, Stewart Alsop, in ibid., May 21, 1950.

North Koreans marched, and liberals were caught in another muzzy situation. Unquestionably, the reform movement as a whole backed the United Nations intervention; within three weeks even Henry Wallace was supporting the move and an estimated half of the Progressives broke with the party leadership when it refused to go along with Wallace.[3] But with the support came questions, the kind of questions Wallace and Willkie had been asking in 1943 now brought to a more fateful focus. "The Asiatics," Max Lerner summarized the worries, "are reaching for a revolutionary nationalism which is a recoil from their colonial status up to now. Can we convince them that our power is not as dangerous to them as the imperialism of Russia? The Asiatics are reaching for new economic and social reform. Can we show them that we can help them get the kind of land reform they want, and then move on to deeper social changes through the method of freedom? Most of all, the Asiatics are deeply distrustful of the racism of the Western world. . . . Can we show them that we too hate racism, that we are moving away from it at home, and that we respect men of all races and colors abroad? Put in this way, what are our chances of success?" [4]

An actual shooting war against Red armies naturally churned the Red-hunt to new furies, and here was an issue on which liberals at least might hope to have a clear-cut position.[5] They

---

[3] Wallace's statement read, in part: "Undoubtedly the Russians could have prevented the attack by the North Koreans and undoubtedly they could now stop the attack at any time they wish. I hold no brief for the past actions of either the United States or Russia but, when my country is at war and the United Nations sanctions that war, I am on the side of my country and the United Nations" (*New York Times*, July 16, 1950). The emergency appropriation bill to pay for American participation passed the Senate unanimously and the lone dissenting vote in the House was that of the fellow-travelling Vito Marcantonio (ibid., July 20, 1950). Wallace estimated the loss of the Progressive Party following on the basis of his mail. "Where I Stand," *New Leader* (August 26, 1950), XXXIII, 3.

[4] *New York Post*, July 25, 1950.

[5] Some of this Red-hunt was a serious concern with potentially dangerous Communists. Much of it, even apart from McCarthy, was so vicious or ridiculous that someday it will make the United States blush furiously. A few illustrative examples should be brought together here and now. United States Senator Andrew Schoeppel, of Kansas, accused the long-time anti-Communist Secretary of the Interior, Oscar Chapman, of a

stood for free speech, and ever since the Red scare of the Twenties most of them had accepted as their criterion of free speech the famous "clear and present danger" dictum of Justice Holmes. Americans were not to be punished for advocating any political doctrine they believed, including the opinion that the government should be overthrown by force. They were to be punished only if their advocacy, quite directly and in an important way, endangered the government. Then, as the Cold War heated up, a New York federal court, acting under the Smith Act, indicted the national directors of the American Communist Party on the grounds that they "did conspire . . . to organize as the Communist Party of the United States of America a society, group, and assembly of persons who teach and advocate the overthrow and destruction of the Government of the United States by force and violence." [6] Promptly the liberals took sides. The cleavage was represented in a public debate between Roger Baldwin and Morris Ernst, two old friends both of whom were officials of the American Civil Liberties Union and both of whom were undoubted liberals in all important respects.

Baldwin had no use for the whole Smith Act. He would not oppose "a federal indictment based upon overt acts," but he emphatically did "oppose action by any governmental body in this country which seeks to punish people for their beliefs and the mere expression of their beliefs." Some Americans, Baldwin

---

"strong and close personal alliance" with the "Russian Soviet cause," and when Chapman completely demolished the charge in a public hearing, the Senator felt no necessity, and apparently little pressure, to apologize (*New York Herald Tribune; New York Post,* September 8, 1950). Ireene Wicker, radio's "Singing Lady," returned from an audience with the Pope, where she was given a special blessing for her work with children, to find her television contract cancelled. The publishers of *Counterattack,* who had brought about the pressure that produced the cancellation, offered this defense: the Communist *Daily Worker* had listed Miss Wicker five years before as a sponsor of a Communist Councilmanic candidate and "the Daily Worker is very accurate; they never make a mistake" (*New York Post,* September 11, 1950). Monogram Pictures canceled a movie about Henry Wadsworth Longfellow. Hiawatha, the studio explained, had tried to stop wars between the Indian tribes, and people might construe the movie as propaganda for the Communist "peace offensive" (*New York Times,* September 17, 1950).

[6] U.S. Court of Appeals, U.S. v. Eugene Dennis et al., IV, 3200.

added with the traditional liberal suspicion of anything smacking of thought-control, "would say that certain ideas are so dangerous, so abhorrent, that the effort to spread them must be suppressed even though no connection with overt acts is shown. . . . Such a notion seems to me dangerous in the extreme. Powerful influences will always tend to say that unpopular ideas are of this character and that advocating them is an illegal conspiracy."

Morris Ernst started by making clear that he believed that "Communists have a right to advocate publicly the overthrow of the government of the United States. I further believe they even have the right to say publicly that if all else failed, they would advocate the ultimate use of violence to change the form of our government. . . . But we are confronted today with a situation where arguments about public statements have no relevance. The question is one, not of public statements, but of secret acts, in the course of a secret conspiracy, which might never become public until it was too late, until democracy no longer had time or the chance to defend itself."

Ernst directly attacked "the shibboleth of liberals," Justice Holmes's dictum. It "assumes that a secret coup succeeds or fails by a mere count of noses. . . . But today we live in a world of such close and intricate technology that under certain circumstances a very small minority may take over a country. . . . Let me ask you: At what time was there a 'clear and present danger' from Quisling in Norway until he came to power? . . . I prefer to the Holmes doctrine that of Justice Brandeis, who said the overriding question is whether, in the given situation, society has a chance to counteract what is being done, has the opportunity to protect itself. If there is a public debate, society certainly has that chance. But the essence of plotting for a revolutionary coup is its secrecy. If the end to be obtained is illegal, and the means are secret, the acts of individuals and groups should be prevented by law whether the size of their effort is large or small." [7]

"Is nothing settled anymore?" one liberal wailed as she read

---

[7] Morris Ernst and Roger C. Baldwin: "Liberals and the Communist Trial," *New Republic* (January 31, 1949), CXX, 7–8.

the Baldwin-Ernst debate.[8] Very little seemed clear as the Communist leaders trooped off to jail amid a liberal squeamishness, an indecisive Korean war turned into highly belligerent truce talks, and Harry Truman prepared to retire with the most mixed record in modern American history.

III

IN THE welter of grayishness, several key facts were incontestable. No matter how much Truman had wavered, no matter what Congress failed to do, no matter Joe McCarthy, the election of 1948 did symbolize liberal triumph. Asia versus Europe, MacArthur versus Truman, could still split the country like a meatcleaver. Americans went on arguing bitterly over specific legislation, and doubt existed whether any very large section of the population genuinely accepted the equalitarian and security doctrines that the New Deal had added to traditional reformism. Yet 1948 shouted a fact which the public opinion polls, even granting a healthy Truman discount for error, had been stating for quite a while. After all the ups and downs, the triumphs that crumbled quickly into disaster, the two fundamentals of modern American reform had taken a hold on the public mind that no discernible event could break. Most Americans now accepted the basic domestic doctrine that generations of reformers since the depression of 1873 had agreed upon and the heart of the foreign policy that they had made their own. The country went along, almost as a matter of course, with the belief that governments, particularly the federal government, should interfere to protect and advance the standard of living and the status of the more depressed groups. It accepted, if without enthusiasm, the argument that the United States should actively participate in an international collective-security organization and should fight, if necessary, to stop any serious aggression.[9]

[8] A Seattle attorney, who prefers not to be named, in a letter to me, February 4, 1949.

[9] As is true in any culture, one of the surest signs of the deep-seated

In an important sense this liberal conquest came as liberalism turned into a form of conservatism. The foreign policy that liberals were espousing in the early Fifties amounted to having the United States serve as the main blockage to the prime revolutionary forces of the day, the Communist ideology and the Red armies. The majorities for Truman were, at least to a large extent, the votes of people who had advanced in income and status during the New Deal and World War II and who feared that Republicanism would take away their gains.

It was no accident that the United States found itself lined up in region after region alongside the representatives of a relatively rightist group, the de Gasperi party in Italy, the Franco government in Spain, or the Nationalist element of Chinese. Nor was it surprising that when interviewers went out to probe the Truman victory, they came back with stories of men and women who voted for the more liberal candidate because they were cautious of change. Dozens of urban communities resembled Arlington, a suburb of Boston, which went Democratic for the first time in 1948. "I own a nice house, have a new car and am much better off than my parents were," the residents explained. ". . . Why change?" Millions of farmers were like the citizens of Guthrie County, Iowa, which had turned in regular Republican majorities even during the Thirties and proceeded to go Democratic in 1948. "I talked about voting for Dewey all summer," one Guthrie farmer put it, "but when voting time came, I just couldn't do it. I remembered . . . all the good things that have come to me under the Democrats." [1]

The very phrases and attitudes that had marked the *avant-*

---

liberal triumph was the way history had come to be written. In 1950 the president of the American Historical Association pointed out: "Fifty years ago, it was difficult to find any general history of the United States that did not present the Federalist-Whig-Republican point of view, or express a very dim view of all Democratic leaders except Cleveland. This fashion has completely changed; it would be equally difficult today to find a good general history of the United States that did not follow the Jefferson-Jackson-F. D. Roosevelt line." Samuel E. Morison: "Faith of a Historian," *American Historical Review* (January 1951), LVI, 272.

[1] Quoted by Lubell, in *Saturday Evening Post* (January 22, 1949), CCXXI, 17, 56.

garde intellectual, his talk of the "common man," "welfare," and "economic democracy," his zest for nonconformity, even his insistence that American culture was devoid of the artistic and his taste for foreign food, were turning into just so many decorations for the status quo. Old George Babbitt, Peter Viereck has remarked, had spawned a son, who calls avoiding unionization "welfare" capitalism, prefers to discuss his Rotary business over *pâté de foie gras* in an adequate little French restaurant, and is enormously smug about his lack of smugness. As for art, Viereck added, George Babbitt merely hated it. Babbitt Junior "hugs it to death." [2]

Not only was liberalism playing something of the conservative's role; the stage had changed drastically. From Henry George's day through the New Deal, the reformer saw his problem as that of a country in which wealth was divided with jarring unevenness, the males were the central concern, the middle classes, whatever their difficulties, still felt themselves the cocks of the walk, and farmers, industrial workers, and the minorities were the gravely depressed groups. But in the United States of the early Fifties, it was estimated that only 18,000,000 family units received incomes of less than $3,000 or more than $10,000, while 21,000,000 were in the middle group. The population contained more females than males; women owned more than sixty per cent of the total national wealth; and they were out working, whether married, single, widowed, or divorced, in astounding numbers, making up 19,000,000 of the total labor force of 63,000,000. Labor, far from being the bedraggled oppressed, was organized so powerfully that it could even stave off many of the effects of a severe inflation, and the unions, performing functions ranging from adult education to a key role in electing Presidents, were giving workers a proud sense of controlling their own empire. All but the unluckiest and least provident of the farmers were living decently, often amid so many machines that a nine-to-five workday, with a television evening, was possible for both husband

[2] Peter Viereck: "Babbitt Revisited," *Harvard Alumni Bulletin* (June 24, 1950), LII, 3–7.

and wife; for the 8,000,000 farm families in the top income group, a year's return of $10,000 was average. Gone completely was the fear of the hayseed charge. "You'll probably think I'm presumptuous," the farmer of the Fifties spoke through Leslie Heiser, of downstate Illinois, "but . . . there isn't a job in New York City that's good enough for me." [3] And certainly the dimensions, if not the seriousness, of the problem of opportunity for the minorities had changed in an era when a Negro captained the Yale football team, all three major candidates for the mayorship of the nation's metropolis were Italian-born, and a Jew headed the federal government's most vital project, the Atomic Energy Commission.[4]

If any one of the large groups felt the kind of unrelieved frustration that had been widespread in the Eighties, that group was the once uppish middle classes. Most of them not only lacked powerful organizations to protect their career security and to fight for salary increases in an inflationary period. Many were in a state that a sociologist has aptly called "status panic," anxious about their ability to keep up with the prestige demands of their class, queasy over their paper-pushing, middleman role in a society that esteemed technological skills so highly.[5] One journalist, writing about "our fear-ridden middle classes," has told of a friend, a graduate of a distinguished university, who gave up his job as an editor on an established publication to become a typesetter. "Two times in the last five years," the friend explained grimly, "I have been kicked out of my job *without any reason being given.* . . . In one case two other men were hired to do what I had previously been doing—and since then they have been fired too. As a salaried editor the most I ever earned was a hundred and twenty-five dollars a week, and I regularly took a

---

[3] Quoted in "The Farmer Goes to Town," *Fortune* (October 1947), XXXVI, 194.

[4] The Negro was Levi Jackson, elected captain of the 1948 team. The three Italian-born candidates in the New York City election of 1950 were Edward Corsi, Vincent Impellitteri, and Ferdinand Pecora. David Lilienthal headed the Atomic Energy Commission from April 1947, to February 1950.

[5] Quoted from C. Wright Mills: *White Collar* (Oxford, 1951), p. 239.

briefcase of material home to work on nights. I can earn that much, without homework, in the workingmen's end of the publication business, and there I can't be kicked out because of a boss' 'change of policy.' . . . My family will have more security, and I will have more self-respect. I am resigning, once and for all, from the most kicked-around class in America—the salaried middle class." [6]

The problems of the middle class were underlined by indications that their position would grow still more vexsome. The rich would be able to take care of themselves; the poor man and the worker or farmer, whether poor or not, were receiving increasing governmental protection. But the position of the middle class was exemplified in the housing field, where, as one expert pointed out, the median group was caught in a " 'no man's land' between those eligible for public housing and those who can pay the high rents required in new private enterprise construction." All the while, the upward thrust of the population to white-collar jobs and expanding educational opportunities were creating a larger, and therefore more vulnerable, middle class. As the Fifties went on, social scientists began envisaging a proletariat of the A.B. degree. By 1969, the Harvard economist Seymour Harris predicted, some two to three college graduates would be applying for every one position considered commensurate with their training.[7]

In this changed America the very meaning of opportunity was undergoing a metamorphosis. It made little sense to worry about the farm hand's opportunity to acquire his own acres when the hand was becoming a "suitcase farmer," motoring from his urban home to well-paid hours in a huge factory-in-the-field. Urban unemployment meant something quite different when the unemployed were likely to be over forty. (From 1900 to 1950, the

[6] Dorothy Thompson: "Our Fear-Ridden Middle Classes," *Ladies' Home Journal* (January 1950), LXVIII, 11. Italics in the original.

[7] The housing expert was Ira S. Robbins, executive vice-president of the New York Citizens Housing and Planning Council, quoted in *New York Times*, January 31, 1949; Seymour E. Harris: *The Market for College Graduates* (Harvard University Press, Cambridge, 1949), Chap. ii.

life expectancy of the white man jumped seventeen years, and it was expected to increase a full twenty years by 1960.) The discussion of how to keep the way open for the starting of small businesses had to take a sharp turn in an era when the Commerce Department was estimating that $6,900 was required to get a hole-in-the-wall restaurant under way, $5,000 for a filling station, and from $7,200 to $34,800 for an apparel shop. The whole problem of providing increasing status satisfactions changed when there was evidence to suggest that a farmer had more prestige in the public eye than a store manager, and a dentist outranked a member of the board of directors of a large corporation.[8]

IV

IF LIBERALISM, triumphant as a kind of conservatism, was not to become merely conservatism, it had to go at the problems of this drastically altered America, and as it wheeled to the task, it ran into even more than its usual number of troubles. All of the new difficulties had a two-sided tortuousness like that of the old ones, so much so that they too approached being dilemmas. If being a Communist leader could mean that you were jailed even when you had committed no actual revolutionary act, liberals like Roger Baldwin asked, what advocate of another unpopular cause was next on the list?[9] "Liberals today," said the former New Deal Secretary of Labor, Frances Perkins, "are too much concerned with enforcing equality by law. . . . If they don't watch out they will be enforcing a situation where everyone is equal, and equally unable to score by individual achievement."[1] Thurman Arnold denounced "those so-called liberals whose principal social value is security for the underdog, rather than opportunity for the individual. For example, one of the popular liberal causes is strong labor organizations. Many liberals would fight for every

[8] "Jobs and Occupations: A Popular Evaluation," *Opinion News* (September 1, 1947), IX, 4–5.
[9] Baldwin, in *New Republic*, CXX, 8.
[1] Interview with Miss Frances Perkins.

strong labor organization until it became a force which restricted production, throttled new enterprise, prevented individual collective bargaining by local units and destroyed democracy in labor." [2] Yet Roger Baldwin would have been the first to agree that the American Communist Party does constitute a potentially dangerous fifth column; Miss Perkins, to acknowledge that equality by law might well be an understandable demand of long-frustrated minorities; and Thurman Arnold, to recognize the importance of the problem of economic security, especially for a population that was aging as rapidly as that of the United States.

All the old difficulties ground ahead. The liberal's "the people," the men and women who were to leap to take advantage of a more democratized government and would use it to advance the general interest, went right on refusing to act their allotted role. By the Fifties, the initiative, referendum, and recall had become quaint; one thought of them, as one remembered Teddy Roosevelt's teeth, in a haze of mezzotint sentimentality. The woman's vote, in a buzz of activity, continued to make little difference. In 1950, on the thirtieth anniversary of the suffrage amendment, a woman surveyed its results in the *New York Times*. Her title was: "What the Women's Vote Has *Not* Done," and the italics were hers. [3]

The process of the atomization of "the people" into special-interest groups had hardly slowed down. The kind of thinking and voting which emphasizes almost exclusively the interests of a particular occupation was becoming so commonplace that few were surprised when the CIO defined politics as "the science of how who gets what, when and why." [4] Dozens of cities were quite familiar with the rabid nationality voting that Buffalo experienced in 1948. Two years before, the Republicans had won

---

[2] Quoted in Eric F. Goldman and Mary Paull: "Liberals on Liberalism," *New Republic* (July 22, 1946), CXV, 72.

[3] Mildred Adams, in *New York Times Sunday Magazine*, August 20, 1950.

[4] Quoted in V. O. Key, Jr.: *Politics, Parties, and Pressure Groups* (Crowell, 1948), p. 1.

the mayor's office, and the Polish-Americans waited, the glint of clan-consciousness in their eyes. Not one of their group was named an important commissioner, and in 1948 the Republicans were thoroughly trounced, with a Polish-American taking a seat in Congress.[5]

Catholic group-centrism was reaching the point where the church conducted a major campaign in behalf of its segregated school system, and conducted it so belligerently that when Mrs. Franklin D. Roosevelt ventured to dissent, Francis Cardinal Spellman publicly accused her of "discrimination unworthy of an American mother." [6] Jewish group-consciousness, spurred ahead by fear of Adolf Hitler, was stimulated still more by the exhilarating last steps in setting up the Israeli state in Palestine. Even Reform rabbis were now reviving long-forgotten resolutions against intermarriage with Christians and most of the American Jewish leadership was noticeably unprotesting when the Israeli Prime Minister, David Ben-Gurion, made it emphatically clear that in the event of any clash between the loyalties of an American Zionist, his loyalties belonged first and foremost to Israel.[7]

[5] Lubell, in *Saturday Evening Post* (January 22, 1949), CCXXI, 17. After World War II, the newest immigrant group, the Puerto Ricans, quickly learned the doctrine of embattled separateness. At word that city officials were looking into the conditions of the Puerto Rican slums in New York City, Abelardo Gonzales, head of one of the airlines that flew the Puerto Ricans in, said: "A long time back everybody was beefing about the Irish when they came over. Then they got themselves a Mayor and a Senator and some Congressmen, and people quit bothering about them. Then came the Jews, and they started kicking about them. They got themselves a Governor and some Congressmen, and they let up on them. Next came the Italians, and they got guys like La Guardia and Marcantonio, and they let up on them. But us? We got nobody, so they pick on us. But just you wait—after a while we'll get some guys, and they'll let up on us, too. That's the way it goes." *New York Herald Tribune,* November 13, 1947.

[6] Quoted in "My Day in the Lion's Mouth," *Time* (August 1, 1949), LIV, 11.

[7] The 1947 meeting of the Central Conference of American Rabbis, a Reformed group, revived a 1909 resolution which stated that mixed marriages should be "discouraged." The convention failed to vote for complete prohibition by only two votes. The trend in thinking was further emphasized by the age cleavage in the voting, most of the older rabbis casting their ballots against the absolute prohibition while most of the younger rabbis voted for it (*New York Times,* January 31, 1947). Ben-Gurion de-

Negro nationalism and racialism did not lag behind. The American Negro population came out of the Fascist invasion of Ethiopia with a flourishing "Ethopian World Federation," dedicated to the Garveyite proposition that American Negroes were not so much Americans as they were part of a world race of black men, and this variety of Garveyism acquired the highly respectable leadership of Finley Wilson, Grand Exalted Ruler of the Negro Elks. A steady stream of best-sellers for the Negro population were being written by J. A. Rogers, a member of Garvey's inner circle who went right on being a Garveyite when he became a columnist for the most influential Negro newspaper in the United States, the *Pittsburgh Courier*. Rogers's pamphlet *100 Amazing Facts about the Negro* enraptured thousands in the Harlems of the United States with the decidedly amazing facts that Beethoven was "without a doubt a dark mulatto," that the founder of the Swedish royal house was a "colored man," and that ancient Negroes laid the basis of "all true culture and civilization." [8] A. Philip Randolph, head of the powerful Pullman Porter's Union and a near-saint in the eyes of many Negroes, did not hesitate to plan a March on Washington which barred, not Communists, but white Communists. "The Negroes," Randolph explained, "need an All-Negro movement, just as the Jews have a Zionist movement. . . ." [9] As for W. E. B. Du Bois, by 1949 he was so much the minority chauvinist that he apologized to a Jewish audience for Ralph Bunche's "misdeeds." Bunche, it seems, had ignored the fact that he was a Negro and treated the Jews, another minority, and the Arabs impartially in his Palestine mediation efforts.[1]

---

fined Zionism, in whatever place it existed, as "complete solidarity with the State and people of Israel," and he added that "Zionists in other countries should have the courage to stand up for the State, even if their governments are against it." "The State and Future of Zionism," *Zionist Newsletter* (May 16, 1950), II, pp. 11, 13.

[8] Rogers: *100 Amazing Facts about the Negro* (E. Vernon Berkeley, New Rochelle, N.Y., 1934), pp. 5, 10, 11.

[9] Roi Ottley: *New World A-Coming* (Houghton Mifflin, 1943), p. 251.

[1] *New York Post*, June 7, 1948. Some influential Negroes who did not approve of racialism nevertheless would not entirely condemn it. Testifying before a Congressional Committee, Hazel Scott explained her support for the Communist, Benjamin Davis, in the New York councilmanic election

In terms of liberalism, the results, of course, were mixed. As always, group-centered thinking, whether occupational, nationality, racial, or religious, could impel a liberal cause along, and it played an important role in electing Truman in 1948. (There is even persuasive evidence that Truman ran more strongly than Roosevelt in some hyphenated districts because the new President, unlike his predecessor, was not especially associated with the war on Germany, had not referred to an Italian "stab in the back" to France, and could not be blamed for the continued Russian control of part of Poland.[2]) Yet when group-centered thinking helped liberalism, the union of the two was accidental, and the postwar was full of important instances when the accident did not happen.

The farm bloc, single-mindedly concerned with keeping agricultural prices high, killed the Administration's Brannan plan, which aimed to bring relief to the consumer.[3] Some Negro organizations, determined to write an antisegregation clause into the Administration's public-housing bill, seriously endangered the chances of the whole program in the Senate; two of the strongest friends of the Negro in Congress, Senators Paul Douglas and Hubert Humphrey, had to work hard to save the generally liberal NAACP from doing the work of the real-estate lobby.[4]

---

of 1943 by saying: "Davis, as the only Negro running, received support he might not otherwise have enjoyed. This may not be healthy; it is a form of racism. But given the facts of Jim Crow—even in the North—such an attitude is understandable" (ibid., September 14, 1950). It is significant, too, that some Negro leaders were no longer using the argument that no such thing as a "Negro vote" exists. For example, Henry L. Moon, the NAACP public-relations man, declared in an interview: "Of course there are racial voting blocs in this country. Any group would be foolish not to try to protect its interests at the ballot box" (ibid., June 7, 1948).

[2] Lubell, in *Saturday Evening Post* (January 22, 1949), CCXXI, 15–17, 54–63.

[3] The opposition of the Farm Bureau to the Brannan plan was so violent that in 1949 the organization broke a tradition by refusing to invite Secretary of Agriculture Brannan to address its convention (*New York Times*, November 18, 1949). In the House vote on a "trial run" of the Brannan plan, even staunch Administration supporters deserted under the terrific farm pressure. Ibid., July 22, 1949.

[4] Ibid., June 30, 1949; *New York Post*, April 25, 1949. Senators Cain and Bricker, two long-time enemies of public housing, were leaders in the fight for the antisegregation amendment. It was estimated that the amend-

The American Medical Association, perennial symbol of the self-centered professional group, impeded efforts to expand the supply of doctors at a time when there were fewer M.D.'s per unit of population than in 1900.[5] Organized labor, still very much Samuel Gompers's labor, was demanding more, more, and then more, unabashed by the evidence that it was contributing to an inflation which injured most of the community.

Catholic-minded Congressmen, attempting to force indirect public funds for parochial schools, jammed the Administration's whole program for federal aid to education in a period of grave school needs.[6] Zionists were at least an important element in killing a Roosevelt-approved plan for spreading all displaced persons around the world which would have brought most liberals up cheering.[7] Then Jewish Congressmen or Congressmen with large numbers of Jewish votes in their districts went after the bane of Zionists, Britain. The group was a major factor in endangering in the House of Representatives the Administration's proposal for a loan to Britain, a proposal that an overwhelming majority of liberals considered important both as a way of helping to keep American factories going and as part of the building

---

ment would swing thirty Southern or border-state votes away from the bill and thus defeat it.

[5] Seymour E. Harris: "Prescription to Meet the Doctor Shortage," *New York Times Sunday Magazine* (May 14, 1950), p. 22. A committee of the conservative American Conference of Academic Deans directly assailed the medical profession on this point, and Dean Simeon E. Leland, of Northwestern, declared that the AMA was dominated by "Petrillo economics. . . . Medicine is the only profession in which the element of competition comes only at the beginning" (*New York Times*, January 10, 1950).

[6] Ibid., March 15, 1950. Typical of the situation was the fact that two ordinarily staunch supporters of Administration legislation who were Catholics from largely Catholic districts—John Lesinski, of Michigan, and John Kennedy, of Massachusetts—went along with the blockage of the bill.

[7] Roosevelt, interested in a plan to spread 500,000 of the beaten peoples of Europe around the world, asked Morris L. Ernst to sound out the British on how many they would take. The British answer was that they would match the United States, man for man. Ernst felt this offer from a small and depleted island would surely break down the resistance of the United States, which was expected to be the chief stumbling-block to the plan. But American Zionist leaders proved violently opposed to the whole idea, and Roosevelt dropped it. Ernst: *So Far So Good* (Harper, 1948), pp. 170–7.

444

of a strong collective-security system. The manner in which group centeredness could impel even long-time liberals to vote against liberalism was dramatically summarized when the Zionist Congressman Adolph Sabath, who had not voted against a New Deal or Fair Deal measure in thirteen years, rose to his feet with a tirade against Britain and an announcement that he would not back the loan. Apparently only great pressure from Jewish leaders of the prominence of Rabbi Stephen Wise and Congressman Sol Bloom (who pointedly reminded his co-religionists that he was backing the measure "as an American, and not as a Jew") swung enough Zionist-minded Congressmen to remove the bill from danger in the House.[8]

Along with the ferocious troubles over groups, another, more institutional problem continued and increased in significance. Now, with their new concerns over enforced equality and economic security, liberals depended more heavily than ever on federal action. Yet here was the federal government using all the powers and prestige which reform efforts had helped give it in a Loyalty Program that deeply disturbed many liberals. The centralization problem was further emphasized by Truman's swings from left to right and his tendency to govern through cronies. Liberals shuddered when the President, in one of those moments when old friendships or old Missouri ways of thinking meant more to him than the Fair Deal, appointed a conservative to head one of the increasingly powerful federal boards.

Whatever the dangers created by Truman's Loyalty Program and his appointing habits, they were nothing compared with the possibilities inherent in the Atomic Energy Commission. "America's Most Radical Law," one expert called the legislation that established the Commission, and certainly the law was unprecedented in the sense that it gave a board of a few men life-and-death powers over American life in the event that atomic

[8] *New York Times*, July 3–10, 1946; *Congressional Record*, 79th Cong., 2nd Sess., XCII, Pt. 7, pp. 8393–6; Stephen Wise: *Challenging Years* (Putnam, 1949), pp. 303–5.

energy was harnessed for peacetime purposes.[9] With complete control over existing and future atomic patents vested in the Commission, a liberal group could remake the country at a rate undreamed of by the most optimistic reformers of previous generations. A different type of board would be able to rush the nation into a freebooter's paradise, complete with cyclotronic profits and highly fissionable morals.

Greater federal powers not only created more potent instruments that could pass into the hands of conservatives or the anti-social. They encouraged graft by making its operations easier and its rewards greater. Shortly before the election of 1952, as the popular outcry over political corruption was nearing its climax, the perceptive liberal, Blair Bolles, hit the point squarely. *How to Get Rich in Washington*, he called his book angrily. Then, with the softer indignation of the thoughtful facing a genuine problem, he expounded his theme. "The centralization of power in the federal government for the purpose of improving the welfare of the laggards in the race for personal security," Bolles wrote, "actually simplifies the task for modern seekers of privilege. Instead of having to take control of the nation, they have only to take control of the nation's government. . . . Lately the welfare state has been undergoing a subtle change into the rich man's welfare state, aiding those who don't need help or who don't deserve it at public expense. The agencies created to end privilege have become bulwarks of privilege. The bureaus which were established originally as balance wheels for segments of the national economy—transportation, communications, land use, etc.—unbalance the economy by distributing the riches unevenly. . . . These agencies have taken to misusing other people's money, at a time when the government has far more money to work with than the Morgans ever touched." [1]

Amid the concern over corruption, like some growl out of the days of the horse and buggy, came the anti-trust speeches.

---

[9] The expert was James R. Newman, counsel for the Senate Committee that drafted the Atomic Energy Act, writing in *Harper's* (May 1947), CXCIV, 436–45.

[1] Bolles: *How to Get Rich in Washington* (Norton, 1952), pp. 12–13.

The Truman Administration, in bursts of cockiness, took on the biggest of the big businesses; one month it was filing a suit against DuPont, and another month, against the A&P. But somehow it was all unreal, as unreal as William Jennings Bryan would have seemed orating to beboppers. The Federal Trade Commission, headed by the impeccably Republican Robert Ewald Freer, announced that the concentration of economic control was reaching the point where, "like Alexander the Great, the modern monopolist may have to bring his merger activities to a halt, owing simply to the imminent absence of 'New Worlds to Conquer.' . . . No great stretch of the imagination is required to foresee that if nothing is done to check the growth in concentration, either the giant corporations will ultimately take over the country, or the Government will be impelled to step in and impose some form of direct regulation in the public interest. In either event, collectivism will have triumphed over free enterprise, and the theory of competition will have been relegated to the limbo of well-intentioned but ineffective ideals." [2] The public went right on delighting in nylon for more and more purposes and deserting the corner grocer for the chrome bargain shelves of the chain supermarket.

Foreign policy, fully as much as domestic policy, continued the old difficulties. The pre-1948 liberal tendency to blame Harry Truman for the foreign debacle, carried over to some extent into the post-election period, was no more an adequate explanation of the failure of the World War II peace settlement than berating Wilson had been in the Twenties. To a considerable extent, Truman had to build on the foundation Roosevelt had laid, and that foundation was none too solid. The fact was that much as Roosevelt tried to avoid Wilson's mistakes, much as he actually did avoid them in some respects, he had not broken with the basic Wilsonian formula. In his statements of war aims he placed greatest emphasis just where Wilson had placed it—on a democracy that was defined primarily as political democracy, on

[2] Federal Trade Commission: *Report of the Federal Trade Commission on the Merger Movement, Summary Report* (1948), pp. 22, 68-9.

447

national self-determination, and on a world organization that was a replica of the League of Nations in its key provisions.

Roosevelt's dependence on appeals to political democracy became ever more conspicuous as the war went on. His earliest public statement of American objectives, the Four Freedoms, included as number three "freedom from want." The Atlantic Charter dedicated Britain and the United States to a world-wide drive for "economic advancement" and "social security." [3] Roosevelt's private statements often indicated that he thought the future peace of the world depended on the economic development of backward regions, and he told a friend that once "this damn war is over, I think Eleanor and I will go to the Near East and see if we can manage to put over an operation like the Tennessee Valley system." [4] Yet his public utterances dealt less and less with economic and social problems. Roosevelt was, above all, concerned with getting on with the war; he dreaded Big Three disunity, either in the war or in the coming peace, and he knew the doggedness of Winston Churchill's conservatism; he was keenly aware how easy it would be to set off a storm in the United States. "Freedom from want" was never implemented in any public statement. As a matter of fact, in the drafting of the original United Nations declaration, any commitment to seek world-wide social security was apparently dropped at Roosevelt's insistence. Probably, Robert Sherwood has speculated, the American President was afraid of home-front charges that he was seeking a global New Deal. [5]

Roosevelt was a genuine Wilsonian in his dependence on national self-determination. The principle was the cornerstone of the Atlantic Charter, and if any one thought was the Roosevelt keynote during the war, that thought was the Atlantic Charter call for the restoration of "sovereign rights and self-government to those who have been forcibly deprived of them." [6] As if in

[3] Samuel Rosenman, ed.: *Public Papers and Addresses of Franklin D. Roosevelt* (Harper, 1950), X, 315.
[4] Frances Perkins: *The Roosevelt I Knew* (Viking, 1946), p. 89.
[5] Robert E. Sherwood: *Roosevelt and Hopkins* (Harper, 1948), p. 453.
[6] Rosenman, X, 315.

symbolism of a Wilsonian concern over national self-determination, the State Department summoned back Isaiah Bowman, the geographer who had been an important figure in redrawing the map of Europe according to nationality demands in 1919. "What a mess we made," Bowman remarked unabashedly as he returned to remaking Europe under the same dictate.[7]

The Roosevelt addiction to self-determination was closely connected with his acceptance of a world organization that was based on completely sovereign nations. Publicly or in the privacy of Big Three counsels, the President never seems to have questioned the assumption that peace could be preserved while leaving each nation free to do as it pleased. His Yalta compromise changed nothing that touched the heart of the matter. The Soviet wanted a veto that would permit each major power to stop the discussion of any matter it did not want brought up in the Security Council. The American compromise made it impossible for a participant to a dispute to block discussion of it, but it left the major powers the veto to stop important action concerning the dispute. Quite clearly, the sovereign veto power on all vital questions had been preserved, and the League of Nations was being re-created.

Just as clearly, this Wilsonian peace produced results that liberals did not want. Vetoes quickly reduced the United Nations to a public forum, useful in airing the world's problems and in bringing to bear what diplomats like to call "the pressure of world opinion," but impotent to stop wars.[8] The Wilson-like emphasis on the glories of national self-determination permitted conservative or fascist-minded regimes to cloak themselves in the prestige of representing "freedom." The process was repeated again and again. It was carried out in the Polish situation, where the "free" government-in-exile was an authoritarian faction, tainted by a record of corruption, indifference to peasant miseries, and a primitive nationalism that included brutal anti-Semitism;

[7] Baltimore *Sun*, March 8, 1944.
[8] It is noteworthy that in the one important mediation effort in which the U.N. succeeded, the Palestine affair, the successful mediation came after one of the parties, the Israeli, had substantially defeated the other by arms.

in Yugoslavia, where the "freedom" forces of Mihailovich were identified with traditional Serbian domination and were widely suspected of collaboration with the Nazis; in Greece, where the "free" government was the royalist dictatorship; in China, where the "free" government of Chiang Kai-shek had continued for more than a decade a dreary dictatorship of war lords and landowners. Each one of these groups grasped for the Roosevelt declarations with unrestrained enthusiasm, and hailed, to use the words of Mihailovich's Ambassador to the United States, "the noble principles which had gained him [Roosevelt] so much prestige with the enslaved peoples." [9]

Roosevelt's identification of the war aims of the United States with political democracy re-created a difficulty of the Wilson approach, and in still more serious form. It gave hostages to the dynamic force that was only a distant threat in 1919. The more Roosevelt concentrated on the importance of purely political democracy, the more the Soviet Union was able to present itself as the one power that was ready to get down to the central concerns of the masses in eastern Europe and Asia—land, higher wages, and the ending of caste. Roosevelt may have remarked airily to one European leader: "You know, I mentioned the matter of our forthcoming American elections to Stalin, and he just couldn't comprehend what I was talking about. I guess he'll never become accustomed to understanding that there is a device known as free elections." [1] Stalin, for his purposes, did not have to understand the democracy of free elections. He was talking the democracy of the full stomach and of the end of social subjugation, and he was finding eager listeners.

In foreign or domestic affairs liberalism's philosophical difficulties, the troubles implicit in Reform Darwinism, continued to plague it. More than ever, the justifying of a means by an end, which Reform Darwinism so easily turned into, had been encouraging liberal acquiescence in means that changed the end. A deal with a Darlan or a Badoglio, which many liberals had

[9] Constantin Fotitch: *The War We Lost* (Viking, 1948), p. 291.
[1] Quoted in Stanislaw Mikolajczyk: *The Rape of Poland* (Whittlesey House, 1948), pp. 59–60.

ultimately glossed over, might well have helped to win World War II more quickly; the war that was won was also changed from a forthright struggle against fascism into a battle against certain kinds of fascists, when they did certain things. The alliances with reaction, including a loan to Franco Spain, which came under Truman and were brushed aside by thousands of the reform-minded, certainly bolstered the West against the East; simultaneously, they made the West not so much the representative of liberal democracy as of mere anti-Sovietism. On the home front a whole series of New Deal and Fair Deal amoralities that were defended by many liberals in the name of expediency certainly accomplished this or that immediate purpose. They also tended to transform the reform movement from one that sought to change American life into one that sought to change everything except the basis, its sense of what is right and wrong. Most obviously, the liberal casualness about political morality that increased so much in the Thirties helped create the situation in which the public, looking at the Fair Deal, saw an infuriating blur of idealistic talk and mink coats, of taxes to advance the public welfare and taxes that stuck to tax-collectors' hands.

All the while, Reform Darwinism's other great danger, extreme relativism, was working its debilitating effects. In 1949 Peter Viereck, an off-beat liberal who enjoys calling himself a conservative, essayed the history of modern reform relativism in three scorching "Chapters":

"*Chapter One*. Burning with innocent leftish enthusiasm, the liberal hacks away at what he calls aristocratic values. . . . Unfortunately, his weapon against the undemocratic values is not a moral democracy . . . but the two-edged sword of relativism: 'All standards, morals, and traditions are relative, merely reflecting self-interest and economics.' . . .

"*Chapter Two*. Next comes the liberal's son. What a clever fellow! Brought up in daddy's emancipated milieu, this Wise Guy knows all the answers; he denies not merely aristocratic values now but—values. Are they not 'all relative'? Have not psychology and semantics proved everything a sentimental, self-deceiving hoax . . .?

"*Chapter Three*. The grandson is the real Realist. No Sunday-school manners in politics for him. None of poor soft grandpa's liberal qualms; none of father's cleverness either ('where does it get you?'); now it's tooth and claw in the struggle of egomaniac self-interests. And what faith he has, is in the state, all other faiths having been discredited. With no tradition of moral restraints to guide him and with the capital exhausted at last, the grandson shouts for a Hitler or a Stalin. And so, in three irresponsible generations, three thousand years of civilization perish to the music of radio lies and clanking chains, chains more efficient and cruel than ever the old ones. . . ." [2]

Viereck's portrayal is obviously shot through with hyperbole. Almost certainly it ends, so far as America is concerned, on the wrong emphasis, because the available evidence indicates that the effect of extreme relativism in the United States has not been to turn young men and women toward totalitarianism but to cause them to flounder in faithlessness.[3] Yet whatever the exaggeration or inaccuracy of Viereck's remarks, unquestionably he was close to the essence of a situation that is hardly a happy one for liberals, whose continued success depends on a new generation which can believe and believe fervidly.

But, as always, the on-the-other-hands were very much present. No doubt Reform Darwinism easily led to troubles. On the other hand, what different ideology, likely to catch on within the American habits of thinking, was potent enough to keep dissolving away conservatism's steel chain of ideas?

No doubt depending on "the people" quickly turned into reliance on self-centered, self-aggrandizing groups. But if "the people" were not to be the basis of political thinking, what was left except some variety of an elite?

---

[2] Viereck: *Conservatism Revisited* (Scribner, 1949), pp. 130–1.
[3] For example, see the fairly typical analysis of the attitudes of American youth at the time made by Miss Sarah Blanding, president of Vassar, who stressed a general "disillusionment and pessimism." *New York Times*, November 9, 1949.

No doubt centralization easily led to infringements on civil liberties and inevitably it established powerful instrumentalities that conservatives, the antisocial, or the corruptionists could use for their own purposes. But how, except by continuing centralization, were the problems of an increasingly centralized economy to be met?

No doubt trust-busting, at least in its traditional forms, was archaic. And if the concentration of industrial power was not halted, how avoid complete corporate domination of American life?

No doubt going along with politically oriented peace aims and a veto-ridden international organization would hardly bring a liberal world. But how do you talk economic interpretation of war and diplomacy and avoid playing into the hands of isolationists? How do you include sweeping economic and social change in your war aims and not, in the middle of desperate situations, split opinion inside the United States and threaten to separate the country from its allies? And is it conceivable that any major power, including the United States, would enter a league that actually abolished the veto?

V

ELLIS ARNALL published *The Shore Dimly Seen* in 1946. In 1948 Seymour Harris brought out *Saving American Capitalism, a Liberal Economic Program.* Then, in rapid succession, came Arthur M. Schlesinger, Jr.'s *The Vital Center,* John Kenneth Galbraith's *American Capitalism, the Concept of Countervailing Power,* Reinhold Niebuhr's *The Irony of American History,* and Samuel Lubell's *The Future of American Politics.* The liberals were hard at it, discussing, debating, probing.

Much of the discussion took the form of facing problems that had been glossed over for decades. The frank reappraisals even carried some of the reform-minded into a consideration of minority chauvinisms, a territory long avoided because any movement toward it so easily produces in the liberal a feeling that he is guilty of illiberal intolerance. The social-minded journalist Roi Ottley produced studies of Negro life that were implied attacks on black racialism, Jewish and non-Jewish reformers joined in a halt-fire to Zionist extremities, and Paul Blanshard, a onetime La Guardia commissioner, published the first important liberal criticism of the way the Catholic hierarchy was functioning in the United States, his *American Freedom and Catholic Power*. But a good deal of the liberal probing went beyond fact-facing in particular fields to a search for sweeping new formulas. In discussions of this type, considerations of TVA's potential significance were easily the most important.

TVA was many things. In part, it was simply a triumph for generations of reformers who had been warring against high electric utility rates. In part, it was a bold conservation measure, pushed by both conservatives and liberals who were concerned over the depletion of American natural resources. In part, it was a victory for a growing school of regionalists, who sought to organize the national life along lines formed by nature and by cultural traditions.[4] Most of all, as it actually worked out, TVA was David Lilienthal, who was peculiarly free-wheeling in his thinking about American problems.

When he was seventeen, the husky Lilienthal had a try at professional boxing, under the tutelage of none other than the "Tacoma Tiger." "He damned near killed me in the process," Lilienthal remembers, "but he taught me something about coming up off the floor and taking more—which has come in handy." [5] That lesson, and a first-hand knowledge of the bottom of American society, was about all the equipment useful to a liberal which

---

[4] The growth of regional thinking in general, and especially among liberals, should be underlined. For example, the Midwestern liberal, Professor William B. Hesseltine, was arguing for recognition of "the basic regionalism of American life. . . . Despite the increasing tendencies to centralization, the problems of the various regions remain different. In truth, a large part of the nation's problems spring from the attempts of dominant groups in some regions to impose their particular programs upon the entire country." "Third Parties," *Progressive* (September 29, 1947), XI, 8.

[5] Quoted in *Current Biography, 1944* (H. W. Wilson), p. 413.

Lilienthal acquired in his youth. Growing up as part of a Czech immigrant family, living in an Illinois factory town, he was far removed both from the influence of the farm or village, which had inclined so many liberals toward the nostalgia of the New Freedom, and from the contacts with books and the world of affairs, which had made others disdainful of trust-busting.

Lilienthal's early manhood added few grooves to his thinking. The Tacoma Tiger's protégé worked his way through Harvard Law School, where he studied under professors deeply committed to the Wilson-Brandeis approach. His first position, serving as an assistant to Donald Richberg, brought him into intimate contact with the man who was trying hard to stop La Follette from campaigning on a Wilson-Brandeis program in the election of 1924. The field to which Lilienthal gravitated, legal and advisory work concerning public utilities, was one in which breaking up monopolies was often transparently unwise, and yet the dangers of monopoly were always plain. Lilienthal went to Tennessee to run the TVA a liberal in-betweener, grinning wide and shrewd, reading with equal pleasure New Freedom and New Nationalist arguments, bundling his family off to a movie whenever his more dogmatic reform associates gave him a trying day.

On the tenth anniversary of TVA, in 1943, Lilienthal started writing *TVA, Democracy on the March*. To some degree, the book was a birthday statement of a father's pride in his child, the thrilling story of excavating holes big enough to bury twenty Empire State Buildings and raising concrete masses more than twelve times the bulk of all the seven great pyramids put together, of gutted hillsides changing into fertile green, of trim prefabricated houses replacing shacks, of the whir of electrical machinery giving tens of thousands the first regular leisure they had ever known. But Lilienthal's book was a good deal more than a summation of specific achievements; it was also the statement of a general program for the future.

"This is a book about tomorrow," he began. ". . . My purpose is to show, by authentic experience in one American region, that . . . our choice need not be between extremes of 'right' and

455

'left,' between overcentralized Big-government and a do-nothing policy, between 'private enterprise' and 'socialism,' between an arrogant red-tape-ridden bureaucracy and domination by a few private monopolies. I have tried in these pages to express my confidence that in tested principles of democracy we have ready at hand a philosophy and a set of working tools that, adapted to this machine age, can guide and sustain us in increasing opportunity for individual freedom and well-being." [6]

Lilienthal's basic approach to economic problems was implicit in TVA itself. The project was government-owned; in that sense it marked a complete break with liberalism of either a New Freedom or a New Nationalist variety and was socialism. Yet Lilienthal had no desire to make TVA an entering wedge for a general system of socialism. It was to serve as a "yardstick," forcing private utility companies to lower prices and improve service by its competition and providing an experimental station that would affect policy in the whole industry (for example, TVA's demonstration that lowered prices could actually raise total profits by increasing enormously the use of electricity). TVA, in short, brushed aside both trust-busting and the New Nationalism for a new way of controlling, or rather nudging, large-scale enterprises toward the public interest.

In discussing the relationship of TVA to the federal government, Lilienthal suggested that the old formulas concerning centralization should be dropped. He vigorously argued the perils of too much centralization and just as vigorously emphasized the need for powerful government in a highly integrated society. The TVA formula, he maintained, went in between, deriving the benefits of big government while avoiding its most serious dangers. It was "decentralized administration of centralized authority." The federal government laid down a general set of objectives to be achieved, and the TVA set out to achieve them, with people working on the spot and with a constant adaptation of the larger objectives to specific local needs or exigencies of the moment. TVA repeated the pattern on the

[6] Lilienthal: *TVA, Democracy on the March* (Harper, 1944), p. xi.

secondary level. It made over-all plans. Then, within the framework of these plans, it rented or sold facilities to towns, farm co-operatives, or other local units and they administered the plans, close, as Lilienthal liked to say, to the "grass roots." [7]

In arguing for the TVA approach, Lilienthal was constantly mindful that it could succeed only if at least some characteristics of the liberal's "people" were brought to the community, only if a clear comprehension of means and ends was maintained, and only if men and women felt a sense of worth-whileness about their efforts. A TVA project, he believed, in and of itself was a gigantic reassertion of keeping the end primary; all the wonders of technology were being directly harnessed to man's well-being. It pulled people together in local planning, and in a kind of planning that constantly cut across group interests. Laborers, Lilienthal reported, frequently came in to complain not about hours and wages but about some situation interfering with "our" dam. Farmers' co-operatives regularly worked with unions in promoting joint projects connected with TVA. Farmers, workers, and businessmen joined to advance some community interest. Only cynics, Lilienthal added, would find these developments surprising. "To those with faith in humankind it is natural enough that when men adopt a common purpose so deep and broad as that of working with nature to build a region's resources there ensue inevitable consequences to the spirit of men." And not the least of these consequences, he concluded, was a sense of the possibilities of the future that ended moral or intellectual defeatism. Proudly Lilienthal quoted the Decatur (Alabama) *Daily*, which said of its region: "We can write of great dams . . . of the building of home-grown industry and of electricity at last coming to the farms of thousands of farm people in the Valley. *Yet the significant advance has been made in the thinking of a people. . . . They have caught the vision of their own powers.*" [8]

If some of Lilienthal's claims for TVA had to be discounted

---

[7] Ibid., pp. 143, 149. Italics have been removed from the phrase "decentralized . . . authority."

[8] Ibid., pp. 36, 87. The italics are Lilienthal's.

as a natural product of overenthusiasm, liberals were increasingly turning to the TVA idea as an exciting general formula for the future.[9] Certainly the concept, even if it did not completely solve liberalism's problems, contributed significantly toward the solutions. What's more, the TVA idea, because of its connection with conservation, was almost certain to prove increasingly attractive to the general public at a time when responsible leaders of opinion were warning that about one quarter of the arable land in the United States was already ruined or severely impoverished and soil losses by erosion alone totaled more than five billion tons annually.

Lilienthal included a chapter on the TVA idea in its international applications, and this type of thinking was also being pushed in liberal circles. Some went so far as to envisage the working out of the Point Four program primarily in terms of a series of TVA projects in the backward parts of the world. Whether liberals went that far or not, most of them were making the carrying out and enlargement of the Point Four concept a cardinal part of their foreign policy, and the more they thought along these lines, the more they were helping themselves get rid of a foreign affairs difficulty that had harassed the movement since 1914.

The natural liberal way of thinking and the one that made them the greatest influence for a liberal peace—a continuing economic interpretation of all proposed American roles in world affairs—had inclined them toward isolationism because the active role was likely to mean, at least in part, protection for private investments and aid to the private pursuit of markets and of raw materials. But with the rise of the Point Four and world TVA

---

[9] The cross-section of liberal opinion showed greater interest in the TVA concept than in any other single new idea. John Fischer has added the suggestion that "because of the liberals' new interest in decentralization, they probably will insist on a large degree of local control for future river valley authorities, rather than sole management by a Washington-appointed directorate of the TVA type ("The Lost Liberals," *Harper's* [May 1947], CXCIV, 391). One of the drafts of a Missouri Valley Authority bill being discussed gives to a local advisory council considerable policy responsibility.

ideas, American activity abroad, no matter how continuous, would not necessarily take the form of imperialism. Much of the money would have to be that of the United States Government and of the United Nations, and the whole program inevitably would take on more of a social and less of a profit orientation. Under these circumstances, the liberal could go on with economic interpretation of foreign policy with no undertow toward isolationism.[1]

While the liberals were helping themselves with this kind of thinking, Joseph Stalin was coming to their aid in other foreign-affairs difficulties. By the fall of 1950, American exasperation over the Korean situation had created a public opinion that made it possible for Secretary of State Dean Acheson to go before the United Nations with some of the boldest proposals ever uttered by a responsible American official. The United States, Acheson declared, recommended that if a veto prevented the Security Council from taking action against an aggressor, the General Assembly, operating free of the veto, should recommend any move it saw fit, including a call to the member nations to use economic sanctions or arms. He urged, further, that as soon as the fighting stopped, Korea should be made the first example of a world-wide economic and social rehabilitation to be undertaken under U.N. auspices, and he pledged that the United States would not remove many of the engineers, doctors, and technicians or much of the material which it had originally sent to Korea for war purposes. "We speak here as the representatives of governments," Acheson concluded, his highly cultivated voice taut with emotion, "but we must also speak the hearts of our countrymen. We speak for people whose deep concern is whether the children are well or sick, whether there is enough food, whether

[1] Throughout the Korean crisis the cross-section of liberal opinion reveals some tendency to go back to moral and political abstractions, but a continued general economic emphasis—a remarkable change from what happened in 1917 and in 1941. Typically, the ADA emphasized again and again that "we must purposefully *use* our strength and prosperity to restore social and economic health to a broken world" (italics in original). Americans for Democratic Action: *Toward Total Peace* (ADA, Washington, n. d.), p. 11.

459

the roof leaks, whether there is peace. . . . This is the task before us." [2]

"Masterful," liberal journalists exclaimed.[3] Then they added quickly: if any serious effort was made to carry out these proposals, would American opinion really stand for a move that edged so close to the surrender of sovereignty? Could so economic-minded a peace actually be carried through without dangerously dividing American opinion in a time of continuing crisis? Yet there they were, proposals that would get liberals out of a cul-de-sac in which they had been struggling through two world peace settlements, duly made by the Secretary of State and not being overwhelmingly repudiated by the opposition.

VI

"THERE IS a mysterious cycle in human affairs," Franklin Roosevelt had told the nation in 1936. "To some generations much is given. Of other generations much is expected. This generation of Americans has a rendezvous with destiny." [4] As the Truman years came to an end amid unprecedented restiveness and dangers around the globe, liberals knew full well that the rendezvous was at hand.

Theirs was an awesome responsibility. Every long-running trend indicated that the broad liberal path was the one in which most of the United States was finding its footing. The country in which liberalism had become so important was, more than any other one power, determining the fate of the world. The world was at a climacteric.

Each era, with the egotism of the present, has seen its age as a turning-point, and often history, with a mocking toss of her head, has decided not to turn. Yet the Fifties know, with unchallengeable certitude, that mankind is hurtling through a

---

2 *New York Herald Tribune*, September 12, 1950.
3 The phrase is Seymour Freidin's, in *New York Post*, September 24, 1950.
4 Rosenman, V, 235.

process that recurs not in centuries but in millenniums. Our civilization began some five thousand years ago in the river valleys of the East. The West, between the fifth and eighteenth centuries, seized dominance. Now the East is reasserting itself. It will reassert itself in co-operation with the West and in aspirations toward the humane democracy that much of the West has achieved, or in a hail of atomic weapons and a snarl of frenzied nationalism and of classphobic change. American liberals of the Fifties have more to achieve and more to let go to disaster than all their predecessors.

How well can modern American liberalism handle its responsibilities? The liberal wonders, his enemies wonder too, and somewhere in that misty realm between hope and fear, where the mistakes of the past deride plans for the future and every day seems a brilliant dawn and an onrushing dusk, the liberal can take strength from one tremendous fact. His is a momentous tradition, all the way from the pre-Civil War Jeffersonian aspirations to which he attached himself, down through the Prince Albert reform of Samuel Tilden, and on to the sidewalk heresies of Harry Truman. For almost a century the modern American reformer has been the gadfly and the conscience, to a large extent the heart and the mind, of the only nation in man's history which has dared to live by the credo that any individual's rendezvous with his destiny is a rendezvous with a better tomorrow.

BIBLIOGRAPHICAL NOTES

THIS BOOK rests in part on manuscript sources and on facts gathered through interviews or correspondence. But primarily it is an attempt at synthesizing and interpreting the vast body of printed materials, the books and the periodical articles, scholarly and popular, the pamphlets and the newspaper pieces, which concern modern American reform.

In most instances, footnotes were used only to identify direct quotations, and these bibliographical notes consequently carry the major burden of supporting my statements. In order to keep the notes within reasonable compass, I have had to be ruthlessly selective. The choices were made with a dual objective—to include the works that most directly buttress this book while simultaneously pointing to the writings most useful for others who may want to read further or do their own writing about the subject under discussion.

The reader has undoubtedly noted that I frequently generalize about the attitudes of reform groups. Naturally, these statements are basically derived from whatever knowledge about the groups I have been able to acquire, but the generalizations also have a more specific rooting which I occasionally refer to in the footnotes as "the cross-section" of reform opinion or "the sampling technique." For each of the major periods of modern American reform, I systematically covered certain sources, carefully chosen for their representativeness and their influence, to check my conception of the attitudes of particular segments of reformers. Varying groups of sources, of course, were used for different periods, and the group for any one period ranged in number from six to fourteen.

In the field of foreign affairs, an additional specific check was undertaken. During the period covered by this book, Congress voted on three especially critical foreign-affairs issues, or groups of issues: American entrance into World War I in 1917, the Lend-Lease legislation of 1941, and the cluster of proposals made after 1945 which represented the developing Truman foreign policy. For each of these three, a chart was prepared which correlated votes on domestic and foreign affairs. (The ballot chosen was not always the final Congressional action; sometimes the vote on an amendment was the critical test or the only significant vote that was on the record.)

Chart I concerns the 6 Senators and 50 members of the House who voted against American entrance into World War I. The degree of progressivism of these men was assessed by their votes on six key domestic measures brought up in Congress between Wilson's Inauguration and the introduction of the war resolution. Chart II concerns the 31 Senators and 165 members of the House who voted against Lend-Lease. Their degree of liberalism in domestic affairs was estimated by their votes on especially meaningful domestic bills (twenty in the case of the Senate, eighteen in the case of the House), which were brought up in Congress from F. D. R.'s Inauguration to March

11, 1941, the day Lend-Lease became law. Chart III was limited to the Senate because the House took too few clear-cut votes on foreign affairs; but, in contrast to the previous charts, the entire membership of the Senate was included. Eleven significant domestic measures were used to gauge each Senator's degree of liberalism in domestic affairs; six critical foreign-affairs votes, to assess his degree of support for the Truman foreign policy. These three charts will be published in their entirety in a scholarly journal.

For interviews and/or correspondence that provided me with helpful, and in some cases with fundamentally important, materials, I am indebted to Ray Stannard Baker, Charles A. Beard, Edward L. Bernays, Edwin M. Borchard, Emerson Brown, Marquis Childs, Mrs. Myron W. Cowen, Elmer Davis, W. E. B. Du Bois, Stephen T. Early, Mrs. James Falconer, Philip S. Foner, Guy Stanton Ford, Felix Frankfurter, Learned Hand, B. H. Hartogensis, Jacob H. Hollander, Herbert Hoover, Austin E. Hutcheson, Harold L. Ickes, Edward L. Israel, Alvin S. Johnson, Hugh S. Johnson, Walter Johnson, Horace M. Kallen, Harry M. Kenin, Alfred A. Knopf, Paul O. Kristeller, Fiorello La Guardia, Sinclair Lewis, Walter Lippmann, Philip Littell, Robert Morss Lovett, Charles McKinley, Edward McMahon, George W. Norris, Mrs. Vernon L. Parrington, Miss Frances Perkins, Ernest Poole, Giuseppe Prezzolini, Richard J. Purcell, Edward A. Ross, William Savery, Mrs. Mary Simkhovitch, Algie M. Simons, George H. Soule, William Allen White, Stephen Wise, and Benjamin F. Wright. For the loan of manuscripts, I am indebted to many of the above men and women and to Jack Abramowitz, Donald R. Come, Kenneth W. Condit, Charles T. Davis, Robert Durden, John W. Gillette, John J. Harmon, John W. Higham, Richard M. Huber, Gordon M. Jensen, Carl Krummel, William J. Newman, Stephen B. Palmer, Thomas Pressly, William S. Rollins, Seymour Shapiro, and Samuel R. Spencer, Jr.

With one exception, the following bibliographical notes use only abbreviations that are self-evident in meaning. The exception is *M. V. H. R.*, standing for the *Mississippi Valley Historical Review*.

Chapter 1

THE RESERVOIR of optimism which Americans brought to the post-Civil War period is discerningly discussed in Louis B. Wright: "Historical Implications of Optimism in Expanding America," *Proc. Amer. Phil. Soc.* (1950), XCIV, and in Arthur A. Ekirch, Jr.: *The Idea of Progress in America, 1815–60* (Columbia U. Press, 1941). Used with recognition of its strong bias against social reform, Ellis P. Oberholtzer: *History of the United States since the Civil War* (5 vols., Macmillan, 1917–37), is a gold mine of materials for what Americans were doing and thinking in the postwar years. Allan Nevins's social history: *The Emergence of Modern America, 1865–1878* (Macmillan, 1927), is less detailed but better organized and fairer. Vernon L. Parrington's classic *Main Currents in American Thought* (3 vols., Harcourt, Brace, 1930) includes a savage portrait of the barbecue atmosphere that was developing, and Thomas C. Cochran and William Miller: *The Age of Enterprise* (Macmillan, 1943), describes it with more balance.

Francis A. Walker: "Some Results of the Census," *Jl. Soc. Sci.* (1873), V, points up the most significant revelations of the census of 1870. The occupational shift is placed within the long-time trend in P. K. Whelpton: "Occupational Groups in the United States, 1820–1920," *Jl. Amer. Stat. Assoc.* (September 1926), XXI. The famous "Second American Revolution" chapter in Charles A. and Mary R. Beard: *The Rise of American Civilization* (2 vols., Macmillan, 1927), powerfully presents the Civil War as a breakthrough for ambitious industrialism, and Henry N. Smith: *Virgin Land: The American West as Symbol and Myth* (Harvard U. Press, 1950), recreates the West as the golden West of dreams. George Creel: *Rebel at Large* (Putnam, 1947), is one of the many autobiographies which emphasize the relative lack of distinctions in the small town. Chris A. De Young: *Introduction to American Public Education* (McGraw-Hill, 1951), and Earle D. Ross: *Democracy's College, The Land-Grant Movement in the Formative Stage* (Iowa State College Press, 1942), treat in detail the key educational developments.

Chapter II

THE STATE of public morality is scourgingly described in Matthew Josephson: *The Politicos, 1865–1896* (Harcourt, Brace, 1938) and *The Robber Barons* (Harcourt, Brace, 1934). The politics of business and of favoritism is solidly worked out in four standard biographies—William D. Foulke: *Life of Oliver P. Morton* (2 vols., Bowen-Merrill, Indianapolis, 1899); W. C. Harris: *Public Life of Zachariah Chandler, 1851–1875* (Michigan Historical Commission, Lansing, 1917); William B. Hesseltine, *Ulysses S. Grant* (Dodd, Mead, 1935); and Henrietta Larson: *Jay Cooke* (Harvard U. Press, 1936). The Tweed episode is told with outrage in Gustavus Myers: *The History of Tammany Hall* (Boni & Liveright, 1917), and with greater calm and scholarship in Alexander C. Flick: *Samuel Jones Tilden* (Dodd, Mead, 1939). William L. Riordan: *Plunkitt of Tammany Hall* (Knopf, 1948), a first-hand document of a Tammany leader who was swiftly rising in 1870, is a fascinating portrayal of the thinking of the post-Civil War politician. Lewis Mumford: *The Brown Decades* (Harcourt, Brace, 1931), sensitively portrays the cultural blight that came with the grabbing.

The liberal movement of 1872 still awaits its historian. The standard account, Earle D. Ross: *The Liberal Republican Movement* (Holt, 1919), is skimpy and unimaginative. The treatment in Josephson: *The Politicos*, is provocative but totally unsympathetic. *The Proceedings of the Liberal Republican Convention in Cincinnati* . . . (Baker & Godwin, New York, 1872) are not particularly informative, and little is added by a contemporary propaganda account, F. G. Welch: *That Convention; or, Five Days a Politician* (F. G. Welch Co., New York, 1872). Thomas S. Barclay: *The Liberal Republican Movement in Missouri, 1865–71* (State Historical Society of Missouri, Columbia, 1926), Carl R. Fish: *The Civil Service and the Patronage* (Harvard U. Press, 1904), Clifford W. Patton: *The Battle for Municipal Reform* (American Council on Public Affairs, Washington, 1940), and Frank M. Stewart: *The National Civil Service Reform League* (U. of Texas Press, 1929), are adequate for their limited subjects.

Especially needed is further analysis of the phenomenon of patrician reform. The subject is approached in two major intellectual histories, Merle Curti: *The Growth of American Thought* (Harper, 1951), and Ralph Gabriel: *The Course of American Democratic Thought* (Ronald, 1940); in Richard Hofstadter's acute volume, *The American Political Tradition* (Knopf, 1948); and in Gabriel A. Almond: "The Political Attitudes of Wealth," *Jl. of Pol.* (August 1945), VII, and Eric F. Goldman: *Charles J. Bonaparte* (Johns Hopkins U. Press, 1943) and "The Presidency as Moral Leadership," *Ann. Amer. Acad. Pol. and Soc. Sci.* (March 1952), CCLXXX.

All liberalism of the 1872 variety is best gone at through biographical and autobiographical volumes, of which the following are especially important for the purpose: Charles F. Adams: *Autobiography* (Houghton Mifflin, 1916); Henry Adams: *Education of Henry Adams* (Houghton Mifflin, 1918); Frederic Bancroft, ed.: *Speeches, Correspondence, and Political Papers of Carl Schurz* (6 vols., Putnam, 1913); Claude M. Fuess: *Carl Schurz* (Dodd, Mead, 1932); George S. Merriam: *Life and Times of Samuel Bowles* (Century, 1885); Stewart Mitchell: *Horatio Seymour of New York* (Harvard U. Press, 1938); Allan Nevins: *Abram S. Hewitt* (Harper, 1935); Rollo Ogden, ed.: *Life and Letters of Edwin Lawrence Godkin* (2 vols., Macmillan, 1907); Henry Watterson: *"Marse Henry"; An Autobiography* (2 vols., Doran, 1919); and Horace White: *Life of Lyman Trumbull* (Houghton Mifflin, 1913).

Tilden's executors combed his papers four times to destroy derogatory materials. The Flick biography is as thorough as it can be under the circumstances. One of Tilden's executors, John Bigelow, edited *The Letters and Literary Memorials of Samuel J. Tilden* (2 vols., Harper, 1908) and *The Writings and Speeches of Tilden* (2 vols., Harper, 1885). The most recent estimate, an unflattering one, is Mark D. Hirsch: "Samuel J. Tilden: The Story of a Lost Opportunity," *Amer. Hist. Rev.* (July 1951), LVI.

Chapter III

THE SHOCK of the depression of 1873 is portrayed in detail in Allan Nevins: *The Emergence of Modern America, 1865–1878* (Macmillan, 1927); Ellis P. Oberholtzer: *Jay Cooke* (2 vols., Jacobs, Philadelphia, 1907) and *History of the United States* (5 vols., Macmillan, 1917–37); and the account written by a contemporary, James F. Rhodes, in *History of the United States* (9 vols., Macmillan, 1928). The standard works on George are Henry George, Jr.: *Life of Henry George* (2 vols., Doubleday, Page, 1911), and George H. Geiger: *The Philosophy of Henry George* (Macmillan, 1933). They have been supplemented by a chatty, though not insignificant, volume by George's younger daughter, Anna De Mille, *Henry George* (U. of North Carolina Press, 1950).

The discontent in the 1880's and 90's is one of the most thoroughly studied phenomena of American history. Exceedingly useful as a general guide is Arthur M. Schlesinger: *The Rise of the City, 1878–1898* (Macmillan, 1933). William D. P. Bliss, ed.: *Encyclopedia of Social Reform* (Funk & Wagnalls, 1897), is chock-full of information on all phases of the dissidence, and Lisle A. Rose is thorough in her "Bibliographical Survey of Economic and Political Writings," *Amer. Lit.* (January 1944), XV.

For the more specifically urban discontent, the starting place is the first-hand, detailed information provided by U.S. Senate Committee on Education and Labor, 48th Cong., 2nd Sess.: *Report . . . upon the Relations be-*

tween Labor and Capital (5 vols., 1885). Also of great value are the contemporary history by Terence Powderly: *Thirty Years of Labor 1859–1889* (Excelsior Publishing House, Columbus, 1890); the warhorse of scholarly labor history, John R. Commons *et al.*: *History of Labour in the United States* (4 vols., Macmillan, 1918–35); the more compressed and analytical study, Norman J. Ware: *The Labor Movement in the United States, 1860–1895* (Appleton, 1929); and the autobiographies of the two major labor figures of the period, Harry J. Carman *et al.*, eds.: *The Path I Trod; The Autobiography of Terence Powderly* (Columbia U. Press, 1940) and Samuel Gompers: *Seventy Years of Life and Labor* (2 vols., Dutton, 1925). Important for specific phases are the deeply informed study of immigrant frustration, Oscar Handlin: *The Uprooted* (Little, Brown, 1951); John W. Higham: "The American Party, 1886–1891," *Pac. Hist. Rev.* (February 1950), XIX, and "European Immigration in American Patriotic Thought, 1885–1925," MS., U. of Wisconsin Library; Donald L. Kemmerer and Edward D. Wickersham: "Reasons for the Growth of the Knights of Labor in 1885–1886," *Indus. and Labor Rel. Rev.* (January 1950), III; a revealing contemporary article, Alice H. Rhine: "Race Prejudice at Summer Resorts," *Forum* (July 1887), III; and Alvin P. Stauffer, Jr.: "Anti-Catholicism in American Politics, 1865–1900," MS., Harvard U. Library.

The standard work on the spread of single-taxism is Arthur N. Young: *The Single Tax Movement in the United States* (Princeton U. Press, 1916). Arthur E. Morgan: *Edward Bellamy* (Columbia U. Press, 1944), does a thorough, if disorganized, job on the rise of Bellamyite Nationalism. Donald D. Egbert and Stow Persons, eds.: *Socialism and American Life* (2 vols., Princeton U. Press, 1952), offers a series of first-rate essays that come close to being the long-awaited fresh history of American socialism, and the second volume is a massive bibliography that ranges far beyond socialism. Morris Hillquit: *History of Socialism in the United States* (Funk & Wagnalls, 1906), though old and thin, should not be overlooked because of the author's intimacy with the party. A close-at-hand feel of these movements at work may be derived from William F. Zornow: "Bellamy Nationalism in Ohio 1891 to 1896," *Ohio State Arch. and Hist. Quar.* (April 1949), LVIII.

Almost all writings on the more specifically rural discontent are closely tied in with the rise of the Populist Party. The standard work, John D. Hicks: *The Populist Revolt* (U. of Minnesota Press, 1931), treats Populism largely as an agrarian movement and has been supplemented by Chester M. Destler: *American Radicalism, 1865–1901* (Collegiate Press, Menasha, Wis., 1946), which emphasizes the interaction of rural and urban discontent. Used together, Arthur M. Schlesinger, Jr.: *The Age of Jackson* (Little, Brown, 1945), and Destler, Chap. i, show the continuity of the "producer class" philosophy from pre-Civil War dissidence into Populism. Vernon L. Parrington's account of his Kansas boyhood in his "Autobiography" (MS., in the possession of Mrs. Parrington) is a vivid portrayal of many facets of the agrarian distress. The Southern phases are admirably treated in two scholarly works of C. Vann Woodward: *Origins of the New South, 1877–1913* (Louisiana State U. Press, 1951) and *Tom Watson* (Macmillan, 1938). Virginius Dabney, *Liberalism in the South* (U. of North Carolina Press, 1932), is rewarding reading for almost any part of the subject of the South's reaction to industrialism.

The more exclusively economic problems of the farmer are studied fruitfully in Lewanda F. Cox: "Tenancy in the United States," *Agr. Hist.* (July

1944), XVIII; Hallie Farmer: "The Economic Backgrounds of Frontier Populism," *M. V. H. R.* (March 1924), X; Paul W. Gates: "The Homestead Law in an Incongruous Land System," *Amer. Hist. Rev.* (July 1936), XLI; and Fred A. Shannon: *The Farmer's Last Frontier* (Farrar & Rinehart, 1945). The non-economic phases are revealed in several contemporary writings, Annie L. Diggs: "The Women in the Alliance Movement," *Arena* (July 1892), VI, Henry J. Fletcher: "The Drift of Population to Cities," *Forum* (March 1895), XIX, Hamlin Garland: *Main Travelled Roads* (Arena Publishing Co., Boston, 1891), and E. V. Smalley: "The Isolation of Life on Prairie Farms," *Atl. Mo.* (September 1893), LXXII; and in the scholarly works, Theodore C. Blegen: *Grass Roots History* (U. of Minnesota Press, 1947), Everett Dick: *The Sodhouse Frontier: 1854–1890* (Appleton-Century, 1939), James S. Ferguson: "The Grange and Farmer Education in Mississippi," *Jl. South. Hist.* (November 1942), VIII, and Walter P. Webb: *The Great Plains* (Ginn, 1931). Lee Benson has written thoughtfully of the panic impact of the "end of the frontier" in "The Historical Background of Turner's Frontier Essay," *Agr. Hist.* (April 1951), XXV.

The agrarian distress has been specifically studied for almost every state. Of these many writings, the following contribute most to the national picture: Alex M. Arnett: "The Populist Movement in Georgia," *Col. U. Stud. in Hist., Econ. and Pub. Law* (1922), CIV; Lucia E. Daniel: "The Louisiana People's Party," *La. Hist. Quar.* (1943), XXVI; R. C. Miller: "The Background of Populism in Kansas," *M. V. H. R.* (March 1925), XI; Gordon B. Ridgeway: "Populism in Washington," *Pac. Northwest Quar.* (October 1948), XXXIX; Daniel H. Robison: "Tennessee Politics and the Agrarian Revolt, 1886–1896," *M. V. H. R.* (December 1933), XX; and William D. Sheldon: *Populism in the Old Dominion* (Princeton U. Press, 1935).

For the Negro's role in Populism, the writings of Woodward can be supplemented by the more detailed studies, Jack Abramowitz: "The Negro in the Agrarian and Populist Movements," MS., in the possession of Mr. Abramowitz; Helen G. Edmonds: *The Negro and Fusion Politics in North Carolina, 1894–1901* (U. of North Carolina Press, 1951); William A. Mabry: "The Disenfranchisement of the Negro in the South," MS., Duke U. Library; Richard L. Morton: *The Negro in Virginia Politics, 1865–1902* (U. of Virginia Press, 1919); and Ralph W. Wardlaw: "Negro Suffrage in Georgia, 1867–1930," *U. of Ga. Bull.* (1932), XXXIII.

The two most important urban figures connected with the Populist upsurge are given biographical treatment in the rambling work, Caro Lloyd: *Henry Demarest Lloyd, 1847–1903* (2 vols., Putnam, 1912), and in the better constructed volume, Harry Barnard: *"Eagle Forgotten," The Life of John Peter Altgeld* (Bobbs-Merrill, 1938). Highly useful for the activities of these men are Destler: *American Radicalism*, and Harvey Wish: "Altgeld and the Progressive Tradition," *Amer. Hist. Rev.* (July 1941), XLVI, and "John Peter Altgeld and the Background of the Campaign of 1896," *M. V. H. R.* (March 1938), XXIV.

The story of the political rise of the farmer-labor parties is told in Nathan Fine: *Labor and Farmer Parties in the United States, 1828–1928* (Rand School of Social Science, New York, 1928), and, more statistically, in Murray S. and Susan W. Stedman, Jr.: *Discontent at the Polls* (Columbia U. Press, 1950). For the Omaha convention, valuable first-hand accounts are the unsympathetic article, Frank B. Tracy: "Menacing Socialism in the Western States," *Forum* (May 1893), XV, and the sympathetic, "official" proceedings included in E. A. Allen: *The Life and Public Services of James Baird Weaver* . . . (People's Party Publishing Company, no p. of p., 1892). Significant details are added to the Omaha story by Mason A. Green: "Edward Bellamy—A Biography of the Author of *Looking Backward*," MS., Harvard U. Library, and John D. Hicks expertly treats a central figure of the convention in "The Political Career of Ignatius Donnelly," *M. V. H. R.* (June–September 1921), VIII.

Key events of the mounting violence of the period are covered in the thorough studies, Henry David: *History of the Haymarket Affair* (Farrar & Rinehart, 1936), Almont Lindsey: *The Pullman Strike* (U. of Chicago Press, 1942), and Donald L. McMurry: *Coxey's Army* (Little, Brown, 1929); and in a superior biography, Ray Ginger: *The Bending Cross, A Biography of Eugene Victor Debs* (Rutgers U. Press, 1949). The relationship of the new violence and discontent to liberalism of the 1872 variety is best approached through the writings of Godkin in the *Nation* and his "Social Classes in the Republic," *Atl. Mo.* (December 1896), LXXVIII, and through Frederic Bancroft, ed.: *Speeches, Correspondence, and Political Papers of Schurz* (6 vols., Putnam, 1913); Alexander C. Flick: *Samuel Jones Tilden* (Dodd, Mead, 1939); Allan Nevins: *Grover Cleveland* (Dodd, Mead, 1932); and Elting E. Morison, ed.: *Letters of Theodore Roosevelt* (4 vols., Harvard U. Press, 1951).

Chapter IV

MOST of the writings discussed on pp. 466–8 contain valuable materials on the difficulties within the attempted labor-farmer coalition. For the Southern Negro-white difficulty, one should add the penetrating observations in V. O. Key, Jr.: *Southern Politics in State and Nation* (Knopf, 1949); Paul Lewinson: *Race, Class, and Party* (Oxford, 1932); and Gunnar Myrdal: *An American Dilemma* (Harper, 1946). The Tillman-Vardaman demagoguery is spelled out in Heber Ladner: "James Kimble Vardaman, Governor of Mississippi, 1904–1908," *Jl. Miss. Hist.* (October 1940), II, and Francis B. Simkins: "Ben Tillman's View of the Negroes," *Jl. South. Hist.* (May 1937), III.

On the agrarian splits within Populism, a useful additional analysis may be found in H. C. Nixon: "The Cleavage within the Farmers' Alliance Movement," *M. V. H. R.* (June 1928), XV. The story of the labor divergence is given greater substance by Gompers's own article: "Organized Labor in the Campaign," *N. Amer. Rev.* (July 1892), CLV; Irving Bernstein, ed.: "Samuel Gompers and Free Silver, 1896," *M. V. H. R.* (December 1942), XXIX; and Louis S. Reed: *The Labor Philosophy of Samuel Gompers* (Columbia U. Press, 1930). The single tax and socialist divergence can be further studied in a contemporary document, Willis J. Abbot: "The Chicago Populist Campaign," *Arena* (February 1895), XI; John J. Harmon: "Algie Martin Simons," MS., Princeton U. Library; J. Martin Klotsche: "The 'United Front' Populists," *Wis. Mag. Hist.* (June 1937), XX; and George H. Knoles: "Populism and Socialism, with Special Reference to the Election of 1892," *Pac. Hist. Rev.* (September 1943), XII. The Populist aversion to the Jew is emphasized in Oscar Handlin: "American Views of the Jew at the Opening of the Twentieth Century," *Publ. Amer. Jew. Hist. Soc.* (June 1951), XL.

Arthur N. Holcombe attempted, with considerable success, the tortuous theme of *The Middle Classes in American Politics* (Harvard U. Press, 1940). Probably the most typical middle-class thinker of the day, William Allen White, has left an informative *Autobiography* (Macmillan, 1946), and he is further revealed in Walter Johnson's skillful volumes: *William Allen White's America* (Holt, 1947) and *Selected Letters of William Allen White, 1899–1943* (Holt, 1947). Mark Sullivan's *Our Times* (7 vols., Scribner, 1926–35) bulges with details of middle-class thinking of the day. Additional suggestive materials can be found in *The Life Stories of Undistinguished Americans as Told by Themselves* (James Pott Co., New York, 1906) and in two delightful books of reminiscence, Henry S. Canby: *The Age of Confidence* (Farrar & Rinehart, 1934), and Clyde B. Davis: *The Age of Indiscretion* (Lippincott, 1950). Edward C. Cassady: "The Business Man in the American Novel," MS., U. of California Library, is pointed in a way useful for understanding the businessman's place in the middle-class credo.

A worthy biography of Bryan is conspicuously lacking. The best available, Paxton Hibben: *The Peerless Leader* (Farrar & Rinehart, 1929), is marred by a leftish condescension. Much of the tone of the 1896 campaign is preserved in William Jennings Bryan: *The First Battle* (W. B. Conkey, Chicago, 1896), and in Bryan and Mary B. Bryan: *The Memoirs of William Jennings Bryan* (Winston, 1925). James A. Barnes: "Myths of the Bryan Campaign," *M. V. H. R.* (December 1947), XXXIV, provides a hardheaded commentary on some crucial phases of the campaign. The most thorough analysis of the results is William Diamond: "Urban and Rural Voting in 1896," *Amer. Hist. Rev.* (January 1941), XLVI.

A good general guide to the hopes and worries of the post-1896 period is Harold U. Faulkner: *The Quest for Social Justice, 1898–1914* (Macmillan, 1930). The role of the Spanish-American War in quieting regional tensions is definitively treated in Paul H. Buck: *The Road to Reunion* (Little, Brown, 1937). Paul H. Douglas: *Real Wages in the United States, 1890–1926* (Houghton Mifflin, 1930), and Willford I. King: *The Wealth and Income of the People of the United States* (Macmillan, 1915), are standard for their subjects. The background of the business leaders of the period is intensively studied in William Miller: "American Historians and the Business Elite," *Jl. Econ. Hist.* (November 1949), IX, "American Lawyers in Business and in Politics," *Yale Law Jl.* (January 1951), LX, and "The Recruitment of the American Business Elite," *Quar. Jl. Econ.* (May 1950), LXIV. The more conciliatory business ideas are included in the biographies of two leaders in the business community, Herbert Croly's deeply researched *Marcus Alonzo Hanna* (Macmillan, 1912), and Richard R. Decker's sketchy "Life of George Walbridge Perkins," MS., Princeton U. Library. Gordon M. Jensen: "The Growth of a Sense of Social Awareness upon the Part of Capital in America," MS., in Mr. Jensen's possession, is the beginning of a thorough study of the new business thinking which Mr. Jensen plans.

The changing position of the farmer is most directly treated in James M. Williams: *The Expansion of Rural Life* (Crofts, 1926). Also useful for the subject are Theodore Saloutos and John D. Hicks: *Agricultural Discontent in the Middle West, 1900–1939* (U. of Wisconsin Press, 1951), and Fred A. Shannon: "The Status of the Midwestern Farmer in 1900," *M. V. H. R.* (December 1950), XXXVII. Specific phases of the changes are described, with the flavor of contemporaneity, in Charles H. Greathouse: "Free Delivery of Rural Mails," *Yearbook of the U.S. Department of Agriculture, 1900,* and Charles M. Harger: "The Prairie Woman: Yesterday and To-Day," *Out-*

look (April 26, 1902), LXX. Paul F. Sharp: "When Our West Moved North," *Amer. Hist. Rev.* (January 1950), LV, covers a much-neglected aspect of "the end of the frontier," the migration to Canada.

For this later phase of socialism, Donald D. Egbert and Stow Persons, eds.: *Socialism and American Life* (2 vols., Princeton U. Press, 1952), can be supplemented by a number of autobiographies, of which the most meaty are Oscar Ameringer: *If You Don't Weaken* (Holt, 1940), Morris Hillquit: *Loose Leaves from a Busy Life* (Macmillan, 1934), and Charles E. Russell: *Bare Hands and Stone Walls* (Scribner, 1933); the biography of Debs, Ray Ginger: *The Bending Cross* (Rutgers U. Press, 1949); the vigorous essays in Charles A. Madison: *Critics and Crusaders* (Holt, 1947); and two especially pertinent scholarly articles, Thomas P. Jenkin: "The American Fabian Movement," *West. Pol. Quar.* (June 1948), I, and David A. Shannon: "The Socialist Party before the First World War," *M. V. H. R.* (September 1951), XXXVIII.

The transition of the patrician dissident to economic and social reform is part of the theme of the perceptive work of Richard Hofstadter: *The American Political Tradition and the Men Who Made It* (Knopf, 1948), and of Eric F. Goldman: *Charles J. Bonaparte* (Johns Hopkins U. Press, 1943). Theodore Roosevelt provides a perfect statement of this later stage of patrician reform in André Tardieu: "Three Visits to Mr. Roosevelt," *Independent* (April 16, 1908), LXIV.

The general hopefulness and respectability of progressivism are pointed up, from interesting angles, in George E. Mowry: "The California Progressive and His Rationale: A Study in Middle Class Politics," *M. V. H. R.* (September 1949), XXXVI, and Boyd C. Shafer: "The American Heritage of Hope, 1865–1940," ibid. (December 1950), XXXVII. Progressivism's connections with feminism are emphasized in Rheta C. Dorr: *What Eight Million Women Want* (Small, Maynard, Boston, 1910); Mary Earhart: *Frances Willard: From Prayers to Politics* (U. of Chicago Press, 1944); and James W. Linn: *Jane Addams* (Appleton-Century, 1935).

Progressivism's mixed feelings about immigrants, and its trend toward genuine acceptance, are thoughtfully detailed in John W. Higham: "European Immigration in American Thought," MS., U. of Wisconsin Library. The progressive Americanization drive is best studied through the general work by a participant, Graham W. Taylor: *Pioneering on New Social Frontiers* (U. of Chicago Press, 1930), and the autobiographies of two important progressive social workers, Jane Addams: *Twenty Years at Hull House* (Macmillan, 1916), and Lillian Wald: *The Home on Henry Street* (Holt, 1915).

The progressive trend toward political centralization is compactly treated in Edward R. Lewis: *A History of American Political Thought from the Civil War to the World War* (Macmillan, 1937). Changing progressive attitudes toward the Negro are pinpointed in Carl Krummel: "The Attitudes of Some of the Leaders of the Progressive Movement, 1890–1914, toward Negroes," MS., in Mr. Krummel's possession. Booker T. Washington's philosophy is expounded in his absorbing autobiography: *Up from Slavery* (Doubleday, Page, 1919), and in an excellent biography, Basil Mathews: *Booker T. Washington* (Harvard U. Press, 1948). The progressive acceptance of the Washington approach is most clearly shown in Ray Stannard Baker: *Following the Color Line* (Doubleday, Page, 1908).

Chapter V

CONSERVATIVE ideology of the period is probed in four major studies of American thought, Henry S. Commager: *The American Mind* (Yale U. Press, 1950); Merle Curti: *The Growth of American Thought* (Harper, 1951); Joseph Dorfman: *The Economic Mind in American Civilization* (3 vols., Viking, 1946–9); and Ralph Gabriel: *The Course of American Democratic Thought* (Ronald, 1940). Robert G. McCloskey: *American Conservatism in the Age of Enterprise* (Harvard U. Press, 1951), is a significant if somewhat polemical discussion.

Bert J. Loewenberg summarized his studies of the American reception of Darwinism in "Darwinism Comes to America," *M. V. H. R.* (December 1941), XXVIII, and the subject is also well delineated in the topical essays of Stow Persons, ed.: *Evolutionary Thought in America* (Yale U. Press, 1950). Basic for the use of Darwinism by conservatives is Richard Hofstadter: *Social Darwinism in American Thought, 1860–1915* (U. of Pennsylvania Press, 1944), though some more recent students have argued that Hofstadter overstresses Darwinism as an element in conservative thinking. Also of considerable usefulness are C. A. Henderson: "Business Men and Social Theorists," *Amer. Jl. Soc.* (January 1896), I; Harris E. Starr: *William Graham Sumner* (Holt, 1925); and Edward L. Youmans: *Herbert Spencer on the Americans and the Americans on Herbert Spencer* (Appleton, 1883).

Commager, Curti, Dorfman, and Gabriel cover the intellectual revolt as well as conservatism. Morton G. White: *Social Thought in America* (Viking, 1949), is an important treatment of the revolt, written from a point of view largely hostile to the emerging school. Samuel Chugerman: *Lester F. Ward, The American Aristotle* (Duke U. Press, 1939), provides a meaty if somewhat disjointed biography of a key figure in Reform Darwinism. The economic interpretation element is treated in specific connections in Eric F. Goldman: *John Bach McMaster* (U. of Pennsylvania Press, 1943), "J. Allen Smith," *Pac. Northwest Quar.* (July 1944), XXXV, and "The Origins of Beard's *Economic Interpretation of the Constitution*," *Jl. Hist. Ideas* (April 1952), XIII.

For suggestive commentaries on Henry George's thinking, the books mentioned on pp. 466–7 can be supplemented by the essay in Daniel Aaron: *Men of Good Hope* (Oxford, 1951), and Albert J. Nock: *Henry George* (Morrow, 1939). George's attack on Conservative Darwinism was continued in all his writings, especially *A Perplexed Philosopher* (Charles L. Webster, New York, 1892) and *Social Problems* (Schalkenbach Foundation, New York, 1934).

Important for the general European influences are W. Stull Holt, ed.: *Historical Scholarship in the United States* (Johns Hopkins U. Press, 1938), and Oscar Cargill: *Intellectual America* (Macmillan, 1941). Specific English influences are sketched in William J. Newman: "American Dissenters in England, 1865–1914," MS., in Mr. Newman's possession. The German scholarly contacts are treated from a nonideological point of view in Charles F. Thwing: *The American and the German University* (Macmillan, 1928), and they emerge a direct reform influence from a number of autobiographies, especially Richard T. Ely: *Ground under Our Feet* (Macmillan, 1938); G. Stanley Hall: *Life and Confessions of a Psychologist*

(Appleton, 1923); and Edward A. Ross: *Seventy Years of It* (Appleton-Century, 1936).

The crackdown in the colleges is discussed, with indignation, in Ross: *Seventy Years of It*, and Thomas E. Will: "A Menace to Freedom; The College Trust," *Arena* (September 1901), XXVI. Merle Curti and Vernon Carstensen: *The University of Wisconsin* (2 vols., U. of Wisconsin Press, 1949), includes an excellent description of the university as a center of progressive thinking. Similar treatments are not available for the other four reform foci universities.

Chapter VI

RELIGIOUS thinking of the period is authoritatively discussed in Arthur M. Schlesinger: "A Critical Period in American Religion, 1875–1900," *Proc. Mass. Hist. Soc.* (June 1932), LXIV. Basic for the emergence of Reform Darwinian Christianity are the memoirs of a pioneer, Washington Gladden: *Recollections* (Houghton Mifflin, 1909), and the scholarly works, Aaron I. Abell: *The Urban Impact on American Protestantism, 1865–1900* (Harvard U. Press, 1943), Charles H. Hopkins: *The Rise of the Social Gospel in American Protestantism, 1865–1919* (Yale U. Press, 1940), and Henry F. May: *Protestant Churches and Industrial America* (Macmillan, 1949). Graham Taylor: "The Rapprochement of the Church and the Working World," *Survey* (July 2, 1910), XXIV, adds a thoughtful contemporary summary.

Dores R. Sharpe: *Walter Rauschenbusch* (Macmillan, 1942), is rhapsodic. A more judicious treatment, but with a limited focus, is provided by Vernon P. Bodein: *The Social Gospel of Walter Rauschenbusch and Its Relation to Religious Education* (Yale U. Press, 1944). The standard account, David Philipson: *The Reform Movement in Judaism* (Macmillan, 1931), is superficial and concerned almost exclusively with doctrinal and organizational developments. It can be filled out by Jerome W. Grollman: "The Emergence of Reform Judaism in the United States," MS., Hebrew Union College Library, which is broader in scope, and by the uneven essays in Bernard J. Bamberger, ed.: *Reform Judaism* (Hebrew Union College Press, 1949). The development of Ethical Culture is sketched in the partially autobiographical book of Felix Adler: *An Ethical Philosophy of Life* (Appleton, 1918), and in the partially historical essays in Horace J. Bridges, ed.: *Aspects of Ethical Religion, Essays in Honor of Felix Adler* (American Ethical Union, New York, 1926). James W. Wise: *Jews Are Like That!* (Brentano's, 1928), includes provocative lookbacks at both Reform Judaism and Ethical Culture.

Objective, broad-ranged studies of the social policies of the American Catholic Church are sorely needed. Useful for understanding the situation in which Father Ryan functioned are Aaron I. Abell: "Origin of Catholic Social Reform in the United States," *Rev. of Pol.* (July 1949), XI, and "The Reception of Leo XIII's Labor Encyclical in America, 1891–1919," ibid. (October 1945), VII; Henry J. Browne: *The Catholic Church and the Knights of Labor*, in *Cath. U. of Amer. Stud. in Amer. Church Hist.* (1949), XXXVIII; Sister M. Joan Leonard: "Catholic Attitudes toward American Labor, 1884–1919," MS., Columbia U. Library; and David J. Saposs: "The Catholic Church and the Labor Movement," *Modern Monthly* (May, June 1933), VII. Ryan's autobiography: *Social Doctrine in Action* (Harper,

1941), is often exceedingly revealing, and Richard J. Purcell: "John A. Ryan, Prophet of Social Justice," *Studies* (Dublin, June 1946), XXXV, is an intimately informed, if totally admiring, study. Especially important among Ryan's many writings are *A Living Wage* (Macmillan, 1906) and *Social Reconstruction* (Macmillan, 1920).

Joseph Dorfman: *The Economic Mind in American Civilization* (3 vols., Viking, 1946-9), is indispensable for the transition in economic thought. The interesting autobiography, John R. Commons: *Myself* (Macmillan, 1934), and Rexford G. Tugwell's incisive study: "The Life and Work of Simon Patten," *Jl. Pol. Econ.* (April 23, 1923), XXXI, add considerably to the picture of reform economics. Ely's octogenarianish autobiography: *Ground under Our Feet* (Macmillan, 1938), is best used along with Sidney Fine: "Richard T. Ely, Forerunner of Progressivism, 1880–1901," *M. V. H. R.* (March 1951), XXXVII. Among Ely's prolific writings, his *Labor Movement in America* (Crowell, 1886) is particularly significant because of its pioneering pro-labor sympathies.

Joseph Dorfman's rich biography: *Thorstein Veblen and His America* (Viking, 1934), can be supplemented by a number of discussions of Veblen or Veblenism, among which I found particularly perceptive R. L. Duffus: *The Innocents at Cedro* (Macmillan, 1944); John S. Gambs: *Beyond Supply and Demand: A Reappraisal of Institutional Economics* (Columbia U. Press, 1946); Max Lerner's introduction to *The Portable Veblen* (Viking, 1948); and Richard V. Teggart: *Thorstein Veblen, A Chapter in Economic Thought*, in *U. of Cal. Publ. in Econ.* (1942), XI.

L. L. and Jessie Bernard: *Origins of American Sociology* (Crowell, 1943), provides the background for Ross's work. His autobiography, *Seventy Years of It* (Appleton-Century, 1936), is almost as much boasting as narration. The only biography of Dugdale is a skimpy memoir, Edward M. Shepard: *The Work of a Social Teacher* (Society for Political Education, New York, 1884). Clarence Darrow's *Story of My Life* (Scribner, 1932) is characteristically forthright and astringent and can be expanded by the warmly admiring biography of Irving Stone: *Clarence Darrow for the Defense* (Doubleday, 1941). Lindsey has left two semi-autobiographical accounts, Lindsey and Harvey J. O'Higgins: *The Beast* (Doubleday, Page, 1917), and Lindsey and Rube Borough: *The Dangerous Life* (Liveright, 1931). Two helpful specific studies are Herbert H. Lou: *Juvenile Courts in the United States* (U. of North Carolina Press, 1927), and Jane Zimmerman: "The Penal Reform Movement in the South during the Progressive Era, 1890–1917," *Jl. South. Hist.* (November 1951), XVII.

The background of the ethnological argument is provided by Robert H. Lowie's standard *History of Ethnological Theory* (Farrar & Rinehart, 1937). Henrietta A. Tolbert: "A Study of the Doctrine of the Inferiority of the Negro in American History," MS., Howard U. Library, is satisfactory for its subject, and Oscar Handlin is suggestive far beyond the limits of his subject in "American Views of the Jew at the Opening of the Twentieth Century," *Publ. Amer. Jew. Hist. Soc.* (June 1951), XL. Paul Radin has an astute essay on Boas in Malcolm Cowley and Bernard Smith, eds.: *Books That Changed Our Minds* (Doubleday, Doran, 1939). Of Boas's own voluminous writings, the most characteristic statements are: "An Anthropologist's Credo," *Nation* (August 27, 1938), CXLVII; *Anthropology* (Columbia U. Press, 1908); "Human Faculty as Determined by Race," *Proc. Amer. Assoc. Advmt. Sci.* (1894), XLIII; and *The Mind of Primitive Man* (Macmillan, 1911).

Phillips has a rambling biographer in Isaac F. Marcosson: *David Graham Phillips and His Times* (Dodd, Mead, 1932), and his feminism is discussed in terms of its trend toward economic environmentalism in Eric F. Goldman: "David Graham Phillips: Victorian Critic of Victorianism," in Willard Thorp, ed.: *The Lives of Eighteen from Princeton* (Princeton U. Press, 1946). The general new emphasis of feminism is shown in a work that was quite influential in its day, Anna G. Spencer: *Woman's Share in Social Culture* (Mitchell Kennerley, New York, 1912).

Chapter VII

RALPH GABRIEL has a masterful discussion of the conservative capture of law and the Constitution in *The Course of American Democratic Thought* (Ronald, 1940), and Edward S. Corwin: "The Constitution as Instrument and as Symbol," *Amer. Pol. Sci. Rev.* (December 1936), XXX, is filled with penetrating observations on the subject. Charles G. Haines: *The Revival of Natural Law Concepts* (Harvard U. Press, 1930), and Benjamin R. Twiss: *Lawyers and the Constitution* (Princeton U. Press, 1942), are solid analyses of the Supreme Court aspects. James W. Hurst: *The Growth of American Law* (Little, Brown, 1950), goes at the point from an unusual institutional angle. Bernard E. Brown: *American Conservatives: The Political Thought of Francis Lieber and John W. Burgess* (Columbia U. Press, 1951), is suggestive beyond its limited subject.

Fred V. Cahill, Jr.: *Judicial Legislation* (Ronald, 1952), is a first-rate general study of the rise of the new attitude toward judicial review. Basic to an understanding of Holmes are Mark D. Howe, ed.: *Holmes-Pollock Letters* (2 vols., Harvard U. Press, 1941), and Holmes's *Collected Legal Papers* (Harcourt, Brace, 1920). Brilliant discussions of his thought may be found in Felix Frankfurter, ed.: *Mr. Justice Holmes* (Coward-McCann, 1931), and Max Lerner, ed.: *The Mind and Faith of Justice Holmes* (Little, Brown, 1943). Paul Sayre: *Life of Roscoe Pound* (State U. of Iowa Press, 1948), is waterish. Especially important for the phases of Pound's thought emphasized in my discussion are his *Interpretations of Legal History* (Macmillan, 1923); "Mechanical Jurisprudence," *Col. Law Rev.* (December 1908), VIII; and "The Scope and Purpose of Sociological Jurisprudence," *Harv. Law Rev.* (June, December 1911, April 1912), XXIV, XXV. Brandeis's *Oregon v. Muller* brief was published under the title *Women in Industry* (National Consumer's League, New York, n.d.), and he has a discerning biographer in Alpheus T. Mason: *Brandeis, A Free Man's Life* (Viking, 1946).

Fulmer Mood is thorough on "The Development of Frederick Jackson Turner as a Historical Thinker," *Trans. Colon. Soc. Mass.* (1943), XXXIV. Of the many superior essays on Turner, George W. Pierson's penetrating, if hostile, articles: "The Frontier and American Institutions," *New Eng. Quar.* (June 1942), XV, and "The Frontier and Frontiersmen of Turner's Essays," *Penn. Mag. Hist. and Biog.* (October 1940), LXIV, especially emphasize considerations pertinent to my discussion. Charles Beard's essay on Turner, in Malcolm Cowley and Bernard Smith, eds.: *Books That Changed Our Minds* (Doubleday, Doran, 1939), is the most important statement of the way Turner served as a bridge to reform-minded economic interpretation. Algie Simons is treated biographically in John J. Harmon: "Algie Martin

Simons," MS., Princeton U. Library; J. Allen Smith, in Eric F. Goldman: "J. Allen Smith," *Pac. Northwest Quar.* (July 1944), XXXV.

The lack of a full-dress biography of Beard is a major hole in American intellectual history. As a teacher, he is discussed in Arthur W. Macmahon: "Charles Austin Beard as a Teacher," *Pol. Sci. Quar.* (March 1950), LXV; Raymond Moley: *27 Masters of Politics* (Funk & Wagnalls, 1949); and Houston Peterson, ed.: *Great Teachers* (Rutgers U. Press, 1946). Biography and analysis are mingled in Bernard C. Borning: "The Political Philosophy of Young Charles A. Beard," *Amer. Pol. Sci. Rev.* (December 1949), XLIII; Merle Curti: "Charles Austin Beard (1878–1948)," *Yearbook Amer. Phil. Soc.* (1948); Hubert Herring: "Charles A. Beard, Free Lance among Historians," *Harper's* (May 1939), CLXXVIII; Matthew Josephson: "Charles A. Beard: A Memoir," *Va. Quar. Rev.* (Autumn 1949), XXV; Horace M. Kallen: "In Remembrance of Charles Beard," *Soc. Res.* (June 1951), XVIII; and Max Lerner: "Charles Beard's Stormy Voyage," *New Rep.* (October 25, November 1, 1948), CXIX. Eric F. Goldman: "The Origins of Beard's *Economic Interpretation of the Constitution*," *Jl. Hist. Ideas* (April 1952), XIII, concentrates on the one book, *An Economic Interpretation*. Richard Hofstadter: "Beard and the Constitution: The History of an Idea," *Amer. Quar.* (Fall 1950), II, moves on from the book to a discussion of Beard's changing Constitutional ideas.

The background for Dewey is illuminated by James K. Angell's early essay: "The Influence of Darwin on Psychology," *Psych. Rev.* (May 1909), XVI; Justus Buchler's lucid *Charles Peirce's Empiricism* (Harcourt, Brace, 1939); Ralph Barton Perry's distinguished *Thought and Character of William James* (2 vols., Little, Brown, 1935); and the two superior studies, Morton G. White: *The Origins of Dewey's Instrumentalism* (Columbia U. Press, 1943), and Philip P. Wiener: *Evolution and the Founders of Pragmatism* (Harvard U. Press, 1949). The best compact guide to Dewey's own thought and activities is Sidney Hook: *John Dewey* (John Day, 1939). His connections with larger social questions are thoughtfully explored in Merle Curti: *The Social Ideas of American Educators* (Scribner, 1935). Two commemorative "John Dewey" issues–the *New Republic*, October 17, 1949, and the *Saturday Review of Literature*, October 22, 1949–are filled with informed observations on Dewey's place in the history of American reform thinking.

Chapter VIII

PROGRESSIVE activity in the early 1900's can be studied through a raft of well-researched writings, many of which are exceedingly lively. Among the especially notable accounts devoted to, or including, the period are Benjamin P. DeWitt's contemporary *The Progressive Movement* (Macmillan, 1915), still valuable for its details concerning the less dramatic aspects; Claude G. Bowers: *Beveridge and the Progressive Era* (Houghton Mifflin, 1932), a distinguished work which fully justifies the second part of its title; John Chamberlain: *Farewell to Reform* (John Day, 1932), a scintillating discussion of ideas and personalities but written with a certain condescension toward progressivism; Harold U. Faulkner: *The Quest for Social Justice, 1898–1914* (Macmillan, 1930), the standard social history; Louis Filler: *Crusaders for American Liberalism* (Harcourt, Brace, 1939), a substantial and spirited treatment that is particularly good on muckraking activities; Richard Hofstadter: *The American Political Tradition* (Knopf, 1948), filled with incisive comments on progressive thinking; Alfred Kazin: *On Native Grounds* (Reynal & Hitchcock, 1942), so broadly gauged that it is much more than literary history; Russel B. Nye: *Midwestern Progressive Politics* (Michigan State College Press, 1951), a cogent account that goes beyond its title in significance; and Mark Sullivan: *Our Times* (7 vols., Scribner, 1926–35), indispensable for catching the atmosphere of this era, as for the whole long span it covers. Many of the local studies of progressivism contribute importantly to the broader picture, especially Walton Bean: *Boss Ruef's San Francisco* (U. of California Press, 1952); Winifred G. Helmes: *John A. Johnson, The People's Governor* (U. of Minnesota Press, 1949); George E. Mowry: *The California Progressives* (U. of California Press, 1951); and Ransom E. Noble, Jr.: *New Jersey Progressivism before Wilson* (Princeton U. Press, 1946).

Of all periods in American history, the progressive era has produced the greatest number of well-wrought autobiographies. The stand-out is the *Autobiography of Lincoln Steffens* (Harcourt, Brace, 1931), so beguiling it must be read with a constant awareness that this is the book of a highly imaginative literary artist and one veering toward a Marxist retake of his progressive days. Among the scores of autobiographies that deserve the adjective "significant," the following are most fruitful for my emphases: Ray Stannard Baker: *An American Chronicle* (Scribner, 1945); George Creel: *Rebel at Large* (Putnam, 1947); Hutchins Hapgood: *A Victorian in the Modern World* (Harcourt, Brace, 1939); Norman Hapgood: *The Changing Years* (Farrar & Rinehart, 1930); Harold L. Ickes: *The Autobiography of a Curmudgeon* (Reynal & Hitchcock, 1948); S. S. McClure: *My Autobiography* (Stokes, 1914); George W. Norris: *Fighting Liberal* (Macmillan, 1945); Gifford Pinchot: *Breaking New Ground* (Harcourt, Brace, 1947); Upton Sinclair: *An American Outpost* (Farrar & Rinehart, 1932); Henry L. Stimson and McGeorge Bundy: *On Active Service in Peace and War* (Harper, 1948); Mark Sullivan: *The Education of an American* (Doubleday, Doran, 1938); Oswald Garrison Villard: *Fighting Years* (Harcourt, Brace, 1939); Brand Whitlock: *Forty Years of It* (Appleton, 1915); and Harvey Wiley: *An Autobiography* (Bobbs-Merrill, 1930).

So many good books have been written about Theodore Roosevelt that another book would be required to comment properly on them. Of the biographies, Henry F. Pringle: *Theodore Roosevelt* (Harcourt, Brace, 1931), is the most generally excellent. Roosevelt's *Autobiography* (Scribner, 1912) cannot be brushed aside. The standard collection of works is Hermann Hagedorn, ed.: *Works of Theodore Roosevelt* (24 vols., Scribner, 1923–6). Elting E. Morison, ed.: *Letters of Theodore Roosevelt* is a skillful editing of the huge correspondence, of which four volumes have appeared (Harvard U. Press, 1951).

La Follette's *Autobiography* (La Follette Publishing Co., Madison, 1920) is superficial, as are Albert O. Barton: *La Follette's Winning of Wisconsin* (no pub., Madison, 1922), and Edward N. Doan: *The La Follettes and the Wisconsin Idea* (Rinehart, 1947). However, La Follette figures in many of the autobiographies and biographies of the period, and his work is informatively, if uncritically, treated in Frederic C. Howe: *Wisconsin, An Experiment in Democracy* (Scribner, 1912), and Charles McCarthy: *The Wisconsin Idea* (Macmillan, 1912). Scholarship is brought to bear on crucial phases of his career in Richard N. Current: *Pine Logs and Politics, A Life of Philetus Sawyer* (State Historical Society of Wisconsin, Madison, 1950); Edward A. Fitzpatrick: *McCarthy of Wisconsin* (Columbia U. Press, 1944); Dorothy Ganfield: "The Influence of Wisconsin on Federal Politics, 1880–1907," *Wis. Mag. Hist.* (September 1932), XV; Robert S. Maxwell, "La Follette and the Election of 1900: A Half-Century Reappraisal," ibid. (Autumn 1951), XXXV; and Wallace S. Sayre: "Robert La Follette, A Study in Political Methods," MS., New York U. Library.

Tom L. Johnson: *My Story* (Huebsch, 1913), is much more rewarding than La Follette's *Autobiography*, but Carl Lorenz: *Tom L. Johnson* (Barnes, 1911), is of value only in occasional spots. Robert H. Bremner: "The Civic Revival in Ohio," MS., Ohio State U. Library (partly published as "Tom L. Johnson," *Ohio State Arch. and Hist. Quar.*, January 1950, LIX), contains quantities of none-too-well digested material on Johnson.

The story of muckraking is detailed in C. C. Regier: *The Era of the Muckrakers* (U. of North Carolina Press, 1932). It can be rounded out by Filler's treatment; the autobiographies of Baker, McClure, Steffens, and Sullivan, and the memoirs of Ida Tarbell: *All in the Day's Work* (Macmillan, 1939); the relevant part of James P. Wood's able study: *Magazines in the United States: Their Social and Economic Influence* (Ronald, 1949); and a specific study of considerable insight, Richard and Beatrice Hofstadter: "Winston Churchill: A Study in the Popular Novel," *Amer. Quar.* (Spring 1950), II.

The general position of the Negro in the early 1900's is described with balance in John H. Franklin: *From Freedom to Slavery* (Knopf, 1947), and E. Franklin Frazier: *The Negro in the United States* (Macmillan, 1949). The reasons for the discontent with the Washington policy are pointed up in the important contemporary article, William E. Walling: "The Race War in the North," *Independent* (September 3, 1908), LXV, and in Mary W. Ovington: *Half a Man, The Status of the Negro in New York* (Longmans, Green, 1911), J. Saunders Redding: *They Came in Chains* (Lippincott, 1950), and Walter White: *A Man Called White* (Viking, 1948). Du Bois's autobiography, *Dusk of Dawn* (Harcourt, Brace, 1940), is one of the most distinguished of the period, and his thinking is described in detail in Samuel R. Spencer: "W. E. B. Du Bois: Apostle of Negro Protest," MS., in Mr. Spencer's possession. Du Bois's criticism of Washington is summarized in his famous essay in *The Souls of Black Folk* (A. C. McClurg, Chicago, 1903), and expanded in a number of later statements, of which a significant example is a 1938 commencement address published as the pamphlet, *A Pageant in Seven Decades*. Ralph L. Bunche includes an incisive statement of the Washington–Du Bois differences in "The Program of Organizations Devoted to the Improvement of the Status of the Negro," *Jl. Negro Educ.* (July 1939), VIII.

The semi-official account, Robert L. Jack: *History of the National Association for the Advancement of Colored People* (Meador Publishing Co., Boston, 1943), is thin. More substantial, but written with a marked anti-Washington point of view, is Jack Abramowitz: "Origins of the NAACP," *Soc. Educ.* (January 1951), XV. The roles of two of the principal white founders are covered in Mark D. Howe: *Portrait of an Independent, Moorfield Storey* (Houghton Mifflin, 1932), and Mary W. Ovington: *The Walls Came Tumbling Down* (Harcourt, Brace, 1947).

American Zionism is very much in need of a historian. Israel Cohen: *The Zionist Movement: Its Aims and Achievements* (Zionist Central Office, Ber-

lin, 1912), contains a weak chapter on the United States. The opposition of
Jews of western European origin is treated in Naomi W. Cohen: "The Re-
action of Reform Judaism in America to Political Zionism (1897-1922),"
Publ. Amer. Jew. Hist. Soc. (June 1951), XL, and understanding of this opposition is enriched by the autobiography of a key Reform leader, David
Philipson: *My Life as an American Jew* (J. G. Kidd & Son, Cincinnati, 1941),
and a study of a closely related subject, Zosa Szajkowski: "The Attitude of
American Jews to East European Jewish Immigration (1881-1893)," *Publ.
Amer. Jew. Hist. Soc.* (March 1951), XL. Chaim Weizmann: *Trial and Error* (Harper, 1949), includes some important American data, and the autobiography of the American leader, Stephen Wise: *Challenging Years* (Putnam, 1949), adds incidents not available elsewhere. Brandeis's conversion is
described in Alpheus T. Mason: *Brandeis* (Viking, 1946), though this section does not come up to the rest of the book in insight. "The Experiences
of a Jew's Wife," *Amer. Mag.* (December 1914), LXXVIII, and Norman
Hapgood's series in *Harper's Weekly* (August 7-21, 1915), LXI, contain invaluable materials for the conditions turning American Jews towards Zionism. Among later publications, the conditions are best treated in Oscar
Handlin's sensitive writings and in Louis Wirth's acute *The Ghetto* (U. of
Chicago Press, 1938).

Chapter IX

AN INTELLECTUAL biography of the Croly family would be a genuine contribution to American cultural history. A start was made in M. James Bol-
querin: "An Investigation of the Contributions of David, Jane, and Herbert
Croly to American Life," MS., School of Journalism Library, U. of Missouri. A small collection of Croly letters was ferreted out by Mr. Thomas
Pressly, of the University of Washington, and generously called to my attention. The letters, mostly from David to Herbert Croly but including
some later correspondence of Herbert, are now in the possession of Mr. Allan Jensen, of Yonkers, N.Y. Much of my information concerning the Crolys
came from interviews or correspondence with men who knew Herbert
Croly, especially from Messrs. Bruce Bliven, Felix Frankfurter, Learned
Hand, Alvin S. Johnson, Horace M. Kallen, Robert Morss Lovett, Ernest
Poole, and George H. Soule (none of whom, of course, is in any way responsible for my interpretations). The kind of Comtean atmosphere in
which the family functioned is sketched in Frederic Harrison: "Auguste
Comte in America," *Positivist Rev.* (June 1, 1901), IX, and given workman-
like treatment in Richmond L. Hawkins: *Auguste Comte and the United
States (1816-1853)* (Harvard U. Press, 1936) and *Positivism in the United
States (1853-1861)* (Harvard U. Press, 1938). As a sociological approach,
American Comteanism forms a good deal of the subject matter of L. L. and
Jessie Bernard: *Origins of American Sociology* (Crowell, 1943). John E.
McGee: *A Crusade for Humanity* (Watts & Co., London, 1931), describes
the "Religion of Humanity" as it was practiced in England at the time. A
scattering of biographical material on Mrs. Croly can be found in *Memo-
ries of Jane Cunningham Croly, "Jenny June"* (Putnam, 1904), and in
Mary I. Wood: *History of the General Federation of Women's Clubs* (General Federation of Women's Clubs, New York, 1912). Sidney Kaplan: "The

Miscegenation Issue in the Election of 1864," *Jl. Negro Hist.* (July 1949), XXXIV, includes an outline of David Croly's life and discusses in detail his extraordinary work, *Miscegenation.* Both the senior Crolys produced a number of writings, most of which are of the type that delights a biographer.

"Herbert Croly, 1869-1930," *New Rep.* (July 16, 1930), LXIII, Pt. II, is filled with biographical and analytical materials by distinguished contributors. Further interesting treatments of Croly may be found in John Chamberlain: *The American Stakes* (Lippincott, 1940); Robert M. Lovett: *All Our Years* (Viking, 1948); David W. Noble: "The New Republic and the Idea of Progress, 1914-1920," *M. V. H. R.* (December 1951), XXXVIII; Russel B. Nye: *Midwestern Progressive Politics* (Michigan State College Press, 1951); and *Walter Weyl, An Appreciation* (privately printed, Philadelphia, 1922).

Provocative materials concerning the progressive difficulties with "the people" concept may be gleaned from Thomas A. Bailey: *The Man in the Street* (Macmillan, 1948); Oscar Handlin: "The Immigrant and American Politics," in David F. Bowers, ed.: *Foreign Influences in American Life* (Princeton U. Press, 1944); Marcus L. Hansen: *The Immigrant in American History* (Harvard U. Press, 1940); Marc Karson: "The Catholic Church and the Political Development of American Trade Unionism (1900–1918)," *Indus. and Labor Rel. Rev.* (July 1951), III; David J. Saposs: "The Catholic Church and the Labor Movement," *Modern Monthly* (May, June 1933), VII; and Arthur M. Schlesinger: *Paths to the Present* (Macmillan, 1949), Chap. iii.

Suggestive for the progressive difficulties inherent in centralization are Robert E. Cushman: *The Independent Regulatory Commissions* (Oxford, 1941), a basic historical work; Harry K. Girvetz's contentious but cogent *From Wealth to Welfare* (Stanford U. Press, 1950); and the sagacious volume, E. Pendleton Herring: *Public Administration and the Public Interest* (McGraw-Hill, 1936). The horns of the trust difficulty are interestingly displayed in a later discussion, Charles A. Beard's article: "The Anti-Trust Racket," *New Rep.* (September 21, 1938), XCVI, followed by the comments in ibid. (October 5, 19, 26, 1938), XCVI, 243, 308, 333.

Among the many trenchant discussions of the progressive difficulties arising from Reform Darwinism or similar thinking, the following tie in especially with my points: Jacques Barzun: *Darwin, Marx, and Wagner* (Little, Brown, 1941); Chester M. Destler: "Some Observations on Contemporary Historical Theory," *Amer. Hist. Rev.* (April 1950), LV; Charles E. Merriam: *The Role of Politics in Social Change* (New York U. Press, 1936); Lewis Mumford: *Faith for Living* (Harcourt, Brace, 1940); Peter Viereck: *Conservatism Revisited* (Scribner, 1949); Richard M. Weaver: *Ideas Have Consequences* (U. of Chicago Press, 1948); and Morton G. White: *Social Thought in America* (Viking, 1949).

Roosevelt from the end of his Presidency to the election of 1912 is intensively covered in George E. Mowry: *Theodore Roosevelt and the Progressive Movement* (U. of Wisconsin Press, 1946). The new business thinking that was joining with Crolyite arguments to influence Roosevelt is discussed in the sources on p. 470. To these can be added, for more specific application to the years 1909–12, a useful contemporary study of Perkins, Harold Kellock: "A Pioneer of Big Business," *Century* (April 1915), LXXXIX; characteristic Perkins arguments, a 1908 Columbia University address published as the pamphlet, *The Modern Corporation*, and "The New South and

the New World," *Market World and Chron.* (May 1, 1915), XCV; a ram
bling biography of Munsey, George Britt: *Forty Years—Forty Millions* (Farrar & Rinehart, 1935); and the scholarly study, Milton N. Nelson: *Open
Price Associations*, in *U. of Ill. Stud. in Soc. Sci.* (June 1922), X. Among the
bedlam of comments on Eddy's *The New Competition*, Alvin Johnson's review in the *Political Science Quarterly* (March 1913), XXVIII, is especially noteworthy.

Chapter X

MOST of the sources cited for Chapter viii, particularly the sweeping accounts and the autobiographical and biographical writings, are equally important for this chapter.

George Mowry: *Roosevelt and the Progressive Movement* (U. of Wisconsin Press, 1946), carries the detailed story of the Bull Moose Party. Key details are added by the participants or first-hand observers, Oscar K. Davis:
Released for Publication (Houghton Mifflin, 1925); George H. Payne: *The
Birth of the New Party* (no pub., 1912); and Henry L. Stoddard: *As I Knew
Them* (Harper, 1927). For the Chicago convention itself, J. M. Striker's
first-hand notes, MS., are in the Harvard U. Library. The best of the contemporary color stories is Richard Harding Davis: "The Men at Armageddon," *Collier's* (August 24, 1912), XLIX, and Claude G. Bowers: *Beveridge
and the Progressive Era* (Houghton Mifflin, 1932), places the convention in
rich perspective.

The transition of Wilson from conservatism to progressivism is percep-
tively described in William Diamond: *The Economic Thought of Woodrow Wilson*, in *Johns Hopkins U. Stud. in Hist. and Pol. Sci.* (1943), LXI,
and William Allen White: *Masks in a Pageant* (Macmillan, 1928) and
Woodrow Wilson (Houghton Mifflin, 1924). It is worked out in greater detail in Arthur Link: *Wilson, The Road to the White House* (Princeton U.
Press, 1947).

Taft's role in the 1912 election is authoritatively handled in Henry F.
Pringle: *The Life and Times of William Howard Taft* (2 vols., Farrar &
Rinehart, 1939). The major Roosevelt-Wilson speeches are published under
the appropriate titles: *The New Nationalism* (Outlook, New York, 1913)
and *The New Freedom* (Doubleday, Page, 1913). Brandeis's ideas received
their best-known expression in *Other People's Money* (Frederick A. Stokes,
New York, 1914), and his brain-truster role in the campaign of 1912 is covered in Alpheus T. Mason: *Brandeis* (Viking, 1946). Meaningful aspects of
the Bull Moose effort are added by Alice P. Campbell: "The Bull Moose
Movement in Michigan," *Mich. Hist.* (Winter 1941), XXV; Herbert Par-
zen: "A Comparative Study of the Progressive Presidential Campaigns of
1912 and 1924," MS., Columbia U. Library; and E. E. Robinson: "Distribution of the Presidential Vote of 1912," *Amer. Jl. Soc.* (July 1914), XX.

The most complete account of Wilson as President is the authorized biography, Ray Stannard Baker: *Woodrow Wilson* (8 vols., Doubleday, Doran,
1927–39). Baker and William E. Dodd edited *The Public Papers of Woodrow Wilson* (6 vols., Harper, 1925–7). Important supplements are John M.
Blum: *Joe Tumulty and the Wilson Era* (Houghton Mifflin, 1951); Charles
Seymour, ed.: *The Intimate Papers of Colonel House* (4 vols., Houghton
Mifflin, 1926–8), though House's exaggeration of his own role must be dis-

counted; and the letters and memoirs of members of the Administration, particularly Josephus Daniels: *The Wilson Era, Years of Peace, 1910–1917* (U. of North Carolina Press, 1944), David F. Houston: *Eight Years with Wilson's Cabinet* (2 vols., Doubleday, Page, 1926), Anne W. Lane and Louise H. Wall, eds.: *The Letters of Franklin K. Lane* (Houghton Mifflin, 1922), and William G. McAdoo: *Crowded Years* (Houghton Mifflin, 1931). Dewey W. Grantham, Jr.: "Southern Congressional Leaders and the New Freedom, 1913–1917," *Jl. South. Hist.* (November 1947), XIII, details a vital circumstance of the Wilson Administrations.

Rich materials for the adjustment problems of minorities can be gathered from the sources mentioned on pp. 467–8 and Thomas C. Blegen: *Norwegian Migration to America, The American Transition* (Norwegian-American Historical Association, Northfield, Minn., 1940); Theodore Maynard: *The Story of American Catholicism* (Macmillan, 1941); and Robert E. Park and Herbert A. Miller: *Old World Traits Transplanted* (Harper, 1921). Louis Filler: *Randolph Bourne* (American Council on Public Affairs, Washington, 1943), is a stimulating biography, and a small segment of diary and a few letters are published as "Letters (1913–1914)," *Twice a Year* (Fall–Winter 1940, Spring–Summer 1941), V, VI, and "Diary for 1901," ibid. Max Lerner: "Randolph Bourne and Two Generations," ibid., and Lewis Mumford: "The Image of Randolph Bourne," *New Rep.* (September 24, 1930), LXIV, are noteworthy essays on Bourne.

William Allen White: *The Old Order Changeth* (Macmillan, 1911), is a perfect expression of the abounding progressive confidence. David E. Weingast: *Walter Lippmann* (Rutgers U. Press, 1949), begins the much-needed study of Lippmann's role in American culture. Lillian Symes and Clement Travers: *Rebel America, The Story of Social Revolt in the United States* (Harper, 1934), and Albert Parry: *Garrets and Pretenders* (Covici, Friede, 1933), chronicle, none too successfully, the revolt against fixedness. Van Wyck Brooks: *America's Coming of Age* (Huebsch, 1915), was a highly influential proclamation, and Malcolm Cowley, ed.: *After the Genteel Tradition* (Norton, 1937), is a sharp lookback. Sinclair Lewis: "A Generation Nourished on H. G. Wells," *New York Herald Tribune Sunday Book Review*, October 20, 1946, is as discriminating as it is readable. The revolt produced scores of superior autobiographies, of which at least the following should be mentioned: Emma Goldman: *Living My Life* (2 vols., Garden City, 1931); Orrick Johns: *Time of Our Lives* (Stackpole, 1937); Alfred Kreymborg: *Troubadour* (Boni & Liveright, 1925); and Harriet Monroe: *A Poet's Life* (Macmillan, 1938).

Of particular value for the Village phenomenon are the first-rate biography, Granville Hicks: *John Reed* (Macmillan, 1936), and the autobiographical writings, Floyd Dell: *Homecoming* (Farrar & Rinehart, 1933); Max Eastman: *Enjoyment of Living* (Harper, 1948); John Reed: *The Day in Bohemia* (privately printed, Hillacre, Conn., 1913); and Art Young: *On My Way* (Liveright, 1928). The early reception of Freudianism in the United States is worked out in considerable detail in William S. Rollins: "The Advent of Freudianism in America, 1909–1920," MS., in Mr. Rollins's possession. Also useful for this subject are A. A. Brill: "The Introduction and Development of Freud's Work in the United States," *Amer. Jl. Soc.* (November 1939), XLV; Frederick J. Hoffman: *Freudianism and the Literary Mind* (Louisiana State U. Press, 1945); and Fritz Wittels: *Sigmund Freud* (Dodd, Mead, 1924).

Bibliographical Notes

The founding of the *New Republic* is sketched in William H. Attwood: "Pathfinders of American Liberalism, The Story of the *New Republic*," MS., Princeton U. Library. Important details are added in the introduction to Groff Conklin, ed.: *The New Republic Anthology, 1915–1935* (Dodge Publishing Co., New York, 1936); Herbert Croly: "The New Republic Idea," *New Rep.* (December 6, 1922), XXXIII, Pt. II, and *Willard Straight* (Macmillan, 1924); "Herbert Croly," *New Rep.* (July 16, 1930), LXIII, Pt. II; and *Walter Weyl, An Appreciation* (privately printed, Philadelphia, 1922).

Chapter XI

GOING at foreign policy from the point of view of trying to distinguish conservative and progressive attitudes, and varying schools within progressivism, is an unusual approach and requires special techniques. For the World War I period, the chart described on p. 463 was essential. Since attention had to be given to the probable importance of hyphenate sentiments, the chart was used along with a study of the nationality backgrounds of the Congressmen and of their constituents. For the latter, of course, the U.S. Census was basic (the 1910 one was used to avoid the population shifts brought by the war). With respect to the German–Americans, the census figures are illuminated by Hildegard B. Johnson: "The Location of German Immigrants in the Middle West," *Ann. Assoc. Amer. Geog.* (March 1951), XLI, and two solid studies of the specific question at hand, Clifton J. Child: *The German–Americans in Politics* (U. of Wisconsin Press, 1939), and Carl Wittke: *German–Americans and the World War* (Ohio State Archaeological and Historical Society, Columbus, 1936). On the Scandinavian–Americans, some revealing materials can be derived from the generalized study, George M. Stephenson: "The Attitude of Swedish Americans toward the World War," *Proc. Miss. Valley Hist. Assoc.* (1918–19), X, and the filiopietistic volume, Olaf M. Norlie: *History of the Norwegian People in America* (Augsburg Publishing House, Minneapolis, 1925).

For the most part, however, progressivism in relation to foreign affairs has to be worked out by using studies written with a quite different focus. Among these, I found most useful John C. Appel: "Labor and American Imperialism, 1895–1905," MS., U. of Wisconsin Library; Thomas A. Bailey: "Was the Presidential Election of 1900 a Mandate on Imperialism?" *M. V. H. R.* (June 1937), XXIV; Herman E. Bateman: "Foreign Affairs and the Presidential Election of 1916," MS., Stanford U. Library; Merle Curti: *Peace or War, The American Struggle, 1636–1936* (Norton, 1936); Fred Harrington: "The Anti-Imperialist Movement in the United States," *M. V. H. R.* (September 1935), XXII; Evelyn Hisz: "The Issue of Imperialism in the Presidential Campaigns of 1900 and 1904," MS., New York U. Library; and Harold C. Syrett: "The Business Press and American Neutrality, 1914–1917," *M. V. H. R.* (September 1945), XXXII.

The first of the three groups of progressives I have singled out, the dogged anti-interventionists, are part of the subject of the acute essay, Samuel Lubell: "Who Votes Isolationist and Why," *Harper's* (April 1951), CCII. Valuable materials concerning them can be gleaned from Merle Curti: *Bryan and World Peace*, in *Smith Coll. Stud. in Hist.* (1931), XVI, and Marie L. Degen: *The History of the Woman's Peace Party*, in *Johns Hopkins U.*

Rendezvous with Destiny

Stud. in Hist. and Pol. Sci. (1939), LVII. Alex M. Arnett: *Claude Kitchin and the Wilson War Policies* (Little, Brown, 1937), treats a key New Freedom anti-war figure. Louis Filler: *Randolph Bourne* (American Council on Public Affairs, Washington, 1943), not only devotes a good deal of space to Bourne's anti-war phase but, along with Oswald Garrison Villard: *Fighting Years* (Harcourt, Brace, 1939), provides a good group picture of the Eastern anti-war progressive intellectuals. Bourne's fragment of an anti-war essay, which was to have influence into the next generation, is included in James Oppenheim, ed.: *Untimely Papers* (Huebsch, 1919).

Naturally, Midwestern isolationism has been most studied, and here the student of progressive foreign policy has the help of two first-rate articles, Ray A. Billington: "The Origins of Middle Western Isolationism," *Pol. Sci. Quar.* (March 1945), LX, and Richard W. Leopold: "The Mississippi Valley and American Foreign Policy, 1890–1941," *M. V. H. R.* (March 1951), XXXVII. Two state studies should not be overlooked, Cedric C. Cummins: *Indiana Public Opinion and the World War, 1914–1917* (Indiana Historical Bureau, Indianapolis, 1945), and Karen Falk: "Public Opinion in Wisconsin during World War I," *Wis. Mag. Hist.* (June 1942), XXV.

For progressive interventionism, Hermann Hagedorn: *The Bugle That Woke America* (John Day, 1940), provides a detailed, if ecstatic, description of Roosevelt's moves toward war. Roosevelt's long-running foreign-policy attitudes are strikingly expressed in André Tardieu: "Three Visits to Mr. Roosevelt," *Independent* (April 16, 1908), LXIV. The general expansive and/or imperialist thinking that was influencing Roosevelt and other progressives is best handled in Claude G. Bowers: *Beveridge and the Progressive Era* (Houghton Mifflin, 1932), and Albert K. Weinberg: *Manifest Destiny* (Johns Hopkins U. Press, 1935). Nonimperialist interventionist progressive thinking is strikingly revealed in two autobiographies, Harold L. Ickes: *The Autobiography of a Curmudgeon* (Reynal & Hitchcock, 1948), and Fiorello H. La Guardia: *The Making of an Insurgent* (Lippincott, 1948).

The general development of the Wilsonian middle-road interventionism is the subject of the substantial volume, Harley Notter: *The Origins of the Foreign Policy of Woodrow Wilson* (Johns Hopkins U. Press, 1937). The less scholarly volumes of Theodore Marburg treat *The Development of the League of Nations Idea* (2 vols., Macmillan, 1932). David Loth: *Woodrow Wilson, The Fifteenth Point* (Lippincott, 1941), is lively and suggestive. An intimate feel of the way Wilson's foreign-policy thinking changed is added by the works mentioned on pp. 481–2 and Josephus Daniels, *The Wilson Era: Years of War and After, 1917–1923* (U. of North Carolina Press, 1946).

The emergence of the *New Republic*'s foreign policy is detailed in David W. Noble: "'One World': The Foreign Policy of the *New Republic* from 1914 to 1920," MS., Princeton U. Library (part of which has been published, with a somewhat different focus, as "The New Republic and the Idea of Progress, 1914–1920," *M. V. H. R.*, December 1951, XXXVII). Walter Lippmann: *Drift and Mastery* (Mitchell Kennerley, New York, 1914) and the *Stakes of Diplomacy* (Holt, 1915), and Walter Weyl: *American World Policies* (Macmillan, 1917), are important contemporary foreign-policy books by *New Republic* editors. Interesting foreign-policy experiences of the *New Republic* group are related in the introduction to Groff Conklin, ed.: *The New Republic Anthology, 1915–1935* (Dodge Publishing Co., New

York, 1936), and my account owes a great deal to information coming from the men listed on p. 479.

The progressive worry and anger over wartime economic trends are vigorously expressed in La Guardia's remarks scattered through the *Congressional Record*, 65th Cong., 1st Sess., LV, Pts. II–IV. Among the many writings that protested the infringements on civil liberties, especially noteworthy are Zechariah Chafee, Jr.: "Freedom of Speech," *New Rep.* (November 16, 1918), XVII; National Civil Liberties Bureau: *War-Time Prosecutions and Mob Violence* (National Civil Liberties Bureau, New York, 1919); Charles D. Stewart: "Prussianizing Wisconsin," *Atl. Mo.* (January 1919), CXXIII; and Norman Thomas: "Justice to War's Heretics," *Nation* (November 9, 1918), CVII. Chafee's later volume, the solid *Free Speech in the United States* (Harvard U. Press, 1941), has become standard.

The closing chapter of William Allen White's novel: *In the Heart of a Fool* (Macmillan, 1918), provides a typical, if floridly worded, expression of the way that progressives were accepting the war as an international extension of progressivism.

Chapter XII

Most of the books mentioned for Chapter xi are equally useful for this one. In addition, I found quite helpful the attention given to various schools of foreign-policy opinion in Thomas A. Bailey: *Woodrow Wilson and the Great Betrayal* and *Woodrow Wilson and the Lost Peace* (Macmillan, 1945), and the intensive analysis of the Senate votes on the Versailles Treaty in W. Stull Holt: *Treaties Defeated by the Senate* (Johns Hopkins U. Press, 1933). Selig Adler: "The War-Guilt Question and American Disillusionment, 1918–1928," *Jl. Mod. Hist.* (March 1951), XXIII, and Richard W. Leopold: "The Problem of American Intervention, 1917," *World Pol.* (April 1950), II, are important for the tie-in between progressive disillusionment and the rise of a revisionist view of World War I. The former, in particular, emphasizes the 1920's and the role of progressives. Specific materials of significance are added by Glenn H. Smith: "Middle Western Attitudes towards World Organization, 1914–1928," MS., U. of Iowa Library, and Edward E. Keso: *The Senatorial Career of Robert Latham Owen*, in *Contr. to Educ., George Peabody Coll. for Teachers* (1938), a sketch of the New Freedomite Senator who made an influential speech in 1923 repudiating the war.

A *New Republic* readers' poll on foreign-affairs attitudes (August 8, 1923, XXXV) is interesting but too badly based to be of much meaning. The *Dial, Freeman, LaFollette's Magazine, Nation*, and *New Republic* of the 1920's are storehouses of articles reflecting the progressive shiftback. Other rewarding materials concerning individuals of importance may be found in the memoirs of the *Freeman* editor, Albert J. Nock: *Memoirs of a Superfluous Man* (Harper, 1943); the autobiographies, Frederic C. Howe: *Confessions of a Reformer* (Scribner, 1925), Ickes: *The Autobiography of a Curmudgeon*, Robert M. Lovett: *All Our Years* (Viking, 1948), George W. Norris: *Fighting Liberal* (Macmillan, 1945), and Lincoln Steffens: *Autobiography* (Harcourt, Brace, 1931); the widely read articles of Lewis G. Gannett: "Documents in Diplomatic Deceit" and "They All Lied," *Nation* (October 11, 1922), CXV; and Walter Weyl's moving essays of disillusionment: *Tired Radicals* (Huebsch, 1921), though Weyl did not turn toward isolationism. R. F. Harrod: *The Life of John Maynard Keynes* (Harcourt, Brace, 1951), provides an intimately informed, if ill-organized, account of Keynes's American influence, and Étienne Mantoux's hostile volume: *The Carthaginian Peace, or The Economic Consequences of Mr. Keynes* (Oxford, 1946), adds materials on the reception of the book.

Harold Stearns has left a none too satisfactory autobiography: *The Street I Know* (Lee Furman, New York, 1935). The mounting prestige for liberals who had been anti-war is well illustrated in Ray Tucker and Frederick R. Barkley: *Sons of the Wild Jackass* (L. C. Page, Boston, 1932), especially in the essay on Norris. The admiration for Bourne reached brilliant climaxes in John Chamberlain: *Farewell to Reform* (John Day, 1933), and in the vignette of Bourne in John Dos Passos: *1919* (Harcourt, Brace, 1932).

Chapter XIII

ANY study of the 1920's can profitably start with the reports of the two Hoover commissions: *Recent Economic Changes in the United States* (2 vols., McGraw-Hill, 1929), and the somewhat less valuable *Recent Social Trends* (2 vols., McGraw-Hill, 1933). The picture of the 1920's as general rampant prosperity is corrected in Preston W. Slosson: *The Great Crusade and After* (Macmillan, 1930), and George Soule: *Prosperity Decade* (Pilot Press, London, 1947). The concentration of industrial control is described in the near-classic work of A. A. Berle, Jr., and G. C. Means: *The Modern Corporation and Private Property* (Macmillan, 1933), and one central aspect of the concentration is authoritatively treated in Fritz Machlup: *The Basing-Point System* (Lippincott, 1949). The agrarian distress is pointed up in the contemporary writings, Bruce Bliven: "Why the Farmer Sees Red," *New Rep.* (November 7, 1923), XXXVI, Arthur Capper: *The Agricultural Bloc* (Harcourt, Brace, 1922), and Henrik Shipstead: "What the Progressive Farmer Wants," *Forum* (April 1924), LXXI, and placed in the larger setting in Robert F. Wallace: "Western Farm Areas in Two World Wars," *Jl. Farm Econ.* (February 1950), XXXII. Its political significance is analyzed in Gilbert C. Fite: "The Agricultural Issue in the Presidential Campaign of 1928," *M. V. H. R.* (March 1951), XXXVII, and Darwin N. Kelley: "The McNary-Haugen Bills, 1924–1928," *Agr. Hist.* (October 1940), XIV. The most important contemporary document relating to labor restlessness is Commission of Inquiry, Interchurch World Movement: *Report on the Steel Strike of 1919* (Harcourt, Brace & Howe, 1920).

The famous work of Robert S. and Helen M. Lynd: *Middletown, A Study in American Culture* (Harcourt, Brace, 1929), best analyzes the business reconquest of thinking. Keith Sward: *The Legend of Henry Ford* (Rinehart, 1948), describes, in a highly critical context, Ford's attitudes and his hold on the public mind. The most thorough treatment of Harding is Harold F. Alderfer: "The Personality and Politics of Warren G. Harding," MS., New York Public Library, and this can be supplemented by Samuel H. Adams's bouncing volume: *Incredible Era, The Life and Times of Warren Gamaliel Harding* (Houghton Mifflin, 1939). Coolidge is more than satisfactorily covered in William Allen White's detailed and mildly ironical *A*

Bibliographical Notes

Puritan in Babylon (Macmillan, 1938). A series of dreary and uncritical biographies of Hoover are being replaced by the ex-President's substantial, if highly contentious, *Memoirs*, of which three volumes have appeared (Macmillan, 1951-2). Important for the drive toward conformity are the contemporary materials, American Civil Liberties Union: "Minutes of the Meetings of the Executive Committee, 1920-1928," 2 vols., MS., Princeton U. Library; Norman Hapgood: *Professional Patriots* (Boni, 1928); Walter Lippmann: *American Inquisitors* (Macmillan, 1928); J. M. Mecklin: *The Ku Klux Klan* (Harcourt, Brace, 1924); Bessie Pierce: *Public Opinion and the Teaching of History in the United States* (Knopf, 1926); and Louis F. Post: *The Deportations Delirium of Nineteen Twenty* (C. H. Kerr, Chicago, 1923). Of the lookbacks, especially notable are the powerful writings, Howard K. Beale: *Are American Teachers Free?* (Scribner, 1936), and G. L. Joughin and Edmund M. Morgan: *The Legacy of Sacco and Vanzetti* (Harcourt, Brace, 1948).

The confused unhappiness of the liberals is best captured through the excellent biography of a litmus-paper figure, Walter Johnson's *William Allen White's America* (Holt, 1947), and a raft of autobiographies, especially Frederic C. Howe: *Confessions of a Reformer* (Scribner, 1925). The attitude that lay behind expatriation is sensitively expressed in Matthew Josephson: *Portrait of the Artist as American* (Harcourt, Brace, 1930). Malcolm Cowley: *Exile's Return* (Norton, 1934), is an intimately informed history of the phenomenon. The trend toward Marxism is most importantly recorded in Lincoln Steffens: *Autobiography* (Harcourt, Brace, 1931), "Bankrupt Liberalism," *New Rep.* (February 17, 1932), LXX, and *Lincoln Steffens Speaking* (Harcourt, Brace, 1936).

A number of writings important for the difficulties clustering around progressive concepts are mentioned on pp. 480-1. To these should be added, for the troubles connected with "the people" concept in this later period, the hardheaded analyses in V. O. Key, Jr.: *Politics Parties and Pressure Groups* (Crowell, 1948). Of the many writings useful for a study of the results of more direct democracy, the following contain materials especially relevant to my points: Claudius O. Johnson: "The Initiative and Referendum in Washington," *Pac. Northwest Quar.* (January 1945), XXXVI; V. O. Key, Jr., and Winston W. Crouch: *The Initiative and the Referendum in California*, in *Publ. U. of Cal. at L. A. in Soc. Sci.* (1939), VI; Charles E. Merriam and Louise Overacker: *Primary Elections* (U. of Chicago Press, 1928); and Arthur M. Schlesinger and Erik M. Eriksson: "The Vanishing Voter," *New Rep.* (October 15, 1924), XL. On the feminist phase, Edna Kenton: "The Ladies' Next Step," *Harper's* (February 1926), CLII, and Stuart A. Rice and Malcolm M. Willey: "American Women's Ineffective Use of the Vote," *Curr. Hist.* (July 1924), XX, are highly suggestive. "Ten Years of Woman Suffrage," *Lit. Dig.* (April 26, 1930), CV, contains unusually interesting quotations.

For the general occupational ingrouping, J. A. C. Grant: "The Gild Returns to America," *Jl. of Pol.* (August, November 1942), IV, is invaluable. American Federation of Labor policy is adequately described in Lewis L. Lorwin: *The American Federation of Labor* (Brookings Institution, 1933), and Louis S. Reed: *The Labor Philosophy of Samuel Gompers* (Columbia U. Press, 1930). An important specific instance of AFL thinking is detailed in E. E. Cummins: "Political and Social Philosophy of the Carpenter's Union," *Pol. Sci. Quar.* (September 1927), XLII. Orville M. Kile: *The Farm*

Bureau Movement (Macmillan, 1921) and *The Farm Bureau through Three Decades* (Waverly Press, Baltimore, 1948), are semi-official histories of the Farm Bureau, and Wesley McCune: *The Farm Bloc* (Doubleday, Doran, 1943), points up the self-interestedness of its thinking. DeWitt C. Wing: "Trends in National Farm Organizations," in *Yearbook of the U.S. Department of Agriculture, 1940*, includes historical sketches of the principal farm organizations. Stuart A. Rice: *Farmers and Workers in American Politics*, in *Col. U. Stud. in Hist., Econ. and Pub. Law* (1924), CXIII, Murray S. and Susan W. Stedman, Jr.: *Discontent at the Polls* (Columbia U. Press, 1950), and P. Alston Waring and Clinton S. Golden: *Soil and Steel* (Harper, 1947), add materials for the problem of farmer-labor collaboration. The attitudes of the American Medical Association are described, with varying degrees of sympathy, in "The American Medical Association," *Fortune* (November 1938), XVIII; Oliver Garceau: *The Political Life of the American Medical Association* (Harvard U. Press, 1941); and James Rorty: *American Medicine Mobilizes* (Norton, 1939).

The mounting group consciousness among minorities is treated, with the emphasis on explaining the reasons for it, in Oscar Handlin: *The Uprooted* (Little, Brown, 1951), and, with venom, in Henry P. Fairchild: *The Melting-Pot Mistake* (Little, Brown, 1926). Edward G. Hartmann: *The Movement to Americanize the Immigrant* (Columbia U. Press, 1948), is thorough on the Americanization drive of the 1920's, and John W. Higham: "European Immigration in American Patriotic Thought," MS., U. of Wisconsin Library, places it within a more subtle complex of forces. Stanley R. Pliska: "American Poles and Poland's Independence Movement, 1914–1919," MS., Columbia U. Library, is a case-study of that type of phenomenon. Additional materials of consequence concerning trends in minority thinking and action can be gathered from the writings mentioned on p. 482 and William F. Ogburn and Nell S. Talbot: "A Measurement of the Factors in the Presidential Election of 1928," *Social Forces* (December 1929), VIII; R. A. Schermerhorn, *These Our People* (Heath, 1949); W. Lloyd Warner and Leo Srole: *The Social Systems of American Ethnic Groups* (Yale U. Press, 1945); Phyllis H. Williams: *South Italian Folkways in Europe and America* (Yale U. Press, 1938); and T. J. Woofter, Jr.: *Races and Ethnic Groups in American Life* (McGraw-Hill, 1933).

Carey McWilliams describes, within an angry economic interpretation, the mounting anti-Semitism in *A Mask for Privilege* (Little, Brown, 1948). A slim sketch of the increasing Zionism is provided by Israel Cohen: *The Zionist Movement* (Zionist Central Office, Berlin, 1912), and the picture is enriched by the autobiographies, Chaim Weizmann: *Trial and Error* (Harper, 1949), Stephen Wise: *Challenging Years* (Putnam, 1949), and especially by the widely read *Upstream* of Ludwig Lewisohn (Boni & Liveright, 1922).

John H. Franklin: *From Slavery to Freedom* (Knopf, 1947), gives a solid account of the worsened position of the Negro. Walter White: *Rope and Faggot* (Knopf, 1929), underlines the increase in lynching, and Gilbert T. Stephenson: "The Segregation of the White and Negro Races in Cities by Legislation," *Nat. Munic. Rev.* (July 1914), III, partially fills in a little-researched phase. Elbert L. Tatum: *The Changed Political Thought of the Negro, 1915–1940* (Exposition Press, New York, 1951), is skimpy but contains some facts otherwise difficult to obtain. The racialism of the Black Renaissance emerges through the lookback of a key intellectual, Carter G. Woodson: "An Accounting for Twenty-five Years," *Jl. Negro Hist.* (October 1940), XXV; a number of autobiographies, of which the most meaty are W. E. B. Du Bois: *Dusk of Dawn* (Harcourt, Brace, 1940), Langston Hughes: *The Big Sea* (Knopf, 1940), and James W. Johnson: *Along This Way* (Viking, 1933); and a scattering of other Negro literary products, particularly James W. Johnson, ed.: *The Book of American Negro Poetry* (Harcourt, Brace, 1922), and Alain Locke, ed.: *The New Negro; An Interpretation* (Boni, 1925). Roi Ottley: *New World A-Coming* (Houghton Mifflin, 1943), includes a vivacious, outspoken treatment of both intellectual and popular racialism.

A history of the Garvey movement would be a decided addition to the knowledge of modern America. Garvey summarized his thought in *Aims and Objects of Movement for Solution of Negro Problem Outlined* (Universal Negro Improvement Association Press, New York, 1924). His wife, Amy Jacques Garvey, edited a slim selection from his utterances: *The Philosophy and Opinions of Marcus Garvey* (Universal Publishing House, New York, 1923). Among the many short studies concerning Garvey, especially useful are Birgit Aron: "The Garvey Movement," *Phylon* (Fourth Quarter, 1947), VIII; Robert H. Brisbane, Jr.: "Some New Light on the Garvey Movement," *Jl. Negro Hist.* (January 1951), XXXVI; W. E. B. Du Bois: "Back to Africa," *Century* (February 1923), CV; Charles I. Glicksberg: "Negro Americans and the African Dream," *Phylon* (Fourth Quarter, 1947), VIII; Rollin L. Hartt: "The Negro Moses," *Independent* (February 26, 1921), CV; the chapter in Claude McKay: *Harlem: Negro Metropolis* (Dutton, 1940); and Truman H. Talley: "Marcus Garvey—The Negro Moses?" *World's Work* (December 1920, January 1921), XLI.

Most of the works cited for the new business thinking on pp. 470 and 480–1 continue to be useful for this later phase of it. Important additions for the 1920's are the earlier sections of the volume by one of Baruch's wartime assistants, Hugh S. Johnson: *The Blue Eagle from Egg to Earth* (Doubleday, 1935), and a polemical book by another ex-assistant of Baruch, George N. Peek: *Why Quit Our Own* (Van Nostrand, 1936); the factual studies, Arthur R. Burns: *The Decline of Competition* (McGraw-Hill, 1936), Leverett S. Lyon and Victor Abramson: *The Economics of Open Price Systems* (Brookings Institution, 1936), and L. E. Warford and Richard A. May: *Trade Association Activities* (Government Printing Office, 1923); and the Hoover *Memoirs*. Additional materials for, or significant comments about, the meaning of these developments may be found in the blasts of the venerable progressives, George W. Norris: "Boring from Within," *Nation* (September 16, 1925), CXXI, and J. Allen Smith: *The Growth and Decadence of Constitutional Government* (Holt, 1930); and in Thurman W. Arnold: *The Folklore of Capitalism* (Yale U. Press, 1937), Stuart Chase: *Government in Business* (Macmillan, 1935), Frank A. Fetter: *The Masquerade of Monopoly* (Harcourt, Brace, 1931), E. Pendleton Herring: *Federal Commissioners* (Harvard U. Press, 1936) and *Public Administration and the Public Interest* (McGraw-Hill, 1936), William A. Orton: *The Economic Role of the State* (U. of Chicago Press, 1950), and George W. Stocking and Myron W. Watkins: *Monopoly and Free Enterprise* (Twentieth Century Fund, New York, 1951).

The rapid spread of Freudianism in the 1920's is treated in the writings mentioned on p. 482 and in Mark Sullivan: *Our Times* (7 vols., Scribner, 1926–35). Provocative materials for the difficulties created by the rising relativism are provided by Oscar Cargill: *Intellectual America* (Macmillan,

1941), and a number of reviews of Lippmann's and Krutch's books, especially Winfred E. Garrison, in *Chris. Cent.* (May 29, 1929), XLVI; Lewis Mumford, in *New Rep.* (May 22, 1929), LIX; Reinhold Niebuhr, in *Chris. Cent.* (May 1, 1929), XLVI; C. M. Perry, in *Inter. Jl. Ethics* (October 1929), XL; Bertrand Russell, in *Nation* (April 10, 1929), CXXVIII; Gilbert Seldes, in *Bookman* (June, 1929), LXIX; and Edmund Wilson, in *New Rep.* (July 10, 1929), LIX.

Kenneth M. MacKay: *The Progressive Movement of 1924* (Columbia U. Press, 1947), is a thorough study of the election of 1924. Stenographic minutes of the convention proceedings, as well as many documents relating to the campaign, may be found in the Library of Congress Manuscripts Division under the heading, People's Legislative Service, "Papers Relating to the La Follette–Wheeler Campaign." Also useful in understanding the campaign are the works mentioned on pp. 487-8; the autobiographies, Arthur G. Hays: *City Lawyer* (Simon & Schuster, 1942), and Donald H. Richberg, *Tents of the Mighty* (Willett, Clark, & Calay, Chicago, 1930); Jane Addams, Herbert Croly, Felix Frankfurter *et al.*: "Why I Shall Vote for La Follette," *New Rep.* (September 10, 1924), XL; Fred E. Haynes: "The Significance of the Latest Third Party Movement," *M. V. H. R.* (September 1925), XII; and Hugh L. Keenleyside: "The American Political Revolution of 1924," *Curr. Hist.* (March 1925), XXI.

Liberalism as a revolt against conformity received a famous expression in Harold Stearns, ed.: *Civilization in the United States* (Harcourt, Brace, 1922). Its spirit is well captured in the distinguished volume of literary criticism which Malcolm Cowley edited, *After the Genteel Tradition* (Norton, 1937), and in the dazzling tour de force, Frederick L. Allen: *Only Yesterday* (Harper, 1931). Fitzgerald is the subject of a first-rate biography, Arthur Mizener: *The Far Side of Paradise* (Houghton Mifflin, 1951). Both of the latest biographies of Mencken, William Manchester: *Disturber of the Peace* (Harper, 1951), and Edgar Kemler: *The Irreverent Mr. Mencken* (Little, Brown, 1950), have their strengths, but Gerald Johnson: "Mencken: Scholar, Wit, One-Man Tornado," *New York Herald Tribune Sunday Book Review*, June 26, 1949, probably best assesses Mencken's place in American culture. Joseph A. Barry: "Sinclair Lewis, 65 and Far from Main Street," *New York Times Sunday Magazine*, February 5, 1950, is an important interview.

Chapter XIV

SOME of the materials which I value most for the period from 1933 on come from interviews or correspondence with participants, but other sources are plentiful. Next to the Administrations of the first Roosevelt, the era of F. D. R. in the White House has produced the richest materials for the student of modern American reform, and the flood of publications is not abating. Basic is Samuel Rosenman, ed.: *The Public Papers and Addresses of Franklin D. Roosevelt* (13 vols., various pubs., New York, 1938-50), the great value of which is enhanced by the Presidential introductions to each volume. Robert S. and Helen M. Lynd continued their penetrating sociological study in *Middletown in Transition* (Harcourt, Brace, 1937). Among the general treatments, extremely useful are the balanced survey, Basil Rauch: *The History of the New Deal, 1933-1938* (Creative Age, 1944); the

Bibliographical Notes

economic history, Broadus Mitchell: *Depression Decade* (Rinehart, 1947); the social history, Dixon Wecter: *The Age of the Great Depression, 1929–1941* (Macmillan, 1948); and a scintillating interpretive essay, Denis W. Brogan: *The Era of Franklin D. Roosevelt* (Yale U. Press, 1950).

The sense of personal shock the depression brought is abundantly documented in R. C. Angell: *The Family Encounters the Depression* (Scribner, 1936); Howard M. Bell: *Youth Tell Their Story* (American Council on Education, Washington, 1938); Clarence J. Enzler: *Some Social Aspects of the Depression* (Catholic U. of America Press, 1939); H. V. Knight: "Poverty in the Farm Belt," *Common Sense* (December 1934), III; and *These Are Our Lives* (U. of North Carolina Press, 1939).

Three discerning books give considerable attention to Roosevelt's pre-Presidential period, John Gunther: *Roosevelt in Retrospect* (Harper, 1950), Gerald Johnson: *Roosevelt: Dictator or Democrat?* (Harper, 1941), and Ernest K. Lindley: *Franklin D. Roosevelt* (Blue Ribbon, New York, 1931). Elliott Roosevelt published many pre-1933 letters in *F. D. R., His Personal Letters* (4 vols., Duell, Sloan & Pearce, 1947–50). Daniel W. Delano, Jr.: *Franklin Roosevelt and the Delano Influence* (James S. Nudi Publications, Pittsburgh, 1946), Eleanor Roosevelt: *This Is My Story* (Harper, 1937), and Sara D. Roosevelt: *My Boy Franklin* (Crown, 1933), are valuable for the family circumstances. James M. Cox: *Journey through My Years* (Simon & Schuster, 1946), contains materials on F. D. R. as a 1920 Vice-Presidential candidate. Gunther: *Roosevelt in Retrospect*, includes a favorable picture of Roosevelt as a patrician, and sharply unfavorable emphases on that theme may be found in Noel F. Busch: *What Manner of Man?* (Harper, 1944), John T. Flynn: *Country Squire in the White House* (Doubleday, Doran, 1940), and Mauritz A. Hallgren: *The Gay Reformer* (Knopf, 1935).

Roosevelt as President and his Administrations are the center of a rapidly increasing body of autobiographical or biographical writings. Of the generally favorable ones, I found most fruitful Marriner S. Eccles: *Beckoning Frontiers* (Knopf, 1951); Edward Flynn: *You're the Boss* (Viking, 1947); Harold L. Ickes: *The Autobiography of a Curmudgeon* (Reynal & Hitchcock, 1948) and "My Twelve Years with F. D. R.," *Sat. Even. Post* (June 5–26, July 3–24, 1948), CCXX; Russell Lord: *The Wallaces of Iowa* (Houghton Mifflin, 1947); Charles Michelson: *The Ghost Talks* (Putnam, 1944); Henry Morgenthau, Jr.: "The Morgenthau Diaries," *Collier's* (September 27–November 1, 1947), CXX; Frances Perkins: *The Roosevelt I Knew* (Viking, 1946); Eleanor Roosevelt: *This I Remember* (Harper, 1949); Samuel I. Rosenman: *Working with Roosevelt* (Harper, 1952); Robert E. Sherwood: *Roosevelt and Hopkins* (Harper, 1948); and the series of reminiscent and analytical articles by Rexford G. Tugwell, in the *Western Political Quarterly* beginning in June 1948. Largely unfavorable writings are fewer in number. Of these, Raymond Moley: *After Seven Years* (Harper, 1939), is by far the most substantial. Of use for certain episodes are George Creel: *Rebel at Large* (Putnam, 1947); James A. Farley: *Jim Farley's Story* (Whittlesey House, 1948); and Jesse H. Jones: *Fifty Billion Dollars, My Thirteen Years with the RFC* (Macmillan, 1951).

One of Tugwell's articles, "The Preparation of a President," *West. Pol. Quar.* (June 1948), I, is excellent on the early relationship between the Brain-Trusters and Roosevelt. Other materials concerning the first group of Brain-Trusters may be found in the able journalism of Ernest K. Lindley: *The Roosevelt Revolution* (Viking, 1934) and *Half Way with Roosevelt*

(Viking, 1936). For Moley specifically, the first section of *After Seven Years* is somewhat autobiographical, and Hume O. Annan, Jr.: "Raymond Moley—From Adviser to Critic," MS., Princeton U. Library, is a sketch of his career and thinking. Tugwell is treated with considerable insight in Russell Lord: "Rural New Yorker," *New Yorker* (March 23, 30, 1935), XI, and certain of his voluminous writings: *The Industrial Discipline and the Governmental Arts* (Columbia U. Press, 1933), *Industry's Coming of Age* (Harcourt, Brace, 1927), *Mr. Hoover's Economic Policy* (John Day, 1932), and "Notes on the Uses of Exactitudes in Politics," *Pol. Sci. Quar.* (March 1939), LIV, are particularly important for an understanding of his complex thinking. A large section of Hugh S. Johnson: *The Blue Eagle from Egg to Earth* (Doubleday, 1935), is autobiographical.

The emergence of Keynesianism and similar thinking is expertly handled in Clarence E. Ayres: "The Impact of the Great Depression on Economic Thinking," *Papers and Proc. Amer. Econ. Assoc.* (May 1946). The timing and extent of its influence on the New Deal itself is a much debated subject, and has to be traced out through the relevant sections of Eccles: *Beckoning Frontiers*; John K. Galbraith: *American Capitalism* (Houghton Mifflin, 1952); Seymour E. Harris: *The New Economics* (Knopf, 1947); R. F. Harrod: *The Life of John Maynard Keynes* (Harcourt, Brace, 1951); Moley: *After Seven Years*; and Tugwell's articles in the *Western Political Quarterly*.

Sherwood: *Roosevelt and Hopkins*, includes a superb treatment of Hopkins in domestic affairs. Hopkins's *Spending to Save* (Norton, 1936) presents his philosophy formally. Donald S. Howard: *The WPA and Federal Relief Policy* (Russell Sage Foundation, New York, 1943), is a sound over-all treatment, and Grace K. Adams: *Workers on Relief* (Yale U. Press, 1939), adds the human material.

Excellent for the background of Triple A are John D. Black: *Agricultural Reform in the United States* (McGraw-Hill, 1929), and Darwin N. Kelley: "The McNary-Haugen Bills, 1924–1928," *Agr. Hist.* (October 1940), XIV. The most connected and detailed story of the origins of the Triple A is told in Lord: *The Wallaces of Iowa.* M. L. Wilson: *Farm Relief and the Domestic Allotment Plan* (U. of Minnesota Press, 1933), is the argument of the chief originator of the Triple A. Robert E. Martin: "The Referendum Process in the Agricultural Adjustment Programs of the United States," *Agr. Hist.* (January 1951), XXV, and Edwin G. Nourse: *Marketing Agreements under the NRA* (Brookings Institution, 1935), treat important techniques developing along with the general program.

The origins of the NRA are described in detail, but with quite different emphases, in Johnson: *The Blue Eagle from Egg to Earth*; Moley: *After Seven Years*; Perkins: *The Roosevelt I Knew*; and Donald R. Richberg: *The Rainbow* (Doubleday, Doran, 1936). John P. Frank: *Mr. Justice Black* (Knopf, 1949), contains additional material on the catalytic role of the Black bill. The first two chapters of Charles F. Roos: *NRA Economic Planning* (Principia Press, Bloomington, 1937), attempt a balanced story of the launching. Business's early favorable attitude toward the NRA is emphasized in John H. Davis: "Business Attitudes toward the New Deal," MS., Princeton U. Library.

William L. Chenery: "Better Days Are Here," *Collier's* (April 29, 1933), XCI, is typical of the hundreds of articles describing the surge of hopefulness as the New Deal got under way. The hold that Rooseveltism was acquiring on the public mind is most concretely seen, with a proper discount for possible error, in the compendium of polls, Hadley Cantril, ed.: *Public Opinion, 1935-1946* (Princeton U. Press, 1951), and in the political statistical study, Edgar E. Robinson: *They Voted for Roosevelt* (Stanford U. Press, 1947). Frederick L. Allen's *Since Yesterday* (Harper, 1940), though not up to *Only Yesterday*, is alive with colorful details marking the swing to economic and social liberalism. Maurice Blinkoff: *The Influence of Charles A. Beard upon American Historiography*, in *U. of Buff. Stud.* (1936), XII, concentrates on a liberal triumph of far-reaching importance. For the new attitudes of youth, see especially "Youth in College," *Fortune* (June 1936), XIII; of literature, Leo Gurko's spirited study: *The Angry Decade* (Dodd, Mead, 1947). Harold E. Stearns, ed.: *America Now* (Scribner, 1938), contrasts meaningfully with his *Civilization in the United States* of the Twenties. George H. Mayer: *The Political Career of Floyd B. Olson* (U. of Minnesota Press, 1951), is a solid story of one of the typical new local leaders, in this case the Governor of Minnesota.

Chapter XV

VIRTUALLY all of the writings listed for Chapter xiv are also valuable for this chapter.

Leverett S. Lyon *et al.*: *The National Recovery Administration* (Brookings Institution, 1935), and Charles F. Roos: *NRA Economic Planning* (Principia Press, Bloomington, 1937), are over-all views of the workings of the NRA. The widespread discontent with NRA is abundantly documented in U.S. Senate Committee on Finance, 74th Cong., 1st Sess.: *Hearings on . . . the National Recovery Administration* (7 parts, 1935). George R. Leighton: "In Search of the NRA," *Harper's* (January 1934), CLXVIII, is one of the better of the innumerable popular statements of the criticisms. The Darrow reports, U.S. National Recovery Review Board: "First, Second, and Third Reports to the President of the United States," were never published but they were mimeographed and are available in most major libraries.

The workings of Triple A are surveyed critically in Joseph S. Davis: *Our Agricultural Policy, 1926-1938* (Stanford U. Press, 1939), and, with more favor, in Edwin G. Nourse: *Government in Relation to Agriculture* (Brookings Institution, 1940) and Nourse *et al.*: *Three Years of the Agricultural Adjustment Administration* (Brookings Institution, 1937). Henry A. Wallace: *New Frontiers* (Reynal, 1934), contains the Secretary of Agriculture's account of the first year's operations. The policy conflict within Triple A is best covered in Russell Lord: *The Wallaces of Iowa* (Houghton Mifflin, 1947), and George N. Peek vigorously stated the case of one side in *Why Quit Our Own* (Van Nostrand, 1936). A wealth of material on the problems Triple A did not solve may be found in Carl C. Taylor *et al.*: *Disadvantaged Classes in American Agriculture* (U.S. Department of Agriculture: *Social Research Report*, No. 8, April 1938), and Arthur F. Raper and Ira De A. Reid: *Sharecroppers All* (U. of North Carolina Press, 1941). U.S. Bureau of Agricultural Economics: *Technology on the Farm* (1940), covers the technological aspects. Charles A. Beard and George H. E. Smith: *The Old and the New Deal* (Macmillan, 1940), makes many acute observations on both the Triple A and the NRA.

The New Popular Front line of the Communist Party was expounded by the then General Secretary of the American party, Earl Browder, in *The People's Front* (International Publishers, 1938) and *What Is Communism?* (Vanguard, 1936). An intensely interesting debate concerning the new line, between Browder and Norman Thomas, was published by the *Socialist Call* as the pamphlet: *Which Road for American Workers—Socialist or Communist?* (1936). The attractions of the new line for liberals is discussed with insight in the opening chapter of Alistair Cooke: *A Generation on Trial, U.S. v. Alger Hiss* (Knopf, 1950); Leslie A. Fiedler: "Hiss, Chambers, and the Age of Innocence," *Commentary* (August 1951), XII; Granville Hicks's essay in Irving Talmadge, ed.: *Whose Revolution?* (Howell, Soskin, New York, 1941); and Arthur M. Schlesinger, Jr.: *The Vital Center* (Houghton Mifflin, 1949). Eugene Lyons: *The Red Decade* (Bobbs-Merrill, 1941), contains a good deal of information, but it is not entirely trustworthy and it is slanted by a vendetta attitude. Valuable materials for the understanding of liberal fellow-traveling may be added from William H. Attwood: "Pathfinders of American Liberalism, The Story of the *New Republic*," MS., Princeton U. Library; Dorothy D. Bromley: "An Ex-Red Tells His Story," *New York Herald Tribune*, June 26, 1949; Richard Crossman, ed.: *The God That Failed* (Harper, 1949); Benjamin J. Davis: "Why I Am a Communist," *Phylon* (Second Quarter, 1947), VIII; Joseph Freeman: *An American Testament* (Farrar & Rinehart, 1936); and Oliver Pilat: "Girl Communist," *New York Post*, November 1-13, 1949.

The details of the Supreme Court fight are covered in a superior piece of journalism, Joseph Alsop and Turner Catledge: *The 168 Days* (Doubleday, Doran, 1938), and liberal attitudes toward Roosevelt's plan are plentifully revealed in U.S. Senate Committee on the Judiciary, 75th Cong., 1st Sess.: *Hearings on . . . Reorganization of the Federal Judiciary* (6 parts, 1937).

The best printed source for the New Deal shiftover to the New Freedom is, despite its marked bias, Raymond Moley: *After Seven Years* (Harper, 1939), and it is well supplemented by the superb journalism of Joseph Alsop and Robert Kintner: *Men around the President* (Doubleday, Doran, 1939). Huey Long's life is presented with keen understanding in Harnett T. Kane: *Louisiana Hayride* (Morrow, 1941); his doctrines emerge from Long: *Every Man a King* (National Book Co., New Orleans, 1933) and *My First Days in the White House* (Telegraph Press, Harrisburg, Pa., 1935). Used cautiously, both Moley: *After Seven Years*, and James Farley: *Jim Farley's Story* (Whittlesey House, 1948), are prime sources for the influence of Long on Roosevelt's policies. Alsop and Kintner are best on the personalities and day-by-day activities of the new group of Brain-Trusters. Helpful details on the leader, Corcoran, may be found in a characteristically shrewd article by Alva Johnston: "White House Tommy," *Sat. Even. Post* (July 31, 1937), CCX.

Edgar Kemler: *The Deflation of American Ideals* (American Council on Public Affairs, Washington, 1941), gathers together the details on the New Deal's casualness concerning politics, but it should be balanced by William S. Carpenter: *The Unfinished Business of Civil Service Reform* (Princeton U. Press, 1952). The authoritative James Farley has written of his processes, with circumspection to be sure, in "Passing Out the Patronage," *Amer. Mag.* (August 1933), CXVI, and *Behind the Ballots* (Harcourt, Brace, 1938). Edward Flynn: *You're the Boss* (Viking, 1947), is a fascinating self-revelation of the new-type political boss.

494

Bibliographical Notes

The great problems that were bringing new emphases to liberalism are best summarized in an extraordinarily successful synthesis: *American Society* (Knopf, 1951), but no one book has yet really contained the complex story. Among the hundreds of important contributions, Abraham Epstein: *Insecurity, A Challenge to America* (Random House, 1938), is basic for its subject; Elton Mayo: *Human Problems of an Industrial Society* (Harvard Graduate School of Business Administration, 1945), is exceedingly provocative; and the "Yankee City" series, published by Yale, is an indispensable reservoir of research-based generalizations. Arnold and Caroline Rose: *America Divided* (Knopf, 1948), is a cogent guide to the minorities. Of the minority groups, the Negroes have been most satisfactorily studied for this period. They are the subject of three superlative sociological studies, St. Clair Drake and Horace W. Cayton: *Black Metropolis* (Harcourt, Brace, 1945), centered on Chicago but far broader in import; E. Franklin Frazier: *The Negro in the United States* (Macmillan, 1949); and Gunnar Myrdal: *An American Dilemma* (Harper, 1944).

Of the many able writers expressing these later phases of liberalism, probably the most influential was Max Lerner, especially his *It Is Later Than You Think* (Viking, 1938) and *Ideas Are Weapons* (Viking, 1939).

Chapter XVI

NATURALLY, many of the writings cited for Chapters xiv and xv continue to be of prime importance for this chapter.

Interesting additional materials concerning F. D. R.'s pre-Presidential foreign-affairs ideas may be gathered from a series of articles he wrote for the *Muskegan* (Mich.) *Chronicle*, September 27–October 14, 1915; a study based on the Roosevelt papers deposited at Hyde Park, Sidney Blaxill: "Franklin Delano Roosevelt: An Introduction to Foreign Policy," MS., Princeton U. Library; and Frank Freidel: "The Haitian Pilot-Plant," *Politics* (March 1944), I. Charles A. Beard: *American Foreign Policy in the Making, 1932–40* (Yale U. Press, 1946), and William C. Bullitt: "How We Won the War and Lost the Peace," *Life* (August 30, September 6, 1948), XXV, emphasize whatever evidence there is that Roosevelt was an isolationist during his early Presidency. Beard's charge that Roosevelt went from isolationism to warmongering is continued in *President Roosevelt and the Coming of the War, 1941* (Yale U. Press, 1948), and answered in detail in Basil Rauch: *Roosevelt from Munich to Pearl Harbor* (Creative Age, 1950). Charles C. Tansill took up the argument that Roosevelt was primarily responsible for American entrance into the war in an extensively researched and bitter volume, *Back Door to War* (Henry Regnery, Chicago, 1952). The critical period is treated from an opposite point of view, and also on the basis of intensive research, in William L. Langer and S. Everett Gleason: *The Challenge to Isolation, 1937–1940* (Harper, 1952). Anne O'Hare McCormick: "As He Sees Himself," *New York Times Sunday Magazine*, October 16, 1938, is an important interview with F. D. R. as he braced himself for the new phase of his Administration. Thomas H. Melohn: "The Election of 1940," MS., Princeton U. Library, includes a detailed study of the foreign-affairs issue during the election.

Roosevelt's desire to avoid Wilson's mistakes is a theme of Robert E. Sherwood: *Roosevelt and Hopkins* (Harper, 1948), a work invaluable for all phases of the developing foreign policy. One part of this Roosevelt aim, the creation of a bipartisan foreign policy, is intimately revealed in Arthur H. Vandenberg, Jr., and Joe A. Morris, eds.: *The Private Papers of Senator Vandenberg* (Houghton Mifflin, 1952). Among the abundance of other useful writings concerning F. D. R.'s foreign policy, I found especially fruitful Cordell Hull: *Memoirs* (2 vols., Macmillan, 1948); Henry L. Stimson and McGeorge Bundy: *On Active Service in Peace and War* (Harper, 1948); Mark S. Watson: *Chief of Staff: Prewar Plans and Preparations* (Historical Division, Department of the Army, 1950); and Sumner Welles: *The Time for Decision* (Harper, 1944) and *Seven Decisions That Shaped History* (Harper, 1950).

The U.S. Senate Special Committee Investigating the Munitions Industry, 73rd Cong., 2nd Sess.: *Hearings . . .* (40 parts, 1934–43), is a storehouse of long-forgotten liberal anti-interventionist attitudes. Among the many let's-stay-out-of-war writings, or writings including that emphasis, by liberals of the period, particularly noteworthy are John Chamberlain: *The American Stakes* (Lippincott, 1940); Jerome Frank: *Save America First* (Harper, 1938); C. Hartley Grattan: *The Deadly Parallel* (Stackpole, 1939); and Maury Maverick: *A Maverick American* (Covici, Friede, 1937). Two bitterly anti-war books, John Dos Passos: *1919* (Harcourt, Brace, 1932), and Laurence Stallings: *The First World War; A Photographic History* (Simon & Schuster, 1933), made a deep impression in liberal circles. The following also include materials useful for studying liberal isolationism: Bruce Catton: *The War Lords of Washington* (Harcourt, Brace, 1948); Wayne S. Cole: "The America First Committee," MS., U. of Wisconsin Library (part of which is published as "The America First Committee," *Jl. Ill. State Hist. Soc.* (Winter 1951), XLIV; Walter Johnson: *The Battle against Isolationism* (U. of Chicago Press, 1944); Allan A. Kuuisto: "The Influence of the National Council for the Prevention of War on United States Foreign Policy, 1935–1939," MS., Harvard U. Library; Harold Lavine and James Wechsler: *War Propaganda and the United States* (Yale U. Press, 1940); and David H. Mickey: "The Isolationist Senatorial Group, 1919–1939," MS., U. of Nebraska Library. Lavine and Wechsler and Benjamin Gitlow: *The Whole of Their Lives* (Scribner, 1948), discuss the influence of shifts in the Communist line, but the latter must be used with great caution.

From 1940 on through World War II, Sherwood: *Roosevelt and Hopkins*, is the best one-book guide to liberal attitudes on foreign policy. It can be supplemented, in book form, by the collected pieces of journalists who both reflected and influenced liberal opinion, Marquis Childs: *I Write from Washington* (Harper, 1942); Mrs. Raymond Clapper, ed., Raymond Clapper: *Watching the World* (McGraw-Hill, 1944); Samuel Grafton: *An American Diary* (Doubleday, Doran, 1943); and Max Lerner: *Public Journal, Marginal Notes on Wartime America* (Viking, 1945).

Chart II (see p. 463) shows the extent of the liberal shift away from isolationism by the time of the passage of the Lend-Lease bill. As in the case of Chart I, the correlation has been used with attention to nationality backgrounds. In the case of Chart II, moreover, religious affiliations of the Congressmen and of their constituencies have been considered (both the nationality and religious checks were made on the statistical basis of the U.S. Census of 1940). The shiftover on foreign policy is also richly documented by the liberal statements in U.S. Senate Committee on Foreign Relations,

77th Cong., 1st Sess.: *Hearings . . . on a bill further to promote the defense of the United States* (3 parts, 1941).

The repudiation of Beardianism is most obvious in the liberal discussions of the Beards' last collaborative work, the *Basic History* (1944), particularly in the comments in the *Saturday Review of Literature* by H[enry] S. C[anby] (November 11, 1944), Lewis Mumford (December 2, 1944), and Dixon Wecter (November 4, 1944), XXVII. Among the many revaluations of liberal thinking being made at the time, especially noteworthy are John Dos Passos: *The Ground We Stand On* (Harcourt, Brace, 1941); Archibald MacLeish: "Post-war Writers and Pre-war Readers," *New Rep.* (June 10, 1940), CII; and Lewis Mumford, *Faith for Living* (Harcourt, Brace, 1940).

Wartime economic developments which disturbed liberals are vigorously detailed in Catton: *The War Lords of Washington*. Other vital materials for the theme can be derived from writings more favorable to the way the economic homefront was conducted: the apologia, Donald M. Nelson: *Arsenal of Democracy* (Harcourt, Brace, 1946); two scholarly studies of major importance, Robert H. Connery: *The Navy and the Industrial Mobilization in World War II* (Princeton U. Press, 1951), and Herman M. Somers: *Presidential Agency, OWMR* (Harvard U. Press, 1950); the skillful synthesis, Eliot Janeway: *The Struggle for Survival* (Yale U. Press, 1951); and the uniquely authoritative treatise, John L. O'Brian and Manly Fleischmann: "The War Production Board Administrative Policies and Procedures," *George Wash. Law Rev.* (December 1944), XIII. John Dos Passos: *State of the Nation* (Houghton Mifflin, 1944), and Selden Menefee: *Assignment: U.S.A.* (Reynal & Hitchcock, 1943), are typical liberal reactions to a variety of wartime social phenomena. The comparative general safety of civil liberties during World War II is reported in American Civil Liberties Union: *Freedom in Wartime* (American Civil Liberties Union, New York, 1943). The Japanese-American situation, which shocked liberals so much, is told from that point of view in Morton Grodzine: *Americans Betrayed* (U. of Chicago Press, 1949).

Mr. Joseph Barnes, a Willkie intimate, is preparing a biography of his late friend, based on the Willkie correspondence. The best study now available is Mary E. Dillon: *The Willkie Legacy* (Lippincott, 1952), which is considerably researched but ax-grinding. Some important first-hand materials are available in Walter White: *A Man Called White* (Viking, 1948). Both a scattering of biographical facts and the early liberal suspicion of Willkie may be found in "This Man Willkie," *New Rep.* (September 2, 1940), CIII, Pt. II. Henry Wallace offers an inviting subject to some biographer with the proper combination of understanding and the lifted eyebrow. Russell Lord: *The Wallaces of Iowa* (Houghton Mifflin, 1947), peters out at the war period. Dwight Macdonald: *Henry Wallace, The Man and the Myth* (Vanguard, 1947), is largely anti-Wallace polemic. Rhapsodically favorable, Kenneth Stewart: "Wallace the Symbol," *PM Picture News Section*, October 26, November 9, 1947, nevertheless contains materials which help to explain Wallace's wartime hold on the liberal public.

Chapter XVII

FROM this chapter on, the book in large measure rests on interviews or on newspaper and magazine articles which have not been collected or redone into books. The articles are mentioned only in rare cases, when they are crucially important, unusually typical, or manage to compress some key point or attitude into a particularly meaningful short piece.

The shock of Roosevelt's death is brilliantly portrayed in Donald P. Geddes, ed.: *Franklin Delano Roosevelt, A Memorial* (Pocket Books, 1945). Rexford G. Tugwell: *The Stricken Land* (Doubleday, 1947), opens with a powerful statement of the foreboding F. D. R.'s death brought to many liberals. Naturally, materials on the Truman Administration are still in the fragmentary stage. Truman has provided an extraordinary half-autobiography, half-private papers in William Hillman: *Mr. President* (Farrar, Straus, & Young, 1952). Jonathan Daniels: *The Man of Independence* (Lippincott, 1950), is a semi-authorized, discriminatingly favorable biography. The major Presidential statements up to 1948, with most space going to the campaign addresses of that year, are collected in M. B. Schnapper, ed.: *The Truman Program* (Public Affairs Press, Washington, 1948).

Two books by thoughtful, liberal-minded journalists, Tris Coffin: *Missouri Compromise* (Little, Brown, 1947), and Jonathan Daniels: *Frontier on the Potomac* (Macmillan, 1946), contain a good deal of material on Washington in the early Truman days, and they also reflect the ambivalent liberal attitude toward the new President. The story of the departing New Dealers is detailed, with revealing quotations, in Richard Wilson: "What's Become of the New Dealers," *Look* (April 27, 1948), XII. The major economic trends that worried liberals so much are authoritatively outlined in Council of Economic Advisers: *First–Third Annual Reports . . . to the President* (1946–8). The voting record of the Eightieth Congress, marked largely by inaction or conservatism, is printed as part of "The Story of the Sold Out 80th Congress," *New Rep.* (September 27, 1948), CXIX.

Probably the best of the discussions of whether the late 1940's were another 1920's by liberal-minded writers is Frederick L. Allen: "This Time and Last Time, Postwar Eras I and II," *Harper's* (March 1947), CXCIV. A group of quotations indicating the doubtings and anger of important liberals are included in Eric F. Goldman and Mary Paull: "Liberals on Liberalism," *New Rep.* (July 22, 1946), CXV. Other noteworthy statements of this type are James B. Conant: "Wanted: American Radicals," *Atl. Mo.* (May 1943), CLXXI; Louis Filler: "The Dilemma, So-called, of the American Liberal," *Antioch Rev.* (Summer 1948), VIII; John Fischer: "The Lost Liberals," *Harper's* (May 1947), CXCIV; William B. Hesseltine: *The Rise and Fall of Third Parties* (Public Affairs Press, Washington, 1948), which is much broader than its title would indicate; Max Lerner: *Actions and Passions* (Simon & Schuster, 1949); the poem of Archibald MacLeish: "Brave New World," *Atl. Mo.* (September 1946), CLXXVII; and Bill Mauldin: *Back Home* (Sloane, 1947). Literary trends offering little solace for liberals are discussed against a long perspective in Malcolm Cowley: "The Young Conquerors," *New Rep.* (June 28, 1948), CXVIII.

Important liberal reviews of Elliott Roosevelt's *As He Saw It* are: Joseph Barnes, in *New York Herald Tribune Sunday Book Review*, October 6, 1946; E. D. Canham, in *Christian Science Monitor*, October 5, 1946; Henry S. Commager, in *New York Times Sunday Book Review*, October 6, 1946; Jonathan Daniels, in *Sat. Rev. Lit.* (October 5, 1946), XXIX. For further significant revelations of the liberal disquietude about foreign affairs, see especially, for Europe, Marshall Knappen: *And Call It Peace* (U. of Chicago Press, 1947), and James S. Martin: *All Honorable Men* (Little, Brown,

1950); for relations with the Soviet, Albert Z. Carr: *Truman, Stalin and Peace* (Doubleday, 1950); and for the general situation, Herman Finer: *America's Destiny* (Macmillan, 1947), Edgar A. Mowrer: *The Nightmare of American Foreign Policy* (Knopf, 1948), and Sumner Welles: *Where Are We Heading?* (Harper, 1946).

The bibliographical notes for the renewed liberal concern over liberty are in the notes for Chapter xviii.

The best way to go at the liberal relationship to the Wallace candidacy is through the publications and statements of the Americans for Democratic Action (anti-Wallace) and of the Progressive Citizens of America (pro-Wallace). Key statements of Wallace (all published in the *New Republic*) are his first editorial for the magazine (October 12, 1946), CXV; "Jobs Peace Freedom" (December 16, 1946), CXV; "The Enemy Is Not Each Other" (January 27, 1947), CXVI; "Farewell and Hail!" (July 19, 1948), CXIX; and his radio address of July 29, 1948, mimeographed and distributed by the Progressive Party. The Progressive Party platform is published in the *Congressional Record*, 80th Cong., 2nd Sess., XCIV, Pt. XII, pp. A5091–6. Rexford G. Tugwell: "Progressives and the Presidency," and Hubert Humphrey: "A Reply to Rex Tugwell," *Progressive* (April 1949), XIII, accurately reflect the discussion going on among the liberal-minded. Dwight Macdonald: "The Wallace Campaign: An Autopsy," *Politics* (Summer 1948 but published in November,) V, and Victor Lasky: "Who Runs Wallace?" *Plain Talk* (June 1948), II, emphasize the Communists' role in the Progressive Party. James A. Wechsler: "My Ten Months with Wallace," *Progressive* (November 1948), XII, is probably the best account of the Wallace campaign, understanding but discriminating.

Chart III (see p. 464) shows the extent of the liberal support for the internationalism of the Truman Administration and the correlation between conservatism in domestic affairs and a neo-isolationism. Cecil J. North, Jr.: "The Development of Conservative Thought in the Republican Party, 1940–1948," MS., Princeton U. Library, is an interesting but not entirely successful attempt to work out what the conservatives were doing in domestic and foreign policy as a "positive" program. Samuel Lubell: *The Future of American Politics* (Harper, 1952), parts of which are cited in the footnotes as articles in the *Saturday Evening Post*, is filled with cogent comments on the new line-ups in foreign policy.

Two of the phases of the first Truman Administration which most pleased liberals, and which are likely to have long-running effects, are the work of his commissions on education and civil rights, the summary reports of which were published as *Higher Education for Democracy* (Harper, 1948) and *To Secure These Rights* (Simon & Schuster, 1947). A typical and delightfully written liberal estimate of Truman as the election of 1948 approached is Richard H. Rovere: "President Harry," *Harper's* (July 1948), CXCVII. The most authoritative explanation yet available of Eisenhower's role in 1948 is Marquis W. Childs: "Why Ike Said No," *Collier's* (August 28, 1948), CXXII.

Chapter XVIII

MOST of the general accounts listed for Chapter xvii carry over in part for the second Truman Administration. The basic foreign-policy documents for

Acheson's tenure as Secretary of State are included in McGeorge Bundy, ed.: *Pattern of Responsibility* (Houghton Mifflin, 1952).

Samuel Lubell: *The Future of American Politics* (Harper, 1952), is far and away the best analysis of the election. Morton Leeds intensively studies one phase of it in "The AFL in the 1948 Elections," *Soc. Res.* (June 1950), XVII, and meaningful details or incisive comments are added by Joseph and Stewart Alsop: "Candidate Truman's Magic Brew," *Sat. Even. Post* (December 31, 1949), CCXXII; Charles G. Ross: "How Truman Did It," ibid. (December 25, 1948), CXX; and Thomas L. Stokes: "Harry Truman, Politician Extraordinary," *New York Times Sunday Magazine*, May 7, 1950.

Lester Markel: "After Four Years: Portrait of Harry Truman," *New York Times Sunday Magazine*, April 10, 1949, is the most balanced picture of Truman's thinking as he entered his second term. John Hersey: "Mr. President," *New Yorker* (April 7–May 5, 1951), XXVII, provides an intimate portrait of Truman in the later days of his Administrations. The extent to which the Fair Deal was enacted up to March 1952 is outlined in Floyd M. Riddick: "The Eighty-First Congress: First and Second Sessions," *West. Pol. Quar.* (March 1951), IV, and "The Eighty-Second Congress; First Session," ibid. (March 1952), V. The restrained enthusiasm of Jonathan Daniels: "H. S. T. and History," *Reporter* (May 13, 1952), VI, is characteristic of the liberal writing being done about Truman as he prepared to retire from the Presidency.

One of the earlier and more searching expressions of the mounting liberal concern over corruption is Marquis Childs: "Will Truman's Friends Ruin Him?" *Look* (June 7, 1949), XIII. Of the enormous mass of liberal literature protesting invasions of civil liberties and debating their proper meaning under the circumstances of the 1950's, the most thoughtful or effective are Alan Barth: *The Loyalty of Free Men* (Viking, 1951); Francis Biddle: *Fear of Freedom* (Doubleday, 1951); Henry S. Commager: "Who Is Loyal to America?" *Harper's* (September 1947), CXCV; William O. Douglas: *Being an American* (John Day, 1948); Thomas I. Emerson and David M. Helfeld: "Loyalty among Government Employees," *Yale Law Jl.* (December 1948), LVIII; Robert H. Jackson: "Justice Jackson on Communism in America," *New York Times Sunday Magazine*, May 21, 1950; and George R. Stewart: *The Year of the Oath* (Doubleday, 1950). The veteran democratic socialist, Norman Thomas, contributed the disturbing essay: "The Dissenter's Role in a Totalitarian Age," *New York Times Sunday Magazine*, November 20, 1949. The most direct liberal thrusts against McCarthyism were the exhaustive study of the methods and effects of the "Red Channels" activity, Merle Miller: *The Judges and the Judged* (Doubleday, 1952), and the sensationally documented series, Charles Wertenbaker *et al.*: "The China Lobby," *Reporter* (April 15, 29, 1952), VI.

The swift and deep changes in the American social scene are described in the writings listed on p. 495. Among the many others of great value for this latest period, a few can be named as especially pertinent to my emphases. On farm life, see Marquis Childs: *The Farmer Takes a Hand, the Electric Power Revolution in Modern America* (Doubleday, 1952), the U.S. Department of Agriculture's meaty yearbook of 1940, *Farmers in a Changing World*, and Carl C. Taylor *et al.*: *Rural Life in the United States* (Knopf, 1949); on urban labor, C. Wright Mills: *The New Men of Power, America's Labor Leaders* (Harcourt, Brace, 1948); on the woman's role, John D. Durand: "Married Women in the Labor Force," *Amer. Jl. Soc.* (November

1946), LII, and H. S., "Women and Money," *Sat. Rev. Lit.* (March 12, 1949), XXXII; on minorities, the compact detailing of the latest findings, Charles F. Marden: *Minorities in American Society* (American Book Co., 1952); on the general economic leveling, U.S. Bureau of the Census: *Current Population Reports, Consumer Income*, Series P-60, No. 9 (1952); on status ratings, Richard Centers: *The Psychology of Social Classes* (Princeton U. Press, 1949), Maethel Deed and Donald G. Paterson: "Changes in Social Status of Occupations," *Occupations* (January 1947), XXV, and Maryon Welch, "The Ranking of Occupations on the Basis of Social Status," ibid. (January 1949), XXVII; and on general attitudes, David Riesman: *The Lonely Crowd* (Yale U. Press, 1950), Riesman and Nathan Glazer: *Faces in the Crowd* (Yale U. Press, 1952), and Samuel A. Stouffer *et al.*: *The American Soldier* (2 vols., Princeton U. Press, 1949).

Rich materials for liberalism as a form of domestic conservatism are included in Lubell: *The Future of American Politics*. Frank Tannenbaum: *A Philosophy of Labor* (Knopf, 1951), is a pioneering essay on the modern American trade-union as a conservative force.

The gold mine for the increasingly pressing problem of the middle classes is C. Wright Mills: *White Collar* (Oxford, 1951). Especially suggestive materials on the theme can be gathered from Catherine Bauer: "The Middle Class Needs Houses Too," *New Rep.* (August 29, 1949), CXXI; a brace of writings basically hostile to the Fair Deal, "Liquidation of the Middle Brackets," *Fortune* (January 1947), XXXV, and Raymond Moley: *How to Keep Our Liberty* (Knopf, 1952), which is focused on what Moley calls the "middle interests"; and two largely factual studies of a key middle-class problem, Seymour E. Harris: *The Market for College Graduates* (Harvard U. Press, 1949), and Ernest Havemann and Patricia S. West: *They Went to College* (Harcourt, Brace, 1952).

Most of the works cited on pp. 480 and 487–90 for the discussion of the inherent difficulties of liberalism continue to be useful for this latest phase. They can be supplemented, with respect to occupational ingrouping, by the trenchant comments of Rexford G. Tugwell: "Is a Farmer-Labor Alliance Possible?" *Harper's* (May 1937), CLXXIV; the vigorously argued essays, Milton Mayer: "The Rise and Fall of Dr. Fishbein" and "The Dogged Retreat of the Doctors," ibid. (November, December 1949), CXCIX, and Russell Smith: "Big Business and the Farm Bloc," *Antioch Rev.* (Summer 1944), IV; and the solid studies, Thomas P. Jenkin: *Reactions of Major Groups to Positive Government in the United States, 1930–1940*, in *U. of Cal. Publ. in Pol. Sci.* (1945), I, and Arnold M. Rose: *Union Solidarity* (U. of Minnesota Press, 1952). Racial and religious ingrouping are illuminated by the anti-Zionist survey: "Mid-Century Inventory," *Menorah Jl.* (Autumn 1950), XXXVIII; Henry L. Moon: *Balance of Power: The Negro Vote* (Doubleday, 1948), and Richard Robbins: "Counter-Assertion in the New York Negro Press," *Phylon* (Second Quarter, 1949), X; and two books concerning Catholicism which amount to a debate, Paul Blanshard: *American Freedom and Catholic Power* (Beacon Press, 1949), and James M. O'Neill: *Catholicism and American Freedom* (Harper, 1952), and a third which goes somewhat in between, Thomas Sugrue: *A Catholic Speaks His Mind on America's Religious Conflict* (Harper, 1952).

Basic to any discussion of liberal difficulties connected with the trusts is the *Summary Report of the Federal Trade Commission on the Merger Movement* (1948). David Lynch's *The Concentration of Economic Control* (Macmillan, 1943) is a troubled probing of the TNEC findings, and Estes Kefauver: "The Coming Showdown," *Progressive* (September 8, 1947), XI, a strident pointing up of the issue. Blair Bolles's alarm-ringing book: *How to Get Rich in Washington* (Norton, 1952), is supplemented by Paul H. Douglas's function-by-function survey of government waste, *Economy in the National Government* (U. of Chicago Press, 1952). Many phases of the progressive troubles connected with centralization are indirectly explored in a basically anti-Fair Deal volume, Sheldon Glueck, ed.: *The Welfare State and the National Welfare* (Addison-Wesley, Cambridge, 1952).

The foreign-affairs difficulties of liberals are made plain in scores of books, two of the most revealing of which are Francis Biddle: *The World's Best Hope* (U. of Chicago Press, 1949), and Paul McGuire: *There's Freedom for the Brave* (Morrow, 1949). Aspects of the difficulties are discussed in many essays, most relevantly to my points in Richard H. Crossman: "Did F. D. R. Escape Wilson's Failure?" *Commentary* (November 1949), VIII, and "Nationalism: Enemy or Ally?" ibid. (July 1950), X; John H. Herz: "Idealist Internationalism and the Security Dilemma," *World Pol.* (January 1950), II; Richard Hofstadter: "The Roosevelt Reputation," *Progressive* (November 1948), XII; Hans J. Morgenthau: *In Defense of the National Interest* (Knopf, 1951); and Frederick L. Schuman: "The Dilemma of the Peace Seekers," *Amer. Pol. Sci. Rev.* (February 1945), XXXIX. Reinhold Niebuhr: *The Irony of American History* (Scribner, 1952), is a penetrating, if at times indirect, commentary on Reform Darwinian types of thinking and their consequences in foreign or domestic affairs.

In addition to the works cited in the text, others noteworthy for their fresh churnings of liberal thinking are Max Ascoli: *The Power of Freedom* (Farrar, Straus, 1949); Horace M. Kallen: *The Liberal Spirit* (Cornell U. Press, 1948); Alexander Meiklejohn: *Free Speech and Its Relation to Self-Government* (Harper, 1948); Irwin Ross: *Strategy for Liberals* (Harper, 1949); and Lionel Trilling: *The Liberal Imagination* (Viking, 1950).

An imaginative biography of Lilienthal would go far toward capturing the whole later-day trend of liberal attitudes. Willson Whitman: *David Lilienthal, Public Servant in a Power Age* (Holt, 1948), is thin and uncritical. Lilienthal's ideas are better approached through his own statements, especially the clearly formulated essay, Lilienthal and Robert H. Marquis: "The Conduct of Business Enterprises by the Federal Government," *Harv. Law Rev.* (February 1941), LIV; *TVA, Democracy on the March* (Harper, 1944); a group of essays, *This I Do Believe* (Harper, 1949); and an important interview with Lilienthal, Archibald MacLeish: "A Progress Report on Atomic Energy," *Life* (September 27, 1948), XXV, which ranges far more broadly than the title would indicate. Also essential for studying the potential meaning of TVA are the trail-breaking study, U.S. National Resources Committee: *Regional Factors in National Planning and Development* (1935), especially Chap. ix, "Federal Regional Authorities—The Tennessee Valley Example"; the thoughtful essays in Merrill Jensen, ed.: *Regionalism in America* (U. of Wisconsin Press, 1951); and the level-headed study, C. H. Pritchett: *TVA: A Study in Public Administration* (U. of North Carolina Press, 1943). Basic to a consideration of the international potentialities of the TVA concept is Herman Finer's careful monograph: *The T. V. A.: Lessons for International Application* (International Labour Office Studies and Reports, Series B, No. 37, 1944). These can be accompanied by a vigorous attack on the whole TVA approach, Frederick L. Collins: *Uncle Sam's Billion-Dollar Baby* (Putnam, 1945).

The publications of the United World Federalists, an organization largely led by liberals, are a clear reflection of the fervid drive on the part of an influential group of liberals for limitations on sovereignty. The book of Vernon Nash, a UWF vice president: *The World Must Be Governed* (Harper, 1949), typifies the viewpoint. Apart from this fringe, the general liberal trend toward a more deeply committed internationalism is plain in a number of passionate writings and it is probably most significantly expressed in Adlai E. Stevenson: "The Challenge of a New Isolationism," *New York Times Sunday Magazine*, November 6, 1949. The increasing liberal emphasis on the importance of international economic and social reform as a basis of American foreign policy can be observed in the publications of the ADA, especially the striking volume it sponsored, Arthur Goodfriend: *The Only War We Seek* (Farrar, Straus, & Young, 1951).

INDEX

�֎

Index

American Medical Association, 294, 444 and n. 5

American Mercury, 21; as organ of liberalism of Twenties, 315–17

American Newspaper Guild, 355

American Protective Association, 36

American Red Cross, 255

American Tragedy, An, 319

Americanism: T.R.'s definition of, 245

Americanization, 314; as program of progressives, 76–9; practice of, in Twenties, 299–300; helps provoke minority chauvinisms, 300; *see also* Immigrants; Melting-pot, the

Americans for Democratic Action: launched as anti-Communist liberal organization, 417; combats Progressive Party (1948), 417–18; quoted on issue of Cold War, 420; some leaders of back Eisenhower for Presidency (1948), 423; economic concern in foreign policy of, 459 n. 1

America's Sixty Families, 366

Ameringer, Oscar, 149

Anarchism, 43; as part of discontent of Eighties, 42

Anderson, Sherwood, 318; quoted on Freud, 311

"Anglo-Saxonism": conservative use of concept of, 89–90; development of Reform Darwinian attack on, 125–8; role of, in foreign policy ideas, 234–5; and progressivism of Twenties, 304

Ann Vickers, 343

Anthony, Susan B., 22

Anthropology: radical use of Morgan's, 85; conservative use of Westermarck's, 86; development of Reform Darwinian interpretation of, 125–8

Anti-Catholicism, *see* Catholics

Anti-Semitism, *see* Jews

Antitrust action, *see* Corporations, tendencies toward trustification; Trusts

A&P: antitrust action against under Truman, 447

Arnall, Ellis G.: *The Shore Dimly Seen*, 453

Arnold, Thurman W., 367; quoted on liberal concern with security for underdog, 439–40

As He Saw It: quoted on World War II foreign policy, 411–13; liberal reactions to, 413–14

Ashurst, Henry F., 358

Asia: F.D.R. on importance of to American security, 374; liberal awareness of in Thirties, 375; Willkie on, 395, 397; Lerner quoted on problems raised by, post-World War II, 431; *vs.* Europe debate, 434; Soviet appeal to, 450; *see also* Foreign policy, liberal (Thirties and during World War II); Foreign policy, liberal (post-World War II)

Associated Press, 32

"Associational Activities," *see* "New business thinking"

Astor, John Jacob, III: supports Tweed, 13

"Atlanta Compromise": advanced by Booker T. Washington, 81–2

Atlanta Cotton Exposition (1895), 81–2

Atlanta University, 178, 179, 182

Atlantic Charter: liberal concern over during World War II, 389–90; call for economic advancement in, 448

Atlantic Pact: liberal Senatorial support for, 420

Atomic bombs, 407; Elliott Roosevelt on, as major threat to Big Three unity, 413; Progressive Party (1948) demand for end of stockpiling of, 417; Bikini test, 422; David Bradley on, 422–3; *see also* Hiroshima

Atomic Energy Commission: battle to keep civilian control of, 410; potential significance of great powers of, 445–6

Autobiography of Lincoln Steffens: influence on depression generation, 356

Babbitt, 319

"Back-to-Africa" movement, 300–2; *see also* Garvey, Marcus A.

ii

Index

Index

Index

Index

Index

Index

Index

Index

Index

A NOTE ON THE AUTHOR

Eric F. Goldman was born in Washington, D.C., and studied at Johns Hopkins University. He first taught there after receiving his Ph.D. in history, then moved in 1940 to Princeton University, where he spent the rest of his teaching career. From 1963 to 1966 he was special adviser to President Lyndon B. Johnson; he later resigned his position and wrote *The Tragedy of Lyndon Johnson*. His other books include *The Crucial Decade* (later revised as *The Crucial Decade—and After*) and *John Bach McMaster, American Historian*. Mr. Goldman became the Rollins Professor of History at Princeton in 1962 and taught modern American history there until his retirement in 1985. He died in 1989.

John Prados, *Presidents' Secret Wars*
Patrick Renshaw, *The Wobblies*
Edward Reynolds, *Stand the Storm*
Louis Rosen, *The South Side*
Richard Schickel, *The Disney Version*
Richard Schickel, *Intimate Strangers*
Richard Schickel, *Matinee Idylls*
Richard Schickel, *The Men Who Made the Movies*
Edward A. Shils, *The Torment of Secrecy*
Geoffrey S. Smith, *To Save a Nation*
Robert W. Snyder, *The Voice of the City*
Bernard Sternsher, ed., *Hitting Home: The Great Depression in Town
    and Country*
Bernard Sternsher, ed., *Hope Restored: How the New Deal Worked
    in Town and Country*
Bernard Sternsher and Judith Sealander, eds., *Women of Valor*
Athan Theoharis, *From the Secret Files of J. Edgar Hoover*
Nicholas von Hoffman, *We Are the People Our Parents Warned Us Against*
Norman Ware, *The Industrial Worker, 1840–1860*
Tom Wicker, *JFK and LBJ: The Influence of Personality upon Politics*
Robert H. Wiebe, *Businessmen and Reform*
T. Harry Williams, *McClellan, Sherman and Grant*
Miles Wolff, *Lunch at the 5 & 10*
Randall B. Woods and Howard Jones, *Dawning of the Cold War*
American Ways Series:
    John A. Andrew III, *Lyndon Johnson and the Great Society*
    Roger Daniels, *Not Like Us*
    J. Matthew Gallman, *The North Fights the Civil War: The Home
    Front*
    Lewis L. Gould, *1968: The Election That Changed America*
    John Earl Haynes, *Red Scare or Red Menace?*
    D. Clayton James and Anne Sharp Wells, *From Pearl Harbor to V-J
    Day*
    John W. Jeffries, *Wartime America*
    Curtis D. Johnson, *Redeeming America*
    Maury Klein, *The Flowering of the Third America*
    Larry M. Logue, *To Appomattox and Beyond*
    Jean V. Matthews, *Women's Struggle for Equality*
    Iwan W. Morgan, *Deficit Government*
    Robert Muccigrosso, *Celebrating the New World*
    Daniel Nelson, *Shifting Fortunes*
    Thomas R. Pegram, *Battling Demon Rum*
    Burton W. Peretti, *Jazz in American Culture*
    Hal K. Rothman, *Saving the Planet*
    John A. Salmond, *"My Mind Set on Freedom"*
    William Earl Weeks, *Building the Continental Empire*
    Mark J. White, *Missiles in Cuba*

European and World History
John Charmley, *Chamberlain and the Lost Peace*
Lee Feigon, *China Rising*
Lee Feigon, *Demystifying Tibet*
Mark Frankland, *The Patriots' Revolution*
Lloyd C. Gardner, *Spheres of Influence*
David Gilmour, *Cities of Spain*
Raul Hilberg, et al., eds., *The Warsaw Diary of Adam Czerniakow*
Gertrude Himmelfarb, *Darwin and the Darwinian Revolution*
Gertrude Himmelfarb, *Marriage and Morals Among the Victorians*

Gertrude Himmelfarb, *Victorian Minds*
Thomas A. Idinopulos, *Jerusalem*
Thomas A. Idinopulos, *Weathered by Miracles*
Allan Janik and Stephen Toulmin, *Wittgenstein's Vienna*
Hilton Kramer and Roger Kimball, eds., *The Betrayal of Liberalism*
Ronnie S. Landau, *The Nazi Holocaust*
Filip Müller, *Eyewitness Auschwitz*
Clive Ponting, *1940: Myth and Reality*
A.L. Rowse, *The Elizabethan Renaissance: The Life of the Society*
A.L. Rowse, *The Elizabethan Renaissance: The Cultural Achievement*
Scott Shane, *Dismantling Utopia*
Alexis de Tocqueville, *Memoir on Pauperism*
Paul Webster, *Petain's Crime*
John Weiss, *Ideology of Death*

Literature, Arts, and Letters
Roger Angell, *Once More Around the Park*
Walter Bagehot, *Physics and Politics*
Stephen Vincent Benét, *John Brown's Body*
Isaiah Berlin, *The Hedgehog and the Fox*
F. Bordewijk, *Character*
Robert Brustein, *Cultural Calisthenics*
Robert Brustein, *Dumbocracy in America*
Anthony Burgess, *Shakespeare*
Philip Callow, *From Noon to Starry Night*
Philip Callow, *Son and Lover: The Young D. H. Lawrence*
Philip Callow, *Vincent Van Gogh*
Anton Chekhov, *The Comic Stories*
Bruce Cole, *The Informed Eye*
James Gould Cozzens, *Castaway*
James Gould Cozzens, *Men and Brethren*
Clarence Darrow, *Verdicts Out of Court*
Floyd Dell, *Intellectual Vagabondage*
Theodore Dreiser, *Best Short Stories*
Joseph Epstein, *Ambition*
André Gide, *Madeleine*
Gerald Graff, *Literature Against Itself*
John Gross, *The Rise and Fall of the Man of Letters*
Olivia Gude and Jeff Huebner, *Urban Art Chicago*
Irving Howe, *William Faulkner*
Aldous Huxley, *After Many a Summer Dies the Swan*
Aldous Huxley, *Ape and Essence*
Aldous Huxley, *Collected Short Stories*
Roger Kimball, *Tenured Radicals*
Hilton Kramer, *The Twilight of the Intellectuals*
Hilton Kramer and Roger Kimball, eds., *Against the Grain*
F. R. Leavis, *Revaluation*
F. R. Leavis, *The Living Principle*
F. R. Leavis, *The Critic as Anti-Philosopher*
Marie-Anne Lescourret, *Rubens: A Double Life*
Sinclair Lewis, *Selected Short Stories*
William L. O'Neill, ed., *Echoes of Revolt: The Masses, 1911–1917*
Budd Schulberg, *The Harder They Fall*
Ramón J. Sender, *Seven Red Sundays*
Peter Shaw, *Recovering American Literature*
James B. Simpson, ed., *Veil and Cowl*
Tess Slesinger, *On Being Told That Her Second Husband Has Taken His First Lover, and Other Stories*

Donald Thomas, *Swinburne*
B. Traven, *The Bridge in the Jungle*
B. Traven, *The Carreta*
B. Traven, *The Cotton-Pickers*
B. Traven, *General from the Jungle*
B. Traven, *Government*
B. Traven, *March to the Montería*
B. Traven, *The Night Visitor and Other Stories*
B. Traven, *The Rebellion of the Hanged*
B. Traven, *Trozas*
Anthony Trollope, *Trollope the Traveller*
Rex Warner, *The Aerodrome*
Rebecca West, *A Train of Powder*
Thomas Wolfe, *The Hills Beyond*
Wilhelm Worringer, *Abstraction and Empathy*
The Shakespeare Handbooks by Alistair McCallum
   Hamlet
   King Lear
   Macbeth
   Romeo and Juliet

Theatre and Drama

Linda Apperson, *Stage Managing and Theatre Etiquette*
Robert Brustein, *Cultural Calisthenics*
Robert Brustein, *Dumbocracy in America*
Robert Brustein, *Reimagining American Theatre*
Robert Brustein, *The Theatre of Revolt*
Stephen Citron, *The Musical from the Inside Out*
Irina and Igor Levin, *Working on the Play and the Role*
Keith Newlin, ed., *American Plays of the New Woman*
Louis Rosen, *The South Side*
David Wood, with Janet Grant, *Theatre for Children*
Plays for Performance:
   Aristophanes, *Lysistrata*
   Pierre Augustin de Beaumarchais, *The Barber of Seville*
   Pierre Augustin de Beaumarchais, *The Marriage of Figaro*
   Anton Chekhov, *The Cherry Orchard*
   Anton Chekhov, *The Seagull*
   Euripides, *The Bacchae*
   Euripides, *Iphigenia in Aulis*
   Euripides, *Iphigenia Among the Taurians*
   Euripides, *Medea*
   Euripides, *The Trojan Women*
   Georges Feydeau, *Paradise Hotel*
   Henrik Ibsen, *A Doll's House*
   Henrik Ibsen, *Ghosts*
   Henrik Ibsen, *Hedda Gabler*
   Henrik Ibsen, *The Master Builder*
   Henrik Ibsen, *When We Dead Awaken*
   Henrik Ibsen, *The Wild Duck*
   Heinrich von Kleist, *The Prince of Homburg*
   Christopher Marlowe, *Doctor Faustus*
   Molière, *The Bourgeois Gentleman*
   The Mysteries: Creation
   The Mysteries: The Passion
   Luigi Pirandello, *Six Characters in Search of an Author*
   Budd Schulberg, with Stan Silverman, *On the Waterfront* (the play)
   Sophocles, *Antigone*

Sophocles, *Electra*
Sophocles, *Oedipus the King*
August Strindberg, *The Father*
August Strindberg, *Miss Julie*
The Shakespeare Handbooks by Alistair McCallum
  Hamlet
  King Lear
  Macbeth
  Romeo and Juliet

Philosophy
Philosophers in 90 Minutes by Paul Strathern
  Thomas Aquinas in 90 Minutes
  Aristotle in 90 Minutes
  St. Augustine in 90 Minutes
  Berkeley in 90 Minutes
  Confucius in 90 Minutes
  Derrida in 90 Minutes
  Descartes in 90 Minutes
  Foucault in 90 Minutes
  Hegel in 90 Minutes
  Hume in 90 Minutes
  Kant in 90 Minutes
  Kierkegaard in 90 Minutes
  Leibniz in 90 Minutes
  Locke in 90 Minutes
  Machiavelli in 90 Minutes
  Marx in 90 Minutes
  Nietzsche in 90 Minutes
  Plato in 90 Minutes
  Bertrand Russell in 90 Minutes
  Sartre in 90 Minutes
  Schopenhauer in 90 Minutes
  Socrates in 90 Minutes
  Spinoza in 90 Minutes
  Wittgenstein in 90 Minutes